VISUAL
COMMUNICATION
AND CULTURE
IMAGES IN ACTION

EDITED BY JONATHAN FINN

OXFORD
UNIVERSITY PRESS

OXFORD
UNIVERSITY PRESS

Oxford University Press is a department of the University of Oxford.
It furthers the University's objective of excellence in research, scholarship,
and education by publishing worldwide. Oxford is a registered trade mark of
Oxford University Press in the UK and in certain other countries.

Published in Canada by
Oxford University Press
8 Sampson Mews, Suite 204,
Don Mills, Ontario M3C 0H5 Canada

www.oupcanada.com

Copyright © Oxford University Press Canada 2012

The moral rights of the author have been asserted

Database right Oxford University Press (maker)

Library and Archives Canada Cataloguing in Publication

Visual communication and culture : images in action / Jonathan Finn, editor.

Includes bibliographical references and index.
ISBN 978-0-19-542662-5

1. Communication and culture—Case studies.
2. Visual communication—Social aspects—Case studies.
3. Visual sociology. I. Finn, Jonathan M. (Jonathan Mathew), 1972–

P94.6.V58 2011   302.2   C2011-903895-1

Cover photo credits, clockwise from top: © iStockPhoto.com/66North;
© iStockPhoto.com/skodonnell; © iStockPhoto.com/webking;
© iStockPhoto.com/JAMCO1; © iStockPhoto.com/MadCircles

Printed and bound in Canada

6 7 8 — 21 20 19

CONTENTS

PREFACE

It is now commonplace to refer to the contemporary world as a visual culture. From MRI scans to oil paintings, and advertisements to maps, images permeate our lives from the personal to the professional. Images teach us; they take us places we cannot physically go, they reveal things we cannot physically see and they shape our memories, histories, and identities. Images can also misinform; they can be used in ways that are racist, sexist, denigrating, or demeaning. As such, it is crucially important that we are able to think critically and communicate about the position and role of images and visual communication in our lives and in the multiple social worlds we inhabit. The essays in this collection bring critical attention to the centrality, import, and impact of images in contemporary life.

A fundamental argument of this book is that images are constitutive elements of human communication. That is, images are not simply supplements to the communication process, nor are they merely self-evident 'windows on the world'. Instead, and as the essays in this book stress, images are complex cultural products with an equally complex set of cultural influences. Just as the beliefs, values, ideologies, and politics of a given culture influence its practices of communication, so too do the resultant images shape the cultures in which they are deployed. The title of the text, *Visual Communication and Culture*, is meant to reflect this reciprocal relationship between images and the cultures within which they are produced, exchanged, and interpreted.

Rather than present a historical trajectory, or a single methodology, theory, or perspective, this book presents a series of case studies related to visual communication and culture. The book addresses *images in action* by offering analyses of visual communication within specific fields of practice including anatomy, law, cartography, museology, and photojournalism. In addition to these fields, cultural conceptions of truth, objectivity, gender, and race, and the many power relations suffused in such notions are investigated throughout the book. The approximately 140 images included in the book mean that the textual and visual are brought together in argument and analysis. Specific sites of analysis include the Visible Human Project, the London Tube Map, Facebook profiles, and Colin Powell's 2003 presentation to the UN. By emphasizing concrete practices and events rather than purely abstract or theoretical perspectives, the book not only offers numerous sites for discussion but also helps to stress the real-world implications of images and visual communication. With specific reference to the examples cited above, such implications include the construction of knowledge of the human body, the ways people conceive of and navigate their geospatial environment, the creation of individual and social identities, and large-scale military campaigns.

This book combines previously published essays with seven original contributions. Perspectives from across the humanities and social sciences in fields such as communication studies, visual studies, cultural studies, and science studies are present in the text; however, the dominant approach is one of interdisciplinarity. Substantial Canadian content brings specific attention to visual communication and culture in Canada, including the representation of First Nations peoples and the development of a national aesthetic. In total, *Visual Communication and Culture: Images in Action*, is intended to encourage readers to analyze and reflect on the importance of images to life, both historically and as they continue to shape our worlds.

Acknowledgements

This collection is the product of many years of thinking about, teaching, researching, and discussing visual communication, and I owe thanks to many people in this regard. Thank you to my colleagues in the Department of Communication Studies at Wilfrid Laurier University and specifically to Paul Heyer, Barbara Jenkins, Anne-Marie Kinahan, Ian Roderick, Peter Urquhart, and Darren Wershler (now at Concordia University). Your suggestions for the book and our ongoing discussions about visual communication have helped shaped this book in significant ways, and I feel indebted to you all. And thank you to my undergraduate and graduate students in visual communication and visual culture, whose voices are very much present in the selection of readings and in the introductions I have written. I am also thankful to my institution, Wilfrid Laurier University, for a book preparation grant that assisted in the production costs for the book.

The editorial and production staff at Oxford University Press have been wonderful to work with. Thank you to Lisa Meschino and Sharron O'Brien for their initial interest in the project and to Dina Theleritis and Andrea Kennedy for their work on early iterations of the manuscript. Jodi Lewchuk and Stephen Kotowych have been helpful and reassuring throughout and I owe a great deal of thanks to Mary Wat for seeing the project through to completion. Leslie Saffrey's copy editing was truly impressive and has made me look like a better writer than I am. I owe great thanks to those who contributed original pieces to the book: Jacqueline Botterill, Karen Engle, Paul Heyer, Anne-Marie Kinahan, Stephen Kline, Lorna Roth, Peter Urquhart, and Ira Wagman. The quality and clarity of your contributions should stand as a model for the students and teachers who use this book.

My biggest thanks are, of course, reserved for my family. None of this would be possible without their continued support. I am fortunate to share a passion for the visual with my wife, Janice Maarhuis. Her insights into the world of visual communication and our conversations of life within and beyond images have played a fundamental role in this project. Finally, I would like to thank our two beautiful daughters, Neve and Naomi, for continually reminding me of the wondrousness of life.

CONTRIBUTORS

Jacqueline Botterill is Assistant Professor in the Department of Communication, Popular Culture and Film at Brock University.

Karen Engle is Associate Professor in the Department of Sociology, Anthropology, and Criminology at the University of Windsor.

Paul Heyer is Professor in the Department of Communication Studies at Wilfrid Laurier University.

Anne-Marie Kinahan is Associate Professor in the Department of Communication Studies at Wilfrid Laurier University.

Stephen Kline is Professor in the School of Communication at Simon Fraser University and Director of the Media Analysis Laboratory.

Lorna Roth is Professor and former Chairperson of the Department of Communication Studies at Concordia University.

Peter Urquhart is Assistant Professor in the Department of Communication Studies at Wilfrid Laurier University.

Ira Wagman is Associate Professor in the School of Journalism and Communication at Carleton University.

INTRODUCTION

Images surround us at work, school, and home and in all places in between. Much of what we know about the world comes from our ability to produce, circulate, and interpret visual representation in a diversity of forms. Textbooks, magazines, professional journals, newspapers, billboards, television, film, the visual arts, and the Internet all depend on images to communicate information. Images teach us, they take us places we cannot physically go, they reveal things we cannot physically see, and they function in the construction of our memory and our history. Images can also misinform: they can participate in the construction and reinforcement of stereotypes and in practices that are racist, sexist, denigrating, or demeaning. As a result it is increasingly important to think critically and communicate about the position and role of images and visual communication in our personal lives and in society at large.

Recognizing the centrality of the visual in daily life, Rudolph Arnheim (1969) argues for increased visual literacy and for specialized training in the visual across the curriculum. For Arnheim, visual representation is a fundamental component not only of communication but of thinking—hence the need for extensive and expansive training in visual literacy. Over the past few decades the visual has attracted increasing critical attention as producers and users of images—academics, professionals, and laypeople alike—have heeded the importance of visual representation in individual and social life. Indeed, the explosion of college and university programs in visual culture, visual communication, visual studies, and related areas over the past two decades is a promising response to Arnheim's call, yet we have only scratched the surface of this tremendously rich and important field of inquiry. This collection of essays contributes to this growing field of study, highlighting the centrality, importance, and impact of images and visual communication in individual and social life.

IMAGES, COMMUNICATION, CULTURE

A central theme of this book is that images both influence and are influenced by culture. Culture is understood in a broad sense to include the belief systems, values, traditions, policies, politics, ideologies, economics, and creative practices of a given social group. Culture is multiple and mutable. That is, one can belong to many cultures simultaneously, and every culture changes over time. My university and my city have particular cultures, as do my province and country, and each of these cultures necessarily changes across time.

Politics, economics, and ideology all influence the production of images. And just as images are influenced by the cultures within which they are produced, so too they influence the cultures in which they are disseminated and interpreted. The hybrid phrase used in the title of this text—*Visual Communication and Culture*—is meant to reflect the reciprocal relationship between images and the cultures within which they are produced, exchanged, and interpreted.

In academic work that utilizes or addresses visual representation, images are too often taken to be supplements to the communication process. Understood in this sense, images are treated either as illustrations in service to textual or oral argument, or as self-evident 'windows on the world'. By contrast, the essays in this book stress that images are not static representations of objects but are active sites in processes of communication. As constitutive elements of human communication, images are central to the production of knowledge and to the meaning-making processes through which we engage with and understand our world. The subtitle of this text, *Images in Action*, stresses this dynamic nature of visual representation.

The academic study of images takes place in a diverse range of fields and under various headings including visual anthropology, visual sociology, visual communication, visual studies, art history, communication studies, media studies, visual culture, film studies, perceptual psychology, design, and architecture. In addition, the study of images takes place across numerous academic fields which do not take the visual as their primary subject area. These include geography, biology, English, and archaeology. In fact, it would be difficult to find an academic field of inquiry which did not include at least a handful of researchers addressing visual representation.

Most academic work that addresses the intersection of visual communication and culture is based in the humanities and social sciences, particularly within the fields of visual culture and visual communication, respectively. The visual culture approach reflects the tradition of art history both as a field of study and in the influence upon it from areas such as cultural studies, film studies, and critical theory. This approach de-emphasizes the literal or practical aspects of the visual in favour of a theoretical analysis of images as cultural objects, particularly as they are tied to power relations and to conceptions of race, class, and gender. By contrast, the visual communication approach emphasizes the formal aspects of images as visual communication as well as the deployment of visual technologies as research tools. Through empirical studies of image production and reception, this approach often addresses the question of how images communicate.

Although myriad contemporary academic fields address the visual, the dedicated study of images has its longest tradition in the field of art history. To better understand the theoretical and methodological approaches of current academic work—including the essays in this book—it is useful to briefly examine some of the dominant currents in the study of images within the humanities and social sciences, paying particular attention to the fields of visual culture and visual communication.

ANALYZING IMAGES

The discipline of art history has its origins in the Renaissance and the publication in 1550 of *Le*

Vite delle più eccellenti pittori, scultori, ed architettori (*Lives of the Most Excellent Painters, Sculptors, and Architects*), by the Italian artist Giorgio Vasari (1511–1574). Vasari's text was encyclopedic: it documented the lives and works of selected Italian painters, sculptors, and architects. In this way, the book promoted the work of some artists—and the artists themselves—as genius. The 'great masters' were portrayed as mythic figures who transcended the general population and whose works were the best society had to offer. This tradition of the artist-as-genius lasted well into the twentieth century and is still present in less-critical accounts of art history and visual culture.

As it developed from the sixteenth through nineteenth centuries, art history was concerned with discussions of style and the development of connoisseurship or iconographic analysis. With respect to style, art works were taken to be representative of a specific historical or cultural style. In this way, art historians could speak of Flemish painting, for example, in contrast to southern or northern Italian painting. Such an approach presupposes that the art object reflects the specific area and time in which it was created. With respect to connoisseurship, art historians developed a specialized model and language for the interpretation of art works. They positioned themselves as having developed a trained eye that enabled them to distinguish the work of one artist from that of another, or a genuine masterpiece (such as one by Rembrandt) from an imitation. These two aspects of studying art—style and connoisseurship—were united in their focus on the art object. Thus, during this phase of the field of art history, art historians took as their central subject matter the work of art itself. The work was understood to have inherent meaning—all that was required was the trained eye of the expert to decipher its content.

The intense focus on the work of art and the notion of the trained eye of the art historian reached its zenith in the modernist period. The meaning of *modernism* varies depending on the particular subject and context of discussion. In art history, it refers to the nineteenth and early twentieth centuries. During this time, art historians were chiefly concerned with authenticity and originality, and the mythic figure of the artist–genius reigned supreme. Also, modernism was based on a belief in the progress of mankind—each society was seen as better and more advanced than its predecessor. These basic tenets of modernism—authenticity and progress—are clearly visible in art-historical writings of the time, particularly in 'survey' texts that offer a linear trajectory of art practice from antiquity to the modern world. This particular version of art history has since been critiqued as inherently elitist and as focused exclusively on male artists of the Western world. To put it more simply, the modern account presented art history as the 'history of dead white guys'.

The development of photomechanical reproduction (photography) in the mid nineteenth century and the subsequent development of film at the beginning of the twentieth century greatly challenged the existing art-historical discourse. Photography and film were popular media; they were used by a diverse range of practitioners and were enjoyed by an equally diverse group. This popularity did not fit well within the discipline of art history, which was considerably more specialized and elitist. Photography also challenged the notion of authenticity that was a hallmark of the study of images. The photomechanical image ushered in an era of reproducibility that problematized notions of authenticity and originality. The tension between authenticity and reproducibility was famously taken up by Walter Benjamin in his 1936 essay, 'The Work of Art in the Age of Mechanical Reproduction'. Benjamin's essay is a careful analysis of the social and political implications of mechanical reproduction, particularly as the technology intersects with artistic production.

Benjamin belonged to a group of scholars known as the Frankfurt School. This group had a lasting impact on scholarly activity through its development of critical theory, which seeks social change through critical, reflexive thought and research. In addition to Benjamin, the Frankfurt School included scholars and theorists such as Max Horkheimer, Theodor Adorno, Herbert Marcuse, and Jürgen Habermas, all of whom were deeply concerned with the then-rapid expansion of industrialization and capitalism. In this way,

scholars of the Frankfurt School were strongly informed by the theories of Karl Marx (1818–1883). Specifically in regard to images and artistic practice, they were interested in the effects of reproducibility on culture. They lamented popular culture and mass media as effectively 'dumbing down' society and as threatening what they perceived to be the best of cultural expression—commonly known as 'high culture'. Although the work of the Frankfurt School is now viewed as elitist, its critique of reproducibility and of the effects of industrialization and capitalism on cultural production is important and has had a lasting impact on scholarly work of the twentieth and twenty-first centuries.

By the mid twentieth century the basic tenets of modernist thought—the importance of authenticity and a belief in progress—had been thoroughly criticized. This criticism opened up new avenues of inquiry for art historians and other scholars interested in visual representation. William Ivins, Jr.'s influential 1953 book, *Prints and Visual Communication* marks a key turning point in the study of images. It examines prints and printmaking practices from antiquity to the modern period as vehicles of communication. This study contrasted dramatically with the then-dominant approach in art history, which examined prints as aesthetic objects. Ivins analyzed prints in relation to changing social patterns, particularly to increasing demand for information.

The image as a mode of communication was also a key concern for a group of mid twentieth century scholars interested in mass media. Paul Lazarsfeld and Harold Lasswell are notable figures in this tradition and are cited alongside Harold Innis and Marshall McLuhan as key figures in the establishment of communication studies as an academic field of practice. Early research on mass media, such as that produced by Lazarsfeld and Lasswell, concentrated on the 'effects' of media such as radio, television, and film. This work shared the concern of the Frankfurt School regarding the power of media to shape and influence public opinion and offered empirical analyses of film, radio, and television in this regard. As with Ivins, and in contrast to the art-historical tradition, mass communication scholars were interested in the communicative capabilities of the image and not in its aesthetic value. Their research foregrounded aspects of image production and reception, focusing on how messages are produced and received through mass media.

Contemporary with the work of 'media effects' researchers, the medium of film was being discussed and theorized by a group of film practitioners and scholars including Sergei Eisenstein and André Bazin. This work sought a humanities-based, aesthetic approach to film, much like that of art historians toward works of visual art. Eisenstein and Bazin were both concerned with the unique properties of film—most specifically its abilities to produce narrative and to represent time through processes of montage. This work was essential to the development of film studies as an academic field of practice, which would fully emerge in the 1960s and 1970s, and also argued for an appreciation of film as an aesthetic practice and as a mode of creative expression. This approach contrasted to perspectives from communication studies and anthropology that emphasized film as a mass medium or as a documentary research tool.

The documentary status of both film and photography was seized on by scholars and researchers in the early twentieth century in order to study objects, artifacts, events, and people. Of primary importance here is the then-emerging field of visual anthropology. In its nascent form, visual anthropology was concerned with the use of visual technologies—primarily photography and film—in ethnography, the empirical study of distinct human cultures or groups. Robert Flaherty's 1922 film, *Nanook of the North*, is a quintessential example of early visual anthropology. As used by Flaherty and his contemporaries, the camera was employed as a documentary tool, and its product—the image—was treated as visual evidence. A central presumption guiding this work was that the camera was an objective recording instrument: in other words, it produced images that were taken to be mirrors of the world.

Beginning in the 1940s and 1950s, anthropologists began to explore a new line of inquiry in relation to visual technologies and visual representation. A central figure in this regard was Margaret Mead. Her work shifted emphasis from the camera as an ethnographic tool to the study of images themselves—often those in the mass media—from an anthropological perspective. Mead's work, and that of her contemporaries, brought a new level of critical attention to the study and use of images and began to question a central assumption of visual anthropology: the documentary status of the camera. The visual communication scholar Sol Worth refers to this as a shift from visual anthropology to the anthropology of visual communication.

Where art historians analyzed images as aesthetic objects, anthropologists treated images as documentary evidence. In the former, the image was seen as a product of creative expression, and analyses offered evaluations of stylistic elements such as colour, shape, line, and composition. In the latter, the image was employed as a research tool, used to document the lives and practices of human cultures. While this distinction between the image as aesthetic object and as documentary evidence is admittedly both simplistic and totalizing, it is nonetheless a useful way to distinguish between the general treatment of images by art historians and anthropologists—and by scholars of the humanities and social sciences more generally—in the early to mid twentieth century.

During what is variously termed the 'linguistic turn', the 'cultural turn', or the 'critical turn' in the 1960s and 1970s, academic work across the humanities and social sciences underwent significant revision. Key components of this 'turn' include the theories of structuralism, post-structuralism, feminism, psychoanalysis, and post-colonialism, and the emergence of cultural studies as a mode of academic inquiry. It is important to note that these components did not emerge sequentially. Rather, they should be seen as contemporaneous, intersecting, and sometimes competing theories. And while there are myriad differences between the theories, as well as nuances within them, as part of the critical turn they all contributed to a radical critique of existing modes of academic inquiry.

Structuralism developed in the work of the Swiss linguist Ferdinand de Saussure, based on the belief that all cultural artifacts are composed of a series of signs and that such a system of signs—its structure—is locatable and identifiable. To this end, structuralists such as de Saussure, Claude Lévi-Strauss, and Roland Barthes used the study of semiotics to put forth distinct methods for analyzing the structures and sign-systems of cultural objects, including images. Understood as a cultural artifact, an image is seen as a collection of distinct signs whose meaning can be discerned through careful analysis. For example, Barthes argued that images had both denotative and connotative levels of meaning. The former refers to the immediate and literal information given off by an image, whereas the latter references the symbolic and culturally specific meaning that we read from the image. In some respects structuralism may seem similar to connoisseurship in art history; however, semioticians differ from art connoisseurs in their emphasis on the image as a cultural product and not as the product of an individual artist–genius.

In contrast to the structuralists, post-structuralists deny any fixed or locatable meaning in an object. This is best exemplified in the work of Jacques Derrida, who asserted that each time someone 'reads' a text, the text is re-made. The term *text* as it is used here highlights the literary origins of much post-structuralist thought and the emphasis on the act of reading or interpreting. Post-structuralism positions buildings, paintings, films, and TV shows as 'texts', to be read and analyzed much in the same way as a traditional written text. The linguistic basis of structuralist and post-structuralist thought proved problematic for the study of images, as is addressed later in this introduction.

Derrida's assertion regarding the reading of texts points to a central feature and result of post-structuralism: a shift in importance from the author to the reader. That is, where modernists were deeply concerned with the presence and centrality of the author in the meaning of a given artifact, post-structuralists largely ignore the notion of the author, focusing attention on the role of the reader as he or she interprets a given object. In the study of images, this focus is a radical departure from earlier academic work—particularly in art history—where the intention of the author or artist was given tremendous importance. A post-

structuralist analysis of an image is more concerned with the interaction between image and viewer than it is with what the image's creator may or may not have intended to communicate.

Feminism developed through the nineteenth and twentieth centuries, but its most significant impact in academic work came in the 1960s and 1970s. During what is called the 'second wave' of feminism, feminist work pointed to the omission of women from a variety of aspects of life, from politics to artistic production. This critique soon expanded to question the very foundation of these practices. Feminist art historians such as Linda Nochlin, Griselda Pollock, and Janet Wolff not only called into question the lack of women in traditional histories of art, but also revealed and challenged the very structure of the discipline as patriarchal. This perspective is illustrated in Nochlin's 1971 essay, 'Why Have There Been No Great Women Artists?' Nochlin's response to that question is a detailed account of how the institutional structures governing the production, display, and critique of art are inherently gendered and exclusionary towards women.

Like feminism, psychoanalysis developed in the nineteenth century and was incorporated into academic work during the 1960s and 1970s. The theory, initially put forth by Sigmund Freud as a therapeutic technique for an array of neuroses, was taken up by scholars—particularly of film—in the 1960s and 1970s as a methodological tool for addressing cultural production, including production of images. As applied to the study of cultural production, psychoanalysis is chiefly concerned with the notion of desire and, in specific reference to visual representation, the pleasure associated with the act of looking, also referred to as scopophilia and 'the gaze'. Laura Mulvey's 1975 essay, 'Visual Pleasure and Narrative Cinema' is a foundational work for the psychoanalytic study of film. Mulvey argues that classic Hollywood cinema places the film viewer in a male subject position, with the female actress on the screen as the object of the viewer's gaze and desire. In this way, Mulvey's analysis is not just psychoanalytic, but also feminist.

Post-colonial theory developed after the peak of activity associated with the critical turn and also had significant influence on the critical study of images. Although it has roots in the 1960s and 1970s, post-colonial theory is most closely associated with Edward Said's 1978 book *Orientalism*. Said's theory of orientalism refers to a culturally constructed divide between the East and West. The divide was perpetuated by the West in a colonialist project of naming and controlling other cultures. As Said notes, by representing and positioning Eastern cultures as less evolved and more primitive and simplistic than their Western counterparts, Western cultures defined themselves as more advanced. Within such a process, the West becomes the dominant or 'normal' culture and other cultures are marginalized and positioned as 'Others'.

This colonialist attitude is illustrated in early art history texts, which present Western artists and movements as being the 'best' in artistic achievement. For example, discussions of the artists Pablo Picasso and Georges Braque, and the Cubist movement of which they were a part, often referenced the 'primitive' cultures of Africa as sources for the 'great' Western artists. Such discourse positions the West at the centre of cultural production, with African, Asian, and other non-Western cultures at the periphery or margins. A chief feature of post-colonial theory is uncovering constructions such as this and promoting the multiplicity of voices and perspectives across the world. Post-colonialism was taken up by numerous scholars in the 1980s and 1990s, notably Gayatri Chakravorty Spivak and Homi J. Bhabha, and is a prominent mode of inquiry in the early twenty-first century.

Cultural studies developed in Britain in the 1960s, specifically through the founding of the Centre for Contemporary Cultural Studies at the University of Birmingham. Cultural studies scholars such as Stuart Hall, Dick Hebdige, and Angela McRobbie were influenced by the Frankfurt School, structuralism, post-structuralism, feminism, and psychoanalysis, and were overtly interdisciplinary in their scholarship. That is, rather than adhering to the theoretical or methodological lines of inquiry from a single discipline, cultural studies scholars employ a range of tools drawn from fields such as psychology,

English, anthropology, sociology, and art history. For the study of images, cultural studies has had at least two primary impacts. First, cultural studies scholars are interested in all forms of cultural production and not just the forms of 'high culture' such as painting, sculpture, and architecture that were typically addressed in academic work. In this way, cultural studies scholarship legitimizes more popular forms of cultural production such as television, graphic novels, and advertising as sites worthy of critical, academic study. The second key impact of cultural studies is its preoccupation with cultural manifestations of gender, race, social class, and power relations. In contrast to much pre-existing and contemporaneous academic work, cultural studies scholars of the 1960s and 1970s were largely uninterested in the aesthetic properties of a cultural product. This new approach to the visual is best illustrated in John Berger's 1972 *Ways of Seeing*, a project at the intersection of art history, media studies, and cultural studies. Initially produced as a BBC television series, *Ways of Seeing* brought a new critical approach to reading images from fine art to mass media. Berger's analysis positioned images in their larger socio-economic and political context to highlight the broad social impact of images.

Combined, structuralism, post-structuralism, feminism, psychoanalysis, post-colonialism, and cultural studies—along with their precursors in critical theory—opened up myriad new avenues of inquiry for the study of images. The traditional practice of art history gave rise to what is referred to as the 'new art history' and a move away from aesthetics towards the economic, social, and cultural networks within which images are produced, shared, and consumed. To put it most simply, *the shift in the study of images from the late nineteenth to the late twentieth century can be best characterized as a shift in focus from the visual object itself to the broad social and technological networks in which images are produced, exchanged, and interpreted.*

NAMING THE DISCIPLINES

The term *visual culture* was used in the 1970s and 1980s by art historians Michael Baxandall and Svetlana Alpers but did not emerge as a distinct academic field of inquiry until the mid 1990s. As a field of study, visual culture grew out of the history of art, and can be seen as largely influenced by the critical turn and the increasingly interdisciplinary nature of scholarship in the late twentieth and early twenty-first century. Visual culture scholars treat an expansive array of visual culture production—from fine art to industrial design—as worthy of critical inquiry, thus extending the broad focus in Berger's *Ways of Seeing*. Despite this considerably more inclusive subject area, it should be noted that most work in visual culture still tends to focus on artistic production. A defining text for the field was published in the 1996 issue of the journal *October*—responses to a questionnaire from artists, art historians, curators, and other scholars interested in art and visual representation. The questionnaire asked about the state of art history and about 'visual culture' as a new field of inquiry, and was an important document in helping to shape the boundaries of visual culture as a field of study.

Two years prior to the *October* questionnaire, W.J.T. Mitchell proposed 'the pictorial turn' in his book *Picture Theory*, and it is worth discussing here. For Mitchell, the linguistic turn, which had influenced all manner of academic work and life in the mid to late twentieth century, was being replaced by the pictorial turn. The critique of logocentrism was fundamental to this transition. *Logocentrism* comes from the Greek *logos*, meaning 'word'. Thus *logocentrism* refers to a belief in the primacy of the word in human thought and communication. The critical or linguistic turn of the 1960s and 1970s was logocentric in that it was based in literary theory and positioned cultural objects and artifacts as 'texts' to be addressed and discussed in the same way as a traditional written text. Subsequently, the resources or 'tool kit' used to analyze imagery was based on language, so that the study of images was always limited by words.

Both linguistic and literary theory presuppose that all thought and communication is structured by language—one cannot think, understand, or communicate outside of language. Critics of this logocentric approach argue that forms of visual communication—such as non-verbal and pictor-

ial communication—can indeed communicate independently of language. Images have immediate, affective, and even universal communicative values that words do not. As such, approaches based in the belief that all thought and behaviour are structured by language cannot account for the unique characteristics of visual communication. What emerged from the debate around logocentrism was a challenge to the traditional text-based model of analysis and a call to identify and analyze the uniqueness of visual representation as independent of text. The uniqueness of images and visual communication remains a central issue to scholars in the twenty-first century.

The field of visual communication developed contemporaneously with visual culture, but is considerably less well defined. While visual culture grew out of the well-established and centuries-long practice of art history, visual communication emerged as an area of interest in anthropology and communication studies. As it developed during its early period, visual communication reflected a basis in the social sciences, specifically in visual anthropology and mass communication research. In the former, scholars such as Sol Worth, Jay Ruby, and Larry Gross extended the work of Margaret Mead and her contemporaries to explore the documentary capabilities of visual technologies and their ability to help in understanding how humans think, make meaning, and communicate. Importantly, and as it was influenced by the 'critical turn', this work was considerably more critical and reflexive towards its use of the camera. This is best illustrated in Sol Worth and John Adair's 1972 project, *Through Navajo Eyes*, which included the production of seven films and a book. In contrast to the traditional practice in anthropology of using cameras to document individuals and groups, Worth and Adair gave cameras to a group of Navajo Indians in order that they could film themselves. The result is a study both of Navajo culture and of the practice of using visual technologies in ethnographic research.

The second basis for visual communication as a field of analysis dates to the mid-century work of Lazarsfeld and Lasswell. As the term implies, mass communication researchers are interested in radio, television, and film. Audience is a particularly important concept in this work, with researchers performing empirical studies on how and to what effect producers of television, radio, and film are able to communicate to their audiences. The specific interest in visual communication within the broader mass communication research agenda was formally addressed in a 1992 special double issue of the journal *Communication* entitled 'Visual Communication Studies in Mass Media Research'. The critical study of visual communication became increasingly formalized in the 1980s and 1990s through the creation of dedicated journals in anthropology and sociology, and through professional associations such as the International Communication Association.

The *Journal of Visual Culture* and the journal *Visual Communication* were founded in the early twenty-first century. In general, these journals emphasize work in the humanities and social sciences respectively, as befitting the historical trajectories of their fields outlined above. However, it is important to note that, despite these differences, there is considerable overlap between the journals and between the fields they represent. Indeed, as we have seen here, scholars of the twenty-first century have a wide array of disciplinary and interdisciplinary perspectives, theories, and methods to draw from when conducting research or analyzing visual material. And while I do not want to negate the many idiosyncrasies and nuances of the approaches identified here—as well as the many others that have been omitted—I want to stress that there is tremendous similarity in work being done by scholars of communication studies, sociology, history, visual culture studies, anthropology, film studies, and other disciplines in the humanities and social sciences. The point of this rough historiography is not to position visual communication and visual culture as incommensurable projects but to stress their similarities and the wealth of perspectives available to students and scholars of the visual.

ABOUT THIS BOOK

Despite the nuances and different institutional trajectories of fields such as visual culture, art history, visual anthropology, and visual sociology among others, contemporary academic work that addresses visual representation assumes that images are more than aesthetic objects and more than supplements to an oral or textual argument. It understands that images are fundamental components in the construction of knowledge and in processes of communication. To this end, rather than aligning itself with a specific methodology, theory, or disciplinary perspective, this book brings together work from across the humanities and social sciences to address the image as cultural product with cultural impact.

There are several high-quality introductory texts that address visual communication and culture. These include Marita Sturken and Lisa Cartwright's *Practices of Looking: An Introduction to Visual Culture*, Nicholas Mirzoeff's *An Introduction to Visual Culture*, John Walker and Sarah Chaplin's *Visual Culture: An Introduction*, Gunther Kress and Theo van Leeuwen's *Reading Images: The Grammar of Visual Design*, Theo van Leeuwen and Carey Jewitt's *Handbook of Visual Analysis*, and Martin Lester's *Visual Communication: Images with Messages*. In addition, the topic is taken up in a series of readers, particularly within the field of visual culture. These books include *The Block Reader in Visual Culture*, Nicholas Mirzoeff's *The Visual Culture Reader*, Jessica Evans and Stuart Hall's *Visual Culture: The Reader*, and Chris Jenks' *Visual Culture*. These collections are considerably more specialized than the introductory books and are often discipline-specific. And, as edited collections, these texts rarely present complete essays but instead offer selections or portions of essays. What is missing, and what this book seeks to address, is an examination of visual communication and culture which complements the dialogue offered in existing introductory texts and allows for advanced discussion across a range of disciplinary practices and perspectives. Further, by including complete essays, rather than smaller selections, this book allows for a thorough and rigorous engagement with each author's argument.

The structure and organization of the book offer a unique perspective on visual communication as a cultural practice. Rather than presenting a historical trajectory or a single methodology or avenue of inquiry, the book presents a series of case studies related to visual communication and culture. The topic is explored in relation to specific disciplines or fields of practice such as anatomy, law, cartography, curatorial work, and photojournalism. Focusing on these areas emphasizes *images in action* and their function in the construction of knowledge. Further, rather than addressing visual communication and culture in a purely abstract or theoretical way, the essays here present careful analyses of distinct objects or events. Theoretical analyses of power, gender, race, and identity are brought to bear on material objects or events. This not only provides concrete examples for discussion but also gives readers a sense of the real implications of visual communication and culture, stressing the importance of a critical engagement with the topic.

The book is further unique in the selection of authors. The essays in this book bring together interesting and divergent perspectives on the visual from numerous disciplines across the humanities and social sciences. In addition to visual communication and visual culture, fields such as history, anthropology, communication studies, science studies, and cultural studies are represented here, each with its own unique perspective and disciplinary tradition. What emerges is less a canon of important authors than a diverse examination of images and image-making practices as inextricably bound with power relations, the construction of knowledge, and cultural formulations such as race, gender, objectivity, expertise, and truth.

Most work in visual communication and culture has come from British and American scholars and institutions. While this work is necessarily represented here, specific attention is also paid to Canadian scholars and Canadian topics. This includes original contributions by eight prominent and emerging Canadian scholars. This material offers some unique points of discussion within the larger field of visual communication and culture.

To unify the book and to assist readers, each part includes a short introduction. The introductions highlight key features of each essay and contextualize the essays and the part as a whole within the book. It is important to note that the primary aim of the part introductions is to assist in developing a shared understanding of content. They are intended only to draw attention to key points and concepts and should not predetermine a specific avenue of inquiry. In addition, each part includes Questions for Reflection that prompt the reader to think beyond the specific subject matter of the essays and often to examine issues raised in the articles as they relate to his or her own life. A central goal, then, of this collection of essays is to raise questions rather than to provide answers. Together, the introductions and Questions for Reflection are intended not to provide a definitive reading of the essays, but to incite critical engagement. A list of further readings accompanies each part, allowing readers to pursue research in areas of specific interest.

There are numerous parameters governing the production of any book: material constraints, the desires of the market, and the needs and mandate of the publisher, as well as production and permission costs. In addition to these parameters, an edited collection of readings such as this necessarily bears the imprint of the specific training and interests of the editor. Recognition and acknowledgement of this editorial process is often missing from collections of essays, an omission which too often leaves readers of the text to infer the specific rationale for the collection and arrangement of essays. As such, and by way of concluding this introduction, it is important that I acknowledge my own editorial bias. The emphasis on images in this book rather than other forms of visual communication, the focus on the Western world, and the inclusion of visual communication in scientific practices reflect my specific educational training in art history and visual and cultural studies and my scholarly work as a teacher and researcher in communication studies. Importantly, these parameters operate primarily at the level of subject matter. Therefore, while the subject matter of the essays reflects a certain editorial bias, the critical questions and issues raised in the readings are applicable throughout the broader field of visual communication and culture and will be of use to scholars in a diverse range of disciplines who concern themselves with the centrality, importance, and role of images in individual and social life.

A final word must be said about the images included in the text. It is now commonplace to refer to the contemporary world as a visual culture. As noted at the beginning of this introduction, the rapid expansion in visual communication and visual culture programs testify to the increased attention being paid to the visual within the academic community. The importance and popularity of images is readily apparent outside the academic community as well. One primary result of this visual turn is that images have become a key commodity in the twenty-first century. As a result, acquiring and reproducing images for publications is becoming increasingly difficult and expensive. To put it simply, books with images are expensive to produce, and difficult to sell because of their high cost. Nonetheless, my aim in this book is to reproduce the essays as they originally appeared—that is, with all their images. The inclusion of high-quality reproductions in their original context is fundamental given a central claim of this text: that images are not supplemental to acts of communication but are fundamental parts of the process. In the end, my hope is that the essays in this book will encourage readers to think about and reflect on the importance of images to life, both historically and as they continue to shape our world. Being able to critically engage with images in all their diverse forms is not just useful but fundamental, given the centrality of visual communication and culture to modern and contemporary life.

FURTHER READING

Arnheim, Rudolph. *Visual Thinking*. Berkeley: University of California, 1969.

Barnhurst, Kevin G., Michael Vari, and Ígor Rodríguez. 'Mapping Visual Studies in Communication'. *Journal of Communication* December (2004): 616–44.

Benjamin, Walter. 'The Work of Art in the Age of Mechanical Reproduction'. *Illuminations* Trans. Harry Zohn. New York: Schoken Books, 1969. 217–51.

Berger, Arthur Asa. *Seeing is Believing: An Introduction to Visual Communication*. 3rd ed. San Francisco: San Francisco State University, 2008.

Berger, John. *Ways of Seeing*. London: British Broadcasting Corporation, 1972.

Bird, John, et al., eds. *The Block Reader in Visual Culture*. New York: Routledge, 1996.

Dikovitskaya, Margarita. *Visual Culture: The Study of the Visual after the Cultural Turn*. Cambridge: MIT Press, 2005.

Elkins, James. *Visual Studies: A Skeptical Introduction*. New York: Routledge, 2003.

Evans, Jessica, and Stuart Hall, eds. *Visual Culture: The Reader*. London: Sage, 1999.

Griffin, Michael. 'Camera as Witness, Image as Sign: The Study of Visual Communication in Communication Research'. *Communication Yearbook* 24 (2001) 433–63.

Ivins, William M. Jr. *Prints and Visual Communication*. Cambridge: MIT Press, 1953.

Jenks, Chris, Ed. *Visual Culture*. London: Routledge, 1995.

Kress, Gunther, and Theo van Leeuwen. *Reading Images: The Grammar of Visual Design*. New York: Routledge, 1996.

Lester, Paul Martin. *Visual Communication: Images with Messages*. 4th ed. Belmont, Calif.: Thomson Wadsworth, 2006.

Messaris, Paul. *Visual Literacy: Image, Mind, & Reality*. Boulder: Westview, 1994.

Mirzoeff, Nicholas. *An Introduction to Visual Culture*. New York: Routledge, 1999.

Mirzoeff, Nicholas, ed. *The Visual Culture Reader*. New York: Routledge, 1998.

Mitchell, W.J.T. 'The Pictorial Turn'. *Picture Theory: Essays on Verbal and Visual Representation*. Chicago: University of Chicago, 1994. 11–34.

Mulvey, Laura. 'Visual Pleasure and Narrative Cinema'. *Screen* 16/3 (1975): 6–18.

Nochlin, Linda. 'Why Have There Been No Great Women Artists'? *Women, Art, and Power and Other Essays*. New York: Harper and Row, 1989.

Rose, Gillian. *Visual Methodologies: An Introduction to the Interpretation of Visual Materials*. 2nd ed. London: Sage, 2007.

Said, Edward. *Orientalism*. New York: Pantheon, 1978.

Sturken, Marita, and Lisa Cartwright. *Practices of Looking: An Introduction to Visual Culture*. New York: Oxford, 2001.

Van Leeuwen, Theo, and Carey Jewitt. *Handbook of Visual Analysis*. London: Sage, 2001.

'Visual Culture Questionnaire'. *October* 76 (1996): 25–70.

Visual Communication Studies in Mass Media Research I & II. Special issues of the journal *Communication* 13/2&3 (1992).

Walker, John, and Sarah Chaplin. *Visual Culture: An Introduction*. New York: St Martin's, 1997.

Worth, Sol. *Studying Visual Communication*. Philadelphia: University of Pennsylvania, 1991.

Worth, Sol, and John Adair. *Through Navajo Eyes: An Exploration in Film Communication and Anthropology*. Bloomington: Indiana University, 1972

IMAGES, COMMUNICATION, AND CULTURE

The opening essays in this reader are from three influential and early figures in the fields of visual communication and visual culture: William Ivins, Jr., Rudolph Arnheim, and Susan Sontag. Their work serves well to foreground many of the ideas that are addressed in this anthology and to introduce the book by examining the interrelationships among images, communication, and culture. In his analysis of printmaking, Ivins highlights the centrality of images in the construction of knowledge and in so doing draws attention to the broad cultural influence and impact of image-making. Arnheim's essay also stresses the importance of images and image-making in the

construction of knowledge; however, rather than emphasize the larger cultural context, Arnheim stresses the extent to which vision is trained and learned through convention. And Sontag identifies the centrality of images in our lives, not just in knowledge production but also in shaping memory and identity. In total, the essays position images and visual communication as fundamental aspects of life.

The first reading, 'Recapitulation', is from Ivins's highly influential book *Prints and Visual Communication*, published in 1953. Ivins's text was unique at that time in that he analyzed printmaking as a practice of communication, rather than a primarily aesthetic endeavour as had been the dominant approach in the field of art history. This is made clear in Ivins's opening remarks: 'Thus the story of prints is not, as many people seem to think, that of a minor art form but that of a most powerful method of communication between men and of its effects upon Western European thought and civilization.' In this way, the passage underscores the intersection of communication and culture that is at the heart of Ivins's text. For Ivins, printmaking developed in response to a cultural demand for information, and the resulting printmaking techniques had their own distinct influence on the cultures in which they were produced and used.

An essential point in the essay is that image-making functions in the development of knowledge. This claim culminates in Ivins's assertion that modern science and technology could not exist without the reproductive capabilities of photography and the half-tone process, both developed in the nineteenth century. It is here that Ivins introduces his now-famous concept of the 'exactly repeatable pictorial statement'. The ability to produce and disseminate images on a mass scale and without the loss of information is, for Ivins, the most important event in the history of communication. The exactly repeatable pictorial statement gave rise to the production of new forms of knowledge; however, Ivins importantly recognizes the problem wrought by such practices, namely the loss of direct experience with the objects of study. Today it is widely acknowledged that we receive most of our information about the world through representation in the form of images, text, and sound. Ivins's work raises important questions about the role of representation—specifically visual representation—in the formation of knowledge, an issue that remains at the forefront of inquiry in visual communication and culture.

The second reading, 'Vision in Education', is from another influential book, *Visual Thinking*, by Rudolph Arnheim, published in 1969. Arnheim's approach to the visual was unique in that he combined his formal training in psychology with an interest in the study of art. Unlike Ivins' book which focused on the chronological development of printmaking as a communicative practice, Arnheim's text is an analysis of the relationship between seeing, thinking, and understanding. A central argument of Arnheim's is that perception (what happens when one looks at an object) cannot be separated from thinking (the process of understanding or making meaning). Some academics, notably the visual communication scholar Sol Worth, have critized Arnheim for his lack of attention to cultural influences on the practice of meaning making as Arnheim was primarily concerned with what happened inside the mind and body of the observer. Nonetheless, in the selection included here, it seems clear that Arnheim's analysis allows for significant cultural influence.

There are two claims in Arnheim's essay that are of particular importance to the present discussion and which are taken up in several other essays in this collection. First, Arnheim positions vision as something that is learned. Chemists, painters, biologists, sculptors, and physicists learn to interpret and produce images in different ways according to different disciplinary conventions. Arnheim then makes the provocative and prescient point that what one sees in a given image depends in large part on what one is looking for, which is itself influenced by one's training. This leads to the second claim: that pictures are propositions. Arnheim's essay underscores the fact that pictures are not illustrations or supplements to a communicative process but that they are a communicative process. Hence Arnheim's wish that we be more visually literate and that visual training take place across the curriculum rather than remain the domain of the fine arts.

The final reading in this part, 'In Plato's Cave', is by scholar and cultural critic Susan Sontag. The essay is the opening chapter of Sontag's famous 1977 book *On Photography*. Sontag offers a broad overview of the medium of photography, specifically emphasizing its interconnections with social relations. She discusses the documentary status of the image, its function in the construction of knowledge and memory, and the power associated with the act of photographing. For Sontag, the photographic image is an inextricable part of life in the twentieth century.

As in her other writings, this essay is rich with thoughtful and provocative claims. For example, early in the essay Sontag writes: 'To collect photographs is to collect the world.' This assertion points to the tremendous power of the photographic image and its ability to stand in as a referent for objects and events in the live world. Like Ivins, Sontag emphasizes the extent to which we gain knowledge and experience through interaction with the photographic image. She writes: 'Ultimately, having an experience becomes identical with taking a photograph of it, and participating in a public event comes more and more to be equivalent to looking at it in photographed form.' And while Sontag was addressing traditional film-based photography in the 1970s, her claim is easily extended to encompass contemporary forms of photographic representation, such as that produced by compact digital cameras, cellphones, and other wireless devices. Indeed, now more than ever our knowledge of and experience in the world comes through the mediation of lens and screen.

The work of William Ivins, Jr., Rudolph Arnheim, and Susan Sontag has been of primary importance in bringing critical analysis to visual representation and visual communication. These scholars' essays effectively highlight the uniqueness of visual representation as a mode of communication as well as the situatedness of image production and reception. Most importantly, the essays rightfully position images and visual communication as inextricably bound to social life and, therefore, as sites that demand dedicated and in-depth study.

1

RECAPITULATION

WILLIAM M. IVINS, JR.

While the number of printed pictures and designs that have been made as works of art is very large, the number made to convey visual information is many times greater. Thus the story of prints is not, as many people seem to think, that of a minor art form but that of a most powerful method of communication between men and of its effects upon western European thought and civilization.

We cannot understand this unless we bear in mind some of the basic factors in communication between human beings.

Whatever may be the psychological and physiological processes which we call knowing and thinking, we are only able to communicate the results of that knowing and thinking to other men by using one or another kind of symbolism. Of the various methods of making such symbolic communication there can be little doubt that the two most useful and important are provided by words and pictures. Both words and pictures have been known to man since the most remote times. In fact, it may be said that until the animal had used them he had not become man.

While both words and pictures are symbols, they are different in many ways of the greatest importance. So little are they equivalent to each other that if communication were confined to either alone, it would become very limited in its scope. All words need definitions, in the sense that to talk about things we have to have names for them. Verbal definition is a regress from word to word, until finally it becomes necessary to point to something which we say is what the last word in the verbal chain of definition means. Frequently the most convenient way of pointing is to make a picture. The word then receives definition, or, if one likes, the thing receives a name, by the association of a sensuous awareness with an oral or visual symbol.

Any legible written word, whether it be drawn painfully by an illiterate or written in flowing calligraphy by a writing master, remains the same word no matter how it may look. The same thing is true of the sound of the spoken word, with all its personal peculiarities and local accents. The reason for this is that any particular specimen, whether spoken, written, or printed, is merely a representative member of a class of arbitrary forms of sounds and visual signs, which we have learned or agreed to regard as having the same meanings. In every instance it is the class of arbitrary forms that has the definition as a word and not any particular oral or visual specimen. Thanks to this it is possible for a word to be exactly repeated, for what is given in repetition is not the same unique specimen but another equally representative member of the same class of arbitrary forms.

Hand-made pictures, to the contrary, we are aware of as unique things; we all see the differences between them and know the impossibility of repeating any of them exactly by mere muscular action. Thus so long as the only way there was of describing objects was by the use of repeatable words and unrepeatable hand-made pictures, it was never possible from an oral or visual description to identify any object as being a particular object and not merely a member of some class. In thinking about this we have to remember that identification of the location, the function, or some particular marking of an object, is not a description of the object.

Except for the words which are proper names or syntactical devices, a word is merely a name for a class of relations, qualities, or actions. The consequence of this is that what we call verbal description is very often no more than the accumulation of a series of class names. It is much like the game we play on board ship when we toss loose rings of rope about a peg. No one of the rings closely fits the peg. If it did we could not toss it over the peg. As it is each ring can go over a great many very different pegs. But by tossing a great many very loose verbal rings over an object we think that we describe the object. Thus when we endeavour to make a full and accurate verbal description of even the simplest things, such for instance as an ordinary kitchen can opener, we accumulate such an enormous and complicated heap of verbal rings that it becomes practically impossible for anyone but a highly trained specialist to understand what we have said. This is the reason the toolmaker wants not a verbal description of the thing he is asked to make but a careful picture of it. It is doubtful if any much more intricate intellectual process can be imagined than the translation of a linear series of verbal symbols, arranged in an analytical, syntactical time order, into an organization of concrete materials, and shapes, and colours, all existing simultaneously in a three-dimensional space. If this is true of such simple abstract forms as those of can openers, it takes little thought to realize what the situation is in regard to the infinitely complex and accidental shapes that occur in nature and in art. It brings home to us the utter necessity of properly made pictures if we wish to convey our ideas in exact and meaningful ways. Certainly, without pictures most of our modern highly developed technologies could not exist. Without them we could have neither the tools we require nor the data about which we think.

Furthermore, science and technology, for their full fruition, need more than just a picture; they need a picture that, like the words of verbal description, can be exactly repeated. A word or a sentence that could not be exactly repeated would have no meaning. Exact repetition is of the essence for words, for without it they would be merely meaningless signs or sounds. Without exact repetition of the verbal symbols there would be no verbal communication, no law, no science, no literature. There would be only animal expression, like that of the barn yard. Over the years a good many people can see a picture, and many pictures can be sent travelling about the world. But, even so, a unique picture can make its communication to very few people, and it can only make it in one place at a time. There is a distinct limit to the number of persons who can seriously see and study and work from any single unique picture. As we have seen, the Greek botanists were fully aware of the limitation upon the use of hand-made pictures as a means of communicating exact ideas of shapes and colours. The reason for this limitation was that the Greeks, like their predecessors and, for many generations, their successors, had no way of making exactly repeatable pictures. They could only make copies of pictures, and when hand-made copies are made from hand-made copies it takes only a small number of copies for the final copy to bear no practically useful resemblance to the original. The meaning of this should be obvious so far as concerns the dissemination of accurate information about forms and shapes. In short, prior to the Renaissance, there was no way of publishing a picture as there was of a text.

While this is never mentioned by the historians of thought and art, of science and technology, it undoubtedly had much to do with the slowness of the development of science and technology and the thought based on them. Communication is absolutely necessary for scientific and especially technological development, and to be effective it must be accurate and exactly repeatable. Science in actual practice is not a dead body of acquired information but an actively growing accumulation of hypotheses put forth to be tried and tested by many people. This trying and testing cannot be done without exact repeatability of communication. What one or two men have thought and done does not become science until it has been adequately communicated to other men.

The conventional exact repeatability of the verbal class symbols gave words a position in the thought of the past that they no longer hold. The only important things the ancients could exactly repeat were verbal formulae. Exact repeatability and permanence are so closely alike that the exactly repeatable things easily become thought

of as the permanent or real things, and all the rest are apt to be thought of as transient and thus as mere reflections of the seemingly permanent things. This may seem a matter of minor moment, but I have little doubt that it had much to do with the origin and development of the Platonic doctrine of Ideas and the various modifications of it that have tangled thought until the present day. The analytical syntax of sentences composed of words certainly had much to do with the origin of the notions of substance and attributable qualities, which has not only played a formative role in the history of philosophy but for long presented one of the most formidable hurdles in the path of developing scientific knowledge. At any rate, until comparatively recent times nominalism, with its emphasis on facts, its distrust of words, and its interest in how things act rather than in what they essentially are, has had little chance, and its great development has coincided remarkably with the ever-broadening development of modern pictorial methods of record and communication.

Some time at the end of the fourteenth or beginning of the fifteenth centuries men in western Europe began to make pictorial woodcuts, but no one knows when or where. For all we know it may have started simultaneously in many different places. By the middle of the fifteenth century men were engraving, and before its end they were etching. Printing from movable types began presumably in the 1440s; by the middle of the 1450s the Gutenberg Bible had been printed; and about 1461 the *Edelstein* came from the press. The *Edelstein* was merely a book of popular tales, but its pages were decorated with woodcuts. At the time they had no informational value or purpose. In 1467 the *Torquemada* was printed. It was a book of devotion, but illustrated with rough woodcuts representing definite particular things—the pictures with which a named and located church had been decorated. In 1472 the *Valturius* appeared. It was full of woodcuts of machinery, which were specifically intended to convey information. Shortly after 1480 the first illustrated botany book appeared. Its woodcuts were the last of a long series of copies of copies that started far back of the ninth century, and in consequence bore no relation to the things they were supposed to represent. In 1485 came the first printed botany book with illustrations drawn at first hand from the plants described in the text. In 1486 Rewich illustrated and printed the first illustrated travel book, the famous *Breydenbach*. Rewich had accompanied the author on his travels and drew the things they saw. In that same year three colours were first used in the printing of illustrations. In 1493 several illustrated catalogues of precious objects in the possession of some of the German cathedrals were printed. These appear to be the first printed illustrated catalogues of any kind of collections. By the middle of the fifteen-hundreds illustrated books about every conceivable kind of subject were coming from the presses of Europe in an ever increasing flood. Conspicuous among them were books about architecture, botany, machinery, anatomy, zoology, costumes, archaeology, numismatics, and, specially, some of the technologies and crafts. The single-sheet print in the various mediums then available had begun its task of carrying across Europe in all directions information about buildings and works of art that themselves never travelled. The rapid pervasion of the Italian Renaissance and Baroque styles was accomplished by the single-sheet print and the illustration.

Nothing like this had ever been known before. The same identical pictorial statements were made in each example of the edition, whether of a single-sheet print or of an illustrated book. While for at least several thousand years men had been accustomed to having texts that repeated the same statements—Pliny the Younger, shortly after AD 100, referred casually to an edition of a thousand copies—now for the first time men were getting accustomed to pictures that repeated the same statements. It began to be possible to convey invariant visual information about things that words were incompetent to describe or define.

With few exceptions, these illustrations prior to the middle of the fifteen-hundreds were what used to be called 'facsimile woodcuts', i.e. woodcuts made by cutting away the surface of a wooden block between the lines drawn on it by a draughtsman. This was not a translation of the draughtsman's lines but a saving of them, as many of the woodcutters were so skilful that the 'hands' of the draughtsmen can be recognized in the prints from the blocks. This skill made it possible for first-hand pictorial statements to appear in books, not only in some volume or volumes but in every copy of the entire edition of a book.

The first-hand pictorial statement by a competent draughtsman has much the same value as the testimony of a first-hand witness. If he is sharp-sighted and observant he can tell us much about an object or an action, but nevertheless his training and habit of seeing and drawing lead him to select certain things for statements and to omit others from them. Each school of art had its scheme for laying lines, and these schemes in time became neither more nor less than grammars and syntaxes which, while making handmade pictorial statements possible, also greatly restricted and influenced their power of statement. Much as he might want to, a German in the fifteenth or sixteenth century could not draw like an Italian, or *vice versa*. This meant that neither could say the same things in his drawings that the other could. We get sharp evidence of this in the copies that each made from the other—the Germans copying Italian engravings and the Italians copying German engravings. Although the specific lines of the original were there before him, the copyist never actually followed them closely in his copy, and rarely made any attempt to do so. Except in the most generalized of ways no two drawings, even one copied from the other, gave the same particularities. Especially was this true when the copy was not only a copy but a translation into another medium. The results of this are perhaps most easily to be seen in the prints after works of art, for in none of them are we able to find the kind of qualitative statement that is necessary for connoisseurship of the work of art itself. As represented in the prints it was impossible to tell the most arrant fake from the original.

However, no matter what its defects might be, the first-hand visual statement in a print had the great advantage that it was exactly repeatable and invariant. This meant that in things like the descriptive sciences, such for instance as botany and anatomy, it was possible to produce what we may think of as representations that were standardized to the extent of the size of the edition. So long as the subject of the print was not a particularity but a generalized statement of the generic traits of some kind of object the situation was good enough. In fact, even today when we want to give a statement not of personal characteristics but of abstracted generic forms we still use drawings for our illustrations.

In the middle of the fifteen-hundreds several very important things happened in print making that were to have unsuspected results. The woodcut broke down under the constant demand for more and more information in the available spaces. To pack more pictorial information in a given space, the lines have to be made finer and closer together. This led to the making of woodblocks with such minutely reticulated surfaces that for practical purposes the printers were unable to get good impressions from the blocks with the paper and the techniques of printing that were then available. Whereas it is easy to find copies of the earlier books containing good impressions of their coarser blocks, it is sometimes exceedingly difficult to find copies of later books that contain good impressions from their finely worked blocks. It is probable that many of the most important picture books of the mid fifteen-hundreds never contained good impressions from their blocks.

The engraving, however, did not suffer from this technical difficulty. Its lines could be very fine and very close together, as compared to those on any wood-block, and still yield a sufficient quantity of clear impressions on the papers then available. I think it can be said that this fact had much to do with the general increase in the use of engraving for illustrations that took place after the middle of the fifteen-hundreds. In any event, by the end of the century the engraving had taken the place of the woodcut in all but very few of the books made for the educated classes. This was not, as has been said, a mere superficial change in fashion, it was a basic change in modes and techniques made in response to an insistent demand for fuller visual information. In so far as there was a fashion as distinct from any need, I believe the fashion merely followed the norm set by the informational demand.

It thus becomes necessary to think about engraving and etching which, from our present point of view, are to be regarded as varieties of the same technique. In the first years of engraving the engravers had been gold- and silversmiths. Then trained draughtsmen began to make engravings and, naturally, they used the linear schemes and syntaxes to which they were accustomed in their pen drawings and those of their schools. The German syntactical scheme was very different from the Italian. In the early years of the sixteenth century Marc Antonio and others after him began to make engravings after drawings, paintings, and sculpture by other men. These prints were made and sold not so much as works of art but rather as informational documents about works of art. Thus Dürer, in his Netherlands diary, refers to prints after Raphael as 'Raphaels Ding', which he knew they were not. Marc Antonio evolved a novel scheme for the translation of sculpture into engraved reproductions. Instead of reporting about the surfaces of objects, their textures, their colour values, and the play of light across them, he devised a linear net which enabled him schematically to indicate their bosses and hollows. The most particular personal characteristics of the original works of art, their brush strokes and chisel marks, were thus omitted, and what was transmitted in the print was little more than an indication of iconography combined with generalized shapes and masses. At the end Marc Antonio used the same linear scheme in engraving Raphael's drawings and paintings that he had worked out for ancient sculpture—the characterless 'Roman copies' of Greek statues. It is important to remember this, for it had momentous consequences.

It is to be noticed that while the early engravers on occasion made prints of late medieval objects, such as Schongauer's 'Censer', it is difficult to find a reproductive print of such an object by any of the engravers who grew up in the linear syntaxes that came after Marc Antonio. For practical purposes it is impossible to find a reproductive print by one of the masters of engraving that represents an early painting or a piece of medieval sculpture. Such medieval statues as were reproduced were reproduced not carefully for their own sakes but merely as hastily indicated details in architectural ensembles. The vast number of these medieval things still in existence shows that they have always been held precious by somebody, if not as works of art at least as examples of skill, as antiquities, or as relics. Thus the lack of engraved reproductions of them cannot be explained simply on the ground of a change in taste or fashion. A much more likely explanation is to be found in the fact that they did not yield themselves to the kind of rendering which was implicitly required by the dominant and highly schematized linear practice of engraving. When you have no vocabulary with which to discuss a subject, you do not talk very much about that subject.

Marc Antonio's method was rapidly adopted and developed by engravers everywhere, for it had the great business advantages that it was easily learned and could be used, no matter how libellously, for many different kinds of subject matter. The very limited average instrument of a very limited average purpose, it became the dominant style of engraving in spite of the fact that it made it impossible for the engraver who used it to catch and hold the particular characteristics that gave the originals their unique qualities. Everything that went through the procrustean engraving shops came out of them in a form that had been schematized and made reasonable—and reasonability meant conformity to the generalized abstract conventional webbing of lines that was an incident of manufacture. As every great work of art is as by definition unconventional in its most important aspects, a representation of it in terms of a convention that leaves out those aspects is by definition a misrepresentation.

Shortly after Marc Antonio began his grammatical or syntactical investigations, the print publisher and dealer began to make his appearance. He was a manufacturer-merchant, and often was not himself an engraver. He employed others to make prints not of subjects that interested them, but of subjects that he thought he might be able to sell. Very often that could have been the only interest that he himself took in them. Some of the publishers had the engravers work for them in their shops, just as though they had been mechanics. As ideas of business

efficiency came in, the engraver gradually ceased to make the drawings after the originals he reproduced. The publishers procured drawings of the objects they wanted to make reproductions of. These were then handed to the engravers, who copied and translated them on to their copper plates, generally without ever having seen the objects their work was supposed to represent. The consequence was that the prints which came out of these efficient shops were at best second- or third-hand accounts of their distant originals, and, not only that, translations of translations as well as copies of copies. The scheme of operation made it impossible to give any pictorial report of such things as the brush work, the chisel strokes or the surfaces, of the originals—which, in fact, were the originals. Moreover, the prints became filled with clichés of representation based on the requirements of the linear syntax that had been adopted by the engraving craft, which interposed a flat veto on the representation of the most personal of all the traits of the original work of art. The linear network varied but little in its general scale, although the objects that were engraved, be they large or small, were all reduced or enlarged to a few typical scales which had no relation to the sizes of the originals. This had important effects on the vision of the people who used the engravings.

Naturally this schematic network of lines became the medium for the exhibition of a great deal of virtuosity, not of keen reporting but of the handling of the lines in the network. The extravagances of the virtuosi had their immediate effect on the day's work of the more humble artisans of the copper plate. The textures of the network became ends in themselves and not merely aids to statement. Form and content were separated, and both got lost.

When engraving became a capitalist enterprise it became important to get as many impressions from the engraved or etched copper plate as possible with as little difference as might be between them. Towards the end of the sixteenth and the beginning of the seventeenth century this problem was worked at with great business acumen by a number of men in different places. Among these men there may be mentioned Rubens, the painter, Callot, the etcher, and Abraham Bosse, who wrote the standard technical treatise on the craft. These men invented and rationalized ways of laying and sinking lines on plates in such a way that the plates would yield very large editions before they wore out. This not only affected the weave of the linear net, but increased its independence from accuracy in reporting.

Rubens, if not actually the first important artist to have a financial interest in the reproduction of his work, was the first to create about himself a school of engravers who specialized in the reproduction of his pictures, and often was himself either the publisher or a partner in the publishing firms. Anthony van Dyck, his famous painter pupil, used the services of a group of these engravers of the Rubens school to produce a set of over a hundred portraits, the first few of which he himself had etched. The set ran through many editions, and its coppers were still being printed from in the present century. The influence of the set can be traced in many engraved portraits until the second half of the nineteenth century. In a way it may be regarded as having provided the norm for much of subsequent portrait-engraving and etching.

In France, the only country that had a single artistic capital, engraving had a popularity perhaps greater than it enjoyed anywhere else. The French engravers of the seventeenth century embarked on a search for linear methods that would be economically efficient and at the same time afford opportunity to show off their skill and agility in the choreography of their self-assumed goose steps. Their skill in these goose steps soon became of more importance than the fidelity with which they reproduced their originals. Some of them engraved in parallel lines, others evolved elaborate schemes of highly artificial cross-hatchings, some became experts in the sheen of satins and metal and the barbering of hair. The subjects to be engraved were undoubtedly chosen to enable them to shine in their specialties. Few of the masterpieces of art did this.

In the eighteenth century the French fashion for framed drawings in interior decoration led to the attempt to give closer reproduction of the superficial qualities of the drawings that the engravers worked from. Up to this time engravings had looked like engravings and nothing else, but now, thanks to the discovery of new techniques, the test of their success began to be the extent to which they looked like something else. Among the new techniques used for this purpose were aquatint and stipple, and soft-ground etching, the crayon manner, and others still. Some of the plates began to be printed in colour the more closely to imitate the drawings and watercolours.In the seventeenth century mezzotinting, a blurry medium devoid of sharp accents, had been invented as a way of reproducing oil paintings in tones instead of in lines. Except in England, where painting was lower in key than in France, it was not much used. One of the curious things about all these new techniques of making prints is that so little original work was ever done in them. Goya was the only great artist ever to produce more than a sporadic essay in aquatint. The best artists to make more than an odd soft-ground etching were Girtin and Cotman. Turner made a few reproductive mezzotints after his own drawings. But I doubt if any great artist has ever regularly used any of the other methods for his firsthand expression. I think it can be said that as a rule the great artist has habitually used only such graphic processes as are comparatively direct, and that the desire for expression is incompatible with the indirections, the technical complexities, and the linear routine that mark most of the reproductive techniques. Direct a process as engraving was in the hands of the primitive masters, and notably in those of such men as Pollaiuolo and Mantegna, it is to be noted that from the point of view of the artist the 'facsimile woodcut' was still easier, for all that he had to do was to make a stylized drawing on the block which was then cut by a skilled mechanic. Even such a complete master of the technique of engraving as Dürer actually designed many more woodcuts than he made engravings, and, if we omit six or eight of his most popular engravings from the count, his most interesting work was done on the block. A further reflection of this easiness of the woodcut is to be seen in the fact that Holbein and Burgkmair made no engravings, and that Baldung and Cranach made but a very few. The wide spread of etching among original artists in the seventeenth century and again in the nineteenth century can probably be accounted for by the fact that it was the most direct and simplest method of making printing surfaces that was known prior to the invention of lithography.

However there is no getting away from the other fact that the easiest way for the original artist was to have his work copied by the professional reproductive engravers. The result was that by the end of the eighteenth century single-sheet prints and book illustrations had, with few exceptions, become mere second- and third-hand statements, in which everything had been reduced to the average common-sense level of craftsman's shop work. By the end of the eighteenth century the first-hand visual statement had practically ceased to exist in the illustration of books, and in the single-sheet print it had become the rare exception. In France, at least, the manufacturing situation in the engraving shops had become even more complicated than it had been in the past, for the printing surfaces were often made by several men, beginning with an etcher, who laid in the outlines of the print from the drawing, and winding up with a finisher-engraver, who went over the etched lines and filled in between and reduced everything to the neat, tidy, characterless, and fashionable, net of rationality of engraving. Sometimes some equivalent of the quality of the drawings for the engraver made a ghostly flicker in the first etched states, but by the time that the finishers had done their work of degradation all qualitative equivalence to the originals and to the drawings for the engraver had completely vanished. The things that counted in public estimation were the brilliant moiré of the damask of the engraved lines and the sentimentality of the general situations represented.

I personally have no doubt that the growth of pictorial reasonability in the eighteenth century was based on the economics and shop practices of the business of print manufacture. Neither have I any doubt that this business had a great effect on the public as well as on the artists, for it was through the engraved picture that the world received its visual notions about most of the things it had not seen and studied with its own eyes—which is to say about most of the things in the world. One might think, if one had not waded through the contents of some of the great historic collections of old prints and illustrated books, that any visual report of a work of art would always tell much the same story about it, no matter where or when it was made, but the fact is that the reproductive prints and illustrations contained far more of the linear syntaxes and shop practices of their places and times of production than they did of the detail or character of the originals they purported to represent. Actually the buyers had come to appreciate prints and illustrations far more for the skill of their makers in the artificial dance steps of the engraver's tool than for any representational fidelity.

Then the poor and the uneducated did not have reproductions. But the rich and the educated did, and their reproductions had a great effect upon their vision, which, as today, was based not so much on acquaintance with originals as on acquaintance with reproductions. I have spoken of the net of engraved lines and all that it omitted, but there was another equally important factor for vision in the old engraved reproductions. The sizes of the printed reproductions bore no necessary relation to the sizes of the originals. In the printed picture the great mural might easily be smaller than a little portrait, a jewel greater in size than a façade. Further, in the handmade reproduction all trace of the handling of his tools by the maker of the original had vanished. There was no difference in the engravings between the texture of a painting by a young Raphael and that by an aged Titian, or between the surfaces of a 'Roman copy', a Greek original, and a Gothic sculpture. The wilful theatrical stroke of Rubens's brush in one of his sketches, like the dominant expressive gouge of Michelangelo's chisel, was smoothed out and obliterated. If the original artist had resorted to shorthand in his statement of any form, the engravers spelled it out at length in terms of the most commonplace vision and cliché of rendering. Had the engravers worked from the originals more than they did, and less from poor sketches by poor draughtsmen, this might not have happened to the same extent. But, whoever might have tried it would still have faced the problem of the longevity of his plates, and that absolutely required the artificial net work of line. Steel facing was not discovered until photography was in use.

As it was, a blighting common sense descended on the vision of the educated world. This showed itself not only in the terms in which that world talked about art but in the contemporary art the world relished. Its principal interest had been diverted by the means of reproduction away from the actual qualities of the originals and works of art and directed to generated notions about their subject matters. Thus the century failed to take account in art, just as so much of it did in writing, of the thing that Pascal in the seventeenth century had pointed out about writing—that the quality of a statement consists more in the choice and arrangement of the particular symbols used in making it than in its general sense (*Les sens recoivent des paroles leur dignité, au lieu de la leur donner*). The eighteenth century talked about harmony, proportion, dignity, nobility, grandeur, sublimity, and many other common-sense abstract verbal notions based upon the gross generalities of the subject matter that came through into the engraved reproductions. The sharp particularities of which works of art are necessarily constructed and which give them their character and value were unknown and unmentioned for they escaped verbal description and were never reproduced in the reproductions. Thus, in spite of Winckelmann's remarks about engravings and the necessity of knowing the originals, the aesthetic doctrine of his *History of Ancient Art* of 1764 may be regarded as the rationalization of a set of values based on the catch of the engraver's net. The same thing can be said of most of the critical discussion in such a standard book as Bosanquet's *History of Aesthetic* which was published in 1892, i.e. at a time when the photomechanical processes were still in a very unsatisfactory state of development. It is amusing to think how few of the great weavers of aesthetic theory had any familiar first-hand acquaintance with works of art and how many of them either, like Lessing, knew the art they talked about only through engravings, or else sieved their ideas out of the empty air. Had it not been for this it is doubtful whether

the Milords who made the grand tours would have been so happy and complaisant about all the poor copies of High Renaissance pictures and all the bad 'Roman' imitations of classical sculpture which they brought back to the North.

We can catch a glimpse of what was going on in still another way. Very few of us ever think to what an extent the painters of the fancy subjects and historical compositions, which were so generally admired during much of the eighteenth century and the first part of the nineteenth century, produced their canvasses to be engraved rather than to be seen in their paint. The sale of the painting was often of less importance than the sale of the prints after it. Hogarth knew this very well. The patronage of Mr. Alderman Boydell, the great print publisher, meant more to many an English painter than did that of His Majesty and a dozen dukes. Today in America we have a curious analogue in the novelists who write for the sale of their 'movie rights' rather than for the sale of their books.

At the end of the eighteenth century a number of things happened which were to have remarkable consequences. Men discovered that, by using the engraver's tool on the end of the grain of the wood instead of a knife on its side, it was possible to produce wood-blocks from which the finest of lines and tints could be printed in great quantities. Paper, smooth paper, began to be made by machinery run by power in a continuous process. Iron printing presses came into being, and in 1815 one was invented that was run by power and not by the strength of men's backs. The number of impressions that could be run off in an hour was greatly multiplied. Stereotyping was remembered and put to practical use. In 1797 Senefelder discovered how to make lithographs; Wedgwood in 1802 announced the first practical step towards Talbot's later discovery of photography. By early in the 1830s the book publishers had discovered that there was a great market for cheap illustrated books, magazines, and cyclopaedias, directed at the man in the street and not at the classically educated gentleman in his elegant library. Among these publications were many that dealt with techniques and the processes of making and doing things, and it was not long before the ordinary man, the uneducated man who used his hands and who knew how to read and to look intelligently at explanatory pictures, was finding out much from which he had been effectually debarred. The crafts instead of being the 'arts and mysteries' of highly restricted trades and guilds were thrown open to anyone who had the ability to teach himself from a book. Out of all this came such a rush of inventions and new processes as had never before been known. The same thing happened in many of the sciences and for much the same reasons. At least in England, which took the lead in all this invention and investigation, the outstanding engineers and scientists for a long time were not the graduates of the classicizing 'public schools' and the universities, but the ingeniously self-educated. It had great moral and ethical results, as well as economic and social ones.

In art, the lithograph made it possible for such artists as Goya and Delacroix to send out into the world their own drawings, not in unique specimens but in editions. Each impression had all their personality and all their daring, unhampered and unspoiled by the intermediary engravers. Things like Goya's 'Bull Fights of Bordeaux' and Delacroix's illustrations for *Faust* blew a great hurricane through the dead air of the single-sheet print and the book illustration in France. It shortly produced Daumier.

In the 1830s Talbot and Daguerre worked out photography and the daguerreotype, and in a little while it became possible for the first time to have reproductions of works of art that had not been distorted and vulgarized by the middleman draughtsman and engraver—to have reports of works of art that had not been reduced to the syntax and the blurring technical necessities of a manufacturing trade and craft. For the first time it became possible to have a reproduction of a drawing or a painting or a piece of sculpture that told enough about the surface of its original for anyone who studied it to tell something about the qualities of the original. By the third quarter of the century many experiments had been made towards getting the photograph translated into printer's ink without the intervention of either the draughtsman or the engraver. About 1860,

Bolton, an English wood-engraver, thought of having a photograph made on his block of wood so that he could engrave a piece of sculpture without having to get a draughtsman to draw it on the block for him. This eliminated one of the two chief obstacles to getting truthful reproductions into the pages of books. Bolton's method remained the principal way of making book illustrations until the end of the century. In the seventies attempts were made to produce what we now call halftones. This came to fruition in the eighties and nineties with the invention of the ruled cross-line halftone screen, a device which made it possible to make a printing surface for a pictorial report in which neither the draughtsman nor the engraver had had a hand. Its great importance lay in the fact that the lines of the process as distinct from the lines of the visual report could be below the threshold of normal human vision. In the old hand-made processes the lines of the process and the lines of the report were the same lines, and the process counted for more than the report in the character of the lines and the statements they made. Until after the two sets of lines and dots, those of the process and those of the report, had been differentiated and separated and the lines and dots of the process had been lost to ordinary vision, as they are in the photograph and the fine halftone, there had been no chance of getting an accurate report. Man had at last achieved a way of making visual reports that had no interfering symbolic linear syntax of their own. In the whole history of human communication it is doubtful if any more extraordinary step had ever been taken than this.

Within a very few years the new method had overrun the world. Not only did it revolutionize printing, but it gave such accuracy of reporting as had never previously been dreamed of. It was prerequisite to the existence of all our popular magazines and of our illustrated newspapers. It has brought about a very complete restudy and rewriting of the accepted history of the arts of the past and more than that it has made all the exotic arts known of the ordinary man. It is interesting to notice how few of the books of connoisseurship published prior to 1880 are still either authoritative or on the shelves for ready reference.

The very vocabulary of art criticism has been changed, as have the qualities for which men look in works of art. Whatever else 'aesthetics' may now be, it is no longer a scholastic quasi-philosophizing whose task is to justify a tradition of forms based in equal measure on obstinate ignorance and sacrosanct revelation.

The flood of photographic images has brought about a realization of the difference between visual reporting and visual expression. So long as the two things were not differentiated in the mind of the world, the world's greater practical and necessary interest in reporting had borne down artistic expression under the burden of a demand that it be verisimilar, and that a picture should be valued not so much for what it might be in itself as for the titular subject matter which might be reported in it.

The photograph and photographic process having taken over the business of visual reporting from the hands of the pictorial reporters and the engravers, the artists suddenly found themselves absolved from any need of verisimilitude in their expression and design. A great many of them, knowing nothing whatever about either expression or design, were lost, for they too had been members of the public and had regarded verisimilitude as the purpose and the justification of their work. Except in the work of the very greatest artists, creation and verisimilitude are incompatible, contradictory aims, and it is only at the hands of these greatest artists that creation has won out in the conflict between the two. With the photograph the magic dance of the creator's hand became for the first time visible in the reports of his work. Thus photographic reproduction of works of art and of what used to be called 'curios' has raised basic questions about the validity of many of the most hard-shelled and firmly entrenched doctrines about both art and beauty. It has changed Asiatic and African Polynesian and Amerindian curiosities into works of art. It has revealed to the public for the first time something of the actual qualities of the Greek and later European arts of the past. It has brought about not only a reconsideration of the curious and ambiguous notion of the masterpiece—which often was no more than the object or picture which

particularly lent itself to the linear net of the engraving—but it has caused many famous and adulated things to fall from grace and bestowed grace upon many unknown ones. It has made the western European world see that 'beauty', as it had known it, so far from being something universal and eternal was only an accidental and transient phase of the art of a limited Mediterranean area. Beauty is no longer the absolute that the pontiffs for so long proclaimed it to be. The photograph has made it obvious that what for four centuries the European world had acclaimed as purpose and beauty in art was no more than a peculiarly local prejudice about subject matter and mode of presentation. I think it is clear that this prejudice was to a great extent based on the methods of reproduction through which artistic and factual report alike had reached the public. For generations that public had been circumscribed and made provincial by the limitations imposed by the syntaxes of its graphic techniques. It is significant, for example, that many line engravings of nudes are 'good', and that very few in any of the other techniques are. The nude was the particular fish for which the net of engraving had originally been devised. In the photograph the nude is more than apt to become either a 'naked' or a vulgarity. The nude has ceased to be the great preoccupation of the artists that it was before the pervasion of photography.

For centuries the European world had been unable to distinguish between factual reporting, with its necessary requirement of verisimilitude (of which perspective was an essential part), and that expression of values, of personality, and of attitude towards life, with which verisimilitude is always at war. As the elder Haldane once remarked, 'it is only through the constant negation of mere appearance that personality realizes itself'.[1] At last, thanks to the photograph, visual dream and expression were no longer required to conform to the informational reportorial demands of the ordinary businesses of life.

In addition to all this, the exactly repeatable pictorial statement in its photographic forms has played an operational role of the greatest importance in the development of modern science and technology of every kind. It has become an essential to most of our industries and to all of our engineering. The modern knowledge of light, like that of the atom, would have been impossible without the photograph. The complete revolution that has taken place in the basic assumptions of physics during the last 50 years could never have been accomplished without the data provided by the photographic emulsion.

The total effect of all these things upon technical philosophy has been remarkable. Many of the old problems, the 'perennial problems of thought', now seem in a way to be resolved by the discovery that at least some of them are little more than accidents of unrecognized, unanalyzed syntaxes of symbolization.

The seriousness of the role of the exactly repeatable pictorial statement in all the long development since about 1450 has escaped attention very largely because that statement has been so familiar that it has never been subjected to adequate analysis. Having been taken for granted it has been overlooked. The photograph, as of today, is the final form of that exactly repeatable pictorial statement or report. Although it has very great limitations, it has no linear syntax of its own and thus has enabled men to discover that many things of the greatest interest and importance have been distorted, obscured, and even hidden, by verbal and pictorial, i.e. symbolic, syntaxes that were too habitual to be recognized. It is unfortunate that most of the world is still unaware of this fact.

In a way, my whole argument about the role of the exactly repeatable pictorial statement and its syntaxes resolves itself into what, once stated, is the truism that at any given moment the accepted report of an event is of greater importance than the event, for what we think about and act upon is the symbolic report and not the concrete event itself.

NOTE

1. Quoted from J.S. Haldane's *Life, Mechanism and Personality,* by permission of Mr. John Murray.

2

VISION IN EDUCATION

RUDOLPH ARNHEIM

Visual perception, far from being a mere collector of information about particular qualities, objects, and events, turned out to be concerned with the grasping of generalities. By furnishing images of kinds of qualities, kinds of objects, kinds of events, visual perception lays the groundwork of concept formation. The mind, reaching far beyond the stimuli received by the eyes directly and momentarily, operates with the vast range of imagery available through memory and organizes a total lifetime's experience into a system of visual concepts. The thought mechanisms by which the mind manipulates these concepts operate in direct perception, but also in the interaction between direct perception and stored experience, as well as in the imagination of the artist, the scientist, and indeed any person handling problems 'in his head'.

If these affirmations are valid, they must profoundly influence our view of art and science, and all the rest of cognitive activity located between these poles. Art has been discussed here principally as a fundamental means of orientation, born from man's need to understand himself and the world in which he lives. As I mentioned before, the various other purposes served by art can be shown to depend on this basic cognitive function. Art, then, approaches the means and ends of science very closely, and for the present purpose it is more important to recognize how much they have in common than to insist on what distinguishes them.

WHAT IS ART FOR?

Perhaps the arts have been prevented in our time from fulfilling their most important function by being honoured too much. They have been lifted out of the context of daily life, exiled by exultation, imprisoned in awe-inspiring treasure-houses. Schools and museums, especially in our own country, have done much to overcome this isolation. They have made works of art more accessible and familiar. But works of art are not the whole of art; they are only its rare peaks. In order to regain the indispensable benefits of art, we need to think of those works as the most evident results of a more universal effort to give visible form to all aspects of life. It is no longer possible to view the hierarchy of art as dominated by the fine arts, the aristocracy of painting and sculpture, while the so-called applied arts, architecture and the other varieties of design, are relegated to the base of the pyramid as impure compromises with utility. The artists of our time have gone a long way in making the old categories inapplicable by replacing the traditional works of the brush and the chisel with objects and arrangements that must merge in the environment of daily life if they are to have any place at all. One more step, and the shaped setting of all human existence becomes the primary concern of art—a setting in which the particular objects of fine art find their particular place.

This broader concept, which the late Ananda K. Coomaraswamy defended so lucidly as 'the normal view of art', must be supplemented by a psychological and educational approach that recognizes art as visual form, and visual form as the principal medium of productive thinking. Nothing less will serve to free art from its unproductive isolation.

At the beginning of this book, I referred to the widespread neglect of art at all levels of our educational system. This situation prevails largely because art educators have not stated their case

convincingly enough. If one looks through the literature on art education one often finds the value of art taken so much for granted that a few stock phrases are considered sufficient to make the point. There is a tendency to treat the arts as an independent area of study and to assume that intuition and intellect, feeling and reasoning, art and science coexist but do not co-operate. If it is found that high school students know little about art history or cannot tell an etching from a lithograph, or an oil painting from a watercolour, the consequences to be drawn will depend, I should think, on how important this sort of knowledge can be shown to be. If it is claimed that the value of the arts consists in developing good taste, the weight of the argument depends on whether taste is a luxury for those who can afford it or an indispensable condition of life. If art is said to be a part of our culture and therefore necessary to the equipment of every educated person, the responsible educator must ask himself whether all parts of this culture are needed for all and are accessible to all, and whether they are all equally relevant. If we hear that the arts develop and enrich the human personality and cultivate creativity, we need to know whether they do so better than other fields of study and why. The battle against one-sided intellectualism cannot be fought by nourishing a Romantic prejudice against the sciences as agents of mechanization. If the present practice of the sciences does indeed impoverish the human mind, the remedy may have to be sought in the improvement of science education and not in an escape from the sciences to the arts as a refuge. Nor are pedantry, sterility, and mechanization found only in the sciences; they are equally present in the arts.

Once it is recognized that productive thinking in any area of cognition is perceptual thinking, the central function of art in general education will become evident. The most effective training of perceptual thinking can be offered in the art studio. The scientist or philosopher can urge his disciples to beware of mere words and can insist on appropriate and clearly organized models. But he should not have to do this without the help of the artist, who is the expert on how one does organize a visual pattern. The artist knows the variety of forms and techniques available, and he has means of developing the imagination. He is accustomed to visualizing complexity and to conceiving of phenomena and problems in visual terms.

PICTURES AS PROPOSITIONS

Artists and art teachers put these talents to good use when they act on the implicit assumption that every art work is a statement about something. Every visual pattern—be it that of a painting, a building, an ornament, a chair—can be considered a proposition which, more or less successfully, makes a declaration about the nature of human existence. By no means need such a declaration be conscious. Few artists would be so able to tell in words what they intend to say, as was, for instance, Van Gogh. Many would refuse to do it, and experience has shown that artists driven by the desire to convey definite messages, such as those of a moral or social nature, are likely to fail. They are in danger of tying their imagery to stereotyped symbols. Correspondingly, insistence on such spelled-out meanings is risky in art education. 'Abstract' representations of concepts, such as *Past, Present, Future*, could fulfill a function very similar to that of doing a portrait, still life, or landscape. They could set a particular pattern of forces as a target. In order to work out an image that truly represents the student's conception of the subject, he must be resourceful, disciplined, insistent; and this is what it takes to produce art and to make its practice educationally fruitful. The rather theoretical themes used in the experiments can be supplemented with more evocative ones, of the kind used by Paul Klee as titles for his pictures: *From Gliding to Rising; Rejuvenation; Beginning Coolness; Pride; Against the Tide; Searching and Finding; Last Hope; Nasty Music.* Such exercises can help the student to realize that no standard of right or wrong can derive from purely formal criteria. Harmony, balance, variety, unity, are applicable only when there is something definite to express, be it consciously explicit or not. The handling of shape and colour is as much a search for this content and its crystallization as it is an effort to render the content clearly, harmoniously, in a balanced, unified

fashion. Exercises of this kind will also suggest to the student that any organized pattern is a carrier of meaning, whether intended or not. Similarly, it follows from this approach that the mere spontaneous outburst, the mere loosening-up and letting-go, is as incomplete a performance artistically as it is humanly. The purely Dionysian orgy, while pleasurable and sometimes needed as a reaction to restraint, calls for its Apollonian counterpart. The outlet of energy aims at the creation of form.

The depicting of natural objects, which has occupied the arts traditionally, is not different in principle from the symbolic representation of concepts. To make a picture of a human figure or a bunch of flowers is to grasp or invent a generic form pattern or structural skeleton. This sort of practice is a powerful aid in establishing the perceptual basis of cognitive functioning. No such training of the mind is accomplished by the mechanical copying of models, aimed at measurable correctness and employing the sense of sight as a measuring tool. Exact reproductions are useful for practical purposes but are made more reliably by machines, and the skill of estimating measurable quantities correctly is insignificant and better entrusted to instruments. The human brain is not suited for mechanical reproduction. It has developed in biological evolution as a means of cognitive orientation and therefore is geared exclusively to the performance of kinds of action and the creation and recognition of kinds of things.

And yet, the days in which faithful copying was considered the main educational purpose of painting and drawing are not all too far behind us. Early in our own century, a leading art educator, Georg Kerschensteiner, stated that the representation of the human figure could not be a suitable objective of drawing in the public schools because the reproductions of which the children are capable would match appearance and shape only partially and, at best, in generic approximation. 'Instruction in drawing, however, can no more be satisfied with mere approximations than can any other field of teaching.'

This purely quantitative criterion of what makes a successful image was, of course, derived from the exact sciences as they had developed since the Renaissance. But it is worth remembering that even in the sciences measurable exactness is not an ultimate value in itself but only a means of ascertaining the nature of relevant facts. The degree of exactness required of measurements depends on the nature of the facts to be identified and distinguished. The quantitative evidence of experiments must be carried far enough to show that the results are not due to accident, that is, to the noise inherent in every empirical situation. The measurements used by Kepler to determine the paths of the planets had to be precise enough to distinguish ellipse from circle with certainty. The same was true for the measurements of Ivan Pavlov, who wanted to find out whether dogs could distinguish ellipses from circles. Pavlov refined his data enough to ascertain how subtly the dogs discriminated shape and how similar the shapes had to be in order to make his subjects uneasy. The range of tolerance in scientific and technological measurements is determined by the nature of the task. Exactness beyond need is pedantry, and the final curiosity of the scientist is not satisfied by numbers. When he learns that the human germ cell contains 46 chromosomes, he wants to know why this is so, and the final answer cannot be a quantity. Both science and art, then, are after qualitative facts, and measurements are means to an end in both.

STANDARD IMAGES AND ART

If the mechanical copying of nature will not do, how about Johann Pestalozzi's ABC of visual understanding (*Anschauung*), which he placed ahead of the ABC of letters because 'conceptual thinking is built on *Anschauung*'? What Pestalozzi had in mind, in those early years of the nineteenth century, deserves our attention:

> I must point out that the ABC of *Anschauung* is the essential and the only true means of teaching how to judge the shape of all things correctly. Even so, this principle is totally neglected, up to now, to the extent of being unknown, whereas hundreds of such means are available for the teaching of numbers and language. This

lack of instructional means for the study of visual form should not be viewed as a mere gap in the education of human knowledge. It is a gap in the very foundation of all knowledge at a point to which the learning of numbers and language must be definitely subordinated. My ABC of *Anschauung* is designed to remedy this fundamental deficiency of instruction; it will ensure the basis on which the other means of instruction must be founded.

For this admirable purpose, however, Pestalozzi forced the children to draw angles, rectangles, lines, and arches, which, he said, constituted the alphabet of the shape of objects, just as letters are the elements of words. His manner of approach had its adherents throughout the nineteenth century. Peter Schmid made his pupils draw accurate likenesses of basic stereometric bodies, spheres, cylinders, slabs, as building stones of the more complex objects of nature, and as late as 1893, Konrad Lange suggested that the teacher put on the blackboard geometrically simplified line drawings of table, chair, flag, bed, or church, to be copied by the children. This use of geometrical guides in drawing goes at least as far back as Villard de Honnecourt's sketchbook, in which this French architect of the thirteenth century showed how to develop human figures or animals from triangles, rectangles, or star patterns.

There is merit in deriving the shape of an image from its underlying structural skeleton. In fact, artists commonly begin their work by sketching the overall patterns, which serve to hold it together. This procedure, however, must be distinguished, on the one hand, from mere trick techniques for the production of stereotyped drawings, and, on the other, from sets of rigidly prescribed forms, to be copied by the faithful student. This latter approach suggests to the student that there is one standardized and objectively correct shape to each kind of object and that the actual specimens encountered in the world are to be considered mere elaborations of this archetype. It is one thing to recognize the core of psychological and physical truth in this conception, and another to base the strategy of art education on it. For through art man acknowledges the full wealth of particular appearance. Instead of imposing pre-established schemata upon these appearances, he searches them for graspable forms and responds with such forms in reaction to what he sees. The form patterns suggested by a landscape or still life relate, when taken in their uniqueness, only quite indirectly to the standard shapes and meanings of trees or farmhouses or artichokes or fishes. The validity such patterns acquire in art is not primarily that of reporting about the subject matter as such but about much more generic patterns of forces reflected by the particular configuration. I mean to say that when van Gogh confronts the figure of a sower with a large, yellow sun, he makes a statement about man and light and labour that takes little more than its terminology from the standard form and character of the objects involved. He would have been hamstrung rather than helped by being required to copy standard figures of sun, man, and tree.

In the arts, then, the student meets the world of visual appearances as symbolic of significant patterns of forces in a manner quite different from the scientific use of sensory information. Sights that are accidental with regard to the objective situation become valid as carriers of meaningful patterns and can be called truthful or false, appropriate or inappropriate by standards not applicable to the statements of science. But art not only exploits the variety of appearances, it also affirms the validity of individual outlook and thereby admits a further dimension of variety. Since the shapes of art do not primarily bear witness to the objective nature of the things for which they stand, they can reflect individual interpretation and invention.

Both art and science are bent on the understanding of the forces that shape existence, and both call for an unselfish dedication to what is. Neither of them can tolerate capricious subjectivity because both are subject to their criteria of truth. Both require precision, order, and discipline because no comprehensible statement can be made without these. Both accept the sensory world as what the Middle Ages called the *signatura rerum*, the signature of things, but in quite different ways. The medieval physicians believed that

yellow flowers cure jaundice and that bloodstone stops hemorrhage; and in a less literal sense modern science still searches the appearance of things for symptoms of their character and virtues. The artist may use those yellows and reds as equally revealing images of radiance or passion; and the arts welcome the multiplicity of world views, the variety of personal and cultural styles, because the diversity of response is as legitimate an aspect of reality as that of the things themselves.

This is why the criteria of exactness in art are quite different from those in science. In a scientific demonstration, the particular appearance of what is shown matters for the validity of the experiment only to the extent to which it is symptomatic of the facts. The shape of containers, the size of dials, the precise colour of a substance may be irrelevant. Similarly, the particular proportions, angles, colours of a diagram may not matter. This is because in science the appearances of things are mere indicators, pointing beyond themselves to hidden constellations of forces. The laboratory demonstration and the diagram in the textbook are not scientific statements but only illustrations of such statements. In the arts the image is the statement. It contains and displays the forces about which it reports. Therefore, all of its visual aspects are relevant parts of what is being said. In a still life, the particular colours and shapes of the bottles and their arrangement are the form of the message presented by the artist.

LOOKING AND UNDERSTANDING

The arts tell the student about the significance of direct experience and of his own response. In this sense, they are complementary to the message of science, where direct experience must be transcended and the individual outlook of each observer counts only to the extent to which it contributes to shaping the one common conception of the phenomenon under investigation. When a student of biology or psychology looks at a piece of nature or a sample of behaviour, he cannot be satisfied with organizing what he sees into a visual image. He must try to relate this direct image to another one, namely, that of some mechanism operative in the perceived object or happening. This relation is not often simple because nature was not shaped with the purpose of disclosing its inner workings and functions to human eyes. Nature was not fashioned by a designer. Its visual appearance is only an indirect by-product of its physical being.

The experienced physician, mechanic, or physiologist looking at a wound, an engine, a microscopic preparation, 'sees' things the novice does not see. If both, experts and laymen, were asked to make exact copies of what they see, their drawings would be quite different. N.R. Hanson has pointed out that such 'seeing' is not simply a matter of tacking different interpretations to one and the same percept,—of requiring visual grist to go into an intellectual mill. The expert and the novice see different things, and different experts see differently also:

> To say that Tycho and Kepler, Simplicius and Galileo, Hooke and Newton, Priestley and Lavoisier, Soddy and Einstein, De Broglie and Born, Heisenberg and Bohm all make the same observations but use them differently is too easy. It does not explain controversy in research science. Were there no sense in which they were different observations they could not be used differently.

But how can the same retinal imprint lead to different percepts? What exactly do different observers see differently? First of all, many sights are ambiguous because they are so vague that they can be organized according to various patterns or because they admit more than one clearcut organization. Every textbook of psychology shows reversible images oscillating between two mutually exclusive versions; but they are only the most obvious demonstration of the fact that most visual patterns can be seen in more than one way. Max Wertheimer gives the example of a geometrical problem solved most easily by the restructuring of a figure (Figure 2.1). The perceptual tendency toward simplest structure favours the view of a square overlaid by an oblique parallelogram; but in order to find the area of square plus parallelogram when lines *a* and *b* are given,

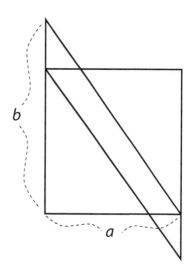

FIGURE 2.1

the figure is better seen as a combination of two overlapping triangles, each with the area $\frac{ab}{2}$. Here the same visual stimulus yields two different percepts through two different groupings of the elements, one of them better suited to the solution of the problem than the other. If the observer happens to have right-angular triangles on his mind, he is likely to hit on the solution more easily. Better still, if he were shown an animated cartoon with two triangles roaming on empty ground and finally coming to rest in the position of Figure 2.1, he should have no trouble at all. A congenial context would guide his perception.

In other instances it is not the grouping of the elements that changes, but the character of the dynamic vectors. The spatial orientation of the reversible cube (Figure 2.2) depends on the direction in which the diagonal vectors are seen to move. Since these perceptual vectors are given only through the shapes, the same figure can often carry more than one pattern of forces.

In many instances, the desired goal pattern can be directly perceived in the problem situation. The two triangles can be seen in Figure 2.1. Armed with the image of what to look for, the hunter, the birdwatcher, the mathematician, or microscopist recognizes it within the complexity of given shapes. Pertinent here are also the instances in which a percept is supplemented or

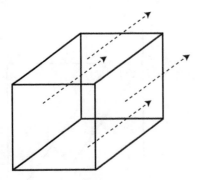

FIGURE 2.2

completed by earlier visual experience. The expert sees a missing part as a gap in an incomplete whole. A footprint in the sand makes us see the foot that is not there. A student who has been told about the continental drift sees the outlines of the African and American continents not as separate, capricious shapes but as fitting together like tongue and groove or male and female. Instead of two masses, he now sees only one, torn apart. The dynamics of the separation of the halves, seen as belonging together like the pieces of a broken pot, are a genuine component of the percept itself, not just an inference.

However, the perceptual solution of a problem does not require that the image on which the crucial thought operation is performed be seen in the problem situation itself. In order to accomplish the heliocentric revolution, it was not necessary for Copernicus, as Hanson assumes, to 'see the horizon dipping, or turning away, from our fixed star'. For thousands of years, astronomical observations had been related to cosmic models of rotating spheres and shells, and the visual transformations needed to establish this relation between direct observation and 'pure shapes' are well within the range of perceptual versatility. Copernicus had to rely on the further image of the relativity of movement, an observation familiar to him from daily experience, and the decisive restructuring consisted in applying the effects of relative motion to the cosmic model, not to what he perceived at sunrise.

Although in such cases the direct observation and the model on which the restructuring is performed are two separate images, they are nevertheless related perceptually. This continuity, which unites all relevant aspects of the phenomenon under investigation is necessary for understanding. Of course, many useful relations can be discovered or learned which connect certain items of experience by mere association. One can stumble on the fact that curare slackens the muscles or learn that the switch of the thermostat changes the temperature, without any conception of the events causing these effects. Much human competence and even some progress derive from the practice of such connections, but since mechanical conditioning lets the mind bypass the relevant facts it does not involve truly productive thinking and surely cannot serve as a model of it.

HOW ILLUSTRATIONS TEACH

When the mind operates in the manner of the scientist, it looks for the one correct image hiding among the phenomena of experience. Education has to bridge the gap between the bewildering complexity of primary observation and the relative simplicity of that relevant image. For the purpose of science, education must do precisely what it needs to avoid in the teaching of art, namely, provide a sufficiently simple version of that final image, whenever the student cannot be expected to discern it by himself in the intricate sight of the real thing. Think of a student trying to understand the shape and functioning of the human heart. The heart's twisted chambers, its tangled arteries and veins, the asymmetry of shapes and locations serving symmetrical functions tax the senses of the observer more confusingly than if he tried to unravel the serpents of the Laocoon group. Eventually the student must learn to see the simple principle in this baroque spectacle; he may even want to understand why nature came to fulfill a simple physiological function with so much contortion. But his road to that goal will be needlessly arduous unless he is given a target image as a sort of template. Figure 2.3 shows a drawing made by Paul Klee to explain to his students the functioning of the human heart. All shape has been radically reduced to the simplest representation of the basic processes. Volume and pathways have been confined to a two-dimensional plane. The chambers, deprived of their internal subdivision, have become symmetrical. Equally symmetrical are the two circuits, the one sending the blood to the lungs for purification and returning it to the heart, the other picking it up and sending it to work through the body and back to the central pump. Some of Klee's anatomical liberties may be misleading; but he has used the freedom of an artist's pictorial imagination to present the basic essentials of the subject with the simplicity of a child's drawing. Once the student has grasped the principle he can move to closer approximations of the intricate real situation.

In the educational practice, learning through perceptual abstraction must be guided by suitable illustrations. This is often done with great ingenuity. For example, the visual information on the pages of the *Scientific American* is consistently excellent. Some textbooks do equally well. Others let their designers get away with 'artistic' embellishments, which serve the misguided self-respect of the commercial artist but confuse the reader. Or again, illustrations may not be geared carefully enough to the particular level of abstraction that fits a student at a given stage of his mental development and of his acquaintance with a given subject matter. Much progress has been made since the medical textbooks of the Middle Ages showed how to apply leeches or treat a bone fracture by depicting doctor and patient in full costume and surrounded with a completely equipped office and dispensary. But the decision of how much to reproduce faithfully and how much to simplify requires educational experience and visual imagination. It must be precisely coordinated with the abstraction level of the teaching. How much detail should a geographical map contain? How much visual complexity can be grasped by the student?

The problem is particularly acute when students are required to make their own drawings. At a level of development at which the

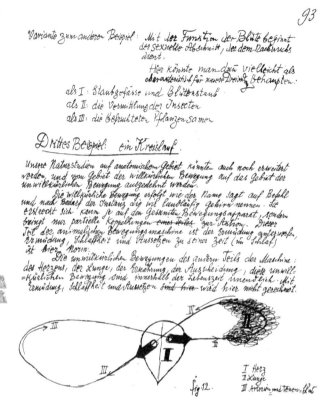

FIGURE 2.3 Paul Klee: Drawing of the human heart.

free artwork of the child still employs relatively simple geometrical shapes, the art teacher may respect his pupils' early stage of visual conception, but in geography class the same children may be compelled, perhaps by the same teacher, to trace the coastlines of the American continent or the irrational windings of rivers—shapes that can be neither perceived nor understood nor remembered. When a college student is asked to copy what he sees under the microscope, he cannot aim, mechanically, for mere accuracy and neatness. He must decide what matters and what types of relevant shapes are represented in the accidental specimen. Therefore, his drawing cannot possibly be a reproduction; it will be an image of what he sees and understands, more or less actively and intelligently. The discipline of intelligent vision cannot be confined to the art studio; it can succeed only if the visual sense is not blunted and confused in other areas of the curriculum. To try to establish an island of visual literacy in an ocean of blindness is ultimately self-defeating. Visual thinking is indivisible.

The lack of visual training in the sciences and technology on the one hand and the artist's neglect of, or even contempt for, the beautiful and vital task of making the world of facts visible to the enquiring mind, strikes me, by the way, as a much more serious ailment of our civilization than the 'cultural divide' to which C.P. Snow drew so much public attention some time ago. He complained that scientists do not read good literature and writers know nothing about science. Perhaps this is so, but the complaint is superficial. It would seem that a person is 'well rounded' not simply when he has a bit of everything but when he applies to everything he does the integrated whole of all his mental powers. Snow's suggestion that 'the clashing point' of science and art 'ought to produce creative chances' seems to ignore the fundamental kinship of the two. A scientist may well be a connoisseur of Wallace Stevens or Samuel Beckett, but his training may have failed nevertheless to let him use, in his own best professional thinking, the perceptual imagination on which those writers rely. And a painter may read books on biology or physics with profit and yet not use his intelligence in his painting. The estrangement is of a much more fundamental nature.

In advocating a more conscious use of perceptual abstraction in teaching, one must keep in mind, however, that abstraction easily leads to detachment if the connection with empirical reality is not maintained. Every thinker is tempted to treat simplified constructs as though they were reality itself. Gerald Holton has vigorously reminded his fellow science teachers that the average lecture demonstration 'is of necessity and almost by definition a carefully adjusted, abstracted, simplified, homogenized, "dry-cleaned" case.' It replaces the actual phenomenon with an analogue, for instance when 'a mechanically agitated tray of steel balls . . . becomes the means of discussing a basic phenomenon (e.g. Brownian motion)—without giving the class a glimpse of the actual case itself.' The phenomenon is torn

out of context as though it were a complete and independent event and is shown, literally or figuratively, 'against a blank background', which eliminates the 'grainy or noisy part' of the actual situation. Neither is the student prepared for the bewildering complexity of the live fact, nor does he experience the excitement of the explorer who tries to clear his path and is unsure of the outcome. Even photographs and films of authentic laboratory or natural situations differ importantly from the direct experiences they replace.

Holton's warnings remind us that science, just as art, can only function if it spans the total range from direct, empirical perception to formalized constructs and maintains continuous interchange between them. Severed from their referents, the stylized images, stereotyped concepts, statistical data lead to empty play with shapes, just as the mere exposure to first-hand experience does not assure insight.

PROBLEMS OF VISUAL AID

The use of so-called visual aids does not provide by itself a sufficiently favourable condition for visual thinking. Lawrence K. Frank has charged that such aids, as the word implies, 'are considered as purely subsidiary to the seemingly all-important verbal communication, the traditional spoken or written representations. Usually visual aids are just that—illustrations; for the words are considered the primary mode of communication.' The mere presentation, by photograph, drawing, models, or live exhibition, of things to be studied, does not guarantee a thoughtful grasp of the subject. The insistence of modern educators on direct experience was certainly a valuable reaction to the remoteness of traditional teaching. But it is not enough to make the objects of study available for direct inspection. Pictures and films will be aids only if they meet the requirements of visual thinking. The unity of perception and conception, which I have tried to demonstrate, suggests that intelligent understanding takes place within the realm of the image itself, but only if it is shaped in such a way as to interpret the relevant features visually. I have put it elsewhere as follows:

> Visual education must be based on the premise that every picture is a statement. The picture does not present the object itself but a set of propositions about the object; or, if you prefer, it presents the object as a set of propositions.

If the picture fails to state the relevant propositions perceptually, it is useless, incomprehensible, confusing, worse than no image at all. In order to do its job, the sight must conform to the rules of visual perception, which tell how shape and colour determine what is seen. Great progress has been made in this respect; but much remains to be done. A few practical examples will make the point.

How much do we know about what exactly children and other learners see when they look at a textbook illustration, a film, a television program? The answer is crucial because if the student does not see what he is assumed to see, the very basis of learning is lacking. Have we a right to take for granted that a picture shows what it represents, regardless of what it is like and who is looking? The problem is most easily ignored for photographic material. We feel assured that since the pictures have been taken mechanically, they must be correct; and since they are realistic, they can be trusted to show all the facts; and since every human being has practised from birth how to look at the world, he can have no trouble with lifelike pictures. Do these assumptions hold true?

In one of the early books on film theory, Béla Balázs tells the story of a Ukrainian gentleman-farmer, who, disowned after the Soviet revolution, lived as the administrator of his estate, hundreds of miles away from the nearest railroad station. For 15 years he had not been in the city. A highly educated intellectual, he received newspapers, magazines, and books and owned a radio. He was up to date, but he had never seen a film. One day he travelled to Kiev and at that occasion saw his first movie, one of the early Douglas Fairbanks features. Around him in the theatre, children followed the story with ease, having a good time. The country gentleman sat staring at the screen with the utmost concentration, trembling of excitement and effort. 'How did you like it?' asked a friend afterwards. 'Enormously interesting,' he

replied, 'but what was going on in the picture?' He had been unable to understand.

The story, authentic or not, makes a valid point. There is much evidence that the comprehension of photographic pictures cannot be taken for granted. Joan and Louis Forsdale have collected examples to show that Eskimos or African tribesmen were unable to perceive such pictures when first introduced to them. In extreme cases, a picture presented by the foreign visitor is a flat object, nothing more. Or a minor detail is the only thing recognized in a longish film. Or a panning shot confuses because it looks as though the houses are moving. Some of these obstacles have been overcome in Western culture; others persist in our own children, unrecognized.

The reactions of African natives reported in one of the studies which the Forsdales cite make it clear that the human mind does not spontaneously accept the rectangular limits of a picture. Visual reality is boundless; therefore when a film showed persons going off the edge of the screen, the audience wanted to know how and why they had disappeared. Interruptions of the continuity of time are equally puzzling. An American filmmaker found that an Iranian audience did not follow the connection between a close-up and a long shot. In order to make it clear that a large isolated eye or foot belonged to the animal shown a moment before, the camera had to present the complete transition in motion.

Many of our own children learn to accept such breaks of spatial or temporal continuity at an early age, although even they will run into the problem when they face unfamiliar conditions. In a useful study of how well pupils in elementary and secondary schools handle geographic maps, Barbara S. Bartz observed that children sometimes assume a country to end where the map ends. She noted that border lines are often so neat as to give a misleading impression of completeness, and that 'bleeding' the picture may do better than the finality suggested by the white margin. The close-up problem can repeat itself when insets are used in maps in order to accommodate a portion of an area for which there is no space on the page otherwise or in order to give a more detailed view of, say, a large city.

Obviously, older children handle this sort of problem better than younger ones, and socio-economic differences also show up clearly. A bright child will do better than a dull one, and some teachers are more skilful than others in training their pupils how to read a map. Teachers must be explicitly aware of the problems that arise because maps differ from the appearance of the ordinary visual world, and they must know the perceptual principles guiding a child's apprehension of visual patterns. The level of abstractness, at which a map is conceived, should be geared, as I suggested earlier, to its purpose and to the user's level of comprehension. As a case in point, Bartz mentions that the graphic scales indicating how many miles correspond to an inch on the map should be no more detailed than appropriate; a high school child needs more division for finer measurement than does a fifth-grader.

Frequently, visual patterns offer difficulties of comprehension, some of which could be avoided if the pertinent perceptual principles were more consciously observed. Scale differences, for example, should be indicated conspicuously because the notion of relative size militates against the primary evidence that a thing is as large as it appears. Hence the temptation to judge the size of two countries by the absolute areas they occupy on two maps of different scale. (Compare here the incurable calamity of lantern slides, which show giant-sized insects, or miniature portraits as large as wall-sized murals.) Map makers have been aware for centuries of the distortions of size and shape that occur when the spherical surface of the earth is projected on flat paper. Also, when the grid lines are curved, the directions of North and South are not the same for all areas of the map but bend at the top and the bottom.

Avoidable difficulties arise frequently in the use of colours. Basically, colours indicate qualitative differences: Spain is blue, France is green, Italy is yellow. But hues also serve as layer-tints to indicate different elevations. W.H. Nault reports:

We have found, for instance, that children associate hue change (as from green to brown to blue) with change in *quality*, and they associate value change (light to dark) with change in *quantity*, amount or intensity. For example, many children said that light blue areas indicated shallower water and dark blue areas indicated deeper water. But when a purplish or reddish-blue was used to depict the deepest water category, two-thirds of the children did not associate this with a further depth change, but rather guessed at all sorts of qualitative changes—islands, coral reefs, and so on. We found hue a difficult factor to handle in map-making. Children have learned many hue-associations before they ever learn to read maps; red is hot, blue is cold, green is grass, blue is water, etc. Thus, what often happens with maps is that colours are spontaneously misinterpreted.

This sort of problem calls for the help of artists, designers, and psychologists, acquainted with the theoretical and practical handling of perceptual principles.

What holds for maps is equally true for every sort of visual presentation in textbooks, models, charts, films, etc. Careful investigations of what the persons see for whom these images are made are indispensable. It is worth noting in this connection that the manuals on audio–visual materials, which abound in technical detail otherwise, tend to dispatch these fundamental problems with the perfunctory recommendation that the pictures be neat, natural, and simple.

A single example may illustrate the visual illiteracy, which still goes largely unnoticed. Jean Piaget, the child psychologist who has been concerned with perceptual problems all his life, used Figure 2.4 to test the comprehension of children. Do they understand how a tap works? When the handle is turned horizontally, the canal is open and lets the water run through; otherwise it is closed. The child's performance will largely depend on whether the drawing is recognizable as a tap and whether it presents the relevant aspects correctly. Is the cross-shaped object in Figure 2.4*a* a tap? The pipe, flat rather than cylindrical, hangs in space. It does not continue on top, nor does it receive water from anywhere. The hatching does not indicate liquid filling a hollow and shows little relation to the dark stripe, meant to be the canal. The canal is in front of the handle

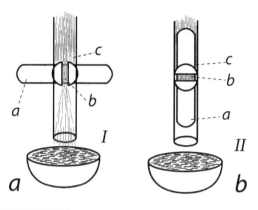

FIGURE 2.4

rather than behind it, and the handle is not in front of the pipe. Does Figure 2.4*b* show a vertical handle outside of a pipe or rather a kind of bob, swallowed by a rectangle or possibly a tube? I am not denying that a person, immunized and warned by years of exposure to mediocre textbook illustrations, mail order catalogues, and similar products of visual ineptness, can figure out the meaning of these drawings, especially if helped by a verbal explanation. But surely, if a child passes the test he does so in spite of the drawing, not with the help of it; and if he fails, he has not shown that he does not understand the working of a tap. He may simply be unable to extricate himself from a visual pitfall.

FOCUS ON FUNCTION

Deficient pictures of this kind can be found at any level of abstractness. The drawings could be much more realistic and still unsuited to present the relevant features of the physical situation. They fail not because they are not lifelike or devoid of detail but because they are ambiguous and misleading. The anatomical drawings of Leonardo da Vinci are so remarkably successful not only because he had the artistic ability to draw what he saw but because he saw every part of the human body as a contraption designed by a fellow inventor. He saw every muscle, bone, or tendon as shaped for its purpose, and represented it as a tool. He used spatial relations in order to show

functional connections. The same holds true, of course, for his technological drawings.

Emanuel Winternitz has discovered remarkable examples of Leonardo's concern with analogies or parallels. One of the drawings 'shows a diagram of tendons and muscles attached to the spine. Leonardo does not draw the muscles in their full width but represents them by thin cords to show clearly and transparently their function in stabilizing the vertebral column. In his comments on the page he compares the spine and its cords to the mast of a ship and its stays.' Leonardo invented a device by which the fingerholes of wind instruments, too widely spaced to be reachable by the human hand, can be controlled by wires, and Winternitz suggests that he took this idea from the tendons of the human hand which permit remote control of the finger tips.

Leonardo was capable of finding analogies among materially distant mechanisms because what he saw in objects of any kind was their 'functional value'. Karl Duncker, who introduced this term into psychology, has shown that all productive thinking discerns between essential principle and accidental embodiment. He experimented, for example, with the following problem:

> Given a human being with an inoperable stomach tumour, and rays which destroy organic tissue at sufficient intensity, by what procedure can one free him of the tumour by these rays and at the same time avoid destroying the healthy tissue which surrounds it?

He gave Figure 2.5 as a first approximation to the problem. With the simplicity of a child's drawing the diagram depicts the essentials: the target within the body, reached by rays. At first, the solution may be sought at a highly abstract level: Use an opening through which the rays can pass without damaging the body! This leads to the next step of searching the anatomy of the body for such an opening. Duncker calls this the approach 'from above'. One can also proceed 'from below', by starting with an inventory of what is given anatomically, in the hope of coming across something that will give the solution. The interaction of both approaches is characteristic

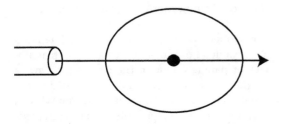

FIGURE 2.5

THE BURDEN OF IT ALL

What I have said may seem all too theoretical. But it contains principles that, if valid, should be constantly on any educator's mind. It is not enough to pay lip service to the doctrine of visual aids; not enough to turn on the movie projector, more or less diffidently, to provide a few minutes of entertainment in the dark. What is needed, it seems to me, is the systematic training of visual sensitivity as an indispensable part of any educator's preparation for his profession. The difference between a picture that makes its point and one that does not can be discerned by anybody whose natural responses to perceptual form have been cultivated rather than stifled.

The experimental and theoretical basis for visual education is being developed in psychology. Practical experience is best provided by work in the arts. It is not good strategy, however, to label perceptual sensitivity as artistic or aesthetic, because this means removing it to a privileged domain, reserved for the talents and aspirations of the specialist. Visual thinking calls, more broadly, for the ability to see visual shapes as images of the patterns of forces that underlie our existence—the functioning of minds, of bodies or machines, the structure of societies or ideas.

Art works best when it remains unacknowledged. It observes that shapes and objects and events, by displaying their own nature, can evoke those deeper and simpler powers in which man recognizes himself. It is one of the rewards we earn for thinking by what we see.

of successful thinking, and they correspond, of course, to the two polar levels of learning material mentioned here earlier: the highly abstract presentation of principle and the complexity of the real-life situation.

At both levels, however, the attention of the observer must be trained upon the functional value embodied in the object. Duncker shows the foolish mistakes that result when someone vaguely remembers the shape of some useful device, without truly realizing the principle served by that shape. Inventors, on the other hand, are concerned with functional values, as the Leonardo drawings indicated. Designers also must be aware of the difference between principle and embodiment, in order to realize where their imagination has freedom and where it is bound. The designer David Pye has shown convincingly that function never prescribes form, although it circumscribes its range. A wheel cannot be square-shaped but allows innumerable variations of the disk. A wedge can assume a hundred shapes, sizes, proportions, and so can a pin, a rod, a hook, a cup; because a function is a principle that does not call for a particular form but for a type of form.

NOTES

What is Art For?
   Coomaraswamy: (4, 5).

Pictures as Propositions
   Kerschensteiner: see Weber (18) p. 56.

Standard Images and Art
   Pestalozzi: (14).
   Schmid and Lange: Weber (18) pp. 26 ff.
   Villard de Honnecourt: (17).

   Signatures: see, e. g., Pauli (13) p. 159.

Looking and Understanding
   Hanson: (9) p. 19.
   Wertheimer: (19).
   Continental drift: Hurley (11).

How Illustrations Teach
   Snow: (16).
   Holton: (10).

Problems of Visual Aid
Frank: (8) p. 456.
Pictures as statements: Arnheim (1) p. 148.
Balázs: (2) p. 2.
Forsdale: (7).
Map reading: Bartz (3) and Nault (12).

Focus on Function
On Leonardo: Winternitz (20, 21).
Functional value: Duncker (6).
Pye: (15) chap. 3.

BIBLIOGRAPHY

1. Arnheim, Rudolf. 'The myth of the bleating lamb'. In Arnheim, *Toward a psychology of art*, pp. 136–50. Berkeley and Los Angeles: Univ. of California Press, 1966.
2. Balázs, Béla. *Der Geist des Films*. Halle: Knapp, 1930.
3. Bartz, Barbara S. *Map design for children*. Chicago: Field Enterprises, 1965.
4. Coomaraswamy, Ananada K. *Christian and oriental philosophy of art*. New York: Dover, 1957. (First published as: Why exhibit works of art? London: Luzac, 1946.)
5. Coomaraswamy, Ananda K. *Figures of speech or figures of thought*. London: Luzac, 1946.
6. Duncker, Karl. 'On problem-solving'. *Psychol. Monographs* 1945, vol. 58, no. 270.
7. Forsdale, Joan Rosengren, and Louis. 'Film literacy'. *Teachers College Record* 1966, vol. 67, pp. 608–17.
8. Frank, Lawrence K. 'Role of the arts in education'. In Eisner and Ecker (eds), *Readings in art education*, pp. 454–9. Waltham, MA: Blaisdell, 1966.
9. Hanson, Norwood Russell. *Patterns of discovery*. Cambridge: Cambridge Univ. Press, 1965.
10. Holton, Gerald. 'Conveying science by visual presentation'. In Kepes (ed.), *Vision and value series: vol. 1 Education and vision*, pp. 50–77. New York: Braziller, 1965/6.
11. Hurley, Patrick M. 'The confirmation of continental drift'. *Scient. Amer.*, April 1968, vol. 218, pp. 52–64.
12. Nault, W.H. 'Children's map reading abilities—a need for improvement'. *New Letter of the Geographic Society of Chicago*, January 1967, vol. 3, no. 5.
13. Pauli, W. *The influence of archetypal ideas on the scientific theories of Kepler*. New York: Pantheon, 1954.
14. Pestalozzi, Johann Heinrich. *Wie Gertrud ihre Kinder lehrt*. Leipzig: Siegismund & Volkening, 1880.
15. Pye, David. *The nature of design*. London: Studio Vista, 1964.
16. Snow, C.P. *The two cultures in the scientific revolution*. Cambridge: Cambridge Univ. Press, 1960.
17. Villard de Honnecourt. *The sketchbook of Villard de Honnecourt*. Bloomington: Univ. of Indiana Press, 1959.
18. Weber, Gert. *Kunsterziehung gestern heute morgen auch*. Ravensburg: Maier, 1964.
19. Wertheimer, Max. 'Ueber Schlussprozesse im produktiven Denken'. In *Wertheimer Drei Abhandlungen zur Gestaltttheorie*. Erlangen: Philos. Akademie, 1925. (English summary in Ellis, Willis D. (ed.). *A source book of Gestalt psychology*, pp. 71–88. New York: Harcourt Brace, 1939.)
20. Winternitz, Emanuel. 'Anatomy the teacher: on the impact of Leonardo's anatomical research, etc.' *Proceedings of the Amer. Philos. Soc.*, August 1967, vol. 111, no. 4, pp. 234–47.
21. Winternitz, Emanuel. 'Leonardo's invention of key-mechanisms for wind instruments'. *Raccolta Vinciana*, 1964, vol. 20, pp. 69–82.

3

IN PLATO'S CAVE

SUSAN SONTAG

Humankind lingers unregenerately in Plato's cave, still revelling, its age-old habit, in mere images of the truth. But being educated by photographers is not like being educated by older, more artisanal images. For one thing, there are a great many more images around, claiming our attention. The inventory started in 1839 and since then just about everything has been photographed, or so it seems. This very insatiability of the photographing eye changes the terms of confinement in the cave, our world. In teaching us a new visual code, photographs alter and enlarge our notions of what is worth looking at and what we have a right to observe. They are a grammar and, even more importantly, an ethics of seeing. Finally, the most grandiose result of the photographic enterprise is to give us the sense that we can hold the whole world in our heads—as an anthology of images.

To collect photographs is to collect the world. Movies and television programs light up walls, flicker, and go out; but with still photographs the image is also an object, light-weight, cheap to produce, easy to carry about, accumulate, store. In Godard's *Les Carabiniers* (1963), two sluggish lumpen-peasants are lured into joining the King's Army by the promise that they will be able to loot, rape, kill, or do whatever else they please to the enemy, and get rich. But the suitcase of booty that Michel-Ange and Ulysses triumphantly bring home, years later, to their wives turns out to contain only picture postcards, hundreds of them, of Monuments, Department Stores, Mammals, Wonders of Nature, Methods of Transport, Works of Art, and other classified treasures from around the globe. Godard's gag vividly parodies the equivocal magic of the photographic image. Photographs are perhaps the most mysterious of all the objects that make up, and thicken, the environment we recognize as modern. Photographs really are experience captured, and the camera is the ideal arm of consciousness in its acquisitive mood.

To photograph is to appropriate the thing photographed. It means putting oneself into a certain relation to the world that feels like knowledge—and, therefore, like power. A now notorious first fall into alienation, habituating people to abstract the world into printed words, is supposed to have engendered that surplus of Faustian energy and psychic damage needed to build modern, inorganic societies. But print seems a less treacherous form of leaching out the world, of turning it into a mental object, than photographic images, which now provide most of the knowledge people have about the look of the past and the reach of the present. What is written about a person or an event is frankly an interpretation, as are handmade visual statements, like paintings and drawings. Photographed images do not seem to be statements about the world so much as pieces of it, miniatures of reality that anyone can make or acquire. Photographs, which fiddle with the scale of the world, themselves get reduced, blown up, cropped, retouched, doctored, tricked out. They age, plagued by the usual ills of paper objects; they disappear; they become valuable, and get bought and sold; they are reproduced. Photographs, which package the world, seem to invite packaging. They are stuck in albums, framed and set on tables, tacked on walls, projected as slides. Newspapers and magazines feature them; cops alphabetize them; museums exhibit them; publishers compile them.

For many decades the book has been the most influential way of arranging (and usually miniaturizing) photographs, thereby guaranteeing them longevity, if not immortality—photographs are fragile objects, easily torn or mislaid—and a wider public. The photograph in a book is, obviously, the image of an image. But since it is, to begin with, a printed, smooth object, a photograph loses much less of its essential quality when reproduced in a book than a painting does. Still, the book is not a wholly satisfactory scheme for putting groups of photographs into general circulation. The sequence in which the photographs are to be looked at is proposed by the order of pages, but nothing holds readers to the recommended order or indicates the amount of time to be spent on each photograph. Chris Marker's film, *Si J'avais quatre dromadaires* (1966), a brilliantly orchestrated meditation on photographs of all sorts and themes, suggests a subtler and more rigorous way of packaging (and enlarging) still photographs. Both the order and the exact time for looking at each photograph are imposed; and there is a gain in visual legibility and emotional impact. But photographs transcribed in a film cease to be collectable objects, as they still are when served up in books.

Photographs furnish evidence. Something we hear about, but doubt, seems proven when we're shown a photograph of it. In one version of its utility, the camera record incriminates. Starting with their use by the Paris police in the murderous roundup of Communards in June 1871, photographs became a useful tool of modern states in the surveillance and control of their increasingly mobile populations. In another version of its utility, the camera record justifies. A photograph passes for incontrovertible proof that a given thing happened. The picture may distort; but there is always a presumption that something exists, or did exist, which is like what's in the picture. Whatever the limitations (through amateurism) or pretensions (through artistry) of the individual photographer, a photograph—any photograph—seems to have a more innocent, and therefore more accurate, relation to visible reality than do other mimetic objects. Virtuosi of the noble image like Alfred Stieglitz and Paul Strand, composing mighty, unforgettable photographs decade after decade, still want, first of all, to show something 'out there', just like the Polaroid owner for whom photographs are a handy, fast form of note-taking, or the shutterbug with a Brownie who takes snapshots as souvenirs of daily life.

While a painting or a prose description can never be other than a narrowly selective interpretation, a photograph can be treated as a narrowly selective transparency. But despite the presumption of veracity that gives all photographs authority, interest, seductiveness, the work that photographers do is no generic exception to the usually shady commerce between art and truth. Even when photographers are most concerned with mirroring reality, they are still haunted by tacit imperatives of taste and conscience. The immensely gifted members of the Farm Security Administration photographic project of the late 1930s (among them Walker Evans, Dorothea Lange, Ben Shahn, Russell Lee) would take dozens of frontal pictures of one of their sharecropper subjects until satisfied that they had gotten just the right look on film—the precise expression on the subject's face that supported their own notions about poverty, light, dignity, texture, exploitation, and geometry. In deciding how a picture should look, in preferring one exposure to another, photographers are always imposing standards on their subjects. Although there is a sense in which the camera does indeed capture reality, not just interpret it, photographs are as much an interpretation of the world as paintings and drawings are. Those occasions when the taking of photographs is relatively undiscriminating, promiscuous, or self-effacing do not lessen the didacticism of the whole enterprise. This very passivity—and ubiquity—of the photographic record is photography's 'message', its aggression.

Images which idealize (like most fashion and animal photography) are no less aggressive than work which makes a virtue of plainness (like class pictures, still lifes of the bleaker sort, and mug shots). There is an aggression implicit in every use of the camera. This is as evident in the 1840s and 1850s, photography's glorious first two decades, as in all the succeeding decades, during which technology made possible an ever-increasing spread of that mentality which looks at the world as a set of potential photographs. Even for

such early masters as David Octavius Hill and Julia Margaret Cameron who used the camera as a means of getting painterly images, the point of taking photographs was a vast departure from the aims of painters. From its start, photography implied the capture of the largest possible number of subjects. Painting never had so imperial a scope. The subsequent industrialization of camera technology only carried out a promise inherent in photography from its very beginning: to democratize all experiences by translating them into images.

That age when taking photographs required a cumbersome and expensive contraption— the toy of the clever, the wealthy, and the obsessed—seems remote indeed from the era of sleek pocket cameras that invite anyone to take pictures. The first cameras, made in France and England in the early 1840s, had only inventors and buffs to operate them. Since there were then no professional photographers, there could not be amateurs either, and taking photographs had no clear social use; it was a gratuitous, that is, an artistic activity, though with few pretensions to being an art. It was only with its industrialization that photography came into its own as art. As industrialization provided social uses for the operations of the photographer, so the reaction against these uses reinforced the self-consciousness of photography-as-art.

Recently, photography has become almost as widely practised an amusement as sex and dancing—which means that, like every mass art form, photography is not practised by most people as an art. It is mainly a social rite, a defence against anxiety, and a tool of power.

Memorializing the achievements of individuals considered as members of families (as well as of other groups) is the earliest popular use of photography. For at least a century, the wedding photograph has been as much a part of the ceremony as the prescribed verbal formulas. Cameras go with family life. According to a sociological study done in France, most households have a camera, but a household with children is twice as likely to have at least one camera as a household in which there are no children. Not to take pictures of one's children, particularly when they are small, is a sign of parental indifference, just as not turning up for one's graduation picture is a gesture of adolescent rebellion. Through photographs, each family constructs a portrait-chronicle of itself—a portable kit of images that bears witness to its connectedness. It hardly matters what activities are photographed so long as photographs get taken and are cherished. Photography becomes a rite of family life just when, in the industrializing countries of Europe and America, the very institution of the family starts undergoing radical surgery. As that claustrophobic unit, the nuclear family, was being carved out of a much larger family aggregate, photography came along to memorialize, to restate symbolically, the imperilled continuity and vanishing extendedness of family life. Those ghostly traces, photographs, supply the token presence of the dispersed relatives. A family's photograph album is generally about the extended family—and, often, is all that remains of it.

As photographs give people an imaginary possession of a past that is unreal, they also help people to take possession of space in which they are insecure. Thus, photography develops in tandem with one of the most characteristic of modern activities: tourism. For the first time in history, large numbers of people regularly travel out of their habitual environments for short periods of time. It seems positively unnatural to travel for pleasure without taking a camera along. Photographs will offer indisputable evidence that the trip was made, that the program was carried out, that fun was had. Photographs document sequences of consumption carried on outside the view of family, friends, neighbours. But dependence on the camera, as the device that makes real what one is experiencing, doesn't fade when people travel more. Taking photographs fills the same need for the cosmopolitans accumulating photograph-trophies of their boat trip up the Albert Nile or their 14 days in China as it does for lower-middle-class vacationers taking snapshots of the Eiffel Tower or Niagara Falls.

A way of certifying experience, taking photographs is also a way of refusing it—by limiting experience to a search for the photogenic, by converting experience into an image, a souvenir.

Travel becomes a strategy for accumulating photographs. The very activity of taking pictures is soothing, and assuages general feelings of disorientation that are likely to be exacerbated by travel. Most tourists feel compelled to put the camera between themselves and whatever is remarkable that they encounter. Unsure of other responses, they take a picture. This gives shape to experience: stop, take a photograph, and move on. The method especially appeals to people handicapped by a ruthless work ethic—Germans, Japanese, and Americans. Using a camera appeases the anxiety which the work-driven feel about not working when they are on vacation and supposed to be having fun. They have something to do that is like a friendly imitation of work: they can take pictures.

People robbed of their past seem to make the most fervent picture takers, at home and abroad. Everyone who lives in an industrialized society is obliged gradually to give up the past, but in certain countries, such as the United States and Japan, the break with the past has been particularly traumatic. In the early 1970s, the fable of the brash American tourist of the 1950s and 1960s, rich with dollars and Babbittry, was replaced by the mystery of the group-minded Japanese tourist, newly released from his island prison by the miracle of overvalued yen, who is generally armed with two cameras, one on each hip.

Photography has become one of the principal devices for experiencing something, for giving an appearance of participation. One full-page ad shows a small group of people standing pressed together, peering out of the photograph, all but one looking stunned, excited, upset. The one who wears a different expression holds a camera to his eye; he seems self-possessed, is almost smiling. While the others are passive, clearly alarmed spectators, having a camera has transformed one person into something active, a voyeur: only he has mastered the situation. What do these people see? We don't know and it doesn't matter. It is an Event: something worth seeing—and therefore worth photographing. The ad copy, white letters across the dark lower third of the photograph like news coming over a teletype machine, consists of just six words: ' . . . Prague . . . Woodstock . . .

Vietnam . . . Sapporo . . . Londonderry . . . LEICA'. Crushed hopes, youth antics, colonial wars, and winter sports are alike—are equalized by the camera. Taking photographs has set up a chronic voyeuristic relation to the world which levels the meaning of all events.

A photograph is not just the result of an encounter between an event and a photographer; picture-taking is an event in itself, and one with ever more peremptory rights—to interfere with, to invade, or to ignore whatever is going on. Our very sense of situation is now articulated by the camera's intervention. The omnipresence of cameras persuasively suggests that time consists of interesting events, events worth photographing. This, in turn, makes it easy to feel that any event, once underway, and whatever its moral character, should be allowed to complete itself—so that something else can be brought into the world, the photograph. After the event ended, the picture will still exist, conferring on the event a kind of immortality (and importance) it would never otherwise have enjoyed. While real people are out there killing themselves or other real people, the photographer stays behind his or her camera, creating a tiny element of another world: the image-world that bids to outlast us all.

Photographing is essentially an act of non-intervention. Part of the horror of such memorable coups of contemporary photojournalism as the pictures of a Vietnamese bonze reaching for the gasoline can, of a Bengali guerrilla in the act of bayoneting a trussed-up collaborator, comes from the awareness of how plausible it has become, in situations where the photographer has the choice between a photograph and a life, to choose the photograph. The person who intervenes cannot record; the person who is recording cannot intervene. Dziga Vertov's great film, *Man with a Movie Camera* (1929), gives the ideal image of the photographer as someone in perpetual movement, someone moving through a panorama of disparate events with such agility and speed that any intervention is out of the question. Hitchcock's *Rear Window* (1954) gives the complementary image: The photographer played by James Stewart has an intensified relation to one event, through his camera, precisely because he has a broken leg and is confined to a wheelchair; being temporarily immobilized prevents him from acting on what he sees, and makes it even more important to take pictures. Even if incompatible with intervention in a physical sense, using a camera is still a form of participation. Although the camera is an observation station, the act of photographing is more than passive observing. Like sexual voyeurism, it is a way of at least tacitly, often explicitly, encouraging whatever is going on to keep on happening. To take a picture is to have an interest in things as they are, in the status quo remaining unchanged (at least for as long as it takes to get a 'good' picture), to be in complicity with whatever makes a subject interesting, worth photographing—including, when that is the interest, another person's pain or misfortune.

'I always thought of photography as a naughty thing to do—that was one of my favourite things about it,' Diane Arbus wrote, 'and when I first did it I felt very perverse.' Being a professional photographer can be thought of as naughty, to use Arbus's pop word, if the photographer seeks out subjects considered to be disreputable, taboo, marginal. But naughty subjects are harder to find these days. And what exactly is the perverse aspect of picture-taking? If professional photographers often have sexual fantasies when they are behind the camera, perhaps the perversion lies in the fact that these fantasies are both plausible and so inappropriate. In *Blowup* (1966), Antonioni has the fashion photographer hovering convulsively over Veruschka's body with his camera clicking, Naughtiness, indeed! In fact, using a camera is not a very good way of getting at someone sexually. Between photographer and subject, there has to be distance. The camera doesn't rape, or even possess, though it may presume, intrude, trespass, distort, exploit, and, at the farthest reach of metaphor, assassinate—all activities that, unlike the sexual push and shove, can be conducted from a distance, and with some detachment.

There is a much stronger sexual fantasy in Michael Powell's extraordinary movie *Peeping Tom* (1960), which is not about a Peeping Tom but about a psychopath who kills women with a weapon concealed in his camera, while photographing them. Not once does he touch his subjects. He doesn't desire their bodies; he wants their presence in the form of filmed images—those showing them experiencing their own death—which he screens at home for his solitary pleasure. The movie assumes connections between impotence and aggression, professionalized looking and cruelty, which point to the central fantasy connected with the camera. The camera as phallus is, at most, a flimsy variant of the inescapable metaphor that everyone unselfconsciously employs. However hazy our awareness of this fantasy, it is named without subtlety whenever we talk about 'loading' and 'aiming' a camera, about 'shooting' a film.

The old-fashioned camera was clumsier and harder to reload than a brown Bess musket. The modern camera is trying to be a ray gun. One ad reads:

> The Yashica Electro-35 GT is the spaceage camera your family will love. Take beautiful pictures day or night. Automatically. Without any nonsense. Just aim, focus and shoot. The GT's computer brain and electronic shutter will do the rest.

Like a car, a camera is sold as a predatory weapon—one that's as automated as possible, ready to spring. Popular taste expects an easy, an invisible technology. Manufacturers reassure their customers that taking pictures demands no skill or expert knowledge, that the machine is all-knowing, and responds to the slightest pressure of the will. It's as simple as turning the ignition key or pulling the trigger.

Like guns and cars, cameras are fantasy-machines whose use is addictive. However, despite the extravagances of ordinary language and advertising, they are not lethal. In the hyperbole that markets cars like guns, there is at least this much truth: Except in wartime, cars kill more people than guns do. The camera/gun does not kill, so the ominous metaphor seems to be all bluff—like a man's fantasy of having a gun, knife, or tool between his legs. Still, there is something predatory in the act of taking a picture. To photograph people is to violate them, by seeing them as

they never see themselves, by having knowledge of them they can never have; it turns people into objects that can be symbolically possessed. Just as the camera is a sublimation of the gun, to photograph someone is a sublimated murder—a soft murder, appropriate to a sad, frightened time.

Eventually, people might learn to act out more of their aggressions with cameras and fewer with guns, with the price being an even more image-choked world. One situation where people are switching from bullets to film is the photographic safari that is replacing the gun safari in East Africa. The hunters have Hasselblads instead of Winchesters; instead of looking through a telescopic sight to aim a rifle, they look through a viewfinder to frame a picture. In end-of-the-century London, Samuel Butler complained that 'there is a photographer in every bush, going about like a roaring lion seeking whom he may devour.' The photographer is now charging real beasts, beleaguered and too rare to kill. Guns have metamorphosed into cameras in this earnest comedy, the ecology safari, because nature has ceased to be what it always had been—what people needed protection from. Now nature—tamed, endangered, mortal—needs to be protected from people. When we are afraid, we shoot. But when we are nostalgic, we take pictures.

It is a nostalgic time right now, and photographs actively promote nostalgia. Photography is an elegiac art, a twilight art. Most subjects photographed are, just by virtue of being photographed, touched by pathos. An ugly or grotesque subject may be moving because it has been dignified by the attention of the photographer. A beautiful subject can be the object of rueful feelings, because it has aged or decayed or no longer exists. All photographs are *memento mori*. To take a photograph is to participate in another person's (or thing's) mortality, vulnerability, mutability. Precisely by slicing out this moment and freezing it, all photographs testify to time's relentless melt.

Cameras began duplicating the world at that moment when the human landscape started to undergo a vertiginous rate of change: While an untold number of forms of biological and social life are being destroyed in a brief span of time, a device is available to record what is disappearing. The moody, intricately textured Paris of Atget and Brassaï is mostly gone. Like the dead relatives and friends preserved in the family album, whose presence in photographs exorcises some of the anxiety and remorse prompted by their disappearance, so the photographs of neighbourhoods now torn down, rural places disfigured and made barren, supply our pocket relation to the past.

A photograph is both a pseudo-presence and a token of absence. Like a wood fire in a room, photographs—especially those of people, of distant landscapes and faraway cities, of the vanished past—are incitements to reverie. The sense of the unattainable that can be evoked by photographs feeds directly into the erotic feelings of those for whom desirability is enhanced by distance. The lover's photograph hidden in a married woman's wallet, the poster photograph of a rock star tacked up over an adolescent's bed, the campaign-button image of a politician's face pinned on a voter's coat, the snapshots of a cabdriver's children clipped to the visor—all such talismanic uses of photographs express a feeling both sentimental and implicitly magical: they are attempts to contact or lay claim to another reality.

Photographs can abet desire in the most direct, utilitarian way—as when someone collects photographs of anonymous examples of the desirable as an aid to masturbation. The matter is more complex when photographs are used to stimulate the moral impulse. Desire has no history—at least, it is experienced in each instance as all foreground, immediacy. It is aroused by archetypes and is, in that sense, abstract. But moral feelings are embedded in history, whose personae are concrete, whose situations are always specific. Thus, almost opposite rules hold true for the use of the photograph to awaken desire and to awaken conscience. The images that mobilize conscience are always linked to a given historical situation. The more general they are, the less likely they are to be effective.

A photograph that brings news of some unsuspected zone of misery cannot make a dent in public opinion unless there is an appropriate context of feeling and attitude. The photographs

Mathew Brady and his colleagues took of the horrors of the battlefields did not make people any less keen to go on with the Civil War. The photographs of ill-clad, skeletal prisoners held at Andersonville inflamed Northern public opinion—against the South. (The effect of the Andersonville photographs must have been partly due to the very novelty, at that time, of seeing photographs.) The political understanding that many Americans came to in the 1960s would allow them, looking at the photographs Dorothea Lange took of Nisei on the West Coast being transported to internment camps in 1942, to recognize their subject for what it was—a crime committed by the government against a large group of American citizens. Few people who saw those photographs in the 1940s could have had so unequivocal a reaction; the grounds for such a judgment were covered over by the pro-war consensus. Photographs cannot create a moral position, but they can reinforce one—and can help build a nascent one.

Photographs may be more memorable than moving images, because they are a neat slice of time, not a flow. Television is a stream of underselected images, each of which cancels its predecessor. Each still photograph is a privileged moment, turned into a slim object that one can keep and look at again. Photographs like the one that made the front page of most newspapers in the world in 1972—a naked South Vietnamese child just sprayed by American napalm, running down a highway toward the camera, her arms open, screaming with pain—probably did more to increase the public revulsion against the war than a hundred hours of televised barbarities.

One would like to imagine that the American public would not have been so unanimous in its acquiescence to the Korean War if it had been confronted with photographic evidence of the devastation of Korea, an ecocide and genocide in some respects even more thorough than those inflicted on Vietnam a decade later. But the supposition is trivial. The public did not see such photographs because there was, ideologically, no space for them. No one brought back photographs of daily life in Pyongyang, to show that the enemy had a human face, as Felix Greene and

Marc Riboud brought back photographs of Hanoi. Americans did have access to photographs of the suffering of the Vietnamese (many of which came from military sources and were taken with quite a different use in mind) because journalists felt backed in their efforts to obtain those photographs, the event having been defined by a significant number of people as a savage colonialist war. The Korean War was understood differently—as part of the just struggle of the Free World against the Soviet Union and China—and, given that characterization, photographs of the cruelty of unlimited American firepower would have been irrelevant.

Though an event has come to mean, precisely, something worth photographing, it is still ideology (in the broadest sense) that determines what constitutes an event. There can be no evidence, photographic or otherwise, of an event until the event itself has been named and characterized. And it is never photographic evidence which can construct—more properly, identify—events; the contribution of photography always follows the naming of the event. What determines the possibility of being affected morally by photographs is the existence of a relevant political consciousness. Without a politics, photographs of the slaughter-bench of history will most likely be experienced as, simply, unreal or as a demoralizing emotional blow.

The quality of feeling, including moral outrage, that people can muster in response to photographs of the oppressed, the exploited, the starving, and the massacred also depends on the degree of their familiarity with these images. Don McCullin's photographs of emaciated Biafrans in the early 1970s had less impact for some people than Werner Bischof's photographs of Indian famine victims in the early 1950s because those images had become banal, and the photographs of Tuareg families dying of starvation in the sub-Sahara that appeared in magazines everywhere in 1973 must have seemed to many like an unbearable replay of a now familiar atrocity exhibition.

Photographs shock insofar as they show something novel. Unfortunately, the ante keeps getting raised—partly through the very proliferation of such images of horror. One's first encounter with the photographic inventory of ultimate horror is a kind of revelation, the prototypically modern revelation: a negative epiphany. For me, it was photographs of Bergen-Belsen and Dachau which I came across by chance in a bookstore in Santa Monica in July 1945. Nothing I have seen—in photographs or in real life—ever cut me as sharply, deeply, instantaneously. Indeed, it seems plausible to me to divide my life into two parts; before I saw those photographs (I was 12) and after, though it was several years before I understood fully what they were about. What good was served by seeing them? They were only photographs—of an event I had scarcely heard of and could do nothing to affect, of suffering I could hardly imagine and could do nothing to relieve. When I looked at those photographs, something broke. Some limit had been reached, and not only that of horror; I felt irrevocably grieved, wounded, but a part of my feelings started to tighten; something went dead; something is still crying.

To suffer is one thing; another thing is living with the photographed images of suffering, which does not necessarily strengthen conscience and the ability to be compassionate. It can also corrupt them. Once one has seen such images, one has started down the road of seeing more—and more. Images transfix. Images anesthetize. An event known through photographs certainly becomes more real than it would have been if one had never seen the photographs—think of the Vietnam War. (For a counter-example, think of the Gulag Archipelago, of which we have no photographs.) But after repeated exposure to images it also becomes less real.

The same law holds for evil as for pornography. The shock of photographed atrocities wears off with repeated viewings, just as the surprise and bemusement felt the first time one sees a pornographic movie wear off after one sees a few more. The sense of taboo which makes us indignant and sorrowful is not much sturdier than the sense of taboo that regulates the definition of what is obscene. And both have been sorely tried in recent years. The vast photographic catalogue of misery and injustice throughout the world has given everyone a certain familiarity with atrocity, making the horrible seem more ordinary—making it appear familiar, remote ('it's only a photograph'), inevitable. At the time of the first photographs of the Nazi camps, there was nothing banal about these images. After 30 years, a saturation point may have been reached. In these last decades, 'concerned' photography has done at least as much to deaden conscience as to arouse it.

The ethical content of photographs is fragile. With the possible exception of photographs of those horrors, like the Nazi camps, that have gained the status of ethical reference points, most photographs do not keep their emotional charge. A photograph of 1900 that was affecting then because of its subject would, today, be more likely to move us because it is a photograph taken in 1900. The particular qualities and intentions of photographs tend to be swallowed up in the generalized pathos of time past. Aesthetic distance seems built into the very experience of looking at photographs, if not right away, then certainly with the passage of time. Time eventually positions most photographs, even the most amateurish, at the level of art.

The industrialization of photography permitted its rapid absorption into rational—that is, bureaucratic—ways of running society. No longer toy images, photographs became part of the general furniture of the environment—touchstones and confirmations of that reductive approach to reality which is considered realistic. Photographs were enrolled in the service of important institutions of control, notably the family and the police, as symbolic objects and as pieces of information. Thus, in the bureaucratic cataloguing of the world, many important documents are not valid unless they have, affixed to them, a photograph-token of the citizen's face.

The 'realistic' view of the world compatible with bureaucracy redefines knowledge—as techniques and information. Photographs are valued because they give information. They tell one what there is; they make an inventory. To spies, meteorologists, coroners, archaeologists, and other information professionals, their value is inestimable. But in the situations in which most people use photographs, their value as information is of the same order as fiction. The information that photographs can give starts to seem very important at that moment in cultural history when everyone is thought to have a right to something called news. Photographs were seen as a way of giving information to people who do not take easily to reading. The *Daily News* still calls itself 'New York's Picture Newspaper', its bid for populist identity. At the opposite end of the scale, *Le Monde*, a newspaper designed for skilled, well-informed readers, runs no photographs at all. The presumption is that, for such readers, a photograph could only illustrate the analysis contained in an article.

A new sense of the notion of information has been constructed around the photographic image. The photograph is a thin slice of space as well as time. In a world ruled by photographic images, all borders ('framing') seem arbitrary. Anything can be separated, can be made discontinuous, from anything else: all that is necessary is to frame the subject differently. (Conversely, anything can be made adjacent to anything else.) Photography reinforces a nominalist view of social reality as consisting of small units of an apparently infinite number—as the number of photographs that could be taken of anything is unlimited. Through photographs, the world becomes a series of unrelated, freestanding particles; and history, past and present, a set of anecdotes and *faits divers*. The camera makes reality atomic, manageable, and opaque. It is a view of the world which denies interconnectedness, continuity, but which confers on each moment the character of a mystery. Any photograph has multiple meanings; indeed, to see something in the form of a photograph is to encounter a potential object of fascination. The ultimate wisdom of the photographic image is to say: 'There is the surface. Now think—or rather feel, intuit—what is beyond it, what the reality must be like if it looks this way.' Photographs, which cannot themselves explain anything, are inexhaustible invitations to deduction, speculation, and fantasy.

Photography implies that we know about the world if we accept it as the camera records it. But this is the opposite of understanding, which starts from *not* accepting the world as it looks. All possibility of understanding is rooted in the ability to say no. Strictly speaking, one never understands anything from a photograph. Of course, photographs fill in blanks in our mental pictures of the present and the past: for example, Jacob Riis's images of New York squalor in the 1880s are sharply instructive to those unaware that urban poverty in late-nineteenth-century America was really that Dickensian. Nevertheless, the camera's rendering of reality must always hide more than it discloses. As Brecht points out, a photograph of the Krupp works reveals virtually nothing about that organization. In contrast to the amorous relation, which is based on how something looks, understanding is based on how it functions. And functioning takes place in time, and must be explained in time. Only that which narrates can make us understand.

The limit of photographic knowledge of the world is that, while it can goad conscience, it can, finally, never be ethical or political knowledge. The knowledge gained through still photographs will always be some kind of sentimentalism, whether cynical or humanist. It will be a knowledge at bargain prices—a semblance of knowledge, a semblance of wisdom; as the act of taking pictures is a semblance of appropriation, a semblance of rape. The very muteness of what is, hypothetically, comprehensible in photographs is what constitutes their attraction and provocativeness. The omnipresence of photographs has an incalculable effect on our ethical sensibility. By furnishing this already crowded world with a duplicate one of images, photography makes us feel that the world is more available than it really is.

Needing to have reality confirmed and experience enhanced by photographs is an aesthetic consumerism to which everyone is now addicted. Industrial societies turn their citizens into image-junkies; it is the most irresistible form of mental pollution. Poignant longings for beauty, for an end to probing below the surface, for a redemption and celebration of the body of the world—all these elements of erotic feeling are affirmed in the pleasure we take in photographs. But other, less liberating feelings are expressed as well. It would not be wrong to speak of people having a *compulsion* to photograph: to turn experience itself into a way of seeing. Ultimately, having an experience becomes identical with taking a photograph of it, and participating in a public event comes more and more to be equivalent to looking at it in photographed form. That most logical of nineteenth-century aesthetes, Mallarmé, said that everything in the world exists in order to end in a book. Today everything exists to end in a photograph.

QUESTIONS FOR REFLECTION

1. How is your own knowledge shaped by images, particularly those reproduced in the textbooks and articles you read?
2. What conventions help to shape your own vision? Are these the conventions of an academic discipline, your family, a sports team, or a social group? Are the conventions formal, informal, or both?
3. Ivins examines the impact of different modes of printmaking on what can and cannot be known (i.e., in the construction of knowledge). Perform a similar analysis on a dominant mode of visual communication in the classroom: PowerPoint. What are the benefits and limitations of PowerPoint and how does the program function in the construction of knowledge?
4. Does the development of digital imaging technologies call into question the 'exactly repeatable pictorial statement' as outlined by Ivins?
5. Sontag says that photography is, among other things, a 'defence against anxiety.' Now, more than 30 years later, do we use photographic and photographic-related technologies in a similar way, as a defence against anxiety? What could such anxiety be and how does it compare to the anxiety described by Sontag?

FURTHER READING

Arnheim, Rudolph. *Art and Visual Perception: A Psychology of the Creative Eye*. Berkeley: University of California, 1954.

Arnheim, Rudolph. *Toward a Psychology of Art*. Berkeley: University of California, 1966.

Arnheim, Rudolph. *Visual Thinking*. Berkeley: University of California, 1969.

Barthes, Roland. *Image, Music, Text*. Trans. Stephen Heath. New York: Hill and Wang, 1977.

Barthes, Roland. *Camera Lucida: Reflections on Photography*. Trans. Richard Howard. New York: Hill and Wang, 1981.

Gombrich, E.H. *Meditations on a Hobby Horse: And Other Essays on the Theory of Art*. London: Phaidon, 1963.

Gombrich, E.H. *The Image and the Eye: Further Studies in the Psychology of Pictorial Representation*. Ithaca, Cornell, 1982.

Gombrich, E.H. *The Uses of Images: Studies in the Social Function of Art and Visual Communication*. London: Phaidon, 1999.

Ivins, William M. Jr. *Prints and Visual Communication*. Cambridge: MIT Press, 1953.

Sontag, Susan. *On Photography*. New York: Anchor, 1990.

Sontag, Susan. *Regarding the Pain of Others*. New York: Picador, 2003.

PART TWO

IMAGES OF THE BODY

Visual representation plays an essential role in the construction of knowledge of the body. Anatomists, radiologists, and biochemists use images to develop disciplinary knowledge about the body, just as children, adults, artists, and marketers create and use images to represent the body to themselves and others. Importantly, and as the essays in this part emphasize, images of the body are never simply representations of bones, organs, bodily systems, or skin; rather, they participate in the construction of cultural conceptions of the body. The essays in this part by Kate Cregan, Lisa Cartwright, and Lorna Roth address this relationship between visual representation, the development

of knowledge, and cultural conceptions of the body. The first two authors address the topic with specific reference to gendered representations of the body in the field of anatomy, while the last emphasizes the racialized body in the more popular arena of wax crayons. The diversity of perspectives and foci in this part point to the myriad ways in which representations of the body both influence and are influenced by culture.

The opening reading in the part, 'Blood and Circuses' by Kate Cregan, examines the public anatomies of the Worshipful Company of Barber Surgeons in seventeenth-century London. Cregan examines the role of anatomy textbooks in the construction of knowledge, specifically as they reflected and reinforced cultural understandings of sex and gender. Further, the author argues that the female body was largely conceived of in terms of its reproductive function and that such cultural presuppositions were made to appear as natural fact through the practice of anatomy.

A central claim of Cregan's is that anatomy theatres functioned as 'sites of discipline' through which attendants learned both anatomical knowledge and also a broad set of social codes associated with the Company, such as hierarchy and status. Anatomical illustration was an essential part of this process; however, the strength of Cregan's analysis is her treatment of the larger visual program of the theatre. She offers an insightful visual analysis of anatomy theatres, comparing them to playhouses and suggesting that both were places to see and be seen. As in the playhouses, architectural space, wall decoration, clothing, and other accoutrements in the anatomy theatre functioned in the process of communication and in the construction of anatomical knowledge of the male and female body. The visual program of the theatre produced information about the body being dissected but also legitimated the authority and expertise of the Company as anatomists.

The second reading in the part is Lisa Cartwright's 'A Cultural Anatomy of the Visible Human Project'. Cartwright is an influential scholar of communication studies and science studies and has written extensively on the body. In this essay, she addresses the Visible Human Project, an initiative of the National Library of Medicine in the United States to create a comprehensive and universal digital anatomical model of the 'normal' male and female bodies to be used by professionals and laypersons alike. What constitutes 'normal' in the project is a question of central importance to Cartwright's essay. The Visible Human Project is ongoing and can be found at: http://www.nlm.nih.gov/research/visible/visible_human.html.

An essential difference between the Visible Human Project and earlier anatomical models, such as those discussed by Cregan, is the public nature of the project. To this end, Cartwright examines the 'cultural narratives' that developed in public discourse around the creation of the Visible Man data set in 1994 and the Visible Woman set in 1995. She notes that the Visible Human Project shares the tradition in anatomy (addressed by Cregan) which positions the male body as the standard or 'normal' body against which the female is compared. And as with Cregan's essay, Cartwright emphasizes the extent to which the female body is defined according to its reproductive capabilities. Importantly, Cartwright's focus on a late twentieth and early twenty-first century practice reminds us that cultural conceptions and misconceptions about the body continue to influence the production of knowledge.

A particularly compelling observation in Cartwright's article is that the Visible Human Project's translation into actual use is problematic. The lack of specific disciplinary conventions in the data set (recall that it was intended to be universal) make the data inadequate for use by individual professions. Chemists, anatomists, or other professionals first have to translate the generic data set into their own specific disciplinary language before it can be of use. In this way the Visible Human Project further highlights vision as a trained practice, an issue which is taken up more fully in Charles Goodwin's essay 'Professional Vision' in Part Three of this collection.

The final essay in this part, 'Flesh in Wax: Demystifying the Skin Colours of the Common Crayon' is by communication studies scholar Lorna Roth. Where Cregan and Cartwright focused on the relationship between anatomy on one hand and sex and gender on the other, Roth addresses the topic of race. Specifically, Roth offers a case study of the Crayola crayon and related children's art materials as tools with which to represent the body. As Roth shows, the colour choices available in Crayola sets function as limitations or constraints on how children can represent their world. This can have a lasting impact on how they conceive of themselves and others as either 'normal' or 'deviant'. The author poses the question, 'Is the apparently politically innocent crayon just a crayon?' and her answer is a compelling account of the intersections between cultural attitudes and beliefs regarding skin colour and everyday products such as the wax crayon. Roth notes that conceptions of race and normalcy are found in such seemingly mundane products and, as such, are important sites of critical analysis.

The now infamous crayon colour similar to that of pale skin, originally called Flesh, is of central importance to Roth's essay. Binney & Smith, makers of Crayola products, introduced the colour in 1949 but renamed it Peach in 1962. This renaming was in large part a response to the growing civil rights movement and the recognition of the multiplicity of skin tones in the world. However—and this is what Roth interrogates—the company took 30 more years to introduce a multicultural set of crayons in 1992, offering a more comprehensive colour spectrum for representing skin colours. Further, while the multicultural set was widely marketed to educators, it remains largely unavailable to the general public. The result is a still-limited set of choices with which to depict the body. Roth concludes by calling for the recognition of a broad skin-colour continuum that would enable children to develop 'cognitive equity' rather than to see the world in terms of black and white. Cognitive equity is a concept developed by Roth and refers to a new way of understanding racial and cultural equity that moves beyond statistics and stresses equity at the level of the everyday—as manifest in the products, advertisements, and technologies that children are exposed to and have at their disposal. Like the essays of Cregan and Cartwright, Roth's paper is important in highlighting the 'embeddedness' of cultural norms such as race in everyday products and practices.

Taken as a whole, the essays in this part provide a convincing account of the reciprocal relationship between visual communication and culture. Images of the body represent the body not so much as natural fact as a specific interpretation of the body. Cultural attitudes and beliefs towards the body, specifically in terms of its sex, gender, and race, influence professional and popular practice from anatomical dissection to childhood education. Such attitudes are disseminated and reinforced in public forums such as the Visible Human Project and in the common Crayola crayon. Within these and other practices, bodily difference becomes naturalized so that what is actually a social construction is seen as a natural fact.

4

BLOOD AND CIRCUSES

KATE CREGAN

Representations of the dead circulated at many levels within early modern English culture. Death was a public and socially performed process, whether as a sacrament or as a punishment: and in the Anatomy Theatre of the Worshipful Company of Barber-Surgeons the deceased human form was both ritualistically, and publicly, explored and explained. In an overtly theatrical pedagogic process barber-surgeons in early seventeenth-century London acted as authorities of delimitation over the discursive construction of the anatomized human body. Bodies were lectured over by 'readers' who referred to illustrated anatomical manuals, outlining in words, with

the aid of visual stimuli, what the audience was to see and understand from the lesson laid before them. It was a lesson that formed the final act in the tragedy of the anatomical subject, frequently a grim product of the public gallows.

The performance of anatomical dissection differentiated and delimited embodiment, utilizing the remains of executed felons to create and propound a gendered ontology. When the classical, scribal authority that characterized earlier models of 'scholastic' education receded before the 'empirical' evidence of Vesalian anatomical practice and illustration, as Johnathon Sawday argues, spectators were no longer limited to seeing what the written word told them to see; they were subjected to the new authority of a protoscientist: the anatomist. 'The confrontation between the body and the anatomist came to replace the tripartite division of textual authority, living authority and the passive authority of the body' (*Body emblazoned* 64–65). To this I would add, a new authority came into being in this dynamic, as powerful as classical textual authority had been: the visual authority of the anatomical illustration. Within the context of a theatrical space, post-Vesalian anatomical illustrations showed the anatomist and his audience what to see. The incorporation of the company in London in 1540 was virtually synchronous with the creation in Italy of Vesalius's richly iconographic pictorial representations of the anatomized human body, which were to have an overwhelming influence on European anatomy for nearly two centuries to come.[1] At the Barber-Surgeons' lectures, conceptions of masculinity and femininity were disseminated, exhorted in pedagogic rhetoric, visually framed by the illustrations embedded in anatomical texts, and mediated through the example on the table.

'WORSE THEN DEAD BODIES'

What are whores?
They are those flattering bels have all one tune
At weddings, and at funerals: your ritch whores
Are only treasuries by extortion fild,
And empt[i]ed by curs'd riot. They are worse,
Worse then dead bodies, which are beg'd at gallowes
And wrought upon by surgeons, to teach man
Wherin hee is imperfect.
—Webster 3.ii.95–102

Cardinal Monticelso abuses Vittoria Corombona in these terms in the trial scene at the centre of *The White Devil* (ca. 1612). Vittoria has been arraigned for infidelity and on suspicion of being an accessory to the murder of her husband. In the

cardinal's biblically inspired rhetoric, whores, and by extension potentially all women, are corrupt and corrupting in the most literal of senses. The allusions to the gallows, anatomical pedagogy, whoredom, and the law contained within this one speech have a direct connection to, and draw together, all the concerns of this chapter. Webster is referring directly to the practices of the Worshipful Company of Barber-Surgeons of London, who retrieved from the gallows at Tyburn, and publicly anatomized, up to four executed felons a year—all within easy walking distance of the Red Bull, where this play was first staged.

The history of one woman is iconic of the nexus of sex, criminality, death, and display at work here. Elizabeth Evans, known as Canberry or Canonbury Besse, and her confederate in life and crime, Countrey Tom (Thomas Sherwood) were hanged in April 1635 for the murder of three men. Tom had bludgeoned the men so they could be robbed, and Besse had assisted him by drawing these 'gulls' in and fleecing them once they had been attacked. H.G.'s (Henry Goodcole's) reporting of the confession and penitence of Countrey Tom demonstrates the kind of submission before God that was considered appropriate behaviour at the gallows.[2] Tom confesses all his crimes, including the murder of one victim for whose death he had not been indicted, and is brought to salvation in his final hours. Even though Goodcole reports that Tom was the one to wield the blows that killed each of the men, the bulk of the moral disapprobation in *Heavens Speedie Hue and Cry* falls to his partner, Besse.[3]

Besse was a disgrace to her 'very good parentage' in Shropshire, because when she was sent into service in London for her improvement, she 'grew acquainted with a young man in London, who tempted her unto folly, and by that ungodly act her suddain ruine insued' (H.G. A.4.v). Her 'ungodly act' was stereotypically lustful: She was sexually incontinent and was a prostitute for the four years before she met Tom. From that time on she was his constant companion until they were apprehended a year later. As a prostitute Besse acted as the 'decoy Ducke' (A.v), using her sexual availability to tempt each of the victims from the main road, at which point Tom could attack them.

Besse's temptation and fall into a lustful life and death is cast in the mould of an Eve tempted by the devil, and in Tom's gallows confession Besse, like Eve, is represented as the source of her partner's downfall. Tom's confession lays the blame for the criminal turn his life took and his imminent execution, squarely at Besse's door: 'admonishing all that did see him that day, to beware of Whores, for they were the worst Company in the World, wishing all to beware by his fall, and not to be seduced, or blind-fold led, as hee was by such bewitching creatures, to irrevocable ruine' (B.4.v). Between the narrative of Tom's confession to the murders and Besse's gallows speech, there are a further two pages, supposedly imparted to Goodcole by Tom, warning both of the ways in which 'lewd' women may approach one, and the places where one can find such women at work.

In her gallows speech, Besse in turn is reported to have expressed 'a perfect hate, and exclamation against all Theeves, which caused her destruction' (C.2.v). In the report of her contrition before her demise, however, Besse is not allowed either the degree of dignity or the detailed reporting accorded Tom. Further, at the moment when she is allowed to express herself, in a very public manner, her words do not form just a confession or a warning, they become a shrewish railing of 'perfect hate'. Like Eve, Vittoria Corombona, and all representations of exorbitant women of her time, Besse is as free with her mouth as she is with her body. Sinfulness, criminality, and corruption are gendered, and Grandmother Eve is at the heart of Besse's, and consequently Tom's, fall. Though she died 'very penitent', she was not spared the fate of many a victim of the Tyburn Tree: she was 'after her execution conveied to Barber Surgions Hal' (C.3.r).

ANATOMY THEATRES

At their incorporation in 1540, Henry VIII granted the Barber-Surgeons of London a perpetual right to the bodies of four executed felons per annum, to be used at their discretion, as anatomical subjects, 'to make incision of the same deade bodies or otherwyse to order the same after

their said discresions at their pleasure for their futher and better knowlage instruction in sight learnyng and experience in the sayd scyence or facultie or surgery' (32 Henry VIII, cap. 12, cited in Beck 18). The barber-surgeons were sanctioned by the sovereign as the 'authorities' who 'delimited, designated, named and established' (Foucault 42) the human subject as an anatomical object.[4] They did this through a process of practical anatomical pedagogy that was carried out, unlike the few anatomical lectures that were held by their rivals the physicians, in English. While these felons were not their only anatomical subjects—private anatomies and post-mortem were also undertaken (with permission) at the expense of individual anatomers (Young 119–120, 180, 331)—these criminal 'persons' were used for their public anatomies: that is, the regular series of lectures held for the benefit of barber-surgical apprentices and their masters, to which curious 'members of the general public were occasionally admitted' (Pepys 59–60).

Initially regular public anatomies were held in the common hall of the company, with temporary scaffolding erected for the accommodation of the crowd of spectators (Young 315). The court records of the company give an early case of the specifications for such a structure:

1st February, 1568. Also yt ys ordayned and agreed by this Courte That there shalbe buyldyngs don and made aboute the hall for Seates for the Companye that cometh unto every publyque anathomy, ffor by cawse that every prsone comyng to se the same maye have good prspect over the same and that one sholde not cover the syght thereof one frome another as here to Blood and Circuses fore the Company have much cõplayned on the same . . . . And also ther shalbe pyllers and Rods of Iron made to beare and drawe Courteynes upon & aboute the frame where wthin the Anathomy doth lye and is wrought upon, for bycawse that no prsone or prsones shall beholde the desections or incysyngs of the body, but that all maye be made cleane and covered wth fayer clothes untyll the Docter shall com and take his place to reade and declare upon the partes desected. (Young 315)

The theatrical implications of this structure, and the participants and properties appertaining to it, are clear. The scaffolding and seats were arranged to allow the optimum view for the audience. They were invited to gaze into the body, even as they were regulated into taking up that position. Once seated their line of sight was drawn, but not restricted, to what was placed on the centrally located dissecting table.

The temporary scaffold structure was superseded by a purpose-built Anatomy Theatre, designed by Inigo Jones and built between 1636 and 1638 (Figure 4.1). In the plans of this theatre one can see a repetition of the attempted regularization of the audience's attention inherent in the design. The seats all face the central platform upon which the body was dissected. The risers ensure that in the crush of a capacity crowd of around two hundred people (Cregan 123–24) those on the higher levels can see over the heads of those below them. The windows that are indicated would have facilitated ample natural light, a factor that was not a feature of most of the continental Anatomy Theatres. It was decorated, like the Leiden Anatomy Theatre and museum, with admonitory examples, flayed skins and prepared skeletons of the bodies of felons. The walls were also painted with 'the figures of seven liberal sciences and the twelve signs of the zodiac' (Dobson and Milnes Walker 81), a decorative effect that had its counterpart in playhouses like the Globe. A female skeleton was placed 'on the Corbell stone of the Signe Libra', punning on blind justice and her scales, while her male counterpart was set above Taurus: Both had 'the planett Venus governeing those twoe signes underneath' (Young 337).

The plans of the Barber-Surgeons' Anatomy Theatre, and the written description of the temporary scaffold theatres that preceded it, reveal a direct homology between their design and those of the playhouses. This is logical enough, the inspiration for their architecture came from a common source—both were designed under the influence of classical and neoclassical architectural principles. They each had areas equivalent to the orchestra or auditorium, the proscaenium, and the arena in their *theatra*. Raked seating

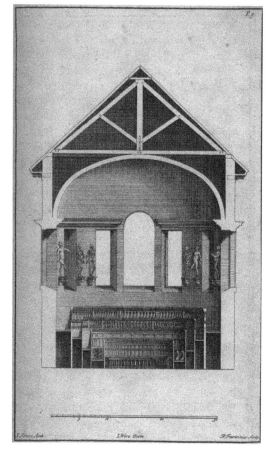

FIGURE 4.1 The Anatomy Theatre at the Worshipful Company of Barber-Surgeons, London, cross-section of the interior, from Isaac Ware's *Designs of Inigo Jones and others* (ca. 1731).

around the margins of each building surrounded a raised central area upon which a formalized scene was enacted on the bodies of subjects scrutinized by an audience prepared to be confronted by a gory spectacle, familiar in the Jacobean playhouses. People went to the public and private theatres to see and be seen. The barber-surgeons went to their theatre to see and to learn a fundamental aspect of their trade. In the ceremonial way in which these anatomies were performed there was also a sense in which the participants were there to be seen. Anatomies were pedagogic apparatuses, but they also functioned as self-legitimating spectacles by which the company asserted and reinforced its position as the sanctioned arbiter of the anatomical subject.

In the early years of the seventeenth century, London was littered with playhouses, from class-inclusive or admixed converted inn yards and baiting houses to the new 'round' public playhouses and the socially segregated private theatres (Gurr 14). Just as in London today one person might be equally at ease in a football stadium, a cinema, or an opera house, an individual theatre patron in the early seventeenth century might frequent all or only one of the Red Bull, the Globe, and the Blackfriars.[5] There are several main features common to the design of all these playhouses. Theatres were first and foremost venues at which the overwhelming imperative was to enable *mass viewing* of the action in play, both on the stage and in the social 'performances' in the galleries and the pit. Auditory considerations work in tandem with this, of course: an actor needs to be seen and heard, particularly in such an aural culture. The construction of the theatres centred, therefore, upon enabling the largest number of people to see the action in progress, with varying degrees of ease and comfort, dependent upon the size of a patron's purse or choice of theatre. In both the public and the private theatres, people were stratified in their physical relation to the stage by their ability to pay, which was also a fair indication of their social rank. A certain measure of attentive behaviour was hoped for if playwright's prefaces are any indication, but, by the same evidence, it was also frequently lacking, with members of the audience taking an active part in voicing their approval or disapproval of what was put before them.

Like the audience of the seventeenth-century public theatres, in the Anatomy Theatre proximity to the 'stage' was determined by professional and/or financial standing, although entry was by invitation rather than payment: High status ensured the best view. In Holland and Italy, where people did pay to attend anatomies, the seats closest to the anatomist were reserved for those who were able to pay for the costlier tickets.[6] In the early seventeenth century the cost of the Barber-Surgeons' anatomies was borne by the company from their general funds, but one's position within the company still regulated one's position within the stands. Apprentices and plebeian visitors were relegated to the stands farthest from the corpse and, like the spectators throwing apple cores or walnut shells onto the playhouse stage from the pit, they could be unruly and call out during the proceedings (Young 366). The more powerful members of the company, like those who took boxes or lords' rooms or sat on the stage in the private theatres, sat closest to the corpse and those who acted upon it.

PERFORMING ANATOMY

Regimens and monetary concerns extended beyond the regulation of behaviour in the theatres. The body at the centre of the theatre was also the product of a series of controlled acts and financial transactions. For at least a century gratuities and regular payments associated with the performance of anatomies formed a significant part of the framework of the company's audit books. The anatomical subject was at the centre of a set of commodifying relations, within which he or she was a consumable object. There were regulations regarding the payment of the beadle and porter for their assistance in collecting the bodies from Tyburn (Young 299, 301, 382).[7] Once the company's right had been claimed, each of the main players had a set fee for taking part in the proceedings.[8] Other payments were also involved in retrieving and eventually disposing of the body. Although the corpse itself was gifted to the company by the sovereign, there were conflicting and competing rights associated with it: for example, the hangman had the right to the clothes of the felon and required recompense if they were not left with him when the body was transported back from Tyburn to Monkwell Square. There were also subsequent costs associated with cleaning up after the anatomy and paying for the burial of the remains. In 1606 the combined burden of these costs led to the suspension of the anatomies for three years because of the poverty of the hall's coffers (Young 327).

The lectures followed a set procedure over three days, given in an order determined by the natural process of decay, with a day devoted to each of the visceral, muscular, and osteological lectures. The public anatomies held on the continent were usually held in the winter months (Ferrari 64–66), which prevented the body from becoming too noisome over the three days' proceedings. Public anatomies at the Barber-Surgeon's Hall followed the same pattern, with lectures given in morning and afternoon sessions (Young 362), but they were held up to four times a year.[9] They fell quarterly, undoubtedly to take advantage of the availability of bodies at the quarterly assizes (Cregan 272).

These performances also had regulations setting out the proper accoutrements for the members of the company and for the linen to be afforded the central players—reader, masters, and stewards. Costume, properties, and setting were manipulated to effect and enhance the pedagogical intent. The terms of these regulations were initially set down in a court minute of '5th March 1555' and were reiterated in 1635 (Young 309, 355). The 1581 portrait of John Banister's anatomy lecture shows the required form of dress in use (Figure 4.2). The title pages of Crooke's ΜΙΚΡΟΚΣΜΟΓΡΑΦΙΑ (1631) and Alexander Read's *The Manuall of the Anatomy or dissection of the body of Man . . .* (1638) also depict ceremonially dressed groups of men in attendance at anatomies.[10]

From the terms of these minutes, the partitioning of anatomical actor from his appreciative audience is clear. Each player in this bloody circus was supposed to behave in an agreed manner and to wear a particular costume that distinguished him in his allotted role.[11] The main performers were not only centrally located within the theatre but their position is also marked out by the 'matte about the harthe in the hall' (Young 309) upon which they stood. The 'ij fyne white rodds appointed for the Docter to touche the body where it shall please him' (Young 309) at once gave the reader the power to point out and describe the

FIGURE 4.2 *The visceral lecture Delivered by Barber-Surgeon Master John Banister Aged 48, Anno Domini 1581.*

body parts being interpreted and allowed him to maintain a distance between himself and the deceased criminal form. Those who dealt with the body had linen 'aprons and sleves every daye bothe white and cleane' (Young 309) that could be changed to avoid begriming their clothes. The barber-surgeons in the audience were supposed to wear caps, hats, and/or gowns signifying their position within the company, just as the populace at large was regulated by wider sumptuary laws. The final character was laid in front of them on a table, upon which the 'business' of the performance was enacted. Even the cadaver had a curtain—later an embroidered pall—in which it was 'clothed' (Young 214). In the raked galleries the 'comon people' observed the spectacle enacted before them. Neglect of these rules attracted fines (Young 335), suggesting a failure to comply with, and an anxiety to ensure, strict adherence to this ritualistic regime.

A small cast of actors played their allotted parts. The reader or doctor, like Prospero in *The Tempest*, governed proceedings, directing the action by declaiming classical authorities on anatomy and appealing to the new authority of the post-Vesalian illustrations that supported them. His attendants, the barber-surgical master and stewards, provided the 'business', laying hands on the body and performing the dissection. The working of this theatre not only shared its layout with the dramatic theatre, it also used analogous spectacular devices to impress its audience. The stewards took care to prepare the body and keep it behind a curtain, confining it to this 'discovery space' until the moment appropriate for its disclosure, when the reader was ready to enter and pronounce over it. In this theatre, however, death was not a ruse. The corpse of the executed criminal, the final actor, was eviscerated, flayed, and the flesh systematically removed from his or her bones.

The material conditions of the Anatomy Theatre at the Barber-Surgeon's hall regulated and disciplined all of the bodies that attended its performances, not just the body of the corpse. They were all subject to a pedagogical regimen, effected through the ritual of the performances that took place in this theatre. Anatomical dissections were

sites of discipline: Both the body and the audience were subject to the authoritative discourse of the anatomy text as pronounced and enacted in this bloody circus. The audience gazed upon the body, which was represented to them by, and mediated through, the word of classical textual authority, declaimed by a lecturer.

The body was framed and represented, defined, monitored, and controlled. The audience who came to view the spectacle of the opened corpse was disciplined within the same dynamic. The anatomical imperative *nosce te ipsum*—'know thyself'—was a literal as well as a metaphoric injunction. The body was not only a reminder of the transience of the flesh; under the anatomical gaze it was also a mirror of the observer, the discursive construction of the corpse reflecting back upon the spectator. As sites that drew spectators, as spaces in which rituals of embodiment were held, the anatomy theatres were also locations where the construction of sex and gender was demarcated as it was in the playhouses. The performance of anatomies was part of the matrix that brought the body into being, under the authority of anatomical illustrations.

'THE FIGURE EXPLAINED'

The painting that commemorates the anatomy lectures given by John Banister in 1581 represents this process of 'authorized' framing in progress. A group portrait, it shows Banister reading a lecture on the viscera, one hand resting on the gut of the opened cadaver, the other holding a 'rod' with which he indicates where those organs would sit in relation to the skeleton, suspended to Banister's right. It stands in the 'case of weynscot made wth paynters worke yr upon', ordered in 1568 (Young 315). To Banister's left, crammed into the upper right quadrant of the painting, are 11 men. One of these figures, by his robes, dignity, and proximity to the body, would appear to be the master of the company. He motions sagely toward the cadaver's head, in a gesture of benediction. Four men, two to Banister's immediate left and two opposite him, are carrying out the actual work of the dissection in the clean white sleeves mandatory for the masters and stewards.

The man immediately to Banister's left holds a probe, the man next to him holds a dissecting knife, their apparel suggesting they are the masters of anatomy. Both rest a proprietorial hand upon the body. The two men on the opposite side of the cadaver appear to be the stewards, who were partially responsible for the procurement and disposal of the body.

The painting shows, on the table at the feet of the corpse, the sort of mess that was complained of as a nuisance to the kitchen: 'hitherto the bodies have been a great annoyance to the tables, dresser boards and utensils of the upper kitchen by reason of the blood, filth, and entrails of these anatomies' (Young 334). Shears, knives, and what appears to be adipose tissue taken from the body litter the lower part of the table. This painting also gives some indication of the kinds of anatomical texts that were in use in this particular Anatomy Theatre. The book that sits on a lectern over Banister's right shoulder is given a dominant position in the painting, higher than the reader himself, and second only in prominence to the skeleton. In this image Banister touches the body and indicates the skeleton, but the text transcribed onto the painting, both in the depiction of the book and the words transposed onto the corpse, makes clear that he has been referring to the book.[12]

Across the opened gut of the cadaver three words appear denoting the upper intestine, the stomach, and the liver. Although the text depicted is unillustrated, apart from its frontispiece, the painter has made the cadaver the anatomical illustration to the text.[13] And in the hierarchy of the participants' scale, which mimics the place of each in the hierarchy of authority (also implicit in the relation between text, skeleton, and reader), Banister is the only character larger than the body of the cadaver. There is a correspondence, too, between the text and the body: What one reads in the book will become clear in and through the form on the table. This painting illustrates how the organs came into being for the audience through the mediating hand of the reader, reinforced by an appeal to the authority of the text. But it goes further by offering the anatomical subject as illustrative evidence, both

within the logic of the painting, as the subject before the assembled audience, and external to the painting, as an illustration to the book on the lectern to the observer of the painting. It is iconic of the shift in the power relation between the anatomist, the body, and the text that was subsequent to the rise of Vesalian illustration.

Anatomy books brought back or imported from the continent, and anglicized for the local classically illiterate market, were illustrated with images infused with the aesthetic mores and theories of Renaissance Italy. Sander Gilman has said, '[I]t is the culturally determined reading of any text or image in its historical (and, indeed, national) context which determines its particular meaning; and one basic aspect of this culturally determined reading of a text is the image of disease which dominates any given culture' (Gilman 155). Gilman's use of the term 'disease' can just as easily be replaced with 'the body'. One of the effects of the migration and multiplication of these continental woodcuts and plates was that some of the factors that influenced their production, such as religious and artistic aesthetics, while not perhaps obtaining directly, were implicit in the dominant discursive representations of the body in England: and they were deeply, stereotypically gendered.

When the patrons of the anatomy theatres of England followed the texts imported from European centres of learning they were taking part in a relatively recent revision of classical anatomical precepts, which saw a shift in authority from the declamatory scholastic tradition to an increasing reliance on empirical observation. Many of the books that were designed to be used at English anatomies as dissection manuals originated in Italy or were based in the practices of educational anatomy as revivified there. Those Englishmen who went on to become the eminent anatomists of the sixteenth and seventeenth centuries had often studied at one or other of the continental universities or had at least visited their Anatomy Theatres (Cook 50–52). Through their aegis, the practice of surgeons, physicians, and anatomists in Padua, Bologna, Paris, and Leiden influenced the practice of surgery and 'physic' in seventeenth-century England.[14] The practice and experience of anatomy in England was infused with both classical anatomical and artistic traditions that had had their rebirth in quattrocento Italy. These drawings were, in turn, permeated by stereotypical assumptions about the 'nature' of 'sex', of sexuality, and of gender: '*Anatomia* operated according to a rigidly gendered set of rules and prohibitions. To those rules and prohibitions, the art, literature, and science of the body were subservient' (Sawday, *Body Emblazoned* 229).

Consider the two figures that appear in the frontispiece and reappear in the body of Helkiah Crooke's ΜΙΚΡΟΚΣΜΟΓΡΑΦΙΑ: *A Description of the Body of Man* (1631): the female gravida figure on the verso and the male *écorché* on the recto. This book is one of the few of which it can be said with certainty that it was in the possession of the Barber-Surgeons: Crooke dedicated it to them and 'donated' a copy of the first edition to the company in 1616 and was granted five pounds for his generosity. It is in English, and it is also known to have been a popular text.[15] These figures are re-engraved from illustrations in Juan Valverde de Hamusco's *Historia de la composición del cuerpo humano* . . . (1556). The female figure originally appeared on the recto of the frontispiece in the first edition as well as in 'The Fourth Booke: Of the Naturall Parts belonging to generation, as well in Man as in Women' (Crooke, *Description* [1615] 197). It shows a pregnant woman with her abdomen partly resected to display a gravid uterus. This illustration had already been reused in Andreas Laurentius's *De anatomice* (1595). Crooke acknowledges his debt to Laurentius and has quite obviously used his re-engraving of the gravid figure rather than Valverde's original. If one compares the three illustrations, Laurentius's and Crooke's are virtually identical, although the engraving in Crooke is a little cruder. That Crooke chose to use Laurentius's version when he obviously knew Valverde's (Crooke 10) is pertinent when one observes their differences. Gesturally, Valverde's original owes much to the penitent nonparous Eve that appears in Vesalius's *Fabrica* and to artistic representations of a newborn, untouched Venus rising from the sea. Valverde's pregnant yet modest Eve covers her right breast and her genitals. There is economy and restraint

in the disposition of her limbs. Her expression is solemn, her eyes properly downcast in shame as she gazes absently to her left.

The reproduction found in Crooke substantially alters the portrayal of the female figure, first and most obviously by reversing her. Other alterations suggest that this is an unrepentant fallen Eve or a lustful Venus. The fingers on the hand that cover the genitals have been splayed further open. This gesture at once suggests concealment and invitation, signifying the characteristic potential for openness or incontinence of even the most chaste woman's body. The left hand covers the left breast, but in straightening the fingers of the hand and moving the point at which the tips of the fingers touch the sternum further across onto the right breast, the figure is made to appear to be erotically presenting her breast to her (male) viewer, much as one presents a nipple to a hungry infant. Not only are the gestures that signify modesty altered, so too are this figure's gaze and expression. When one combines the gestural codes with her direct smiling gaze looking out of the plane of the picture at the viewer, we see another version of Eve or Venus: the seductress. And she is soon to undergo the fulfillment of God's curse: 'I will greatly multiply your pain in childbearing; in pain you shall bring forth children' (Gen. 3:16).

The majority of illustrations used in Crooke's text show little sign of emendation. Where they are adapted they portray the female figures as sexually available and reinforce the casting of male figures as pitiable martyrs. The central male figure of the frontispiece appears in the body of the text in the first edition but is brought to prominence on the title page of this, the second. It shows a man who has seemingly obliged his audience and his anatomist by flaying himself.[16] It is generally accepted that the depiction of this figure has been influenced by representations of the Ethiopian Christian martyr, Saint Bartholomew. Samuel Edgerton has noted the striking similarity between the flayed skin that Valverde's figure holds and that held by Michelangelo's depiction of Saint Bartholomew in the *Last Judgment* (215–19). This obliging fellow is, like the female figure, adapted from Valverde by Crooke's engraver, but in this case only by the introduction of some crude changes to his musculature. His expression and stance portray the nobility of bearing and saintly forbearance that characterizes the original and which is typical of the depiction of the vast majority of male anatomical figures. The only discernible difference is in the ghostly visage of the flayed skin. In Crooke's version it appears to be looking out at the reader, and its expression is more pitiable than the fiercer-looking original. One could take this as a shift in emphasis from the stance of a proud Christian martyr to the resignation of a secularly punished criminal, like Tom.

The choice of these two figures as the opening illustration to the book is appropriate. Like the Adam and Eve given as examples of surface anatomy adapted by Thomas Geminus directly from Vesalius, the male/masculine body is portrayed as repentant, thoughtful, and forbearing; the female/feminine body as sexual. There was in fact some controversy surrounding Crooke's first edition, over the explanation of generation and the illustrations used in this book, on the grounds that they were lewd. Crooke, rightly, argued that the illustrations had been in use for decades, that 'they are no other then those which were among our selves dedicated to three famous Princes, the last a Mayden-Queene' (Crooke 10). Crooke's politically motivated detractors, who alluded to 'Aretine's' postures, had a point, however: the representations of the female form in anatomical illustrations are, like the sexual figures that accompanied Pietro Aretino's sonnets, highly eroticized.

Crooke's text was large and expensive and most probably intended to be the reader's reference on the lectern. This would seem to limit the influence of these illustrations to the privileged few close enough to the centre of the theatre to see them clearly. But these illustrations were more accessible in a vernacular pocket edition, specifically designed for use by barber-surgical apprentices crowded into the raked standings.[17] Alexander Read's *Description of the Body of Man* was an epitome of Crooke's text, which contained the same illustrations and was directly indexed to it, making it a valuable pedagogic tool.[18] The volume is much smaller than Crooke's and designed to be portable and affordable. It is the pedagogical function of Read's text more than the illustrations that appear in it that warrant some comment. The page on which each of Read's figures appears in Crooke's book is given for all the plates, with directions to seek them in 'the History of this Booke at large'. Read's illustrations follow Crooke's in all essential points. The text is severely pared down, however, containing only brief explanatory information on the indicated structures.

In Read's preface he justifies his distillation of Crooke's compilation of the work of others by pointing out some of the disadvantages of large anatomies and the advantages of his own:

> [I]n the aforesaid Authors, the descriptions of the parts being interposed betweene the Figures, distract the minde, and defraud the store house of memory; besides this the volumes are not portable: Whereas by the contrarie, this small volume presenting all the partes of the body of man by continuation to the eie, impresseth the Figures firmly in the mind, and being portable may be carried without trouble to the places appointed for dissection: where the collation of the Figures, with the Descriptions, cannot but affoord greate contentment to the minde. The Printer therefore of the former great volume, hath published this small Manuell, hoping it will proove profitable and delightful! to such as are not able to buy or have no time to peruse the other (Read, *Description* A3r-A3v)

Read's lauding of the lack of complex written explanation and disputation is intriguingly empiricist. Read privileges the 'Figures' or illustrations, over the learned text, in essence because the written text is unnecessary. Written descriptions 'distract the minde' from the images that are clearly understandable to the observing eye. An illustration impresses the 'Figures more firmly in the mind', it aids in committing them to memory more forcefully: an anatomical picture is worth a thousand words. This privileging of the visual image over the written word is also inherent in the title of Read's *The Manuall of the Anatomy or dissection of the body of Man* (1638): the 'Anatomy or dissection' is not explained, it is 'shewed' so that it can be 'methodically digested' and thereby reconstructed.

Read merely states explicitly what is already implicit in the whole process of theatrically displayed anatomies: that the evidence of the eyes and the comparison of figure in the book with figure on the table, or the figure on the corbel stone, will yield up the truth of embodiment itself. That 'truth' comes tied to a wealth of cultural presuppositions. The anatomized female is always seen in terms of her gender, her culture, and her sexual availability. The male form is predominantly shown as an *écorché*, flayed to varying degrees, like a martyred Saint Bartholomew or Marsyas. The female body is *never* shown without some drapery of skin. The muscular, skeletal, and nervous systems are almost exclusively depicted on the male body, as are all the organs common to both males and females. The female body is depicted in these anatomical texts, together with the proliferation of small pamphlets that were indebted to them, solely in terms of its generative function. The effect, then, is to propagate the idea that all the gendered, cultural, gestural, and aesthetic codings that are present in these representations of the bodies of women are in fact true and *essential*.[19]

Sawday argues that the trope of presenting the anatomical subjects as seemingly live creates the effect that the cadaver is complicit in the act of dissection. He argues that the cadaver in the frontispiece of Vesalius's *Fabrica*, a female subject, looks toward Vesalius compliantly, yielding to the act, as if she *'desires* dissection' ('Fate of Marsyas' 123). To which I would add she is also positioned with her genitals facing the reader, her legs parted, breasts bared, and in a position that invites entry. Laqueur states 'she comes out at us from the plane of the picture' (172) and argues that the rhetorical strategy of this frontispiece may be read as 'an assertion of male power to know the female body and hence to know and control feminine Nature' (73). I would argue that it is not so much that the corpse desires dissection but that even in death the feminine body is sexually charged. How could a Renaissance

man conceive of a naked woman who does not express her sexual desires, those irresistible forces by which he believed she was ruled?

As the body is dissected it both becomes an 'anatomy' and reveals anatomy. The title page from Read's *Manuall* exemplifies the slippage between these two terms. Anatomy and dissection are interchangeable, but the act of anatomization is part of the production of anatomy. The body is, then, both the site of a corpus of knowledge and also names and gives meaning to the corpus of knowledge itself. The body, the gendered body, is the product of a set of attributions, properties, and appearances, which are decided upon and shaped by the authority of delimitation that is viewing and describing it. The 'passive authority' of the body is dependent on the discursive construction of meaning within which it is itself constructed. Anatomical illustration forms a part of that discursive constitution of the ontological.

'BEG'D AT GALLOWES'

Canberry Besse came to form an integral part of that ontology in the Barber-Surgeons' Anatomy Theatre. Unlike the majority of felons anatomized by the company, Besse was never accorded the final dignity of being interred. She is, however, mentioned in the Barber-Surgeons' court minutes for 29 March 1638: 'It is ordered that Edward Arris and Hen: Boone shall have libertie to sett up in or Theater a Sceleton by them wrought on when they were Masters Anatomysts on the body of Cañbury besse to be placed on the Corbell stone of the Signe of Libra' (Young 337). The notoriety of her crimes undoubtedly influenced her anatomists to make her a permanent exhibit. Convicted, condemned, and executed, Besse was dissected at the Barber-Surgeons and mounted as a permanent display above their regular public anatomical lectures. The gibbeted remains of her confederate, Countrey Tom—'martyred' at a public crossroads in a manner that made his anatomization, like Saint Bartholomew, virtually redundant—were retrieved at some later date for exhibition opposite her.

Partners in life, crime, and death, Besse and Tom became the two skeletal figures set upon the corbel stones adorned with the symbols of Libra and Taurus, respectively, 'the planett Venus governeing those twoe signes underneath' (Young 337). In death, as in life, Besse was represented as an icon of feminine corruption. When one takes into account her crimes, as relayed in the 'gallows confession' pamphlet, the punning significance of placing her anatomized remains above the Libran scales of justice and her partner in life and in crime above Taurus become clearer. It reinforces the logical end of their physical and criminal partnership. The way in which the Barber-Surgeons chose to display their remains casts them as eternally portraying the lust and corruption that they penitently regretted at the gallows.

Eve was set above Libra, Adam above Taurus. Their skeletal remains, like the cadaver in the Banister painting, were an adjunct to the pedagogical workings of the theatre, a pair of three-dimensional anatomical illustrations. In anatomical illustrations, as on the early modern stage, explicit connections are frequently made between the corrupting nature of a woman's sexual organs, death, and anatomy. Besse became a desiccated exemplar of the dangers of the pleasures of the flesh, reinforcing the pedagogic message that was proffered in the anatomical illustrations before the apprentices. She was such a perfect example of corrupt femininity one assumes she was still there in 1666 and was one of the skeletons whose safe return to the Anatomy Theatre was compensated for after the confusion of the Great Fire (Young 414).

Besse is the only readily traceable body anatomized by the Barber-Surgeons prior to the Restoration, and it is significant that she is a female and a felon. Her criminality, sinfulness, and sexuality are inextricable from her representation both within the Anatomy Theatre and in the reporting of her demise. Hers is also the only body in the surviving records of felons who were anatomized whose ultimate fate is also recorded with the narrative of her crimes and her execution. The rhetoric surrounding her death and her anatomization casts her fate as a just end to a sinful career. Is it any wonder that, though she 'died very penitent,' she was 'after her execution conveied to Barber Surgions Hal for a Skeleton

having her bones reserved in a perfect forme of her body which is to beseene and now remaines in the aforesaid Hall' (H.G. C3.r). And this is applauded, at least by Goodcole.

The anatomization of an individual person in such obvious and direct connection with the workings of justice does not reappear until well into the eighteenth century with the passing of the Murder Act (1752), which made anatomization a legal adjunct to a sentence of death. Legal justice is not particularly important to Besse's narrative. The judicial process through which she and Tom passed, their imprisonment in Newgate and trial at the Sessions House, is dealt with and disposed of in little more than a paragraph. Rather, she is receiving God's judgment and his punishment for a sinful life. It is a just punishment upon an aberrant, exorbitant woman. Not only is her grisly fate relayed along with the reporting of her confession, it is repeated, with less sympathy and more relish, at the end of the pamphlet: 'the Coy-duck, or divellish allurer to sinne and confusion, was dissected and her dryed Carkase or Sceleton of Bones and Gristles is reserv'd, in proportion to be seene in Barber Surgeons Hall' (H.G. C.4.r). This rider is, in effect, an advertisement for the admonitory exhibition she became, set up 'to teach man, / Wherein hee is imperfect.'

Sawday allies the venally explicit representation of the female body to a preoccupation with categorization and control: the illustrations in anatomy manuals that were used as guides to the body bear this out. But Sawday conflates a socially diffuse preoccupation with female sexuality with an apparently heightened enactment of that preoccupation. That the *only* way that the female form was 'seen' was in relation to its sexual availability and venal propensities does not mean that the bodies of women need have been particularly common as anatomical subjects. It just means that when a woman *was* anatomized the motivating factor for doing so was to examine the organs of generation. The same can be said of the allying of femininity, criminality, and the subject of dissection. Amongst those convicted of serious crimes, men grossly outnumbered women: Even on the most extravagant estimate women could not have accounted for more than 20 per cent of those who underwent capital punishment in the seventeenth century (Cregan 247–51).

Certainly the idiosyncratic manner in which William Shepherd, the humorist clerk of the Parish of Saint Olaves, consistently recorded the unnamed burials of publicly dissected persons seems to display a fascination with the anatomization of females, through a decided feminization of the anatomical subject's remains (Register of Baptisms). In the variable orthography characteristic of the period, An or Ann Athomy[20] was buried approximately 18 times in the space of four and a half years between 1644/5 and 1649/50. The facetious use of this pseudonym for the remains of a dissection suggests at once a desire to conceal the fact of the burial of anatomies within the churchyard, scattering them through the register amongst the other Anns late of this parish, and a feminization of the generic subject of the slab. It also hints at a wider fascination, at least for this clerk, with the female subject of the Anatomy Theatre: for him, the splayed and eviscerated female body was seemingly indissociable from the general act of anatomy.

William Shepherd, like the barber-surgeons, anatomists, illustrators, and playwrights of his day, knew the 'truth' of embodiment. Even in the unity of death, at which point logically all bodies suffer the same fate, it is differentiated, and in that difference it is erotically and morally weighted.

NOTES

This chapter is a distillation of the first part of my dissertation. The section titled 'The Figure Explained' is taken from an illustration of a female gravida figure in Jane Sharp's *The Midwives Book* (1671). Here I have to confine my analysis to a single example of the gendering at work in anatomical illustrations, but in my doctoral thesis I have given detailed analysis of over fifty illustrations and surveyed hundreds printed between 1400 and 1700. I would like to thank Jonathan Carter, Denise Cuthbert, and Paul James for their generosity in reading an earlier draft of this work and for their acute insights, comments, and suggestions.

1. See Cushing for a bibliography of the books in which Vesalius's work appears.
2. See Sharpe on the rhetoric of the penitent 'good death' at the gallows.
3. In this respect, as Langbein argues, it is a fairly representative example of its genre (46).
4. Foucault uses madness as an example of an object constructed through and by an authorized discourse, namely medicine: '(as an institution possessing its own rules, as a group of individuals constituting the medical profession, as a body of knowledge and practice, as an authority recognized by public opinion, the law, and government) [it] became the major authority in society that delimited, designated, named and established madness as an object' (42).

5. These three theatres, respectively a converted inn yard, a public playhouse, and a private theatre, are rough equivalents of the sports stadium, cinema, and opera house. The ability to enter these different arenas was, of course, also governed by price: admission varied from one pence to six pence in the public playhouses, but seats in the private theatres were rated in shillings (Gurr 26).
6. See Heckscher (42–3) for Holland and Ferrari (82–4) for Italy.
7. From 1715 this was no easy matter as there were many riots at Tyburn over the removal of bodies, and beadles often found themselves injured in the affray. It is often erroneously assumed that this was always the case, usually by mis-citing Peter Linebaugh's seminal article on eighteenth-century anatomy, 'The Tyburn Riots Against the Surgeons', in Hay et al. Linebaugh is perfectly correct in his argument, but as I have demonstrated in 'Microcosmographia', the same case does not obtain before the eighteenth century.
8. Between 1604 and 1620 the master and stewards received six pounds for performing their duties (*Audit Book*).
9. I have demonstrated conclusively that unlike the continental pre-Lenten public anatomies, the Barber-Surgeons performed their public anatomies virtually all year around, although far fewer were performed in the summer months (Cregan 256–72).

10. Both these books were dedicated to the company so it is fair to assume that these illustrations are intended to reflect their intended recipients to some degree, although in the case of Crooke's work the scene displayed on the verso to the frontispiece does not show the scaffolding used at public anatomies, which by the company's accounts were definitely in use when this reprint of his 1615 *magnum opus* was published (Cregan, appendix 5). It may, however, depict a private anatomical lecture.

11. While there were females who paid their quarterage to the company and female apprentices who may have attended, none were ever office bearers and therefore would not have taken an active role in the public anatomies, much as women did not tread the boards in this period.

12. This has been identified as an octavo edition of Realdus Columbus's *De re anatomica* (Paris, 1572), opened at the section on the viscera (Power 77–8).

13. The imposition of text onto a painting, particularly free-floating banderoles, mottoes, or dates, was far from unusual in English art at this period. The fact that it is imposed on a body is unusual: this is the sort of labelling reserved for maps, like John Speede's, or the adaptation of Saxton's Atlas on which Queen Elizabeth I stands in the 'Ditchley' portrait (Strong 134–6). It is more typical of older (fourteenth- and fifteenth-century) traditions of European anatomical illustration, of 'wound men' and 'frog posture' fugitive sheets.

14. For a brief (if a little jumbled) account of the interrelationship of the practices of Anatomy Theatres in Italy, Holland, England, and France, see van Rupp.

15. I have chosen to be conservative in my choice of texts and selected those I thought were the most accessible and/or the most prolific publi-cations, for the following reasons. Just because an image is striking and rich in metaphor or iconography does not mean that the message being transmitted by it was a widely received or a commonly accepted one. For example, whilst the images in *De dissectione* that Laqueur sets such store by are rich and remarkable, the book was expensive, and I would argue that any implied message in its images reached far fewer people on the continent than would have been the case for those published by Read or Crooke in England. A 'king may go a progress through the guts of a beggar' (*Hamlet* 4.3.30–31), but a lavishly produced, illustrated anatomical text by a physician, who from 1546 was also the printer to King Francis I, would not necessarily reach and influence the perceptions of a beggar, or a barber-surgeon.

16. Sawday reads this figure as Marsyas, flayed by Apollo ('Fate of Marsyas' 126).

17. 'Pocket' editions and fugitive sheets available to the apprentice allowed him or her the agency to observe and interpret the image within the pedagogical process, but the interpretation of those images was directed by the reader, and they also carried with them stereotypical assumptions about gendered attributes.

18. Crooke's full-format book went through six issues and two editions as well as being abridged by Read as his *Description* and further adapted as *The Manuall of the Anatomy or dissection of the body of Man* (London 1638), both of which went through multiple print runs (Russell xxiii, 161–3).

19. This is not the same as saying they are biologically determined; it is more an affirmation of the 'nature of woman' as taught by the Church.

20. The (female) name An or Ann appears in Shepherd's hand with proper surnames throughout the period he kept the register.

WORKS CITED

Audit Book 1659–1674. MS D/2/2 Barber-Surgeon's Hall, Monkwell Square, London.
Beattie, J.M. *Crime and the Courts in England, 1660–1800.* Oxford: Clarendon Press, 1986.
Beck, R. Theodore. *The Cutting Edge: Early History of the Surgeons of London.* London: Lund Humphries, 1974.
Cook, Harold J. *The Decline of the Old Medical Regime in Stuart London.* Ithaca, N.Y.: Cornell University Press, 1986.
Cregan, Kate A. 'Microcosmographia: Seventeenth-Century Theatres of Blood and the Construction of the Sexed Body'. Diss. Monash University, 1999.

Crooke, Helkiall. ΜΙΚΡΟΚΣΜΟΓΡΑΦΙΑ: *a Description of the Body of Man*. London: William Jaggard, 1615.

——. ΜΙΚΡΟΚΣΜΟΓΡΑΦΙΑ: *A Description of the Body of Man*. London, 1631.

Cushing, Harvey W. *A Bio-Bibliography of Andreas Vesalius*. London: Archon Books, 1962.

Dobson, Jessie, and R. Milnes Walker. *Barbers and Barber-Surgeons of London: A History of the Barber's and Barber-Surgeon's Companies*. Oxford: Blackwell Scientific, 1979.

Edgerton, Samuel Y., Jr. *Pictures and Punishment: Art and Criminal Prosecution During the Florentine Renaissance*. Ithaca, N.Y.: Cornell University Press, 1985.

Ferrari, Giovanna. 'Public Anatomy Lessons and the Carnival in Bologna'. *Past and Present* 117 (1987): 57–107.

Foucault, Michel. *The Archaeology of Knowledge*. London: Routledge, 1994.

Geminus, Thomas. *Compendiosa Totius Anatomie Delineatio . . .* Trans. Nicholas Udal. London: 1553.

Gilman, Sander L. *Disease and Representation: Images of Illness from Madness to AIDS*. Ithaca, N.Y.: Cornell University Press, 1988.

G[oodcole]., H[enry]. *Heavens Speedie Hue and Cry Sent After Lust and Murder*. London: N. and I. Nokes, 1635.

Gurr, Andrew. *Play going in Shakespeare's London*. Cambridge: Cambridge University Press, 1991.

Heckscher, William S. *Rembrandt's Anatomy of Dr. Nicolaas Tulp: An Iconological Study*. New York: New York University Press, 1958.

Langbein, John H. *Prosecuting Crime in the Renaissance: England, Germany, France*. Cambridge, Mass.: Harvard University Press, 1974.

Laqueur, Thomas. *Making Sex: Body and Gender from the Greeks to Freud* Cambridge, Mass.: Harvard University Press, 1992.

Laurentius, Andreas. *De Anatomice . . .* Paris: 1595.

Linebaugh, Peter. 'The Tyburn Riots Against the Surgeons'. *Albion's Fatal Tree: Crime and Society in Eighteenth Century England*. Ed. D. Hay, et al. London: Allen Lane, 1975. 65–118.

Pepys, Samuel. *The Diary of Samuel Pepys*. Ed. R.C. Latham and W. Matthews. Vol. 4. London: G. Bell and Sons, 1971.

Power, Sir D'Arcy. *Selected Writings 1877–1930*. Oxford: Clarendon Press, 1931.

Read, Alexander. *cor a Description of the Body of Man*. London: William Jaggard, 1616.

——. *The Manuall of the Anatomy or dissection of the body of Man . . .* London, 1638.

Register of Baptisms, Marriages and Burials, Parish of St. Olaves Silver Street 1561–1770 . MSS 6534 and 6534A Guildhall Library, Aldermanbury, London.

Roberts, K. B., and J. D. W. Tomlinson. *The Fabric of the Body: European Traditions of Anatomical Illustration*. Oxford: Clarendon Press, 1992.

Russell, K. F. *British Anatomy 1525–1800: A Bibliography of Works Published in Britain, America and on the Continent*. Winchester, Hamps.: St. Paul's Bibliographies, 1987.

Sawday, Jonathan. *The Body Emblazoned: Dissection and the Human Body in Renaissance Culture*. London: Routledge, 1995.

——. 'The Fate of Marsyas: Dissecting the Renaissance Body'. *Renaissance Bodies: The Human Figure in English Society C.1540–1660*. Ed. Lucy Gent and Nigel Llewellyn. London: Reaktion Books; 1990. 111–35.

Shakespeare, William. *The Complete Works*. Ed. S. Wells and G. Taylor. Oxford: Oxford University Press, 1986.

Sharpe, J. A. ''Last Dying Speeches': Religion, Ideology and Public Execution in Seventeenth Century England'. *Past and Present* 107 (1985): 144–67.

Strong, Roy. *Gloriana: The Portraits of Queen Elizabeth I*. London: Thames and Hudson, 1987.

Valverde de Hamusco, Juan. *Historia de la composición del cuerpo humano . . .* Rome: Antonio de Salamanca, 1556.

5

A CULTURAL ANATOMY OF THE VISIBLE HUMAN PROJECT

LISA CARTWRIGHT

In 1986, a long-range planning committee of the National Library of Medicine, a division of the National Institutes of Health, speculated about a coming era when the library's widely used bibliographic and factual database services would be complemented by libraries of digital images, distributed over high-speed computer networks and by high-capacity media. The committee encouraged the library to investigate the feasibility of producing a biomedical images library of its own. The Planning Panel on Electronic Image Libraries was formed and in 1990 proposed the ground plan for

a first project: building a digital image library of volumetric data representing a complete, normal adult male and female. This Visible Human Project will include digitized photographic images for cryosectioning, digital images derived from computerized tomography, and digital magnetic resonance images of cadavers.[1]

The library's speculation about the future flow of digital biomedical images was remarkably prescient. In 1986 the application of digital imaging in clinical settings was largely limited to specialized areas, and a computer interface that could link text, graphics, video, and audio on computers around the world was still just the fantasy of a few computer entrepreneurs. By 1994, the year the Visible Human Project's first completed database, dubbed the Visible Man, was unveiled to a global audience of World Wide Web users, digital imaging had become ubiquitous in US medicine, and digital anatomical programs were available in relative abundance on the Web and elsewhere. The National Library of Medicine already provided access to a searchable database of nearly 60,000 images. The website titled 'Anatomical Imaging Sites on the World Wide Web' now lists over 100 destinations, and a single company, A.D.A.M. Software, Inc., whose acronym stands for Animated Dissection of Anatomy for Medicine, advertises over 15 anatomical multimedia programs tailored to users ranging from physicians and scientists to schoolchildren and families. Why, among these images, was press coverage of the Visible Man so extensive? Why the fanfare surrounding its completion in 1994 and the Visible Woman's in 1995? What makes the Visible Man and Woman so different from previous anatomical models and previous ways of organizing biomedical knowledge?

This essay takes up these questions about the project's reception and its difference through an analysis of its various images, texts, and techniques. My central concern is sex difference and other aspects of cultural difference as they are (or are not) represented in the project. In their study of representations of male and female anatomy in texts for US medical students, Susan C. Lawrence and Kate Bendixen show that in the century from 1890 to 1989, anatomy texts remained consistent in their disproportionate use of male figures or male-specific structures to illustrate or describe human anatomy. In these texts, the normal human body is pervasively presented as male, making it impossible to learn female anatomy without first learning male anatomy (e.g., 'the clitoris is commonly described as "homologous with the penis in the male"').[2] By presenting the female body as a variation on the male, or by presenting the male body as a standard for gender-neutral medical information (as was sometimes the case), these texts contributed to the neglect of

health conditions specific to women and the tacit perception of female-specific aspects of anatomy as innately abnormal. Adriane Fugh-Berman, a physician who attended Georgetown Medical School in the mid-1980s, writes about the place of female-specific anatomy in medical teaching: 'The prevailing attitude toward women was demonstrated on the first day of classes by my anatomy instructor, who remarked that our elderly cadaver "must have been a Playboy bunny" before instructing us to cut off her large breasts and toss them into the 30-gallon trash can marked "cadaver waste".'[3]

The salient point here is not that the instructor has a prurient interest in sexualized body parts, but that he views with professional contempt and dismissal parts of the female body precisely because they bear sexual meanings not tied to reproduction. Fugh-Berman's anecdote suggests that anatomy's treatment of the female body may be seen, in this case at least, as the repressive side of a broader cultural tendency to privilege women's bodies as objects of visual pleasure. Terri Kapsalis's recent analysis of gynecology texts cogently demonstrates how such popular conventions of representing sexuality as pornography can serve to make visible that which medicine refuses to image. Kapsalis quotes a female gynecologist: 'When I was in medical school, a fellow student had never seen a naked woman and would start sweating anytime anybody mentioned a pelvic exam . . . A bunch of us bought him a copy of *Penthouse* so he would know what he was going to be looking at.'[4]

In light of these accounts, the National Library of Medicine's decision to make the female body visible rather than opting to create a singular Visible Human on the basis of a male body sounds progressive. As a branch of the National Institutes of Health, the Library had reason to ensure representation of female anatomy. As Anne Eckman explains the NIH was taken to task in a 1990 Government Accounting Office report to Congress for failing to meet a research protocols policy stipulating that biomedical research should emphasize conditions and diseases unique to, or more prevalent in, women. In the wake of the publicity that surrounded this report, women became the focus of new initiatives by the NIH and other medical entities, with one result that in 1991 the term *women's health* entered the *Index Medicus*, the National Library of Medicine's widely used bibliographic index of medical knowledge, signalling among other changes a pervasive recognition of the need to endow women 'with a fully visible and complete set of organs'.[5] The Visible Woman may be seen as one example of this initiative to make women's bodies visible.

The act of making women visible, however, does not in itself address the complex question of how gender difference is constructed and given value in medicine.[6] Lisa Jean Moore and Adele E. Clarke document historical changes in what (if anything) counts as 'the clitoris' in twentieth-century anatomy texts, demonstrating among other things the heterogeneity of representations of, and the contests of definition over, this body part where it is made visible.[7] Thus, it becomes necessary to analyze the ways that difference is assigned to bodies and their parts, and is encoded in medical images. My analysis focuses on the cultural and technical conventions used to produce the Visible Man and Visible Woman. A $1.4 million government-sponsored project that aims to foster the creation of a universally acknowledged set of anatomical images of designated normal male and female bodies, the Visible Human Project promises, in the words of one journalist, to make it possible for scientists to 'study human bodies in ways never before possible'.[8] According to the Center for Human Simulation at the University of Colorado, the team that contracted with the library to produce the project database, the images were created 'to provide a universally-accessible, national resource for anatomical information for researchers, educators, medical professionals, as well as the general public'.[9] How will universal concepts about what is normal anatomy—and which bodies may serve as a standard in medicine—hold up against the specific physicality and history of the citizens on whose bodies the Visible Human Project is based? Moreover, how does this new standard compare to anatomy's past representational practices? My angle on these broad questions is to retrace the acquisition and presence of these images in their current incarnations on the Web and in various commercial productions. My goal is to demonstrate that this massive and universalizing project replicates certain well-known characteristics of older anatomical paradigms, notably the taking of a male body as the standard in medical research and the use of the cadavers of criminals for anatomical dissections, but with an ironic twist: against earlier anatomical practices that identified the criminal body as innately pathological, the body of the Visible Man, based on the cadaver of a convicted felon, is now the basis for a medical norm. A second example of this return to earlier anatomical paradigms is the project's use of older and more broadly familiar conventions of photography and surface modelling in conjunction with more abstract image processes to produce this new anatomical standard. As I demonstrate below, this combination of strategies results in a unique kind of realism[10] that is difficult to reconcile with the range of applications imagined for the project. My overall aim is to show that the Visible Human Project, promoted through the rhetoric of new technologies and advanced scientific knowledge, ultimately is confounded in its goals of creating a new standard for medical research and education.

THE VISIBLE HUMAN PROJECT'S DIFFERENCE

A number of factors set the Visible Human Project apart from the plethora of digital anatomical resources on the market. Most important is its paradoxical status as the last word in virtual-body imaging and the closest thing to an actual living body. The most striking example of the latter is the project's use of 'corpses' (a term used to refer specifically to bodies in the early period after death) rather than 'cadavers' (a term generally applied to bodies preserved for anatomical study).[11] As Paula Treichler notes,

Traditional anatomy texts and classes are based on photographs or illustrations or (more recently) computer-generated images of dissections of cadavers in various stages of preservation and decomposition—and most often cadavers are old people, sick people, or people with lots of pathology. So the Visible Man represents for the first time a young, healthy, 'normal' guy whose tissues and organs are the closest thing possible to a living body. Medical students often describe the shock of seeing living tissues and organs in surgery that look nothing like what they saw dissecting cadavers. The Visible Man and Visible Woman will change that.[12]

The Visible Man and Visible Woman are the closest thing possible to fresh, healthy living tissue and organs because the people used to produce them died in states of relative health and their bodies were immediately frozen rather than chemically preserved. The Visible Man consists of 24-bit digitized computed tomography, magnetic resonance, and photographic images of over 1,800 1.0-millimetre cross-sectional slices of a male corpse, and the Visible Woman is composed of 5,000 images of .33-millimeter slices of a female corpse.

The Visible Man and Visible Woman are regarded as realistic not only because they are based on the closest thing to a living body, but because they are the closest medicine has come to creating accurate and detailed virtual bodies using advanced biomedical imaging techniques. Writing about anatomical representations published between 1900 and 1991, Moore and Clarke note that 'precisely because anatomy is *not* cutting edge biomedical science and has supposedly been comparatively stable, we can see its (re) constructions more vividly'.[13] The Visible Human Project is a watershed in anatomy because it uses advanced biomedical imaging techniques, and in doing so it dramatically breaks away from the relatively stable view of bodily structure presented in prior anatomical constructions. The corpses used to produce the Visible Man and Visible Woman were subjected to computerized tomography and magnetic resonance imaging. It is widely reported (in project literature and press accounts) that the research team that produced the data sets embedded in gelatin and deep-froze the two corpses, then sawed them each into four

large chunks and passed these through a cryogenic macrotome—a kind of high-tech meat slicer. Then, as they milled away[14] each body from head to toe in ultrathin increments, a colour photograph was taken of each of the flat cross-sectional planes exposed on the face of the remaining frozen block (Figure 5.1).[15] These thousands of cryographs were then numbered in series and scanned into a computer animation program, which would eventually allow users to stack, disassemble, and volume-render discrete parts or whole bodies. Programs based on the data sets allow users to move optically through these highly detailed images of body sections via hypermedia links, three-dimensional reconstructions, and fly-through animations in which one can construct and travel through the minute spaces of various systems from a range of vantage points.

The image of slicing fresh bodies evokes earlier anatomical techniques—the messy practice of physically unlayering bodies through hands-on dissection, for example. For users of the project database, however, actual contact with the viscera of corpse, cadaver, or living body is conveniently replaced by virtual contact. Participants in the many interactive and virtual reality programs designed using Visible Human data are able to see and manipulate fresh organs and tissue carefully simulated to approximate living structures so closely that surgical techniques may be practised upon them with great precision. As one project program advertisement suggests, users may 'explore an entire human body with the click of a mouse!'[16]

The rhetoric of the virtually real appears frequently throughout discussions about the project. The Center for Human Simulation states that its goal is to enable the user to interact with the Visible Human imagery 'in very real ways', asserting in a caption beneath one Visible Man rendering that 'the tattoo [visible in the image] and all of the colors are real' and 'this is not a photograph!!' but a computer-generated view created directly from Visible Man body slices.[17] Ben Schneiderman, head of the Human-Computer Interaction Laboratory at the University of Maryland at College Park, also emphasizes the

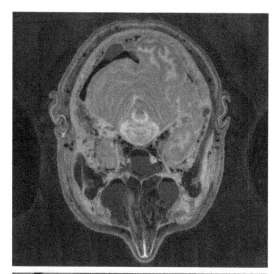

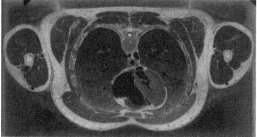

FIGURE 5.1 Photographic cryosections of head and thorax of the Visible Man.

realism of the Visible Man as compared to other anatomical renderings; 'Medical textbooks give us a highly interpreted view of the human body, emphasizing key organs. This [the Visible Man database] was a raw and fresh perspective that told me things about my own body that I never knew before.'[18] A Women's Wire news story re-iterates the premium placed on realism in the non-scientific press, revealing details about the woman whose body was used to make the Vis-ible Woman data set in order to support the assertion that 'the images are not artificially created forms'.[19] The combination of raw, fresh (unpreserved) flesh and virtual imaging thus confers on the Visible Man and Visible Woman a level of authenticity well beyond that conferred on the photograph of the cadaver, the digital

image, or most any other mode of anatomical documentation prior to the Visible Human Pro-ject's inception.

What further sets the project apart from other contemporary anatomical programs is its perva-sive presence in both public as well as profes-sional settings. The stated goal of the Center for Human Simulation is to 'enable the user, from the 12-year-old science student to the practicing surgeon', to use the database.[20] Although the im-ages are not in the public domain, a sampling of them can be downloaded from the Web by anyone without revealing one's identity, and the entire data sets can be downloaded, for a fee, through a licensing agreement.[21] The Visible Man's 400-plus licensees include physicians in the US Army, who are using the Visible Man to simulate the passage of shrapnel through flesh and bone; an interdisciplinary team at the State University of New York at Stony Brook, which has created an interactive fly-through anima-tion of the Man's colon as a step toward de-veloping a scanning test for colon cancer; the publishing company Mosby, Inc., which is cre-ating a commercial CD-ROM and printed atlas in conjunction with a computer animation com-pany; and teachers and students at Smoky Hill High School, who are creating their own Visible Human Digital Anatomy Project. The project's global scope is indicated by the presence on the Web of its Far East site, based at the University of Singapore.[22] The National Library of Medicine is working on imaging transmission technolo-gies that would broaden this already wide base of licensees in much the same way it now makes accessible to countless medical professionals 8.6 million text-based records dating back to 1966 and an index of articles from over 3,800 biomedical journals (through database services such as Medline). As a featured project of the federal entity that brings us Medline, the self-proclaimed 'premier bibliographic database cov-ering the fields of medicine, nursing, dentistry, veterinary medicine, the health care system, and the preclinical sciences',[23] the Visible Hu-man Project stands a strong chance of becom-ing the international gold standard for human anatomy in coming years.

The current high profile of the Visible Man goes beyond medicine proper. His appearances in 1995 through 1996 included a gallery exhibition in Japan, where Visible Man images were displayed alongside body renderings by Leonardo Da Vinci, as if to suggest that this model is the new paradigm of human anatomy. The Man also served as a model for ergonomic furniture: designers studied the range of his motion to design more comfortable seating.[24] Each month new videos, interactive videodisks, and CD-ROMs based on both the male and female data sets are introduced through websites and advertisements placed in journals ranging from *Science* to *Wired*. Stories about the Man have been featured in venues ranging from international news wires and National Public Radio to local newspapers and the *Chronicle of Higher Education*. The Visible Man's public profile is high in part because his was the first data set to be completed (because an appropriate male cadaver became available first, not because a male body was deemed more necessary to the database). A more significant source of his celebrity, though, is the fact that the press revealed information about the identity of the man whose corpse was used to make the male data set. The story behind this breach of donor privacy is significant to my consideration of sexual and cultural difference in at least two ways. First, whereas medical accounts of the actual and potential uses of the Visible Man represent him as a universal anatomical norm, medical accounts of the Visible Woman highlight factors about her body and identity that potentially limit her data set's applicability to research that is not universal, and not even universally female. While the recognition of the specificity of bodies is not a bad thing, this discrepancy of treatment raises several questions: Why are the attributes of sex made prevalent only in the case of the female body? And how do researchers justify elevating the Visible Man to a universal standard while specifying the need (as we shall see) for more than one female model? Second, while the Visible Man has attained an honourable public profile, whether as modern-day hero or martyr to science, the Visible Woman has been much less glamorously received.

THE VISIBLE COUPLE: INTERNET ANGEL AND POSTMENOPAUSAL HOUSEWIFE

It seems only natural that a project that so strongly foregrounds the real of the bodies involved would invite cultural narratives about those bodies. This tendency has extended to the ascription to the project of conventional heterosexual family models, not only by the press but by project personnel. 'The Visible Man has been an incredibly big success', states Donald Lundberg, director of the National Library of Medicine. 'But you have to have a female body to go with the male'.[25] The prevalence of this view that the female body is necessary only after, 'to go with', the male is evident in accounts of the project that refer to the Visible Woman as a 'mate' (as in *Science*'s news story, 'Visible Man Gets High Resolution Mate') or to the data sets collectively as 'the Visible Couple' or a 'digital Adam and Eve'.[26] The implication, of course, is that female anatomical information is necessary for the analysis of reproductive anatomy. Accordingly, the Visible Woman is the basis for such projects as a grant proposal to the Women's Health Research Program of the Department of Defense involving use of the images for virtual reality training in gynecologic and reproductive health care.[27]

In at least one respect, however, this particular configuration of the Visible Couple doesn't quite mesh with the larger family picture imagined by the Center for Human Simulation. The discrepancy hinges on the age-appropriateness of the Visible Woman for her role as partner to the Man. Whereas the Visible Man is based on the corpse of a 39-year-old, the Visible Woman's source was 59 when she died. How age is deemed medically relevant has bearing on the construction of cultural norms and standards in the project. Where the Visible Man's age is mentioned, it is cited as evidence of his status as an exemplar of normal (healthy and fit) male anatomy. Victor Spitzer, head of the Center for Human Simulation, describes the middle-aged 39-year-old corpse in terms of youth and fitness: 'In a younger body', he explains, there is good muscle tone, and you can see the anatomy. In an older body things get smaller.'[28] Press coverage also tends to overstate the Man's youth (39 is hardly young) and fitness, suggesting that these characteristics are central to collective mythologies about the normal male body. Wheeler notes that Ben Schneiderman, the person who learned about his own body from the Man data, 'was surprised . . . by the way the images revealed the strength of the thighs'.[29] Even the Man's weight (199 lbs.) is referenced only in passing, not as a factor in assessing whether his body does, in fact, constitute a norm.

The project's presentation of the Visible Woman suggests different criteria for normal female anatomy. The Visible Woman is represented as older, her age is linked to her sex and reproductive function, and specifically it is implied that she is postmenopausal. Victor Spitzer, a member of the team that produced the data sets, states the team's intention to seek further subjects—identified as 'a fetus and a premenopausal woman'—to complete the data bank, implying that unlike the Man the current Visible Woman is not an adequate standard because she is postmenopausal and presumably therefore unsuited to demonstrating processes of reproduction.[30] The Visible Woman comes into being not only as a counterpart to the male model, but as an incomplete one at that. A premenopausal woman and a fetus are needed to make the Visible Family a viable reproductive unit. In their study of gender and sex bias in anatomy and physical diagnosis text illustrations, Kathleen Mendelsohn and colleagues found that women are dramatically under-represented in illustrations of normal, non-reproductive anatomy, with one outcome that students may develop an incomplete knowledge of normal female anatomy except with respect to the reproductive system, which is not under-represented; because 'society has traditionally valued women most for their reproductive function and their role as mothers, it is not surprising that scientists and physicians would share this bias'.[31] Similarly, women become visible in the Visible Human Project primarily on the basis of their reproductive function. The current and future Visible Women exist in relationship to menopause, a term that does the double duty of inscribing age and reproductive ability as essential aspects of normal women's anatomy.

Perhaps ironically, women probably stand to benefit from the availability of more specific models for medical research and teaching. As Lawrence and Bendixen note, the neglect of representations of women's anatomy leads to a lack of training in health conditions specific to women. They conclude that more images are better. The project's treatment of difference, however, is clearly problematic because the difference at issue, in concept at least, primarily seems to be reproductive anatomy. The prospect of gender-neutral uses of images (i.e., illustrations in which gender is not made obvious by the image or the caption) is worth considering since the Man data set in particular has been used for a number of projects, such as the colon fly-through, in which gender is not apparently a central issue. As by far the more detailed of the two image sets, however, the Visible Woman is likely to become the more useful model for programs requiring detailed data (virtual reality renderings for surgical simulations, for example). Mendelsohn and colleagues note that the use of apparently neutral illustrations poses an interesting dilemma: 'Although neutral illustrations avoid bias by portraying neither sex', they explain, 'they do not address the known physical and functional differences between the sexes' beyond those of the reproductive system. They conclude that 'neutral illustrations should be avoided in favor of equal representations of both sexes'.[32] It remains to be seen whether the existing Woman data set will also be used to support sex-specific research on subjects other than reproduction, and whether the Man data set will be identified as sex-specific in research that is not about the reproductive system. The outcome of these questions will be determined not by the producers of the database alone, of course, but collectively by the vast range of federal and commercial entities using the image sets for discrete research and educational programs.

The dilemma of neutrality posed by Mendelsohn and colleagues is indeed an interesting one with reference to the Visible Human Project since professional and popular accounts rarely fail to identify not only the gender but other aspects of the cultural identity of the respective bodies.

At this point, each data set bears a considerable amount of cultural baggage, so that even in the most scientific of applications it would be difficult for those involved to overlook the identities inscribed in the images. Shortly after the Visible Man's Web debut, the press identified him as John Paul Jernigan, a 39-year-old convicted felon executed by the State of Texas who had willed his body to science. In 1981, Jernigan was caught by surprise in the midst of a home burglary in which he stabbed and fatally shot the homeowner. Texas courts found Jernigan guilty of murder and sentenced him to death by lethal injection. Twelve years after the crime, prison workers attached an IV catheter to Jernigan's left hand and administered a drug that effectively suppressed the brain functions that regulate breathing. As journalist David Ellison has put it, the drug made Jernigan forget how to breathe.[33]

Jernigan may have led a life of crime, but on at least one count, he was a model citizen: He had signed a donor consent authorizing scientific use of his body upon death. Jernigan's generous intentions might have been thwarted by the fact that the cause of his death was lethal injection, a process that left his organs contaminated and hence useless for transplant into another (living) body. However, his age, body type, and health condition suited perfectly the needs of the researchers from the University of Colorado at Boulder who had won a contract from the National Library of Medicine to produce the Visible Human database.[34] A relatively healthy corpse in such fine condition is hard to get. The team, which had been searching for over a year, seized the chance to acquire Jernigan's corpse for the part of the Visible Man.

Neither the library nor the Center for Human Simulation meant for Jernigan's identity to become public knowledge. Michael Ackerman, library head of the Visible Human Project, explains that 'the cadavers which the project receives are anonymous donations. In the case of the male cadaver, he died of court-ordered lethal injection in Texas on August 3, 1994. From this information the press tracked down his life story.'[35] The Visible Man raised the historical spectre of anatomy's use of the cadavers of charges of the state—principally criminals and the insane—for autopsy.[36] Some of the press broached this issue (minus the historical perspective) as an ethical question, ironically overlooking the questionable ethics of their own decision to broadcast Jernigan's name and life history. National Public Radio delicately posed the question of using a prisoner's body while noting the project's technological achievements. David L. Wheeler's article in the *Chronicle of Higher Education* recounts minor details of Jernigan's story (such as the contents of his last meal), dubbing him an 'Internet angel' and even proposing a narrative of divine retribution through service to science. 'In his life, he took a life,' Wheeler writes. 'In his death, he may end up saving a few.'[37] (Though the article was published a few months after the release of the Visible Woman, she is mentioned only in passing.) That the story's appeal is Jernigan is made clear from the lead pull quote, the ethical implications of which are never pursued in the article text: 'From the cadaver of an executed murderer, scientists produce digital anatomical images.'[38]

If Jernigan's public persona is Internet angel, the Visible Woman might be said to have the less stellar title of Internet housewife. Although the donor whose body became the Visible Woman remains anonymous as per her legal instructions, certain facts about her identity and health have become public knowledge: she was a 59-year-old Maryland housewife; she had 'never been sick a day in her life'; she died in her sleep of a myocardial infarction. According to one account, her husband, who had read a news story about the project, specifically requested that her body, which she had left to science, be donated for the part of the Visible Woman. Gender is thus at issue in the public construction of the Visible Woman's persona as well, with her husband acting as broker, not only volunteering her body for the job but providing the information he deemed suitable to the press.[39]

The project's highly touted realism poses another interesting dilemma vis-à-vis neutrality versus specificity: that of markers of racial identity (or their absence) in the data sets. Surprisingly, Jernigan's racial identity has not been discussed alongside his other vital statistics in descriptive accounts. Given the disproportionately high per-centage of black men in prison populations, it is surprising that Jernigan's racial identity has not come up along with his other vital statistics in descriptive accounts. His mug shot, which has been published (in monochrome not colour), would suggest that he is white; however, a de-termination based on appearances can only be speculation. This guess is reinforced by some of the imagery associated with the project. One of the options of a volume-rendering program based on the Visible Man and Visible Woman is to allow the user not only to reassemble the form of the body, but to reconstitute its containing organ, the skin. The Visible Man and Woman's optically and physically decomposed bodies are uncannily reconstituted quite literally in the flesh, using a high-resolution 3-D surface-construction algo-rithm called Marching Cubes.[40] These full-body surface models include dimensional renderings of the face, a part typically concealed in medical images in order to maintain the anonymity of the subject (Figures 5.2 and 5.3). The conventional photographic clarity of these images differs dra-matically from the kind of realism and clarity associated with the photographic cross-sections. Here we see body images that eerily resemble con-ventional full-body photographs of living bodies. The fact that these images are accessible on the Web poses obvious problems for the mainten-ance of subject anonymity and, moreover, raises questions about the encoding of racial difference that have been entirely unaddressed. In its col-ourized appearance on screen, this rendering has a uniform pinkish beige tone, matching precisely the old Crayola crayon whose label 'flesh' implied that whiteness is the norm and this particular hue is the standard skin tone. Certainly this almost comical cliché of flesh tone is not an example of the program's highly touted realism; the com-puter rendering can't possibly match the corpses' actual skin tone. Is it an example, then, of the project's idea of what constitutes viable stan-dards and norms? The decorative tattoo on the Man's chest present and highlighted in the cap-tion of the image described on page 62 has been erased from this rendering, suggesting that it is not meant to replicate the specificity of Jernigan's

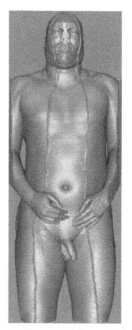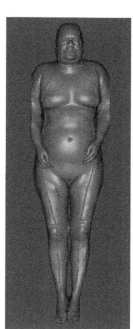

FIGURES 5.2 and 5.3

body. Regarding the project's quest for a detailed anatomical model, we must ask which aspects of the body matter and which aspects are permitted to remain in the realm of crude stereotype.

A UNIVERSAL STANDARD OR A 'CATALOGUER'S NIGHTMARE'?

The project's rhetoric of realism merits closer examination with respect to its agenda of fa-cilitating anatomical knowledge. A Center for Human Simulation document notes that 'the current knowledge explosion in biomedical sci-ences necessitates greater efficiency in training, data search, and testing for all health care profes-sionals' in the area of anatomy, which 'provides much of the fundamental vocabulary of the health care professional' but poses difficulties in dimensional visualization.[41] While the Center sees the Visible Human database as a means to greater efficiency in the organization and dis-semination of anatomical knowledge, there is evidence that the project may be introducing unanticipated degrees of complexity to the field.

Spitzer has remarked, 'The Visible Man is useful if you already know anatomy. It's difficult to learn any anatomy from him.'[42] This is a rather startling statement, given that the aim of the project is precisely to teach and to clarify anatomy. It appears that the project's emphasis on detailed realism has paradoxically confounded its goal of furthering anatomical knowledge. Wheeler writes that 'as scientists moved beyond their initial aesthetic reactions to the images . . . they were quickly confronted with the Visible Man's most important failing', that is, the absence of labels showing which organs are where among the thousands of images in the data set. As Ackerman puts it, 'For a librarian, this is very unsettling. It's like having books lying all over the place not indexed or cataloged.'[43] This disarray is exacerbated by the incommensurability of written and visual data in computer programs and by the fact that the photographic cross-sections were not shot at uniform intervals and with consistent magnification levels, adding to the difficulty of correlating information from one body slice to the next. These problems of organizing the data and standardizing the images are certain to be addressed as programs fostering image-text compatibility are developed and as the data continue to be processed by program licensees. However, it is unclear whether these problems will be resolved or exacerbated as hundreds of project users bring their respective organizing principles, needs, and aesthetics to the job. The following Web posting by radiation oncologists at the University of North Carolina at Chapel Hill indicates how far the project might be from its goal of standardization and efficiency:

> We (the Radiation Oncology department at UNC, not NLM) are dealing with the frozen Male CT scans and have found many errors. We think that the information we have gathered about the images is important and so are sharing it. We are also sharing the corrected images at this time (cf. license agreement) but do not have sufficient resources to spend much time doing this!
>   . . . [W]e needed to strip the arms from the body because they are not in normal scanning position for a pelvic study. We also needed all

of the scans in the head & neck area to be of identical zoom (magnification factor). We will make some of these reworked scans available to other institutions, free of charge over a network connection, after the recipient signs a license agreement with the NLM. Of course, this depends on our current work-load.[44]

Problems of image standardization and organization suggest that anatomical knowledge is not always commensurable across fields, and hence a universal anatomical model is not viable. The problem of commensurability is undoubtedly aggravated by the proliferation of medical subspecialties, which include a multitude of imaging modalities, each with its own conventions for rendering and interpreting data and its own idea of what constitutes realism. The range of images (computed tomography, magnetic resonance, and photographic) that comprise the Visible Human Project suggests that the disarray of the database goes beyond lack of unity within each body set to include (potential) lack of translation or correspondence across modalities. The Center for Human Simulation sets as its general goal facilitation of collaboration among an impressive list of specialists, but the length of this list in itself indicates the potential for problems of commensurability of knowledge and goals. It includes anatomists, radiologists, computer scientists, bioengineers, physicians, educators, mathematicians, pathologists, anthropologists, medical information specialists, and library scientists.[45] Ironically, the very proliferation of new technologies that has made the Visible Human Project so appealing has also created needs so specific that a universal database, much less universal bodies, cannot adequately serve them.

This crisis of commensurability can be characterized in terms of a paradox of visibility: The Visible Human Project was devised in part in answer to a demand for anatomical images providing greater and more detailed information about the human body. In filling this demand, the project has generated a level of quantity and detail beyond that which its users are equipped to process. Moreover, as the UNC case above demonstrates, the very specificity of the data precludes its universality. This paradox suggests that it would be fruitful to consider more closely the techniques used to produce and interpret the Visible Man and Visible Woman.

In their analysis of anatomical representations of the clitoris, Moore and Clarke note that two kinds of images were predominant in texts published between 1981 and 1991: photography of cadavers—a technique whose introduction they describe as resulting in 'a new vivid realism'—and the newer techniques of computer-generated imaging—which, they argue, 'delete the range of variation' among bodies and, moreover, 'delete the body itself' insofar as computer-generated images are more difficult to translate than conventional photographs.[46] Moore and Clarke express concern that computer images' deletion of specific characteristics of gender, race, class, and culture along with their general dematerialization of the body may ultimately eliminate women from the anatomical picture, much as they have been disappearing in reproductive discourses.[47] The Visible Human images fit and exceed the categories described by Moore and Clarke, suggesting a new paradigm for the 1990s. I have cited numerous sources suggesting that the project's colour photographs of corpses introduce a new realism even more vivid—and certainly more vivified—than cadaver photography. And the computed tomography scans, magnetic resonance images, and cryographs all involve computer-imaging techniques that make it difficult even for trained researchers to visualize the whole body on the basis of these images (the 'nightmare' of uncatalogued cryographs). The computer-generated graphics noted by Moore and Clarke, however, are essentially line drawings. They do not share the Visible Human images' detailed correspondence with actual bodies. Whereas the graphics Moore and Clarke describe fail to evoke a body because they are schematic and abstract, the Visible Human images fail to evoke a body because they detail 'parts' so minute and so arbitrarily segmented that they preclude ready recognition and categorization. For instance, a single 0.33-millimetre cross-section of the Visible Woman's torso might provide a bit of data about any number of structures including the breasts, the lungs, the heart,

the skeletal system. Though the data are highly detailed, they may be hard to place in context of an entire body because (a) the slice does not correspond to conventional ways of dividing the body for anatomical study (according to systems or organs, for example); and (b) the wealth of minute detail makes it difficult to determine which aspects of the data field matter and which do not. The very aspect of the project lauded by Schneiderman—the fact that its computer renderings are not highly interpreted like other anatomical images—becomes a factor in its lack of 'face recognition'. Ironically, close attention to anatomical detail—to differences right down to the cellular level—is a factor in the apparent failure of individual images in isolation from the set to evoke the material body. At this point in time, the images may take on embodied life for some after significant modification (as in the various interactive and virtual reality programs that give the Visible Man and Visible Woman attributes such as dimensionality, wholeness, and flesh colour). But, of course, it is only a matter of time until those working with the project in their laboratories, secondary school classrooms, and home computer workstations encode and enliven the discrete images with new cultural meanings. What those meanings will be vis-à-vis gender, race, and other differentials remains to be seen.

CONCLUSION

It is striking that the Visible Human Project, a federal initiative to generate a universal set of anatomical norms, was launched at a moment when the government also began to subsidize the Human Genome Project, an even broader-based (and more heavily funded) international search for a detailed universal encoding of life. The projects share the paradox of seeking to create a universal archive through which to represent and to know human biology, while rendering their respective body models with a level of specificity that may ultimately confound goals such as the establishment of a norm. Both projects are beset with the difficulty of determining what data are relevant from among the surfeit of information represented. However, while genome research is largely the province of official science, the Visible Human Project exists in a somewhat more ambiguous zone between medicine, media, and science. Available on the Web and through a relatively inexpensive licensing fee, the Visible Human database approximates shareware (computer programs distributed widely and for free) when compared to the findings of genome research. As such, the Visible Man and Woman may be viewed, used, and altered in ways neither anticipated nor approved by the National Library of Medicine and the Center for Human Simulation. This factor suggests that there is no singular Visible Human Project, but rather a heterogeneous range of project applications and, moreover, that the possibility exists for using the data in unexpected ways.

How will this potential play out with regard to the representation of sexual difference? I noted above that women may benefit from the availability of more specific models for medical research and teaching. But one could easily argue from either perspective: that an army of Visible Women would better support research on diseases with manifestations particular to age, genetic makeup, or any other set of characteristics and conditions; or that such research might foster wrongful designations of sex-based pathology. The relevant question, however, is not whether more or fewer images of women will aid or offset the inadequate regard of women in medicine, but what agendas the current and future Visible Women will serve, and how anatomical difference will be constructed through the various imaging techniques used to render these models. Will the highly touted realism of the simulations based on the Visible Human data sets always replicate conventional views of the gendered body, or will they introduce new ways of seeing, ultimately shaking anatomy's static paradigms of binary sexual difference? Are anatomy's visible women likely to be biomedical Stepford wives, supporting research that reinforces historical views of women as exceptions to (male) anatomical norms and creating new needs for women on the basis of iatrogenic anxieties about their difference being pathological (e.g., the need for hormone therapy)? Or will more detailed and diversified anatomical models support inquiry into sex-specific factors of health and disease including and beyond conditions linked to reproduction? Moreover, will the project eventually recognize the limits of its current familial model and generate a range of male and transgendered as well as female anatomical specimens? The current disarray of the images, the mix of project licensees and website image poachers, and the range of potential applications of the data make it difficult to place a bet on any one answer. For the moment, the heterogeneity and confusion of this 'universal' database makes these questions remain promisingly open.

NOTES

1. National Library of Medicine (US) Board of Regents, 'Electronic Imaging, Report of the Board of Regents', US Department of Health and Human Services, Public Health Service, National Institutes of Health, 1990. NIH Publication 90–2197.

2. Susan C. Lawrence and Kate Bendixen, 'His and Hers: Male and Female Anatomy in Anatomy Texts for US Medical Students', *Social Science and Medicine* 35.7 (October 1992): 925–33. Citation from 925.

3. Adriane Fugh-Berman, 'Man to Man at Georgetown; Tales Out of Medical School', *Nation* (January 20, 1992): 1, 54.

4. See Chapter 4 of Terri Kapsalis, *Public Privates: Performing Gynecology from Both Ends of the Speculum* (Durham, NC; Duke UP, 1997) 81–111. Quotation from 81. This is not to imply that women's sexual organs are not represented in medical textbooks. On this point see Lisa Jean Moore and Adele E. Clarke, 'Clitoral Conventions and Transgressions: Graphic Representations in Anatomy Texts, c. 1900–1991', *Feminist Studies* 21.2 (Summer 1995): 255–301.

5. Anne K. Eckman, 'Beyond 'The Yentl Syndrome': Making Women Visible in Post-1990 Women's Health Discourse', The Visible Woman: Imaging Technologies, Gender, and Science. Eds. Paula

A. Treichler, Lisa Cartwright and Constance Penley New York: NYU, 1998 130–68.

6. Evidence that making women visible will not in itself address this larger issue can be found in the numerous critical studies of scientific and medical representations of the body which have shown that historically where bodies and their parts are identified as sex- or race-specific these models have often been used to support arguments about the biological bases of pathology to the exclusion of environmental and social factors. The literature on the construction of sexual and racial difference in anatomy, science, and medicine is extensive. It includes: Nancy Leys Stepan, *The Idea of Race in Science: Great Britain, 1800–1960* (Hamden, CT; Archon Books, 1982); Ludmilla Jordanova, *Sexual Visions: Images of Gender in Science and Medicine between the Eighteenth and Twentieth Centuries* (Madison: U of Wisconsin P, 1989); Thomas Laqueur, *Making Sex: Body and Gender from the Greeks to Freud* (Cambridge; Harvard UP, 1990); Cynthia Eagle Russett, *Sexual Science: The Victorian Construction of Womanhood* (Cambridge: HarvardUP, 1989); Londa Schiebinger, *The Mind Has No Sex? Women in the Origins of Modern Science* (Cambridge: Harvard UP, 1989); Sander Gilman, *Pathology and Difference: Stereotypes of Sexuality, Race, and Madness* (Ithaca; Cornell UP, 1985); Elizabeth Fee, 'Nineteenth-Century Craniology: The Study of the Female Skull', *Bulletin of the History of Medicine* 53 (1979): 415–33; David Horn, 'This Norm Which Is Not One: Reading the Female Body in Lombroso's Anthropology', in *Deviant Bodies*, Jennifer Terry and Jacqueline Urla, eds. (Bloomington: Indiana UP, 1995) 109–128; Allan Sekula, 'The Body and the Archive', *October* 39 (1986): 3–64; Thomas Forbes, 'To Be Dissected and Anatomised', *Journal of the History of Medicine and Allied Sciences* 36 (1981); 490–2; Giuliana Bruno, 'Spectatorial Embodiments: Anatomies of the Visible and tile Female Bodyscape', *Camera Obscura 28* (1992): 239–61. For opposing discussions of more recent findings regarding biological difference, see Simon LeVay, *The Sexual Brain* (Cambridge: MIT Press, 1993); and Jennifer Terry, 'Anxious Slippages Between 'Them' and 'Us': A Brief History of the Scientific Search for Homosexual Bodies', in *Deviant Bodies*, Urla and Terry, eds.

7. Moore and Clarke 255–301.

8. Jacqueline Stenson, '"Visible Woman" Makes Debut on the Internet', *Medical Tribune* News Service, November 28, 1995.

9. From the website of the Center for Human Simulation, February 2, 1996.

10. I'd like to clarify my use of the term 'realism' since much of this essay takes issue with its use. In their classic introductory film studies textbook, David Bordwell and Kristin Thompson argue against using the term realism as a standard of value in judging films because the conventions associated with realism vary according to historical period, genre, and other aspects of context (*Film Art*, 5th ed. [New York: McGraw Hill, 1996]). The same argument can be made about realism in science and medicine. It is worth asking whether conventions of realism are in fact the most useful means of 'learning more' about, or 'better representing' the body in anatomy. Catherine Waldby provides a more extended discussion of the Visible Human Project in terms of conventions of realism and representation in 'Revenants: The Visible Human Project and the Digital Uncanny', *Body and Society* 3.1 (March 1997): 1–160.

11. My definitions of 'corpse' and 'cadaver' are drawn from *Dorland's Illustrated Medical Dictionary*, 27th ed. (Philadelphia: W.B. Saunders, 1988), 383 and 251.

12. Paula Treichler, in a personal note.

13. Moore and Clarke 257.

14. I use the term 'mill away' rather than 'slice' because the latter implies that the material cut away is intact, whereas I believe the material cut away is so thin that it probably could not be maintained as an intact slice.

15. Accounts of the process appear in numerous sources. See the Visible Human Project website, Project Overview, http://www.nlh.nih.gov/research/visible_human.html.

16. From the website of Micron BioSystems' Visible Productions, advertising the Visible Human Male Videodisc.

17. From the website of the Center for Human Simulation, February 2, 1996: http://www.uchsc.edu/sm/chs. The image has since been replaced by another rendering of the visible man. A 1996 Web advertisement for the first CD-ROM to be based on Visible Human Project data em-

phasizes the Visible Man's unique wholeness and accessibility, inviting potential clients to '[i]magine exploring an entire body with the click of a mouse!' (Micron BioSystems' Visible Productions advertising the Visible Human Male CD-ROM).

18. Quoted in David L. Wheeler, 'Creating a Body of Knowledge', *Chronicle of Higher Education*, February 2, 1996: A6, A7, A14. Quotation from A7, A14.

19. Web archive of the Women's Wire News for November 28, 1995.

20. From the website of the Center for Human Simulation.

21. The cost is $1,000 in the United States, Canada, and Mexico, and $2,000 elsewhere.

22. Visible Human Project Far East site at the University of Singapore, http://medweb.nus.sg/vhp/vhp.html

23. From the Medline homepage, http://www.nlm.nih.gov/databases/databases.html

24. Wheeler A14.

25. Donald Lundberg quoted by Jacqueline Stenson, '"Visible Woman" Makes Debut on the Internet', MEDTRIB, the *Medical Tribune* News Service, November 1995.

26. See Constance Holden, '"Visible Man' Gets High Resolution Mate', *Science* 270 (1995): 1927; Gary Stix, 'Habeas Corpus: Seeking Subjects to be a Digital Adam and Eve', *Scientific American* 268.1 (1993): 122–3.

27. From the Center for Human Simulation website.

28. Quoted in Wheeler A7.

29. Wheeler A14.

30. Quoted in Women's Wire news for November 28, 1995. This report also notes that the Visible Woman may at some point be used to demonstrate processes of aging.

31. Kathleen Mendelsohn, Linda Z. Nieman, PhD, Krista Isaacs, Sophia Lee, and Sandra Levison, MD, *Journal of the American Medical Association* 272.16 (October 26, 1996): 1267–70, citation from 1269.

32. Mendelsohn et al. 1270.

33. David Ellison, 'Anatomy of a Murderer', *21-C* (March 1995): 20–5.

34. From the website of the Center for Human Simulation.

35. Quoted by Amy Friedlander, editor of *D-Lib Magazine*, in response to online queries about Ackerman's 'Accessing the Visible Human Project', *D-Lib Magazine*, October 1995. (The magazine's tagline is 'the magazine of digital library research'.)

36. See, for example, Ruth Richardson, 'A Dissection of the Anatomy Act', *Studies in Labor History* 1 (1976): 1–13.

37. Wheeler A14.

38. Wheeler A6.

39. See Stenson, '"Visible Woman' Makes Debut on the Internet'; brief from the National Library of Medicine, *Gratefully Yours* (a newsletter published by the NLM), September/October 1995; and Bill Lorensen, 'Marching Through the Visible Woman' website (http://www.graphics.stanford.edu/-lorensen/vw/vw.html). Lorensen works for the GE Imaging and Visualization Laboratory.

40. See Lorensen, 'Marching Through the Visible Woman' and 'Marching Through the Visible Man'; and W. E. Lorensen and H. E. Cline, 'Marching Cubes: A High Resolution 3D Surface Construction Algorithm', *Computer Graphics* 21.3 (July 1987): 163–9.

41. From the website of the Center for Human Simulation.

42. Quoted in Wheeler A14.

43. Wheeler A14.

44. Gregg Tracton, Web posting of August 16, 1996, http://www.radonc.unc.edu/visiman/what-ishere.html

45. From the website of the Center for Human Simulation.

46. Moore and Clarke 289.

47. Moore and Clarke 289. On the disappearance of women in reproductive discourses, see Valerie Hartouni, *Cultural Conceptions: On Reproductive Technologies and the Remaking of Life* (Minneapolis: University of Minnesota Press, 1997) and Carole Stabile, 'Shooting the Mother: Fetal Photography and the Politics of Disappearance', chapter 5 in this volume.

6

FLESH IN WAX: DEMYSTIFYING THE SKIN COLOURS OF THE COMMON CRAYON[1]

LORNA ROTH

> Billy: What's your favorite color?
> Ellen: Flesh, like the Crayola color.
> Billy: Didn't the NEA [National Endowment for the Arts] cut off funding for that color?
>
> Excerpt from an exchange between two characters on ABC's *thirtysomething* episode broadcast in New York on 22 January 1991 (Dubin 1992: 316–7).

In the very early part of the twentieth century, when modern North American crayons were developed by Binney & Smith, makers of the Crayola brand (1903), visual materials and technologies aiming to represent or embellish human flesh tones had been commonly perceived as value-neutral, devoid of ideology—they were simply considered to be extensions or expressions of instrumental rationality. Over time, it has been revealed that this is simply not true (Comolli 1971, 1986; Winston 1996; Dyer 1997; Roth 2009). In this essay, I demonstrate that even in seemingly innocent tools of visual representation for children—art supplies such as crayons, markers, clay, and paint, used for decades to portray or depict people—we can distinguish an invisible norm of racial whiteness. This ideological norm has often become the barometer against which the flesh tones of Blacks, Asians, First Peoples, and other Peoples of Colour can be read as a deviation.

The material in this chapter forms part of my larger book project, *Colour Balance: Reflections on Race, Representation and 'Intelligent Design'*, which examines the ways in which skin tones have been imagined, embedded, and colour-adjusted over time as manufacturers of technologies, software, and beauty products began to recognize that not all skin colours are within the Caucasian range.

How do manufacturers respond to globalization and to the current discursive politics of cultural and racial diversity? What can this study of the common crayon, which at first glance seems trivial, tell us about the politics of skin colour in North America?

Binney & Smith,[2] with headquarters in Easton, Pennsylvania, is a particularly interesting company to analyze in this regard, given its lengthy history and its initiative in the early 1990s to adapt its products to a multicultural and multiracial[3] society. In this essay I describe and analyze the process by which Binney & Smith decided on several socially and politically important colour adjustments. Evidence from the Binney & Smith case is further used to argue that the way in which skin colour has been represented in our technologies and tools of visual imagery needs to be explicitly unpacked and examined, and then transformed to better reflect the multicultural and multiracial populations using these products. This is an ethical as well as a marketing issue. How long can a product stay in circulation when at a very deep cognitive level it promotes a vision of whiteness, an absence of any alternative skin tone possibilities? At what point does a manufacturer decide to recognize 'Otherness' as an essential design component of its products and media of representation?

BINNEY & SMITH: A HERITAGE COMPANY

In 1903, Binney & Smith launched its first box of eight Crayola wax crayons. Over time, the company extended its product lines to include poster, watercolour, and acrylic paints; fingerpaint; markers and pencils; modelling clay; paste and glue; and new assortments of crayons and chalk.

Colour *heritage* is an important foundation of users' commitment to Binney & Smith products, which the company has used to its competitive advantage. For example, its managers consider that the company gains *value* from the longevity of the visual design and colours of its famous yellow and green Crayola Crayon box. The names of Binney & Smith's product colours, and the company's reputation for representing such traditional virtues as education, play, and safety are perceived as valuable

assets as well.[4] And, very important for sales in the crayon industry, Binney & Smith crayons have a highly nostalgic odour—an odour which triggers memories for adults of having grown up colouring their favourite images with these crayons. According to a study at Yale University, cited in an article in *Colors* magazine, 'Crayola wax crayons have the eighteenth most recognized smell in the USA' (December 98–January 99: 38).[5] It is partially for these reasons, these associative links for adults, who want their children to recreate wonderful experiences with the same crayons they used themselves in their earlier years, that Binney & Smith often faces consumer resistance (and sometimes strong protest) to retiring or changing a colour, or changing the name of a colour.

In the last few decades, the company has become aware of the historical, social, and cultural implications of how its crayon colours are named. At the same time, managers and marketers have evolved a dual consciousness on product quality: (1) producing a consistently good colouring product and distributing it widely on the international market; and (2) ensuring that the product's social, cultural, political, and other symbolic connotations reflect current levels of skin-colour awareness. This essay focuses on some of the company's more public and controversial adjustments to colours of the common crayon. But first, I would like to situate Binney & Smith in relation to one of its main groups of supporters and critics—teachers.

BINNEY & SMITH AND ITS ENGAGEMENT WITH EDUCATORS

In the early twentieth century, Binney & Smith developed a subtle, yet very powerful in-service education and marketing strategy, which succeeded in firmly yoking together the smell of the wax crayon and the name Crayola. The company hired highly qualified art consultants, who visited schools to help teachers develop their art pedagogy. Of course, these consultants brought Binney & Smith products to the schools. Thus for the teachers, using Binney & Smith art products became associated with personal relationships and positive social experiences. One of Binney & Smith's former presidents describes the company's historical relationship with educators:

> Ultimately, the teachers are what built Crayola . . . . Years ago, we had fifteen or so art consultants that went around the country . . . ladies who were part educators. They would spend three days putting on an art seminar on how to use the product. They didn't sell the product, they didn't promote Binney & Smith per se, but they used Binney & Smith products. They would show how to use crayons and water colours and how to paint. The teachers used to love that. We would have groups of fifty taking the workshop.
>
> Having done that for twenty years, the reputation among schools of Binney & Smith, with teachers coming into their classrooms, was positive. These activities helped to build a gigantic network of loyalty. That is what made the Crayola crayon, not advertising. Crayola really grew out of the educational establishment. That lingers today. We don't have the fifteen people going around anymore. It is strictly trade advertising and shows these days, but that heritage has hung on (Jack Kofed, former president of Binney & Smith, personal interview, 12 June 1996).

Teachers and their national organizations have always been of primary importance to Binney & Smith. Although it no longer sponsors art workshops, except by special request,[6] the company still uses teachers' comments and feedback to stimulate innovation and to re-align key products to reflect changing social and cultural norms. Children, whose use and enjoyment of art materials informs teachers of their preferences and tastes, also provide information directly to Crayola designers and manufacturers. In an activity room at the Crayola Factory, 'a combination museum, interactive theme park and simulacrum of the actual factory' (Patton and Wojcik 1995: 45), children test new products and play with existing ones.[7] But it is ultimately teachers who act as multi-channel informants to the company, identifying new trends in children's art preferences and practices, and pointing out appropriate moments for strategic social shifts in product names and marketing policies.

CRAYOLA'S COLOUR ADJUSTMENTS OVER THE YEARS—AN OVERVIEW

Several instances of colour adjustments stand out in Binney & Smith's history.[8] These shifts are listed below, with the company's stated reasons, followed by a more focused analysis of context and implications related most directly to skin colour.

Prussian Blue Becomes Midnight Blue (1958)

The name Prussian Blue was changed to Midnight Blue because teachers and students were no longer familiar with Prussian history.

Flesh Becomes Peach (1962)

As quoted in just about all of Binney & Smith literature, 'the Crayola colour called "flesh" was renamed "peach" in 1962, partly as a result of the civil rights movement' (Binney & Smith information pamphlet). This significant name change is analyzed in detail later in the chapter.

Eight Traditional Colours Replaced with New Colours (1990–1991)

Eight colours were 'retired' in both Canada and the US to a Crayon Hall of Fame in 1990, and were replaced by eight 'hot' colours in 1991. According to Binney & Smith's market research, the retired colours were not popular enough to warrant continued production. In the words of Jack Kofed,

> So you cut the ones that are dead and slowing down. Before they die, you give them a nice burial. If you wait until they die, then you have done damage to your brand.

To be current with peoples' feelings towards colours, you have to move into what they like. You try to anticipate that or be *with* it and not be behind it, because then some other guy does it while you are still putting out the old colours and your business goes down (Personal interview with Jack Kofed, 12 June 1996).

The retirement of the eight traditional colours 'from active duty' (personal interview with Eric Zebley, 10 June 1996) caused a public uproar. At least three grassroots groups lobbied to retain the colours. These were CRAYON—the Committee to Re-establish All Your Old Norms; the National Campaign to Save Lemon Yellow; and the Raw Umber and Maize Preservation (RUMP) Society. They petitioned the company, organized letter campaigns, and even picketed outside the company headquarters on the day that the colours to be retired were announced (personal interview with Eric Zebley, 10 June 1996). Eventually, Binney & Smith brought the crayons back for nine months in 1991, in response to requests from the public for special, limited-time availability. It featured the box of 64 current colours along with the box of eight retired colours in a collector's set (ibid.). This strategy seemed to appease most protesters.

The retired colours are no longer available—in Eric Zebley's words, 'They are history' (ibid.). What does the fuss about their retirement tell us? What does it say about a desire for the restoration of a symbolic social order akin to the perceived normative structures of a certain kind of childhood? What does it tell us about tradition? About conservatism? About the role of the nostalgic in ordinary lives?

The 'People Pack Multination'/'My World Colours' Collection Introduced (1991–1992)

Beginning in the late 1980s, educators had asked Binney & Smith to produce a line of multicultural art products, to portray a full range of skin tones, since people are not black and white. In 1991, a 'People Pack Multination' collection of 'My World Colours' (later known as 'Multicultural') crayons

was designed and launched. Binney & Smith had to rename its product, because another crayon manufacturer had had the same idea and had already trademarked the name 'People Pack'.

Crayola multicultural products include:

- crayon colours—Sepia, Burnt Sienna, Mahogany, Tan, Peach (formerly known as Flesh), Apricot, Black, and White for blending
- washable paint colours—Brown, Mahogany, Terra Cotta, Olive, Bronze, Tan, Beige, and Peach
- washable markers—Sienna, Mahogany, Terra Cotta, Bronze, Tawny, Golden Beige, Beige, and Tan.

The introduction of the multicultural crayon collection is analyzed in more detail later in the chapter.

Indian Red Becomes Chestnut (1999)

Binney & Smith held a contest to select a less contentious, more politically correct name for Indian Red. Indian Red, introduced in 1949, was

> . . . originally based on a reddish-brown pigment commonly found near India. But the manufacturer has gotten complaints from teachers who say students think the colour has to do with North American Indians.
>
> 'Little children take words and names very literally', said Louise Cosgrove, an art teacher in Allentown. 'They think Indian red is the colour of a Native American's skin'. (Associated Press 1999)

In June 1999, it announced that Chestnut was the winner in the contest to rename Indian Red.

THE STORY OF HOW FLESH BECAME PEACH[9]

A key question in this case study focused on the degree to which changing the colour name Flesh to Peach was driven by concerted efforts of organized lobby groups of various peoples of colour, whose skin tones clearly did not match that of the crayon called Flesh. This crayon was a whitish, peachy colour that harmonized very well with a wide range of Caucasian skin tones. In fact, the name suggested an equation between skin itself and whiteness, and in no way could the crayon be used to colour African-American, Asian, Hispanic, North American Indian, or Inuit skin tone ranges. When I approached Binney & Smith, I found that they, like most companies, had not kept an archive of textual materials from the 1960s (for example, letters from customers or company policy records), so I have had to rely on oral histories as my main source of information for my investigation. These multiple narratives have been woven together into this partially coherent perspective of the period.

The first name change, in 1962, from Flesh (named in 1949) to Peach seems more important than Binney & Smith's other colour adjustments, perhaps because it was the first public recognition of the embeddedness of the notion of race in such an ordinary product as the wax crayon. Clearly, the decision to change the name was made not only because market research indicated a 'preference' for one name over the other. The situation was more complicated.

As I researched the network of people involved in this decision, I was told about Rosemarie P. Mandarino, an art consultant working for Binney & Smith at the time. In a letter, she responded to my queries about the name change:

To the best of my recollection, the change took place sometime in the mid fifties. The Civil Rights movement was in full flood with great stress on raising self-esteem in the Black community. 'Black is beautiful' was a phrase used repeatedly and especially to Black children. When these children opened their boxes of crayons to colour with, they, their teachers and parents, became very aware that the colour called Flesh did not represent theirs.

As a consequence, the mail being received at the corporate offices of Binney & Smith, Inc., then located in New York City, included many letters protesting the use of Flesh as a colour name since it portrayed a Caucasian skin tone, which obviously was not theirs. The officers of the company, after consultation with and input from their staff of artists, colour chemists, and art consultants, agreed they had a valid point and made the decision to change the name.

The colour itself was not part of the basic 16-colour Colour Wheel, but one of the additional colours that filled a particular need. Since blending tints and shades of colours with wax crayon is difficult, especially for children, colours such as Flesh, Sky Blue and others, were formulated and added to the various assortments. Colour names such as Red, Blue, and Yellow were taken from the colour spectrum. Prussian Blue, Carmine Red etc. came from artist paint colours; some from their resemblance to flowers and fruits and some for direct usage; to colour sky or skin. I assume the colour name Flesh was formulated to depict a Caucasian skin tone in a time when that was considered correct as a way to answer a specific need for colouring with a wax crayon.

The selection of the name Peach to replace Flesh was chosen after referring to the United States Catalogue of Standardized Colour Names. I'm not sure of the title of this volume but I know it was part of the colour labs and the library and was heavily relied upon. There were a number of names listed to describe the colour. One of these was Peach. It was chosen after a consensus of opinions from the aforementioned staff. Since that time, names for many of the crayon colours have changed. You will no longer find Prussian Blue or Carmine Red. In some instances, the actual colour was reformulated to answer the changing needs and tastes of the users; the teachers, artists and, most importantly, the children (Rosemarie P. Mandarino, retired colour/arts consultant, Binney & Smith, personal correspondence, 9 July 1996).

The change from Flesh to Peach was made essentially for reasons of social justice and racial equity, and it made good moral sense in a period of United States history in which the civil rights movement was beginning to make political and

constitutional gains. The retirement of Flesh recognized a clear ideological and racial bias embedded in the product concept, and Binney & Smith
sought to correct it.

This is not to say that Binney & Smith deliberately or consciously designed its products with a
racist bias. My point, rather, is to identify a pervasive dominant cognitive belief system around
race, a racial *unconsciousness* embedded within
North American business and manufacturing
practices at the time. Corporate America, until
very recently, has created and marketed products
of colour reflecting 'white flesh' tones as if they
were the only existing ones. Binney & Smith, in
its interpretation of the colour Flesh as white,
was little different from the majority of North
America- and Europe-based companies producing
consumer items for a market that was mostly Caucasian. Indeed, compared with manufacturers of
other products such as flesh-tone bandages and
nylon stockings—whose selection of flesh colours
for the longest time reflected a range of Caucasian
skin tones—or with popular US-based cosmetics
companies, which only relatively recently added
an array of shades for Peoples of Colour, Binney
& Smith was quick to shift its social contours in
response to public pressures circulating in the
late 1950s and early 1960s. Of course, from a
marketing perspective, it made impeccable sense
to correct the labelling of the colour Flesh and
acknowledge the physical, material evidence that
the product had indeed been misnamed in the
first instance.

THE MULTICULTURAL CRAYON COLLECTION—A CHANGE IN THE SPIRIT OF THE TIMES

'As far as I and other people in the company
knew, it was just a decision that we decided
to make in the spirit of the times' (Telephone
interview with Tad Girdler, 25 June 1996).

Having renamed the colour Flesh in 1962, Binney & Smith might have been expected to soon
produce a series of other colours to further reflect its public recognition of diverse skin tones.

However, there was a notable gap of almost 30
years between the re-labelling of Flesh to Peach
and the launching of the 'multicultural' products. Why did it take so long for Binney & Smith
to mark race as an integral feature of its colour
palettes? Furthermore, what was it that con-
vinced the company that the early 1990s was the
right time to adapt its merchandise to more diverse representational practices?

To the best of my knowledge, based on document research, interviews, and textual analysis,
there was no concerted *formal* lobby group made
up of members of the general public that mounted a campaign to persuade Binney & Smith to
make its products reflect a multicultural and
multiracial world. User groups did interact with
Binney & Smith public relations officers, but in
an ad hoc manner. In this interview extract, an
employee at the time remembers the kind of public feedback he heard about in the 1980s:

Typically, the general public would call in and
say, 'Why don't you come up with some crayons that would be appropriate for People of Colour?' or something like that. Nothing beyond
that. There was no mass lobbying or anything,
or people protesting . . . (Personal interview
with Eric Zebley, 10 June 1996).

But there were letters and comments from
teachers, with whom Binney & Smith did have a
special relationship and who strongly contributed to the company's decision-making processes.

How many phone calls and letters were needed
for the company to pay attention to its consumers'
requests? At what point did the company's recognition of such a progressive subject as diversity
become a positive offering of a range of alterna-
tives, rather than a negative and passive retreat
from potential criticism? What critical factors led
Binney & Smith to consider changing corporate
policy so that their products would reflect a shift
in the cultural, racial, and social norms of society? In other words, why at that time?

The colours useful in representing the skin,
eyes, and hair of all peoples were already available
in several Binney & Smith boxed crayon collections. Why, then, did the company market these

colours as a separate multicultural package in the early 1990s? Unfortunately, I cannot provide a definitive response. I can remind the reader, however, that multiculturalism was in the air at the time; that the civil rights movement had made important inroads into the education system; that in the mid 1980s educational curricula began to incorporate African-American, First Peoples, and various other ethnic, historical, and cultural studies; that, as non-Caucasian stories and people began to be privileged within the media, norms of whiteness began to be challenged as exclusionary; and that the logic of capitalism in a global market entailed a necessary colour adjustment to accommodate the multi-coloured bodies and biases of people around the world. Perhaps also, what Raymond Williams calls the 'structures of feeling' of the period contributed to Binney & Smith's decision to multiply its tools of skin-tone reproduction (Williams 1977: 128–35). Certainly, all these factors point to an irreversible social and perceptual shift. Binney & Smith moved with the spirit of the time, but it only moved so far . . . and then waited for consumer responses.

Company planning for multicultural products began in 1990, and by 1991, boxes of crayons appropriate for various colours of skin, hair, and eyes were ready to be launched. Their first targeted market was educators; their second was retail customers, where the new collection 'lasted about a year and a half' (Personal interview with Eric Zebley, 10 June 1996).

From my interviews, it is clear that teachers' requests were a decisive factor in Binney & Smith's decision to produce the collection, so that children would be able to accurately draw, paint, and mark their own images in all their varieties of skin colour. In a prominent leaflet outlining their multicultural products, subtitled *Helping Children See Themselves and their World*, Binney & Smith describe educators' reasons for wanting the collection:

> Educators have asked Binney and Smith to produce a line of multicultural art products, in a full range of skin tones, since people are not black and white. It strengthens children's comfort with who they are when they can draw

themselves in colours that truly reflect their complexions. When children are given boxes of crayons and markers that have a variety of skin tones, it enables and encourages them to draw a diverse community, recognizing the ethnic diversity around them (*Crayola Multicultural Products: Helping Children See Themselves and their World*, n.d.: 1).

To facilitate art teachers' use of the new collection, pedagogical materials were developed by Binney & Smith consultants, which were distributed in schools throughout North America. These materials include lesson plans, model designs, and other curricular variations for lessons on diversity issues, which teachers have found very useful.

Less understandable is Binney & Smith's decision not to market these same products more aggressively to the retail market, by providing similar support materials to parents and families. Thus, although Binney & Smith is to be praised for its positive social intervention in what appears to have been a low-profile lobbying effort by educators, one wonders about the lack of proactive marketing to retail customers.

WHAT IS THE MESSAGE OF THE FLESH-IN-WAX PRODUCT LINE?

What can we conclude from the Binney & Smith case study in light of Marshall McLuhan's well-known comment that 'the medium is the message'? What is the message of Binney & Smith's visual art materials over the last several decades, and what does it say about our perceptions of our bodies as colour-marked citizens in North American society? What racial colour options could we have used to draw before 1962, and then again, before 1992? What colours can we now choose with which to represent ourselves?

The decision to rename Flesh in 1962 and the 1992 launching of the multicultural collection opened up many possibilities for non-Caucasian users of Crayola products. First, it indicated the potential to reconceptualize the colour of one's body on paper. Second, it legitimized body colours that in the past had been marginalized, those of brown and black bodies. Finally, broader notions of pigment variation suggested new ways of looking at and critiquing our societies' white-biased body norms. These alternative strategies of seeing may thus provoke a concurrent shift in our standards of beauty regarding colour and race.

What can we conclude from Binney & Smith's initially passive retail marketing strategy? Was diversity to exist only within the walls of the schoolhouse? What happens to multiculturalism at home? Why was there a two-tiered system of integration—one for the school and one for the streets? Was this sectoralism a wise strategy? Although the multicultural crayon collection is now slightly more available to the average consumer than when it was launched, it is still not widely visible. One has to hunt to find them in ordinary venues where crayons are sold. I have not yet seen a box of multicultural crayons in a pharmacy or a dollar store in Montreal. When will notions and products reflecting a multicultural and multiracial perspective permanently and visibly migrate into storefront North America?

Binney & Smith's colour adjustments are historically significant. They may seem small and trivial, but they denote a powerful shift in the tools used to study, draw, and represent the human body on paper. The products are generally targeted at children of a vulnerable age, when they first begin to record their perceptions of the social, cultural, and political bodies and institutions in which they live. Splitting the colour palette in two—for the educational and the retail sectors—may very well, though not necessarily, have triggered a corresponding split in race consciousness with deeper implications for future socio-cultural and political relations.

Is the apparently politically innocent crayon just a crayon? My contention in taking on this topic is that it is more than just a crayon. When notions of skin colour are embedded within an everyday object such as a crayon, we begin to see what society is teaching its children. Its values and dominant perspectives on race and culture become apparent. Margaret Visser (1986) notably writes: 'The extent to which we take everyday objects for granted is the precise extent to which they govern and inform our lives.' If we read a society symptomatically, that is, if we look at the range of products, signs, and symbols on its surface in search of a deeper meaning, we can begin to take seriously what at first appear to be insignificant play tools, one of which is the common crayon.

COGNITIVE EQUITY: TOWARD AN EMBEDDED NORMATIVE RANGE OF SKIN TONES

Reaching beyond the current critique of whiteness (Winston 1996 and Dyer 1997, for example), this case study begins to document evidence for an original conceptual notion that I am calling 'cognitive equity'—a new way of understanding racial and cultural equity. This notion doesn't revolve around statistics and access to institutions, but rather inscribes a vision of skin colour equity into technologies, products, and body representations in a range of visual media. It is particularly important that cognitive equity be designed into young children's visual culture and commodities to reinforce multiculturalism and multiracialism, because stereotypes and racisms are formed and reinforced very early in a child's cognitive and cultural development.

Finally, to allow current technologies and visual portrayals to represent a wide range of skin tones, my work suggests two strategies that would better enable children to develop racial and cognitive equity: (1) design technologies, images, and products so that it becomes easier to capture and reproduce a continuum of skin tones without having to resort to (often unsatisfactory) methods of compensation; and (2) develop a wider range of skin-colour norms in body representations, so that this broad range itself becomes the standard, the new norm, for portraying and depicting bodies in the arts, in business, and in all media—whether virtual or two- or three-dimensional.

As more and more manufacturers and creative producers explicitly acknowledge the skin-tone values they are working with and reinforcing in the minds of their customers and audiences, and as they begin to tackle the complexities of the colour adjustment process, we hopefully shall note a wider public recognition and acceptance of multiracialism. Of course, there are no guarantees that implementing my suggested strategies of change in design prototypes would automatically help children to develop cognitive equity. This development would also require complementary changes in school curricula, in the global manufacturing economy, and in discourses about diversity at school, at home, on the streets, in stores, and in the media.

As challenging as it may be to achieve this shift, the establishment of a colour continuum—rather than the retention of whiteness as a default reference point for skin colour reproduction—would be an important starting point from which children could begin to perceive, categorize, and think about race and ethnicity differently. Most importantly, it would further promote an environment where stereotypical notions of skin colour, however unconscious, could be eliminated from the moment of inscription, so that they may no longer be so easily repeatable (Greenberg 2009).[10]

APPENDIX A

Crayola Crayon Colour History[11]

Colours Available in 1903

Black	Green	Violet
Blue	Orange	Yellow
Brown	Red	

Colours Available 1949–1957

Apricot	Lemon Yellow	Red Violet
Bittersweet Gray	Magenta	Salmon
Black	Mahogany	Sea Green
Blue	Maize	Silver
Blue Green	Maroon	Spring Green
Blue Violet	Melon	Tan
Brick Red	Olive Green	Thistle
Brown	Orange	Turquoise Blue
Burnt Sienna	Orange Red	Violet (Purple)
Carnation Pink	Orange Yellow	Violet Blue
Cornflower	Orchid	Violet Red
Flesh*	Periwinkle	White
Gold	Pine Green	Yellow
Green	Prussian Blue**	Yellow Green
Green Blue	Red	Yellow Orange
Green Yellow	Red Orange	

Colours Available 1958–1971
All 48 colours previously listed plus the following 16 colours added in 1958.

Aquamarine	Goldenrod	Raw Sienna
Blue Gray	Indian Red***	Raw Umber
Burnt Orange	Lavender	Sepia
Cadet Blue	Mulberry	Sky Blue
Copper	Navy Blue	
Forest Green	Plum	

* Name voluntarily changed to Peach in 1962, partially as a result of the Civil Rights Movement.
** Name changed to Midnight Blue in 1958 in response to teachers' requests.
*** Name changed in 1999 to Chestnut.

Colours Available 1972–1989
All colours previously listed plus the following fluorescent colours added in 1972.

Chartreuse	Ultra Green	Ultra Red
Hot Magenta	Ultra Orange	Ultra Yellow
Ultra Blue	Ultra Pink	

Fluorescent colour names changed in 1990

Atomic Tangerine	Laser Lemon	Shocking Pink
Blizzard Blue	Outrageous Orange	Wild Watermelon
Hot Magenta	Screamin' Green	

Colours Available 1990–1992
All 72 colours previously listed plus the following eight fluorescent colours.

Electric Lime	Neon Carrot	Sunglow
Magic Mint	Radical Red	Unmellow Yellow
Purple Pizzazz	Razzle Dazzle Rose	

Retired Colours
In 1990, Binney & Smith (US) retired eight colours and introduced eight new ones. Around the same time, Binney & Smith (Canada) conducted a national poll asking consumers to decide which eight colours should be retired. In February 1992, eight colours were retired in each country; in Canada three of the eight were different from those retired in the US.

Canada Retired Colours	US Retired Colours	New Colours
Blue Gray	Blue Gray	Cerulean
Cadet Blue	Green Blue	Dandelion
Goldenrod	Lemon Yellow	Fuchsia
Maize	Maize	Jungle Green
Orange Red	Orange Red	Royal Purple
Orange Yellow	Orange Yellow	Teal Blue
Raw Umber	Raw Umber	Vivid Tangerine
Yellow Orange	Violet Blue	Wild Strawberry

Colours Available in 1993

All 80 colours previously listed plus the following 16 colours added in 1993, named by US and Canadian consumers, for a grand total of 96 colours.

Asparagus	Pacific Blue	Timber Wolf
Cerise	Purple Mountain's Majesty	Tropical Rain Forest
Denim	Razzmattazz	Tumbleweed
Granny Smith Apple	Robin's Egg Blue	Wisteria
Macaroni and Cheese	Shamrock	
Mauvelous	Tickle Me Pink	

Colours Available 1998

24 new colours added

Almond	Cotton Candy	Piggy Pink
Antique Brass	Desert Sand	Pink Flamingo
Banana Mania	Eggplant	Pink Sherbet
Beaver	Fern	Purple Heart
Blue Bell	Fuzzy Wuzzy Brown	Shadow
Blush	Manatee	Sunset Orange
Canary	Mountain Meadow	Torch Red
Caribbean Green	Outer Space	Vivid Violet

Colours Available 2000

All colours previously listed with the following exceptions: Thistle was removed from the 120-count assortment to make room for Indigo; Torch Red was renamed Scarlet.

Colours Available 2003

4 new colours added, 4 retired
Number of Colours: 120

New Colours	**Retired Colours**
Inch Worm	Blizzard Blue
Jazzberry Jam	Magic Mint
Mango Tango	Mulberry
Wild Blue Yonder	Teal Blue

NOTES

1. This essay is an expanded version of 'Home on the Range: Kids, Visual Culture, and Cognitive Equity', originally published in *Cultural Studies and Critical Methodologies* 9, 2 (April 2009), 141–8.
2. Although Binney & Smith's name is now officially Crayola and has been so since 2007, I am using its original name, since the events described in this essay all took place before it was renamed.
3. In my own work, I differentiate between the terms *multicultural* and *multiracial* in the following way. *Multicultural(ism)* can refer to cultural and ethnic backgrounds exclusively and does not include the range of skin colours, that is covered in the term *multiracial(ism)*. However, the way in which the term is used by Binney & Smith, and many others I might add, indicates a conflation of the two terms under the heading of multiculturalism.

4. According to a 1995 article in *The International Design Magazine*, Binney & Smith's Crayola crayons have a 99 per cent brand recognition and higher sales than any electronic toy sold in the US up to that time (Patton and Wojcik 1995: 41).
5. For interest's sake, the first two are coffee and peanut butter (ibid.).
6. This cutback on in-service training was due mainly to two factors: a) the fact that a large pool of school teachers, involved in the American Federation of Teachers began to refuse to do extra work, unless they got paid for it; and b) it became increasingly hard to find a room in the schools that could be closed off from all other activities for three days to do the workshops (personal interview with Tad Girdler, 25 June 1996).
7. Prior to the opening of the Crayola Factory in mid 1996, designers' main source of children's feedback was derived from school visits to the actual factory located in Easton, Pennsylvania.
8. For a complete list of Crayola Crayon's colour names and the years in which they developed as part of Binney & Smith's colour palette, see Appendix A.
9. In June of 1996, I visited the Binney & Smith headquarters in Easton, Pennsylvania, to interview the staff and to attain a richer and deeper understanding of the complexities involved in the colour-change decisions made in relation to skin colours. Much of the material that I detail in this essay is derived from these personal conversations, as well as from phone interviews with retired employees undertaken at a slightly later time, and written correspondence.
10. This statement by Reesa Greenberg (2009) was her response to my notion of cognitive equity that she initially read about in my first version of this article. I found it to be quite fascinating and useful in furthering my own thinking about the concept.
11. Source: http://www.crayola.com/colorcensus/history/chronology.cfm.

WORKS AND DOCUMENTS CITED

Associated Press. 1999. 'Crayola renames touchy shade of red'. *The Gazette* (Montreal) March 11: C-3.

Binney & Smith. 'Crayola Crayon Chronology'. Available at: http://www.crayola.com/colorcensus/history/chronology.cfm.

———. n.d. Crayola Information Pamphlet.

———. n.d. *Crayola Multicultural Products: Helping Children See Themselves and their World.*

Comolli, Jean-Louis. 1971. 'Technique et Idéologie: Caméra, perspective, profonduer de champ'. *Cahiers du Cinéma* 229 (May): 4–21; 230 (July): 51–7; 231 (August–September): 42–9; 233 (November): 39–45; 234–5 (December, January, February): 94–100.

———. 1977. 'Technique and Ideology: Camera, Perspective, Depth of Field'. In Patricia Erens and Bill Horrigan (eds), *Film Reader 2*: 128–40. Evanston, Illinois: Northwestern University.

Dubin, Steven C. 1992. *Arresting Images: Impolitic Art and Uncivil Actions.* New York: Routledge Press.

Dyer, Richard. 1997. *White.* London: Routledge, 1997.

Greenberg, Reesa. 2009. '"Remembering Exhibitions": From Point to Line to Web'. *Tate Papers* (Autumn). Available at: http://www.tate.org.uk/research/tateresearch/tatepapers/09autumn/greenberg.shtm. Accessed June 2010.

Patton, Phil, and James Wojcik. 1995. 'The Business of Colour'. *The International Design Magazine* (November): 40–7.

'Race. Flesh'. 1999. *Colors* December 1998–January 1999: 38.

Roth, Lorna. 2009. 'Home on the Range: Kids, Visual Culture, and Cognitive Equity'. *Cultural Studies and Critical Methodologies* 9, 2 (April): 141–8.

Visser, Margaret. 1986. *Much Depends on Dinner.* Toronto: McClelland & Stewart.

Williams, Raymond. 1977. *Marxism and Literature.* Oxford: Oxford University Press.

Winston, Brian. 1996. *Technologies of Seeing: Photography, Cinematography and Television.* London: British Film Institute.

Personal interviews at Binney & Smith headquarters in Easton, Pennsylvania

Dana Conover, 10 June 1996
Brett Wilson, 10 June 1996
Eric Zebley, 10 June 1996
Herman Reich, 11 June 1996
Rachel Strauss, 11 June 1996
Jack Kofed, 12 June 1996

Telephone interview with former employee

Tad Girdler, 25 June 1996

Correspondence with former employee

Rosemarie P. Mandarino, 9 July 1996

QUESTIONS FOR REFLECTION

1. Is your own classroom, house, school, office, or other space a 'site of discipline' in the sense described by Cregan? How, and to what effect?

2. In what other ways has sexual, gender, and racial difference been naturalized and made to appear as fact?

3. Do we actively look for difference between bodies, according to sex, gender, race, or other criteria? Is this way of seeing 'natural' or learned? What are the implications of this practice?

FURTHER READING

Cartwright, Lisa. *Screening the Body: Tracing Medicine's Visual Culture*. Minneapolis: University of Minnesota, 1995.

Gilman, Sander. *Pathology and Difference: Stereotypes of Sexuality, Race, and Madness*. Ithaca, Cornell, 1985.

Green, David. 'Veins of Resemblance: Photography and Eugenics'. *Oxford Art Journal* 7.2 (1985): 3–16.

Horn, David G. *Social Bodies: Science, Reproduction, and Italian Modernity*. Princeton: Princeton University Press, 1994.

Jordanova, Ludmilla. *Sexual Visions: Images of Gender in Science and Medicine between the Eighteenth and Twentieth Centuries*. Madison: University of Wisconsin, 1989.

Laqueur, Thomas. *Making Sex: Body and Gender from the Greeks to Freud*. Cambridge: Harvard University, 1990.

Roth, Lorna. 'Looking at Shirley, the Ultimate Norm: Colour Balance, Image Technologies, and Cognitive Equity.' *Canadian Journal of Communication* 34.1 (2009): 111–136.

Schiebinger, Londa. *The Mind Has No Sex? Women in the Origins of Modern Science*. Cambridge: Harvard, 1989.

Sekula, Allan. 'The Body and the Archive'. *October* 39 (Winter 1986): 3–64.

Terry, Jennifer, and Jacqueline Urla. *Deviant Bodies: Critical Perspectives on Difference in Science and Popular Culture*. Bloomington: Indiana University, 1995.

Treichler, Paula A., Lisa Cartwright, and Constance Penley, Eds. *The Visible Woman: Imaging Technologies, Gender, and Science*. New York: New York University, 1998.

Warner, John Harley, and James M. Edmonson. *Dissection: Photographs of a Rite of Passage in American Medicine: 1880–1930*. New York: Blast, 2009.

PART THREE

VISUAL EVIDENCE

Images are often deployed as visual evidence of an object or event in the natural world. Images function as evidence in a wide array of practices ranging from the hard sciences to the fine arts, and from the professional to the personal. However, as emphasized in the Introduction, even in the most seemingly objective fields of practice images are never free from subjective influence. The essays in Parts Two and Four of this collection exemplify this point particularly well and highlight the inextricable bond between images and the cultures within which they are produced and used. Indeed, contrary to the notion of objectivity that is often associated with the use of visual representation, the production and interpretation of images are never immune to the influence of cultural beliefs and attitudes. The readings in this part interrogate the use of images as visual evidence.

In the first article of this part, 'Professional Vision', the linguistics scholar Charles Goodwin deconstructs how professional expertise, what he calls 'professional vision', is constructed and reinforced through disciplinary practice. Of particular importance in this essay is Goodwin's emphasis on images as a fundamental component in the construction of disciplinary knowledge and expertise. Goodwin proposes a model to address the construction of professional vision according to three constituent parts: coding, highlighting, and producing and articulating material representations. He then performs a case study of an archaeological dig through which he documents the ways in which its participants develop and reinforce their own vision as archaeologists, a central feature of which is the production of images.

Most of Goodwin's article is dedicated to an examination of the controversial 1992 trial *California v. Powell*, in which four Los Angeles Police Department officers were accused of beating motorist Rodney King. Goodwin applies his model of professional vision to examine the use of the central piece of evidence in that case: a videotape of the beating taken by a nearby observer. The prosecution's strategy was to let the jurors see the evidence for themselves by simply playing the videotape. In so doing the prosecution upheld a cultural belief as old as photography itself—that the photomechanical image is an objective record, one that can speak for itself. By contrast, the defence meticulously deconstructed the videotape and rebuilt an interpretation that was consistent with their own assertion that the officers had acted appropriately and professionally. Due in large part to the defence's effective use of images, the four officers were acquitted in a verdict that led to wide-scale rioting in Los Angeles.

The deployment of images in legal trials is also the focus of the second essay in this part, 'Visual Literacy in Action' by law professor Richard Sherwin. The author opens the essay by noting the increasing importance of visual representation in courts of law. Sherwin stresses that lawyers now routinely turn to images in building their arguments and in trying to persuade jurors and judges. Of particular importance here is Sherwin's emphasis on the influence of popular culture on legal proceedings. He argues that cultural production in the form of television and film has had a significant impact on the legal process. Jurors expect trials to proceed according to what they have seen in television programs and movies, and lawyers incorporate accepted popular cultural conventions when using visual representation at trial.

Borrowing from psychological and social-psychological studies, Sherwin positions images as unique communication vehicles. Compared to words, which are more precise and limited in meaning, and which depend largely on their appearance as part of a sequence, images provide a wealth of information, and they do so instantaneously. Images are taken to indicate reality (at least better than words do) and they evoke emotions in ways words do not. As such, Sherwin urges law students to be more visually literate, to be able to understand and use images more effectively in making and critiquing legal arguments. To this end he identifies four rules of thumb for visual legal rhetoric: simplify the complex; exploit the iconic; emulate the generic; and respect the medium. Sherwin's concluding remarks mirror a central argument of this book: images both influence and are influenced by culture. As he writes: 'When the life of the law imitates art, aesthetics are not ancillary to legal reality. They are constitutive.'

Whereas Goodwin and Sherwin examine the use of images in formal, legal proceedings, in 'The Pleasures of Looking: The Attorney General's Commission on Pornography versus Visual Images', Carole S. Vance addresses the topic as manifest in public, governmental hearings. Specifically, Vance analyzes the discourse surrounding visual representation, including its influence and power, during the US Meese Commission on pornography in 1985–1986. Headed by Attorney General Edwin Meese III, the commission sought to regulate the production, circulation, and consumption of pornographic images. To this end, the commission produced a 2000 page report recommending tighter police controls over images and strict penalties for actions deemed pornographic. Importantly, and as Vance highlights, the commission was in fact a collection of distinguished conservative figures, and its proceedings were decidedly not investigative, but rather proscriptive.

The treatment and use of images in the Meese Commission is a tremendously fruitful site for the analysis of visual communication and culture. As Vance highlights, the commission attributed significant power to the image, defining a causal relationship between representation and action (what Vance identifies as a 'monkey-see, monkey-do' attitude). This being the case, the commission sought to regulate human behaviour through the regulation of images. Vance summarizes: 'Part of the charm of regulating pornography is that sexual images in the public arena can be banished more reliably than sexual impulses in the individual psyche.' The deployment of the image in the control of populations is taken up more fully by J.B. Harley in Part Four of this reader; here it is sufficient to note that while images were ostensibly the subject of the commission, in actual fact the group was interested in influencing cultural values and beliefs.

In its use of images during the six public hearings, the commission produced a carefully scripted visual argument in a manner similar to that described by Sherwin in the preceding essay. Only the most extreme examples of pornographic imagery were shown during the hearings; the images were divorced from any contextual information; no experts on visual representation or pornography were called to speak; and the display of images took place in a public setting (in direct contrast to the usual private viewing of pornography). In sum, the commission created an environment that 're-inforced sexual secrecy, hypocrisy, and shame'. What was purported to be an open, public investigation of pornographic imagery was instead a highly scripted, predetermined attempt to regulate public behaviours and attitudes. Ironically, although visual representation played a central role in the Meese Commission, Vance shows that the commission was less about images than it was about cultural attitudes towards sex, obscenity, and morality.

The final essay in the part, by communication studies scholar Ira Wagman, is an examination of the roles of photographs-as-evidence that are uploaded and viewed on the popular social networking site Facebook. Wagman points to a paradox in contemporary society: the simultaneous desire for both privacy and publicity. In an era when citizens are increasingly concerned with intrusions of privacy, why do the same citizens engage in self-promotion and disclose vast amounts of personal information via social networking sites such as Facebook? Wagman's essay, 'The Suspicious and the Self-Promotional', examines the popular website as a way to explore this question and the underlying tension between privacy and publicity in the contemporary world.

Wagman emphasizes two key roles of the photographic image as used on Facebook: its capacity to arouse suspicion, and its capacity as a self-promotion tool. In the former, the evidentiary power of the photograph functions as a tool of surveillance. Whether employed by the state (through the police), by insurance companies, or by individuals taking and sharing images of others engaged in suspicious or deviant activity, the photograph can be used as evidence of one's actions. For self-promotion, a Facebook user exploits the evidentiary capability of the image to present a particular public identity. Key to Wagman are the vast differences from one person to the next in technological competence and know-how, or what he terms 'literacy'. He argues that some users of Facebook are often unaware of the consequences of posting images and details of their lives in an online forum, while others are quite knowledgeable and actively exploit the site and image manipulation technologies to offer up highly fabricated identities. The author concludes that what is needed is not greater control over the flow of images but greater visual literacy or, in his words, 'understanding [of] the power and limitations of the image, and understanding the technologies that produce, distribute, and display images'. Wagman's essay is an important investigation of the power of images to shape our lives as well as their tremendous import in a surveillance society.

In his articulation of vision as a shared practice, Goodwin's essay offers a concrete model for the type of visual practice that is addressed throughout this book. Anatomists, archaeologists, cartographers, lawyers, jurors, and others learn to see and visually communicate in ways that are guided by both formal and informal conventions. Even in settings prized for their neutrality and objectivity—such as a court of law—images are never free from subjective influence, nor do they have a singular, fixed meaning. Vance's call to action serves well to summarize a key argument of the readings in this part, one that must be seen as fundamental to a critical engagement with images and visual communication. She writes: 'We need to offer an alternative frame for understanding images, one that rejects literalist constructions and offers in their place multiplicity, subjectivity, and the diverse experience of viewers.'

7

PROFESSIONAL VISION

CHARLES GOODWIN

Discursive practices are used by members of a profession to shape events in the domains subject to their professional scrutiny. The process creates the objects of knowledge that become the insignia of a profession's craft: the theories, artifacts, and bodies of expertise that distinguish it from other professions. Analysis of the methods used by members of a community to build and contest the events that structure their lifeworld contributes to the development of a practice-based theory of knowledge and action.[1] In this article, I examine two contexts of professional activity: archaeological field excavation and legal argumentation. In each of these contexts, I investigate three practices: (1) *coding*, which transforms phenomena observed in a specific setting into the objects of knowledge that animate the discourse of a profession; (2) *highlighting*, which makes specific phenomena in a complex perceptual field salient by marking them in some fashion; and (3) *producing and articulating material representations*. By applying such practices to phenomena in the domain of scrutiny, participants build and contest *professional vision*, which consists of socially organized ways of seeing and understanding events that are answerable to the distinctive interests of a particular social group.

In the 1992 trial of four white police officers charged with beating Mr Rodney King, an African-American motorist who had been stopped for speeding, a videotape of the beating (made without the knowledge of the officers by a man in an apartment across the street) became a politically charged theatre for contested vision. Opposing sides in the case used the murky pixels of the same television image to display to the jury incommensurate events: a brutal, savage beating of a man lying helpless on the ground versus careful police response to a dangerous 'PCP-crazed giant' who was argued to be in control of the situation. By deploying an array of systematic discursive practices, including talk, ethnography, category systems articulated by expert witnesses, and various ways of highlighting images provided by the videotape, lawyers for both sides were able to structure, in ways that suited their own distinctive agendas, the complex perceptual field visible on the TV screen.

The Rodney King trial provides a vivid example of how the ability to see a meaningful event is not a transparent, psychological process but instead a socially situated activity accomplished through the deployment of a range of historically constituted discursive practices. It would, however, be quite wrong to treat the selective vision that is so salient in the King trial as a special, deviant case, merely a set of lawyers' tricks designed to distort what would otherwise be a clear, neutral vision of objective events unambiguously visible on the tape. All vision is perspectival and lodged within endogenous communities of practice. An archaeologist and a farmer see quite different phenomena in the same patch of dirt (for example, soil that will support particular kinds of crops versus stains, features, and artifacts that provide evidence for earlier human activity at this spot). An event being seen, a relevant *object of knowledge*, emerges through the interplay between a *domain of scrutiny* (a patch of dirt, the images made available by the King videotape, etc.) and a set of *discursive practices* (dividing the domain of scrutiny by highlighting a figure against a ground, applying specific coding schemes for the constitution and interpretation of relevant events, etc.) being deployed within a *specific activity* (arguing a legal case, mapping a site, planting crops, etc.). The object being investigated is thus analogous to what Wittgenstein (1958:7) called a *language game*, a

'whole, consisting of language and the actions into which it is woven'.

MY OWN PRACTICES FOR SEEING

It is not possible to work in some abstract world where the constitution of knowledge through a politics of representation has been magically overcome. The analysis in this article makes extensive use of the very same practices it is studying. Graphic representations, including transcripts of talk, diagrams, and frame grabs of scenes recorded on videotape, are annotated and highlighted in order to make salient specific events within them. Such highlighting guides the reader to see within a complex perceptual field just those events that I find relevant to the points I am developing. Applying a category such as *highlighting*, *graphic representation*, or *coding scheme* to diverse practices in different environments is itself an example of how coding schemes are used to organize disparate events into a common analytical framework. It is thus relevant to note briefly why I made the representational choices that I did.

To analyze how practice is organized as a temporally unfolding process encompassing both human interaction and situated tool use, I require as data records that preserve not only sequences of talk but also body movements of the participants and the phenomena to which they are attending as they use relevant representations. I use videotapes as my primary source of data, recognizing that, like transcription, any camera position constitutes a theory about what is relevant within a scene—one that will have enormous consequences for what can be seen in it later—and what forms of subsequent analysis are possible. A tremendous advantage of recorded data is that they permit repeated, detailed examination of actual sequences of talk and embodied work practices in the settings where practitioners actually perform these activities. Moreover, others can look at—and possibly challenge—my understanding of the events being examined.

As part of continuing fieldwork focusing ethnographically on how scientists actually do their work, activities at one archaeological field school in Argentina and two in the United States were videotaped. All the material analyzed in this article is drawn from one of the American field schools. Tapes of the first Rodney King trial were made from broadcasts of Court TV. I was unable to record the entire trial, so my own recordings were supplemented by an edited summary of the trial purchased from Court TV. The second trial was not broadcast on either radio or television. I was able to get into the courtroom only for the prosecution's closing arguments.

Practices of transcription constitute one local site within anthropology where the politics of representation emerge as a practical problem.[2] For a journal article, the rich record of complicated vocal and visual events moving through time provided by a videotape must be transformed into something that can silently inhabit the printed page.

Both linguistic anthropologists and conversation analysts have devoted considerable complementary and overlapping attention to questions of how talk should be transcribed, including the issue of how speakers themselves parse the stream of speech into relevant units. A major analytic focus of conversation analysis is the description of the procedures used by participants in the midst of talk-in-interaction to construct the events that constitute the lived lifeworld within ongoing processes of action.[3] This has required developing methods of transcription that permit detailed analysis of actors' changing orientations as events unfold though time. Linguistic anthropologists, concerned with maintaining the complex structure of oral performance, have argued that the division of talk into lines within a transcript should make visible to the reader how the speaker organized his or her talk into relevant units.[4] I have tried to do that in this article, breaking lines at intonational units and indenting the continuation of units too long to fit within the page margins. Given the rich interplay of different kinds of units in the stream of speech, the divisions I've made should not be treated as anything more than a provisional attempt to deal with a very complicated issue. In all other respects, my transcription uses the system developed by Gail Jefferson[5] for the analysis

of conversation. The conventions most relevant to the analysis in this article include the use of **_bold italics_** to indicate talk spoken with special emphasis, a left bracket ([) to mark the onset of overlapping talk, and numbers in parentheses—for example, (1.2)—to note the length of silences in seconds and tenths of seconds. A dash marks the cut-off of the current sound. An equal sign indicates 'latching', signifying that there is no interval between the end of one unit and the beginning of a next. Transcribers' comments are italicized in double parentheses; single parentheses around talk indicate a problematic hearing. Punctuation symbols are used to mark intonation changes rather than as grammatical symbols: a period indicates a falling contour; a question mark, a rising contour; and a comma, a falling-rising contour, as might be found in the midst of a list.

CODING SCHEMES

Central to the organization of human cognition are processes of classification. _Coding schemes_ are one systematic practice used to transform the world into the categories and events that are relevant to the work of the profession (Cicourel 1964, 1968). For example, linguists classify sounds in terms of phonetic distinctions; sociologists classify people according to sex and class.

The pervasive power of coding schemes to organize apprehension of the world is demonstrated in particularly vivid fashion in scientific work. Ethnographic analysis of what is usually considered the epitome of abstract, objective, universal, disembodied cognition—Western science—has revealed it to be a patchwork of situated, disparate, locally organized cultures in which knowledge is constituted through a variety of social and political processes.[6] Central to the cognitive processes that constitute science are both material objects (tools and machines of many different types) and writing practices quite unlike those typically studied by anthropologists investigating literacy. In order to generate a data set, collections of observations that can be compared with each other, scientists use coding schemes to circumscribe and delineate the world

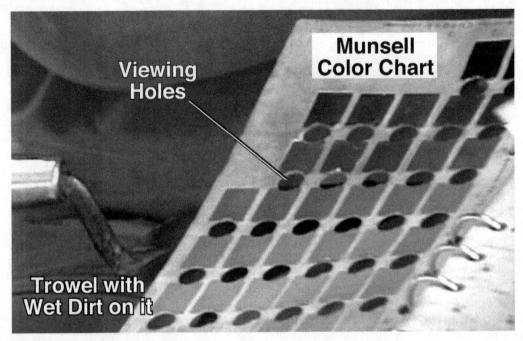

FIGURE 7.1 Munsell colour chart

they examine. When disparate events are viewed through a single coding scheme, equivalent observations become possible.

Let us briefly investigate this process using the example of a field school for young archaeologists. The medium in which archaeologists work is dirt. Students are given a form that contains an elaborate set of categories for describing the colour, consistency, and texture of whatever dirt they encounter. They are even expected to taste a sample of the dirt to determine how sandy it is. Moreover, some of the categories are supported by additional tools of inscription, such as a Munsell colour chart, used by archaeologists all over the world as a standard for colour descriptions.

The process of filling in the form requires physical, cognitive, and perceptual work. Thus, in order to determine the colour of a specimen of dirt, the students must obtain a sample with a trowel, highlight it by squirting it with water, and then hold the sample under the holes in the Munsell colour chart (see Figure 7.1). The Munsell book encapsulates in a material object the theory and solutions developed by earlier workers faced with this task of classification (Hutchins 1993). The pages juxtapose colour patches and viewing holes that allow the dirt to be seen right next to the colour sample, providing a historically constituted architecture for perception.

Though apparently distant from the abstract world of archaeological theory and from the debates that are currently animating the discipline, this encounter between a coding scheme and the world is a key locus for scientific practice, the place where the multifaceted complexity of 'nature' is transformed into the phenomenal categories that make up the work environment of a scientific discipline. It is precisely here that nature is transformed into culture.

Despite the rigorous way in which a tool such as this one structures perception of the dirt being scrutinized, finding the correct category is not an automatic or even an easy task (Goodwin 1993). The very way in which the Munsell chart provides a context-free reference standard creates problems of its own. The colour patches on the chart are glossy, while the dirt never is, so that the chart colour and the sample colour never look exactly the same. Moreover, the colours be-ing evaluated frequently fall between the discrete categories provided by the Munsell chart. Two students at the field school looking at exactly the same dirt and reference colours can and do dis-agree as to how it should be classified. However, the definitiveness provided by a coding scheme typically erases from subsequent documentation the cognitive and perceptual uncertainties that these students are grappling with, as well as the work practices within which they are embedded.

The use of such coding schemes to organize the perception of nature, events, or people within the discourse of a profession carries with it an array of perceptual and cognitive operations that have far-reaching impact. First, by using such a system, a worker views the world from the perspective it establishes. Of all the possible ways that the earth could be looked at, the perceptual work of stu-dents using this form is focused on determining the exact colour of a minute sample of dirt. They engage in active cognitive work, but the param-eters of that work have been established by the system that is organizing their perception. Inso-far as the coding scheme establishes an orienta-tion toward the world, it constitutes a structure of intentionality whose proper locus is not an isolated, Cartesian mind but a much larger or-ganizational system, one that is characteristically mediated through mundane bureaucratic docu-ments such as forms. Forms, with their coding schemes, allow a senior investigator to inscribe his or her perceptual distinctions into the work practices of the technicians who code the data. Such systems provide an example of how distrib-uted cognition is organized through the writing practices that coordinate action within an organ-ization (Smith 1990:121–2).

HIGHLIGHTING

Human cognitive activity characteristically oc-curs in environments that provide a compli-cated perceptual field. A quite general class of cognitive practices consists of methods used to divide a domain of scrutiny into a figure and a ground, so that events relevant to the activity of the moment stand out. For example, forms and other documents packed with different kinds of information are a major textual component of many work environments. Faced with such a dense perceptual field, workers in many settings *highlight* their documents with coloured markers, handwritten annotations, and stick-on notes. In so doing they tailor the document so that those parts of it which contain information relevant to their own work are made salient. Psychologists have long talked about figure/ground relations as a basic element of human perception. Situating such processes not only within the mind but as visible operations on external phenomena has a range of significant consequences. As we will see in subsequent examples, through these practices structures of relevance in the material environ-ment can be made prominent, thus becoming ways of shaping not only one's own perception but also that of others.

Highlighting will be examined first in the work practices of archaeologists. In looking at the earth, archaeologists attend to an array of colour distinc-tions in order to discern the traces of past human structures. For example, even though a post that supported a roof of an ancient house has long since decayed, the earth where it stood will have subtle colour differences from the dirt around it. Archaeologists attempt to locate *features* such as these post moulds[7] by scrutinizing the earth as they dig. Categories of relevance to the profession, such as post moulds, are thus used to structure interpretation of the landscape. When a possible feature is found, the archaeological category and the traces in the dirt that possibly instantiate it are each used to elaborate the other in what has been called the *documentary method of interpreta-tion*.[8] Thus the category 'post mould' provides a texture of intelligibility that unifies disparate patches of colour into a coherent object. These patches of colour in turn provide evidence for the existence in this patch of dirt of an instance of the object proposed by the category.

Features can be difficult to see. In order to make them visible to others, the archaeologist outlines them by drawing a line in the dirt with a trowel (see Figure 7.2). By doing this the archae-ologist establishes a figure in what is quite lit-erally a very amorphous ground. This line in the

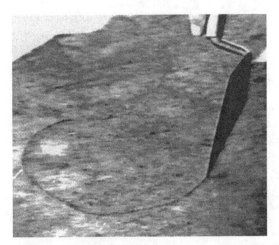

FIGURE 7.2 Post mould

sand has very powerful persuasive consequences. As a visible annotation of the earth, it becomes a public event that can guide the perception of others while further reifying the object that the archaeologist proposes to be visible in the colour patterning in the dirt. The perceptual field provided by the dirt is enhanced in a work-relevant way by human action on it. Through such highlighting and the subsequent digging that it will help to organize, the archaeologist discursively shapes from the materials provided by the earth the phenomenal objects—that is, the archaeological features—that are the concerns of his or her profession.

GRAPHIC REPRESENTATIONS AS EMBODIED PRACTICE

Most linguists analyzing literacy have focused on the writing of words, sentences, and other written versions of spoken language. However, graphic representations of many different types constitute central objects in the discourse of various professions. Scientific talks and papers are best seen not as a purely linguistic text but as a reflexive commentary on the diagrams, graphs, and photographs that constitute the heart of a presentation.[9] More generally, since the pioneering work of Latour and Woolgar (1979), the central importance of *inscriptions* in the organization

of scientific knowledge has become a major focus of research. A theory of discourse that ignored graphic representations would be missing both a key element of the discourse that professionals engage in and a central locus for the analysis of professional practice. Instead of mirroring spoken language, these external representations complement it, using the distinctive characteristics of the material world to organize phenomena in ways that spoken language cannot—for example, by collecting records of a range of disparate events onto a single visible surface.

To explore such issues and prepare the ground for investigation of how lawyers articulated graphic representations in the Rodney King trial, the practices that archaeologists use to make maps will now be investigated. This will allow us to examine the interface between writing practices, talk, human interaction, and tool use as these professionals build representations central to the work of their discipline. A team of archaeologists is at work producing a map (see Figure 7.3). This particular map is of a *profile*, the layers of dirt visible on the side of one of the square holes that are dug to excavate a site. Maps of this sort are one of the distinctive forms of professional literacy that constitute archaeology as a profession.

To demarcate what the archaeologist believes are two different layers of dirt, a line is drawn between them with a trowel. The line and the ground surface above it are then transferred to a piece of graph paper. This is a task that involves two people. One measures the length and depth coordinates of the points to be mapped, using a ruler and a tape measure. He or she reports the measurements as pairs of numbers, such as 'At forty, plus eleven point five' (see Figure 7.4). A second archaeologist transfers the numbers provided by the measurer to a piece of graph paper. After plotting a set of points, he or she makes the map by drawing lines between them. What we find here is a small activity system that encompasses talk, writing, tools, and distributed cognition as two parties collaborate to inscribe events they see in the earth onto paper.

The activity of inscription that we will now examine begins with a request from Ann, the writer, to Sue, the measurer (lines 1–2):

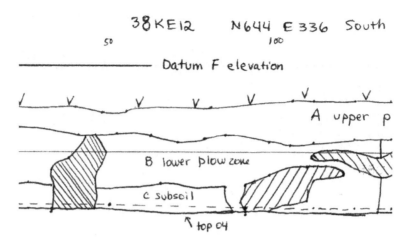

FIGURE 7.3 Map scan

> 1 Ann: Give me the ground surface over here
> 2 to about **nine**ty.

3 (1.7)

4 Ann: No– No– Not **at** ninety.=

5 From you to about ninety.

However, before Sue has produced any numbers, indeed before she has said anything whatsoever, Ann, who is her professor, challenges her, telling her that what she is doing is wrong (lines 4–5). How can Ann see that there is something wrong with a response that has not even occurred yet? Crucial to this process is the phenomenon of *conditional relevance* (Schegloff 1968). A first utterance creates an interpretive environment that will be used by participants to analyze whatever occurs after it. Here no subsequent talk has yet been produced. However, providing an answer in this activity system encompasses more than talk: before speaking the set of numbers, Sue must first locate a relevant point in the dirt and measure its coordinates. Both her movement through space and her use of tools such as the tape measure are visible events.[10]

As Ann finishes her directive, Sue is holding the tape measure against the dirt at the left or zero end of the profile. However, just after hearing 'ninety',

Sue moves both her body and the tape measure to the right, stopping near the 90 mark on the upper ruler. By virtue of the field of interpretation opened up through conditional relevance, Sue's movement and tool use as elements of the activity she has been asked to perform can now be analyzed by Ann and found wanting. Immediately after this Ann produces her correction (lines 4–5).

Additional elements of cognitive operations that Ann expects Sue to perform in order to make her measurements are revealed as the sequence continues to unfold. Making the relevant measurements presupposes the ability to locate where in the dirt measurements should be made. Sue's response to the correction calls this presupposition into question and leads to Ann telling her explicitly, in several different ways, what she should look for in order to determine where to measure. The process begins after Ann tells Sue to measure points between 0 and 90 (line 5). Sue does not immediately move to this region but instead hesitates for a full second (line 6) before replying with a weak 'Oh'.

> 1 Ann: Give me the ground surface over here
> 2 to about **nine**ty.

3 (1.7)

"At forty
Plus eleven point five"

Ruler

FIGURE 7.4 Measuring and writing for an archaeological chart

4 Ann: No– No– Not *at* ninety.=
5 From you to about ninety.
6 Sue: (1.0) Oh.
7 Ann: Wherever there's a change in slope.
8 Sue: (0.6) Mm kay.

In line 7 Ann moves from request to instruction by telling Sue what she should be looking for in the landscape: 'Wherever there's a change in slope.' Though most approaches to the study of meaning in language focus on the issue of how concepts can best be defined (for example, componential analysis and other approaches to semantics), Wittgenstein (1958:242) notes that 'If language is to be a means of communication there must be agreement not only in definitions but also (queer as this may sound) in judgments.' In the present case, in order to use what Ann

has just said to pursue the task they are collaboratively engaged in, Sue must be able to find in the dirt what will count as 'a change in slope'. As the party who has set her this task, Ann is in a position to evaluate her success. Sue again moves her tape measure far to the right (see Figure 7.5, image A). At this point, instead of relying on talk alone to make explicit the phenomena that she wants Sue to locate, Ann moves into the space that Sue is attending to (image B) and points to one place that should be measured while describing in more vernacular language what constitutes 'a change in slope': 'where it *stops* being flat' (line 11). She then points to additional places for measurement (lines 13–17).

Labelling what Ann does here either deictic gesture or ostensive definition does not do adequate justice to its complexity. Analysis of the gesture

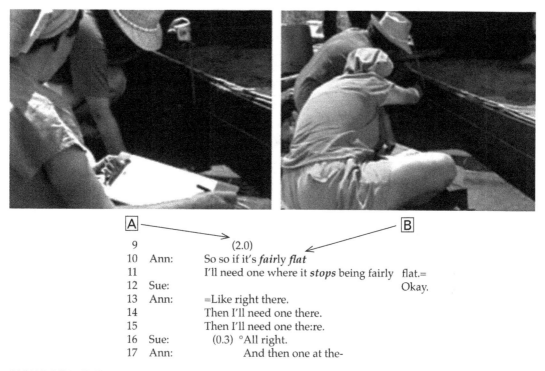

9		(2.0)
10	Ann:	So so if it's *fairly flat*
11		I'll need one where it *stops* being fairly flat.=
12	Sue:	Okay.
13	Ann:	=Like right there.
14		Then I'll need one there.
15		Then I'll need one the:re.
16	Sue:	(0.3) °All right.
17	Ann:	And then one at the-

FIGURE 7.5 Talk and gesture mutually elaborate each other

cannot focus on the gesture alone or on some possible mental state of the speaker it is externalizing (effectively drawing an analytic bubble at the skin of the actor); it requires simultaneous attention to the environment that the hand is highlighting, the talk that sets the coding problem for the addressee, and the activity that these participants are working to accomplish. Talk and gesture mutually elaborate on each other within a framework of action that includes at least three components: (1) a semantic description, such as 'a change in slope'; (2) a complex perceptual field where an instantiation of that category is to be located; and (3) the hand of an actor moving within that perceptual field. The activity in progress, including the sequence of talk within which these ostensive demonstrations emerge, provides a relevant language game that can be used to make inferences about precisely which features of the complex perceptual field being pointed at should be attended to. What Sue is being taught is not something that falls within the scope of language as an isolated system—not a definition (she already knows what a 'change in slope' is in the abstract)—but a mode of practice, how to code a relevant perceptual field in terms of categories that are consequential for her work. In turn this process is embedded within the larger activity of doing archaeological fieldwork, as well as a local interactive field that structures participants' mutual access to both each other and the domain of scrutiny where relevant work is being done. Within such an interactive field, the actions that Sue is expected to perform enable Ann to evaluate her comprehension and, where relevant, to take remedial action in subsequent moves. The cognitive activities occurring here are situated, distributed, and interactively organized. In this process coding tasks (Sue is set the problem of finding an example of a particular category in the materials she is looking at) and highlighting (the movement of Ann's hand that displays where a solution to Ann's problem is to be found) function together in the production of a relevant graphic representation (the map).

One of the things that is occurring within this sequence is a progressive expansion of Sue's understanding as the distinctions she must make to carry out the task assigned to her are explicated and elaborated. In this process of socialization through language,[11] growth in intersubjectivity occurs as domains of ignorance that prevent the successful accomplishment of collaborative action are revealed and transformed into practical knowledge—a way of seeing that is sufficient to complete the job at hand—in a way that allows Sue to understand what Ann is asking her to do and make an appropriate, competent response to her request.

It would, however, be quite wrong to see the unit within which this is lodged as being simply two minds coming together to do the work at hand. Instead, the distinctions being explicated, the ability to see in the very complex perceptual field provided by the landscape to which they are attending those few events that count as points to be transferred to the map, are central to what it means to see the world as an archaeologist and to use that seeing to build the artifacts, such as this map, that are constitutive of archaeology as a profession. All competent archaeologists are expected to be able to do this; it is an essential part of what it means to be an archaeologist,[12] and it is to these professional perceptual standards that Sue is being held accountable. The relevant unit for the analysis of the intersubjectivity at issue here is thus not these individuals as isolated entities but archaeology as a profession, a community of competent practitioners, most of whom have never met each other but nonetheless expect each other to be able to see and categorize the world in ways that are relevant to the work, tools, and artifacts that constitute their profession.

This sequence brings together an important range of cognitive phenomena relevant to the organization of human action, including interaction with both other human beings and the world itself, talk as a form of social action, writing practices, and the construction of cognitive artifacts that provide relevant representations of the world. These inscription practices are accomplished through the appropriate use of artifacts such as graph paper, rulers, and tape measures.

Supporting such tool use are sets of perceptual structures, the ability to see what and where to measure. Moreover, we are able to glimpse how these structures are passed on from one generation to the next through apprenticeship.

CONTESTED VISION

The use of coding schemes, highlighting practices, and the articulation of graphic representations to organize perception will now be examined in another professional setting: the courtroom. On March 3, 1991, an amateur video photographer taped a group of Los Angeles police officers administering a very violent beating with metal clubs to an African-American motorist, Mr Rodney King, who had been stopped for a traffic violation. When the tape was broadcast on television, there was public outrage, and four police officers involved in the beating were put on trial for excessive use of force. The principal piece of evidence against them was the tape of the beating. The violence it showed was so graphic that many people assumed that a conviction was almost automatic. However, the jury found the police officers innocent, a verdict that triggered the Los Angeles uprising. At a second federal trial a year later, two of the four officers were convicted of violating King's civil rights and two were acquitted.

Perhaps surprisingly, the main evidence used in the defence of the police officers was the tape showing them beating King. Indeed, one of the officers convicted in the second trial, Sergeant Stacy Koon, spent much of his time between the two trials watching and rewatching the tape, seeing how it looked when projected on different walls in his house. Rather than wanting to minimize the events on the tape, he told a reporter that

if we had our way, we'd go down to Dodger Stadium and rip off that big-screen Mitsubishi and bring it into the courtroom and say, 'Hey, folks, you're in for the show of your life because when this tape gets blown up it's awesome.' (Mydans 1993d:A10)

For Rodney King the experience of looking at the tape was quite different: 'It's sickening to see it. It makes me sick to my stomach to watch it' (Newton 1993a:A16).

At the first trial the prosecution presented the tape of the beating as a self-explicating, objective record. Thus the chief prosecutor said,

> What more could you ask for? You have the videotape that shows objectively, without bias, impartially, what happened that night. The videotape shows conclusively what happened that night. It can't be rebutted. (Mydans 1993b:A7)

But the lawyers defending the police officers did not treat the tape as a record that spoke for itself. Instead they argued that it could be understood only by embedding the events visible on it within the work life of a profession. The defence proposed that the beating constituted an example of careful police work, a form of professional discourse with the victim in which he was a very active co-participant—indeed, the party who controlled the interaction.

To successfully make this claim, the defence provided the jury with ethnography about police practices and with a coding scheme to be used to analyze the events on the tape. The power of coding schemes to control perception in this fashion was central to the defence strategy. The defence contended that if the police officers could legitimately see King's actions as aggressive and a threat to them, then the police were entitled to use force to protect themselves and take him into custody. The central point debated within the trial was what the police officers who beat King perceived him to be doing. These perceptions were treated not as idiosyncratic phenomena lodged within the minds of individual police officers but as socially organized perceptual frameworks shared within the police profession.

These assumptions about the conventions maintained by the police had two consequences for the organization of discourse within the courtroom: (1) police perceptions, as a domain of professional competence, can be described and analyzed through use of highlighting, coding schemes, and graphic representations; (2) in that these perceptions are not idiosyncratic

phenomena restricted to individuals but frameworks shared by a profession, *expert testimony* is possible. An expert who was not present at the scene can describe authoritatively what police officers could legitimately see as they looked at the man they were beating.

Expert testimony is given a very distinctive shape within the adversarial system of the American courtroom.[13] Each side hires its own experts and attacks the credibility of its opponents' experts. Moreover, the use of expert witnesses intersects with rules establishing what counts as adequate proof. Reasonable doubt can be created by muddying the water with a plausible alternative. In the words of the lawyer for Officer Theodore Briseno, one of the defendants:

> Your experts really don't have to be better than their [the prosecution's] experts. All you've got to have are experts on both sides. I think [jurors] wonder: 'How could we as lay people know beyond a reasonable doubt, when the experts can't decide?' (Lieberman 1993b:A32).

Such a strategy can be quite successful. One of the jurors who acquitted the police officers in the first King trial said, 'Our instructions of how we could consider evidence stated . . . if there are two reasonable explanations for an event, we had to pick the one that points to innocence, not the one that points to guilt' (Lieberman 1993b:A32).

CODING AGGRESSION AS PROFESSIONAL PRACTICE

Allowing expert testimony on the use of force by the police had the effect of filtering the events visible on the tape through a police coding scheme, as articulated by an expert who instructed the jury how to see the body movements of the victim in terms of that system. What one finds in the trial is a dialogic framework encompassing the work of two different professions, as the discourse of the police with one of their suspects is embedded within the discourse of the courtroom.

In order to measure police perception, a coding scheme for the escalation of force was applied to the tape: (1) if a suspect is aggressive, the proper police response is escalation of force in order to subdue him; (2) when the suspect co-operates, then force is de-escalated. When an expert applies this coding scheme to the tape, a new set of finely differentiated events is produced, described through appropriate language drawn from the social sciences. In the words of one expert:

Expert: There were,
ten distinct (1.0) uses of force.
rather than one single use of force.
. . .
In each of those, uses of force
there was an escalation and a de
escalation, (0.8)
an assessment period, (1.5)
and then an escalation and a de-
escalation again. (0.7)
And another assessment period.

The massive beating is now transformed into ten separate events, each with its own sequence of stages. The use of this category system radically transforms the images visible on the tape by placing them within an expert frame of reference. Thus when King is hit yet another blow, this is transformed from a moment of visible violence—what the prosecution in the second trial will instruct the jury to see as 'beating a suspect into submission'—into a demonstration that the 'period of de-escalation has ceased':

B

Defence: Four oh five, oh one.
We see a blow being delivered. =
Is that correct.
Expert: That's correct.
The- force has been again escalated
(0.3)
to the level it had been previously,
(0.4)
and the de-escalation has ceased.
. . .
Defence: And at-
At this point which is,
for the record four thirteen twenty
nine, (0.4)
We see a blow being struck

and thus the end of the period of,
de-escalation?
Is that correct Captain.
Expert: That's correct.
Force has now been elevated to the previous level, (0.6) after this period of de-escalation.

A reader looking at this sequence might argue that what the expert is saying is a mere tautology: if someone is being hit again, then—almost by definition—any period of de-escalation of force (the moments when the suspect is not being hit) has ceased. However, much more than tautology is involved. By deploying the escalation/de-escalation framework, the expert has provided a coding scheme that transforms the actions being coded into displays of careful, systematic police work. One of the defence lawyers said that what he wanted to show the jury was that 'what looks like uncontrolled uh brutality and random violence is indeed a very disciplined and controlled effort to take King into custody' (interview with Court W, CRT 018:03:30). A major resource for affecting such a perceptual transformation is the use of coding schemes such as the one articulated above by the defence's expert witness. Such schemes provide the jury with far from neutral templates for viewing and understanding in a particular way the events visible on the tape.

These structures also define the instruments of violence visible on the tape. Earlier it was noted how the conditional relevance of an utterance creates a context that shapes interpretation of the events it points to. When the escalation framework was first introduced, the defence attorney showed the jury a chart of *tools* used by the police that included not only the batons with which they were beating him but also the kicks that they administered:

C

Defence: And this chart will show you the **tools** that Sergeant Koon had available to him on March third.
. . .
The next tool up, (1.9)
Is: (0.3) a side handle baton. (0.8)

> a metal (0.3) baton. (1.0)
> is: a tool (0.8)
> to protect yourself (0.9)
> and to take people into custody. (1.0)
> And in addition to that (0.3)
> on the same level with this (0.5)
> the experts will tell you as well as
> Sergeant Koon, (0.4)
> that there are **ki**cks,

A coding scheme, classifying phenomena visible on the tape as tools required for the work of a particular occupation, is deployed to move what the prosecution described as brutal 'cowardly stomps' inflicted on a prone, beaten man into a domain of professional police work.

The escalation/de-escalation framework was taught in the police academy as a guide for appropriate action when applying force. It generated a second coding scheme focused on the suspect's body. Central to the case made by the defence was the proposal that the police officers themselves were required to evaluate King's actions as either *aggressive* or *co-operative* in order to decide whether to escalate or de-escalate force—that is, whether they should hit him again. The key perceptual decision posed in the analysis of the tape thus becomes whether the police officers can legitimately see the suspect as aggressive, in which case, it is argued, they are justified in applying further force. The following is from the cross-examination of defendant Laurence Powell, the officer who landed the most blows on King:

Prosecutor: You can't look at that video and say that every one of those blows is reasonable can you. (1.0)
Powell: Oh I **can** if I put my perceptions in.

Crucially, the defence argues that an interpretive framework focused on the suspect's actions vests control of the situation in the victim, since his actions control the response of the police:

Defence: Rodney **King** and Rodney King alone was in control of the situation.

The net effect of buying into this category system as a framework for the interpretation of the tape is a most consequential structuring of the dense and complicated perceptual field provided by the tape, with the suspect/victim King becoming the figure, the focus of minute scrutiny, while the officers performing the beating recede into the background.

EXPERT TESTIMONY: AN ETHNOGRAPHY OF SEEING

To analyze the tape in these terms, the defence calls Sergeant Charles Duke from the Los Angeles Police Department as an expert on the use of force by the police (see Figure 7.6). Commentators on the first trial considered Duke to be the most important and persuasive witness in the case.

At the point where we enter the following sequence, the prosecutor has noted that King appears to be moving into a position appropriate for handcuffing him and that one officer is in fact reaching for his handcuffs—the suspect is being co-operative.

1 Prosecutor: So uh would you,
2 again consider this to be:
3 a non-aggressive, movement by Mr. King?
4 Sgt. Duke: At this time no I wouldn't. (1.1)
5 Prosecutor: It is aggressive.
6 Sgt. Duke: Yes. It's starting to be. (0.9)
7 This foot, is laying flat, (0.8)
8 There's starting to be a **bend**. in uh (0.6)
9 this leg (0.4)
10 in his butt (0.4)
11 The buttocks area has started to rise. (0.7)
12 which would put us,
13 at the beginning of our **spec**trum again.

Here the process of coding events within a relevant perceptual field becomes an open contest as prosecution and defence use a range of discursive practices to debate whether body movements

FIGURE 7.6 Sergeant Duke analyzes the Rodney King video tape. Historical still of the Rodney King Beating courtesy of George Holliday.

of King visible on the videotape should be coded as co-operative or aggressive. By noting both the submissive elements in King's posture and the fact that one of the officers is reaching for his handcuffs, the prosecutor has tried to make the case that the tape demonstrates that at this point the officers perceive King as co-operative. If he can establish this point, hitting King again would be unjustified and the officers should be found guilty of the crimes they are charged with. The contested vision being debated here has very high stakes.

To rebut the vision proposed by the prosecutor, Duke uses the semantic resources provided by language to code as aggressive extremely subtle body movements of a man lying face down beneath the officers (lines 7–11). Note, for example, not only his explicit placement of King at the very edge, the beginning, of the aggressive spectrum (line 13) but also how very small movements are made much larger by situating them within a prospective horizon through repeated use of 'starting to' (lines 6, 18, 11), for example, 'The buttocks area has started to rise.' The events

visible on the tape are enhanced and amplified by the language used to describe them.

This focusing of attention organizes the perceptual field provided by the videotape into a salient figure, the aggressive suspect, who is highlighted against an amorphous background containing non-focal participants, the officers doing the beating. This structuring of the materials provided by the image is accomplished not only through talk but also through gesture. As Duke speaks, he brings his hand to the screen and points to the parts of King's body that, he is arguing, display aggression (see Figure 7.7). In looking at how the senior archaeologist pointed to where examples of the categories her student was searching for could be found, it was noted how a category, a gesture, and the perceptual field that it was articulating mutually elaborated on each other. Here the touchable events on the television screen provide visible *evidence* for the description constructed through talk. What emerges from Duke's testimony is not just a *statement*, a static category, but a *demonstration* built through the active interplay between

FIGURE 7.7 Sergeant Duke shows display of aggression by Rodney King. Historical still of the Rodney King Beating courtesy of George Holliday.

the coding scheme and the domain of scrutiny to which it is being applied. As talk and image mutually enhance each other, a demonstration that is greater than the sum of its parts emerges. Simultaneously, King, rather than the officers, becomes the focus of attention as the expert's finger, articulating the image, delineates what is relevant within it.

By virtue of the category systems erected by the defence, the minute rise in King's buttocks noted on the tape unleashes a cascade of perceptual inferences that have the effect of exonerating the officers. A rise in King's body is interpreted as aggression, which in turn justifies an escalation of force. Like other parties faced with a coding task, the jury members were led to engage in intense, minute cognitive scrutiny as

they looked at the tape of the beating to decide the issues at stake in the case. However, once the defence's coding scheme is accepted as a relevant framework for looking at the tape, the operative perspective for viewing it is no longer a layperson's reaction to a man lying. on the ground being beaten but instead a microanalysis of the movements being made by that man's body to see if it is exhibiting aggression.

The expert witnesses for the defence simultaneously construct actions as both rational and without moral responsibility, in the case of the police, and as mindlessly mechanical and morally responsible, in the case of Rodney King.[14] Thus references to phenomena such as 'an assessment period' imply rational deliberation on the part of the police without individual moral responsibility in terms other than the correctness of assessment—for example, the agentless passive voice of 'We see a blow being delivered', 'The force has again been escalated', and 'kicks' as tools of the trade. On the other hand, King is characterized both as an almost mindless, moving force—for example, 'The buttocks area has started to rise'—and as being 'in control of the situation'. This is accomplished in part by the disassembly of King's body from a responsible agent into a bunch of moving parts that become the triggering mechanism for a typified process to which, it is argued, the police are required to respond in a disciplined, dispassionate way. Discourses of rationality, of mechanism, and of moral responsibility are simultaneously, but strategically and selectively, deployed.

In the first trial, though the prosecution disputed the analysis of specific body movements as displays of aggression, the relevance of looking at the tape in terms of such a category system was not challenged. Observers considered this to be a very serious mistake (Lieberman 1993a:A26). A key difference in the second trial, which led to the conviction of two of the officers, was that there the prosecution gave the jury alternative frameworks for interpreting the events on the tape. These included both an alternative motive for the beating, namely that the police officers were teaching a lesson to a man who had been disrespectful to them (Mydans 1993c), and an alternative interpretation of the movements of King's body that Sergeant Duke highlighted, namely as normal reactions of a man to a beating rather than as displays of incipient aggression. In the prosecution's argument, King 'cocks his leg' not in preparation for a charge but because his muscles naturally jerk after being hit with a metal club. The prosecution's alternative interpretive template also instructed the jury to look at the physical behaviour of the police officers who were not hitting King, portraying them as nonchalantly watching a beating rather than poised to subdue a still dangerous suspect. Instead of restricting focus to the body of King, the prosecution drew the jury's attention to the slender stature of Officer Briseno, the officer sent in alone at the end of the beating to handcuff the man that the defence was portraying as a dangerous giant. The prosecutor in the second trial also emphasized to the jury inherent contradictions in the arguments being made by the defence. The defence had portrayed King as both a cunning martial arts expert, scanning the scene to plot his next move, and as a man crazed by drugs. Instead, the prosecution argued, he was simply a beaten man who fell helplessly to the ground.[15] Though most of the evidence used in the two trials was the same (most crucially the tape), the prosecutors in the second trial were able to build discursively their own interpretive frameworks to counter those that had been so effectively deployed by the defence, and thus provide their jury with ways of looking at the tape that had not been available to the first jury.

The perspectival framework provided by a professional coding scheme constitutes the objects in the domain of scrutiny that are the focus of attention. By using the coding scheme to animate the events being studied, the expert teaches the jury how to look at the tape and how to see relevant events within it (Shuy 1982:125). He provides them with an ethnography of seeing that situates the events visible on the tape within the worklife and phenomenal world of a particular work community. Here this ethnographer is not an outside anthropologist but an actual member of the community whose work is being explicated. Expert testimony in court forces members of a discourse community to become metapragmatically aware of the communication practices that organize their work, including, in this case, violence as a systematic mode of discourse capable of being described scientifically as professional practice in minute detail.

Insofar as the courtroom provides a dialogic framework encompassing the discourse of two different professions, scrutiny is occurring on a number of distinct levels: first, police scrutiny of the suspect's body as a guide for whether to beat him; second, scrutiny by those in court, including the jury and expert witnesses, as they assess the scrutiny of the police;[16] and third, within the framework of this article, our scrutiny of how those in the courtroom scrutinize the police scrutinizing their victim.

FIGURE 7.8 Use of white lines to highlight King's body. Historical still of the Rodney King Beating courtesy of George Holliday.

GRAPHIC DEMONSTRATIONS AND MATERIAL ARTIFACTS: THE BIRTH OF RODNEY KING AS A VISIBLE ACTOR

The perceptual field provided by the tape was manipulated and enhanced in other ways as well. At the very beginning of the tape, while the camera was still slightly out of focus, King ran toward the officers. On the tape itself, this event is hard to see: it happens very quickly and is difficult to discern in the midst of a dark but very complex perceptual field filled with other events, including numerous police officers, a police car, and King's own car, which, because of its light colour and lack of movement, is the most salient object in the frame—indeed, the only item that can be easily recognized. The images visible on the tape are made even more difficult to see by the movement of the zooming camera and its lack of focus.

One of the defence attorneys in the first trial had photographs made from individual tape frames. The photos were cropped, enlarged, and pasted in sequence to form a display over a metre long that was placed in front of the jury on an easel. The salience of King in these images was amplified through use of *highlighting*. As the defence attorney unveiled his display, he placed clear overlays with large white lines outlining King's body on top of the photos (see Figure 7.8). Earlier we saw an archaeologist weave a post mould into existence by drawing a line through subtle patches of colour differences in a bit of dirt. Here the defence attorney uses similar procedures for enhancing objects in the domain of scrutiny to call forth from the murky pixels on the video screen the discursive object that is the point of his argument, a large, violent, charging African-American man who was so dangerous that hitting him 47 times with metal clubs was reasonable and justified. By virtue of the figure/ground relationship established through such highlighting, the police officers, all situated beyond the boundaries of the lines drawn by the lawyer, recede into the background.

When videotape is used as the medium for displaying King's movements, a sense of what is happening as events unfold rapidly through time can be obtained only by replaying the tape repeatedly while trying to select from the confusing images on the screen that subset of visible events on which one is trying to concentrate. The work of the viewer is radically changed when these scenes are transformed into the photographic array. Movement through time becomes movement through space, that is, the left-to-right progression of the cropped frames. Each image remains available to the viewer instead of disappearing when its successor arrives, so that both the sequence as a whole and each event within it can be contemplated and rescanned at leisure. Much of the visual clutter[17] in the original images is eliminated by cropping the photos.

In his analysis of similar representational practices in scientific discourse, Lynch (1988) wrote about them providing an *externalized retina*. The defence lawyer makes precisely the same argument, stating that by enhancing the image in this way, he is able to structure the world being scrutinized so that it reveals what his client perceived (lines 5–8):

1 Defence: Rodney King, (0.4) in the very beginning, (1.0)
2 in the first six frames, (2.2)
3 of this incident, (2.4)
4 *Went* (4.7) from the ground, (0.4) to a charge. (1.2)
5 And what Sergeant Koon will tell you=
6 =*this* is his rendition, (0.4) of *what* he saw. (0.7)
7 ((Laying White Line Overlays on Top of Photos))
8 *This* is how he perceived it. (3.6)
9 But once he saw Rodney King,
10 *rise* to his feet, (1.2) and attack at Powell, (1.4)
11 That in **Koon**'s mind, (0.9) in charge of his officers (1.2)
12 that Rodney King has set the tone. (1.6)
13 **Rod**ney King, (1.1) was trying to get in that position.

Once again talk and visual representation mutually amplify each other. Descriptors such as 'a

charge' (line 4) provide instructions for how to see the highlighted sequence on the easel, while that very same sequence provides seeable proof for the argument being made in the defence attorney's talk. (At the second trial, King testified that he ran after one of the officers said, 'We're going to kill you nigger. Run.') At line 13 the defence attorney points with his finger toward the last photo in the series, the one where King is actually making contact with Officer Powell. This deictic gesture establishes that image as the referent for 'that position' at the end of line 13— the attacking position that the defence is arguing Rodney King was repeatedly trying to gain. Traditional work on gesture in interaction (and deixis in linguistics) has drawn a bubble around the perimeters of the participants' bodies. The body of the actor has not been connected to the built world within which it is situated. In these data the graphic display that receives the point is as much a constructed discursive object as the pointing finger or the spoken words; all three mutually elaborate on each other. Theoretical frameworks that partition the components of this process into separate fields of study cannot do justice to the reflexive relationship that exists between the talk, the gesture, and the artifacts that have been built and put in place precisely to receive that pointing. It is necessary to view all these phenomena as integrated components of a common activity.

THE POWER TO SPEAK AS A PROFESSIONAL

I will now briefly investigate the phenomenal structure and social organization that provide the ground from which the power to speak as a professional emerges.

Expert witnesses, such as Sergeant Duke, are entitled to speak about events in the courtroom because of their membership in a relevant community of practitioners. Duke's voice can be heard because he is a police officer, an expert on police use of force, and thus someone who can speak about what the police officers on the tape are perceiving as they look at King writhing on the ground. The structure of Duke's expertise, which gives him his right to speak authoritatively, creates a situated perspective from which events on the tape are viewed.

D

After demonstrating by playing the videotape that Mr. King appears to be moving his right hand behind his back with the palm up.

1	Prosecutor:	That would be the position you'd want him in.=
2		=Is that correct. (0.6)
3	Sgt. Duke:	Not, (0.2) Not with uh:, (0.2) the way he is. (0.6)
4		His uh:, (0.4) His leg is uh
5		Is bent in this area. (0.6)
6		Uh:, (0.2) Had he moved in this hand here being uh:
7		(0.4) straight up and down.
8		That causes me concern (0.7)
9	Prosecutor:	Uh does it also cause you concern that
10		someone's stepped on the back of his neck.
11	Sgt. Duke:	(0.6) No it does not.

Here, as in the data examined earlier, Duke displays intense concern about very small movements of King's leg and hand (lines 4–8). However, when asked about the fact that an officer has stepped on the back of King's neck (see Figure 7.9), Duke states in effect that violent actions performed by police officers against their suspect cause him no concern at all (lines 9–11). The events on the tape are being viewed and articulated by Duke from a local, situated perspective—that of the police who are beating King—which is precisely his domain of expertise.

Insofar as the perceptual structures that organize interpretation of the tape are lodged within a profession and not an isolated individual, there is a tremendous asymmetry about who can speak as an expert about the events on the tape and thus structure interpretation of it. Here Duke states that his training makes it possible for him to 'perceive the perceptions' of the police officers, but that he has no access to the perceptions of

the man they are beating, since Duke himself has 'never been a suspect':

E

1	Sgt. Duke	They're taught to evaluate.
2		And that's what they were doing in the last two
3		frames.
4		Or three frames.
5	Prosecutor:	Can you read their mind uh, (1.4) Sergeant Duke.
6		(1.3)
7	Sgt. Duke:	I can, (0.4) form an opinion based on my training.
8		and having trained people,
9		what I can perceive that their perceptions are.
10		(0.6)
11	Prosecutor:	Well what's Mr. King's perceptions at this time.
12		(0.6)
13	Sgt. Duke:	I've never been a suspect.
14		I don't know.

While administering a beating like this is recognized within the courtroom as part of the work of the police profession, no equivalent social group exists for the suspect. Victims do not constitute a profession. Thus no expert witnesses are available to interpret these events and animate the images on the tape from King's perspective. In the second trial, King was called as a witness, but he could not testify about whether the police officers beating him were using unreasonable force since he lacked 'expertise on the constitution or the use of force' (Newton 1993a:A16).

The effect of all this is the production of a set of contradictory asymmetries. Within the domain of discourse recorded on the videotape, it is argued that King is in control of the interaction, and that is what the first jury found. But within the discourse of the courtroom, no one can speak for the suspect. His perception is not lodged within a profession and thus publicly available to others as a set of official discursive procedures. Within the discourse of the trial, he is an object to be scrutinized, not an actor with a voice of his own. However, within the discourse

FIGURE 7.9 Sergeant Duke discusses officer stepping on King's neck. Historical still of the Rodney King Beating courtesy of George Holliday.

made visible on the tape, he is constituted as the controlling actor.

The way in which professional coding schemes for constituting control and asymmetry in interaction are used by the police to justify the way that they beat someone alerts us to ethical problems that can arise when we put our professional skills as social scientists at the service of another profession, thereby amplifying its voice and the power it can exert on those who become the objects of its scrutiny.

CONCLUSION

Central to the social and cognitive organization of a profession is its ability to shape events in the domain of its scrutiny into the phenomenal objects around which the discourse of the profession is organized: to find archaeologically relevant events such as post holes in the colour stains visible in a patch of a dirt and map them or to locate legally consequential instances of aggression or co-operation in the visible movements of a man's body. This article has investigated three practices used to accomplish such professional vision—coding schemes, highlighting, and the production and articulation of graphic representations—in the work settings of two professions: an archaeological field excavation and a courtroom.

Such work contributes to efforts by linguistic anthropologists, practice theorists, and conversation analysts to develop anthropologically informed analyses of human action and cognition as socially situated phenomena, activities accomplished through ongoing, contingent work within the historically shaped settings of the lived social world. In this process some traditional dichotomies that have isolated subfields from each other, such as the assignment of language and the material world to separate domains of inquiry, disappear. The ability to build and interpret a material cognitive artifact, such as an archaeological map, is embedded within a web of socially articulated discourse. Talk between co-workers, the lines they are drawing, measurement tools, and the ability to see relevant events in the dirt all mutually inform each other within a single coherent activity. Simultaneously, the practices clustered around the production, distribution, and interpretation of such representations provide the material and cognitive infrastructure that make archaeological theory possible.

Within such a framework, the ability to see relevant entities is lodged not in the individual mind but instead within a community of practitioners. This has a range of consequences. First, the power to authoritatively see and produce the range of phenomena that are consequential for the organization of a society is not homogeneously distributed. Different professions—medicine, law, the police, specific sciences such as archaeology—have the power to legitimately see, constitute, and articulate alternative kinds of events. Professional vision is perspectival, lodged within specific social entities, and unevenly allocated, The consequences that this had for who was entitled to instruct the jury about what was happening on the Rodney King videotape support Foucault's (1981) analysis of how the discursive procedures of a society structure what kinds of talk can and cannot be heard, who is qualified to speak the truth, and the conditions that establish the rationality of statements.

Second, such vision is not a purely mental process but instead is accomplished through the competent deployment of a complex of situated practices in a relevant setting. An earlier generation of anthropologists, influenced by Saussure's notion of *langue*, brought precision and clarity to their analytic projects by focusing on the grammars of cultural phenomena such as category

systems and myths while ignoring the courses of practical action within which categories and stories were articulated in the endogenous scenes of a society's everyday activities. The procedures investigated in this article move beyond the mind of the actor to encompass features of the setting where action is occurring. Through practices such as highlighting, coding, and articulating graphic representations, categories (post moulds, aggression) are linked to specific phenomena in a relevant domain of scrutiny, creating a whole that is greater than the sum of its parts—for example, an actual instantiation of a post mould or a visible demonstration of aggression. As argued by Wittgenstein (1958), a category or rule cannot determine its own application; seeing what can count as a 'change of slope' or 'aggression' in a relevant domain of scrutiny is both a contingent accomplishment and a locus for contestation—even a central site for legal argument. Categories and the phenomena to which they are being applied mutually elaborate each other.[18] This process is central among those providing for ongoing change in legal and other category systems.

Third, insofar as these practices are lodged within specific communities, they must be learned (Chaiklin and Lave 1993; Lave and Wenger 1991). Learning was a central activity in both of the settings examined in this article, but the organization of that learning was quite different in each. Like students in an anthropology class being lectured about events in another culture, the jury at the Rodney King trial was instructed by an expert about what a police officer (someone who they would never be) could see in the events visible on the tape (see Figures 7.10 and 7.11). On the other hand, the young archaeologist, crouching in the dirt and struggling to determine where in it to properly position one of the tools of her profession, was learning to be a competent practitioner. The dirt in front of her was a locus for embodied practice, not an object of contemplation.

Consistent with recent research in conversation analysis on the interactive organization of work settings (Drew and Heritage 1992), different ways of learning and their associated modes of access to the phenomena being scrutinized were constituted in each setting through the

FIGURES 7.10 and 7.11 Instruction by experts: Sergeant Duke showing police officer perspective; archaeologist showing measurement technique.

alternative ways that human interaction was organized. Though ultimately the jury decided the case, throughout the trial its members never had the chance to question the expert witnesses who were lecturing them, but instead sat week after week as a silent audience. They had the opportunity to use the tools relevant to the analysis that they were charged with performing—that is, the opportunity to play the tape themselves—only when they were alone in the jury room. By way of contrast, Ann, the senior archaeologist, was positioned to monitor not only the dirt her student was studying but also embodied actions of that student within a field of relevant action.[19] Instead of being positioned as an expert lecturing to an audience, Ann's own ability to perform a relevant next action was contingent on the competent performance of her student; Ann could not mark her map until Sue had produced a necessary measurement. Each was dependent on the other for the moment-by-moment accomplishment of a common course of action. To make that happen, Ann first provided Sue with successive descriptions of what to look for and then got down in the dirt to point to relevant phenomena, thus adjusting in detail to the problems her student was visibly facing. The necessity of collaborative action not only posed tasks of common understanding as practical problems but also exposed relevant domains of ignorance, a process crucial to their remedy. In brief, though instruction was central to what both the archaeologists and the expert witnesses in the courtroom were doing,

within each setting learning processes, encompassing participation frameworks, and modes of access to relevant phenomena were shaped in to quite different kinds of events by the alternative ways that interaction was structured.

Despite very marked differences in how each setting was organized, common discursive practices were deployed in both. There seem to be good reasons why the configuration of practices investigated in this article are generic, pervasive, and consequential in human activity. First, processes of classification are central to human cognition, at times forming the basic subject matter of entire fields such as cognitive anthropology. Through the construction and use of coding schemes, relevant classification systems are socially organized as professional and bureaucratic knowledge structures, entraining in fine detail the cognitive activity of those who administer them, producing some of the objects of knowledge around which the discourse in a profession is organized, and frequently constituting accountable loci of power for those whose actions are surveyed and coded. Second, though most theorizing about human cognition in the twentieth century has focused on mental events—for example, internal representations—a number of activity theorists, students of scientific and everyday practice, ethnomethodologists, and cognitive anthropologists have insisted that the ability of human beings to modify the world around them, to structure settings for the activities that habitually occur within them, and to build tools, maps, slide rules, and other representational artifacts is as central to human cognition as processes hidden inside the brain. The ability to build structures in the world that organize knowledge, shape perception, and structure future action is one way that human cognition is shaped through ongoing historical practices. Graphic representations constitute a prototypical example of how human beings build external cognitive artifacts for the organization and persuasive display of relevant knowledge. This article has investigated some of the ways in which relevant communities organize the production and understanding of such representations through the deployment of situated practices articulated within ongoing processes of human interaction.[20] Human activity characteristically occurs in environments that provide a very complicated perceptual field. A quite general class of cognitive practices consists of methods for highlighting this perceptual field so that relevant phenomena are made salient. This process simultaneously helps classify those phenomena, for example, as an archaeological feature rather than an irrelevant patch of colour in the dirt,

or as an aggressive movement. Practices such as highlighting link relevant features of a setting to the activity being performed in that setting.

In view of the generic character of the issues that these practices address, it is not surprising that they frequently work in concert with each other, as when Sergeant Duke's pointing finger linked a category in a coding scheme to specific phenomena visible in a graphic representation. The way in which such highlighting structures the perception of others by reshaping a domain of scrutiny so that some phenomena are made salient, while others fade into the background, has strong rhetorical and political consequences. By looking at how these practices work together within situated courses of action, it becomes possible to investigate quite diverse phenomena within a single analytical framework. As these practices are used within sequences of talk-in-interaction, members of a profession hold each other accountable for—and contest—the proper perception and constitution of the objects of knowledge around which their discourse is organized.[21]

ACKNOWLEDGEMENTS

I am very deeply indebted to Gail Wagner and the students at her archaeological field school for allowing me to investigate the activities in which they were engaged. Without their openness and support, the analysis being reported here would not be possible. I owe a tremendous debt to Lucy Suchman for demonstrating to me how important the way in which participants tailor and reshape objects in work settings in order to accomplish local tasks is to any understanding of human cognition and action (see, for example, Suchman 1987). I wish to thank Christopher Borstel, Lisa Capps, Aaron Cicourel, Janet Keller, John Heritage, Bernard Hibbits, Cath-

ryn Houghton, Hugh Mehan, Curtis Renoe, Lucy Suchman, Patty Jo Watson, and most especially Candy Goodwin for helpful and insightful comments on an earlier version of this analysis. I thank Court TV for granting permission to use the images from their broadcast.

An earlier version of this article was presented as a plenary lecture at the International Conference on Discourse and the Professions, Uppsala, Sweden, August 28, 1992, and in colloquia at UCLA, the University of California at Santa Barbara, the University of California at San Diego, and the University of South Carolina.

NOTES

1. See Bourdieu 1977, Chaiklin, and Lave 1993, Hanks 1987, and Lave and Wenger 1991 for contemporary work on practice theory. Analyses of how cognition makes use of phenomena distributed in everyday settings can be found in Lave 1988, Rogoff 1990, Rogoff and Lave 1984, and Suchman 1987. Hutchins (1993) provides a very clear demonstration of how cognition is not located in the mind of a single individual but is instead embedded within distributed systems, including socially differentiated actors and external representations embodied in tools.

Dougherty and Keller (1985) demonstrate how cognitive frameworks and material features of a setting mutually constitute each other. Recent work by linguistic anthropologists on the discursive constitution of context can be found in Duranti and Goodwin 1992. Work on activity theory (Engestrom 1987; Wertsch 1985) growing out of the pioneering work of Vygotsky (1978) has long stressed the mediated, historically shaped character of both cognition and social organization. Though focused on the organization of sequences of talk rather than tool-mediated cognition, the field of conversation analysis (Atkinson and Heritage 1984; Drew and Heritage 1992; Sacks 1992; Sacks et al. 1974) has developed the most powerful resources currently available for the analysis of the interactive organization of emerging action with actual settings (Goodwin 1990), including the way in which each next action relies on prior action for its proper interpretation while simultaneously reshaping the context that will provide the ground for subsequent action.

2. For example, see Ochs 1979 and Scheiffelin and Doucet 1994.

3. See Heritage 1984 and Sacks et al. 1974.

4. For further discussion, see Du Bois et al. 1993, Gumperz 1982, Sherzer and Woodbury 1987, and Tedlock 1987.

5. An elaboration of this system can be found in Sacks et al. 1974 on pp. 731–3.

6. See Haraway 1989, Latour 1987, Latour and Woolgar 1979, Lynch 1985, Lynch and Woolgar 1988, and Pickering 1992.

7. Archaeologists distinguish between post moulds and post holes. In order to place a post that will support a roof or other structure, people frequently dig a pit substantially larger than the post itself. After the post is in place, dirt is packed around it to support it. The larger pit is called a post hole, while the hole created by the post itself is called a post mould.

8. See Garfinkel 1967, Goodwin 1992, and Heritage 1984.

9. For analysis of how graphic representations are articulated in the mist of scientific practice, see Goodwin 1990 and Ochs et al. 1994. The more general issue of graphic representations in the discourse of science has been an important topic in the sociology of scientific knowledge (for example, Lynch 1988 and Lynch and Woolgar 1988).

10. For analysis of how participants read the movement of another's body through socially defined space, see Duranti 1992.

11. For extensive analysis of the reflexive relationship between socialization and language, see the work of Ochs and Scheiffelin (for example, Ochs 1988; Ochs and Schieffelin 1986; Scheiffelin 1990; Scheiffelin and Ochs 1986).

12. The practices at issue here have consequences for not only the production of such maps but also their reading. Competent archaeologists know that the dots on a map, the only points in the landscape that have actually been measured, have a different status than the lines connecting the dots. Thus they will sometimes discard the lines and rely only on the dots for subsequent analysis.

13. See Drew 1992, pp. 472–4, and Shuy 1982.

14. I am deeply indebted to Lucy Suchman for bringing the phenomena discussed in this paragraph to my attention.

15. The prosecution arguments at the second trial noted here are drawn from my notes made at the closing argument and from newspaper reports.

16. The ability to record events on videotape and replay them in the court created baroque possibilities for layering and framing the perception of events. At the second trial, one of the defendants, Officer Briseno, chose not to testify. However, the prosecution received permission to play for the jury videotape of his testimony at the first trial in which he criticized the actions of the other defendants. 'That placed jurors in the federal trial in the unusual position of watching a defendant on one videotape describe yet another videotape' (Newton 1993b:A25). The jury was able to watch 'as the taped Officer Briseno spoke from the monitor accompanied by the word *Live*, while the real Officer Briseno sat passively with the other defendants, following his own year-old words on a transcript' (Mydans 1993a:A14).

17. The notion of what events constitute 'clutter' to be eliminated is of course an important political decision being made by the party who reshapes the image for presentation to the jury.

18. See Goodwin 1992, Heritage 1984, and Keller

and Keller 1993.

19. The most thorough analysis of how archaeology is learned as a mode of embodied practice can be found in Edgeworth 1991.
20. See also Goodwin 1990.
21. Professional settings provide a perspicuous site for the investigation of how objects of knowledge, controlled by and relevant to the defining work of a specific community, are socially constructed from within the settings that make up the lifeworld of that community—that is, endogenously, through systematic discursive procedures. This should not, however, be taken to imply that such processes are limited to professional discourse. The way in which we reify our realities through practices such as highlighting and coding are pervasive features of human social and cognitive life.

REFERENCES CITED

Atkinson, J. Maxwell, and John Heritage, eds. 1984. *Structures of Social Action*. Cambridge: Cambridge University Press.

Bourdieu, Pierre. 1977. *Outline of a Theory of Practice*. Richard Nice, trans. Cambridge: Cambridge University Press.

Chaiklin, Seth, and Jean Lave, eds. 1993. *Understanding Practice: Perspectives on Activity and Context*. Cambridge: Cambridge University Press.

Cicourel, Aaron V. 1964. *Method and Measurement in Sociology*. New York: Free Press.

————. 1968. *The Social Organization of Juvenile Justice*. New York: Wiley.

Dougherty, Janet W.D., and Charles Keller. 1985. 'Taskonomy: A Practical Approach to Knowledge Structures'. In *Directions in Cognitive Anthropology*. J.W.D. Dougherty, ed. Pp. 161–74. Urbana: University of Illinois Press.

Drew, Paul. 1992. 'Contested Evidence in Courtroom Examination: The Case of a Trial for Rape'. In *Talk at Work: Interaction in Institutional Setting*. P. Drew and J. Heritage, eds. Pp. 470–520. Cambridge: Cambridge University Press.

Drew, Paul, and John Heritage, eds. 1992. *Talk at Work: Interaction in Institutional Settings*. Cambridge: Cambridge University Press.

Du Bois, John, Stephen Schuetze-Coburn, Danae Paolino, and Susanna Cumming. 1993. 'Outline of Discourse Transcription'. In *Talking Data: Transcription and Coding Methods for Language Research*. J.A. Edwards and M.D. Lampert, eds. Hillsdale, NJ: Lawrence Erlbaum.

Duranti, Alessandro. 1992. *Language and Bodies in Social Space: Samoan Ceremonial Greetings*. American Anthropologist 94(3):657–91.

Duranti, Alessandro, and Charles Goodwin, eds. 1992. *Rethinking Context: Language as an Interactive Phenomenon*. Cambridge: Cambridge University Press.

Edgeworth, Matthew. 1991. 'The Act of Discovery: An Ethnography of the Subject-Object Relation in Archaeological Practice'. Doctoral thesis, Program in Anthropology and Archaeology, University of Durham.

Engeström, Yrjö. 1987. *Learning by Expanding: An Activity-Theoretical Approach to Developmental Research*. Helsinki: Orienta-Konsultit Oy.

Foucault, Michel. 1981. 'The Order of Discourse'. In *Untying the Text: A Post-Structuralist Reader*. R. Young, ed. Pp. 48–78. Boston: Routledge, Kegan, Paul.

Garfinkel, Harold. 1967. *Studies in Ethnomethodology*. Englewood Cliffs, NJ: Prentice-Hall.

Goodwin, Charles. 1990. 'Perception, Technology and Interaction on a Scientific Research Vessel'. Paper presented at the Annual Meeting of the American Anthropological Association, New Orleans.

————. 1992. 'Transparent Vision'. Paper presented at the Workshop on Interaction and Grammar, Department of Applied Linguistics, UCLA, May 1, 1992. (*Interaction and Grammar*, Elinor Ochs, Sandra Thompson, and Emanuael Schegloff, eds., forthcoming [published as: Ochs, Elinor, Emanuel E. Schegloff, and Sandra A. Thompson, Eds. *Interaction and Grammar*. Cambridge UK: University of Cambridge, 1996. Pp 370–404].)

————. 1993. 'The Blackness of Black: Color Categories as Situated Practice'. In *Proceedings from the Conference on Discourse, Tools and Reasoning: Situated Cognition and Technologically Supported Environments, Lucca, Italy, November 2–7*. Lauren Resnick, Clotilde Pontecarvo, and Roger Saljo, eds.

Goodwin, Marjorie Harness. 1990. *He-Said-She-Said: Talk as Social Organization among Black Children*. Bloomington: Indiana University Press.

Gumperz, John J. 1982 Discourse Strategies. Cambridge: Cambridge University Press.

Hanks, William. 1987. *Discourse Genres in a Theory of Practice*. American Ethnologist 14(4):668–92.

Haraway, Donna. 1989. *Primate Visions: Gender, Race, and Nature in the World of Modern Science*. New York: Routledge.

Heritage, John. 1984. *Garfinkel and Ethnomethodology*. Cambridge: Polity Press.

Hutchins, Edwin. 1993. 'Learning to Navigate'. In *Understanding Practice: Perspectives on Activity and Context*. S. Chaiklin and J. Lave, eds. Pp. 35–63. Cambridge: Cambridge University Press.

Keller, Charles, and Janet Dixon Keller. 1993. 'Thinking and Acting with Iron'. In *Understanding Practice: Perspectives on Activity and Context*. S. Chaiklin and J. Lave, eds. Pp. 125–43. Cambridge: Cambridge University Press.

Latour, Bruno. 1987. *Science in Action: How to Follow Scientists and Engineers through Society*. Cambridge, MA: Harvard University Press.

Latour, Bruno, and Steve Woolgar. 1979. *Laboratory Life: The Social Construction of Scientific Facts*. London: Sage.

Lave, Jean. 1988. *Cognition in Practice*. Cambridge: Cambridge University Press.

Lave, Jean, and Etienne Wenger. 1991. *Situated Learning: Legitimate Peripheral Participation*. Cambridge: Cambridge University Press.

Lieberman, Paul. 1993a. 'King Case Prosecutors Must Scale Hurdles of History'. *The Los Angeles Times*, February 7, pp. A1, A26.

——. 1993b. 'King Trial May Come Down to a Case of Expert vs. Expert'. *The Los Angeles Times*, April 4, pp. A1, A32.

Lynch, Michael. 1985. *Art and Artefact in Laboratory Science*. London: Routledge and Kegan Paul.

——. 1988. 'The Externalized Retina: Selection and Mathematization in the Visual Documentation of Objects in the Life Sciences'. *Human Studies* 11:201–34.

Lynch, Michael, and Steve Woolgar, eds. 1988. *Representation in Scientific Practice*. Cambridge, MA: MIT Press.

Mydans, Seth. 1993a. 'Defendant on Videotape Gives Trial an Odd Air'. *The New York Times*, April 7, p. A14.

——. 1993b. 'Prosecutor in Beating Case Urges Jury to Rely on Tape'. *The New York Times*, April 21, p. A7.

——. 1993c. 'Prosecutor in Officers' Case Ends with Focus on Beating'. *The New York Times*, April 9, p. A8.

——. 1993d. 'Their Lives Consumed, Los Angeles Officers Await Trial'. *The New York Times*, February 2, p. A10.

Newton, Jim. 1993a. '"I Was Just Trying to Stay Alive", King Tells Federal Jury'. *Los Angeles Times*, March 10, pp. A1, A16.

——. 1993b. 'King Jury Sees Key Videotape; Prosecutors Rest'. *The Los Angeles Times*, April 7, pp. A1, A25.

Ochs, Elinor. 1979. 'Transcription as Theory'. In *Developmental Pragmatics*. E. Ochs and B.B. Schieffelin, eds. pp. 43–72. New York: Academic Press.

——. 1988. *Culture and Language Development: Language Acquisition and Language Socialization in a Samoan Village*. Cambridge: Cambridge University Press.

Ochs, Elinor, Patrick Gonzales, and Sally Jacoby. 1994. '"When I Come Down, I'm in a Domain State": Grammar and Graphic Representation in the Interpretive Activity of Physicists'. In *Interaction and Grammar*. E. Ochs, E.A. Schegloff, and S. Thompson, eds. Forthcoming [published as: Ochs, Elinor, Emanuel E. Schegloff, and Sandra A. Thompson, Eds. *Interaction and Grammar*. Cambridge UK: University of Cambridge, 1996. Pp. 328–69].

Ochs, Elinor, and Bambi B. Schieffelin. 1986. *Language Socialization across Cultures*. New York: Cambridge University Press.

Pickering, Andrew, ed. 1992. *Science as Practice and Culture*. Chicago: The University of Chicago Press.

Rogoff, Barbara. 1990. *Apprenticeship in Thinking*. New York: Oxford University Press.

Rogoff, Barbara, and Jean Lave. 1984. *Everyday Cognition: Its Development in Social Context*. Cambridge, MA: Harvard University Press.

Sacks, Harvey. 1992. *Lectures on Conversation*. 2 vols. Gail Jefferson, ed. Oxford: Basil Blackwell.

Sacks, Harvey, Emanuel A. Schegloff, and Gail Jefferson. 1974. *A Simplest Systematics for the Organization of Turn-Taking for Conversation*. Language 50:696–735.

Schegloff, Emanuel A. 1968. 'Sequencing in Conversational Openings'. *American Anthropologist* 70:1075–95.

Schieffelin, Bambi B. 1990. *The Give and Take of Everyday Life: Language Socialization of Kaluli Children*. Cambridge: Cambridge University Press.

Schieffelin, Bambi B., and Rachelle Charlier Doucet. 1994. 'The "Real" Haitian Creole: Metalinguistics and Orthographic Choice'. *American Ethnologist* 21(1):176–200.

Schieffelin, Bambi B., and Elinor Ochs. 1986. 'Language Socialization'. In *Annual Review of Anthropology*. B.J. Siegel, A.R. Beals, and S.A. Tyler, eds. Pp. 163–246. Palo Alto: Annual Reviews, Inc.

Sherzer, Joel, and Anthony C. Woodbury, eds. 1987. *Native American Discourse: Poetics and Rhetoric*. Cambridge: Cambridge University Press.

Shuy, Roger. 1982. 'The Unit of Analysis in a Criminal Law Case'. In *Analyzing Discourse: Text and Talk*. D. Tannen, ed. Washington, DC: Georgetown University Press.

Smith, Dorothy E. 1990. *Texts, Facts and Femininity*. London: Routledge.

Suchman, Lucy A. 1987. *Plans and Situated Actions: The Problem of Human Machine Communication.* Cambridge: Cambridge University Press.

Tedlock, Dennis. 1987. 'Hearing a Voice in an Ancient Text: Quiche Maya Poetics in Performance'. In *Native American Discourse: Poetics and Rhetoric.* J. Sherzer and A.C. Woodbury, eds. Pp. 140–75. Cambridge: Cambridge University Press.

Vygotsky, L.S. 1978. *Mind in Society: The Development of Higher Psychological Processes.* Cambridge: Harvard University Press.

Wertsch, James. 1985. *Culture, Communication, and Cognition: Vygotskian Perspectives.* Cambridge: Cambridge University Press.

Wittgenstein, Ludwig. 1958. *Philosophical Investigations.* G.E.M. Anscombe and R. Rhees, eds. G.E.M. Anscombe, trans. 2nd edition. Oxford: Blackwell.

8

VISUAL LITERACY IN ACTION: LAW IN THE AGE OF IMAGES

RICHARD K. SHERWIN

In this essay, I explore how a deeper appreciation of visual strategies helps students to grasp the various ways in which legal advocates invoke their audiences' intuitive beliefs and how the right image can help move decision-makers toward a desired outcome in a given case. I will present a range of images to illustrate the kind of visual legal rhetoric that is now being deployed both in American courtrooms and in the court of public opinion.[1] These images dispel traditional notions of an autonomous legal domain dominated by linear-causal rationality[2] and draw attention to the role of alternative cognitive and cultural models in the legal meaning-making process.[3]

Consider, for example, a criminal trial in which a home video depicting police officers surrounding and beating a lone civilian is digitally replotted to 'demonstrate' how the civilian's movements 'caused' the police to beat him. When George Holliday's fortuitously captured images of a group of white Los Angeles police officers repeatedly striking black motorist Rodney King with their batons were broadcast on the television news, public sympathy for King was strong. What could justify that kind of concerted violence against an unarmed civilian?

Indeed, the prosecutor in the state criminal case that was subsequently brought against the officers seemed to echo this popular sentiment. 'Just watch the videotape', he repeatedly told the jurors. But his trust in the simplicity of visual truth turned out to be misplaced. Locked into his own naïve realist perspective, the prosecutor never paused to consider the persuasive impact on the jury of the defence's strategy. By digitizing Holliday's images, the defence team gained significant control over the representation and renarratization of what the jurors saw at trial. For one thing, slowing down and isolating specific visual frames defused the violence of the police blows. Even more importantly, however, by altering the sequential flow of the images, the defence managed to reverse causation in the jurors' minds. The premise was simple. Psychologists have long known that when we see two objects come together and one immediately move away, our mind reads causation into the scene. It looks as if one object *caused* the other to move. Similarly, when jurors watched the digital version of George Holliday's videotape first, they saw Rodney King's body rise up off the ground (in direct violation of the officers' instructions), then they saw the officers' batons come down upon his body. When King resumed the prone position, the police batons rose up again. And so the pattern continued, with King rising up and batons coming down.

In short, the defence had effectively renarrated the scene to establish that King's own movements caused the batons to strike him. Instead of the prosecutor's story about white racist cops beating an innocent black motorist, jurors now 'saw' a series of images in which police officers carefully (and professionally) 'escalated and deescalated' levels of force in direct response to King's aggressive resistance of arrest.

Or consider the case in which a closing argument was presented in court *entirely on video*. This was a civil dispute involving the largest accounting firm in the world: Price Waterhouse. In arguing their case, the plaintiff's lawyers used a visual montage showing a broad range of visual images, borrowing from both documentary and feature film sources. The central image, however, remained the same throughout. There on the screen was the unsinkable *Titanic*, the largest ocean-going vessel in the world at the time

FIGURE 8.1

FIGURE 8.2

(see Figure 8.3). Why the *Titanic*? The plaintiff's case theory was as simple as it was ingenious. Price Waterhouse had been hired to investigate the financial standing of a bank that the plaintiff wanted to take over. In the course of their analysis, however, Price Waterhouse made numerous accounting errors, and their carelessness caused the plaintiff to unwittingly take on massive unsecured loans. The upshot? Price Waterhouse might be the largest accounting firm in the world, but just like the *Titanic*, being the largest is no guarantee against carelessness and disaster.

As a matter of everyday practice, in courtrooms across the United States, legal and non-legal realities are being visually projected in a variety of ways inside the courtroom:

- from 'day in the life' documentaries in personal injury lawsuits,

FIGURE 8.3

- to reality-based police surveillance and security videos,
- to amateur and news journalist videos (together with their digitized reconstruction),
- to computer graphics and digitally reconstructed accidents and crime re-enactments, and
- to video montage as a form of legal argumentation (including the interweaving of documentary and feature film images, as occurred in the *Titanic* closing argument).

As electronic screens proliferate in both public and private domains, the mind's adaptation to novel forms of information packaging proceeds apace. We have learned to simultaneously view multiple 'windows' onto the real and the virtual, we have come to accept simulations of reality interspersed with real-life documentation, and we have willingly absorbed narratives with fragmented timelines shaped by non-linear ('associative') forms of logic that flaunt self-reflexive allusions to the interpretive process of meaning making itself. In short, human perception and cognition are rapidly adapting to the nature and demands of new communication technologies.

In contemporary, visually literate, multimodal societies, the meaning-making codes of television, film, and, to an increasing extent, the Internet have become a part of our visual common sense; that is, they have been unconsciously assimilated. The seamless blending of fantasy and reality that we often find on film, television, and computer screens is a notable feature of this visual common sense. Of course, this is not an isolated phenomenon. Recent studies in cognitive psychology have shown that our world knowledge is often scripted a mixture of fictional and non-fictional claims.[4]

Law is not exempt from popular meaning-making processes. Nor should this prove surprising. To succeed in the business of persuasion, lawyers (especially trial lawyers) must operate within the available bandwidth of popular culture. This means that they must learn to emulate common patterns of thinking, speaking, and seeing. If persuasion is a matter of mobilizing the categories and meaning-making tools that people commonly carry around in their heads, where else would lawyers turn but to the screen? As Philip Meyer has written, '[J]urors seem to make sense out of increasingly complex simulations through references to *other* imagistic stories.' Based on his own in-court observations, Meyer claims that there is a newly emerging, open-ended legal storytelling style that is 'remarkably influenced by the conventions of contemporary popular imagistic storytelling'.[5] In short, the visual storytelling practices of contemporary popular culture are finding their way into courts and the legal culture proper.

The blurring of Hollywood fictions and legal reality is also occurring in the stories trial lawyers tell. Consider the prosecutors in *real* homicide cases who compare the accused to film characters from Francis Ford Coppola's *The Godfather* or Oliver Stone's *Natural Born Killers*, or the state's attorney who establishes a 'knowing and voluntary' waiver of Miranda rights based on the defendant's familiarity with a popular TV show.[6]

The law's assimilation of popular content takes other forms as well. Consider in this regard the movies and television shows that we watch. They tend to cycle and recycle through our minds, and the more compelling among them end up as templates for understanding and belief. This helps to explain social phenomena like the so-called Perry Mason effect, referring to the early, highly popular American TV show that led some jurors in real cases to expect to hear a confession from the witness stand at some point during the trial. These jurors experienced doubt when the expected admission of guilt was not forthcoming. Or consider the *People's Court* phenomenon, referring to the spate of popular American reality judge shows that has led some jurors to conclude that if the judge is not shouting her skepticism from the bench, she must find the witness on the stand credible. Or consider the more recent *CSI* phenomenon, referring to a cluster of popular American television shows featuring 'criminal science investigators' armed with new forensic technologies, like DNA analysis. These shows have led some jurors to experience doubt when the prosecution's science falls short. 'Where's the DNA evidence?' some jurors have been heard to protest. 'Something must be wrong with the state's case.'[7]

Lawyers have no choice but to adapt to the cognitive environment in which they work. This is why prosecutors who do *not* have DNA evidence to present (and, contrary to the popular impression film and television may create, forensic evidence is not collected at every crime scene) may feel compelled to explain why 'real law' is not like 'TV law'. Of course, it may also be with TV law in mind that a shrewd defence attorney might harp on the state's 'missing' evidence.

Today, savvy lawyers know and are putting to practical use what advertisers and politicians have known and practiced for quite some time: how to get the message out, how to tailor content to medium, and how to spin the image, edit the bite, and seize the moment on the screen and in the mind of the viewer.[8] Lawyers are storytellers, and the best, most compelling stories are the ones that adapt familiar narrative forms featuring recognizable character types driven by ordinary human emotions, motives, and desires. Advocates who can weave their legal theory into an effective story form, and play it out in court within evidentiary constraints, are more likely to be persuasive before a jury than those who simply state the facts and recite the applicable rule.

Reliance upon the strength of deductive and inductive logic alone will not do—not when characters need to be evoked, motives understood,

and states of mind laid bare. This kind of persuasion requires the fictional method, the imaginary ground plot, and the apt image—fruits of the advocate's facility with the raw materials out of which meanings are made, and made to *stick* in the decision-maker's mind. In short, legal persuasion requires familiarity with the narrative resources of popular culture.[9]

It warrants noting here that the rise of digital technology and the proliferation of visual mass media are double-edged swords when it comes to law. On the one hand, digital technology inside the courtroom makes it possible to depict objects and events with previously unimaginable clarity. Images offer an immediacy of access to trained as well as untrained eyes. Yet, precisely because of their ease of access and credibility ('seeing is believing'), visual images introduce new challenges—as the unwary American prosecutor in the Rodney King case would have done well to note.

Of particular concern in this regard is the peculiar efficacy of visual representation and visual persuasion. There are three factors to consider. First, because photographs, films, and videos can appear to resemble reality, they tend to arouse cognitive and especially emotional responses similar to those aroused by the real thing depicted. Movies, television, and other image-based entertainments have overwhelmed text-based media in popularity largely because they *seem* to simulate reality more thoroughly, engulfing the spectator (or, in the case of interactive computer and video games and immersive virtual environments, the participant) in vivid, lifelike sensations. To the extent that persuasion works through emotion as well as reason, images persuade more effectively than words alone. Second, because images appear to offer a direct, unmediated view of the reality they depict, they tend to be taken as credible representations of that reality. Unlike words, which are obviously constructed by the speaker and thus are understood to be at one remove from the reality they describe, photograph, film, and video images (whether analog or digital) appear to be caused by the external world, without the same degree of human mediation and hence interpretation; images thus seem to be better evidence for what they purport to depict.[10] Third, when images are used to communicate propositional claims, at least some of their meaning always remains implicit. Images cannot be reduced to explicit propositions. In this respect, images are well suited to leaving intended meanings unspoken, as would-be persuaders may prefer to do,[11] especially when evidentiary rules forbid making a given claim explicitly.

Images, therefore, do not simply 'add' to the persuasive force of words; they transform argument and, in so doing, have the capacity to persuade all the more powerfully. Unlike words, which compose linear messages that must be taken in sequentially, at least some of the meaning of images can be grasped all at once. This rapid intelligibility permits visual messages to be greatly condensed (it takes a lot less time to see a picture than to read a thousand words), and allows the image creator to communicate one meaning after another in quick succession. Such immediacy of comprehension enhances persuasion. When we think we've gotten the whole message at once, we are disinclined from pursuing the matter further. And, increasingly, rapid image sequences disable critical thinking because the viewer is too busy attending to the present image to reflect on the last one. For both reasons, the visual message generates less counterargument, and is therefore more likely to retain our belief. Images, moreover, convey meaning through an associational logic that operates in large part subconsciously, and through its appeal to viewers' emotions. Finally, images readily lend themselves to intertextual references that link the communication to other works and other genres, enabling arguments to draw on the audience's presumed familiarity with those other works and genres and thus to appropriate meaning from the culture at large. An audience's pleasure in the familiar, their belief that they are perceiving reality, combined with quick and easy comprehension make it more fun to watch than to read. And because viewers are occupied and entertained, they are both less able and less willing to respond critically to the persuasive visual message. Hence, the message is more likely to be accepted.

The dissemination of popular culture in a virtual flood of visual images has had an impact on law in the United States and beyond. The rapid globalization of commerce has sped the exportation of American popular culture together with its representations of law and the legal process. Consider, for example, the Canadians who insist on being told their Miranda rights when stopped by Canadian police. Having been virtually 'naturalized' by an inundation of American law films and popular TV shows, these Canadian citizens apparently feel entitled to the same constitutional rights and protections as the characters who appear on the screen. Or consider German lawyers who rise in court to contest rulings from the bench or who dramatically cross-examine witnesses on the stand. Here, too, the habitual consumption of American popular legal culture, together with the adversarial norms that it embodies, *seems* to have led some jurists to forget the inquisitorial (non-adversarial, dossier-oriented) character of their own Continental legal tradition.[12] Such developments lead one to speculate whether the transnational appeal of adversarial legal melodrama, a genre prominently featured within Anglo-American popular culture,[13] might be reconstituting global common sense about legal process and the search for truth inside the courtroom.[14]

In a schematic sense, one might express the premise of these remarks as shown below. Four 'rules of thumb' may help us think about law's life on the screen.

'Rules of thumb' for law on the screen
- 'simplify the complex'
- 'exploit the iconic'
- 'emulate the generic'
- 'respect the medium'

Consider the first rule of thumb: *simplify the complex*. New digital simulation technologies enable lawyers to accurately represent complex phenomena with compelling clarity. For example, in a recent class action against some of the world's largest tobacco companies, plaintiffs' lawyers contended that the defendant companies were being deceitful when they denied knowledge of the addicting properties of nicotine. At trial, a simple simulation demonstrated how nitrogen molecules had been added to cigarettes for the sole purpose of facilitating the rapid intake of nicotine (see Figure 8.4). The colour-coded images made plain that the tobacco companies had designed their product as a maximally efficient nicotine delivery system. Through their use of this cogent and simple visual simulation, the plaintiffs were able to immediately distill for the jury the essence of their claim.

Let us turn next to the second rule of thumb: *exploit the iconic.* The term *iconic* in this context is meant to convey the strategic use in court of familiar pop cultural templates. For example, consider the illustrative visual that was used in an insider trading case involving Martin Siegel, who was accused of providing Ivan Boesky with inside information about a bank takeover. Possession of this non-public information allowed both Siegel and Boesky to profit handsomely, albeit unlawfully, by buying undervalued stock shares and selling them at a significantly increased market value once news of the takeover had been made public.

At the trial, the plaintiff's made effective use of videotaped depositions (i.e., pre-trial interviews) of the defendants. Indeed, at one point in their closing argument, the jury saw Marty Siegel's image replicated on the screen in three rows of three—precisely the design of the old, popular television game show called *Hollywood Squares* (see Figure 8.5). In that show, celebrities (somewhat past their prime) took their seat in a large-scale tic-tac-toe board. In the trial version, Siegel was the sole player, and in each of nine exchanges he had but one thing to say: 'On advice of counsel, I invoke my fifth amendment right against compelled self-incrimination.' The effect of hearing and seeing nine Marty Siegels simultaneously invoking the right to silence while ensconced in nine boxes inside a tic-tac-toe board is comical. It was just the humorous effect needed to take the edge off of the real strategy that these images deploy: demonizing the defendant for refusing to explain himself in his own words from the witness stand at trial. An iconic cultural template, a popular TV show instantly familiar to most members of the television-watching served the plaintiffs well, for it instantly and wittily

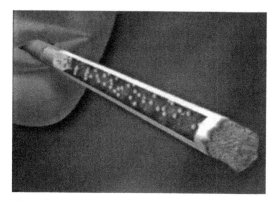

FIGURE 8.4

FIGURE 8.5

communicated the character of the man the jurors had been asked to condemn.

Consider next the third rule of thumb: *emulate generic fictions (to produce truth).* This rule reflects insights from recent social studies. These studies have shown that different sources of information are not always kept neatly separated in people's minds. Truth readily intermingles with fiction. Our world knowledge is often scripted by a mixture of fictional and non-fictional claims. In fact, the credibility of a particular image or story may depend on its faithful emulation of fictional storytelling techniques that fulfill popular expectations about what reality looks like on the screen. Consider in this regard the credibility of the 'home video' aesthetic. Several years ago, this low-tech style was exploited in a popular American horror film called *The Blair Witch Project.* In this film, three amateur filmmakers go off into the woods in search of a fabled witch. The rough, ill-lit images produced by an unsteady camera, the off-centre framing, and seemingly unscripted exchanges all contribute to an enhanced sense of immediacy and visual truthfulness (see Figure 8.6).

What began as a distinct cinematic visual style, however, may have serious consequences outside the realm of popular entertainment when the chief evidence in a law case is a film. Consider a recent criminal case prompted by an 'amateur' video that was made by a group of college students (see Figure 8.7). They used a camcorder to film what state prosecutors called a kidnapping and assault of a young woman, and what defence lawyers described as nothing more than an amateur horror film.

Is it real horror, or is it staged? If this case had gone to trial,[15] a jury would have been called upon to watch and judge for themselves the 'truth' or 'simulation' of what they saw on the screen. This would be a criminal trial that turned on a jury's response to aesthetic cues, where the jurors' perception of truth might just depend on the degree to which visual evidence effectively emulated a popular fictional genre. This case may be unique in the vividness with which it presents the fiction/non-fiction dilemma, but it is not an isolated example. Trial lawyers, judges, jurors, and the lay public must deal with similar challenges as visual evidence and visual storytelling become more commonplace in courtrooms, and elsewhere where legal meanings are being disseminated.

My last illustration addresses the fourth rule of thumb: *respect the medium*. Whenever we shift to a new medium, whether it is print, film, or massive multiplayer online gaming, we not only encounter new content but also become accustomed to new ways of experiencing content. Just as the cultural templates and cognitive heuristics that we learn from early childhood on help to shape and inform the way we perceive the world outside our skin, so too digital image-making machines embody an underlying program that helps to shape our sense of reality. Once our minds learn these artificial programs, they become 'second nature' to us. Their common-sense logic is immediately at hand and 'invisible' unconscious). Like the classic 'restaurant script' in Roger Schank and Robert Abelson's seminal study,[16] once a cognitive template is internalized as a norm, every time we confront the same or a sufficiently similar situation, we expect the same script to play out. I believe we encounter a similar expectation with respect to technology-based templates.

This applies to our expectations generated from interactive popular computer software and video gaming (an industry that has now exceeded film sales among the younger generation). In the early days of the Internet, there was a saying: 'information wants to be free'. In light of subsequent

FIGURE 8.6

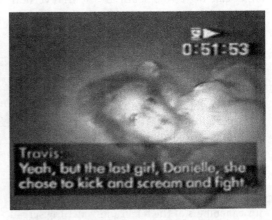

FIGURE 8.7

developments, particularly in the sphere of massive multiplayer online gaming, one might propose a slight revision: 'information wants to be played with'. People expect to be able to interact with data on the screen. And, indeed, this norm has begun to play out in the law.

In a recent, highly publicized homicide case in England, the trial judge satisfied this expectation. I have in mind the notorious Soham murder trial. This was a circumstantial evidence case. The heart of the state's case was fibres—sweater fibres from the clothing worn by the two young female victims at the time of their disappearance. The jurors not only got to see in court digital representations of those fibers, but the judge also gave them a DVD to play during their deliberations. The DVD contained images of not only sweater fibres, but also the sweaters they came from, the crime scene, the girls' route home, videotaped witness testimony, as well as other evidentiary material.

During their deliberations, the jurors got to move freely among this digital evidence. In this way, the trial judge 'respected the digital medium', and fulfilled ordinary expectations about multimodal, on-screen images. That expectation says that we should be able to interact with what we see on the screen. How this might have opened up the lawyers' carefully crafted narrative frameworks to new juror-inspired replottings, and with what impact on the outcome, is but one more question that the introduction of new visual technologies in the courtroom raises. It is a matter that warrants further study.

I will close with a final thought. As film and television genres, video games, and mass media advertisements converge with visual legal evidence and persuasion inside the courtroom, it becomes imperative for law students and teachers alike to appreciate that the making and display of images are not simply matters of aesthetics. When the life of the law imitates art, aesthetics are not ancillary to legal reality. They are constitutive.

The stakes here could not be higher, for law always implicates the use (and legitimacy) of force

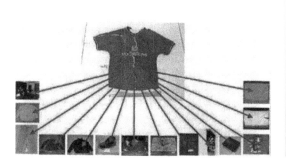

FIGURE 8.8

FIGURE 8.9

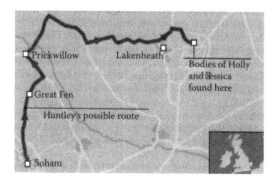

FIGURE 8.10

FIGURE 8.11

in its name. In this sense, then, helping students become more visually literate is essential to doing justice, and to the continued flourishing of participatory democracy in contemporary society.

ENDNOTES

1. See, generally, Richard K. Sherwin, *When Law Goes Pop: The Vanishing Line between Law and Popular Culture* (Chicago: University of Chicago Press, 2000); see also Christina O. Spiesel, Richard K. Sherwin, and Neal Feigenson, 'Law in the Age of Images' in *Contemporary Issues of the Semiotics of Law*, ed. Anne Wagner, Tracey Summerfield, and Farid Samir Benavides Vanegas (Oxford: Hart Publishing, 2005).

2. As stated by Judge Jack Weinstein, forensic courtroom teaching is expected to be grounded in the real world. Evidence of that world is produced, and from that evidence, using hypotheses, generally based on knowledge the to the case, opinions are formed. They are based upon rational syllogisms, leading to conclusions about statements of fact that are material propositions (sometimes called operative facts) defined by the law. (Verizon Directories Corporation v. Yellowbook USA, Inc, 338 Federal Supplement 2d 422 [2004]).

3. See G. Amsterdam and Jerome Bruner, *Minding the Law* (Cambridge, Mass.: Harvard Press, 2000); and Dorothy Holland and Naomi Quinn, *Cultural Models in and Thought* (Cambridge: University Press, 1987).

4. Richard Gerrig, *Narrative Worlds* (New Haven, Conn.: Yale University Press, 1993); and Gilbert, 'How Mental Systems Believe', *American Psychologist* 46 (1992): 107–19.

5. See Philip N. Meyer '"Desperate for Love": Cinematic Influences upon a Defendant's Closing Argument to a Jury', 18 Vt. L Rev. 721 (1994).

6. See Thomas M. Kemple, 'Litigating Illiteracy: The Media, the Law, and The People of the State of New York v. Adelbert Ward', *Canadian Journal of Law and Society* (1995): 1. See also Adam Liptak, 'New Trial for a Mother Who Drowned 5 Children', *New York Times*, January 7, 2005.

Andrea Yates, the Texas woman convicted of drowning her children in a bathtub, was granted a new trial by an appeals court in Houston yesterday. The court ruled that a prosecution expert's false testimony about the television program 'Law & Order' required a retrial.

Ms. Yates, who had received diagnoses of postpartum depression and psychosis, confessed to the police in 2001 that she had drowned her five children, ages 6 months to 7 years. A Houston jury convicted her of murder the next year for three of the drownings, rejecting her insanity defence. The case ignited a national debate about mental illness, postpartum depression and the legal definition of insanity. Yesterday's ruling was narrow and novel. It turned on testimony by Dr. Park Dietz, a psychiatrist who was the prosecution's sole mental health expert. Dr. Dietz testified that Ms. Yates was psychotic at the time of the murders but knew right from wrong. The latter conclusion meant that she was not insane under Texas' unusually narrow definition of legal insanity. On cross-examination, Dr. Dietz was asked about his work as a consultant on 'Law & Order', a program Ms. Yates, the appeals court said, 'was known to watch'. He was asked whether any of the episodes he had worked on concerned 'postpartum depression or women's mental health'.

'As a matter of fact,' he answered, 'there was a show of a woman with postpartum depression who drowned her children in the bathtub and was found insane, and it was aired shortly before the crime occurred.'

That statement was false: There was no such episode. The falsehood was discovered after the jury convicted Ms. Yates.

7. See Jamie Stockwell, 'Defense, Prosecution Play to New 'CSI' Savvy: Juries Expecting TV-Style Forensics', *Washington Post*, May 22, 2005, A01,

which stated, 'Prosecutors say jurors are telling them they expect forensic evidence in criminal cases, just like on their favorite television shows, 'CSI: Crime Scene Investigation'. . . . [I]ncreasingly, jurors are reluctant to convict someone without [forensic evidence], a phenomenon the criminal justice community is calling the CSI effect'.

8. See, e.g., G. Christopher Ritter, *Creating Winning Trial and Graphics* (Chicago: American Bar Association, 2004). See also Bernd H. Schmitt, David Rogers, and Karen Vrotsos, *There's No Business That's Not Show Business* (Upper Saddle River, N.J.: Prentice Hall, 2004). See, generally, Stuart Ewen, *PR! A History of Spin* (New York: Basic Books, 1996).

9. See Sherwin, *When Law Goes Pop.*

10. See S. Kassin and M. Dunn, 'Computer-Animated Displays and the Jury: Facilitative and Prejudicial Effects', *Law and Human Behavior* 21 (1997): 269–81.

11. For example, in his 1988 presidential campaign, George Bush ran television ads accusing his opponent, Massachusetts governor Michael Dukakis, of being soft on crime. The ads prominently featured the face of an African American man named Willie Horton, a convicted murderer who raped a white woman and stabbed her fiancé while on furlough from a Massachusetts prison. A number of commentators believed that the Bush campaign was playing racial fears by using Horton's face as a symbol of the threat that black posed to innocent whites. See Susan Estrich, 'The Politics of Race: When George Bush Made Willie Horton Part of His Campaign Team, the Issue Wasn't Just Crime—It Was Racial Fear. Michael Dukakis' Campaign Manager Saw It Happening, and Blames Herself for Not Speaking Out', *Post*, April 23, 1989, magazine section, W20. See generally Paul Messaris, *Visual Persuasion: The Role of Images in Advertising* (Thousand Oaks, Calif: Sage, 1997).

12. See Stefan Machura and Stefan Ulbrich, 'Law in Film: Globalizing the Hollywood Courtroom Drama', *Journal of Law and Society* 28 (2001): 1117–32.

13. See Carol Clover, 'Law and the Order of Popular Culture', in *Law in the Domains of Culture*, ed. Austin Sarat and Thomas R. Kearns (Ann Arbor: University of Michigan Press, 2000), 97–119.

14. See Edward S. Herman and Robert W. McChesney, *The Global Media* (London: Cassell, 1997).

15. According to Elba County, Michigan, prosecutor Byron Konschuh, the defendants in this case chose to plead guilty to attempted kidnapping and felonious assault. They spent two months in jail. Konschuh learned that the victim had not given her consent to partake in this prank. Apparently, the defendants could not get their story straight. They did not unanimously assert the 'amateur horror movie' defence. And when one defendant pled guilty, this prompted the other to follow suit. Telephone conversation with Byron Konschuh, March 1, 2004.

16. Roger Schank and Robert Abelson, *Scripts, Plans, Goals, and Understanding: An Inquiry into Human Knowledge Structures* (New York: Halsted, 1977).

9

THE PLEASURES OF LOOKING: THE ATTORNEY GENERAL'S COMMISSION ON PORNOGRAPHY VERSUS VISUAL IMAGES

CAROLE S. VANCE

The Attorney General's Commission on Pornography, a federal investigatory commission appointed in May 1985 by then–Attorney General Edwin Meese III, orchestrated an imaginative attack on sexual pleasure and desire. The chief targets of its campaign were sexually explicit images, dangerous, according to the logic of the commission, because they might encourage sexual desires or acts. The commission's public hearings in six US cities during 1985 and 1986, lengthy executive sessions, and an almost two-thousand-page report[1] constitute an extended rumination about visual images and their power. Although the term *representation* was not in its vocabulary, the panel of commissioners tenaciously clung to and aggressively advanced implicit theories of visual representation. More important, the commission took every opportunity to show sexually explicit images during its public hearings, using them to promote its point of view, to document the alleged nature of pornography, to offer a compelling interpretive frame, and to intensify a climate of sexual shame that made dissent from the commission's viewpoint almost impossible.

To enter a Meese Commission public hearing was to enter a time warp, an inviolable bubble in which the 1950s were magically recreated. Women were virgins, sex was dirty, shame and secrecy were rampant. Consider the testimony of self-described 'victim of pornography' Larry Madigan.[2] He testified earnestly that at age 12 he was a 'normal, healthy boy and my life was filled with normal activities and hobbies', when his life was radically disrupted by exposure to a deck of pornographic playing cards: 'These porno cards highly aroused me and gave me a desire I never had before.' Soon after that, he started to masturbate. Later, he went on to have 'promiscuous' sex with two women and almost ended up 'a pervert, an alcoholic, or dead', until he found Christ and was born again. How can we explain that this testimony was received in 1985 by several hundred people in a federal courthouse in a major American city without a single, publicly audible laugh? The answer lies in the commission's use of visual images to create a logical and emotional climate in which such claims were not only plausible, but convincing.

Appointed during President Ronald Reagan's second term, the commission paid a political debt to conservatives and fundamentalists who had been clamouring for action on social issues, particularly pornography, throughout his term of office. Pornographic images are symbols of what more conservatives want to control: sex for pleasure, sex outside the regulated boundaries of marriage and procreation. Sexually explicit images are dangerous, conservatives believe, because they have the power to spark fantasy, incite lust, and provoke action, as well as convey undesirable information. What more effective way to stop sexual immorality and excess, they reason, than to curtain sexual desire and pleasure at its source—in the imagination.

Conservatives also project their intense feelings about sexuality and gender politics onto pornography. Pornography, to them, is a stand-in for destructive sexual impulses that, left uncontrolled, threaten to destroy the stability of the family, the authority of men over women, and the power of parents over children. Sexual pleasure is always suspect and usually dangerous, unless harnessed within marriage, reproduction, and God's plan. Stirrings of desire, as well as individuals who would encourage or defend it, constitute a moral lapse and a personal threat. The battle against unruly sexual impulses is a never-ending struggle, even for those with strong convictions. Part of the charm of regulating pornography is that sexual images in the public arena can be banished more reliably than sexual impulses in the individual psyche.

The campaign against pornography comes at a time when moral conservatives' control over sexual behaviour is shrinking. The past century has seen a relentless increase in the frequency and acceptance of sexual behaviour outside the confines of marriage and even hetereosexuality.[3] Contemporary controversies about sexuality—teen pregnancy, lesbian and gay rights, sex education in the schools, abortion, and AIDS—make it obvious that traditional moral standards no longer hold absolute sway. Sexuality is an actively contested terrain, where diverse constituencies struggle over definitions, law, and policy. Amid this flux, regulation of visual images gives the illusion of control: visual images can still be regulated, although the actual sexual behaviour they depict usually cannot be. Visual images remain an easy target, since many who participate in sexual pleasure in private remain unwilling and ashamed to defend images of it in public.

The goal of the Meese Commission was to implement a repressive agenda on sexually explicit images and texts: vigorous enforcement of existing obscenity laws coupled with the passage of draconian new legislation. The commission's 92 recommendations continue to pose a serious threat to free expression.[4] They include appointing a high-powered Justice Department task force to coordinate obscenity investigations and prosecutions nationwide, developing a computer bank to collect data on individuals and businesses 'suspected' (as well as convicted) of producing obscene materials, mandating high fines and long jail sentences for offences, and using punitive RICO legislation (the Racketeer Influenced and Corrupt Organizations Act, originally developed to fight organized crime) to confiscate the personal property— cameras, darkroom equipment, computers, even homes and cars—of anyone convicted of the 'conspiracy' of producing or distributing pornography. Performers and producers of sexually explicit photos and films should be prosecuted under existing prostitution and pimping laws, the panellists reasoned, since money changes hands in exchange for sexual services. They regretfully noted a large body of sexually explicit images beyond prosecutorial reach, since the images could not be judged obscene by current legal standards. The commission endorsed citizen action crusades, providing pages of detailed instructions for neighbourhood watchdog groups to target and remove material in their communities that 'some citizens may find dangerous or offensive or immoral'.[5]

For imagemakers, the impact of the commission is significant in generating more aggressive prosecutions at the federal, state, and local levels, in encouraging passage of new legislation that implements the commission's recommendations, and in increasing caution and self-censorship among those who produce sexually explicit visuals. In 1988, officials arrested artist Alice Sims at her home in Alexandria, Virginia, for allegedly producing child 'pornography', photographs of two naked little girls, one of them her one-year-old daughter. The photofinishing lab had reported her, as required by new laws, for developing 'sexually explicit' material using children (a felony charge with a maximum penalty of 10 years in jail). Officials—including US Postal Inspector Robert Northrup, who testified before the Meese Commission—searched Sims's house, carted away three bags of 'evidence' (her art), and removed her children, including the still breast-feeding daughter, to foster care.[6]

In another instance of the commission's impact, Congress passed, by an overwhelming majority, the 1988 Child Protection and Obscenity Enforcement Act, which contained several Meese Commission recommendations. Retroactive to 1978, the act would have required producers and distributors of material that depicted 'frontal nudity' or 'actual sexually explicit conduct' (not necessarily obscene) to obtain and maintain for an indefinite period of time proof of the model's age. Opponents challenged the law, arguing that such burdensome record-keeping provisions and severe forfeiture penalties would, in effect, ban constitutionally protected art books, photography, and motion pictures that have sexual content. The federal court agreed and struck down

the legislation, though the government considered redrafting the legislation or appealing.

The commission's unswerving support for aggressive obscenity law enforcement bore the indelible stamp of the right-wing constituency that brought the panel into existence. Its influence was also evident in the belief of many commissioners and witnesses that pornography leads to immorality, lust, and sin. But the commission's staff and the Justice Department correctly perceived that an unabashedly conservative position would not be persuasive outside the right wing. For the commission's agenda to succeed, the attack on sexually explicit material had to be modernized by couching it in more contemporary arguments, arguments drawn chiefly from social science and feminism. So the pre-eminent harm that pornography was said to cause was not sin and immorality, but violence and degradation. In practice, the coexistence of these very different frameworks and languages proved uneasy, and modernized rhetoric at best disguised, but never replaced, the persistent bias of the commission.

I. PROCEDURES AND BIAS

Appointed to find 'new ways to control the problem of pornography', the panel was chaired by Henry Hudson, a vigorous anti-vice prosecutor from Arlington, Virginia, who had been commended by President Reagan for closing down every adult bookstore in his district. Hudson was assisted by his staff of vice cops and attorneys and by executive director Alan Sears, who had a reputation in the US Attorney's Office in Kentucky as a tough opponent of obscenity.[7] Prior to convening, seven of the eleven commissioners had taken public stands opposing pornography and supporting obscenity law as a means to control it. These seven included a fundamentalist broadcaster, several public officials, a priest, and a law professor who had argued that sexually explicit expression was undeserving of First Amendment protection because it was less like speech and more like dildos.[8] The smaller number of moderates sometimes curbed the staff's conservative bent, but their efforts were modest and not always effective.

The commission had a broad mandate to examine a wide range of sexually explicit texts and images, including pornography as well as the much smaller category of obscenity. Obscenity, a legally meaningful term, had been defined by a series of court decisions determining that obscene expression fell outside normal First Amendment protection and thus could be regulated in a manner that most speech could not.[9] Laws that restrict sexually explicit speech may do so only if the material meets the definition of obscenity established by the courts, as interpreted by judges and juries. Pornography, on the other hand, has no legal definition, is not regulated by law, and comprises a much wider range of material. Material can be sexually explicit and even pornographic without being obscene. Thus, the panel's challenge: how to control or eliminate the large body of material called pornography, when the available legal weapons targeted only obscenity? (One solution was to encourage extralegal citizen action against material that was merely pornographic. A second was to invent a new category of pornography—'violent pornography', which was so pernicious, the panel argued, that it should be assimilated into the category of obscenity and subjected to its harsher penalties.)

The conservative bias continued for 14 months, throughout the panel's more than 300 hours of public hearings in six US cities and lengthy executive sessions. The list of witnesses was tightly controlled: 77 per cent supported greater control, if not elimination, of sexually explicit material. Heavily represented were law-enforcement officers and members of vice squads (68 of 208 witnesses), politicians, and spokespersons for conservative antipornography groups like Citizens for Decency through Law and the National Federation for Decency. Great efforts were made to find 'victims of pornography' to testify,[10] but those reporting positive experiences were absent. Witnesses were treated unevenly, depending on whether the point of view they expressed facilitated the commission's ends. There were several glaring procedural irregularities, including the panel's attempt to withhold drafts and working documents from the public and its effort to name major corporations such as Time Inc., Southland,

CBS, Coca-Cola, and K-Mart as 'distributors of pornography' in the final report, repeating unsubstantiated allegations made by Rev. Donald Wildmon, executive director of the National Federation for Decency. These irregularities led to several lawsuits against the commission.[11]

The barest notions of fair play were routinely ignored in gathering evidence. Any negative statement about pornographic images, no matter how outlandish, was accepted as true. Anecdotal testimony that pornography was responsible for divorce, extramarital sex, child abuse, homosexuality, and excessive masturbation was entered as 'evidence' and appears as supporting documentation in the final report's footnotes. Chairman Hudson's hope that social science evidence could provide the smoking gun linking pornography to violence was dashed by social scientists' testimony, which cautioned against drawing such hasty conclusions. When it became clear that social science would not provide the indictment of pornography that he wanted, the chair announced that harm should be evaluated according to two additional tiers of evidence: 'the totality of the evidence', which included victim testimony, anecdotal evidence, expert opinion, personal experience, and common sense; and 'moral, ethical, and cultural values'. Pornography could thus still be convicted on two out of three tiers, despite the lack of more objective data.

The commission concentrated on sexually explicit images, although obscenity law applies to both texts and images. This marks a notable departure from the past century of obscenity regulation and moral crusades, when a significant part of censorship efforts were directed against written material.[12] During the period bracketed by 1933 (when the Supreme Court upheld the publication of *Ulysses*) and 1966 (when it ruled in favour of *Fanny Hill*), however, literary prosecutions became relatively unsuccessful, with all but the most zealous prosecutors losing interest in these doomed, and increasingly ridiculed, efforts. Conservatives like to explain their current emphasis on censoring sexually explicit images in terms other than the practical, maintaining that visual images have a special power to influence behaviour. In addition, they argue that pornography has become increasingly visual and influential, due to the swelling numbers of hard-core magazines, new technologies like home video and cable television, and more audacious content. They complain that 'porn' is flooding the nation, and now everyone can see it, even illiterates. This alarm signals a concern about the availability of visuals across boundaries of class, youth, and gender. This same concern fuelled nineteenth-century attempts to restrict literature, when reformers worried that cheap printing processes and penny-papers would put pornography, formerly available only to classically schooled aristocrats, within reach of the barely literate masses.[13] The arguments made against pornographic visuals today are virtually the same as those made against pornographic texts in the late nineteenth and early twentieth centuries, even though twentieth-century arguments against sexually explicit texts have fallen into total disrepute.

Despite their overriding concern with visual images, the commissioners invited few recognized experts on representation to testify. The small number included social psychologists reporting on their laboratory experiments on imagery and aggression, though their testimony concentrated on scientific questions and only briefly mentioned the stills or short video clips they had fashioned as experimental stimuli. More typical was a grandiosely titled lecture, 'The History of Pornography', delivered by a vice detective. He provided a brief history of pornographic images in the twentieth century, illustrating his lecture with slides from adult magazines and films. No specialists were invited to discuss the history of representing nudity, the body, or eroticism. It proved easy for the commissioners to falsely claim that their efforts to regulate commercial pornography would have no impact on the fine arts: their refusal to consider artistic material made it difficult to see the connections between them.[14]

Although few experts were called to testify, most witnesses—particularly vice cops, politicians, and moral majoritarians—offered clear statements about the effect of visual images and their mechanisms of influence. Most were

adherents of the 'monkey see, monkey do' school of representation: viewers simply imitated the sexual behaviour they saw in pornography. Most important, visual images were presented as having the capacity to arouse sexual desire and fantasy in a visceral and immediate way. Bypassing logic and moral standards, explicit pictures stimulated lust, which then demanded immediate satisfaction through masturbation, perverted sex, or rape. The effect was cumulative and addictive, with viewers purportedly graduating from reading more socially acceptable men's magazines such as *Playboy* and *Penthouse* to hard-core magazines depicting fetishism and child pornography. Soon, as the story went, viewers were dependent on pornography for the supercharged arousal it offered, causing ordinary sex to pale in comparison. The path could go only downhill, ending in sexual addiction, antisocial behaviour, and personal ruin. Sexually explicit visuals also communicated information about unfamiliar behaviour—anal sex, bestiality, group sex—which enterprising and curious viewers would be inclined to try for themselves, thus expanding the perverse forms desire might take. In this manner, pornography served to influence norms, suggesting that hedonism, sex for pleasure, and promiscuity were acceptable. The proof of this was easily seen, witnesses claimed, offering personal and professional anecdotes as evidence. The social scientists who testified about what they had discovered to be the thin connection between sexually explicit material and sexual violence were easily overwhelmed by melodramatic recitations of personal anecdote and assertions of moral certainty.

No visual artists or art groups were called to testify.[15] The absence of spokespersons for the visual arts community was striking, given the commission's intense preoccupation with images and the potentially serious impact of its restrictive recommendations on imagemakers. A moderate panellist, *Woman's Day* editor Ellen Levine, occasionally raised questions about the relationship between the images found in the photography of Bruce Weber, Robert Mapplethorpe, and Helmut Newton and the pornographic images under discussion, asking about the impact of new regulation on their work. Since most commissioners seemed unfamiliar with contemporary work, the discussion never developed. But unlike writers' groups who vigorously testified about the possible impact of censorship on their writing, visual and graphic arts groups, as well as individual artists, were silent. The only testimony given on behalf of groups connected to the actual production of visual images was offered by trade organizations (the Motion Picture Association of America, the Adult Film Association of America, and the National Cable Television Association), a freelance porn producer, and representatives of several men's magazines, but they rarely addressed issues of interpretation and meaning. It is unclear if visual groups were absent because of their unwillingness to testify or their ignorance of the proceedings, but their absence was a serious loss.

II. INTERPRETING VISUAL IMAGES

The commission's campaign against sexually explicit images was filled with paradox. Professing belief in the most naïve and literalist theories of representation, the commissioners nevertheless brilliantly used visual images during the hearings to establish 'truth' and manipulate the feelings of the audience. Arguing that pornography had a singular and universal meaning that was evident to any viewer, the commission staff worked hard to exclude any perspective but its own. Insisting that sexually explicit images had great authority, the commissioners framed pornography so that it had more power in the hearing than it could ever have in the real world. Denying that subjectivity and context matter in the interpretation of any image, they created a well-crafted context that denied there was a context.

The foremost goal of commission was to establish 'the truth' about pornography, that is, to characterize and describe the sexually explicit material that was said to be in need of regulation. Pornographic images were shown during all public hearings, as witnesses and staff members alike illustrated their remarks with explicit, fleshy, often full-colour images of sex. The reticence to view this material that one might have

anticipated on the part of fundamentalists and conservatives was nowhere to be seen, though the anomaly was not lost on wags in the audience, who jokingly referred to 'the federally funded peep show'. The commission capitalized on the realistic representational form of still photos and movie and video clips, stating that the purpose of viewing these images was to inform the public and themselves about 'what pornography was really like'. Viewing was carefully orchestrated, and a great deal of staff time went toward organizing the logistics and technologies of viewing. Far from being a casual or minor enterprise, the selection and showing of sexually explicit images constituted one of the commission's major interventions.

In fact, visual images dominated the hearings at all times. During screenings, pornographic images consistently captured the audience's attention with a reliability that eluded the more long-winded witnesses. The images were arresting, vivid, memorable, and, one had to suspect, not infrequently arousing. A rustle of excitement swept through the audience at the announcement of each showing. The chance to see forbidden material had obvious appeal. In between slide shows, the images of sex still loomed large, as witnesses testified under a blank projection screen whose unblinking, steady eye served as a reminder of the pornography whose nature had been characterized with seemingly documentary precision. Residual effects were palpable, too, in the aroused emotional state of the audience and commissioners, which made dissent not only unwelcome, but incomprehensible and personally discrediting as well.[16]

The structure of viewing was an inversion of the typical context for viewing pornography. Normally private, this was public, with slides presented in federal courthouse chambers before hundreds of spectators in the light of day. The viewing of pornography, usually an individualistic and libidinally anarchic practice, was here organized by the state—the Department of Justice, to be exact. The normal purpose in viewing, sexual pleasure and masturbation, was ostensibly absent, replaced instead by dutiful scrutiny and the pleasures of condemnation.

These pleasures were intense. Some had called the commission a show trial in which pornography was to be found guilty, but if so, it seemed scripted by the staff of *Saturday Night Live*. The atmosphere throughout the hearings was one of excited repression: witnesses alternated between chronicling the negative effects of pornography and making sensationalized presentation of 'it'. Taking a lead from feminist antipornography groups, everyone had a slide show: the FBI, the US Customs Service, the US Postal Service, and sundry vice squads. At every 'lights out', spectators would rush to one side of the room to see the screen, which was angled toward the commissioners. Were the hearing room a ship, we would have capsized many times.

Alan Sears, the executive director, told the commissioners with a grin that he hoped to include some 'good stuff' in their final report, and its two volumes and 1,960 pages faithfully reflect the censors' fascination with the thing they love to hate. Although the commission stopped short of reproducing sexually explicit images in a government document, the enthusiastic voyeurism that marked the hearings is evident in the report. It lists in alphabetical order the titles of material found in sixteen adult bookstores in six cities: 2,370 films, 725 books, and 2,325 magazines, beginning with *A Cock between Friends* and ending with *69 Lesbians Munching*. A detailed plot summary is given for the book *The Tying Up of Rebecca*, along with descriptions of sex aids advertised in the books, their cost, and how to order them. The report describes photographs found in 10 sexually explicit magazines, for example, *Tri-Sexual Lust*, *Bizarre Climax No.9*, *Every Dog Has His Day*, and *Pregnant Lesbians No. 1*. The interpretive approach may not be on the cutting edge of photographic criticism, but here it earnestly slogs along for 33 pages ('one photograph of the female performing fellatio on one male while the other male's erect penis rests on her cheek' and 'one close-up photograph of a naked Caucasian male with the testicles of another naked Caucasian male in his mouth').[17]

The commission viewed a disproportionate amount of atypical material, which even moderate commissioners criticized as 'extremely violent and degrading'.[18] To make themselves sound contemporary and secular, conservatives needed to establish that pornography was violent rather than immoral and, contradicting social science evidence, that this violence was increasing.[19] It was important for the panel to insist that the images presented were 'typical' or 'average' pornography. But typical pornography—glossy, mainstream porn magazines directed at heterosexual men—does not feature much violence, as the commission's own research (quickly suppressed) confirmed.[20] Yet the slide shows did not present many carefully airbrushed photos of perfect females or the largely heterosexual gyrations (typically depicting intercourse and oral sex) found even in the more hard-core adult bookstores. The commission concentrated on atypical material, produced for private use or for small, special-interest segments of the market, or confiscated in the course of prosecutions. Slides featured subjects guaranteed to have a high shock value: excrement, urination, homosexuality, bestiality (with over 20 different types of animals, including chickens and elephants), and especially sadomasochism (SM). Child pornography was frequently shown (with no effort made to disguise the identity of the children), despite repeated testimony from the commission's own expert witnesses that severe penalties had made this material virtually unobtainable in the commercial market.

Predictably, the commission relied on the realism of photography to amplify the notion that the body of material shown was accurate, that is, representative. The staff also skillfully mixed atypical and marginal material with pictorials from *Playboy* and *Penthouse*, rarely making a distinction between types of publications or types of markets. The desired fiction was that extreme images were found everywhere and that all pornography was the same. Images existed in a timeless pornographic present, 'with little attention given to describing an image's date, provenance, conditions of production, intended market, or producer. Although representatives from major men's magazines testified, taking pains to distance what they called the 'healthy adult entertainment' in their publications from the sleazy and degraded images, which they agreed deserved censorship, the mud-slinging only reinforced the idea that sexual images were suspect.

The panel's effort to modernize the case against pornography led to complex symbolic and rhetorical gymnastics. The most successful effort was the appropriation of the term *degrading*. Used by some antipornography feminists to describe sexist images, the term was rapidly appropriated to cover images of all sexual behaviour that might be considered immoral, since in the conservative worldview, immorality degraded the individual and society. 'Degrading' was freely applied to visual images that portrayed homosexuality, masturbation, and even consensual heterosexual sex. Even images of morally approved marital sexuality were judged 'degrading', since public viewing of what should be a private experience degraded the couple and the sanctity of marriage.

A more difficult enterprise for the commission was managing the contradiction between the heavy emphasis on 'violent' or 'degrading' pornography in the hearings and the commission's concerns about more typical sexually explicit images, that is, the *Playboy* problem. Strategically, the panel emphasized atypical material to build a strong case against pornography. But even successful attempts to restrict these images (child pornography, SM, bestiality) would in fact have little impact on pornography available, because they constitute such a small fraction of the market. This reality surfaced in panel discussions periodically, and members' frustration exposed the panel's enduring interest in restricting all sexually explicit material, including mainstream magazines that had never been judged obscene by the courts. Commissioners complained that the overemphasis on extreme material incorrectly implied that the worst harm of pornography was found at the edges of the porn industry. To the contrary, they stated, the real danger of pornography was in its most acceptable guise, the men's magazine, which endorsed hedonism, promiscuity, and sex without responsibility in homes throughout America.

The visuals, including commentaries, descriptions, and instructions about how to read them, were a crucial part of the commission's discourse.

Yet the commission's strategic manoeuvres and assertions about sexual images were covert and therefore exempt from argument. Many have commented on the way all photographic images are read as fact or truth because the images are realistic. This general phenomenon is true for pornographic images as well, but it is intensified when the viewer is confronted by images of sexually explicit acts that he or she has little experience viewing in real life. Shock, discomfort, fascination, repulsion, arousal all operate to make the image have an enormous impact and seem undeniably real.

But any photographic image, of course, reflects choice, perspective, intention, and conventions of production. And any collection of images said to represent a body of work—say, a slide show—bears the mark of an editing hand and an organizing intelligence or intentionality. Yet the ritual showing of pornographic images with their accompanying voice-overs throughout the course of the hearings erased the commission's editing hand, guaranteeing that many images and their interpretations would be given the status of unassailable truth. It is difficult to argue with a slide show.

The commission's frame was always a literal one. The action depicted was understood as realistic, not fantastic or staged for the purpose of producing an erotic picture. Thus, images that played with themes of surrender or domination were read as actually coerced. A nude woman holding a machine gun was obviously dangerous, because the gun could go off (an interpretation not, perhaps, inaccurate for the psychoanalytically inclined reader). Images of obviously adult men and women dressed in exaggerated fashions of high school students were called child pornography. Although meaning was said to be self-evident, nothing was left to chance.

Sadomasochistic pornography had an especially strategic use in establishing that sexually explicit imagery was 'violent'. The intervention was effective, since few (even liberal critics) have been willing to examine the construction of SM in the panel's argument. Commissioners saw a great deal of SM pornography and found it deeply upsetting, as did the audience. Photographs included images of women tied up, gagged, or being 'disciplined'. Viewers were unfamiliar with the conventions of SM sexual behaviour and had no access to the codes participants use to read these images. The panel provided the frame: SM was non-consensual sex that inflicted force and violence on unwilling victims. Virtually any claim could be made against SM pornography and, by extension, SM, which remains a highly stigmatized and relatively invisible sexual behaviour. Stigma and severe disapproval ensure that one normal channel of information about the unfamiliar, discussion with friends and peers about behaviour they engage in, is closed, because the cost to participants is too high. As was the case for homosexuality until recently, invisibility reinforces stigma, and stigma reinforces invisibility in a circular manner.

The redundant viewing and narration of SM images reinforced several points useful to the commission: pornography depicted actual violence; pornography encouraged violence; and pornography promoted male dominance and the degradation of women. Images that depicted male domination and female submission were often shown. An active editorial hand was at work, however, to remove reverse images of female domination and male submission; these images never appeared, though they constitute a significant portion of SM imagery. Amusingly, SM pornography elicited hearty condemnation of 'male dominance'; the only sphere in which conservative men were moved to critique it throughout the course of the hearing.

The commission called no witnesses to discuss the nature of SM, either professional experts or typical participants. Given the atmosphere, it was not surprising that no one defended it. Indeed, producers of more soft-core pornography joined in the condemnation, perhaps hoping to direct the commission's ire to more stigmatized groups and acts.[21] The commission ignored a small but increasing body of literature that documents important features of SM sexual behaviour, namely consent and safety.[22] Typically the conventions we use to decipher ordinary images are suspended when it comes to SM images. When we see war movies, for example, we do not leave the theatre believing that the carnage was real or that the performers were injured making the films. But the commissioners assumed that images of domination and submission were both real and coerced.

In addition, such literalist interpretations were evident in the repeated assertions that all types of sexual images had a direct effect on behaviour. Witnesses provided the evidence: rapists who were said by arresting officers to have read pornography, and regretful swingers who said their careers were started by exposure to pornography. According to the commission, the danger in sexually explicit images was that they inspired literal imitation, as well as more generalized and free-flowing lust. The less diversity and perversity available for viewing, the better.

The commission downplayed the most common use of pornography—for arousal during masturbation. To fully acknowledge this use would put the entire enterprise dangerously close to seeming to attack masturbation, a distinctly nineteenth-century crusade that would seem to defy most forms of rhetorical modernization. The idea that sexual images could be used and remain on a fantasy level was foreign to the commission, as was the possibility that individuals might use fantasy to engage with dangerous or frightening feelings without wanting to experience them in real life. This lack of recognition is consistent with fundamentalist distrust and puzzlement about the imagination and the symbolic realm, which seem to have no autonomous existence; for fundamentalists, imagination and behaviour are closely linked. For these reasons, the commission was deeply hostile to psychoanalytic theory, interpretation, or the notion of human inconsistency, ambiguity, or ambivalence. If good thoughts lead to good behaviour, a sure way to eliminate bad behaviour was to police bad thoughts.

The voice-over for the visual segments was singular and uniform, which served to obliterate the actual diversity of people's response to pornography. But sexually explicit material is a contested ground precisely *because* subjectivity matters. An image that is erotic to one individual is revolting to a second and ridiculous to a third. The object of contestation *is* meaning. Age, gender, race, class, sexual preference, erotic experience, and personal history all form the grid through which sexual images are received and interpreted. The commission worked hard to eliminate diversity from its hearings and to substitute instead its own authoritative, often uncontested, frequently male, monologue.

It is startling to realize that many of the Meese Commission's techniques were pioneered by antipornography feminists between 1977 and 1984. Claiming that pornography was sexist and promoted violence against women, antipornography feminism had an authoritative voice-over, too, though for theorists Andrea Dworkin and Catharine MacKinnon and groups like Women Against Pornography, the monologic voice was, of course, female.[23] Although antipornography feminists disagreed with fundamentalist moral assumptions and contested, rather than approved, male authority, they carved out new territory with slide shows depicting allegedly horrific sexual images, a technique the commission happily adopted. Antipornography feminists relied on victim testimony and preferred anecdotes to data. They, too, shared a literalist interpretive frame and used SM images to prove that pornography was violent. It was not a total surprise when the panel invited leading antipornography feminists to testify at its hearings, and they co-operated.

In the Meese Commission's monologue, even dissenting witnesses inadvertently co-operated by handing over the arena of interpretation to the commission. Not a single anticensorship witness ever showed a slide, provided a competing frame of visual interpretation, or showed images he or she thought were joyful, erotic, and pleasurable.[24] All lost an important opportunity to present another point of view, to educate, and to interrupt the fiction of a single, shared interpretive frame. Visual images remained the exclusive province of the censors and the literalists. This further cemented the notion that the visual 'evidence' was uncontested and indeed spoke for itself. Why did the anticensorship community not do better?

The Meese Commission was skilled in its ability to use photographic images to establish the so-called 'truth' and to provide an almost-invisible interpretative frame that compelled agreement with its agenda. The commission's true genius, however, lay in its ability to create an emotional atmosphere in the hearings that facilitated acceptance of the commission's worldview. Its strategic use of images was a crucial component of this emotional management. Because the power of this emotional climate fades in the published text, it is not obvious to most readers of the commission's report. Yet it was and is a force to be reckoned with, both in the commission and, more broadly, in all public debates about sexuality that involve the right wing. Though the commission was not infrequently ridiculed by journalists for its lack of objectivity and its overzealous puritanism, logical objections to its manipulations often faded in the hearing room.

III. CREATING A CLIMATE OF SEXUAL SHAME

The commission relentlessly created an atmosphere of unacknowledged sexual arousal and fear. The large amount of pornography shown, ostensibly designed to educate and repel, was nevertheless arousing. The range and diversity of images provided something for virtually everyone, and the concentration on taboo, kinky, and harder-to-obtain material added to the charge. Signs were evident in nervous laughter, rapt attention, flushed cheeks, awkward jokes, throat clearing and coughing, squirming in seats, and a charged, nervous tension in the room. Part of the discomfort may have come from the unfamiliarity of seeing sexually explicit images in public, not private, settings, and in the company of others not there for the express purpose of sexual arousal. But a larger part must have come from the problem of managing sexual arousal in an atmosphere where it was condemned.

The rhetoric of the commission suggests that pornographic material is degrading and disgusting and that no decent person would seek it out or respond to it. Although it is obvious that millions of people buy pornography, none of them appeared in the hearing room to defend it. And, as the testimony elicited by the panel suggested that porn consumers are likely to be rapists, raving maniacs, and perverts easily detected by their flapping raincoats and drooling saliva, certainly no one present at the hearing was willing to admit to feeling sexually aroused. As a result, anyone who experienced any arousal to the images shown felt simultaneously ashamed, abnormal, and isolated, particularly in regard to homosexual or SM imagery, which had been characterized as especially deviant.

The commission's lesson was a complex one, but it taught the importance of managing and hiding sexual arousal and pleasure in public, while it reinforced sexual secrecy, hypocrisy, and shame. The prospect of exposure brought with it fear, stigmatization, and rejection. Sexual feelings, though, did not disappear; they were split off as dangerous, alien, and hateful, projected onto others, where they must be controlled. Unacknowledged sexual arousal developed into a whirlwind of confused, repressed emotion that the Meese Commission channelled toward its own purpose.

Dissenting witnesses rarely attacked the commission's characterization of pornography. Although they made important arguments about censorship, they left the commission's description of pornography, interpretive frame, and account of subjectivity unchallenged. The commission's visual interventions and narrative voice-over remained powerful because no one pointed to their existence or the mechanisms through which they were created.

No one offered a deconstruction of the commission's visual techniques or offered images that would problematize its constructions. A counter slideshow might have included erotic images from the fine arts as well as from advertising, calling into question the neat category of 'the pornographic'. It could have historicized sexually explicit imagery by relating images to time, place, genre, audience, and conditions of production. It might have included images of similar bodies and body parts whose context made all the difference in meaning, or included viewers talking about the diversity of their responses to the same image. And it could have included artists talking about erotic creativity. To show positive images of sexual explicitness would have been a radical act.

To be fair, it was extraordinarily difficult to offer a dissenting perspective. The overwhelming emotional climate created by the hearings turned anyone who disagreed into a veritable monster, a defender of the most sensational and unpalatable images shown. The frame demonized pornography, but it also tarnished the reputation of anyone who questioned the commission's program. Most prospective dissenting witnesses correctly perceived that the atmosphere was closer to a witchcraft trial than a fact-finding hearing. Some declined to testify, and others moderated their remarks, anticipating a climate of intimidation.[25]

Indeed, an important aspect of the commission's work was the ritual airing and affirmation of sexual shame in a public setting, a practice that was embedded in the interrogatory practices of the chair. Witnesses appearing before the commission were treated in a highly uneven manner. Commissioners accepted virtually any claim made by antipornography witnesses as true, while those who opposed restriction of sexually explicit speech were often met with rudeness and hostility. Visual images proved to be the Achilles' heel of anticensorship witnesses, since the witnesses were often asked if they meant to defend a particularly stigmatized image that had just been flashed on the screen, such as *Big Tit Dildo Bondage* or *Anal Girls*. The witnesses were often speechless, and their inarticulateness about images often undercut their testimony.

Sexual shame was also ritualized in how witnesses spoke about their personal experience with images. 'Victims of pornography' told in lurid detail of their use of pornography and eventual decline into masturbation, sexual addiction, and incest. Some testified anonymously, shadowy apparitions behind translucent screens. Their first-person accounts, sometimes written by the commission's staff,[26] featured a great elaboration of the sexual damage caused by visual images. To counter these accounts there was nothing but silence: descriptions of visual and sexual pleasure were absent. The commission's chair even noted the lack and was fond of asking journalists if they had ever come across individuals with positive experiences with pornography. The investigatory staff had tried to identify such people to testify, he said, but had been unable to find any. Hudson importuned reporters to please send such individuals his way. A female commissioner helpfully suggested that she knew of acquaintances, 'normal married couples living in suburban New Jersey', who occasionally looked at magazines or rented X-rated videos with no apparent ill effects. But she doubted that they would be willing to testify about their sexual pleasure in a federal courthouse, with their remarks transcribed by a court stenographer and their photos probably published in the next day's paper as 'porn-users'.

Though few witnesses chose to expose themselves to the commission's intimidation through visual images, the tactics used are illustrated in the differential treatment of two female witnesses, former *Playboy* Playmate Micki Garcia and former *Penthouse* Pet of the Year Dottie Meyer. Garcia accused Playboy Enterprises and Hugh Hefner of encouraging drug use, murder, and rape (as well as abortion, bisexuality, and cosmetic surgery) in the Playboy mansion. Her life was endangered by her testimony, she claimed. Despite the serious nature of her charges and the lack of any supporting evidence, her testimony was received without question.[27] Meyer, on the other hand, testified that her association with *Penthouse* had been professionally and personally beneficial. At the conclusion of her testimony, the lights dramatically dimmed and large blow-ups of several *Penthouse* pictorials were flashed on the screen, with rapid-fire questions the chair demanded that she explain sexual images he found particularly objectionable. Another commissioner, prepared by the staff with copies of Meyer's nine-year-old centrefold, began to pepper her with hectoring questions about her sexual life: Was it true she was preoccupied with sex? Liked sex in cars and alleyways? Had a collection of vibrators? Liked rough-and-tumble sex?[28] His cross-examination was reminiscent of that directed at a rape victim made vulnerable and discredited by an image of her own sexuality.

The commission's success in maintaining and intensifying a climate of sexual shame depended on the inability of witnesses to address the question of sexuality and pleasure. Most witnesses who opposed greater restriction of sexually explicit material framed their arguments in terms of the dangers of censorship, illustrating their points by examples of literature that had been censored in previous, presumably less enlightened, times. Visual examples were rare. Speakers favoured historical, rather than contemporary, examples around which a clear consensus about value had formed. Favoured examples were the plays of Eugene O'Neill and D. H. Lawrence's *Lady Chatterley's Lover*. The frame was cultured and high-minded, calling on general principles like free speech and the Bill of Rights.

The motives behind this strategy differed. The small number of witnesses directly associated with the sex industry (producers of X-rated films, books, or magazines) believed that their disreputable image could be uplifted by associating themselves with higher, unassailable principles that had a minimal connection with sexuality. Although they had practical experience with visuals, they judged it a wiser course to say little about their real-world connection. The second group, a much larger number of witnesses representing literary, artistic, and anticensorship organizations, was totally unprepared to talk about visuals. They had thought little about questions of representation or sexually explicit images, often shared the same unsophisticated premises as the commissioners, and appeared to feel that association with sexuality was potentially discrediting.

The second group was fair game for the chair. Relying on his well-honed prosecutorial abilities, he was selectively relentless. He went right to the heart of witnesses' reluctance to associate themselves with anything sexual, visual, or pleasure-filled. Pointing to the latest slide or holding aloft the latest exhibit, he questioned them about their organization's position on *Hot Bodies of Split Beavers*. Did their members produce such images? Did their organization mean to defend such material? Did they think such material should be available?

Like vampires spying crosses and garlic cloves, witnesses shrank back. Having never seen the sexually explicit material or thought about it, having no well-developed position about sexuality or visual representation, and sensing the increasingly dangerous turf they were being lead into, they said, 'No'. They were unprepared, speechless, and unwilling to defend anything so patently sexual. The chair had proven his point: even anticensorship advocates would not defend visual pornography. He politely excused them, with bland, if inaccurate, assurances that antipornography efforts would target only indefensible sleaze, not worthy high culture. More important, he appeared to establish a consensus, which included even liberals, that sexually explicit visuals were beyond the pale. Despite their valiant effort, the testimony of anticensorship witnesses never succeeded in deconstructing or interrupting the Meese Commission's rhetorical and symbolic strategies. The right wing's commitment, however, to controlling symbols means that there will be other times, other battles in which to elaborate a richer, more complex response.

IV. SPEAKING SEXUAL AND VISUAL PLEASURE

The antidote to the Meese Commission—and by extension all conservative and fundamentalist efforts to restrict sexual images, whether in pornography, sex education, or AIDS information—is a complex one, requiring vigorous response that goes beyond appeals to free speech. Free expression is a necessary principle in these debates because of the steady protection it offers to all images, but it cannot be the only one. We need to offer an alternative frame for understanding images, one that rejects literalist constructions and offers in their place multiplicity, subjectivity, and the diverse experience of viewers. We must challenge the conservative monopoly on visual display and interpretation. The visual arts community needs to employ its interpretive skills to unmask the modernized rhetoric conservatives use to justify their traditional agenda, as well as deconstruct the 'difficult' images fundamentalists pick to set their campaigns in motion. Despite their uncanny intuition for choosing culturally disturbing material, their focus on images also contains many sleights of hand, even displacements, which we need to examine. Images even we allow to remain 'disturbing' and unconsidered put us anxiously on the defensive and undermine our own response. To do all this, visual artists and arts groups need to be willing to enter public debate and activism, giving up the notion that art or photography is somehow exempt from right-wing crusades against images.

The most robust and energetic response, however, must be to take courage and begin to speak to what is missing, both in the Meese Commission's monologue and in the anticensorship reply: desire, sexuality, and pleasure. Truly dissenting voices and speakers must start to say in public that sexual pleasure is legitimate and honourable, a simple statement that few witnesses in the commission's dealings dared to make. If we remain afraid to offer a public defence of sex and pleasure, then even in our rebuttal we have granted the right wing its most basic premise: sexuality is shameful and discrediting. The rigid, seemingly impenetrable symbolic and emotional facade constructed by the Meese Commission can, in fact, be radically undermined by insistently confronting it with what it most wants to banish—the tantalizing connection between visual and sexual pleasure.

ACKNOWLEDGEMENTS

I am grateful to many individuals for helpful discussions, comments on early drafts, and encouragement, especially Ann Snitow, Frances Doughty, Sharon Thompson, Lisa Duggan, David Schwartz, and Gil Zicklin. Special thanks to Frances Doughty for insightful and invaluable suggestions about writing. Thanks to Carol Squiers for editorial suggestions and to Gayle Rubin for last-minute help.

NOTES

1. Attorney General's Commission on Pornography, *Final Report*, 2 vols. (Washington, D.C.: US Government Printing Office, July 1986).

   Public hearings were organized around preselected topics in six cities: Washington, D.C. (general), Chicago (law enforcement), Houston (social science), Los Angeles (production and distribution), Miami (child pornography), and New York (organized crime). Each public hearing typically lasted two full days. Commission executive sessions were held in each city, usually for two working days, in conjunction with the public hearings. Additional work sessions occurred in Washington, D.C., and Scottsdale, Arizona. All the commission's executive sessions were open to the public, following the provision of sunshine laws governing federal advisory commissions. Commissioners were specifically enjoined from discussing commission business or engaging in any information deliberations outside public view.

   My analysis is based on direct observations of the commission's public hearings and executive sessions, supplemented by many interviews with participants.

2. Larry Madigan, 'former consumer of pornography', testified as the Miami hearings. He was introduced by his therapist, Dr. Simon Miranda, who claimed that most of his own clinical work was with patients whose problems were caused by pornography. 'Larry,' he stated, 'has informed me recently that, in fact, he can trace many of the problems that he has had life long, to an encounter with pornography' (Miami hearing transcript, 21 November 1985).

3. For changes in sexual patterns in the last century, see (for England) Jeffrey Weeks, *Sex, Politics, and Society: The Regulation of Sexuality Since 1800* (New York: 1981), and (for America) John D'Emilio and Estelle B. Freedman, *Intimate Matters* (New York: Harper and Row, 1988)

4. See *Final Report*, pp. 433–58, for a complete list of the panel's recommendations.

5. *Final Report*, p. 420. See also, pt. 4, chap. 7, 'Citizen and Community Action and Corporate Responsibility'. These instructions are significant because they outline a powerful, extralegal strategy for eliminating materials that are 'non-obscene but offensive', that is, normally immune from legal action under obscenity law. Suggestions include forming antipornography activist groups and collecting detailed information on sexually explicit materials available in local stores, movie theatres, hotels, and through video, cable, and computer channels. A detailed checklist is provided for citizens to conduct 'a thorough survey of these establishments and media'. Citizens are also encouraged to pressure police and public officials, conduct court watches, picket and boycott local stores, and monitor rock music heard by their children. Commissioners also recommend that institutions that are taxpayer supported prohibit the 'production, trafficking, distribution, or display of pornography on their premises or in association with their institution'. Conservative politicians and right-wing decency groups used this strategy in 1989 to attack the National Endowment for the Arts for indirectly funding an exhibit of Robert Mapplethorpe's photographs, some of which were erotic, some sexually explicit, at the Corcoran Gallery, Washington, DC (For an account of the NEA–Mapplethorpe controversy: see Carole S. Vance, 'The War on Culture', *Art in America*, September 1989, pp. 39–45.)

6. The children were returned home the next day, as social-service officials determined there was no evidence that the children were in danger. Charges were eventually dropped by the state of Virginia because of local protest, but the US Postal Service has not officially closed the case. According to Sims, while searching her house Agent Northrup told her, 'Art is anything you can get away with', and referring to her work, 'This is all filth.' Later, in an interview with *Village Voice* art critic Elizabeth Hess, he said, 'Artistic people are funny. Mrs. Sims's house was not like Ozzie and Harriet's.' He asked, 'How do you differentiate between an artist and a pedophile?' For a more complete account of the case, see 'Snapshots, Art, or Porn?' *Village Voice*, 25 October 1988, pp. 31–2. Thanks to Jeff Weinstein for this citation.

7. Alan Sears went on to become the executive director of Citizens for Decency through Law, a major conservative antipornography group.

(The group later changed its name to the Children's Legal Foundation).

8. Besides Hudson, the commission panel included the following: James Dobson, head of the fundamentalist organization Focus on the Family: 'I have a personal dislike for pornography and all it implies', he told the *Washington Post*. Judge Edward Garcia, recently appointed by then-President Reagan to the Federal District Court in California; Garcia prosecuted obscenity cases before becoming a judge. Diane Cusack, a member of the Scottsdale, Arizona, City Council; Cusack urged residents to take photographs and license numbers of patrons entering the local adult theatre. Father Bruce Ritter, a Franciscan priest; Ritter directed Covenant House, a home for runaways in New York's Time Square area, and was an outspoken critic of pornography. Attorney Harold (Tex) Lazar; Lazar played an instrumental role in setting up the commission as an aide to Reagan's first attorney general, William French Smith. Frederick Schauer, a law professor at the University of Michigan; Schauer has written extensively on obscenity. The four members of the panel with no public positions on pornography included Park Elliott Dietz, a psychiatrist at the University of Virginia and a consultant to the Federal Bureau of Investigation, who specialized in the subject of sexual deviations ('paraphilias'); Judith Becker, a Columbia University psychologist known for her research on rapists and rape victims; Ellen Levine, a vice president of CBS and editor of *Woman's Day*; and Deanne Tilton, head of the California Consortium of Child Abuse Councils.

9. A variety of state laws had resulted in prosecutions and convictions for obscenity in the nineteenth and twentieth centuries. In response to a challenge of one such law, the Supreme Court in 1957 articulated the First Amendment standard for what could be prosecuted as 'obscene' in *Roth v. United States* (354 U.S. 476 [1957]). The court decided that the normal protections given to constitutionally protected speech need not be given to legally obscene material.

The most recent attempt to define what is 'obscene' in a constitutionally permissible manner is found in a 1973 case *Miller v. California* (413 US. 15 [1973]). According to *Miller*, material is obscene if an three of the following conditions are met:

1. The average person, applying contemporary standards, would find that the work, taken as a whole, appeals to the prurient interest, and
2. the work depicts or describes, in a patently offensive way, sexual conduct specified by the statute, and
3. the work, taken as a whole, lacks serious literary, artistic, political, or scientific value.

10. Victims of pornography, as described in the *Final Report*, included 'Sharon, formerly married to a medical professional who is an avid consumer of pornography', 'Bill, convicted of the sexual molestation of two adolescent females', 'Dan, former Consumer of Pornography [*sic*]', 'Evelyn, Mother and homemaker, Wisconsin, formerly married to an avid consumer of pornography', and 'Mary Steinman, sexual abuse victim'.

11. In February 1986, the executive director at the commission announced that in the future no drafts or working papers could be released to the press or public. The American Civil Liberties Union sued the commission for violating access and the commission settled before the case got to court, agreeing to release these documents to the public (see the *Washington Post*, 7 March 1986; 4 April 1986; 12 April 1986).

When some commissioners objected to repeating unsubstantiated allegations in the final report, the staff sent letters to the corporation on Department of Justice letterhead, noting that 'the Commission received testimony alleging that your company is involved in the sale or distribution of pornography.' The letter noted that the companies had 30 days to respond and that 'a lack of reply would indicate they did not differ' with the allegations. Some corporations strenuously protested these methods. Others, however, caved in. Southland Corporation, which owns 4500 7-Eleven convenience stores, announced that it would no longer carry *Playboy*, *Penthouse*, and *Forum* magazines. Bob Guccione, *Penthouse* publisher, called the move 'blacklisting' and launched lawsuits against the commission. The commission settled one by agreeing not to publish the allegations in the report, but Guccione continued his suit for economic damages against the commission and individual commissioners

(*New York Times*, 15 April 1986, p. B5; *Newsweek*, 26 April 1986, pp. 38–9).

12. For accounts of the history of regulating indecency and obscenity in the United States and England, see Edward J. Bristow, *Vice and Vigilance: Purity Movements in Britain since 1700* (New Jersey: Rowman and Littlefield, 1977); David Pivar, *Purity Crusade: Sexual Morality and Social Control: 1868–1900* (Westport, Conn.: Greenwood Press, 1972); Walter Kendrick, *The Secret Museum* (New York: Viking, 1987); John D'Emilio and Estelle B. Freedman, *Intimate Matters* (New York: Harper and Row, 1988).

13. See Walter Kendrick, *The Secret Museum*, for a discussion of the class concerns that motivated nineteenth-century obscenity regulation.

14. The falsity of this claim is made evident by the right-wing attack on the National Endowment of the Arts over the 'blasphemy' and 'obscenity' contained in the work of Andres Serrano and Robert Mapplethorpe.

15. In contrast to visual artists, print and literary groups turned out in force. The commission heard testimony from the National Writers Union, Writers Guild, Association of American Publishers, the American Library Association, the Freedom to Read Committee, Bantam Books, and Actors Equity Association.

16. A number of potential witnesses told me that they were afraid to testify, in some cases declining actual invitation and in other cases deciding against requesting to speak. They feared hostile and humiliating cross-examination and, for producers of sexually explicit material, police retaliation in the form of harassment, investigation, and potential prosecution. Fear of reprisal was among the freelance, and often more innovative, producers of sexually explicit material, whether pornography or radical political graphics. As they could not rely on large parent organizations to offer legal protection and financial backing (and, some implied, payoffs to corrupt vice cops). With only modest financial resources at hand, the prospect of disrupted business or costly legal battles (even if ultimately victorious) spelled financial disaster. Most small producers felt it was prudent not to testify, leaving the job to mainstream men's magazines not known for radical sex politics or innovative graphics.

17. Descriptions of magazine photographs can be found in the *Final Report*, pp. 1614–46. Videos and movies are also described, though the narrative concentrates primarily on plot and dialogue. The narrative reproduces long sections of dialogue verbatim, arguably constituting a copyright violation.

18. *Final Report*, statement of Judith Becker and Ellen Levine, p. 199. In addition, they wrote: 'We do not even know whether or not what the Commission viewed during the course of the year reflected the nature of most of the pornographic and obscene material in the market; nor do we know if the materials shown us mirror the taste of the majority of consumers of pornography . . . . While one does not deny the existence of this material, the fact that it dominated the materials presented at our hearings may have distorted the Commission's judgment about the proportion of such violent material in relation to the total pornographic material in distribution.'

19. Recent empirical evidence does not support the often-repeated assertion that violence in pornography is increasing. In their review of the literature, social scientists Edward Dormerstein, Daniel Linz, and Steven Penrod conclude, 'at least for now, we cannot legitimately conclude that pornography has become more violent since the time of the 1970 obscenity and pornography commission' (in *The Question of Pornography: Research Findings and Policy Implications* [New York: The Free Press, 1987], p. 91).

20. The only original research conducted by the commission examined images found issues of best-selling men's magazines (*Cheri, Chic, Club, Gallery, Cui, Penthouse, Playboy, Swank*). The study found that 'images of force, violence, or weapons' constituted less than 1 per cent of all images (0.6 per cent), hardly substantiating the commission's claim that violent imagery in pornography was common. Although the results of this study are reported in the draft, they were excised from the final report.

The study found that the most common acts portrayed were 'split beaver' poses (20 per cent), other imagery including touching (19 per cent), oral–genital activity (12 per cent), and activities between two women (12 per cent). According to the Audit Bureau of Circulation (ABC) the

13 top-selling mainstream magazines sold 12 million copies per month (4.2 million copies for *Playboy*, 3.3 million copies for *Penthouse*), with a monthly sales value over $38 million (1984 data).

21. The proclivity of mildly stigmatized groups to join in the scapegoating of more stigmatized groups is explained by Gayle Rubin in her discussion of the concept of sexual hierarchy ('Thinking Sex: Notes for a Radical Theory of the Politics of Sexuality', in *Pleasure and Danger: Exploring Female Sexuality*, ed. Carole S. Vance [Boston: Routledge & Kegan Paul. 1984], pp. 267–319).

22. For recent work on SM, see Gini Graham-Scott, *Dominant Women, Submissive Men* (New York: Praeger,1983); Thomas Weinberg and G.P. Levi Kamel, *S and M: Studies in Sadomasochism* (Buffalo: Prometheus Books, 1983); and Caroline Greene, *S-M: The Last Taboo* (New York: Grove Press, 1974); Michael A. Rosen, *Sexual Magic: the S/M Photographs* (San Francisco: Shaynew Press, 1986); Geoff Mains, *Urban Aboriginals* (San Francisco: Gay Sunshine Press, 1984); Samois, ed., *Corning to Power*, 2nd ed, (Boston: Alyson Press, 1982)

23. Major works of antipornography feminism include Andrea Dworkin, *Pornography: Men Possessing Women* (New York: G.P. Putnam and Sons, 1979); Laura Lederer, ed., *Take Back the Night* (New York: William Morrow, 1930);

Catharine A. MacKinnon, 'Pornography, Civil Rights, and Speech:' *Harvard Civil Rights—Civil Liberties Law Review* 20 (Cambridge, Mass.: Harvard University, 1985), pp. 1–70.

Opinion within feminism about pornography was, in fact, quite diverse, and it soon became apparent that the antipornography view was not hegemonic. For other views, see Varda Burstyn, ed. *Women against Censorship* (Vancouver: Douglas and McIntyre, 1985), and *Caught Looking: Feminism, Pornography, and Censorship* (New York: Caught Looking, Inc., 1986).

24. These witnesses included legal scholars, representatives from the American Civil Liberties Union, the Freedom to Read Committee, and publishers' and authors' groups.

25. Some producers of sexually explicit material declined to testify because the commission had no authority to immunize witnesses from criminal prosecution. They feared that their testimony would be used by law enforcement officials to investigate or prosecute them. This was especially true during the Los Angeles hearing devoted specifically to the sex industry, since local officials were just then conducting an especially vigorous effort against producers.

26. Statement of Alan Sears, Executive director (Washington, D.C., transcript, 18 June 1985).

27. Los Angeles hearing, 17 October 1985.

28. New York City hearing, 22 January 1986.

10

THE SUSPICIOUS AND THE SELF-PROMOTIONAL: ABOUT THOSE PHOTOGRAPHS WE POST ON FACEBOOK

IRA WAGMAN

This chapter explores one of the central contradictions in popular discourses about living in a digital culture. On the one hand, there is significant interest in issues of privacy, in the ways that digital technologies—and the companies, governments, and institutions that own them—collect and store information about ourselves and distribute it to others, often without our prior knowledge. On the other hand, however, we see users of those same technologies promoting themselves to others. It is not hyperbolic to suggest that more people have access to more forms of self-promotion, especially through media technologies and platforms, than ever before. Some

see this as one of the virtues of living in a digital age, in which individuals are not only consumers of culture, but also producers and distributors of works that form part of the marketplace of ideas. Here the concern is something different—how to communicate oneself in a world of abundant media, images, and opinions.

This tension may well be grounded in the here and now, but it is also a longstanding feature of communication technologies—from paper to iPad—that have made it possible to frame, record, and distribute images that represent people, places, and things. Discourses about the ability of digital technologies to 'snoop on us' and to 'speak for us' draw attention to questions about the status of the images themselves. Who controls images of us? Who decides how images of us are used?

To illustrate this tension between society's concern for *privacy* and its interest in *publicity*, this chapter focuses on the use of photographs on the social networking website Facebook. With over 500 million users, Facebook is one of the most popular websites on the Internet. By some estimates, there are over 15 billion photographs on the site, with users adding photos at a rate of 850 million per month.[1] If this number is correct, Facebook is arguably one of the largest repositories of photographs in the world. In a perfect example of 'old' media technologies being re-born with the arrival of new technologies, a process Bolter and Grusin call 're-mediation', the photograph—the 'new' medium of early modernity—clearly now is a critical part of the Facebook experience (Bolter and Grusin).

This chapter focuses on how those photographs are put into action by Facebook users. Given the numbers of users and of photographs, what follows in this chapter is hardly a comprehensive list of possible uses. Indeed, I have here drawn mainly from media coverage of celebrated case studies, as well as my own experience on the site. At the same time, this chapter makes only modest judgments on the aesthetic properties of digital photographs, a subject too broad to be taken up here. Instead, I wish to draw attention to two dominant aspects of photographic practice that can help us understand the use of photography on Facebook, as well as to reflect broadly on the place of the photograph within digital culture.

The first dominant aspect is the photograph's ability to arouse suspicion, in being used online to *frame* or point out things that people do and shouldn't be doing. This phenomenon is often a function of a user's lack of competence on the website and his or her unawareness of what the site can and cannot do. In other cases, it is a function of ubiquitous photography, of numerous people taking pictures of others without their prior consent. Here we see how photographs have been used to root out criminals, to catch people

'in the act', and to draw attention to things many seem to miss in real life. The second mode of use is what I wish to characterize as *self-promotional*. By this term I refer to someone using Facebook—and indeed, using the photographs posted on his or her page—to communicate a particular image of him- or herself to others. The tensions created by these uses of photographs—between privacy and publicity, between user competence and incompetence, and between authorized and unauthorized use of imagery—are a major cause of the anxious discourse that characterizes aspects of digital culture.

I conclude by suggesting that while the overwhelming emphasis is on the control of images, we should rather try to gain a better understanding of how to live in a world of abundant media—a question that draws attention to making sense of media, rather than controlling it.

FACEBOOK, PHOTOGRAPHY, AND THE DIGITAL IMAGE

As many of us know, Facebook is a type of website that performs tasks we commonly term 'social networking'. The company claims that 50 per cent of its users log into the site at least once a day, and the site is available in over 60 languages. At the time of writing, there are over 15 million user accounts attributed to Canadians, making Canada one of the most 'Facebooked' nations in the world.[2] In total, users are logged into the site for an average of 700 million minutes per month and each month they consume over 30 billion units of what the company calls 'pieces of content', ranging from video games to photographs.

While Facebook is arguably the most popular form of social networking, it is hardly the first or the only website to offer such a service. The number of such sites has grown; a partial list would include early online pioneers such as Friendster or Typepad, to those that entered the market around the same time as Facebook, such as MySpace, Bebo, and LinkedIn. While each site has different characteristics, or may be targeted towards a specific audience, all social networking sites share many essential properties. They require users to establish a profile that contains their name and contact information, as well as some data about their hobbies, interests, political leanings, religious views, or preferences in popular culture. That information is then 'fenced in' to the site itself; depending on the site, users can adjust their settings to restrict their information from public view, or viewing information may be restricted to other members (boyd and Ellison).

The inspiration for the modern-day Facebook can be found offline. Many American universities would distribute 'facebooks', pamphlets or bound volumes containing information about both the institution and the incoming class. Here one could find a student's 'profile': contact information, expressions of likes and dislikes, and photographs of the student and his or her colleagues. In many ways, a facebook is similar to a high-school yearbook, the publication distributed to students at the end of the school year. The major difference between the two is temporal. If the yearbook serves a memorial purpose, a souvenir of one's time at school, the facebook serves more short-term goals—to stimulate sociality, to 'break the ice' between strangers. If one recognized a classmate's face and already knew that one shared his or her tastes in music, for example, one could bypass the awkward hurdles associated with first meetings.

In its beginnings in online form, only students registered at Harvard University could get into the Facebook. This exclusivity was short-lived; the site's membership expanded to include students at other American universities, then those at universities in other countries, then those in certain organizations, and finally any individuals. Now anyone with a valid email account can be a member of a club once restricted by status and age. After initial howls of protest from students that their parents were now on Facebook, we have reached a state in which it seems everyone—students, parents, governments, businesses, and elements of popular culture—populates the site.

In the online version of Facebook, once a profile is established, the user builds her or his social network, attempting to make connections with other users on the site. This process may take a few different forms. The user may contact a friend he or she knows is a member of the network, ask to be 'friends', and, if successful, make a connection. Typically, that connection is announced to other members of a user's social network. Other people become aware that the two people are friends, and then include the newest entry into the social network. A network may consist of a few friends or may have participants numbering into the thousands. Once a network is established, members of the group are notified of the goings-on of other members of the network, either through public postings of information, or through internal messaging services, such as the Mail function on Facebook. Those announcements may tell of memberships in fan clubs or subscriptions to 'pages', which represent informal groups of like-minded people, or which are devoted to products, political parties, musicians, movies, and so on, and which distribute information to all members of that particular page.

Facebook's user-friendly interface and uncluttered design make social networking extremely easy. The site's other features, like web searching and its mail function, allow people to do lots of things on Facebook, making it the primary platform for many of its users to perform numerous activities on the World Wide Web, including posting photographs. Such photographs, ranging from the banal to the *risqué*, may be sent from one online friend to another; they may be posted on one's Facebook page for all to see; and users may learn of other people's pictures through 'tags' on photographs that identify people in the pictures.

Historical developments in the art of photography influence how we take pictures today. Photography as we know it today has evolved through a long process, one characterized by the increasingly wide availability of cameras, the rise of snapshot photography, and, as Susan Murray points out, the proliferation of media outlets, from tabloid newspapers to magazines like *Life*, that made photographs a vital part of the news narrative (Murray 152). At the same time, the story is one of technological innovation. The switch from images captured on film to digital images, and the introduction of digital cameras equipped with massive storage capacity—developments that have largely happened since

1995—make it possible for us to take pictures without concern for cost, availability, or even style. While we once had cameras that were disposable or that offered immediate processing—think of the Polaroid—the film itself was valuable. We could take relatively few shots before running out of film. In addition, the costs of development limited how many pictures we could afford to take. Now, with digital cameras, even when we reach the limit of pictures the memory card can hold, a quick 'dump' of the images onto a computer frees up space to continue to take pictures. As well, the software—we used to call it 'artificial intelligence'—on many digital cameras does much of the work once relegated to experts and enthusiasts, setting the aperture size, shutter speed, and focus for each shot. Many digital cameras can record video with sound, a move that converts the apparatus used to make still photography into something capable of shooting short films. Then there are the various photo editing applications, most famously Adobe Photoshop, which allow us to edit images with varying levels of precision.

Such developments mean that cameras once made to take pictures now perform other tasks, like shooting movies; it is also true that almost any electronic device can be outfitted to take still images. Cameras are now present on a range of devices, from desktop computers equipped with webcams, to laptop computers, to cellular phones. One might just as profitably argue that even aspects of the physical environment, like buildings or bank machines, have been turned into cameras, or better yet, into picture-takers, through the ubiquity of surveillance cameras that now dot the urban landscape.

The proliferation of photographic devices and the massive amounts of memory those devices now offer are only part of the picture (if you will). Many cameras can be plugged directly into computers, allowing us to view photos on the larger screen and to organize masses of pictures in different ways. Photographic software, such as Iphoto or PhotoShare—sometimes included in the basic package of an operating system—makes it possible to coordinate picture archives. Finally, photo-sharing websites, such as Picasa, Flickr, and,

of course, Facebook, allow distribution of images in the absence of a physical *photograph*. Although printing a photograph is now relatively inexpensive, most photographs today are never printed.

Just as the 'life' of a physical photograph is always threatened by elements such as fire, rain, or sunlight, the survival of a digital photograph may well be subject to availability of electricity and quality of computer code. A power failure or a breakdown of a server on which many photographs are stored threatens to effectively eliminate those photographs from the historical record. As I will argue later, this may not be an unwanted outcome, since most photographs serve an immediate, rather than a memorial, purpose.

The effect of the large quantities of photographs and the numerous photographic devices and platforms is important. It is part of a broader transformation, one that began with the availability of inexpensive film and development and continued with cheap, more disposable cameras which transformed amateur photography from something driven by memorialization into something more documentary—an adjunct to the routines of daily life. This is what Ori Schwarz means when he describes photography using camera-phones as a far more personal form than that using traditional cameras, enabling what he calls 'spontaneous, costless photography' (Schwartz 353). The effect is to move photography into the realm of the everyday, or make it, as Susan Murray put it, 'about an immediate, rather fleeting display of one's discovery of the small and mundane (such as bottles, trees, debris and architectural elements)' (Murray 151). If Schwartz's observation describes the effect of digitization on photographic practice, and if Murray's observation is a meditation on the nature of digital photography, what remains to be discussed is how the photograph functions as evidence, as a way of communicating about someone or something in the service of a broader argument. It is to this question that this essay now turns.

THE SUSPICIOUS IMAGE

Natalie Blanchard, a resident of Granby, Quebec, was once employed by the high-technology giant IBM. She took sick leave from the company when she was diagnosed with depression. Her doctor advised her to take medication, seek therapy, and pursue opportunities to socialize with friends. This treatment involved taking a vacation to a sunny destination and heading out on the town. Photos of these events, including a shot of Blanchard in a bikini, were posted on her Facebook page. Employees of the insurance company that paid her sick-leave benefits saw this photo, deemed that Blanchard was healthy enough to work, and stopped her sick-leave payments. This decision attracted considerable attention in the press, briefly making Natalie Blanchard a media celebrity in 2009. Although the insurance company maintained that it would never base a decision to cut off benefits based solely on a Facebook photograph, it admitted that it used the photograph in its investigation as to whether benefits to Blanchard should continue (CBC News).

Let us turn to a second case. A story in the *New York Times* reported the use of Facebook by traffic police in New Delhi, India, in detecting traffic violations. Citizens were encouraged to become volunteer deputy traffic officers—to take pictures of vehicles making illegal turns, drivers using cellphones, and vehicles parked improperly—and post the photos on Facebook. In the first two months of the campaign, more than 3000 photographs were posted, and police issued over 600 tickets (Timmons).

The cases of Nathalie Blanchard and the Delhi Traffic Police illustrate how Facebook images are used to catch people 'in the act'. Such stories also remind us of the ways in which traditional photography has aided surveillance, whether by police forces or insurance companies auditing or monitoring people. Arguably the best example is the police mug shot, an innovation of the late nineteenth century. In 1886, the chief of police of New York City, Thomas Byrnes, authored a coffee-table–sized book featuring the faces of criminals. The book featured over 200 photographs, as well as other information about the criminals, including a detailed record of the dates of robberies committed across the United States during the previous 20 years, and a list of murders and executions (Cole 21). The book was intended to improve

recognition and recall of the faces of criminals by those most in contact with them, from police constables to hotel employees and bank tellers. The book is a printed version of the 'rogues' gallery', a collection of criminal photographs posted at a police station for the public to view. The establishment of rogues' galleries began in the mid 1800s; by the 1870s, cities like New York, Moscow, and London used them (Cole 21).

Photography made it possible for policing to extend to places beyond the reach of individual constables. With pictures of criminals, everyday citizens could become deputy officers—turn-of-the-century crime-stoppers, if you will—rooting out crime where they saw it happening. Such efforts were necessary to organize societies that were becoming both urbanized and massified. As Tom Gunning notes, the need for photographs in police work resulted from a citizenry made increasingly mobile by the then new form of transportation, the train (Gunning).

Photography, then, helps hold criminals in place. Of course, the major difference between photography in police work and in the examples of Natalie Blanchard and the Delhi Traffic Police may well be considered a matter of consent. Whereas criminals are well aware of being photographed, the drivers on the streets of New Delhi may be unaware that their photos are being taken to be used as evidence against them. This may be true of Natalie Blanchard as well, but a very different explanation in her case is possible: she may have been unaware of who can see, or what others might do with, images posted on Facebook. Here Blanchard is not alone; user unawareness (and indeed, user naïveté) figures prominently in popular press accounts of the misadventures of young people on the site, who learn of the consequences of their behaviour at the most inopportune time, such as when they apply for university or hit the job market.

These examples show that what we are experiencing—our anxieties over privacy—are in a way a continuation of another story, a vestige of the 'democratization' of photography. With so many people now capable of taking pictures from anywhere they happen to be, all places and spaces are open for amateur photographers. Many have noted this development goes back to the beginning of the last century; Stephen Kern writes of how the mass production of cheap cameras and inexpensive film in the early twentieth century inspired articles in American newspapers expressing concern about invasions of privacy from 'Kodakers lying in wait' (Kern 187). Susan Sontag characterized the camera as a 'predatory weapon', like a car or a gun, used to shred the boundaries between private and public space (Sontag 14). A theme common to the newspaper coverage at the beginning of the twentieth century and Sontag's analysis in the middle of the same century is the massification and convenience of cultural production. That photography is *easy* to do and that *anyone* can do it are causes for alarm. Of course, both Kern and Sontag imply that photography is used recklessly, that the photographer is unaware of the power of the tool he or she is wielding. While such a claim may provoke an immediate negative reaction, one that we might associate with elitism or snobbery, the examples above remind us that photographs can be used in ways not intended by the photographer or the subject.

John Tagg shows that this possibility is an extension of a longer history of the democratization of the visual image—Tagg uses the term 'the era of throwaway images'—which dates back to the advent of the tabloid newspaper. In tabloids, photographs of celebrities, once available only to few people, could now be seen by many. 'No longer would it seem remarkable,' Tagg wrote, 'to possess an image of someone well-known or powerful' (Tagg 56). As we will see in the next section, the distinctive characteristic of the 'era of throwaway images' may well be the extension of practices once limited to celebrities to 'regular' people like you and me.

THE SELF-PROMOTIONAL IMAGE

Writing in the 1960s, Marshall McLuhan notes the power of photography to produce what he calls a 'transformation of sense-awareness'. A heightened sense-awareness involves what McLuhan calls 'a development of self-consciousness that alters facial expression and cosmetic makeup as immediately as it does our bodily stance, in

public or in private' (McLuhan 177). In other words, self-consciousness is part of photography's role as a promotional vehicle, one that communicates images of ourselves to others. Awareness of the power of images—even our own—is built into the way we present ourselves to others—the way we pose for pictures or mug for the camera. Photographs, then, are important conduits for communicating who we are. Such ideas are implicit in the second form of the social use of Facebook photographs, namely, to display and promote the self to others in the social network.

Stewart Ewen observes that one of the features of living in a highly mobile society, 'where first impressions are important and where selling oneself is the most highly cultivated "skill", the construction of appearances becomes more and more imperative' (Ewen 85). Media systems, Ewen argues, provide the signposts, the basis on which people fashion their images. Although Ewen is talking about commercial photography, his sentiments can easily apply to the use of photography in Facebook. Of course, it is not only first impressions that matter, but also the continued maintenance of those impressions—the management of image in much the same way that celebrities, political parties, and corporations do.

In his article on the use of photography on an Israeli social networking site, Ori Schwarz observes that a particular style of photograph—the self-portrait—represents one of the dominant image forms of the online presentation of self (Schwartz). This is typically a photograph one takes of oneself holding the camera at arm's length. The Urban Dictionary, a user-driven website of Internet slang, characterizes the typical Facebook photo as

> An 'I look so good from this angle' pose that people pull when someone is taking a picture of them that is likely to appear on Facebook. Such pictures are usually taken at a concert/party/club and are posted for no reason other than to make people appear successful or popular and like they have a life. (Urban Dictionary)

Indeed, such photographs may likely be used mostly by younger users of the site, but there are

FIGURE 10.1 Self-portrait of author, plus 'Pop Art effect'

other forms of self-portraiture that are ubiquitous throughout the site. These include taking a picture of oneself in a mirror or some reflective surface, or using a webcam or built-in computer camera. The website AllFacebook, a leading blog about the site, claims, perhaps with tongue placed firmly in cheek, that there are up to 30 different Facebook photo types, ranging from those that include pets or children to those that articulate one's political position, and from those that use animation to those that are manipulated using various kinds of applications, such as a version of that shown in Figure 10.1 (AllFacebook).

In a recent article on the 'consuming self', Jefferson Pooley characterizes Facebook as 'a calculated authenticity machine', and part of a long tradition of the culture of personality which runs deep in the North American cultural imagination (Pooley 85). Here, Pooley notes that most users of the site are well aware of its limitations and act so as to present only a positive version of themselves to their friends and neighbours. My own social network, for example, consists of friends who are mostly academics with young families,

and who share my socio-economic status. My social network, then, is decidedly middle-class. Thus, the forms of self-presentation on the site—my own as well as others'—communicate value within that social network. These include professional developments (such as new publications and appearances at conferences), travel stories, new purchases of things like houses or phones, links to articles of shared interest, complaints about things like waiting in line and the cost of parking, cooking exploits, and, of course, photographs of these things and activities.

Such activities are part of the communication of one's *habitus*, to use Pierre Bourdieu's term, which, broadly speaking, details the forms, languages, and modes of taste that frame social behaviour in different social settings (Bourdieu). Thus, one is careful about what one communicates to others in the network, given the social and professional stakes of 'posting'. Given my cultural status, certain kinds of content which could appear on my Facebook page—such as a description of a fight with my spouse, an inappropriate thought, a disparaging word about a colleague, discussions of my personal finances, a story about a child's tantrum, expressions of laziness, or evidence of lavish expenditures on consumer products—are 'off limits'. What remains, then, is content that is either self-promotional or that serves as self-maintenance, keeping the apple cart in place rather than upsetting it. This use of a social networking site is not all that surprising; and yet, it stands in contrast to much of the discourse about the ability of new technologies to fashion new forms of identity and self-presentation. Given that the stakes involved in being a Facebook user have become more serious, play-acting, once the prominent tone on the site, has given way to a more serious posture, meaning that, at least for many adults, the online presentation of oneself is either 'played with' only in small and insignificant ways or is remarkably similar to the self that exists in the material world.

CONCLUSION: IMAGE MANAGEMENT IN THE INFORMATION AGE

At first glance, Facebook's popularity and the massive number of photos in its archive appear to be evidence of a culture of extreme openness, an international phenomenon in which people freely share information about themselves with others. Yet we appear to be living in a time of heightened concern about privacy. For every user that posts pictures on the site, there appear to be others who take information away, attempting to close their accounts, to tighten their privacy settings, and even to wean themselves off the site altogether. Countries such as Canada and Germany have pushed Facebook to change its privacy policies. Others have called for more aggressive measures to manage all of this information. Viktor Mayer Schönberger suggests that information available online, including photographs, should have expiry dates, to avoid what he considers the Internet's greatest deficiency—its capacity for eternal memory (Schönberger).

While such a proposal may appear to calm anxieties associated with the two themes discussed here—privacy and publicity—such suggestions also reveal their common characteristic

—a desire for control of images. The idea that one should have control over one's image appears in discussions around the cultural or creative industries, usually through the language of intellectual property or copyright, but gets lost in discussions over the uses of digital photography—uses that drive us toward discussion of privacy or of the extent to which, to use Christopher Lasch's famous phrase, we live in 'a culture of narcissism'. But what such discussions obscure, and what this essay hopefully makes clear, is a larger, broader social anxiety about living in an age of abundant information. This anxiety exists across the spectrum of digital culture, even though digital technology hardly stands as a 'new' medium. As Michael Newman notes, current fascination with the extent to which new media affect our 'attention span' is not new; it can be found at various stages throughout the history of media technologies. In addition, it serves less as an insight into cognitive processes and more as a means for coping with the unknown, a way of making sense of something which is both strange and new (Newman 593).

Similar tendencies are evident in the way we make sense of information in digital culture. Perhaps we are right to be concerned about the fact that we leave traces wherever we go online, and that this information can be used by others without our permission. Furthermore, we should be concerned about a society that rewards those who excel at self-promotion rather than those who are most worthy. Clearly, the anxiety about photographs on Facebook is not only over the strangeness of the technology, but over the varying levels of competence in its use. Many are rightly concerned that some people have a better understanding of how to use the site, and maximize their use of it, than others do. Seen this way, saying very little about one's personal life on Facebook or sticking to one's expected habitus may well reflect one's technological competence more than one's sense of prudence.

Competence is less about control than about literacy—a matter of teaching people how to 'read' images; how photographic processes work; how images can be edited, managed, and replaced; and how organizations that house or store images can use them. Such an approach may have several effects. Perhaps the most important effect is to educate us about the role of photographs as evidence of various forms of social behaviour and about the role—problematic as it may be—of visual imagery in making sense of the world around us. In addition, an attention to visual literacy—in short, understanding the power and limitations of the image, and understanding the technologies that produce, distribute, and display images—may well teach us what those who study other areas of the sensorium, such as sound, taste, touch, or smell have known for years: that while there is much to learn, there is also more to life than just what we see in a photograph.

NOTES

1. The number of Facebook photographs and the rate of addition comes from an article published by TechCrunch, a leading new technology blog, from 2009 (Schonfeld). The reporter of the piece attributes the figure to numbers provided by the company. In a book review published in *The New Republic* early in 2010, author Richard Posner claims the number is as high as 30 billion (Posner).

2. For an additional discussion about Facebook in Canada, see Wagman.

REFERENCES

AllFacebook. 'The 30 Standard Facebook Styles'. Available at: http://www.allfacebook.com/facebook-photo-styles-2009-03. Accessed 19 July 2010.

Bolter, Jay David, and Richard Grusin. 2000. *Remediation*. Cambridge: MIT Press.

Bourdieu, Pierre. 1984. *Distinction: A Social Critique of the Judgement of Taste*. Cambridge: Harvard University Press.

boyd, danah, and Nicole Ellison. 2007. 'Social Networking Sites: Definition, History and Scholarship'. *Journal of Computer Mediated Communication* 13 (1). Available at: http://jcmc.indiana.edu/vol13/issue1/boyd.ellison.html. Accessed 10 August 2010.

CBC News. 2009. 'Depressed Woman Loses Benefits over Facebook Photos'. CBCnews.ca, November 21. Available at: http://www.cbc.ca/canada/montreal/story/2009/11/19/quebec-facebook-sick-leave-benefits.html. Accessed 14 July 2010.

Cole, Simon. 2002. *Suspect Identities: A History of Fingerprinting and Criminal Identification*. Cambridge: Harvard University Press.

Ewen, Stewart. 1999. *All Consuming Images*. New York: Basic Books.

Gunning, Tom. 1995. 'Tracing the Individual Body: Photography, Detectives, and Early Cinema'. In Vanessa Schwartz and Leo Charney (eds), *Cinema and the Invention of Modern Life*. Berkeley: University of California Press: 15–45.

Kern, Stephen. 1983. *The Culture of Time and Space, 1880–1918*. Cambridge: Harvard University Press.

Lasch, Christopher. 1979. *The Culture of Narcissism: American Life in an Age of Diminishing Expectations*. New York: W.W. Norton.

McLuhan, Marshall. 1964. *Understanding Media*. New York: Signet.

Murray, Susan. 2008. 'Digital Images, Photo-Sharing, and Our Shifting Notions of Everyday Aesthetics'. *Journal of Visual Culture* 7 (2): 147–63.

Newman, Michael. 2010. 'New Media, Young Audiences, and Discourses of Attention: From *Sesame Street* to "Snack Culture"'. *Media, Culture, and Society* 32 (4): 581–96.

Pooley, Jefferson. 2010. 'The Consuming Self: From Flappers to Facebook'. In M. Aronczyk and D. Powers (eds), *Blowing Up the Brand: Critical Perspectives on Promotional Culture*, 73–91. New York: Peter Lang.

Posner, Richard. 2010. 'Just Friends'. *The New Republic*. July 21. Available at: http://www.tnr.com/article/books-and-arts/magazine/76433/facebook-privacy-mark-zuckerberg. Accessed 22 August 2010.

Schönberger, Viktor Mayer. 2009. *Delete: The Nature of Forgetting in the Digital Age*. Princeton: Princeton University Press.

Schonfeld, Erick. 2009. 'Who Has the Most Photos of Them All? Hint: It is Not Facebook'. *TechCrunch*. April 7. Available at: http://techcrunch.com/2009/04/07/who-has-the-most-photos-of-them-all-hint-it-is-not-facebook/. Accessed 30 June 2010.

Schwartz, Ori. 2009. 'Good Young Nostalgia: Camera Phones and Technologies of Self among Israeli Youths', *Journal of Consumer Culture* 9 (3): 348–76.

Sontag, Susan. 2001. *On Photography*. New York: Picador.

Tagg, John. 1993. *The Burden of Representation: Essays on Photographies and Histories.* Minneapolis: University of Minnesota Press.

Timmons, Heather. 2010. 'In India, Using Facebook to Catch Scofflaw Drivers'. *New York Times*, August 1. Available at: http://www.nytimes.com/2010/08/02/technology/02traffic.html?_r=1&ref=global-home. Accessed 10 August 2010.

Urban Dictionary. 'Facebook Pose'. Available at: http://www.urbandictionary.com/define.php?term=facebook%20pose. Accessed 1 June 2010.

Wagman, Ira. 2009. 'Log On, Goof Off and Look Up: Facebook and the Rhythms of Canadian Internet Use'. In B. Beaty, D. Briton, G, Filax, and R. Sullivan (eds), *How Canadians Communicate III: Contexts of Popular Culture*, 55–77. Athabasca: Athabasca University Press.

QUESTIONS FOR REFLECTION

1. As the title of his article implies, Goodwin addresses 'professional vision'. Could his model be used to analyze the construction of shared vision in non-professional practices such as your own participation on a sports team, or membership of a church, political party, or club? What could be gained from such an exercise?

2. Is it possible to be critical of claims to authority or expertise in highly specialized fields such as law without having specialized knowledge in that field? How could we be critical of such practices in a meaningful way, and what could we hope to achieve?

3. In what other public forums have you seen the power of images debated? Following the analysis of Vance, how were these debates framed? How were images discussed and used, and to what effect?

4. What guides your own participation in social networking sites? Are you aware of the potential ramifications associated with the images and material you make available? In what ways do you use images on Facebook and similar sites, and what is your level of literacy about such practices?

FURTHER READING

Daston, Lorraine, and Peter Galison. 'The Image of Objectivity'. *Representations* 40 (1992): 81–128.

Finn, Jonathan. *Capturing the Criminal Image: From Mug Shot to Surveillance Society*. Minneapolis: University of Minnesota, 2009.

Galison, Peter. 'Judgment Against Objectivity'. *Picturing Science Producing Art*. Eds. Caroline A. Jones and Peter Galison. London: Routledge, 1998. 327–59.

Goodwin, Charles. 'Action and Embodiment Within Situated Human Interaction'. *Journal of Pragmatics* 32 (2000): 1489–522.

Iles, Chrissie and Russell Roberts, Eds. *In Visible Light: Photography and Classification in Art, Science, and The Everyday*. Oxford: Museum of Modern Art, 1997.

Lynch, Michael. 'The Externalized Retina: Selection and Mathematization in the Visual Documentation of Objects in the Life Sciences'. *Representation in Scientific Practice*, Eds. Michael Lynch and Steve Woolgar. Cambridge: mit Press, 1988. 85–121.

Mitchell, William J. *The Reconfigured Eye: Visual Truth in the Post-Photographic Era*. Cambridge: mit Press, 1992.

Mnookin, Jennifer. 'The Image of Truth: Photographic Evidence and the Power of Analogy'. *Yale Journal of Law and the Humanities* 10.1 (1998): 1–74.

Phillips, Sandra S., Mark Haworth-Booth, and Carol Squiers, Eds. *Police Pictures: The Photograph as Evidence*. San Francisco: Chronicle, 1997.

Tagg, John. *The Burden of Representation: Essays on Photographies and Histories*. London: Macmillan, 1988.

MAPS, CHARTS, AND DIAGRAMS

How information is communicated has a significant impact on the message being communicated. This is the basis of the famous maxim, 'the medium is the message', by Canadian communication studies scholar Marshall McLuhan. In areas such as advertising or the fine arts, this statement is obvious to the most casual observer. An advertiser's choices of models, props, lighting, and angle in a photograph, or a painter's choice of medium, subject matter, colour, line, and composition all contribute to the meaning of the finished work. However, in modes of communication that are less clearly subjective, the impact of such choices on message content is often unacknowledged. The essays in Part Four address visual communication in such practices and show how communication in the form of maps, charts, and diagrams is susceptible to subjective, cultural influence and can have distinct, even fatal, consequences on the cultures within which they are deployed.

The opening reading in this part, 'Deconstructing the Map', is from the highly influential geographer J.B. Harley, who was a leading figure in bringing critical, theoretical analysis to the field of cartography. In this essay, he argues that maps are not objective representations of the world, but subjective statements about it. For

Harley, maps are the products of complex relationships between patrons and cartographers, their individual and disciplinary histories, and the social networks within which they interact. Writing within the context of the 'literary turn' as outlined in the Introduction to this book, Harley positions the map as a 'text' to be deconstructed—a cultural product that employs devices such as metaphor and rhetoric to persuade its readers. This leads Harley to his central argument: Maps are power. Maps function as power for cartographers by reinforcing the legitimacy of their discipline in a process similar to developing professional vision described by Goodwin in Part Three. Maps also function as power in a more abstract, social way. Just as Cregan and Cartwright in Part Two argue that anatomical illustrations can reinforce existing social codes and power structures, so too does Harley stress that maps participate in the regulation and control of populations. In this latter sense, maps function in the disciplining and normalizing of society.

Importantly, Harley's essay is not simply about the process of mapmaking; another dominant concern of his paper is the way in which maps shape our understanding of the world. In a manner reminiscent of Ivins's argument in Part One, Harley notes that maps assist in 'shaping mental structures, and in imparting a sense of the places of the world'. In other words, much of our knowledge of the world comes through our exposure to its representation in the form of maps. And, as Harley so effectively shows, such maps are not mirrors of the world but are arguments about it.

The map's function in 'shaping mental structures, and in imparting a sense of the places of the world' is the basis of the second essay of this part, 'Mind the Gap', by Janet Vertesi. While Harley argues the need to understand maps as cultural products, Vertesi is interested in the map's role in shaping its users' knowledge and experience of the locale that is represented. She analyzes the London Underground Map not for its accuracy in relation to the physical city, but as a technology that mediates users' lived experience in that space.

Vertesi rightly notes that the London Underground Map is a modern icon, one which represents more than a transit system—it represents the city itself. One of the most interesting aspects of the essay is the author's ethnographic research, specifically, her inclusion of Londoners' own representations of their city. Vertesi asked selected Londoners to draw their city and found that almost all instinctively based their drawings on the London Underground Map. The point is not just that Londoners treat the map as synonymous with the city itself, but also that the map participates in the development of knowledge, experience, and social life. The map is thus not a supplement to its user's lived experience—it does not simply direct the user from point A to point B; rather, it is an active site in the construction of its user's lived experience. Further, and parallel to Harley's discussion of maps, Vertesi shows that one's location on or off the map carries distinct ties to power and social status. Vertesi's analysis of the London Underground Map raises numerous important questions about the role of maps in our own lives and in our experiences of the places we live, work, and play.

The final essay in this part, 'Powell's Point: "Denial and Deception" at the UN' is an examination of the use of visual representation in Colin Powell's infamous 2003 presentation to the United Nations Security Council. Drawing from Charles Goodwin's theory of professional vision, Jonathan Finn argues that Powell was unable to convince Security Council members to see what he claimed to see in his visual evidence. Finn performs a close visual and textual analysis of the presentation to argue that the central problem of the presentation was the conflation of different forms of visual representation. Maps, file photographs, and computer-generated images were presented as synonymous forms of visual evidence; for Finn, this presentation raises numerous questions about the meaning of the images.

A primary argument of the essay is that different modes of visual representation—illustrations, computer-generated images, photographs, and so on—have different communicative capabilities. In order to communicate effectively, one must be aware of such differences and choose methods of representation accordingly. In this way, Finn shares the concern of Sherwin about the uniqueness of visual representation. However, where

Sherwin stressed the uniqueness of images as compared to text, Finn argues that each medium of visual representation is unique and that the idiosyncratic features of maps, drawings, photographs, and other forms of representation play fundamental roles in the process of communication. The essay concludes with an important reminder of the power of images. As Finn notes, although Powell's presentation was ultimately unsuccessful, his visual evidence was intended to garner United Nations support for a war that has taken tens of thousands of lives.

The essays in this part emphasize the varied powers of images: they direct us, they influence us, they create a sense of place and space, and they are used in the control of populations. As forms of visual representation, maps, charts, and diagrams are subject to the same cultural influence as other, more overtly subjective forms of visual communication. By extension, these forms of representation should be subject to the same critical attention given to the usual subjects of visual communication and visual culture scholars: television, film, advertising, and art. As Harley rightly points out, the seemingly mundane map is actually a complex, culturally informed argument about the areas, people, and objects it represents.

11

DECONSTRUCTING THE MAP

J.B. HARLEY

> A map says to you, 'Read me carefully, follow me closely, doubt me not.' It says, 'I am the earth in the palm of your hand. Without me, you are alone and lost.'
>
> And indeed you are. Were all the maps in this world destroyed and vanished under the direction of some malevolent hand, each man would be blind again, each city be made a stranger to the next, each landmark become a meaningless signpost pointing to nothing.
>
> Yet, looking at it, feeling it, running a finger along its lines, it is a cold thing, a map, humourless and dull, born of calipers and a draughtsman's board. That coastline there, that ragged scrawl of scarlet ink, shows neither sand nor sea nor rock; it speaks of no mariner, blundering full sail in wakeless seas, to bequeath, on sheepskin or a slab of wood, a priceless scribble to posterity. This brown blot that marks a mountain has, for the casual eye, no other significance, though twenty men, or ten, or only one, may have squandered life to climb it. Here is a valley, there a swamp, and there a desert; and here is a river that some curious and courageous soul, like a pencil in the hand of God, first traced with bleeding feet.
>
> Beryl Markham, 1983[1]

The pace of conceptual exploration in the history of cartography—searching for alternative ways of understanding maps—is slow. Some would say that its achievements are largely cosmetic. Applying conceptions of literary history to the history of cartography, it would appear that we are still working largely in either a 'premodern' or a 'modern' rather than in a 'postmodern' climate of thought.[2] A list of individual explorations would, it is true, contain some that sound impressive. Our students can now be directed to writings that draw on the ideas of information theory, linguistics, semiotics, structuralism, phenomenology, developmental theory, hermeneutics, iconology, marxism, and ideology. We can point to the names in our footnotes of (among others) Cassirer, Gombrich, Piaget, Panofsky, Kuhn, Barthes, and Eco. Yet despite these symptoms of change, we are still, willingly or unwillingly, the prisoners of our own past.

My basic argument in this essay is that we should encourage an epistemological shift in the way we interpret the nature of cartography. For historians of cartography, I believe a major roadblock to understanding is that we still accept uncritically the broad consensus, with relatively few dissenting voices, of what *cartographers* tell us maps are supposed to be. In particular, we often tend to work from the premise that mappers engage in an unquestionably 'scientific' or 'objective' form of knowledge creation. Of course, cartographers believe they have to say this to remain credible but historians do not have that obligation. It is better for us to begin from the premise that cartography is seldom what cartographers say it is.

As they embrace computer-assisted methods and Geographical Information Systems, the scientistic rhetoric of mapmakers is becoming more strident. The 'culture of technics' is everywhere rampant. We are told that the journal now named *The American Cartographer* will become *Cartography and Geographical Information Systems*. Or, in a strangely ambivalent gesture toward the nature of maps, the British Cartographic Society proposes that there should be two definitions of cartography, 'one for professional cartographers and the other for the public at large.' A definition 'for use in communication with the general public' would be 'Cartography is the art, science and technology of making maps'; that for 'practising cartographers' would be 'Cartography is the science and technology of analyzing and interpreting geographic relationships, and communicating the results by means of maps.'[3] Many may find it surprising that 'art' no longer exists in 'professional' cartography. In the present context, however, these signs of ontological schizophrenia can also be read as reflecting an urgent need to rethink the nature of maps from different perspectives. The question arises as to whether the notion of a progressive science is a myth partly created by cartographers in the course of their own professional development. I suggest that it has been accepted too uncritically by a wider public and by other scholars who work with maps.[4] For those concerned with the history of maps it is especially timely that we challenge

the cartographer's assumptions. Indeed, if the history of cartography is to grow as an interdisciplinary subject among the humanities and social sciences, new ideas are essential.

The question becomes how do we as historians of cartography escape from the normative models of cartography? How do we allow new ideas to come in? How do we begin to write a cartographic history as genuinely revisionist as Louis Marin's 'The King and his Geometer' (in the context of a seventeenth-century map of Paris) or William Boelhower's 'The Culture of the Map' (in the context of sixteenth-century world maps showing America for the first time)?[5] These are two studies informed by postmodernism. In this essay I also adopt a strategy aimed at the deconstruction of the map.

The notion of deconstruction[6] is also a password for the postmodern enterprise. Deconstructionist strategies can now be found not only in philosophy but also in localized disciplines, especially in literature, and in other subjects such as architecture, planning and, more recently, geography.[7] I shall specifically use a deconstructionist tactic to break the assumed link between reality and representation which has dominated cartographic thinking, has led it in the pathway of 'normal science' since the Enlightenment, and has also provided a ready-made and 'taken for granted' epistemology for the history of cartography. The objective is to suggest that an alternative epistemology, rooted in social theory rather than in scientific positivism, is more appropriate to the history of cartography. It will be shown that even 'scientific' maps are a product not only of 'the rules of the order of geometry and reason' but also of the 'norms and values of the order of social . . . tradition'.[8] Our task is to search for the social forces that have structured cartography and to locate the presence of power—and its effects—in all map knowledge.

The ideas in this particular essay owe most to writings by Foucault and Derrida. My approach is deliberately eclectic because in some respects the theoretical positions of these two authors are incompatible. Foucault anchors texts in socio-political realities and constructs systems for organizing knowledge of the kind that Derrida loves to dismantle.[9] But even so, by combining different ideas on a new terrain, it may be possible to devise a scheme of social theory with which we can begin to interrogate the hidden agendas of cartography. Such a scheme offers no 'solution' to a historical interpretation of the cartographic record, nor a precise method or set of techniques, but as a broad strategy it may help to locate some of the fundamental forces that have driven mapmaking in both European and non-European societies. From Foucault's writings, the key revelation has been the omnipresence of power in all knowledge, even though that power is invisible or implied, including the particular knowledge encoded in maps and atlases. Derrida's notion of the rhetoricity of all texts has been no less a challenge.[10] It demands a search for metaphor and rhetoric in maps where previously scholars had found only measurement and topography. Its central question is reminiscent of Korzybski's much older dictum 'The map is not the territory'[11] but deconstruction goes further to bring the issue of how the map represents place into much sharper focus.

Deconstruction urges us to read between the lines of the map—'in the margins of the text'—and through its tropes to discover the silences and contradictions that challenge the apparent honesty of the image. We begin to learn that cartographic facts are only facts within a specific cultural perspective. We start to understand how maps, like art, far from being 'a transparent opening to the world', are but 'a particular human way . . . of looking at the world'.[12]

In pursuing this strategy I shall develop three threads of argument. First, I shall examine the discourse of cartography in the light of some of Foucault's ideas about the play of rules within discursive formations. Second, drawing on one of Derrida's central positions I will examine the textuality of maps and, in particular, their rhetorical dimension. Third, returning to Foucault, I will consider how maps work in society as a form of power-knowledge.

THE RULES OF CARTOGRAPHY

One of Foucault's primary units of analysis is the discourse. A discourse has been defined as 'a system of possibility for knowledge'.[13] Foucault's method was to ask, it has been said,

> what rules permit certain statements to be made; what rules order these statements; what rules permit us to identify some statements as true and others as false; what rules allow the construction of a map, model or classificatory system . . . what rules are revealed when an object of discourse is modified or transformed. . . . Whenever sets of rules of these kinds can be identified, we are dealing with a discursive formation or discourse.[14]

The key question for us then becomes, 'What type of rules have governed the development of cartography?' Cartography I define as a body of theoretical and practical knowledge that mapmakers employ to construct maps as a distinct mode of visual representation. The question is, of course, historically specific: The rules of cartography vary in different societies. Here I refer particularly to two distinctive sets of rules that underlie and dominate the history of Western cartography since the seventeenth century.[15] One set may be defined as governing the technical production of maps and are made explicit in the cartographic treatises and writings of the period.[16] The other set relates to the cultural production of maps. These must be understood in a broader historical context than either scientific procedure or technique. They are, moreover, rules that are usually ignored by cartographers so that they form a hidden aspect of their discourse.

The first set of cartographic rules can thus be defined in terms of a scientific epistemology. From at least the seventeenth century onward, European mapmakers and map users have increasingly promoted a standard scientific model of knowledge and cognition. The object of mapping is to produce a 'correct' relational model of the terrain. Its assumptions are that the objects in the world to be mapped are real and objective, and that they enjoy an existence independent of the cartographer; that their reality can be expressed in mathematical terms; that systematic observation and measurement offer the only route to cartographic truth; and that this truth can be independently verified.[17] The procedures of both surveying and map construction came to share strategies similar to those in science in general: cartography also documents a history of more precise instrumentation and measurement; increasingly complex classifications of its knowledge and a proliferation of signs for its representation; and, especially from the nineteenth century onward, the growth of institutions and a 'professional' literature designed to monitor the application and propagation of the rules.[18] Moreover, although cartographers have continued to pay lip service to the 'art and science' of mapmaking,[19] art, as we have seen, is being edged off the map, It has often been accorded a cosmetic rather than a central role in cartographic communication.[20] Even philosophers of visual communication—such as Arnheim, Eco, Gombrich, and Goodman[21]—have tended to categorize maps as a type of congruent diagram—as analogs, models, or 'equivalents' creating a similitude of reality—and, in essence, different from art or painting. A 'scientific' cartography (so it was believed) would be untainted by social factors. Even today many cartographers are puzzled by the suggestion that political and sociological theory could throw light on their practices. They will probably shudder at the mention of deconstruction.

The acceptance of the map as 'a mirror of nature' (to employ Richard Rorty's phrase[22]) also results in a number of other characteristics of cartographic discourse even where these are not made explicit. Most striking is the belief in progress: that, by the application of science ever more precise representations of reality can be produced. The methods of cartography have delivered a 'true, probable, progressive, or highly confirmed knowledge'.[23] This mimetic bondage has led to a tendency not only to look down on the maps of the past (with a dismissive scientific chauvinism) but also to regard the maps of other non-Western or early cultures (where the rules of mapmaking were different) as inferior to European maps.[24] Similarly, the primary effect of the scientific rules was to create a 'standard'—a successful version of 'normal science'[25]—that enabled cartographers to build a wall around their citadel of the 'true' map. Its central bastions

were measurement and standardization and beyond there was a 'not cartography' land where lurked an army of inaccurate, heretical, subjective, valuative, and ideologically distorted images. Cartographers developed a 'sense of the other' in relation to nonconforming maps. Even maps such as those produced by journalists, where different rules and modes of expressiveness might be appropriate, are evaluated by many cartographers according to standards of 'objectivity', 'accuracy', and 'truthfulness'. In this respect, the underlying attitude of many cartographers is revealed in a recent book of essays on *Cartographie dans les medias*.[26] One of its reviewers has noted how many authors attempt to exorcise from

> the realm of cartography any graphic representation that is not a simple planimetric image, and to then classify all other maps as 'decorative graphics masquerading as maps' where the 'bending of cartographic rules' has taken place . . . most journalistic maps are flawed because they are inaccurate, misleading or biased. [27]

Or in Britain, we are told, there was set up a 'Media Map Watch' in 1984. 'Several hundred interested members [of cartographic and geographic societies] submitted several thousand maps and diagrams for analysis that revealed [according to the rules] numerous common deficiencies, errors, and inaccuracies along with misleading standards.'[28] In this example of cartographic vigilantism the 'ethic of accuracy' is being defended with some ideological fervour. The language of exclusion is that of a string of 'natural' opposites: 'true and false'; 'objective and subjective'; 'literal and symbolic'; and so on. The best maps are those with an 'authoritative image of self-evident factuality'.[29]

In cases where the scientific rules are invisible in the map we can still trace their play in attempting to normalize the discourse. The cartographer's 'black box' has to be defended and its social origins suppressed. The hysteria among leading cartographers at the popularity of the Peters' projection,[30] or the recent expressions of piety among Western European and North American mapmakers following the Russian admission that they had falsified their topographic maps to confuse the enemy give us a glimpse of how the game is played according to these rules. What are we to make of the 1988 newspaper headlines such as 'Russians Caught Mapping' (*Ottawa Citizen*), 'Soviets Admit Map Paranoia' (*Wisconsin Journal*), or (in the *New York Times*) 'In West, Map Makers Hail "Truth"' and 'The rascals finally realized the truth and were able to tell it, a geographer at the Defense Department said'?[31] The implication is that Western maps are value free. According to the spokesman, our maps are not ideological documents, and the condemnation of Russian falsification is as much an echo of Cold War rhetoric as it is a credible cartographic criticism.

This timely example also serves to introduce my second contention that the scientific rules of mapping are, in any case, influenced by a quite different set of rules, those governing the cultural production of the map. To discover these rules, we have to read between the lines of technical procedures or of the map's topographic content. They are related to values, such as those of ethnicity, politics, religion, or social class, and they are also embedded in the map-producing society at large. Cartographic discourse operates a double silence toward this aspect of the possibilities for map knowledge. In the map itself, social structures are often disguised beneath an abstract, instrumental space, or incarcerated in the coordinates of computer mapping. And in the technical literature of cartography they are also ignored, notwithstanding the fact that they may be as important as surveying, compilation, or design in producing the statements that cartography makes about the world and its landscapes. Such an interplay of social and technical rules is a universal feature of cartographic knowledge. In maps it produces the 'order' of its features and the 'hierarchies of its practices'.[32] In Foucault's sense the rules may enable us to define an *episteme* and to trace an archaeology of that knowledge through time.[33]

Two examples of how such rules are manifest in maps will be given to illustrate their force in structuring cartographic representation. The first is the well-known adherence to the 'rule of ethnocentricity' in the construction of world maps. This has led many historical societies to place their own territories at the centre of their cosmographies or world maps. While it may be dangerous to assume universality, and there are exceptions, such a rule is as evident in cosmic diagrams of pre-Columbian North American Indians as it is in the maps of ancient Babylonia, Greece, or China, or in the medieval maps of the Islamic world or Christian Europe.[34] Yet what is also significant in applying Foucault's critique of knowledge to cartography is that the history of the ethnocentric rule does not march in step with the 'scientific' history of mapmaking. Thus, the scientific Renaissance in Europe gave modern cartography coordinate systems, Euclid, scale maps, and accurate measurement, but it also helped to confirm a new myth of Europe's ideological centrality through projections such as those of Mercator.[35] Or again, in our own century, a tradition of the exclusivity of America was enhanced before World War II by placing it in its own hemisphere ('our hemisphere') on the world map.[36] Throughout the history of cartography ideological 'Holy Lands' are frequently centred on maps. Such centricity, a kind of 'subliminal geometry',[37] adds geopolitical force and meaning to representation. It is also arguable that such world maps have in turn helped to codify, to legitimate, and to promote the world views which are prevalent in different periods and places.[38]

A second example is how the 'rules of the social order' appear to insert themselves into the smaller codes and spaces of cartographic transcription. The history of European cartography since the seventeenth century provides many examples of this tendency. Pick a printed or manuscript map from the drawer almost at random and what stands out is the unfailing way its text is as much a commentary on the social structure of a particular nation or place as it is on its topography. The mapmaker is often as busy recording the contours of feudalism, the shape of a religious hierarchy, or the steps in the tiers of social class,[39] as the topography of the physical and human landscape.

Why maps can be so convincing in this respect is that the rules of society and the rules of measurement are mutually reinforcing in the same image. Writing of the map of Paris, surveyed in

1602 by Jacques Gomboust, the King's engineer, Louis Marin points to 'this sly strategy of simulation-dissimulation':

> The knowledge and science of representation, to demonstrate the truth that its subject declares plainly, flow nonetheless in a social and political hierarchy. The proofs of its 'theoretical' truth had to be given, they are the recognisable signs; but the economy of these signs in their disposition on the cartographic plane no longer obeys the rules of the order of geometry and reason but, rather, the norms and values of the order of social and religious tradition. Only the churches and important mansions benefit from natural signs and from the visible rapport they maintain with what they represent. Townhouses and private homes, precisely because they are private and not public, will have the right only to the general and common representation of an arbitrary and institutional sign, the poorest, the most elementary (but maybe, by virtue of this, principal) of geometric elements; the point identically reproduced in bulk.[40]

Once again, much like 'the rule of ethnocentrism', this hierarchicalization of space is not a conscious act of cartographic representation. Rather it is taken for granted in a society that the place of the king is more important than the place of a lesser baron, that a castle is more important than a peasant's house, that the town of an archbishop is more important than that of a minor prelate, or that the estate of a landed gentleman is more worthy of emphasis than that of a plain farmer. Cartography deploys its vocabulary accordingly so that it embodies a systematic social inequality. The distinctions of class and power are engineered, reified, and legitimated in the map by means of cartographic signs. The rule seems to be 'the more powerful, the more prominent'. To those who have strength in the world shall be added strength in the map. Using all the tricks of the cartographic trade—size of symbol, thickness of line, height of lettering, hatching and shading, the addition of colour—we can trace this reinforcing tendency in innumerable European maps. We can begin to see how maps, like art, become

a mechanism 'for defining social relationships, sustaining social rules, and strengthening social values'.[41]

In the case of both these examples of rules, the point I am making is that the rules operate both within and beyond the orderly structures of classification and measurement. They go beyond the stated purposes of cartography. Much of the power of the map, as a representation of social geography, is that it operates behind a mask of a seemingly neutral science. It hides and denies its social dimensions at the same time as it legitimates. Yet whichever way we look at it the rules of society will surface. They have ensured that maps are at least as much an image of the social order as they are a measurement of the phenomenal world of objects.

DECONSTRUCTION AND THE CARTOGRAPHIC TEXT

To move inward from the question of cartographic rules—the social context within which map knowledge is fashioned—we have to turn to the cartographic text itself. The word 'text' is deliberately chosen. It is now generally accepted that the model of text can have a much wider application than to literary texts alone. To non-book texts such as musical compositions and architectural structures we can confidently add the graphic texts we call maps.[42] It has been said that 'what constitutes a text is not the presence of linguistic elements but the act of construction' so that maps, as 'constructions employing a conventional sign system',[43] become texts. With Barthes we could say they 'presuppose a signifying consciousness' that it is our business to uncover.[44] 'Text' is certainly a better metaphor for maps than the mirror of nature. Maps are a cultural text. By accepting their textuality we are able to embrace a number of different interpretive possibilities. Instead of just the transparency of clarity we can discover the pregnancy of the opaque. To fact we can add myth, and instead of innocence we may expect duplicity. Rather than working with a formal science of communication, or even a sequence of loosely related technical processes, our concern is redirected to a history and anthropology of the image, and we learn to recognize the narrative qualities of cartographic representation[45] as well as its claim to provide a synchronous picture of the world. All this, moreover, is likely to lead to a rejection of the neutrality of maps, as we come to define their intentions rather than the literal face of representation, and as we begin to accept the social consequences of cartographic practices. I am not suggesting that the direction of textual enquiry offers a simple set of techniques for reading either contemporary or historical maps. In some cases we will have to conclude that there are many aspects of their meaning that are undecidable.[46]

Deconstruction, as discourse analysis in general, demands a closer and deeper reading of the cartographic text than has been the general practice in either cartography or the history of cartography. It may be regarded as a search for alternative meanings. 'To deconstruct', it is argued,

is to reinscribe and resituate meanings, events and objects within broader movements and structures; it is, so to speak, to reverse the imposing tapestry in order to expose in all its unglamorously dishevelled tangle the threads constituting the well-heeled image it presents to the world.[47]

The published map also has a 'well-heeled image' and our reading has to go beyond the assessment of geometric accuracy, beyond the fixing of location, and beyond the recognition of topographical patterns and geographies. Such interpretation begins from the premise that the map text may contain 'unperceived contradictions or duplicitous tensions'[48] that undermine the surface layer of standard objectivity. Maps are slippery customers. In the words of W.J.T. Mitchell, writing of languages and images in general, we may need to regard them more as 'enigmas, problems to be explained, prison-houses which lock the understanding away from the world'. We should regard them 'as the sort of sign that presents a deceptive appearance of naturalness and transparence concealing an opaque, distorting, arbitrary mechanism of representation'.[49] Throughout the history of modern cartography in the West, for

example, there have been numerous instances of where maps have been falsified, of where they have been censored or kept secret, or of where they have surreptitiously contradicted the rules of their proclaimed scientific status.[50]

As in the case of these practices, map deconstruction would focus on aspects of maps that many interpreters have glossed over. Writing of 'Derrida's most typical deconstructive moves', Christopher Norris notes that

deconstruction is the vigilant seeking-out of those 'aporias', blindspots or moments of self-contradiction where a text involuntarily betrays the tension between rhetoric and logic, between what it manifestly *means to say* and what it is nonetheless *constrained to mean*. To 'deconstruct' a piece of writing is therefore to operate a kind of strategic reversal, seizing on precisely those unregarded details (casual metaphors, footnotes, incidental turns of argument) which are always, and necessarily, passed over by interpreters of a more orthodox persuasion. For it is here, in the margins of the text the 'margins', that is, as defined by a powerful normative consensus—that deconstruction discovers those same unsettling forces at work.[51]

A good example of how we could deconstruct an early map—by beginning with what have hitherto been regarded as its 'casual metaphors' and 'footnotes' is provided by recent studies reinterpreting the status of decorative art on the European maps of the seventeenth and eighteenth centuries. Rather than being inconsequential marginalia, the emblems in cartouches and decorative title pages can be regarded as *basic* to the way they convey their cultural meaning,[52] and they help to demolish the claim of cartography to produce an impartial graphic science. But the possibility of such a revision is not limited to historic 'decorative' maps. A recent essay by Wood and Fels on the Official State Highway Map of North Carolina[53] indicates a much wider applicability for a deconstructive strategy by beginning in the 'margins' of the contemporary map. They also treat the map as a text and, drawing on the ideas of Roland Barthes of myth as a semiological system,[54] develop a forceful social critique of cartography which though structuralist in its approach is deconstructionist in its outcome. They begin, deliberately, with the margins of the map, or rather with the subject matter that is printed on its verso:

> One side is taken up by an inventory of North Carolina points of interest—illustrated with photos of, among other things, a scimitar horned oryx (resident in the state zoo), a Cherokee woman making beaded jewelry, a ski lift, a sand dune (but no cities)—a ferry schedule, a message of welcome from the then governor, and a motorist's prayer ('Our heavenly Father, we ask this day a particular blessing as we take the wheel of our car . . .'). On the other side, North Carolina, hemmed in by the margins of pale yellow South Carolinas and Virginias, Georgias and Tennessees, and washed by a pale blue Atlantic, is represented as a meshwork of red, black, blue, green and yellow lines on a white background, thickened at the intersections by roundels of black or blotches of pink. . . . To the left of . . . [the] title is a sketch of the fluttering state flag. To the right is a sketch of a cardinal (state bird) on a branch of flowering dogwood (state flower) surmounting a buzzing honey bee arrested in midflight (state insect).[55]

What is the meaning of these emblems? Are they merely a pleasant ornament for the traveller or can they inform us about the social production of such state highway maps? A deconstructionist might claim that such meanings are undecidable, but it is also clear that the State Highway Map of North Carolina is making other dialogical assertions behind its mask of innocence and transparence. I am not suggesting that these elements hinder the traveller getting from point A to B, but that there is a second text within the map. No map is devoid of an intertextual dimension and, in this case too, the discovery of intertextuality enables us to scan the image as more than a neutral picture of a road network.[56] Its 'users' are not only the ordinary motorists but also the State of North Carolina that has appropriated its publication (distributed in millions of copies) as

a promotional device. The map has become an instrument of State policy and an instrument of sovereignty.[57] At the same time, it is more than an affirmation of North Carolina's dominion over its territory. It also constructs a mythic geography, a landscape full of 'points of interest', with incantations of loyalty to state emblems and to the values of a Christian piety. The hierarchy of towns and the visually dominating highways that connect them have become the legitimate natural order of the world. The map finally insists 'that roads really *are* what North Carolina's all about'.[58] The map idolizes our love affair with the automobile. The myth is believable.

A cartographer's stock response to this deconstructionist argument might well be to cry 'foul'. The argument would run like this: 'Well after all it's a state highway map. It's designed to be at once popular and useful. We expect it to exaggerate the road network and to show points of interest to motorists. It is a derived rather than a basic map.'[59] It is not a scientific map. The appeal to the ultimate scientific map is always the cartographers' last line of defence when seeking to deny the social relations that permeate their technology.

It is at this point that Derrida's strategy can help us to extend such an interpretation to all maps, scientific or non-scientific, basic or derived. Just as in the deconstruction of philosophy Derrida was able to show 'how the supposedly literal level is intensively metaphorical'[60] so too we can show how cartographic 'fact' is also symbol. In 'plain' scientific maps, science itself becomes the metaphor. Such maps contain a dimension of 'symbolic realism' which is no less a statement of political authority and control than a coat-of-arms or a portrait of a queen placed at the head of an earlier decorative map. The metaphor has changed. The map has attempted to purge itself of ambiguity and alternative possibility.[61] Accuracy and austerity of design are now the new talismans of authority culminating in our own age with computer mapping. We can trace this process very clearly in the history of Enlightenment mapping in Europe. The topography as shown in maps, increasingly detailed and planimetrically accurate, has become a metaphor for a utilitarian philosophy and its will to power. Cartography inscribes this cultural model upon the paper and we can examine it in many scales and types of maps. Precision of instrument and technique merely serves to reinforce the image, with its encrustation of myth, as a selective perspective on the world. Thus maps of local estates in the European *ancien regime*, though derived from instrumental survey, were a metaphor for a social structure based on landed property. County and regional maps, though founded on scientific triangulation, were an articulation of local values and rights. Maps of the European states, though constructed along arcs of the meridian, served still as a symbolic shorthand for a complex of nationalist ideas. And world maps, though increasingly drawn on mathematically defined projections, nevertheless gave a spiralling twist to the manifest destiny of European overseas conquest and colonization.[62] In each of these examples we can trace the contours of metaphor in a scientific map. This in turn enhances our understanding of how the text works as an instrument operating on social reality.

In deconstructionist theory the play of rhetoric is closely linked to that of metaphor. In concluding this section of the essay I will argue that notwithstanding 'scientific' cartography's efforts to convert culture into nature, and to 'naturalize' social reality,[63] it has remained an inherently rhetorical discourse. Another of the lessons of Derrida's criticism of philosophy is 'that modes of rhetorical analysis, hitherto applied mainly to literary texts, are in fact indispensable for reading *any* kind of discourse'.[64] There is nothing revolutionary in the idea that cartography is an art of persuasive communication. It is now commonplace to write about the rhetoric of the human sciences in the classical sense of the word *rhetoric*.[65] Even cartographers—as well as their critics—are beginning to allude to the notion of a rhetorical cartography but what is still lacking is a rhetorical close-reading of maps.[66]

The issue in contention is not whether some maps are rhetorical, or whether other maps are partly rhetorical, but the extent to which rhetoric is a universal aspect of all cartographic texts. Thus for some cartographers the notion of 'rhetoric' would remain a pejorative term. It would be an 'empty rhetoric' which was unsubstantiated in the scientific content of a map. 'Rhetoric' would be used to refer to the 'excesses' of propaganda mapping or advertising cartography or an attempt would be made to confine it to an 'artistic' or aesthetic element in maps as opposed to their scientific core. My position is to accept that rhetoric is part of the way all texts work and that all maps are rhetorical texts. Again we ought to dismantle the arbitrary dualism between 'propaganda' and 'true', and between modes of 'artistic' and 'scientific' representation as they are found in maps. All maps strive to frame their message in the context of an audience. All maps state an argument about the world and they are propositional in nature. All maps employ the common devices of rhetoric such as invocations of authority (*especially* in 'scientific' maps[67]) and appeals to a potential readership through the use of colours, decoration, typography, dedications, or written justifications of their method.[68] Rhetoric may be concealed but it is always present, for there is no description without performance.

The steps in making a map—selection, omission, simplification, classification, the creation of hierarchies, and 'symbolization'—are all inherently rhetorical. In their intentions as much as in their applications they signify subjective human purposes rather than reciprocating the workings of some 'fundamental law of cartographic generalisation'.[69] Indeed, the freedom of rhetorical manoeuvre in cartography is considerable: The mapmaker merely omits those features of the world that lie outside the purpose of the immediate discourse. There have been no limits to the varieties of maps that have been developed historically in response to different purposes of argument, aiming at different rhetorical goals, and embodying different assumptions about what is sound cartographic practice. The style of maps is neither fixed in the past nor is it today. It has been said that 'The rhetorical code appropriates to its map the style most advantageous to the myth it intends to propagate.'[70] Instead of thinking in terms of rhetorical versus non-rhetorical maps it may be more helpful to think in terms of a theory of cartographic rhetoric which accommodated this fundamental aspect of representation in all types of cartographic text. Thus, I am not concerned to privilege rhetoric over science, but to dissolve the illusory distinction between the two in reading the social purposes as well as the content of maps.

MAPS AND THE EXERCISE OF POWER

For the final stage in the argument I return to Foucault. In doing so I am mindful of Foucault's criticism of Derrida that he attempted 'to restrict interpretation to a purely syntactic and textual level',[71] a world where political realities no longer exist. Foucault, on the other hand, sought to uncover 'the social practices that the text itself both reflects and employs' and to 'reconstruct the technical and material framework in which it arose'.[72] Though deconstruction is useful in helping to change the epistemological climate, and in encouraging a rhetorical reading of cartography, my final concern is with its social and political dimensions, and with understanding how the map works in society as a form of power-knowledge. This closes the circle to a context-dependent form of cartographic history.

We have already seen how it is possible to view cartography as a discourse—a system which provides a set of rules for the representation of knowledge embodied in the images we define as maps and atlases. It is not difficult to find for maps—especially those produced and manipulated by the state—a niche in the 'power/knowledge matrix of the modern order'.[73] Especially where maps are ordered by government (or are derived from such maps) it can be seen how they extend and reinforce the legal statutes, territorial imperatives, and values stemming from the exercise of political power. Yet to understand how power works through cartographic discourse and the effects of that power in society further dissection is needed. A simple model of domination and subversion is inadequate and I propose to draw a distinction between *external* and *internal* power in cartography. This ultimately derives from Foucault's ideas about power-knowledge, but this particular formulation is owed to Joseph Rouse's recent book on *Knowledge and Power*,[74] where a theory of the internal power of science is in turn based on his reading of Foucault.

The most familiar sense of power in cartography is that of power *external* to maps and mapping. This serves to link maps to the centres of political power. Power is exerted *on* cartography. Behind most cartographers there is a patron; in innumerable instances the makers of cartographic texts were responding to external needs. Power is also exercised *with* cartography. Monarchs, ministers, state institutions, the Church, have all initiated programs of mapping for their own ends. In modern Western society maps quickly became crucial to the maintenance of state power—to its boundaries, to its commerce, to its internal administration, to control of populations, and to its military strength. Mapping soon became the business of the state: cartography is early nationalized. The state guards its knowledge carefully: maps have been universally censored, kept secret, and falsified. In all these cases maps are linked to what Foucault called the exercise of juridical power.[75] The map becomes a juridical territory': it facilitates surveillance and control. Maps are still used to control our lives in innumerable ways. A mapless society, though we may take the map for granted, would now be politically unimaginable. All this is power *with* the help of maps. It is an external power, often centralized and exercised bureaucratically, imposed from above, and manifest in particular acts or phases of deliberate policy.

I come now to the important distinction. What is also central to the effects of maps in society is what may be defined as the power *internal* to cartography. The focus of inquiry therefore shifts from the place of cartography in a juridical system of power to the political effects of what cartographers do when they make maps. Cartographers manufacture power: They create a spatial panopticon. It is a power embedded in the map text. We can talk about the power of the map just as we already talk about the power of the word or about the book as a force for change. In this sense maps have politics.[76] It is a power that intersects and is embedded in knowledge. It is universal. Foucault writes of

The omnipresence of power: not because it has the privilege of consolidating everything under its invincible unity, but because it is produced from one moment to the next, at every point, or rather in every relation from one point to another. Power is everywhere; not because it embraces everything, but because it comes from everywhere.[77]

Power comes from the map and it traverses the way maps are made. The key to this internal power is thus cartographic process. By this I mean the way maps are compiled and the categories of information selected; the way they are generalized, a set of rules for the abstraction of the landscape; the way the elements in the landscape are formed into hierarchies; and the way various rhetorical styles that also reproduce power are employed to represent the landscape. To catalogue the world is to appropriate it,[78] so that all these technical processes represent acts of control over its image which extend beyond the professed uses of cartography. The world is disciplined. The world is normalized. We are prisoners in its spatial matrix. For cartography as much as other forms of knowledge, 'All social action flows through boundaries determined by classification schemes.'[79] An analogy is to what happens to data in the cartographer's workshop and what happens to people in the disciplinary institutions— prisons, schools, armies, factories—described by Foucault:[80] In both cases a process of normalization occurs. Or similarly, just as in factories we standardize our manufactured goods so in our cartographic workshops we standardize our images of the world. Just as in the laboratory we create formulaic understandings of the processes of the physical world so too, in the map, nature is reduced to a graphic formula.[81] The power of the mapmaker was not generally exercised over individuals but over the knowledge of the world made available to people in general. Yet this is not consciously done and it transcends the simple categories of 'intended' and 'unintended' altogether. I am not suggesting that power is deliberately or centrally exercised. It is a local knowledge which at the same time is universal. It usually passes unnoticed. The map is a silent arbiter of power.

What have been the effects of this 'logic of the map' upon human consciousness, if I may adapt Marshall McLuhan's phrase ('logic of print')?[82]

Like him I believe we have to consider for maps the effects of abstraction, uniformity, repeatability, and visuality in shaping mental structures, and in imparting a sense of the places of the world. It is the disjunction between those senses of place, and many alternative visions of what the world is, or what it might be, that has raised questions about the effect of cartography in society, Thus, Theodore Roszac writes

The cartographers are talking about their maps and not landscapes. That is why what they say frequently becomes so paradoxical when translated into ordinary language. When they forget the difference between map and landscape— and when they permit or persuade us to forget that difference—all sorts of liabilities ensue.[83]

One of these 'liabilities' is that maps, by articulating the world in mass-produced and stereotyped images, express an embedded social vision. Consider, for example, the fact that the ordinary road atlas is among the best selling paperback books in the United States[84] and then try to gauge how this may have affected ordinary Americans' perception of their country. What sort of an image of America do these atlases promote? On the one hand, there is a patina of gross simplicity. Once off the interstate highways the landscape dissolves into a generic world of bare essentials that invites no exploration. Context is stripped away and place is no longer important. On the other hand, the maps reveal the ambivalence of all stereotypes. Their silences are also inscribed on the page: Where, on the page, is the variety of nature, where is the history of the landscape, and where is the space-time of human experience in such anonymized maps?[85]

The question has now become: do such empty images have their consequences in the way we think about the world? Because all the world is designed to look the same, is it easier to act upon it without realizing the social effects? It is in the posing of such questions that the strategies of Derrida and Foucault appear to clash. For Derrida, if meaning is undecidable so must be, *pari passu*, the measurement of the force of the map as a discourse of symbolic action. In ending, I prefer to align myself with Foucault in seeing all knowledge[86]—and hence cartography—as thoroughly enmeshed with the larger battles which constitute our world. Maps are not external to these struggles to alter power relations. The history of map use suggests that this may be so and that maps embody specific forms of power and authority. Since the Renaissance they have changed the way in which power was exercised. In colonial North America, for example, it was easy for Europeans to draw lines across the territories of Indian nations without sensing the reality of their political identity.[87] The map allowed them to say, 'This is mine; these are the boundaries.'[88] Similarly, in innumerable wars since the sixteenth century it has been equally easy for the generals to fight battles with coloured pins and dividers rather than sensing the slaughter of the battlefield.[89] Or again, in our own society, it is still easy for bureaucrats, developers, and 'planners' to operate on the bodies of unique places without measuring the social dislocations of 'progress'. While the map is never the reality, in such ways it helps to create a different reality. Once embedded in the published text the lines on the map acquire an authority that may be hard to dislodge. Maps are authoritarian images. Without our being aware of it maps can reinforce and legitimate the status quo. Sometimes agents of change, they can equally become conservative documents. But in either case the map is never neutral. Where it seems to be neutral it is the sly 'rhetoric of neutrality'[90] that is trying to persuade us.

CONCLUSION

The interpretive act of deconstructing the map can serve three functions in a broad enquiry into the history of cartography. First, it allows us to challenge the epistemological myth (created by cartographers) of the cumulative progress of an objective science always producing better delineations of reality. Second, deconstructionist argument allows us to redefine the historical importance of maps. Rather than invalidating their study, it is enhanced by adding different nuances to our understanding of the power of cartographic representation as a way of building order into our world. If we can accept intertextuality then we can start to read our maps for alternative and sometimes competing discourses. Third, a deconstructive turn of mind may allow map history to take a fuller place in the interdisciplinary study of text and knowledge. Intellectual strategies such as those of discourse in the Foucauldian sense, the Derridian notion of metaphor and rhetoric as inherent to scientific discourse, and the pervading concept of power-knowledge are shared by many subjects. As ways of looking at maps they are equally enriching. They are neither inimical to hermeneutic enquiry nor antihistorical in their thrust. By dismantling we build. The possibilities of discovering meaning in maps and of tracing the social mechanisms of cartographic change are enlarged. Postmodernism offers a challenge to read maps in ways that could reciprocally enrich the reading of other texts.

ACKNOWLEDGEMENTS

These arguments were presented in earlier versions at 'The Power of Places' Conference, Northwestern University, Chicago, in January 1989, and as a 'Brown Bag' lecture in the Department of Geography, University of Wisconsin at Milwaukee, in March 1989. I am grateful for the suggestions received on those occasions and for other helpful comments received from Sona Andrews, Catherine Delano Smith, and Cordell Yee. I am also indebted to Howard Deller of the American Geographical Society Collection for a number of references and to Ellen Hanlon for editorial help in preparing the paper for press.

NOTES

1. Beryl Markham, *West with the Night*. New York: North Point Press, 1983.
2. For these distinctions see Terry Eagleton, *Literary Theory: An Introduction*. Minneapolis: University of Minnesota Press, 1983; for an account situated closer to the direct concerns of cartog-

raphy see Maurizio Ferraris, 'Postmodernism and the Deconstruction of Modernism', *Design Issues* 4/1 and 2, Special Issue, 1988: 12–24.

3. Reported in *Cartographic Perspectives: Bulletin of the North American Cartographic Information Society* 1/1, 1989: 4.

4. Others have made the same point: see, especially, the trenchantly deconstructive turn of the essay by Denis Wood and John Fels, 'Designs on Signs/Myth and Meaning in Maps', *Cartographica* 23/3, 1986: 54–103.

5. Louis Marin, *Portrait of the King*, trans. Martha M. Houle, *Theory and History of Literature* 57. Minneapolis: University of Minnesota Press, 1988: 169–79; William Boelhower, *Through a Glass Darkly: Ethnic Semiosis in American Literature*. Venezia: Edizioni Helvetia, 1984: esp. 41–53. See also, Boelhower's 'Inventing America: A Model of Cartographic Semiosis', *Word and Image* 4/2, 1988: 475–97.

6. Deriving from the writings of Jacques Derrida: for exposition see the translator's Preface to Jacques Derrida, *Of Grammatology*, trans. Gayatri Chakratvorty Spivak. Baltimore: The John Hopkins University Press, 1976: ix–lxxxvii; Christopher Norris, *Deconstruction: Theory and Practice*. London: Methuen, 1982; and Christopher Norris, *Derrida*. Cambridge, Mass.: Harvard University Press, 1987.

7. On architecture and planning see, for example, *The Design Professions and the Built Environment*, ed. Paul L. Knox. London: Croom Helm, 1988; Derek Gregory, 'Postmodernism and the Politics of Social Theory', *Environment and Planning D: Society and Space* 5, 1987: 245–48; on geography see Michael Dear, 'The Postmodern Challenge: Reconstructing Human Geography', *Transactions, Institute of British Geographers* (New Series), 13, 1988: 262–74.

8. Marin, *Portrait of the King*, 173, the full quotation appears later in this article.

9. As an introduction I have found to be particularly useful Edward W. Said, 'The Problem of Textuality: Two Exemplary Positions', *Critical Inquiry* 4/4, Summer 1978: 673–714; also the chapters 'Jacques Derrida' by David Hoy and 'Michel Foucault' by Mark Philp in Quentin Skinner, ed., *The Return of Grand Theory in the Human Sciences*. Cambridge: Cambridge University Press, 1985: 41–64: 65–8.

10. On the other hand, I do not adopt some of the more extreme positions attributed to Derrida. For example, it would be unacceptable for a social history of cartography to adopt the view that nothing lies outside the text.

11. Alfred Korzybski, *Science and Sanity: An Introduction to Non-Aristotelian Systems and General Semantics*, 3rd ed. with new pref. Lakeville, Connecticut: The International Non-Aristotelian Library Pub. Co., 1948:58,247,498,750–1.

12. H.G. Blocker, *Philosophy and Art*, New York: Charles Scribner's Sons, 1979: 43.

13. Mark Philp, 'Michel Foucault', in Skinner, *The Return of Grand Theory*: 69.

14. *Ibid.*

15. 'Western cartography' is defined as the types of survey mapping first fully visible in the European Enlightenment and which then spread to other areas of the world as part of European overseas expansion.

16. The history of these technical rules has been extensively written about in the history of cartography, though not in terms of their social implications nor in Foucault's sense of discourse: see, for example, the later chapters of G.R. Crone, *Maps and Their Makers: An Introduction to the History of Cartography*, 1st ed., 1953, 5th ed. Folkestone, Kent: Dawson; Hamden, Conn.: Archon Books, 1978.

17. For a discussion of these characteristics in relation to science in general see P.N. Campbell, 'Scientific Discourse', *Philosophy and Rhetoric* 6/1, 1973; also Steve Woolgar, *Science: The Very Idea*. Chichester, Sussex: Ellis Horwood, 1988, esp. Chapter 1, and R. Hooykaas, 'The Rise of Modern Science: When and Why?' *The British Journal for the History of Science* 20/4, 1987; 453–73, for a more specifically historical context.

18. For evidence see John A. Wolter, 'The Emerging Discipline of Cartography', Ph.D. Diss., University of Minnesota, 1975; also, 'Cartography—an Emerging Discipline', *The Canadian Cartographer*, 12/2, 1975: 210–216.

19. See, for example, the definition of cartography in International Cartographic Association, *Multilingual Dictionary of Technical Terms in Cartography*, ed. E. Meynen. Wiesbaden: Franz Steiner Verlag, 1973, 1, 3: or, more recently, Helen M. Wallis and Arthur H. Robinson, eds. *Cartographical Innovations: An International*

Handbook of Mapping Terms to 1900. Tring, Herts: Map Collector Publications and International Cartographic Association, 1987, xi, where cartography 'includes the study of maps as scientific documents and works of art'.

20. See the discussion in J. Morris, 'The Magic of Maps: The Art of Cartography', M.A. Diss., University of Hawaii, 1982.

21. Rudolf Arnheim, 'The Perception of Maps', in Rudolf Arnheim, *New Essays on the Psychology of Art*. Berkeley: University of California Press, 1986: 194–202; Umberto Eco, *A Theory of Semiotics*. Bloomington: Indiana University Press, 1976: 245–57; E. Gombrich, 'Mirror and Map: Theories of Pictorial Representation', *Philosophical Transactions of the Royal Society of London* Series B, vol. 270, Biological Sciences, 1975: 119–49: and Nelson Goodman, *Languages of Art; An Approach to a Theory of Symbols*. Indianapolis and New York: Bobbs-Merrill, 1968: 170–1; 228–30.

22. Richard Rarty, *Philosophy and the Mirror of Nature*. Princeton, 1979.

23. Larry Laudan, *Progress and Its Problems: Toward a Theory of Scientific Growth*. Berkeley: University of California Press, 1977: 2.

24. For a discussion of these tendencies in the historiography of early maps see J.B. Harley. 'L'Histoire de la cartographie comme discours', *Prefaces* 5 December 1987–January 1988: 70–5.

25. In the much-debated sense of Thomas S. Kuhn, *The Structure of Scientific Revolutions*. Chicago: The University of Chicago Press, 1962. For challenges and discussions, see Imre Lakatos and Alan Musgrave, eds., *Criticism and the Growth of Knowledge*. Cambridge: Cambridge University Press, 1970.

26. *Cartographie dans les medias*, ed. M. Gauthier. Quebec: Presses de l'Université du Quebec, 1988.

27. Sona Karentz Andrews, review of *Cartography in the Media* in *The American Cartographer*, 1989, forthcoming [published in vol. 16, no. 3 (July 1989): 219–20].

28. W.G.V. Balchin, 'The Media Map Watch in the United Kingdom', in *Cartographie dans les medias*, 1988: 33–48.

29. The phrase is that of Ellen Lupton, 'Reading Isotype', *Design Issues* 3/2, 1986, 47–58 (quote on page 53).

30. Arno Peters, *The New Cartography*, New York: Friendship Press, 1983. The responses included John Loxton, 'The Peters Phenomenon', *The Cartographic Journal* 22/2, 1985: 106–8; 'The So-called Peters Projection', in *ibid.*, 108–10; A.H. Robinson, 'Arno Peters and His New Cartography', *American Cartographer* 12, 1985: 103–11; Phil Porter and Phil Voxland, 'Distortion in Maps: The Peters' Projection and Other Devilments', *Focus* 36, 1986: 22–30; and, for a more balanced view, John P. Snyder, 'Social Consciousness and World Maps', *The Christian Century*, February 24, 1988: 190–2.

31. 'Soviet Aide Admits Maps Were Faked for 50 Years' and 'In West, Map Makers Hail "Truth"', *The New York Times* September 3, 1988; 'Soviets Admit Map Paranoia', *Wisconsin State Journal* Saturday, September 3, 1988; 'Soviets Caught Mapping!' *The Ottawa Citizen* Saturday, September 3, 1988; 'Faked Russian Maps Gave the Germans Fits', *The New York Times* September 11, 1988; and 'National Geo-glasnost?' *The Christian Science Monitor* September 12, 1988.

32. Michel Foucault, *The Order of Things: An Archaeology of the Human Sciences*. A translation of *Les mots et les choses*. New York: Vintage Books, 1973, xx.

33. *Ibid.*, xxii.

34. Many commentators have noted this tendency. See, for example, Yi-Fu Tuan, *Topophilia. A Study of Environmental Perception, Attitudes, and Values*. Englewood Cliffs, New Jersey: Prentice-Hall, 1974, Chapter 4, 'Ethnocentrism, Symmetry, and Space', 30–44. On ancient and medieval European maps in this respect see J.B. Harley and David Woodward, eds., *The History of Cartography*, vol. I, *Cartography in Prehistoric, Ancient, and Medieval Europe and the Mediterranean*. Chicago: The University of Chicago Press, 1987. On the maps of Islam and China see J.B. Harley and David Woodward, eds., *The History of Cartography*, vol. 2, *Cartography in the Traditional Islamic and Asian Societies*, Chicago; The University of Chicago Press, forthcoming [published as *The History of Cartography vol. 2, Cartography in the Traditional Islamic and South Asian Societies*. Chicago: University of Chicago, 1992].

35. Arno Peters, *The New Cartography, passim*.

36. For the wider history of this 'rule' see Arthur P. Whitaker, *The Western Hemisphere Idea: Its*

Rise and Decline. Ithaca, New York: Cornell University Press, 1954; also S. Whittemore Boggs, 'This Hemisphere', *Department of State Bulletin* 12/306, May 6, 1945: 845–50; Alan K. Henrikson, 'The Map as an "Idea": The Role of Cartographic Imagery During the Second World War', The American Cartographer 2/1, 1975: 19–53.

37. J.B. Harley, 'Maps, Knowledge, and Power', in *The Iconography of Landscape*, ed. Denis Cosgrove and Stephen Daniels, Cambridge: Cambridge University Press, 1988: 289–90.

38. The link between actual mapping, as the principal source of our world vision, and *mentality* still has to be thoroughly explored. For some contemporary links see Alan K. Henrikson 'Frameworks for the World', Preface in Ralph E. Ehrenberg, *Scholars' Guide to Washington, D.C. for Cartography and Remote Sensing Imagery*. Washington, D.C: Smithsonian Institution Press, 1987, viii–xiii. For a report on research that attempts to measure this influence in the cognitive maps of individuals in different areas of the world see Thomas F. Saarinen, *Centering of Mental Maps of the World*. Department of Geography and Regional Development, Tucson, Arizona, 1987.

39. For a general discussion see Harley, 'Maps, Knowledge, and Power', 292–4; in my essay on 'Power and Legitimation in the English Geographical Atlases of the Eighteenth Century', in *Images of the World: The Atlas Through History*, ed. John A. Wolter. Washington, D.C.: Library of Congress, forthcoming [published as *Images of the World: The Atlas Through History*. Eds. John Amadeus Wolter and Ronald E. Grim. New York: McGraw-Hill, 1997. Pp 161–204]; these 'rules of the social order' are discussed in the maps of one historical society.

40. Marin, *Portrait of the King*, 173.

41. Gifford Geertz, 'Art as a Cultural System' in *Local Knowledge: Further Essays in Interpretive Anthropology*. New York: Basic Books, 1983, 99.

42. This is cogently argued by D.F. McKenzie, *Bibliography and the Sociology of Texts*. London: The British Library, 1986, esp. 34–9, where he discusses the textuality of maps. Robinson and Petchenik, 1976, p. 43, reject the metaphor of map as language: they state that 'the two systems, map and language are essentially incompatible', basing their belief on the familiar

grounds of literality that language is verbal, that images do not have a vocabulary, that there is no grammar, and the temporal sequence of a syntax is lacking. Rather than isolating the differences, however, it now seems more constructive to stress the *similarities* between map and text.

43. McKenzie, *Bibliography*: 35.

44. Roland Barthes, *Mythologies: Selected and Translated from the French by Annette Lavers*. London: Paladin, 1973: 110.

45. The narrative qualities of cartography are introduced by Denis Wood in 'Pleasure in the Idea: The Atlas as Narrative Form', in *Atlases for Schools: Design Principles and Curriculum Perspectives*, ed. R.J.B. Carswell, G.J.A. de Leeuw, and N.M. Waters, *Cartographica* 24/1, 1987: 24–45 [Monograph 36].

46. The undecidability of textual meaning is a central position in Derrida's criticism of philosophy: see the discussion by Hoy, 'Jacques Derrida' in Skinner, *The Return of Grand Theory*, 1985: 54–8.

47. Terry Eagleton, *Against the Grain*. London: Verso, 1986: 80. Quoted in Edward W. Soja, *Postmodern Geographies*. London: Verso, 1989, 12.

48. Hoy, 'Jacques Derrida', 540.

49. W.J.T. Mitchell, *Iconology: Image, Text, Ideology*. Chicago: The University of Chicago Press, 1986: 8.

50. J.B. Harley, 'Silences and Secrecy: The Hidden Agenda of Cartography in Early Modern Europe', *Imago Mundi* 40, 1988: 57–76.

51. Christopher Norris, *Derrida*. Cambridge, Mass.: Harvard University Press, 1987: 19.

52. Most recently, C.N.G. Clarke, 'Taking Possession: The Cartouche as Cultural Text in Eighteenth-Century American Maps', *Word and Image* 42, 1988: 455–74; also Harley, 'Maps, Knowledge, and Power', esp. 296–99 and J.B. Harley, 'Meaning and Ambiguity in Tudor Cartography', in *English Map-Making, 1500–1650: Historical Essays*, ed. Sarah Tyacke. London: The British Library Reference Division Publications, 1984: 22–45; and 'Power and Legitimation in the English Geographical Atlases of the Eighteenth Century', in *Images of the World: The Atlas Through History*, ed. John A. Wolter, Washington, D.C.: Library of Congress, Center for the Book, forthcoming [published as *Images of the*

World: The Atlas Through History. Eds. John Amadeus Wolter and Ronald E. Grim. New York: McGraw-Hill, 1997. Pp 161–204].

53. Wood and Fels, 'Designs on Signs', 1986.
54. Roland Barthes, 'Myth Today', in Barthes, *Mythologies*: 109–59.
55. Wood and Fels, 'Designs on Signs', 1986: 54.
56. On the intertextuality of all discourses—with pointers for the analysis of cartography—see Tzvetan Todorov, *Mikhail Bakhtin: The Dialogical Principle*, trans. Wlad Godzich. Minneapolis: University of Minnesota Press, 1984: 60–74; also M.M. Bakhtin, *The Dialogic Imagination: Four Essays*, ed. Michael Holquist, trans. Caryl Emerson and Michael Holquist. Austin: University of Texas Press, 1981. I owe these references to Dr. Corden Vee, History of Cartography Project, University of Wisconsin at Madison.
57. Wood and Fels, 'Designs on Signs', 1986: 63.
58. *Ibid.*, 60.
59. The 'basic' and 'derived' division, like that of 'general purpose' and 'thematic', is one of the axiomatic distinctions often drawn by cartographers. Deconstruction, however, by making explicit the play of forces such as intention, myth, silence, and power in maps, will tend to dissolve such an opposition for interpretive purposes except in the very practical sense that one map is often copied or derived from another.
60. Hoy, 'Jacques Derrida' in Skinner, *The Return of Grand Theory*, 1985: 44.
61. I derive this thought from Eagelton, *Literary Theory*, 135, writing of the ideas of Roland Barthes.
62. These examples are from Harley, 'Maps, Knowledge, and Power', 1988: 300.
63. Eagelton, *Literary Theory*, 1983: 135–6.
64. Christopher Norris, *Deconstruction*, 19.
65. See, for example, Donald N. McCloskey, *The Rhetoric of Economics*. Madison: The University of Wisconsin Press, 1985; and *The Rhetoric of the Human Sciences: Language and Argument in Scholarship and Public Affairs*, ed. John S. Nelson, Allan Megill, and Donald N. McCloskey. Madison: The University of Wisconsin Press, 1987.
66. For a notable exception see Wood and Fels, 'Designs on Signs', 1986. An interesting example of cartographic rhetoric in historical atlases is described in Walter Goffart, 'The Map of the Barbarian Invasions: A Preliminary Report' *Nottingham Medieval Studies* 32, 1988: 49–64.
67. *Ibid.*, p. 99, the examples are given for topographical maps of reliability diagrams, multiple referencing grids, and magnetic error diagrams; on thematic maps 'the trappings of F-scaled symbols and psychometrically divided greys' are a similar form of rhetorical assertion.
68. The 'letter' incorporated into Gomboust's map of Paris, as discussed by Marin, *Portrait of the King*, 169–74, provides an apposite example.
69. This is still given credence in some textbooks: see, for example, Arthur H. Robinson, Randall D. Sale, Joel L. Morrison and Phillip C. Muehrcke, *Elements of Cartography* 5th ed. New York: John Wiley & Sons, 1984, 127.
70. Wood and Fels, 'Designs on Signs', 1986, 71.
71. Hoy, 'Jacques Derrida' in Skinner, *The Return of Grand Theory*, 1985: 50; for further discussion see Norris, *Derrida*, 1987: 213–20.
72. Hoy, 'Jacques Derrida': 60.
73. Philp, 'Michel Foucault', in Skinner, *The Return of Grand Theory*, 1985: 76.
74. Joseph Rouse, *Knowledge and Power: Toward a Political Philosophy of Science*. Ithaca: Cornell University Press, 1987.
75. Michel Foucault, *Power/Knowledge: Selected Interviews and Other Writings, 1972–1977*, ed. Colin Gordon, trans. Colin Gordon, Leo Marshall, John Mepham, Kate Sopher. New York, Pantheon Books, 1980, 88; see also Rouse, *Knowledge and Power*: 209–10.
76. I adapt this idea from Langdon Winner, 'Do Artifacts have Politics?', *Daedalus* 109/1, 1980: 121–6.
77. Michel Foucault, *The History of Sexuality: Vol. I: An Introduction*, trans. Robert Hurley. New York: Random House, 1978: 93.
78. Adapting Roland Barthes, 'The Plates of the *Encyclopedia*', in *New Critical Essays*. New York: Hill and Wang, 1980: 27, who writes much like Foucault, 'To catalogue is not merely to ascertain, as it appears at first glance, but also to appropriate.' Quoted in Wood and Fels, 'Designs on Signs', 1986: 72.
79. Robert Darnton, *The Great Cat Massacre and Other Episodes in French Cultural History*. New York: Basic Books, 1984: 192–3.
80. Rouse, *Knowledge and Power*: 213–26.
81. Indeed, cartographers like to promote this

metaphor of what they do: read, for example, Mark Monmonier and George A. Schnell, *Map Appreciation*. Englewood Cliffs, New Jersey: Prentice Hall, 1988: 15. 'Geography thrives on cartographic generalization. The map is to the geographer what the microscope is to the microbiologist, for the ability to shrink the earth and generalize about it. . . . The microbiologist must choose a suitable objective lens, and the geographer must select a map scale appropriate to both the phenomenon in question and the "regional laboratory" in which the geographer is studying it.'

82. Marshall McLuhan, *The Guttenberg Galaxy: The Making of Typographic Man*. Toronto: University of Toronto Press, 1962, *passim*.

83. Theodore Roszak, *Where the Wasteland Ends: Politics and Transcendence in Postindustrial Society*. New York: Doubleday, 1972, 410; Roszak is using the map as a metaphor for scientific method in this argument, which again points to the widespread perception of how maps represent the world.

84. Andrew McNally, 'You Can't Get There from Here, with Today's Approach to Geography', *The Professional Geographer* 39, November, 1987: 389–92.

85. This criticism is reminiscent of Rolande Barthes' essay on 'The *Blue Guide*', Mythologies: 74–77, where he writes of the *Guide* as 'reducing geography to the description of an uninhabited world of monuments' (we substitute 'roads'). More generally, this tendency is also the concern of Janos Szego, *Human Cartography: Mapping the World of Man*, trans. Tom Miller. Stockholm: Swedish Council for Building Research, 1987. See also Roszak, *Where the Wasteland Ends*, 1972, where he writes p. 408, that 'We forfeit the whole value of a map if we forget that it is *not* the landscape itself or anything remotely like an exhaustive depiction of it. If we do forget, we grow rigid as a robot obeying a computer program; we lose the intelligent plasticity and intuitive judgement that every wayfarer must preserve. We may then know the map in fine detail, but our knowledge will be purely academic, inexperienced, shallow.'

86. See *The Foucault Reader*, ed. by Paul Rabinow. New York: Pantheon Books, 1984: 6–7.

87. J.B. Harley, 'Victims of a Map: New England Cartography and the Native Americans'. Paper read at the Land of Norumbega Conference, Portland, Maine, December, 1988.

88. Boelhower, *Through a Glass Darkly*, 47, quoting Francois Wahl, 'Le desir d'espace', in *Cartes et figures de la terre*. Paris: Centre Georges Pompidou, 1980: 41.

89. For a modern example relating to Vietnam see Phillip C. Muehrcke, *Map Use: Reading, Analysis, and Interpretation*, 2nd ed. Madison: J.P. Publications, 1986, 394, where, however, such military examples are classified as 'abuse' rather than a normal aspect of actions with maps. The author retains 'maps mirror the world' as his central metaphor.

90. There is a suggestive analogy to maps in the example of the railway timetable given by Robin Kinross, 'The Rhetoric of Neutrality', *Design Issues*, 2/2, 1985: 18–30.

12

MIND THE GAP: THE LONDON UNDERGROUND MAP AND USERS' REPRESENTATIONS OF URBAN SPACE

JANET VERTESI

When he had first arrived, he had found London huge, odd, fundamentally incomprehensible, with only the Tube map, that elegant multicolored topographical display of underground railway lines and stations, giving it any semblance of order. (Gaiman, 1996: 8)

Most of what we call 'abstraction' is in practice the belief that a written inscription must be believed more than any contrary indications from the senses. (Latour, 1990: 51)

Along with Tower Bridge and Big Ben it is the most widely recognized symbol of London. (Halliday, 2001: 145)

No visitor to London can avoid the ubiquitous London Underground Map (Figure 12.1); like many public transit maps, it is regularly posted on city streets outside stations, and strategically placed inside train cars and on platforms at regulated locations and angles for maximum exposure. But the map exceeds the confines of the transit system: the famous design is plastered all over the city on tourist trinkets such as T-shirts, mugs, umbrellas, lighters, and postcards, and an estimated 95 per cent of Londoners are said to have a copy at home.[1] It is no wonder that this map is often referred to as a modern icon, a symbol of London, representing not just the subway but even the city itself. Recognizing this fact, officials at the city's transport authority office, Transport for London, are always careful to call it a 'network diagram' or a 'journey planner', and they point to its trademark design principles, laid down by Harry Beck in 1932,[2] as the reason for its fame in the design world, its influence on subway maps worldwide, and its ease of use.[3] But this representation does other work for the Londoners and users of London I spoke with during my own study of the map in London. They call it 'the Tube Map', and while these users were

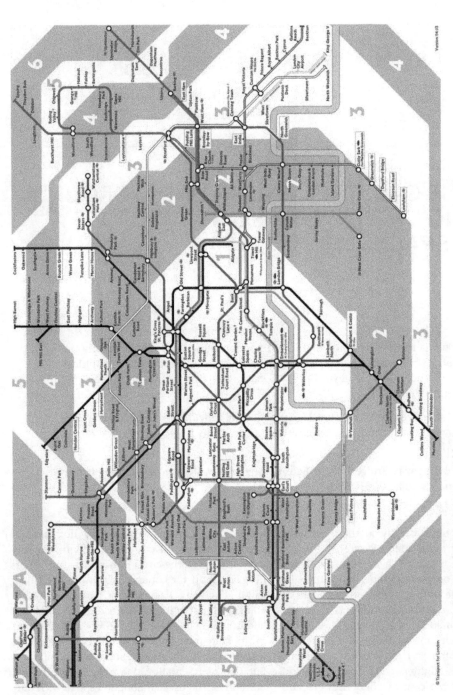

FIGURE 12.1   The London Underground Map.

careful to state outright that it did not properly represent the geography of London, this paper will examine how they rely on this representation to tame and enframe the chaotic city above ground. Thus, while the famous call to 'Mind the gap' usually refers to the gap between the train and the platform, this paper will recall another gap: between the iconic, abstract London Underground Map, and users' stories and practices of navigating, experiencing, and representing the city of London.

We rarely see a city as a whole without some kind of technological mediation: We walk, bike, or drive through the tangle of streets; we stand on top of tall buildings or at a publicly developed lookout point to gain a city-sanctioned view, or we peer down at the landscape from airplane windows.[4] But another essential technology that mediates between the city and its users is a technology of representation: the map. Whether walking or driving along city streets, maps show us where to go and how to get there, serving as sites of interaction and active interpretation as well as wayfinding devices *in loco*.[5] But do these representations structure our expectations, narratives, or even our interactions and interventions with the city itself? If so, what traces of this relationship between representations of and interactions with the city can we discern?

The London Underground Map presents a unique case through which to explore these issues. Unlike Paris or New York, London aboveground presents few organizing principles: There is no Rive Gauche or Central Park, no grid or *arrondissement* system that provides the critical landmarks for wayfinding and making sense of the urban geography. The tangled medieval core of the city, rebuilt with few changes after the Great Fire of 1666, remains intact, and as of 1996 there were more than 50,000 streets registered (Ackroyd, 2000). The subway map itself is further unlike those of Paris or New York: Lines are traced on a blank background instead of superimposed on a map of the city with streets and major landmarks, and the cartographic projection is non-traditional, inflating the centre and conflating the periphery. The map is also highly stable in this singular view: it is so heavily copyrighted and controlled by the London Underground Limited branding regulations that alternative views of the network are strictly prohibited and rarely seen by Londoners.[6] Further, the abstract diagram is always presented alone, unlike other subway maps which may present a Londonesque diagram alongside or drawn atop a street map: a representational move that recalls Michael Lynch's (1990) comparison of microbial photographs and schematized drawings. Thus the London Underground Map presents an interesting case for science and technology studies, both in establishing a fruitful analogy to scientific illustration, and paying close attention to the ways in which a subway system map can make a city 'imageable' (Lynch, 1960).

CRITICAL QUESTIONS

Studying the map of an urban subway network brings together several strands of research in science and technology studies and urban geography. Seminal works in cultural studies of geography emphasize and illustrate the knowledge, power, and politics inherent in maps and mapmaking.[7] To discuss the constructions of urban space, we can point to De Certeau's work on 'walking the city' (1984), or the recent addendum by Thrift on 'driving in the city' (2004). Schivelbusch's (1986) classic book on nineteenth-century railway systems established a way to talk about how technology may transform the physiological and psychological experience of geography, themes which echo in Bull's (2000) contemporary work on the use of personal stereos in the urban environment. Subway networks themselves draw our attention not only because they constitute a 'large technological system' (Hughes, 1987), but also because of the considerable skill, coordination, and 'heterogeneous engineering' (Law, 1987) needed to operate them.[8] In another vein, Thomas Gieryn (2006) explores the city as 'truth-spot' for the Chicago School of Urban Studies, while Anique Hommels (2005), and Eduardo Aibar and Wiebe Bijker (1997) have discussed the city as a large and complex socio-technological system, Hommels arguing for the application of STS principles to the study of cities in general.[9]

While I am indebted to these sources in too many ways to detail, this study of the Tube Map will speak primarily to critical issues in representation in science. As such, it parallels Lynch & Law's (1999) study of bird watching: exploring a site of analysis that may appear tangential or extra-scientific, but which has significant implications for how we understand complex uses of the visual in science. Two particular themes are at stake here.

First, this paper explores how inscriptions work *in the world*, not just at their sites of production. Latour (1986), Lynch (1990), Knorr-Cetina & Amann (1990) have described the use of images at the lab bench, and Rudwick (1976) has discussed disciplinary visual languages in formation, but it is also important to study how images are employed *outside* of an inner circle of experts by an active public with a particular kind of user expertise.[10] In this move into a more public space, even such a stable image as the Underground network diagram—with more than 15 million pocket versions printed each year[11]—may remain unchanged, but take on new meaning in a strange twist of the usual 'immutable mobile' story.[12] The map is therefore not another story of 'bringing the object back' from the periphery, as La Perouse's charts did to the 'centres of calculation' in France; instead it provides a case study of local, everyday interactions and encounters with an image that affects users' own calculations about their trajectory within, and understanding of, civic space.

Second, this paper explores the complex relationship between representing and intervening through an empirical study of practical activity with images. This duality was famously explored by philosopher Ian Hacking in support of a pragmatic realism about scientific entities in the philosophy of science, shifting focus towards 'intervening' to break out of the hermeneutical circle of representation and the hope to 'hook-up with the world' (Hacking, 1983: 140). However, this paper inverts Hacking's move by asking how much intervening is in fact predicated upon representing, and uses an empirical study to examine how representations stage, structure, and justify object interventions. The critical question is located in practice: viz., how do iconic or otherwise highly stable representations of scientific objects guide our interactions with those objects?

This is a difficult topic to explore in the social studies of science, as many scientific objects are made visible, representable, and interactable through instrumental means. If we want to explore how iconic images of the atom, such as the Bohr model, quantum cloud, or nano-scale spheres, affect how chemists, theoretical physicists, or nano-technologists interact with atoms, we ought first to grapple with the complexities of lasers, electron microscopes, or scanning tunnelling microscopes.[13] But the Tube Map presents a fascinating case where the mediating technology in question is, effectively, the image itself. Conversations with users reveal that the map is not only an interface to the subway system, but is also metonymically used as an interface to the city as a whole, establishing a virtual space in which the analog urban environment can be explored, constructed, narrated, and understood. Further, we may bypass fruitless discussion of whether or not the represented object is actually 'there' or represented 'accurately'; the city is clearly both tangible and constructed, and in its myriad experiential forms it does not necessarily always 'line up' with its many representations. The question thus changes from *whether* or *how well* the visualization represents the object, to *how the visualization constructs the object for interaction.*

Turning from the philosophy of representation to practices of interaction follows Michael Lynch's (1994: 149) suggestion that if we wish to produce meaningful analyses of images in science, we ought to cease comparing representations with 'reality' and focus our attention on 'what people do when they engage in an activity that makes one or another "representation" perspicuous'. However, it is still important to note the Tube Map's divergence from a classic geographical projection or even from urban experience, if only because this contrast reveals one of the map's most significant and pervasive practices, and its importance for the study of representation in science: that is, it is through familiarity with this iconic image that topology and topography become intertwined, enmeshed, and confused in everyday practices of interaction.[14] As this paper will show, the represented properties of the network, its nodes and corridors, are incorporated into users' *spatial* mapping and wayfinding practices, narratives, and representations as essential properties of London. Comparing the Tube Map with London above-ground, then, is neither due to naïveté about the illustration's 'inaccuracy' when measured up to 'reality', nor to a lack of expertise or understanding about the map's functions and limitations.[15] Rather, the comparison enables the analyst to probe the specific role and power of the iconic image for envisioning and directing interactions with represented objects; and it is precisely this complex relationship between representing and intervening that this paper explores.

METHODS

The subway is a disconnected nether world, and it is intriguing to speculate what means might be used to mesh it into the structure of the whole . . . . A detailed analysis of the imageability of subway systems, or of transit systems in general, would be both useful and fascinating. (Lynch, 1960: 57, 74)

This paper presents the results of fieldwork conducted in London in the summer of 2004, when I designed a study to probe the effects of the iconic Tube Map on stories, representations, and interactions with London. This study involved three different methods. First, I conducted interviews with staff at London Underground Limited, its larger umbrella group Transport for London (the organization under the Mayor's Office which administers all forms of London transit, from buses to the Tube to the driving tariff in the inner city), and general Tube enthusiasts, complemented with archival research at the London Transport Museum. Through these traditional methods, I aimed to get a sense of the official history and use of the Tube Map, as well as some alternate views of the system, past and present. Second, I explored another class of interactions, which involved asking for directions and distances to

places in London, both above ground and underground. I asked questions of pedestrians across the city, such as, 'How far is it to St Paul's?' or 'How do I get to the British Museum?' Alternating between destinations with eponymous Tube stops and places without clear ties to the subway, I aimed to elicit how the map plays a role outside its traditional journey-planner mode for wayfinding, navigation, and calculating urban space and time.

Third, I conducted more than 20 extended sit-down interviews with a variety of Londoners. Each interview began with the request, 'Draw me London', eliciting a variety of rich accounts and pictures of the city. This technique, called 'cognitive mapping', was first introduced by Kevin Lynch in his now-classic text in urban studies, *The Image of the City* (1960), in which the urban planner asked subjects in Jersey City, Boston, and Los Angeles to draw their city for him to get a sense of what he called 'the image of the city'.[16] Cognitive mapping has since enjoyed popularity in urban planning, geographical information systems design, and cognitive psychology research into 'mental maps'.[17] However, while this study follows Lynch's (1960: 57, 74) suggestion that the 'disconnected nether world' of the subway's influence on a city's image be explored, I am not interested here in how best to design a city, or whether or not people actually hold a mental map of London in their heads that more or less adequately corresponds to the cityscape. Rather, I am interested in cognitive mapping as a practical activity that brings at least three methodological benefits to Science and Technology Studies (STS). First, it presents a fruitful qualitative method of study: Asking people to draw an object that they work with produces not only remarkable and unique images, but also rich stories about the images as they evolve and develop under their pens. Here, understanding image-making as an active process is as important as looking at the final product: Sometimes *how* informants drew London was just as important as *what* they drew. Second, the technique focuses on what Lynch (1960: 9) calls the 'imageability' of the city: 'that quality in a physical object which gives it a high probability of evoking a strong image in any given observer'. To avoid essentialism, this might alternatively be read as tracing the *representations* or *instrumental experiences* of a physical object that give it a high probability of evoking a strong image in any given observer. Third, cognitive mapping may present STS with an alternative, literal way of doing epistemography, which Peter Dear (2001) identifies as the main task of Science Studies: a method of describing—or in this case, inscribing—epistemological themes or frameworks in historical and cultural situations. Asking people to draw an object is a powerful way to elicit stories about what they know about that object, presenting the possibility of accessing the effects of disciplinary education, theory-laden observation and representation, and the everyday gestalt switches between representations and objects. In these three kinds of interactions, the Tube Map clearly influenced representations of the city of London, both imagistic and narrative: It also enabled interventions or interactions with the city, both above- and below-ground, and provided a way to distinguish normalcy from distortion, user expertise from resistance.[18] This paper will therefore explore these three themes—representing, intervening, and resisting—in order to draw conclusions about the potential influences of the iconic, stable visual language on patterns of representation and interaction in science.

PRACTICES OF REPRESENTING

'If I asked you to draw London, what would you draw?' 'The Tube Map!' (Interview 4)

'It's the Tube Map. I'm drawing the Tube Map!' (Interview, Peter Wilson)

'It's on the Tube Map, therefore it must be London', exclaimed one interviewee (Interview 3), echoing a common claim that, by showing what is 'on' or 'off' the map, the Tube Map defines what is and what isn't London. This same respondent was keen to discuss how she chose an expensive flat over a cheaper one because it was close to a Tube station—not because she used the subway to commute, but because her friends would be more

likely to visit if she were 'on the map'. This association between station names and London locations runs so deep that whole neighbourhoods, such as Queensbury, gain their identities from the naming of a local station: Turnham Green even shifted location from the site of its namesake park to the area around the eponymous station a few miles down the road. It also has political implications, as many of the poorest areas of the city in the south-east do not have underground stops: several of my respondents noted that this makes these neighbourhoods even more disadvantaged, as being 'off the map' divorces them from civic culture and political discourse. However, the definition of what constitutes London is not derived from the physical structural elements of the subway network, but rather from the structural elements of its famous map. This influence goes beyond the station names, which link the analog city to its virtual representation, like geographical Lacanian 'anchor points'.[19] When I asked her to draw me London, one respondent began by tracing a rectangle on her paper, declaring, 'This is the Tube Map, the big one that they have on the walls in the stations' (Interview 9; see Figure 12.2). Most respondents did not directly articulate the Tube Map's influence on their ideas of the city's boundaries, but the majority chose to draw only central London: Zones 1 and 2 as depicted on the inset maps in the subway cars, centred on the junction between the Northern Line and the Central Line instead of around their own neighbourhoods, or even traditional centres of civic power, such as the City, the Walls or Gates, or the Parliament buildings.

Many respondents articulated the River Thames as the 'backbone' of the city, and set about inscribing the river into their maps, Yet, without exception, they expressed considerable confusion about 'how the river actually goes', pens pausing or tracing a variety of curved lines over the paper, 'I know it [the Thames] does some funny stuff down here . . .', claimed one long-time Londoner (Interview 6). After tracing the river upon their pages, most were unsatisfied, dismissing the squiggle with a comment like, 'This is the wrong scale' (Interview 2). It is not insignificant that the river Thames is the only above-ground

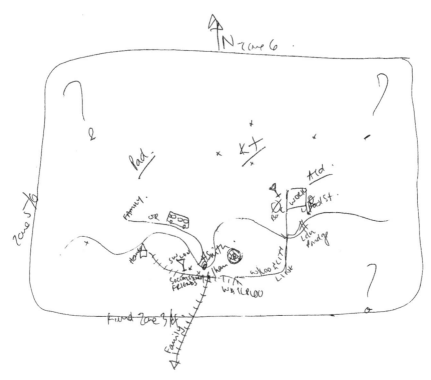

FIGURE 12.2 The map denotes boundaries: note 'here be dragons' question marks, the sketched Thames, and the subway lines on the above-ground space (Interview 9).

feature pictured on the Tube Map, but while Londoners in early user-surveys insisted it remain on the map, its abstracted form has changed shape even over the past few years, Thus the Tube Map's abstract and geometric pattern for the Thames informed mappers that it was 'there' and essential, but even 'walking the river' along the South Bank's popular new pedestrian passage was not enough to provide them with an alternative view of 'how it actually goes'.

The map also lends an underlying axis or structure to the city through the most familiar Tube lines: the Central, Northern, Piccadilly, and Circle Lines, In an interesting example, one respondent who had lived in London for three years stated outright, 'I think of it [London], surprisingly enough, as a grid'. He then proceeded to draw an x/y axis on his paper, labelling it with station names, from Ealing to Mile End and Barnet to Clapham (Figure 12.3), When

I asked him where the Central Line was on his map, he pointed to the x axis: 'And this [pointing at y axis], this is the Northern Line.' He spoke about how he judged the position of other London locations with reference to this grid, a practice he demonstrated later, when I asked him to place Paddington Station and the River Thames on his map. This technique also translated into his above-ground interactions: he described how he remained aware of the location of Tottenham Court Road Station (the intersection of x and y) when moving through the city, so that he would 'know where I am at all times' (Interview 14).

While this interviewee thought of London as a grid, another claimed, 'I think of London as . . . lots of little centres stuck together . . . it's something I think about the way the city fits together' (Interview 2). This was not an uncommon way to talk about London, as a collection of disparate and distinct localities. One respondent even

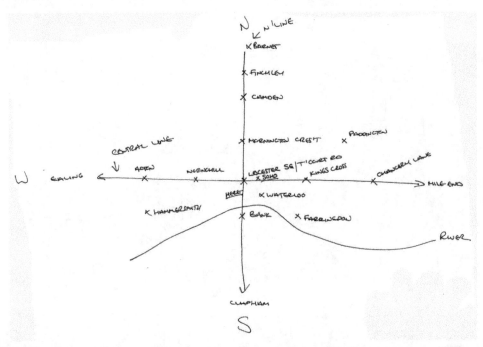

FIGURE 12.3 Tube lines as structure: London as x/y axis of the Northern and Central lines (Interview 14).

drew London as round, open circles, scattered about the page, including little sketches of what one might do or see above ground at any given place: a boat at Greenwich, for example, or a sun-tanning figure at Hampstead Heath (Interview 11; Figure 12.4). On the one hand, this image of London is an artifact of the city's popular history, a story of a growing metropolis that subsumed or cobbled together a number of small villages. The city does not have a single 'downtown', and different neighbourhoods cultivate particular personalities, attract particular clientele and types of residents, and maintain their own festivals or markets. But it is a view of the city that is supported and maintained by the Tube Map, with echoes of the subway experience in general: localities become 'stops' on the map; spaces to surface from the warp of the underground and encounter the above-ground locality. Most of my interviewees described this experience of the city as a matter of not knowing where anything is: One occasional London visitor sighed, 'I have no

idea where anything is . . . I remember spending some time in Trafalgar Square once, but I don't know where that is' (Interview 6).[20] However, another long-time resident let go of above-ground geography entirely in her approach to subway travel: 'There's no north, south, east, west down there, there's just Tube lines. All you're aware of is destination: direction isn't relevant' (Interview 1). Still another heavy subway commuter changed his approach to the city in order to combat this mentality: 'I had a sense of dots, I didn't know where they were. That was a problem for me, so I stopped using [the Tube]. Now they are where I thought they were' (Interview 15).

This latter informant understood London by privileging above-ground geography over 'dots' on the Tube Map, but for many others, the essential elements to understanding the city were the coloured lines between these station dots:

[While drawing,] I just see lots of blue and brown and yellow lines, but to think where everything is [is impossible] . . . . [Why?] Because

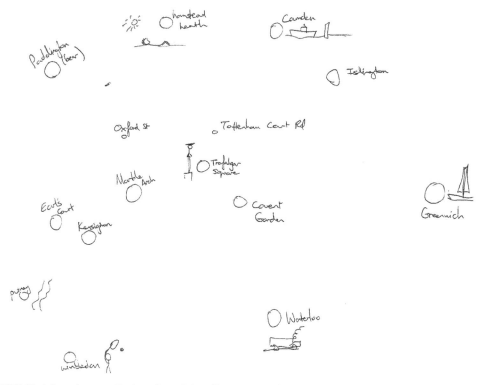

FIGURE 12.4 London as distinct localities (Interview 11).

of the Underground Map. Because that's how I know London. I can't even show you where Piccadilly Circus is, I'd just get on the Piccadilly Line and get off there or at Heathrow [the end of the line]. (Interview 7)

These lines were sometimes drawn onto the map, but were usually traced with a finger in order to place a locality on their map. The artifacts of this process remain inscribed in their drawings, such as Figure 12.5, in which the respondent's pen followed the Northern Line (including its branch north of King's Cross) without actually tracing the line, but rather placing station names along this well-travelled route. I also asked my interviewees to place King's Cross and Paddington Station on their maps: The majority placed King's Cross just north of centre, and followed the straight line of the Circle Line out to the left, placing Paddington at a right angle to King's Cross and the Central Line. This is consistent

with Paddington's placement on the Tube Map, where the western side of the city is heavily distorted. If my informants had been heavily influenced by driving, riding buses, or looking at 'geographical' projections of the city, they might instead have placed Paddington to the south-west of King's Cross, not level with it.[21]

The placement exercise echoed a common task that Londoners perform in and about their city, a task articulated by one informant invoking an early-modern mapmakers' convention, with the phrase, 'Here be dragons'. As the Tube Map defines what is and what isn't London, it also provides a framework for anticipation: Places that are familiar only from their stop on the map give a sense of what one ought to find should one go there, while spaces not colonized by station dots or Tube lines present uncharted and perhaps dangerous territory. This 'here be dragons' approach is well illustrated in Figure 12.2, where

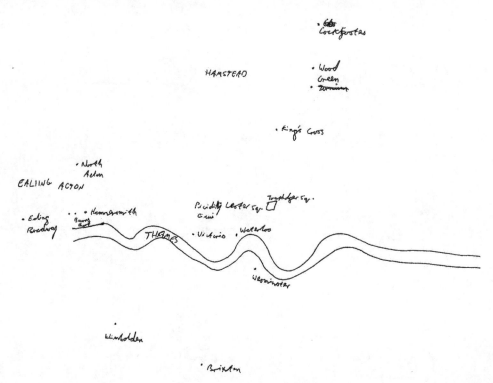

FIGURE 12.5 Tracing the Northern line upwards, placing stops along its path (Interview 19).

large question marks appear on parts of London about which the mapmaker has little knowledge aside from the fact that they are on the Tube Map. Wandering too far away from the familiar Underground Roundel, one might still be 'on the map', but somehow disconnected or located in a magical, uncharted space.

PRACTICES OF INTERVENING

I probably know London better by Tube than I do above ground, because when I'm walking without a map and then I hit a Tube stop, then I know where I am. So I sort of live in an underground world. (Interview 18)

Moving from representation to interaction, respondents reconciled the virtual space of the map with the analog space of the city in their navigational experiences and practices. Several common

methods and stories emerged when they spoke of the practical task of getting from point A to point B.[22] In these stories, the map is not only an object to think with (Turkle, 2007) or an object connected with a centre of calculation (Latour, 1987), it also provides, like personal stereos in the city, a 'technologized site of experience' (Bull, 2000: 157): a virtual space in which experiences of the city are lived and interpreted.

One way in which the virtual representation bled into the analog experience of the city is through effects on the sense of urban space and time. The effects of 'railroad space and railroad time' have been well discussed by Schivelbusch (1986), and Hadlaw (2003) even goes so far as to discuss the London Underground Map itself as a manifesto of modernist space and time.[23] These historical and theoretical approaches are here complemented by an inquiry based in practice, in which the effects of this modern representation of space and time are clearly and keenly experienced when navigating, explaining, and wayfinding in the city.

One such effect is in the computation of time and distance in London, whether above ground or underground. When calculating a journey, the two most common 'algorithms' I heard from Londoners were either 'three minutes per stop, five minutes to change' or 'five minutes per stop'. Another approach was more holistic, based on approximations of larger units of space, such as zones or inches across the map. Proponents of such an approach were likely to say something like, 'that will take you 20 minutes'. When pushed to explain this calculation outside of a direction-giving interaction, one interviewee claimed, 'It's [timing] a very intuitive thing and it's not consistent. I don't have a mathematical formula' (Interview 18), while another stated, ' . . . the only way I can tell how far things are is the number of stops or what zone they're in; it's my only reference, really' (Interview 6). Interestingly, these distance measurements were often the same regardless of whether the interviewee was approached above or below ground. Above-ground direction givers were just as likely to answer a question such as, 'How far is it to St Paul's?' with 'Five stops', or an equivalent 'Fifteen minutes': Only after a puzzled look from the questioner were they likely to qualify this statement with, 'by Tube'.[24]

Interviewees also reconciled their above- and below-ground experience of the city by correcting the Underground Map when they knew from personal experience that it was in error. Many of them performed a pinching gesture at the map, attempting to squish stops together that they knew from urban experience were close-by above-ground: Queensway and Bayswater, and Leicester Square and Covent Garden were consistently subject to such squishing gestures, whereas Monument and Bank were spread apart with an opposing gesture to indicate that they were not as close together as they appeared on the map. Thus the above-ground can be used to correct the Underground Map, which in these cases was held accountable to above-ground experience of space in spite of its own proclaimed a-geographicity.

Yet the above-ground experience was not complete without reference to the underground. One

of my mappers, in the middle of drawing an exclusively above-ground map, suddenly exclaimed, 'I gotta have the Northern Line [on my map] but I don't know where it comes from!' (Interview 6). He thus drew it in the straight north-south style of the Tube Map, running just east of Trafalgar Square and crossing the river (Figure 12.6). Others sometimes placed station markers in the middle of rich above-ground illustrations of their neighbourhoods or work areas alongside local restaurants, banks, or homes, and some even traced a subway line or the imagined trajectory of their underground commute onto their maps. Thus the underground bled into the above-ground in their representations of London.

Turning to street-level interactions with London, the story would not be complete without some discussion of the A-to-Z (the street map book published for more than 100 years by the London Geographical Society), which can be purchased pocket-sized, large map-book style, or for mobile devices. Most Londoners speak of the A-to-Z as crucial for getting around London, and rumour has it that even taxi drivers, London's most expert wayfinders, are lost without it. Examined from the point of view of representational fidelity or even ownership statistics, the A-to-Z would seem to present a challenge to a story of the Tube Map as key to making sense of London. However, from the point of view of practice, it quickly becomes clear that the two are complementary. In spite of many possible scripts for using a city map, I witnessed one Londoner after another perform a back-and-forth flip between the close-up street maps inside the book, and the Tube Map printed on the back cover. The two pieces of the puzzle were linked through station names, the only above-ground Tube presence on the street maps. My informants would usually thumb the index for a location, flip to that page to see the above-ground map, and then locate the closest Tube stations on the page. From there, they would turn to the back of the book to place that piece of London 'on the map'—the Tube Map, that is. The reverse practice, beginning with a station on the Tube Map and finding its location on the street map, was also extremely common. That is, the Tube Map provides the framework into which pieces

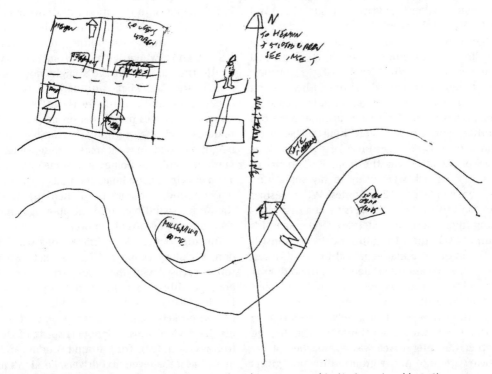

FIGURE 12.6 The Northern line drawn onto the above-ground in its imagined location (Interview 6).

of the street map are inserted and adjusted, like pieces in a jigsaw puzzle. A London Underground employee summed up the situation based on research conducted after an advertising campaign: 'What we found was people use the Tube Map more than the A-to-Z, even if they're not using the Tube. They'll think, "I can walk from Gloucester Road to South Kensington" . . . stations that look close together on the Tube Map, but which the A-to-Z will show as a long walk apart.[25]

The Tube Map is also entrenched in both direction-giving and wayfinding in the 'analog' city above ground. A particularly rich example comes from an interaction with a clerk at a store in Covent Garden:

1. **J.V.:** Excuse me, I'm a little turned around. How do I get to Tottenham Court? (*Presents her London A-to-Z*)
2. **Clerk:** (*Looks at the back of the A-to-Z, at the Tube Map*): Well, you won't want to take

the Tube from here because you'll have to change lines . . .
3. **J.V.:** (*Pointing to A-to-Z*): I think Covent Garden is on page 14 . . .
4. **Clerk:** (*opens the book and consults page 14*): Okay, come with me to the door and I'll point you on your way. (*Goes to doorway, R follows. He points.*) Okay walk out here and down this street to Covent Garden Tube Station, the Tube Station, and take a left. Walk down that street until you get to Leicester Square Tube station, you'll come to the Tube, then go right, up that street and you'll come to Tottenham Court Road Tube Station at the top of the road and there you are.
5. **J.V.:** You mean up Charing Cross Road?
6. **Clerk:** Yes. Go left at the Tube, right at the Tube, and there you are.[26]

It is interesting to note that the clerk assumed I was asking for Tottenham Court Road Station, not simply the street, which I would have encountered before the station; he also resisted my references to the above-ground, such as Charing Cross Road, or even the suggestion to look inside the A-to-Z. Further, the Tube here is playing the role of landmark, with stations acting as the means by which people can judge their location and their route. Interviewees often spoke of the Tube station as 'a meeting place, a reference point, even if you're on foot' (Interview 2), and of the disorientation of turning a corner and running into a station that you didn't expect to see, and then realizing that you're in a different part of the map than you had thought. But most fascinating is the route the clerk directed me to follow. Instead of choosing a direct path between the two points, which would lead a tourist through the charming streets and shops of lower Soho, he had me walk the lines of the Tube above ground: tracing out the Piccadilly, then the Northern lines to get to Tottenham Court Road. Thus the imagined, virtual lines of the underground map linked the above-ground station points in routes that made sense, regardless of their fidelity to any train lines below.

PRACTICES OF RESISTANCE

> Well really, the only map of London there is, is the Tube Map. (Interview 13)

The majority of my informants made a point of mentioning that the Tube Map is a distortion. It is common knowledge in London that the map's strange geography, expanding the centre of the city and contracting the suburbs in towards the centre, does not employ any standard geographical projection to make sense of the disorder above ground.[27] Ironically, however, respondents came to identify the Tube Map holistically as a 'normal' image of London, with the above-ground portrayal constituting the distortion. One of them articulated this switch clearly: 'Something I've always wanted to do is take a map of London and draw out where the Tube lines actually go. It's such a familiar shape and map, it'd be like stretching it over a balloon' (Interview 2). She thus identified

FIGURE 12.7 A unique view of Piccadilly Line, from London Marketing.

the above-ground cityscape as distorted, judging its geographical projection against the standard of the Underground Map. As another interviewee simply stated, 'The Tube Map, you know it's wrong but you know *how* it's wrong' (Interview 13).

My informants exhibited a grotesque fascination with the movement between the above-ground and the underground, watching the familiar shapes become distorted. For example, the Piccadilly Line administration was puzzled by the success of London Marketing's unique poster, 'Above Ground: A GlobalVision Perspective' (Figure 12.7), which draws the blue line of the subway meandering through a partial above-ground view of London, complete with landmarks. The Real Tube Map, produced by Sam Rich and posted on the London Underground site, gets thousands of hits, as do other home-made graphics which attempt to place the lines of the subway on a satellite image of the city.[28] This kind of disorientation or sense of not knowing 'where the stops are' is reflected in the popular BBC radio show, *Mornington Crescent*, which takes an absurdist approach to the map, asking contestants to rattle off station names based on association or stream of consciousness.[29]

Moving away from the map towards the surface, coming to know '*how* it's wrong', is not just an exercise in cognitive dissonance; it constitutes an important step towards establishing expertise in London. The urban legend of the tourist who takes the Tube from Leicester Square to Piccadilly Circus was often repeated to illustrate what you wouldn't know if you had just arrived in London: the tacit skills of city navigation that come with time and experience. Another cognitive mapper began his response to 'Draw me London' with: 'I'm thinking of the subway map first of all, but that isn't a very useful map for the above-ground . . . so I'm putting myself on street corners that I know in my mind and I'm thinking how would I get there from here' (Interview 16), revealing that he was expert enough to know when and where it was appropriate to use the Tube Map. Some 'users' of London spoke of 'weaning their way off' the map either purposefully or unintentionally. During a Tube strike, one interviewee was surprised to find that she lived closer to her workplace than she had thought, and that it was both easy and enjoyable to walk home from work; she thus made a habit of walking from then on. Thus a clear hierarchy of users emerged, in which exclusive reliance on the Tube Map to get around London demonstrated inexperience with the city, while the more experienced spoke of a cumulative above-ground competency and displayed an ability to use the Tube Map selectively as a tool.[30] Such advanced users even revealed an anthropomorphic familiarity with the Underground, speaking of individual lines' 'personalities'. However, even those who had grown up in London still used the 'Here be dragons' technique to identify places they had not visited: This held true for Londoners who avoided using the Underground system as well, preferring instead to bike or walk. The pervasive nature of such practices supports Sally Wyatt's (2003: 76) claim that both active and passive non-use of a technological system may be partial and not necessarily holistic.

Although familiarity with the above-ground cityscape may demonstrate expertise, pushed too far it can be seen as an aberration. For example, a cognitive psychologist at a British university insists that the hallowed design principles of the Tube Map are counterintuitive for human psychological hardwiring (Roberts, 2007). According to his extensive research on the perception of different geometries, as well as his own well-honed geographical sensibilities, the map's characteristic angles and shapes make the city more, not less, difficult to understand. A Tube enthusiast himself, he set about building a new Tube Map to conform to alternative guidelines generated from his studies, painstakingly constructing it from pieces of the original using Microsoft Paint. But when he showed the result (Figure 12.8) to an official at London Underground Limited, the response was telling:

> You should entitle it The Devil's Map. It satanically undermines all that is good, clean, pure about Beck's sacred qabbalistic [sic] map. Seriously, though, I think it's psychologically very disturbing to see London messed around in this way.[31]

This is not an uncommon response to Dr. Roberts' alternate map. Instead of finding it easier to understand, the majority of viewers consider his map incomprehensible or display the same fascination they do for the abovementioned alternative views: few are converts to his way of seeing the city. As he points out, 'The real irony is that I've messed about with London much less than the standard Underground map does!'[32] But, as Latour (1990: 51) suggests, abstracted inscriptions may inspire stronger belief than 'any contrary indications from the senses', or even from experience. Perhaps the final irony is that the standard,

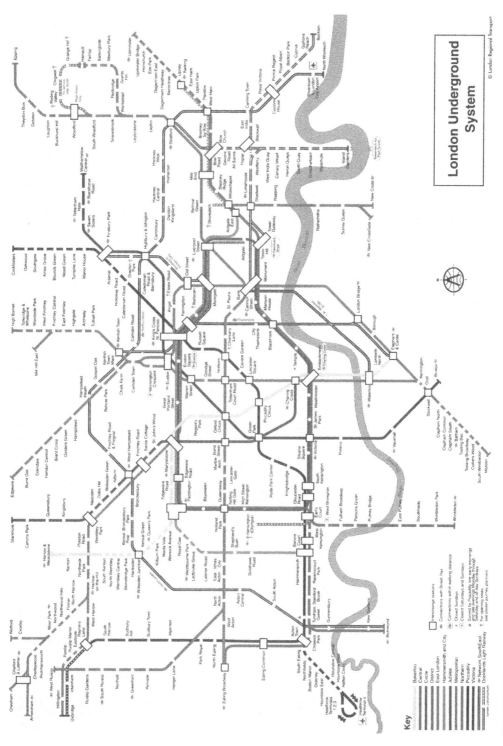

FIGURE 12.8 A proposed view.

abstracted Underground map constitutes such an important way of understanding London that it is no longer seen as a distortion: it has instead become the measuring stick by which normalcy, expertise, and resistance in picturing and interacting with the city are judged.

CONCLUSIONS

When we consider the map as a visual technology in action,[33] mediating between the user and the complex socio-technological system of the city, the effects of representing on intervening become more easily discernible. A stable, iconic representation such as the Tube Map may convey a general sense of structure, establish points of interaction, and enable further representations and narratives about the object. It can act as a reference point for practices of navigation and wayfinding, affording judgments of normalcy and degrees of expertise or resistance. It may also, through its mapping of topological connections, be read not only as a subway map but as a useful way of representing the city in general: an object it does not pretend to represent. The Tube Map thus becomes something of a graphical user interface to the city, presenting and concealing opportunities for engagement, and making sense of the city to its users.

This paper began by claiming a tie between the Underground map and iconic or stable imagery in science, and some final comments on that analogy are in order. First of all, the above discussion suggests that we should expect to see some correlation between the properties of representation, intervention, and resistance, not only with regard to subway maps, but in scientific representations as well. It is important to note that the map is not the *only* technology for experiencing a city: urban residents may walk, bike, bus, or have many other mediated experiences. Similarly, scientists may look through a variety of microscopes or scanning devices, or perform a number of technologically mediated experiments on a represented object. If pushed, they too refer to the representation as a kind of shorthand, or unpack the technology of representation ('this isn't really what an atom "looks like"'). But recalling

that even seasoned users have strong ties to the Tube Map, using it to put London together and put themselves 'on the map', the present study suggests that even expert users may maintain general reference to an iconic image, as a way to structure explanations or to extrapolate to the unknown.[34] As such, methods for understanding varying uses of stabilized representations might be useful for exploring how citizens and scientists use visual icons as map-like interfaces to their objects of interest.

Further, when following an immutable mobile from its site of production to its site of mass use, we notice that the mutability is not necessarily in the image's physical form or delineation, as Adrian Johns has famously critiqued.[35] Rather, the mutability lies in the *representational referent*, the image's indexicality, which changes in an appropriated (but still expert) context of use. In what we might call a 'visual language game', the visual language of the map is sensically interpreted such that the image comes to represent not just the subway network, but also London itself.[36] Extending this Wittgensteinian approach, we might note that the gestalt switch between seeing the map as the subway network and seeing it as London is both effected by and has tangible effects upon narratives, representations, and practices of civic navigation. This is not a naive gestalt switch, an example of reading a duck as a rabbit by accident or due to misunderstanding, but rather a necessary navigation between object and representation, subway, and city, with implications for object interactions and interpretations. As analysts of science, we ought especially to look out for the locations of this representational turn and its subsequent effects on object interactions in scientific practice. For example, just as Dumit (2003) considers the effects of positron emission tomography (PET) scans on a patient's sense of identity, we can identify a location of practical scientific activity in which it makes sense to say of an image like a brain scan: 'Now I see it as distributed brain activity; now I see it as a depressed person'. We ought to be attuned to similarly sensical expressions that allow easy gestalt movement between representation and object, virtual and analog environment.

This study also demonstrates that modes of representation should be treated analytically as inseparable from a community's interactions with (and within) a technological system: that is, *the study of representations in interaction* is *critical to the study of technological systems in action.* Such representations are more than passive illustrations or things-to-think-with, they are also *things-to-act-with*—and interact with—in subsequent access of the represented object. A departure from questions of accuracy, even if judged 'in terms of pragmatic utility' (Gieryn, 1999: 11), enables the analyst to move towards questions of how different communities of users define and draw their objects of study, with what effects on or relationships to their practice. As such, we are challenged to examine the representation as distinct from a discussion of ontology, topology, utility, or mimetic fidelity—against which the Tube Map would surely fail as an 'accurate' representation of London above-ground—to analyze the concrete ways in which representational organization enables narratives of movement and manipulation and, most important, to locate the boundaries and points of interaction *for particular communities of users.*

In 2003, London Underground Limited launched a widespread advertising campaign aimed to establish a strong connection between the subway system and London. The memorable advertisements featured Londoners enjoying activities associated with particular parts of the city made accessible by Tube, but in incongruous locations: a university professor giving a lecture dressed in Portobello Road carnival gear (I ♥ Notting Hill), or a typist in an office surrounded by exotic flowers (I ♥ Kew Gardens). At the end of the advertisement, a split-second scene of the arrival of a subway train replaces the *You* and the heart in the phrase 'You ♥ London' with the word *We* and the Underground roundel respectively, implying that the Underground comprises the essential fabric of the city, tying its disparate locations together and making the distant present. Londoners responded positively to the 'Love London' advertisements, but a post-advertisement survey was puzzled to find that the majority of those surveyed did not know what the advertisements were for. For them, the advertisements simply stated the obvious. The same survey also found that Londoners overwhelmingly responded that they 'Could not imagine London without the Underground', ranking the statement between 7.1 and 8 points out of 10 regardless of whether they used the Tube or not.[37] This paper may provide some clues to understanding why such results are not surprising in the least. The advertisement was beaten to the punch by a technology as essential to forging the intimate connection between the Tube and the city of London as the physical, steel lines of the subway itself: the London Underground Map.

NOTES

My sincere thanks to Michael Lynch, Trevor Pinch, and Ron Kline for their support and guidance throughout this project; I am also grateful to Shay David, Tarleton Gillespie, Jofish Kaye, Rachel Prentice, Phoebe Sengers, and Ron Smith for their comments on earlier presentations of this material, and to the paper's reviewers for their thought provoking and helpful comments. Many people and organizations made my fieldwork in London rich and informative, especially Paul Amlani-Hatcher, Seppe Embrechts, David Leboff, and Richard Smith of London Underground Limited, Peter Wilson of the TubeGuru, Helen Kent at the London Transport Museum library, Peter McLeod of Demos UK, Max Roberts of the University of Essex, Barry Brown of Glasgow University, and Isabel Dedring at Transport for London. Earlier versions of this paper were presented at the 'Engaging the City' workshop at the ACM Conference on Computer-Human Interaction (CHI; Portland, 2005), the Society for Social Studies of Science (Pasadena, 2005), the Cornell/MIT/RPI Graduate Student Conference (Ithaca, 2005), and the Science & Technology Studies Department at Cornell University (Ithaca, 2004 and 2005). Finally, my thanks to Transport for London, Max Roberts, and London Marketing for permission to reproduce copyright images, and to the Social Sciences and Humanities Research Council of Canada for the

Doctoral Program grant (752–03–0451) that made this research possible.

1. See Moss (1996) for London Underground Limited (LUL) placement regulations in the train and on the platform, and Ratmer (2003: 39–40) for recent Journey Planner statistics.

2. It is, unfortunately, beyond the scope of this paper to pursue the historical development of the Tube Map. Interested readers are referred to Ken Garland's (1994) definitive work on Beck; also Leboff & Demuth (1999), Leboff (1985), and Roberts (2005); on general Underground history, see Halliday (2001), and Day & Reed (2001). On current design principles, see the London Underground Limited's standards document (1993), wherein the company's view on the image is stated: 'the diagram itself is termed a "Journey planner" as it is not a literal representation of distance and geography, therefore it should not be called a map' (p. 4).

3. Edward Tufte is a proponent of the Tube Map's simple but effective design strategy (see his website at www.edwardtufte.com); it is also taught in a popular Human-Computer Interaction conference class on designing graphical interfaces (see Mullet & Sano, 1995).

4. The seeds for this project were sown several years ago when, in an interminable holding pattern over Heathrow Airport, the clouds below my plane parted, and I saw London from the air for the first time. It took me a long time to figure out what I was seeing, and I was disconcerted by my extreme disorientation caused by this sudden, holistic view of the city from above. This mimics the visitor's disorienting experience with the ceramic model of Paris in the Samaritaine in Latour & Hermant's, *Paris: Ville Invisible* (1998)—the title a play on Calvino's (1974) *Invisible Cities*, the story of Marco Polo relating the world to the great Khan. Seeing, representing, and narrating the city are key themes in the current discussion.

5. The map as site of wayfinding interactions is explored in Brown & Laurier (2005). I thank Barry Brown for making a manuscript available before its publication.

6. Interestingly, the only alternative maps of the subway network in public circulation are independently produced by travel guide companies, who, restricted from printing London Underground intellectual property for independent financial gain, are forced to come up with their own images. A comparative study of these alternate views by Roberts (2005) is underway, but it would be interesting to explore tourists' interactions with the system based on these guidebook images.

7. The literature on the meaning of maps is extensive, Important critical approaches to the material from the science studies perspective are Cosgrove (1984) on symbolic landscapes, Harley (1988) on Foucauldian themes of knowledge and power, Turnbull (1996) on knowledge spaces, and Wood's (1992) excellent introduction to maps in general. David Turnbull (2006) has also, very recently, written about the Tube Map, and I thank him for sharing this paper with me during the final stages of my project.

8. King's College London's 'Work, Interaction and Technology' group has studied the skills, 'situated actions' and material object interactions involved in operating a Tube line (Luff & Heath, 2000; Hindmarsh & Heath, 2000; Heath & Hindmarsh, 2000).

9. Aibar & Bijker (1997) discuss Barcelona as a socio-technical artifact of the technology of town planning; Hommels (2005) introduces city-planning and reconstruction as a theme for STS applications to urban studies; Latour (1996) discusses a city's construction of a subway system from the point of view of the subway train, and other implicated actors.

10. This paper will continue to use the term 'users', derived from Human–Computer Interaction studies, to refer to people who interact with London, as well as users of the London Underground network. While there is significant overlap between these two categories, they are not identical: many Londoners resist using the Tube or take alternative forms of transit, but those I spoke with still resorted to the Tube Map when wayfinding in London. An excellent collection of critical scholarship on 'users' as a category is included in Pinch & Oudshoorn (2003).

11. Interview, R. Smith, London Underground Limited, 21 June 2004.

12. The original source on immutable mobiles is Latour (1990 [1986]).

13. It is therefore not surprising that Hacking (1983, ch. 11) spends considerable time deconstructing the constructivist claims about the microscope to show that we *can* have direct access to the natural world even through a mediating technology. See Dennis (1989) for an excellent constructivist discussion of representation and instrumentality with regard to microscopes.

14. For a particularly illustrative early discussion of topology, the non-Euclidean 'social space' of relationships between components in an actor-network, see Mol & Law (1994).

15. This is Law and Lodge's (1984) assumption. They write: 'Clearly this map [the Tube Map] is not a proper representation of the London Underground System *except for certain purposes*. It has, in fact, been specifically designed with one major purpose in mind: to allow travellers to plan routes through the system with the greatest possible efficiency . . . . And when the system is running properly, this reading of the map is right' (62–3). However, this paper will show that there are other purposes to which the map is routinely put.

16. Note that the researcher did *not* ask their subjects to draw a *map* of London: the question was *always* 'Draw me London.' The result was, however, always a 'cognitive map' approach to illustrating the city.

17. For current trends in cognitive mapping in psychology, see Freundschuh & Kitchin (1999) and Kitchin & Freundschuh (2000). On cognitive maps and geographical information systems (GIS), see Freundschuh & Egenhofer (1997) and Brown & Perry (2002).

18. It is worth noting here that this study is not ethnographic. While I observed others and participated in reading the map and riding the Tube, it would be impossible to try to witness above-ground interactions in which the conventions of the Tube Map confront the activity of navigating above ground: people cannot walk through buildings and personal disorientation is rarely expressed overtly or advertised publicly in a large city. Thus, this project focused on representations and narratives about interactions, the ways in which people talked about and drew the city. It is here that the rich stories about interacting with London came

out, as well as tracing the lines of the Underground Map in their stories and drawings, and here where I believe we might best access the ways in which the virtual and analog spaces of map and city are breached and reconciled.

19. I am grateful to Rachel Prentice for alerting me to this connection.

20. He may also have been confused because Trafalgar Square, although it is a London landmark, has no eponymous Tube Station: it is framed, instead, by Charing Cross and Leicester Square. It is worth noting that some respondents attempted the interesting trick of showing me where above-ground landmarks 'were' on the Tube Map, such as Green Park, Hyde Park, or Trafalgar Square. They did so by filling in the blank spaces between the lines of the map, but never coloured outside the lines.

21. Interviewees usually chose the Northern Line as the city's meridian, labelling 'north' and 'south' at its extremes, and placing east and west on either side of the Central Line like the cardinal points of a compass. While this geometricity conforms to the right angles of the Tube Map, it does not reflect the positioning of the city more generally.

22. Perhaps I should state the obvious: people use the Tube Map to use the subway. A major site of interactivity occurs in front of the official maps placed in the stations, on the subway platforms, or inside the carriages, where people stand in front of the map alone or in groups) peer at it, argue over the best way to go, point at it, and trace pathways across the city, counting stops and calculating their exchanges. Viewing these interactions, an official London Underground study called the Journey Planner 'the definitive reference document' (London Underground Limited, 1997). While these interactions are interesting, it was impossible to get anyone to explain to me what they were doing: using the map is so assumed and so widespread that passengers gave me incomprehensible stares (or dirty looks) when I asked for clarification. Further, it was not entirely clear what asking for such information could mean: this is not, after all, a study of people using the map for the purposes for which it was constructed, but rather of using or re-appropriating the map to explain, narrate, and otherwise represent an

object for which it was not intended. With re-gard to getting people to verbalize the mental arithmetic they do in front of a map, I found the technique of asking for distances and time estimates more fruitful, that is, asking a fellow traveller how much time they thought a par-ticular journey might take. For a conversation analysis approach to direction-giving inter-actions, see Psathas (1991).

23. See especially chapter 3 of Schivelbush (1986). Hadlaw (2003: 35) reads the Tube Map as a cap-italist depiction of both space and time that is 'orderly, lucid, regular, efficient, and entirely functional'.

24. This recalls Annemarie Mol's (2003) inter-action with an atherosclerosis pathologist who similarly qualifies his statement of visual fact with 'Through a microscope'; indeed, we might see the Underground Map as one representa-tion of enacting London, representative of one of London's multiple—and oft-enacted—ontol-ogies.

25. Interview, P. Amlani-Hatcher, London Under-ground Limited, 21 June 2004.

26. 11 May 2004, 1:15 pm in the Body Shop store at Covent Garden.

27. There is a political history to this choice. Before 1932, the underground lines snaked across a full-sized map of London and its environs, re-quiring a lot of paper to manage in transit if a traveller wanted to double-check their route. Beck therefore chose to inflate the centre and conflate the periphery in order to fit all the sta-tions on a single, manageable map. His design was turned down when presented to the man-agement, but taken up a year later when the individual, privately owned Underground lines merged into a new, single, public company. Along with ownership of the train lines came ownership of the land the lines were built on (outside of the city centre, that is), and the pos-sibility for property development. To advertise new communities such as Golder's Green as vi-able neighbourhoods for London professionals, Beck's map was ideal: it promoted the new de-velopments by placing them 'on the map', made it seem that these suburban locations were close to the city centre, and encouraged regular use of the Tube in daily commutes. See Garland (1994) and Halliday (2001).

28. Rich's creation is now part of the London Underground official site: www.tfl.gov.ukltube/maps/realunderground/realunderground.html. (S, Rich, personal correspondence).

29. See the unofficial site of this long-running BBC radio game show at http://www.morningtoncrescent.org/. Peter Wilson's TubeGuru system takes ad-vantage of the ties between Tube Map and street map, using the Network Diagram as interface to cross-listings from clubs and restaurants, and the A-to-Z street map, maintaining the integrity of each representation to bring station-focused events to users: see the Tube Guru online at www.visitlondon.com/tubeguru/.

30. On such a scale, taxi drivers were often revered, thought to possess an almost magical sense of where things are and how to get there exclu-sively above ground.

31. Psychologist, personal correspondence.

32. Psychologist, personal correspondence.

33. This visual technology may be a complement to the literary technology for virtual witness-ing, uniting citizens in a shared, virtual view of their urban environment much as Boyle's literary technology rallied a shared view of an experiment. See Shapin (1984) on literary tech-nology, and Shapin & Schaffer (1985) on vir-tual witnessing.

34. While it is beyond the scope of this paper to engage in the structuration debate, it is worth noting that as the icon or the map both enable and restrict classes of object interactions, these may present a kind of technological 'frame', in Bijker's (1995: 191–2) terms, which can 'provide actors with the goals, the ideas, and the tools needed for action. [Frames] guide action and interaction . . . . But at the same time the build-ing up of a technological frame will constrain the freedom of members of the relevant social group.' On structure and action, Gieryn (1992) is particularly helpful.

35. Johns (1998) critiques the immutability of the immutable mobile in his detailed history of pir-acy in the seventeenth-century book trade.

36. This, of course, plays off of Wittgenstein's (1958) terminology to suggest a contextually organized environment of activities that es-tablish sensical and non-sensical visualizations in a local setting. Lynch & Law (1999) develop the notion of the 'literary language game' as a

method of using a text in the organized practice of an activity.

37. 'Unlocking London' (London Underground Limited, 2004: 22, 35).

REFERENCES

Ackroyd, Peter (2000) *London: the Biography* (London: Chatta and Windus).

Aibar., Eduardo & Wiebe E. Bijker (1997) 'Constructing a City: The Cerda Plan for the Extension of Barcelona', *Science, Technology, & Human Values* 22(1): 3–30.

Bijker, Wiebe (1995) *Of Bicycles, Bakelites and Bulbs: Toward a Theory of Sociotechnical Change* (Cambridge, MA: MIT Press).

Brown, Barry & Eric Laurier (2005) 'Maps and. Journeys: An Ethnomethodological Investigation'. *Cartographica* 40(3): 17.

Brown, Barry & Mark Perry (2002) 'Of Maps and Guidebooks: Designing Geographical Technologies'. *Proceedings of Designing Interactive Systems* (London: ACM Press).

Bull, Michael (2000) *Sounding Out the City: Personal Stereos and the Management of Everyday Life* (New York: Berg).

Calvina, Italo (1974) *Invisible Cities*, W. Weaver (trans.) (New York: Harcourt Brace Jovanovich).

Cosgrove, Denis E. (1984) *Social Formation and Symbolic Landscape* (Madison, WI: University of Wisconsin Press).

Day, John R. & John Reed (2001) *The Story of London's Underground* (Middlesex: Capital Transport Publishing).

De Certeau, Michel (1984) *The Practice of Everyday Life* (Berkeley) CA: University of California Press).

Dear, Peter (2001) 'Science Studies as Epistemography', in Jay A. Labinger & Harry Collins (eds), *The One Culture? A Conversation about Science* (Chicago, IL: University of Chicago Press): 128–42.

Dennis, Michael A. (1989) 'Graphic Understanding: Instruments and Interpretation in Robert Hooke's *Micrographia*', *Science in Context* 3: 309–64.

Dumit, Joseph (2003) *Picturing Personhood: Brain Scans and Biomedical Identity* (Princeton, NJ: Princeton University Press).

Freundschuh, Scott M. & Max J. Egenhofer (1997) 'Human Conceptions of Spaces: Implications for GIS, *Transactions in gis* 2(4): 361–75.

Freundschuh, Scott M. & Rob Kitchin (1999) 'Contemporary Thought and Practice in Cognitive Mapping Research: An Introduction', *Professional Geographer* 19(4): 507–10.

Gaiman, Neil (1996) *Neverwhere* (New York: Avon Books).

Garland, Ken (1994) *Mr. Beck's Underground Map: A History by Ken Garland* (Middlesex: Capital Transport Planning).

Gieryn, Thomas F. (1992) 'Riding the Action/Structure Pendulum with those Swinging Sociologists of Science', in S, Jasanoff (ed.), *The Outlook for Science and Technology Studies (sts): Report on an sts Symposium and Workshop* (Ithaca, NY: Cornell University): 23–34.

Gieryu, Thomas F. (1999) *Cultural Boundaries of Science: Credibility on the Line* (Chicago, IL: University of Chicago Press),

Gieryu, Thomas F. (2006) 'City as Truth-spot: Laboratories and Field-sites in Urban Studies', *Social Studies of Science* 36(1); 5–38.

Hacking, Ian (1983) *Representing and Intervening: Introductory Topics in the Philosophy of Natural Science* (Cambridge: Cambridge University Press).

Hadlaw, Janin (2003) 'The London Underground Map: Imagining Modern Time and Space', *Design Issues* 19(1): 25–35.

Halliday, Stephen (2001) *Underground to Everywhere: London's Underground Railway in the Life of the Capital* (London: Sutton Publishing, London Transport Museum).

Harley, John Brian (1988) 'Maps, Knowledge and Power') in D. Cosgrove & S. Daniels (eds.), *The Iconography of Landscape: Essays on the Symbolic Representation, Design, and Use of Past Environments* (Cambridge: Cambridge University Press): 277–312.

Heath, Christian & Jon Hindmarsh (2000) 'Configuring Action in Objects: From Mutual Space to Media Space', *Mind, Culture and Activity* 7: 81–104.

Hindmarsh, Jon & Christian Heath (2000) 'Embodied Reference: a Study of Deixis in Workspace Interaction', *Journal of Pragmatics* 32(12); 1855–78.

Hommels, Anique (2005) *Unbuilding Cities* (Boston, MA: MIT Press).

Hughes, Thomas P. (1987) 'The Evolution of Large Technological Systems', in W. Bijker, T. Hughes & T, Pinch (eds.), *The Social Construction of Technological Systems* (Cambridge, MA: MIT Press): 51–82.

Johns, Adrian (1998) *The Nature of the Book* (Chicago, IL: Chicago University Press).

Kitchen, Rob & Scott M. Freundschuh (eds) (2000) *Cognitive Mapping: Past, Present and Future* (New York: Routledge).

Knorr-Cetina, Karin & Klaus Amann (1990) 'Image Dissection in Natural Scientific Inquiry', *Science,*

Technology, & Human Values 15(3): 259–83.

Latour, Bruno (1986) 'Visualization and Cognition: Thinking with Eyes and Hands', *Knowledge and Society* 6: 1–40.

Latour, Bruno (1987) *Science in Action: How to Follow Scientists and Engineers through Society* (Cambridge, MA: Harvard University Press),

Latour, Bruno (1990 [1986]) 'Drawing Things Together', in M. Lynch & S. Woolgar (eds), *Representation in Scientific Practice* (Cambridge, MA: MIT Press): 19–68.

Latour, Bruno (1996) *Aramis, or the Love of Technology* (Cambridge, MA; Harvard University Press).

Latour, Bruno & Emilie Hermant (1998) *Paris: Ville Invisible* (Paris: La Decouverte). Virtual text available in multiple languages at www.ensmp.fr/-latour/virtual/index.html.

Law, John (1987) 'Technology and Heterogeneous Engineering: The Case of Portuguese Expansion', in W. Bijker, T, Hughes & T. Pinch (eds.), *The Social Construction of Technological Systems* (Cambridge, MA: MIT Press); 111–34.

Law, John & Peter Lodge (1984) *Science for Social Scientists* (London: MacMillan Press),

Leboff, David (1985) *The London Underground Map*. MSc Thesis, Oxford Polytechnic.

Leboff, David & Timothy Demuth (1999) *No Need To Ask! Early Maps of London's Underground Railways* (Middlesex: Capital Transport Publishing).

London Underground Limited (1993) *London Underground Journey Planner and Line Diagram Standards*, internal report (London: London Underground Limited).

London Underground Limited (1997) *Tube Guide Research: Qualitative Stage*, internal report (London: Business & Market Research Limited).

London Underground Limited (2004) *'Unlocking London': Advertising Research Dip 4 Report of Findings*, internal report (London: Synovate Research).

Luff, Paul & Christian Heath (2000) 'The Collaborative Production of Computer Commands in Command and Control', *International Journal of Human–Computer Studies* 52 (4): 669–99.

Lynch, Kevin (1960) *The Image of the City* (Cambridge, MA: MIT Press).

Lynch, Michael (1990) 'The Externalized Retina: Selection and Mathematization in the Visual Documentation of Objects in the Life Sciences', in M. Lynch & S. Woolgar (eds), *Representation and Scientific Practice* (Cambridge, MA; MIT Press); 153–86.

Lynch, Michael (1994) 'Representation is Overrated; Some Critical Remarks about the Use of the Concept of Representation in Science Studies', *Configurations* 2(1): 137–49.

Lynch, Michael & John Law (1999) 'Pictures, Texts and Objects; The Literary Language Game of Birdwatching', in M, Biagioli (ed.), *The Science Studies Reader* (London: Routledge): 317–41.

Mol, Annemarie (2003) *The Body Multiple: Ontology in Medical Practice* (Durham, NC: Duke University Press).

Mol, Annemarie & John Law (1994) 'Regions, Networks, and Fluids: Anaemia and Social Topology', *Social Studies of Science* 24(4): 641–71.

Moss, Paul (1996) *Train Interior Design Guidelines*, A.D. Consultants for London Underground Limited (London: London Underground Limited).

Mullet, Kevin & Darrell Sano (1995) *Designing Visual Interfaces: Communication Oriented Techniques* (New Jersey: Prentice Hall).

Pinch, Trevor & Nellie Oudshoorn (eds.) (2003) *How Users Matter* (Cambridge, MA: MIT Press).

Psathas, George (1991) 'The Structure of Direction-giving in Interaction', in D. Boden & D.H. Zimmerman (eds), *Talk and Social Structure: Studies in Ethnomethodology and Conversation Analysis* (Berkeley, CA: University of California Press): 195–216.

Rattner, Helen (2003) *All You Ever Wanted to Know about Customer's View on Customer Information*, internal marketing and planning report, July 2003 (London: London Underground Limited).

Roberts, Maxwell J. (2005) *Underground Maps After Beck* (Harrow Weald: Capital Transport).

Roberts, Maxwell J. (2007) *Henry Beck Rules, Not Okay? Breaking the Rules of Diagrammatic Map Design*. Unpublished manuscript, Department of Psychology, University of Essex.

Rudwick, Martin (1976) 'The Emergence of a Visual Language for Geological Science 1760–1840', *History of Science* 14: 149–95.

Schivelbusch, Wolfgang (1986) *The Railway Journey: The Industrialization of Time and Space in the 19th Century* (Berkeley, CA: University of California Press).

Shapin, Steven (1984) 'Pump and Circumstance; Robert Boyle's Literary Technology', *Social Studies of Science* 14: 481–520.

Shapin Steven & Simon Schaffer (1985) *Leviathan and the Air Pump: Hobbes, Boyle and the Experimental Life* (Princeton, NJ: Princeton University Press).

Thrift, Nigel (2004) 'Driving in the City', *Theory, Culture and Society* 21(4): 41–59.

Turkel, Sherry (ed.) (2007) *Evocative Objects: Things We Think With* (Cambridge, MA: MIT Press).

Turnbull, David (1996) 'Cartography and Science in Early Modern Europe: Mapping the Construction of Knowledge Spaces', *Imago Mundi* 48: 5–24.

Turnbull, David (2006) 'Templates and Maps in Learning to See: Chartres Cathedral and the London Underground as Examples of Performing

Design', in Cristina Grasseni (ed.), *Skilled Visions: Between Apprenticeship and Standards* (New York: Berg Press): 125–44.

Wittgenstein, Ludwig (1958) *Philosophical Investigations* (G.E.M. Anscombe, trans.) (Oxford: Basil Blackwell).

Wood, Denis (1992) *The Power of Maps* (London, Guilford Press).

Wyatt, Sally (2003) 'Non-Users Also Matter: The Construction of Users and Non-Users of the Internet', in T. Pinch & N. Oudshoorn (eds), *How Users Matter* (Cambridge, MA: MIT Press): 67–79.

13

POWELL'S POINT: DENIAL AND DECEPTION AT THE UN

JONATHAN FINN

In the opening minutes of his presentation to the United Nations Security Council on 5 February 2003, Colin Powell spoke directly to the collective vision of Security Council members: 'What you will see is an accumulation of facts and disturbing patterns of behavior,' Powell claimed, adding, 'Indeed, the facts and Iraq's behavior show that Saddam Hussein and his regime are concealing their efforts to produce more weapons of mass destruction.'[1] The purpose of Powell's speech was to convince Security Council members that Iraq was in violation of that Council's Resolution 1441 and that it was in possession of and continuing to develop weapons of mass destruction. What

was to be a spectacular display of imagery from the world's leading super-power turned out to be a weak and discontinuous PowerPoint slide show.

Studies of opinion and editorial columns in major US newspapers following Powell's presentation found increasing public support for war with Iraq (Jurkowitz, 2003). In contrast to the public's positive reaction to the presentation, Security Council members remained divided on the convincingness of Powell's evidence (Preston, 2003; Weisman, 2003). In the months following the presentation it became clear that the evidence presented was faulty, based on poor intelligence and that only evidence that favoured a war with Iraq was presented. Powell himself was suspicious enough of the supposed evidence that he ordered a secret review of the intelligence and information documented in the speech prior to his 5 February delivery (Goldenberg et al., 2003). More recently, Powell has referred to the speech as 'painful' and as something that will leave a permanent stain on his record as a member of the United States Administration (Weisman, 2005).

The success or failure of Powell's speech depended in large part on the presentation of visual evidence. In this way, the images used in the 5 February presentation were not simply illustrations of Powell's point, they were his point: they were to stand as irrefutable visual evidence of Iraq's failure to comply with Resolution 1441. Because of its unique reliance on images, Powell's speech is particularly fertile ground for an investigation of images as visual communication. Rather than analyze the presentation through its political, economic or ideological underpinnings I want to confine the focus to the use of visual representation in the PowerPoint slides. I borrow from Goodwin's (1994) theory of professional vision to argue that Powell's presentation failed to develop a shared vision of the material presented. I argue that a central flaw of the presentation in this regard was the conflation of different forms of visual representation. Satellite photographs, transcripts of intercepted conversations, and file photographs were presented as synonymous forms of visual evidence. As a result, the dozens of images that were to prove Iraq's non-compliance appeared instead as a random collection of visual material.

PROFESSIONAL VISION

Goodwin's essay problematizes the understanding of seeing or vision as an inherent, natural phenomenon. He identifies professional vision as 'socially organized ways of seeing and understanding events that are answerable to the distinctive interests of a particular social group' (p. 606). For Goodwin, archaeologists, chemists, geologists, lawyers, psychologists, and any other professionals learn to see through discipline-specific practices. What one sees as a member of

a specific group or participant in a given activity is determined through the interrelation of pre-existing disciplinary practices and the context in which viewing takes place. He writes: 'an event being seen, a relevant *object of knowledge*, emerges through the interplay between a *domain of scrutiny* . . . and a set of *discursive practices* . . . being deployed within a *specific activity*' (p. 606, emphases in original).

Goodwin identifies three discursive practices which function in the construction of professional vision. First, coding refers to the translation of the natural environment into the specific language of a given group. Goodwin argues that it is within this stage that 'nature is transformed into culture' (p. 608). As an example he cites the Munsell colour chart used by archaeologists to classify and categorize soil. The second discursive practice—highlighting—establishes a figure/ground relationship and in so doing identifies specific features as salient within the larger field of observation. Pointing to, outlining, or marking an object in some way exemplifies the act of highlighting. Finally, producing and articulating graphical representations serves as the third discursive practice and is self-explanatory. Importantly, the three discursive practices are not mutually exclusive, nor are they sequential; instead, coding, highlighting, and producing and articulating material representations continually interact in the construction of professional vision.

Given its specificity, Goodwin's theory lends itself to being represented diagrammatically. To this end, and for the purposes of this article, I want to propose a model for understanding and applying Goodwin's theory as in Figures 13.1 and 13.2. The former shows the model in its abstract form, while the latter identifies the three discursive practices. The purpose of representing Goodwin's theory visually is two-fold; first, it helps to further elucidate the theory, identify its constituent parts, and show their interrelations; second, as a model, Goodwin's theory is more easily adopted for use in examining other visual practices.

Goodwin addresses two very different practices to investigate the construction of professional vision: an archaeological dig and a legal trial. In the former, he performs an ethnographic study of a

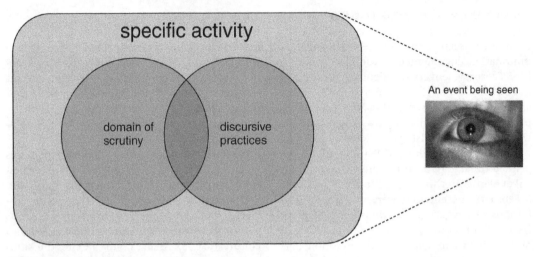

FIGURE 13.1 Goodwin's model (abstract)

particular dig. In this case, Ann, a professor, and Sue, her student, employ the discursive practices of coding, highlighting, and talk (articulation) in the production of a material representation in the form of a cross-section map of soil. Through this network of activity, Ann and Sue learn to see the same thing in the soil, thereby building their professional vision as archaeologists.

The majority of Goodwin's analysis is directed towards the trial *California v. Powell et al.*, in which four LAPD officers were accused of beating Rodney King. In this case, Goodwin illustrates the defence's success in convincing the jury to see with them—to see that the beating was not brutal and excessive but that it was the product of careful, systematic police work. Confident of the veridical power of the videotape, the prosecution chose to let the visual material speak for itself. By contrast, the defence meticulously deconstructed and reconstructed the videotape evidence. By

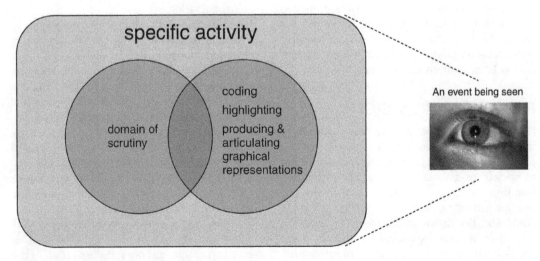

FIGURE 13.2 Goodwin's model (expanded)

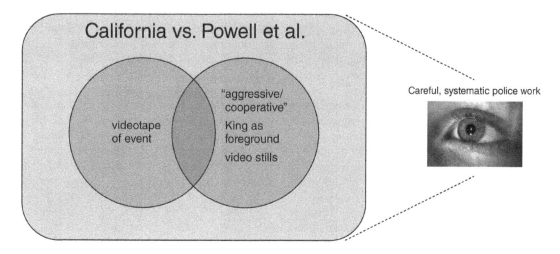

FIGURE 13.3 Juror's vision during *California v. Powell et al.*

highlighting King's body in video stills and employing coding schemes such as 'aggressive' and 'co-operative' to describe King's actions, the defence effectively turned the focus of jurors from the actions of the police officers to the movements of Rodney King. The effect was to position King as in control of his own actions, with officers simply responding to King's movements.

Figure 13.3 illustrates the construction of professional vision in *California v. Powell et al.* through recourse to Goodwin's model. Jurors' viewing of the videotape is mediated through the particular setting and a series of discursive practices employed by the defence. Rather than seeing for themselves (the prosecution's tactic), the defence effectively taught jurors to see what they and their numerous witnesses and experts saw: police officers performing a systematic and controlled attempt to subdue an aggressive and unco-operative suspect.

Goodwin's theory forms part of a growing and diverse literature on the construction of shared vision within specific disciplines or fields of practice. For example, Latour and Woolgar (1979) have analyzed the process within an endocrinology laboratory, Amann and Knorr-Cetina (1988) have examined the practice within DNA analysis, Cole (1998) within fingerprinting, Cregan (2004) within anatomy, and Harley (1989) and

Wood (2002) within cartography. Like Goodwin, these authors dispel the mythic notion of the distanced, objective professional as well as the assumption that images have inherent and fixed meaning. Rather, this work positions vision as something that is socially constructed and which is tied to the needs or mission of specific groups.

I want to stress that Goodwin's theory of professional vision and his analysis of *California v. Powell et al.* are particularly pertinent for addressing Powell's speech. Both the trial and Powell's speech were unidirectional modes of communication and both were heavily dependent on visual representation. As with the trial, Powell's presentation can be addressed as an attempt to achieve a shared understanding or vision of visual material. In both cases, coding, highlighting, and the production and articulation of material representations are deployed in a one-way communication process in an attempt to persuade a diverse audience. Whereas in the King case, the defence was successful in persuading the jury to see with them. Powell was ineffective in developing such a shared vision.

In analyzing *California v. Powell et al.*, Goodwin focused solely on the videotape evidence. In her essay 'The Eye of Everyman: Witnessing DNA in the Simpson Trial', Jasanoff (1998) points to a curious omission in Goodwin's analysis, namely the judge's role in determining the admissibility or inadmissibility of visual evidence and expert testimony in the trial. For Jasanoff, such determinations are essential in framing what can and cannot be seen by the jury. With specific emphasis on visual representation, we could extend Jasanoff's critique to note other omissions in Goodwin's article. Photographic enlargements of police reports, graphical reconstructions of the car chase preceding Mr King's beating, and live demonstrations of police use of force were all offered as visual evidence alongside the videotape but were not addressed by Goodwin. A complete understanding of the defence's success in building a shared vision in the trial should account for the entire visual program.

As with *California v. Powell et al.*, Colin Powell's UN speech could also be analyzed for its complete visual program. Such an analysis would include not just the PowerPoint slides but other modes of visual representation including the particular positioning and size of the projection screen, Powell's live demonstration of a vial during his discussion of chemical warfare as well as alterations made to the material environment, notably the decision to cover up a copy of Picasso's famous anti-war painting, 'Guernica', which hangs in front of the Security Council chambers (Dowd, 2003; Walsh, 2003).

Analyses of the complete visual programs in *California v. Powell et al.* and Powell's presentation would undoubtedly produce multiple sites for fruitful discussion; however, such analyses are well beyond the scope of a single paper. The respective foci of Goodwin's account and that of the present discussion are understandable and justifiable given the primacy of the videotape in the trial and of the slideshow. The specific focus of the latter is further justified given that no experts, laypersons, professionals, or any other body was called to speak on behalf of the evidence. As noted in the introduction to this article, Powell's slides were not supplements to his point, they were his point.

THE EFFECTIVE USE OF IMAGES

To foreground what I want to argue was a central flaw in Powell's presentation, I first address his most compelling and effective use of imagery, namely the series of aerial satellite images. Nine satellite images were used to offer proof that Iraq was producing and storing extensive chemical and biological munitions and that they were evading the mandated UN inspections. The images combine the seeming objectivity of unmediated mechanical observation with coding and highlighting to produce an effective visual demonstration. A close examination of the first two satellite photographs used is sufficient to identify the strength of these images in Powell's presentation.

Before projecting the first of the satellite images, Powell offered the following disclaimer:

> Let me say a word about satellite images before I show a couple. The photos that I am about to show you are sometimes hard for the average person to interpret, hard for me. The painstaking work of photo analysis takes experts with years and years of experience, poring for hours and hours over light tables. But as I show you these images, I will try to capture and explain what they mean, what they indicate to our imagery specialists.

He then went on to explain slides 12 and 13 (represented here in Figures 13.4 and 13.5).

> Let's look at one. This one [slide 12] is about a weapons munition facility, a facility that holds ammunition at a place called Taji (ph) . . .
> Here, you see 15 munitions bunkers in yellow and red outlines. The four that are in red squares represent active chemical munitions bunkers.
> How do I know that? How can I say that? Let me give you a closer look.
> Look at the image on the left [slide 13].
> On the left is a close-up of one of the four chemical bunkers. The two arrows indicate the presence of sure signs that the bunkers are storing chemical munitions. The arrow at the top that says 'Security' points to a facility that is the signature item for this kind of bunker . . . .
> The truck you also see is a signature item. It's a decontamination vehicle in case something goes wrong. . .

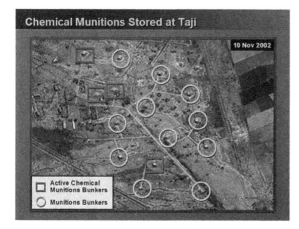 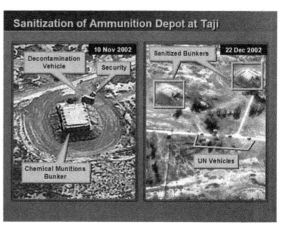

FIGURES 13.4, 13.5 Slides 12 (left) and 13 (right) of Powell's presentation

Now look at the picture on the right [slide 13]. You are now looking at two of those sanitized bunkers. The signature vehicles are gone, the tents are gone, it's been cleaned up, and it was done on the 22nd of December, as the UN inspection team is arriving, and you can see the inspection vehicles arriving in the lower portion of the picture on the right.

The bunkers are clean when the inspectors get there. They found nothing.

As with any specialized imaging practices, satellite images necessitate some form of human translation or articulation; this is made clear in Powell's disclaimer to the satellite imagery. In his articulation of slides 12 and 13, Powell employs coding schemes to translate the generic visual information of satellite images into a representation of Iraq's non-compliance with Resolution 1441. What are architectural structures, vehicles, and pathways to the naked eye become *munitions bunkers*, *weapons munitions facilities*, and *decontamination* and *UN inspection vehicles*. Importantly, Powell's use of terminology serves a second function: It not only translates nature into culture but also provides a necessary temporal component to the images. Bunkers are described as *active* and others as *sanitized*, thus translating these static images into representations of an active program of *denial and deception*, itself a coding scheme used in the presentation.

The formal features of the images complement the language used by Powell and employ highlighting to reinforce the issue at hand. The surrounding blue frame of each slide links the two slides and serves to foreground the black and white satellite photographs. Circles, squares, and directional text boxes identify the salient features of the visual field. As with Powell's coding schemes, the practices of highlighting also perform a secondary, more symbolic function through the particular use of colour. The use of red in slide 12 underscores the urgency of the perceived threat posed by 'active' bunkers and the use of yellow offers a cautionary tone for the presumably inactive bunkers. In total, the compositions are clear and uncluttered. There is no extraneous information or 'chart junk' to use Tufte's (1997: 26) term; instead, the use of legends and labels is economical, marking only the relevant information in the pictures: munitions bunkers, decontamination vehicles and UN inspection vehicles.

As with the oral part of the presentation, the representation of time is of central importance in the images. Slide 12 shows numerous munitions bunkers in a photograph that is dated 10 November 2002. This same date reappears in the left image of slide 13, reinforcing Powell's verbal claim that this is a close-up of one of the bunkers depicted in the previous slide. The date of 22 December 2002 in the right photograph of slide 13

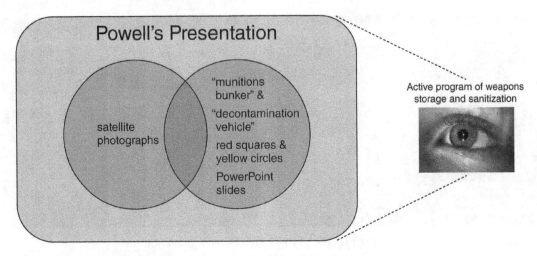

FIGURE 13.6 The construction of shared vision of satellite imagery

makes the necessary temporal link between the storage of munitions and their sanitization. The titles of the slides perform a similar function, uniting the two slides by location (Taji) while emphasizing their difference over time (storage to sanitization). Finally, the highlighting of UN inspection vehicles in slide 13 further reinforces the point—the sanitization of munitions bunkers in advance of UN weapons inspectors.

Practices of coding and highlighting are present throughout Powell's presentation although nowhere more effectively than with the use of satellite imagery. These images and their corresponding articulation by Powell conform neatly to Goodwin's model of professional vision (Figure 13.6). Coding ('munitions bunker' and 'decontamination vehicle'), highlighting (red squares and yellow circles), and talk come together in these images to guide the viewer through a shared understanding of their content. UN Security Council members are encouraged to see what Powell purports to see in the images: an active program of weapons storage and their sanitization in advance of inspections.

THE INEFFECTIVE USE OF IMAGES

In contrast to the effective use of satellite imagery, the majority of Powell's images were treated with much less careful attention. This is exemplified in Figures 13.7 and 13.8, which shows slides 11 and 31 of the presentation. In contrast to the careful coding, highlighting, and articulation of the satellite images, these are offered as generic representations of a person and a metallic tube. The title of slide 11, 'Documents Found in Home of Iraqi Scientist', raises more questions than it answers: Are these the documents that were taken from the home of the Iraqi scientist? Is this a representation of the documents being removed? Is this the Iraqi scientist? And what is the significance of the Reuters credit in the bottom right corner of the image? Powell's articulation of this image answers some but not all of the questions:

> Thanks to intelligence they were provided, the inspectors recently found dramatic confirmation of these reports. When they searched the home of an Iraqi nuclear scientist, they uncovered roughly 2,000 pages of documents. You see them here being brought out of the home and placed in UN hands. Some of the material is classified and related to Iraq's nuclear program.

Powell's comments point specifically to the image and seek to identify it as a representation of documents being removed from the scientist's home. However, the lack of reference to a specific

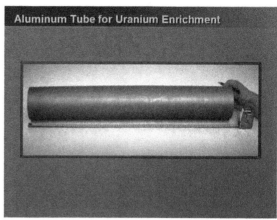

Documents Found in Home of Iraqi Scientist

Aluminum Tube for Uranium Enrichment

FIGURES 13.7, 13.8 Slides 11 (left) and 31 (right) of Powell's presentation

document, a specific house, a specific scientist or UN inspector severely detracts from the evidentiary weight of the image. The fallibility of the claims being made through slide 11 and its articulation are further complicated by the Reuters credit in the lower right corner of the image. Why, in a presentation rich with claims to confidentiality and secrecy, is a key piece of visual evidence taken from a popular news photo agency?

Slide 31 is prone to the same errors as described earlier and commits the additional error of letting the image speak for itself. The title of the slide, 'Aluminum Tube for Uranium Enrichment', attempts to identify both the item shown and its eventual use. However, Powell's corresponding talk addresses neither of these features and is worth citing in its entirety:

> Saddam Hussein is determined to get his hands on a nuclear bomb. He is so determined that he has made repeated covert attempts to acquire high-specification aluminum tubes from 11 different countries, even after inspections resumed.
>
> These tubes are controlled by the Nuclear Suppliers Group precisely because they can be used as centrifuges for enriching uranium. By now, just about everyone has heard of these tubes, and we all know that there are differences of opinion. There is controversy about what these tubes are for.

Most US experts think they are intended to serve as rotors in centrifuges used to enrich uranium. Other experts, and the Iraqis themselves, argue that they are really to produce the rocket bodies for a conventional weapon, a multiple rocket launcher.

> Let me tell you what is not controversial about these tubes. First, all the experts who have analyzed the tubes in our possession agree that they can be adapted for centrifuge use. Second, Iraq had no business buying them for any purpose. They are banned for Iraq. I am no expert on centrifuge tubes, but just as an old Army trooper, I can tell you a couple of things: first, it strikes me as quite odd that these tubes are manufactured to a tolerance that far exceeds US requirements for comparable rockets.
>
> Maybe Iraqis just manufacture their conventional weapons to a higher standard than we do, but I don't think so.[2]

Nowhere in this discussion is the slide specifically addressed. In the absence of any specific articulation, the image is left to speak for itself and its interpretation is left to Security Council members. As with slide 11, the image and its corresponding talk raise more questions than they answer. Is this an aluminum tube? Where is it? Who took the photograph, when and why? What US experts? What other experts? Who were the experts that examined the tubes? And, most

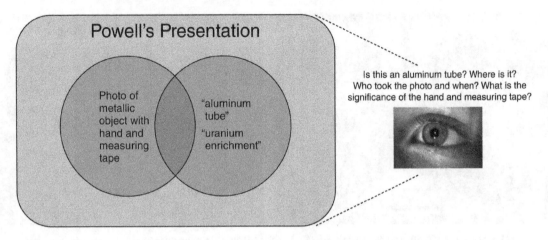

FIGURE 13.9 Powell's slide 31 through Goodwin's model. Rather than building a shared vision, the poor coding and lack of highlighting and talk raise a series of questions about the image.

curiously, why the inclusion of a hand holding a pencil and a measuring tape in the image?

The lack of careful attention in these images as well as in their articulation detracts from their value as evidentiary statements. To return to Goodwin's model, these images do not bring together coding, highlighting, and articulation in an attempt to achieve shared vision. Figure 13.8 illustrates the point. The title of the slide attempts to code the image as an aluminum tube that is used in the process of uranium enrichment. However, such coding schemes are not reinforced or substantiated through highlighting or articulation. The inclusion of the hand and measuring tape only complicates the matter. These elements suggest that the length of the tube is of primary importance, a fact that is not addressed in the presentation and is indeed irrelevant to the discussion. In sum, where the satellite images were presented in conjunction with relevant coding schemes, practices of highlighting and articulation, the image of the metallic tube and that of the man with paper are left to speak for themselves and what they have to say is decidedly unclear.

The lack of specificity in slides 11 and 31 exemplifies a recurring problem in the presentation: a failure to ground or substantiate the claims being made in the speech and supposedly represented in

the imagery projected on the screen. As Goodwin (1994) identifies, a central part of the defence's success in the Rodney King trial was their employment of legally sanctioned experts to speak on behalf of the videotape evidence. In this way, jurors were asked not to believe the words of the defendants or the lawyers arguing the case but to believe those of experts, with all the claims to objectivity and impartiality that that title brings. No such experts were called upon in Powell's speech, a fact which might be explained by the particular confines of the venue (a UN speech). However, expert authority is not even named in Powell's speech; instead, he continually defers to an abstract category of 'human sources'. Consider the following five appeals to authority:

1. 'My colleagues, every statement I make today is backed up by sources, solid sources. These are not assertions. What we're giving you are facts and conclusions based on solid intelligence. I will cite some examples, and these are from human sources.'

2. 'Numerous human sources tell us that the Iraqis are moving, not just documents and hard drives, but weapons of mass destruction to keep them from being found by inspectors.'

3. 'Let me just tell you what a number of human sources have told us.'

4. 'Ladies and gentlemen, these are not assertions. These are facts corroborated by human sources, some of them sources of the intelligence services of other countries.'

5. 'What we know comes largely from intercepted communications and human sources who are in a position to know the facts.'

These five passages are indicative of a failure to substantiate the evidentiary claims being made that is pervasive in Powell's presentation. Without grounding in a relevant expert community, satellite imagery, intercepted telephone conversations, and computer-generated graphics are left to speak for themselves. Had Powell been able to identity or even call upon specific individuals, the information collected from non-human sources could have been corroborated and further explained. Returning to slide 31 of the presentation (Figure 13.8), Powell refers to 'experts' three times without citing or calling on an actual, identified expert to reinforce his point. This lack of support is exacerbated by Powell's own admission that he himself is not an expert in centrifuge tubes. With no one to identify or articulate slide 31, the net effect of this continued deferral to an unnamed expert community is to leave the image to speak for itself. Even the satellite images, which I have argued were the most effective, were produced and interpreted by unidentified 'image experts'. Like the prosecution in *California v. Powell et al.*, Powell's presentation let the images speak for themselves, a tactic which raised more questions than it answered.

VISUAL EVIDENCE AND THE 'FUNCTIONAL ADEQUACY' OF IMAGES

The preceding two sections show the extent to which Goodwin's model of professional vision is useful in addressing the effective or ineffective use of individual images. In this sense, individual slides of Powell's presentation can be positioned as distinct domains of scrutiny within which the discursive practices of coding, highlighting, and talk are deployed. Despite its effectiveness in this regard, to address the individual satellite images or any other specific images as discrete entities ignores their participation as part of a sequence within a larger program of visual communication. Similarly, to treat the different types of imagery offered as an aggregate category or single domain of scrutiny would be to ignore key differences between media and modes of representation.

In examining *California v. Powell et al.*, Goodwin emphasizes the transformation of the videotape as a single, continuous document, to its dissection into a series of still images. As he identifies, the still images and video shown in the trial have important temporal and material differences which necessarily impact the communication process. On the transformation between moving and still images he writes:

Movement through time becomes movement through space, that is, the left-to-right progression of the cropped frames. Each image remains available to the viewer instead of disappearing when its successor arrives, so that both the sequence as a whole and each event within it can be contemplated and rescanned at leisure. (p. 622)

As Goodwin rightly notes, the still images enabled the defence to quite literally highlight Rodney King's body, bringing him to the foreground, simultaneously pushing the actions of the officers (the actual subject of the trial) into the background. The static, material nature of the photographic stills allowed the defence to construct a reading of the videotape that was not possible with the continuous stream of the videotape.[3]

As a visual artifact, Powell's slideshow is considerably more complex than the videotape in *California v. Powell et al.* Despite the unique features of the videotape and still photographs in the trial, these modes of representation share the same source, subject and content. Both the video and still images are mechanical forms of representation and, as its products, the still images remain inextricably bound to the videotape. The same cannot be said of the imagery used in Powell's presentation. Powell's slideshow is a highly complex visual artifact, one that is composed of a series of disparate images that differ in important ways, both in terms of form and content. The presentation included multiple forms of visual representation such as still photographs, video, maps, computer-generated illustrations, and text. Just as the differences between still images and videotape were a factor in *California v. Powell et al.*, so too do the multiple modes of visual representation in Powell's slides impact on the message being communicated.

In 'The Photographic Message', Barthes (1977 [1961]) notes that the meaning or connotation of an individual image is altered when that image is presented as part of a sequence. He writes: 'the signifier of connotation is then no longer to be found at the level of anyone of the fragments of the sequence but at that . . . of the concatenation' (p. 24). Following Barthes, the interpretation of any one image in Powell's presentation is necessarily impacted by the interpretation of other images and of the sequence as a whole. And it is precisely at the level of the concatenation that Powell's presentation fails most significantly. With the possible exception of the satellite images, Powell's presentation failed to address or acknowledge the differences between modes of representation. Excerpts from manuscripts and transcribed conversations were presented in sequence with computer-generated simulations, file photographs, and maps as synonymous forms of visual evidence.

Conflating photographs, drawings, maps, and images of text as an aggregate category of visual evidence denies the unique properties of a given medium, including the particular circumstances of their production and reception as well as their cultural status as modes of representation. Work in the field of medium theory, notably that of Innis (1950, (1951) and McLuhan (1977[1964]), emphasizes the extent to which any given medium has unique properties and idiosyncrasies which influence the process of communication. As this work shows, the content of a message cannot be separated from the medium of its transmission. And so it is with Powell's presentation: the message being communicated through the slides is influenced both by the medium and format of the presentation (light, electricity, and Power-Point) and the various media used in the individual slides. A comprehensive account of Powell's presentation would necessarily address both form and content as well as multiple other 'semiotic resources' (Goodwin, 2000) such as talk, gesture, expression, and body movement. Here I am primarily concerned with the differences between modes of visual representation used in the Power-Point slides.

Photographs, drawings, maps, charts, video, and computer-generated imagery all have properties—formal and cultural—which distinguish them from each other and from other modes of visual representation. Formally, technical capabilities and compositional properties such as resolution, focus, perspective, colour, and contrast contribute to the message being conveyed. Culturally, any given medium carries with it certain values that have been ascribed to it across time and these necessarily influence the interpretation of messages conveyed through that medium.

Photographic representation provides an effective example of the intersection of a medium's formal and cultural attributes and their impact on the communication process. On a formal level, the verisimilitude of photographs is unparalleled by other modes of representation: the camera provides uniform, consistent, high-resolution images. However, the camera can only capture a limited visual field and is restricted to a singular perspective (Crary, 1990; Mitchell, 1992). Culturally, the photomechanical image has a privileged history of use as being associated with truth and objectivity (Barthes, 1981; Batchen, 1997[1990]; Sekula, 1986; Tagg, 1988; Trachtenberg, 1980). The photograph's chemical and mechanical basis was often taken as proof of its documentary capability by a myriad of artistic, social-scientific and scientific practices during the nineteenth and twentieth centuries. Combined, these formal and cultural attributes contribute to the photograph's unique claims to veracity.

I do not want to privilege the mechanical over non-mechanical forms of representation, nor to claim that certain forms of representation are inherently more objective than others. The work of Batchen (1997 [1990]), Mnookin (1998), Daston and Galison (1992), and Galison (1998) has done much to dispel this belief. As this work rightly notes, the veracity, accuracy, or truthfulness of a given image is produced through a confluence of forces, including the context of use, its formal and technical properties, and its cultural status, including its histories of use. Similarly, I do not want to suggest that the particular properties of a given medium predetermine its use or interpretation. This is exemplified in *California v. Powell et al.* where a seemingly objective, unedited videotape was translated into a highly specialized visual artifact that required expert interpretation. Rather, I stress that individual media carry unique formal and cultural attributes and that such attributes function as key variables in the communication process.

Powell's presentation included 45 slides that are represented here in Figure 13.10. The slides can be classified as follows:

- 9 title slides
- 9 depicting transcripts of intercepted conversations
- 9 satellite photographs of various locations in Iraq
- 4 organizational charts, including mugshots
- 3 computer-generated images depicting mobile production facilities for biological agents
- 2 maps
- 1 text excerpt from United Nations Security Council Resolution 1441
- 1 video clip of an Iraqi F-I Mirage Jet during a test flight
- 7 still photographs documenting the following:
  - the declaration documents presented to the UN from Iraq
  - an individual removing documents from the home of an Iraqi scientist
  - a UN reconnaissance plane
  - 122-mm chemical warheads found by UN inspectors
  - an aluminum tube

- crates of aluminum tubes
- an unmanned aerial vehicle (UAV)

The images presented to the Security Council differed in important ways both in terms of their formal characteristics and in their cultural status as modes of representation. Highly verisimilar images were contrasted by more symbolic representations, machine-made images contrasted with human-made, colour with black and white, and static with dynamic.

Photographs are inherently different from maps, which are different from computer-generated images, which are different from video. The particular impact of these differences will vary depending on the particular setting in which they are deployed—what Goodwin (2000), in a subsequent essay, refers to as the 'contextual configuration'. Nonetheless, to successfully employ different modes of visual representation in an act of communication, one must be open to these differences and cognizant of their impact on the communication process. This is what the defence in *California v. Powell et al.* was able to seize upon and what was largely ignored in Colin Powell's presentation. Figures 13.11 and 13.12 exemplify the problem of the latter.

Understanding the content of a satellite image requires acceptance only of the coding schemes applied by Powell (Figure 13.11). The verisimilitude of the photographic image and its legacy of objectivity lend significant evidentiary weight to the satellite image. The image establishes a sense of *having-been-there* (Barthes, 1977[1964]) or the *this-has-been* (Barthes, 1981), which other forms of representation cannot. As a result, we do not question that there are buildings, vehicles, and pathways in the image, only that these are munitions bunkers and decontamination vehicles and that this is a specific location in Iraq.

By contrast, understanding a computer-generated image of a truck or rail car (Figure 13.12) as a mobile production facility for biological agents requires acceptance of the coding schemes provided but also that this is a representation of an actual truck and rail car. In other words, the computer-generated image does not convey the *having-been-there* of the satellite images or the other

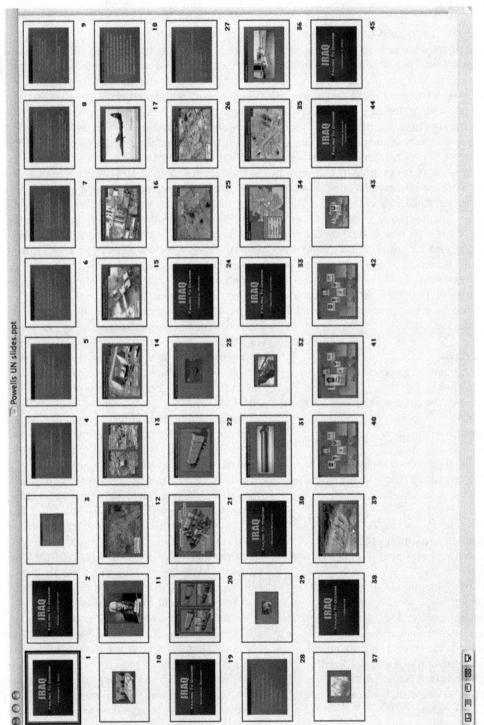

FIGURE 13.10 Powell's 45 slides

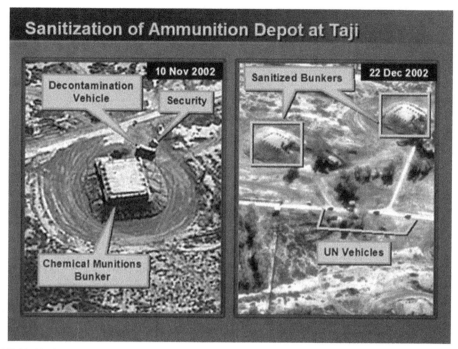

FIGURE 13.11 Slide 13 of Powell's presentation

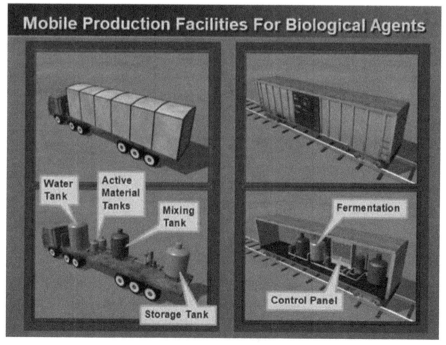

FIGURE 13.12 Slide 20 of Powell's presentation

photographs used in the presentation. There is a further level of mediation at work in the image which is not addressed in the oral presentation. Powell acknowledges that these were drawn according to the descriptions of 'human sources' on the ground; however, no such source is ever called upon or identified. Rather, viewers are simply asked to defer to an abstract, unnamed source, to accept that this type of truck and rail car exist, and that this is an accurate representation of such vehicles.

The lack of evidentiary weight in slide 20 (Figure 13.12) is further jeopardized through its particular display. Given its overtly manufactured nature, the information presented in the slide requires some form of grounding and evidentiary support. As already noted, this was absent in the oral presentation. Importantly, it was also absent visually. Slide 20 would have been much more effective had it been presented in conjunction with a photomechanical image documenting an actual truck and rail car. Appropriate coding and highlighting could then locate the images within a visual argument about the production of biological weapons in Iraq. Instead, slide 20 was presented as part of a five-slide sequence on biological weapons which included a title slide (slide 19), two slides of computer-generated images similar to that in slide 20 (slides 21 and 22) and an isolated photograph of an airplane (slide 23). These images were not presented as part of an argument in conjunction with careful practices of coding, highlighting, and talk; rather, they were offered up as abstract, unsubstantiated, and unarticulated pictures.

Presenting a computer-generated image alongside a photomechanical image would seize on the unique powers of each: the ability of the former to isolate, mark, and identify features in a noiseless visual field and the latter's cultural status as an objective mode of representation. Presented together, the images would support each other in a manner similar to that described by Lynch (1990 [1988]) in 'The Externalized Retina'. In his discussion of split-screen displays of biological specimens, Lynch notes that when the oversimplified image of the diagram is presented alongside the 'raw' photomechanical image, the two representations support one another in a convincing visual display.[4] Within such a

context, the diagram appears less as a subjective illustration and more as an enhanced and in some ways more accurate version of the data captured by the camera. Had Powell recognized and seized upon the differences between photographs and computer-generated images, he would have been able to produce a visual sequence whose evidentiary weight is greater than that of its parts.

In his book *The Reconfigured Eye: Visual Truth in the Post-Photographic Era* (1992), Mitchell offers an insightful method for addressing images, one that is useful in analyzing Powell's presentation but also in examining visual communication as a whole. As the title implies, Mitchell's book addresses the topic of visual representation in the wake of digital imagery and the then purported 'death of photography'. What emerges from Mitchell's text is an emphasis on the function of the image, its unique properties and its context of use. He writes: 'pictures—like other types of physical artifacts—must be fit for the particular uses to which they are put. They must have the properties that assure their functional adequacy' (p. 221). For Mitchell:

image-production processes make certain representational commitments: they record certain kinds of things and not others, and they record some kinds of things more completely and accurately than others. These representational commitments determine in a very obvious way the limits of a resulting images' potential uses in acts of communication. (p. 221)

This leads Mitchell to a key conclusion:

Just as you must understand the different uses afforded marshmallows and hammers if you want to perform physical tasks successfully, so you must distinguish between the varying functional capabilities of paintings and drawings, photographs, and digital images produced under various different circumstances in order to use these different types of images felicitously. (p. 223)

Mitchell's argument is particularly useful in that it points to the situatedness of interpretation and meaning-making practices and the mutable roles of images within such practices. Within such a framework, successful acts of visual communication bring together the formal and cultural attributes of a given image with the idiosyncrasies of the context in which it is being deployed, assuring its 'functional adequacy' to the task at hand. By contrast, unsuccessful acts of visual communication fail to address the unique features of medium and/or context. By not attending to such features and not recognizing the unique attributes of his images, Powell failed to assure their functional adequacy.

To reiterate, I do not want to privilege the photomechanical image or to suggest that computer-generated simulations, maps, and projections of text cannot function as effective visual evidence (Al Gore's use of imagery in *An Inconvenient Truth* provides an interesting counter-example to Powell's presentation in this regard).[5] Rather, my point is that to effectively use any image in an act of visual communication one must acknowledge the unique properties of the image and deploy the discursive practices of coding, highlighting, and articulation accordingly. Of the multiple variables at play in the communication process, this article has emphasized the importance of recognizing differences between modes of representation. This is not to deny differences within modes of representation (i.e. between one photograph and another) but to stress that computer-generated images, maps, photographs, and drawings have unique properties—formal and cultural—that function in the communication process. Understanding that photographs are different from computer-generated images which are different from drawings, would have enabled Powell to address and use each image more felicitously, to use Mitchell's word. In not accounting for the representational choices made, key questions were left unanswered: Why satellite imagery in one instance but not in another? Why a computer-generated image of a mobile production facility but a file photograph of a reconnaissance plane? Why a Reuters news agency photograph of a man holding documents but a United Nations Special Commission (UNSCOM) photograph of a UAV? By not fully recognizing and accounting for the

unique properties of his images, Powell's 45 slides appeared less as a coherent argument than as a weak and discontinuous PowerPoint slide show.

CONCLUSION

The purpose of Powell's presentation was to convince United Nations Security Council Members that Iraq was in violation of that Council's Resolution 1441. The images used in the presentation were not supplements to the verbal argument; rather, they were the argument. As an act of visual communication, Powell's presentation failed in that he was unable to convince Council members to see what he claimed to see in the images presented: he failed to construct a shared vision.

The point of this article is not to reconstruct the 5 February presentation in a more effective way or simply to lament the sloppy treatment of images on that day. Rather, I stress that the use of imagery in Powell's presentation serves as an instructive example to scholars of visual communication in at least three ways. First, it reiterates the central point highlighted in *California v. Powell et al.* that meaning and understanding are not inherent in images but are manufactured through discipline and context-specific practices. A key failure of Powell's in this regard was that he did not utilize and incorporate the images as part of his argument; instead, he often left the images to speak for themselves, a tactic which left their interpretation to the discretion of Security Council members. Second, the presentation illustrates that one's choices in visual representation—the decision to use a photograph, a drawing, a map or a computer-generated image—function as key variables in the communication process. As I have argued here, a central flaw in Powell's presentation was not taking account of and articulating the differences between modes of representation. Instead, Powell's slides presented maps, drawings, text excerpts, and satellite photographs as synonymous forms of visual representation. Powell's presentation is instructive in a third way in that it underscores the centrality of images in contemporary life and highlights their power to impact on the lives of individuals and groups. Although unsuccessful, it should not be forgotten that these

45 images were intended to garner UN support for a military campaign that has taken the lives of tens of thousands of individuals.

I want to conclude by suggesting another reason why Powell's presentation is particularly useful to scholars of visual communication, particularly as read through Goodwin's theory of professional vision. In *Visual Thinking* (1969), Arnheim argued the need for increased visual literacy and called for specialized training in the visual across the curriculum. For Arnheim, the visual was inextricably bound to thought and was therefore of central importance to life. This being the case, Arnheim lamented the trend of its critical study being largely confined to the Fine Arts. Over the past few decades, the visual has seen an increasing amount of attention—critical and otherwise—from academics, practitioners, and the private sector, a fact which suggests that an expanding array of citizens have heeded the importance of visual representation and visual communication in individual and social life. Within the academy, the continued development of college and university programs in visual communication, visual culture, and in cognate areas over the past two decades can be read as a promising response to Arnheim's call.

Nonetheless, and despite the increased attention being paid to the visual, I would argue that it is still largely under-examined and its importance under-acknowledged. Even within disciplines in which the visual features as primary subject area, images are too often used as supplements to the textual or oral argument being made. Our classrooms, conferences, journals, and other professional venues are increasingly mediated by images, yet within these spaces the image remains largely an accoutrement to the communication process. And it is here that Powell's presentation speaks most loudly. Both in its successes and failures, Powell's presentation highlights the need to be more critically aware of our own representational choices, particularly as we produce and articulate images in the construction of our own profession's vision.

NOTES

1. Powell's speech, including the slides, can be found at: http://www.whitehouse.gov/news/releasesI2003/02120030205-l.html. The site includes full audio of the speech and a transcript, which includes the images. This site served as the basis for the analysis presented here.

2. The start of the projection displaying the aluminum tube cannot be exactly determined from the videostream available. The image is removed and replaced by another when Powell begins his second of two personal comments on centrifuge tubes. Due to the length of the passage, I have included the breaks in the text as presented on the website.

3. In a subsequent essay, Goodwin (2000) offers a more elaborate and nuanced theory of human action and meaning making, taking into account multiple 'semiotic fields' and 'contexts of configuration'. His focus in 'Professional Vision' is decidedly less broad, attending to the specific discursive practices through which shared vision is achieved.

4. I am not suggesting that the photographic image is 'raw' and without its own mediations. Rather, and like Lynch, the point is that, relative to the computer-generated image, the photograph has an appearance of being more genuine, unedited and 'raw'.

5. It is worth noting that the presentation of visual evidence in *An Inconvenient Truth* may be no more 'accurate' than that of Powell's. My point here is that Gore used his images effectively and, as such, was able to build a convincing, even compelling argument.

REFERENCES

Amann, K. and Knorr Cetina, K. (1988) 'The Fixation of (Visual) Evidence', in Michael Lynch and Steve Woolgar (eds) *Representation in Scientific Practice*, pp. 85–121. Cambridge, MA: MIT Press.

Arnheim, Rudolf (1969) *Visual Thinking*. Berkeley: University of California Press.

Barthes, Roland (1977 [1961]) 'The Photographic Message', in *Image, Music, Text*, pp. 15–31, trans. Stephen Heath. New York: Hill and Wang.

Barthes, Roland (1977 [1964]) 'Rhetoric of the Image', in *Image, Music, Text*, trans. Stephen Heath, pp. 32–51. New York: Hill and Wang.

Barthes, Roland (1981) *Camera Lucida: Reflections on Photography*, trans. Richard Howard. New York: Hill and Wang.

Batchen, Geoffrey (1997[1990]) *Burning with Desire: The Conception of Photography*. Cambridge, MA: MIT Press.

California v. Powell et al.: What the Jury Saw (1992), Court TV, VHS recording.

Cole, Simon (1998) 'Witnessing Identification: Latent Fingerprint Evidence and Expert Knowledge', *Social Studies of Science* 28(5–6): 687–712.

Crary, Jonathan (1990) *Techniques of the Observer: On Vision and Modernity in the Nineteenth Century*. Cambridge, MA: MIT Press.

Cregan, Kate (2004) 'Blood and Circuses', in Elizabeth Klaver (ed.) *Images of the Corpse: From the Renaissance to Cyberspace*, pp. 39–62. Madison: University of Wisconsin Press.

Daston, Lorraine and Galison, Peter (1992) 'The Image of Objectivity', *Representations* 40: 81–128.

Dowd, Maureen (2003) 'Powell Without Picasso', *The New York Times*. URL (consulted 22 Sept 2008): http://query.nytimes.com/gstlfullpage.html ?res=9F02E2DB IF38F936A35751 COA9659C8B63.

Galison, Peter (1998) 'Judgment Against Objectivity', in Caroline A. Jones and Peter Galison (eds) *Picturing Science Producing Art*, pp. 327–59.London: Routledge.

Goldenberg, Suzanne, Norton-Taylor, Richard, and Heslop, Katy (2003) 'Weapons Row: Powell's Doubts over CIA Intelligence on Iraq Prompted Him to Set Up Secret Review: Specialists Removed Questionable Evidence about Weapons from Draft of Secretary of State's Speech to UN', *The Guardian*, 2 June: 3.

Goodwin, Charles (1994) 'Professional Vision', *American Anthropologist* 96(3): 606–33.

Goodwin, Charles (2000) 'Action and Embodiment within Situated Human Interaction', *Journal of Pragmatics* 32: 1489–522.

Harley, J.B. (1989) 'Deconstructing the Map', *Cartographica* 26(2): 1–20.

Innis, Harold (1950) *Empire and Communications*. Oxford: Clarendon Press.

Innis, Harold (1951) *The Bias of Communication*. Toronto: University of Toronto Press.

Jasanoff, Sheila (1998) 'The Eye of Everyman: Witnessing DNA in the Simpson Trial', *Social Studies of Science* 28(5–6): 713–40.

Jurkowitz, Mark (2003) 'The Media: Powell's UN Speech Proves Persuasive for Commentators', *The Boston Globe*, 13 February: B12.

Latour, Bruno and Woolgar, Steve (1979) *Laboratory Life: The Social Construction a/Scientific Facts*. Beverley Hills, CA: Sage.

Lynch, Michael (1990[1988]) 'The Externalized Retina: Selection and Mathematization in the Visual Documentation of Objects in the Life Sciences', in Michael Lynch and Steve Woolgar (eds) *Representation in Scientific Practice*, pp. 85–121. Cambridge, MA: MIT Press.

McLuhan, Marshall (1964) *Understanding Media: The Extensions of Man*, 2nd edn. New York: New American Library.

Mitchell, William J. (1992) *The Reconfigured Eye: Visual Truth in the Post Photographic Era*. Cambridge, MA: MIT Press.

Mnookin, Jennifer (1998) 'The Image of Truth: Photographic Evidence and the Power of Analogy', *Yale Journal of Law and the Humanities* 10(1): 1–74.

Preston, Julia (2003) 'Threats and Responses: Diplomacy; U.N. Envoys Said to Differ Sharply in Reaction to Powell Speech', *The New York Times*, 7 February: A10.

Sekula, Allan (1986) 'The Body and the Archive', *October* 39: 3–64.

Tagg, John (1988) *The Burden of Representation: Essays on Photographies and Histories*. Basingstoke: Macmillan.

Trachtenberg, Alan (ed.) (1980) *Classic Essays on Photography*. New Haven, CT: Leete's Island Books.

Tufte, Edward R. (1997) *Visual Explanations: Images and Quantities, Evidence and Narrative*. Cheshire, CT: Graphics Press.

Walsh, David (2003) 'UN Conceals Picasso's "Guernica" for Powell's Presentation', *World Socialist*, 8 February. URL (consulted 22 Sept. 2008): http://www.wsws.org/articles/2003/feb2003/guer-f08.5html

Weisman, Steven R. (2003) 'Threats and Responses: Security Council; Powell, in U.N. Speech, Presents Case to Show Iraq has not Disarmed', *The New York Times*, 6 February: A1.

Weisman, Steven R (2005) 'Powell Calls UN Speech a Blot on his Record', *The Globe and Mail*, 10 September.

Wood, Denis (2002) 'The Map as a Kind of Talk', *Visual Communication* 1(2): 139–61.

QUESTIONS FOR REFLECTION

1. Examine maps of your own university or college campus and your own city. How are these maps arguments about your campus and city? Beyond instructing how to get from point A to point B, what is the 'message' of these maps? How is that message conveyed (through line, shape, colour, scale, etc.)?

2. Following from Vertesi, draw your campus or city. How do your representations differ from those of others (professionals and lay-persons)? What do such differences suggest or reveal?

3. How do your own instructors and fellow students use images in presentations? Are they able to construct a shared vision? Do they employ different modes of representation and, if so, to what effect? Do they use their images 'felicitously'?

FURTHER READING

Hadlaw, Janin. 'The London Underground Map: Imagining Modern Time and Space'. *Design Issues* 19.1 (Winter 2003): 25–35.

Jacobson, Robert, Ed. *Information Design*. Cambridge: MIT Press, 1999.

Laxton, Paul, Ed. *The New Nature of Maps: Essays in the History of Cartography*. Baltimore: Johns Hopkins, 2001.

Mijksenaar, Paul. *Visual Function: An Introduction to Information Design*. Princeton: Princeton Architectural Press, 1997.

Monmonier, Mark. *Spying with Maps: Surveillance Technologies and the Future of Privacy*. Chicago: University of Chicago, 2002.

Tufte, Edward. *Beautiful Evidence*. Cheshire Conn: Graphics Press, 2006.

Tufte, Edward. *Visual Explanations: Images and Quantities, Evidence and Narrative*. Cheshire Conn: Graphics Press, 1997.

Tufte, Edward. *Envisioning Information*. Cheshire, Conn: Graphics Press, 1990.

Tufte, Edward. *The Visual Display of Quantitative Information*. Cheshire, Conn: Graphics Press, 1983.

Wood, Denis. *Rethinking The Power of Maps*. New York: Guilford Press, 2010.

Wood, Denis. 'The Map as a Kind of Talk'. *Visual Communication* 1.2 (2002): 139–61.

Wood, Denis, and John Fels. *The Power of Maps*. New York: Guilford Press, 1992.

PART FIVE

IMAGES IN THE NEWS: PHOTOJOURNALISM

We receive the news through a variety of media, each with its own unique benefits and limitations. We turn to newspapers, magazines, television, radio, and the Internet to see and hear about events in our community, city, country, and world. The essays in this part focus on the relationship between images, journalism, and news, and specifically that in print form. Images are essential and powerful components of news, yet in discussing newspapers, news magazines, or journals, one speaks of a favourite newspaper, or favourite writer, reporter, or editor; however, one rarely, if ever, speaks of a favourite news photographer. This is not a natural phenomenon—there is nothing inherent in the news photo that would bring about the subordination of image to word in journalism. Rather, this relationship has been built through journalistic practice and the particular adoption of images by news media during the late nineteenth and early twentieth centuries. The rapid emergence of digital imaging technologies and the twenty-first–century conglomeration of news photo agencies into archives such as Getty and Corbis further problematizes the curious relationship between images and the news. The essays in this part offer historical and contemporary analyses of the image and its complicated relationship to journalism and the news.

The opening essay of this part is by the communication studies scholar Dona Schwartz. The essay, 'To Tell the Truth: Codes of Objectivity in Photojournalism', positions the truthfulness or objectivity of the news photograph as a social construct. In other words, and as the author stresses, the news image is not an inherently accurate 'window on the world' but is instead the product of a series of professional codes and practices which make it appear as an objective, truthful rendering of a live event. Schwartz analyzes several of the major instruction books in photojournalism to see how the code of objectivity is built into the profession. The result is a compelling critical analysis of disciplinary conventions that guide photojournalists. In this way, Schwartz's essay mirrors the concerns addressed by Cregan, Goodwin, Harley, and others in this text about the professionalization of vision.

A central feature of Schwartz's essay is the emphasis on both the form and content of news photographs. She writes: 'With news photographs, *what* is represented and *how* it is represented give the image its impact'. Schwartz contends that while photojournalists argue that the content of the image is its primary message, its form is of equal communicative import. The production of news imagery is governed by a series of conventions such as the rule of thirds, minimalist composition, lack of clutter, selective focus, and leading lines that indicate direction. Importantly, and as Schwartz argues, such formal elements have become naturalized parts of the practice and are not considered constitutive parts of the image and its message. Schwartz deconstructs the news photograph to show that it is not a spontaneous capturing of an event but a carefully constructed representation.

The second reading in this part, 'Photojournalism and the Tabloid Press' by Karin E. Becker, traces the co-development of photography and tabloid newspapers. The author begins by noting, as is highlighted in Part One, that text has a privileged history as a medium of communication. Becker points out that within journalism, the image has traditionally been understood as supplemental to the news or even as a form of entertainment. Such a belief presupposes that 'real' news is conveyed textually and not visually. The essay first examines the historical development of photographs as they were used in the press in order to foreground an analysis of contemporary tabloids.

Becker locates the adoption of photography into newspapers and journals as part of a larger competition for readership. The captivating photo and large, bold headlines common in today's papers have their history in the late nineteenth and early twentieth centuries and the competition for readership. It was within this climate that the photograph came to be equated with sensationalism rather than with serious or trustworthy news. In an effort to attract readers, newspaper editors turned to shocking or titillating images and bold headlines for their front pages. For Becker, understanding this historical tradition is essential in analyzing contemporary tabloids. As she argues, tabloids utilize the same formal conventions as mainstream newspapers (as also discussed by Schwartz), only in different or 'inverted' ways. Therefore, studying visual representation in tabloids reveals not only the underlying communication processes of those papers but of mainstream photojournalism as well.

The final reading in the part, 'Miller's Crossing: War, Surrealism, and *Vogue*', is a case study of the photojournalist Lee Miller by Karen Engle. Miller, an accomplished photographer, was strongly influenced by the surrealist movement, often bridging the seemingly distinct areas of artistic and documentary photography. In this essay, Engle addresses Miller's photojournalistic work during the Second World War, and specifically the images she took documenting the liberation of concentration camps at Dachau and Buchenwald. The author begins with a striking image of a dead Nazi soldier floating in a canal and questions why this image was never published. What follows is a careful deconstruction of Miller's war photography for *Vogue* magazine, which reveals the complex series of relationships at work in producing news stories. Engle summarizes: 'The finished magazine story presents a focused picture that does not reflect its complex origins'.

The essay highlights the reciprocal relationship between images and the cultures within which they are produced and used. The US and UK offices of *Vogue* ran dramatically different stories of the war, with the US opting to show images by Miller that were much more gruesome than the ones selected for publication in the UK. For Engle this reflects a larger cultural desire in the US to put a face on an enemy that was an ocean away. Nonetheless, and despite their differences, both US and UK offices ran 'straight' photographs in their stories, that is, images without any clear signs of artifice or aesthetic beauty. As the author notes, this is a common photojournalistic tactic, one that might be added to the list of conventions offered by Schwartz in the opening essay of this part. Thus, Engle concludes that the image of the floating soldier was not published because it is, perhaps paradoxically, an aesthetically beautiful image. She further argues that this particular photograph forces the viewer to consider his or her own relationship to the dead, floating body and in so doing, brings the viewer's own identity and relationship to the war into question.

Such an effect would not have been amenable to readers of *Vogue*. Engle's essay emphasizes the constructedness of news stories and is also an important examination of the affective capabilities of the photographic image.

What we see and read in newspapers, news magazines, and other forms of journalism is a carefully constructed account of an event or events. And because we rely on news for our knowledge of much of the world, it is imperative that we understand news 'stories' as such. Disciplinary conventions, material limitations, authorial and editorial choices, and intended audience are among the many facets at work in the production of news. The images we see, which are meant to represent the people, events, and places of the world, are selections: They are choices among many possible choices and are used in conjunction with text and layout to construct the news. Understanding what these choices are and how they were made makes creates a more informed audience and helps to reveal the possibilities and limitations of images in the news.

14

TO TELL THE TRUTH: CODES OF OBJECTIVITY IN PHOTOJOURNALISM

DONA SCHWARTZ

Recent mass media scholarship has shed considerable light on journalistic objectivity as a social construct. Seminal studies by researchers like Tuchman (1978), Gans (1979), Epstein (1973), and Fishman (1980) have revealed the relationships among work routines, professional norms and values, and the institutional contexts in which newsmaking takes place. Examining news production as a social activity has helped to place objectivity within an appropriate cultural frame, allowing us to see it as a professional value and a set of communicative strategies employed by journalists. While the newsmaking routines associated with print and broadcast journalism have received significant scholarly attention, surprisingly little

scrutiny has been directed towards news photography, or photojournalism.

Both history and popular lore have encouraged us to view photographs as direct, unmediated transcriptions of the real world, rather than seeing them as coded symbolic artifacts whose form and content transmit identifiable points of view. Statements of the kind made by Lady Elizabeth Eastlake, published in the *London Quarterly Review* for 1857, represent the enduring popular attitude towards the medium of photography:

[Photography] is the sworn witness of everything presented to her view. What are her unerring records in the service of mechanics, engineering, geology, and natural history, but facts of the most sterling and stubborn kind? . . . Facts which are neither the province of art nor of description, but that of a new form of communication between man and man—neither letter, message, nor picture—which now happily fills up the space between them?

Since the introduction of photography, viewers have invested the medium with a level of authority and credibility unparalleled by other modes of communication. The iconic similarity of the photograph to its subject masks the distinction between image and reality, and obscures the significance of the picture-making process in the construction of a photographic message. Like Lady Eastlake, most contemporary viewers continue to think of the photograph as a transparent window on the world, capturing the reality in front of the camera lens.

The facticity attributed to the photographic image contributed to the emergence of its reportorial use in the latter part of the nineteenth century. During this period of photographic experimentation, energetic camera operators explored a variety of uses for this new medium. They employed photographs for artistic, commercial, and scientific purposes at the same time that the use of the photograph as a documentary record was expanding. In the United States, Jacob Riis is the most frequently cited pioneer of photojournalism, utilizing photography as a part of his reportorial apparatus to cover the 'police beat' in New York City during the 1880s and 1890s. During the late 1800s it also became clear to newspaper publishers that using illustrations boosted the circulations of their periodicals. The reluctance of editors and publishers to sensationalize or cheapen their publications with photographs gave way with the development of increasingly reliable and standardized reproduction technology and the prospect of increased sales. By the 1920s photographs became a regular part of the news diet.

Tension between the natural and the symbolic is an inherent aspect of photography.[1] To viewers possessing little familiarity with the processes of photographic image-making and the choices

shaping the appearance of the final printed photograph, the image seems unquestionably truthful, generated by the subject matter itself, rather than the agency and the intent of the photographer. However, when the many variables involved in the photographic production process are examined, the conventionally constructed, symbolic character of photography becomes undeniable. The iconic linkage of subject and image causes an ontological conundrum unique to photography. For this reason, photography offers a productive focus for the study of objectivity as a social phenomenon.

Photojournalists, highly skilled manipulators of the medium, must negotiate the tension between the natural and the symbolic in photography during the course of their everyday work routines. Although photojournalists are constantly involved in the manufacture of imagery and they actively employ a set of learned codes and conventions, they still must work to legitimize photography as a medium that 'captures' the news. They must insist on the objectivity of their pictures at the same time that they attempt to demonstrate their mastery of the craft.[2] Thus, the relationship between content and form plays a pivotal role in defining photojournalism. As an objective newsgathering activity, photojournalists view content as primary, while form serves as its vehicle, imperceptibly transporting content to the viewer. The rhetoric surrounding the practice of photojournalism configures form as transparent, and thereby neutral. For example, Frank Hoy, a photojournalism professor, advises aspiring photojournalists:

> The practical test of any compositional device is whether the viewer can understand the content. When the viewer notices a form or composition, it has called attention to itself at the expense of the message. Content must communicate with the viewer so clearly that the viewer doesn't even notice the compositional devices (Hoy, 1986: 169)

Hoy's advice suggests that photojournalists learn to integrate the dualism of photography into a single conceptual package rendering news photographs simultaneously natural and symbolic through a communicational code of *naturalism*. As I use the term, naturalism refers to a communicative strategy which seeks to obscure the articulatory apparatus utilized in the production of a message, diminishing the perceived presence of an author and the significance of intent or point of view. To quote Hoy (1986: 76),

> In many instances the photograph is *interpretive*, in that it can also present a *point of view*—the photographer's personal intellectual stance, opinion, or unique attitude toward the subject. At its best, however, the single photograph overcomes its 'one-view' disadvantage by communicating the significance of a scene or event. To do this the photojournalist must know the story and how much to include in the frame. He or she must question the resulting photograph, asking whether it is true to the nature of the particular news.

This approach to photography exploits the iconic nature of the medium and suggests that photographs are authored by the subject matter they depict, with the able assistance of the skilled photojournalist.

Working from the assumption that news photographs are socially constructed artifacts, their appearance shaped by the institutional context of the mass media organization in which they are produced (cf. Rosenblum, 1978), this discussion examines how the code of journalistic objectivity is expressed in photographic terms and the symbolic strategies photojournalists are taught to employ in order to make pictures that tell the truth.

DEFINING PHOTOJOURNALISM

A comprehensive catalogue of the communicative codes of photojournalism is readily available in photojournalism textbooks. Written by journalism school faculty members (most of whom have come from the ranks of professional photojournalists) photojournalism textbooks detail the photo-techniques, typical work routines, professional ethics, and visual aesthetics of news photography. These how-to-do-it manuals offer the aspiring photojournalist a complete introduction

to canons of professional practice, framed within in a distinctive set of values and beliefs which school the reader in the culture of the profession. An analysis of these texts reveals one mechanism by which professional practices and codes are perpetuated.

In an attempt to explicate the role of photography in journalism I have analyzed the eight photojournalism textbooks currently listed in *Books in Print*. The high degree of correspondence found among these texts, expressed in recurrent professional rhetoric and aesthetic prescriptions, underscores the existence of a functioning code of photojournalistic practice. Examples from these sources will be used to construct a composite view of photojournalists' approach to objectivity.

A common presupposition found in these texts is that photojournalism's primary responsibility is to engage and inform a non-specialized mass readership. Frank Hoy (1986: 5–7) lists a set of characteristics defining photojournalism that illustrate these ideas.

> . . . photojournalism is communication photography. The communication can express a photojournalist's view of a subject, but the message communicates more than personal self-expression.

> The aim of the photojournalist is to communicate a clear message so the viewer can understand the situation quickly. The power of a great photograph is the power of an immediately understood message. The simpler the composition, the better the photograph . . .

> . . . photojournalism *reports* . . . you should report news so readers wish they had been there . . .

> . . . photojournalism deals with people. To succeed, the photojournalist must have a great interest in people. People are the prime ingredient in both ends of the photojournalistic message—they are the subjects and the viewers . . .

> . . . photojournalism communicates to a mass audience. This means that the message must be

concise and immediately understood by many different people. Private images or meanings have no place in photojournalism. A photojournalist can produce lasting images, even art, but the immediate message must effectively communicate to a mass audience.

Photojournalism texts are rife with inferences about the needs and desires of readers, although the characterizations are rarely supported by any explicit evidence. Instead, photojournalists carve out their roles and responsibilities in response to an audience constructed on the foundation of 'occupational wisdom' and common sense.[3]

CONTENT: FIRES, ACCIDENTS, AND CRIME

Content plays a major role in defining photojournalism, and the code of photojournalism includes a conception of what is and what is not news photography. Photojournalists adhere to a conception of news values espoused by print journalists, and because their images often illustrate reporters' stories a clear parallel can be found between the kinds of stories newspapers run and the kinds of images staff photographers produce. Photojournalists recognize a finite set of picture-making categories, categories which are formalized through National Press Photographers Association (NPPA) competitions, held nationally each month. Picture categories include: spot news, general news, features, sports action, sports feature, portrait/personality (close-ups), environmental portraits, pictorial, food illustration, fashion illustration, and editorial illustration.

News photography categories warrant particular concern here, because news pictures demand the photographer's reportorial skills as an impartial observer.[4] Photojournalists distinguish between two types of news assignments, and these distinctions are routinely discussed in photojournalism texts. Spot news refers to the coverage of unanticipated events, photographed as they happen or soon afterwards. Disasters, acts of violence, and conflict predominate. General news, in contrast, refers to planned news events, such as press conferences, speeches, ceremonies, or parades.

Kobre (1980: 100) defines news in contradistinction to feature photography, writing that

A news picture portrays something new. News is timely. Therefore news pictures get stale quickly.

Feature pictures, on the other hand, are expected to exhibit a quality of timelessness, depicting subject matter not necessarily defined by a specific time or place. Features pictures record commonplace occurrences, while

A news picture accrues value when (1) its subject is famous, (2) the event is of large magnitude, or (3) the outcome is tragic (Kobre, 1980: 101).

According to Kobre (1980: 102) even the act of shooting a news photo differs from shooting a feature photo in that photographers surrender control to the news event itself:

With hard news the event controls the photographer. Photographers jump into action when their editor assigns them to cover a plane crash or a train wreck. When they reach the scene, they limit their involvement to *recording* the tragedy. They certainly would not rearrange the bodies and wreckage for a more artistic picture angle.

Despite the assertion that photojournalists *record* events when they cover news assignments, photo texts give clear instructions detailing how a news event *should be photographed* in order to produce the most complete narrative re-telling. Kobre, in particular, gives lengthy descriptions of three major types of spot news assignments— fires, accidents and disasters, and crime—and he offers both a rationale for the newsworthiness of each and a list of specific photo possibilities, described in detail. His advice reads like a film storyboard, pre-scripting the visual narrative.

Why should photojournalists shoot fire pictures? Because, explains Kobre, even though 'they have read the news about fires, people want to see pictures of the disaster', and photographs 'can show not only the emotions of the participants, but also the size of the fire better than words can describe it' (Kobre, 1980: 52). Photo coverage should include:

1. a record shot;
2. an overall shot, perhaps from a high angle, in order to establish the location and the size of the fire;
3. the human side of the tragedy;
4. firefighters at work;
5. the psychological attraction of the fire ('the crowd stares with wide eyes and open mouths, seemingly transfixed');
6. the economic angle—the type of building burning, its proximity to other buildings in the neighbourhood, the extent of the damage, the cause of the fire, investigators at work;
7. the scene of the fire on the following day—charred buildings, residents returning to examine belongings.

The list of photos Kobre suggests makes possible the construction of a visual narrative filled with drama, excitement, and pathos. While the newsworthiness of the report receives significant attention in Kobre's text, the importance of *emotional impact* is a recurring theme in this and other discussions of spot news photography (see especially Rothstein, 1979 and Hoy, 1986). Because photojournalists assert that photography operates primarily at the level of emotional response, pictures exemplifying good news photography are said to 'grab at the heartstrings of the reader' (Kobre, 1980: 55).

Like fires, 'accidents make news' so photojournalists need to know how to photograph them. Kobre (1960: 61–3) offers four reasons for shooting accidents and disasters. First, 'accidents and disasters occur' and to 'record what goes on in the city and to keep readers informed about what's happening constitute two of the major roles of the press'. Second, 'readers are curious about accidents'. Third, 'people want to see what they read about'. And fourth, 'accident pictures grab the emotional side of the reader . . . the picture brings the tragedy home'. Kobre acknowledges that while accidents are all different, they also 'have certain points in common for the photographer

to look for'. As before, he generates a list of shots the photographer can make.

Kobre advises photographers to 'concentrate on the human element of any tragedy', because 'readers relate to people pictures'. A straightforward record shot should be made because 'the viewer wants to see the relationship of the cars to one another and to the highway'. Symbolic pictures can be used to imply what occurred, affording editors the option of using a picture lacking literal (gory) detail. Photographers can sometimes make pictures that show the cause of an accident, and they should attempt to portray its effect on people in the surrounding area (e.g., traffic jams). A follow-up story might look at the frequency of accidents in the area. To round out the coverage, the photographer should try to portray people's responses, 'how they adapt to their misfortune' (Kobre, 1980: 63–4).

While crimes may be difficult to photograph as they occur, Kobre (1980: 67, 70) suggests that a 'photographer with good news sense can learn to predict some situations that might erupt into violence', an important skill because 'crime, almost any kind, makes a printable story in most newspaper offices throughout the country'. According to Kobre, photos of crime personalize the meaning of 'abstract crime figures' for readers. Newsworthiness aside, photojournalists should shoot crime pictures because they 'rivet the attention of the viewer'. Kobre (1980: 70) substantiates his claim by citing the popularity of TV cop shows. News photography differs from TV representations, however, in that

> [a]ctual news photos take the viewer from the fantasy realm of television to the real crisis in the streets. Crime photos in the paper remind the viewer that felonies don't stop at 11 P.M.; they can't be switched to another channel, or turned off at bedtime.

Building on what he considers to be evidence of public interest in crime photographs, Kobre (1980: 70) asserts further:

> The public's insatiable curiosity about crime photos accounts also for editors' continued

use of such photos. Few readers can resist inspecting a photo of a mugging in progress or a grocery store hold-up.

Perhaps readers' curiosity for crime pictures lies in a deep-seated belief that criminals look different from regular people. Even though psychologists have disproved the notion of the 'criminal face', the reader checks to see if the convict has close-set eyes or a lowered brow—just as the reader suspected . . .

The circular reasoning exhibited here legitimizes crime as a worthy spot news subject, and the photojournalist's (and editors') responsibility to satisfy perceived viewer interest perpetuates this type of photographic coverage.

News as narrative. With the three examples of spot news coverage Kobre offers, the importance of narrative becomes clear. In each case, photojournalists are directed to compile a set of photographs which will allow an editor to assemble a sequential visual representation of a news event, telling the story 'as it occurred'. Since very few stories utilize more than a single photograph, each individual image should be able to tell something significant about the event in case it is used alone. In each example reviewed, the photographic strategy includes making a shot to establish the scene; photographs of participants, whether victims or authorities; representing the nature and extent of conflict, injury, or damage; photographs showing the *modus operandi*; and photos representing the effect of the incident. In all cases, photographers are instructed to seek out opportunities to represent the affective dimensions of the stories they shoot, personalizing the news and allowing for reader identification and empathy.[5] As the suggested photo possibilities make clear, drama is an important story element because drama draws and holds viewer attention, provoking a more emphatic impact and legitimizing the utility of visual illustrations.

Kobre compares the photojournalist's job with that of the movie director: when *Gone with the Wind* was shot, the director carefully planned each shot. Photojournalists do the same thing, but they 'work under the pressure of the moment' without the luxury of retakes. Going

beyond notions of appropriate content, Kobre suggests a specific formal approach to 'directing' a photo assignment, assuring visual variety and complete coverage of the event. The establishing shot should be taken front a high angle using a wide angle lens. Medium shots 'contain all the 'story-telling' elements of the scene . . . compressing the important elements into one image'. The close-up adds drama and 'slams the reader into eyeball-to-eyeball contact with the subject'. The close-up 'elicits empathy in the reader'.

Utilizing these strategies allows the photojournalist to produce a dramatic visual narrative. The fact that Kobre employs comparisons from entertainment media—television and film—warrants note. By invoking these comparisons, Kobre implicitly frames news photographs within the domain of narrative fiction. Like a good movie or television show, photojournalism benefits from conflict, excitement, action, and emotion. Pictures exhibiting these qualities are assumed to satisfy readers' visual appetites. The photographic strategies Kobre recommends require a simultaneous conception of news photographs as impartial recordings of events and as dramatic photoplays. This conceptual merger resembles the format of docudrama, an emergent genre of television entertainment that packages fact in the conventions of narrative fiction.

Extending this further, Kobre advises that even general news assignments can take on the drama and excitement of spot news if the photojournalist approaches them in a way that demonstrates the *uniqueness* of the event. The photographer can portray the 'flavour' of a meeting:

through the creative application of framing techniques, catching the moment, and using long lens and light, the photographer can help portray for the reader the excitement, the tension, the opposition, and the resolution of the meeting (Kobre, 1980: 79).

Similarly, Hoy writes that with general news the photographer is

still aiming to get a spontaneous photo, so look for candids as the event unfolds. After you have covered a number of similar events, you can anticipate the action (1986: 66).

While explicit manipulation may violate professional norms, setting out with a pre-conceived storyboard does not. Prior knowledge about news events and the conventions guiding editors' decisions elicit from photojournalists a routine work strategy that ensures predictability and aesthetic continuity.

People and posing. Because people pictures are a staple of photojournalism, photo texts offer extensive advice on establishing rapport with subjects. To pose or not to pose people when shooting an awards ceremony, a mug shot, or an environmental portrait raises questions of professional ethics. Hoy (1979: 44) addresses the issue in this way:

> Perhaps one of the most confusing myths of photojournalism is that posing or directing a subject is unethical. The second most confusing myth is that the vast majority of good photographs you see in magazines and newspapers are totally candid. The old photojournalism saying, 'make a picture, don't just take one' applies to imaginative thinking. It also applies to the many situations where some posing of the subject is needed to get more than a snapshot . . .
>
> A working photojournalist cannot consistently cover assignments without being willing and able to pose, direct, or otherwise enlist the cooperation of subjects. It is ethical to do all of this to get a better, more story-telling, photograph.

Tips for making subjects look natural abound: when photographed in familiar surroundings a subject is more likely to 'be himself'; look for gestures that give an informal appearance; coax people to do what they normally do; when there is too little time to wait for a natural response or to establish rapport, provoke a reaction; ask for a demonstration to 'elicit the natural ham in people'; or tell the subject exactly what to do. Rothstein (1979: 44) echoes Hoy when he addresses the ethics of re-enactments in his text:

> The re-enactment of a news event is a problem for every photographer's conscience. It can be

resolved only when the photographer honestly believes that his directions are creating a true picture of what actually happened. Direction by the photographer supposes a conception of what the final print will be like. It should add to the realism of each picture by coordinating the events or subjects before the camera to make the visual impact more effective. Direction has its greatest value when it is least discernible.

Kobre suggests that photojournalists ask subjects to wear professional costumes (a lab coat, for example), and to pose them in front of identifying props that will indicate their significance. He also spells out the meanings viewers will attach to different kinds of lighting and compositions. High-key light will be perceived as 'upbeat', while shadows will lead to a sombre image. A balanced composition will suggest stability, while an off-balance composition will produce tension. Close-ups suggest intimacy.

A constant admonition underlying the discussions of useful strategies is that the use of these picture-making techniques should not be discernible to the viewer. Photojournalists strive to construct naturalism; the pictures they make need not actually *be* spontaneous or candid, but they should *appear as if they record actual behaviour.* The photographer bears responsibility for the honesty of his or her portrayals of individuals and events. If the image is true to the *spirit* of the subject, the means to that end are justified—the photograph must tell the story.

Form. While the range of subjects appropriate to news photography contribute to the communicative codes of photojournalism, form plays an important role in distinguishing photojournalism from other kinds of photographic practice. Photojournalists strive to make form transparent, an unobtrusive vehicle for content. Yet despite the prominence of this notion, formal codes can be readily identified by examining news photographs. The aesthetics of photojournalism require the active manipulation of form in order to maintain the illusion of naturalism.

In his discussion of techniques of good composition, Kerns (1980: 76) offers this advice:

Economy of visual elements within the frame is primary to visual success. Convey the most information or emotion with the fewest visual elements possible. When this guideline is followed, there is little to confuse the reader.

Likewise, Hoy (1986:163) recommends 'simplicity of design':

Even when reporting a complex idea or scene, your design should be simple and effective.

As is frequently the case, the needs of the reader are invoked in these calls for simplicity. The recurring assumption in photo texts is that readers cannot adequately deal with images requiring active, extended scrutiny. Good news photographs communicate their messages directly and immediately. As Geraci (1984: 122) writes:

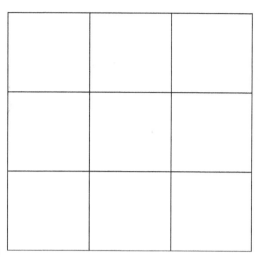

FIGURE 14.1

In simplicity, as in brevity, there is usually strength. So it is with photographs. The less cluttered, the more readily the eye of the beholder can grasp the full meaning of a photograph. The quicker it gets to the reasoning center of the brain, the quicker a reader can register approval or disapproval. If a photograph is too cluttered, the reader may move on to something else without really comprehending the subject of the photograph at all.

Simplicity of design is achieved by following a set of regularly cited rules. In a well-designed photograph, the 'centre of interest', the main subject of the picture, must be clearly discernible to the viewer. This may be accomplished through framing, selective focus, or the use of leading lines in the composition. Photojournalism texts uniformly recommend use of the 'rule of thirds' in order to frame the subject in such a way as to assure a dynamic composition. Using the rule of thirds, the pictorial frame is divided into three equal sections, horizontally and vertically, as though a tic-tac-toe board were drawn within the edges of the frame. The grid produced by this partitioning yields four points of intersection, all of them off centre. The main subject is placed at one of these four points of intersection in order to

produce an active composition with visual interest. At all costs, photographers are enjoined from placing the subject in the middle of the frame, because centred compositions inevitably produce a 'static image'. To achieve pictorial balance, Kerns (1980) recommends that photographers place the largest object in the frame at one point of intersection on the rule of thirds grid, and the smallest object at another.

Rothstein (1979) discusses selection and focus as key elements of composition. According to Rothstein, photographers should select the proper moment, the right lens, and the best viewpoint in order to emphasize the centre of interest in the image. Manipulating the focus within the frame allows specific areas of the photograph to remain discernibly sharp, while others blur. Varying focus makes it possible for the photographer to direct the viewer's attention to a particular part of the photograph, passing over others. Choosing when and how to shoot a picture, the photographer controls which elements within the visual field will receive viewer attention.

'Distracting' backgrounds and foregrounds can plague photojournalists, diluting the immediate impact of their pictures. Framing and selective focus are used to draw attention away from 'inessential' objects or activities in the foreground or background. Photographers can either move in closer to eliminate unwanted elements from the frame, or they can throw them out of focus by manipulating the depth of field of the camera lens they have chosen. Distracting elements, known as 'clutter', draw viewers' attention in different directions, detracting from the simplicity of the composition, and making it more difficult for the reader to instantly apprehend the significance of the image. Kerns (1980: 81) writes:

> Our pictures may have more than one area of interest, but it should be instantly clear what the most important center of interest is.

Because professionals assert that photojournalism communicates immediately and emotionally, too much visual information appearing within the frame undermines the efficacy of the image.

The use of 'leading lines' also helps establish the photograph's centre of interest. Leading lines result from the presence of objects within the frame that impart a sense of directionality. For instance, the appearance of a roadway from lower left to upper right within the frame would tend to draw the viewer's gaze in a diagonal direction through the picture. Photojournalists recognize the utility of these directional elements and frame their pictures so as to exploit the graphic emphasis leading lines offer. Hoy (1986) suggests the use of leading lines to point to the picture's centre of interest. He mentions lines in the shape of 'a' 'c', and 'l', and a 't', as well as 's-curves', 'pluses', and 'radials'.[6]

Taken together, these three formal strategies—the rule of thirds, selective focus, and the use of leading lines—allow the photojournalist to construct a successful image capable of communicating 'at a glance'. Hoy (1986: 167) offers a list of related semiotic equations photojournalists should keep in mind:

simplicity of design = visual impact
visual impact = action or possibility of action
close up = intimacy or emphasis
long shot = isolation or aloneness
subject facing into frame = leads to object of
    gaze
subject facing out of frame = mystery

sharpness of detail = reality
softness of focus = mystery or non-reality
lightness of print = happiness
darkness of print = sadness or foreboding
facial expression = best for showing emotion

Because many of the circumstances confronting photojournalists demand split-second responses, these formal decisions are often made tacitly, carried out as a part of the routine of the job. Unlike other photographers, photojournalists usually have little time to consider a variety of approaches. They rely upon the codes of photojournalism, internalized through professional practice, to guide the process of making pictures.

GOOD NEWS PHOTOGRAPHS

The qualities attributed to good news photos recur across photojournalism texts. The criteria used to evaluate news photographs are criteria invoked with regard to judging other kinds of picture-making as well. That is, photojournalists respond not only to the norms and conventions of newsmaking, but also to the norms and conventions of picture-making. Some of the values ascribed to good paintings, good movies, good television shows, and good photographs also influence what is considered to be a good news *picture*. Geraci's (1984: 115) view is illustrative:

> Photographs, to be good photojournalism, must be a 'slice of life' lifted from reality and transferred to silver in such a manner that the viewer senses some of the spontaneity and excitement of the original scene. If the subject looks uncomfortable, the viewer will feel this discomfort. If the subject is static, 'posing for the camera', the viewer will soon lose interest and move on to another thing. If the subject appears commonplace, viewed from eyelevel and lacking action or some other visual appeal, the picture will not long command the attention of the viewer.

Beyond truthfulness then, good news photographs must have 'visual appeal', an ephemeral quality attributed to pictures that people seem to enjoy looking at. Geraci associates visual appeal with impact and emotion. Kobre (1980: 208) calls good news photos 'eye stoppers', pictures that have interesting patterns, strong contrasts in tonal value, pictures that lend themselves to unique cropping, and hold viewers' interest. Photojournalists agree that photographs with visual appeal are well composed, pleasing to the eye. Beyond the recipes offered for good composition, well-made photographs trigger an intuitive positive response. 'If it looks right, chances are a photo *is* well composed' (Geraci, 1984: 116).

For Geraci (1984: 85,86), visual appeal also requires dramatic action, real or implied:

> To be interesting, a photograph must convey a sense of the expectant . . . In most photographs action is an asset and it is indispensable in news photographs . . . . Action and viewer interest are intertwined. A photograph lacking action is probably one lacking interest, certainly universal interest, and very likely should not be used in a publication.

As a storytelling medium, stories told in an exciting way are valued above stories told matter-of-factly. Dramatic angles, framing, and lighting add to the impact of the image, presumably piquing viewer interest. Emotion is prized; news photos wring emotional response from viewers as no other medium can. Action, drama, and emotion are conveyed through the content of the image, but these qualities are also conveyed through the formal treatment given to the image. With news photographs, *what* is represented and *how* it is represented give the image its impact. Despite the insistence on the pre-eminence of content, form plays a crucial role.

CODES OF OBJECTIVITY

Photojournalism relies upon the notion that photography captures an objective record of reality for viewers. Yet, at the same time, a clearly defined system of rules and conventions governs the professional practice of photojournalism, delimiting the range of appropriate images and shaping the form those images take. Paradoxically, news photographs are valued as neutral records at the same time that they are admired as carefully crafted pictures. Photojournalists earn kudos not only for what they show, but also for how well they show it. Photo competitions pitting photojournalists against one another in the quest for the best telling of the story attest to the importance of craft in the photojournalistic enterprise.

Photojournalists operate within a conceptual framework and within an institutional context that determines what subjects warrant attention. Conventions of framing, composition, lighting, and colour or tonal value guide the translation of newsworthy subjects into the two-dimensional photographic image. But the representational devices employed by photojournalists are designed to be transparent. If an image is dramatic, it is the subject that appears to produce the drama, not the representational skill of the photographer. In their careful crafting of images, photojournalists ascribe to a formal code of naturalism, preserving the objective aura cast around the photographic image.

Well schooled in the techniques and the conventions of photojournalism, the photographer can approach any event, object, or individual and translate actuality into imagery. In an important sense, the practice of photojournalism supersedes its objects: the codes of professional practice make it possible to translate real life's complexity into a visual representation 'immediately understandable' to the viewer. The simplicity of the translation, a quality valued by photojournalists, provokes an emotive response. The dramatic stories told by good news photographs are meant to be apprehended viscerally. The narrative frame cast around news events encourages readers to identify with the story, the dilemmas and situations of its starring actors, masking complexity and diffusing critical response. Photojournalism, cloaked in its mantle of objectivity, offers the viewer a vision of the world easily consumed and digested, while its naturalism perpetuates its legitimacy as an objective bearer of the news.

NOTES

1. Worth and Gross (1974) distinguish between natural and symbolic events and the interpretational strategies they provoke. When viewers encounter natural events they need only recognize that they exist—natural events require no interpretive response. Symbolic events are assumed to have been intentionally created for the purpose of communicating meaning. Once a viewer identifies a symbolic event, it behooves him or her to attend to the purposeful ordering and structuring of that event in order to interpret the message it advances. Photographs are often mistaken for natural events, requiring no interpretation, and to a very large degree photojournalism depends upon this misapprehension.

2. The conflict endemic to managing this dichotomy is not unique to photographers. Wordsmiths have also developed strategies for naturalizing the newswriting process, transforming authored accounts into objective reports. Photojournalism parallels newswriting in this regard, but the degree to which subject matter, or content, is thought to determine form is especially salient in photography.

3. Muriel Cantor (1971) discusses 'old line' Hollywood TV producers' similar common sense knowledge about the desires and needs of the television viewing audience, and says that they make programming decisions based upon this intuitive understanding of the public.

4. Sports action photography is considered to proceed from objective sports reporting skills, like news photography. Portraiture should also reflect or reveal the real personality of the sitter, according to photojournalism texts, and the photographer's job requires that he or she come to some kind of understanding of the nature of the subject in order to succeed at making the portrait.

5. The recommendations offered by Kobre substantiate Hall's (1981) claim that news photographs present a view that disarms readers' critical apparatus by personalizing events and encouraging an empathetic response to the image.

6. The compositional rules offered in photojournalism textbooks bear a strikingly close resemblance to the rules followed by amateur camera club photographers. And an examination of literature distributed by Eastman Kodak Company—how-to-do-it manuals and books on photography—yields the same set of recipes for successful picture making. This confluence of conceptions of good photography is related to the pivotal role played by the photographic industry in generating consumer markets and setting standards for photographic practice. (See Schwartz and Griffin, 1987.)

REFERENCES

Cantor, Muriel (1971). *The Hollywood tv Producer.* New York: Basic Books.

Edam, Clifton C. (1976). *Photojournalism: Principles and Practices.* Dubuque: Wm. C. Brown Company Publishers.

Epstein, Edward J. (1973). *News from Nowhere: Television and the News.* New York: Random House.

Feinberg, Milton (1969). *Techniques of Photojournalism.* New York: Wiley-Interscience.

Fishman, Mark (1980). *Manufacturing in the News.* Austin: University of Texas Press.

Gans, Herbert (1979). *Deciding What's News.* New York: Pantheon.

Geraci, Philip C. (1984). *Photojournalism: New Images in Visual Communication.* Dubuque: Kendall/Hunt Publishing Company.

Hall, Stuart (1981). 'The Determinations of News Photographs'. *The Manufacture of News: Deviance, Social Problems and the Mass Media.* London: Constable. 226–43.

Hoy, Frank P. (1986). *Photojournalism: The Visual Approach.* Englewood Cliffs, New Jersey: Prentice-Hall.

Hurley, Gerald D. and Angus McDougall (1971), *Visual Impact in Print.* Chicago: American Publishers Press.

Kerns, Robert L. (1980). *Photojournalism: Photography with a Purpose.* Englewood Cliffs, New Jersey: Prentice-Hall

Kobre, Kenneth (1980). *Photojournalism: The Professionals' Approach.* Boston: Focal Press.

Rosenblum, Barbara (1978). 'Style as Social Process'. *American Sociological Review.* 43(June): 422–38.

Rothstein, Arthur (1979). *Photojournalism*. Garden City, New York: Amphoto.

Schwartz, Dona and Michael Griffin (1987). 'Amateur Photography: The Organizational Maintenance of an Aesthetic Code'. *Natural Audiences: Qualitative Research of Media Uses and Effects*, Thomas Lindlof ed. New York: Ablex. 198–224.

Tuchman, Gaye (1978). *Making News: A Study in the Construction of Reality*. New York: Free Press.

Worth, Sol and Larry Gross (1974). 'Symbolic Strategies'. *Journal of Communication*. 24: 27–39.

15

PHOTOJOURNALISM AND THE TABLOID PRESS[1]

KARIN E. BECKER

Photography has a long and uncomfortable history within Western journalism. Despite its very visible presence in the daily and weekly press of the past century, photography is rarely admitted to settings in which journalism is discussed, investigated, and taught. Whenever the distinction is drawn between information and entertainment, or the serious substance of a journalism appealing to an intellectual reading public is defended against the light, trivial appeal of the popular, photography falls within the popular, excluded from the realm of the serious press. Nowhere are the consequences of this position more evident than in the pages and discussion of the tabloid press. There the display and presumed appeal of the photographs are used as criteria for evaluating, and ultimately dismissing, tabloid newspapers as 'merely' popular.

The history of this link between photography and the tabloid press can be traced to photography's successive adoption by three distinct types of publications: first in the elite periodical press with its established tradition of illustration; then in the tabloid press with a more popular appeal; and almost simultaneously, in weekly supplements to the respected organs of the daily press. Examining this history reveals the development of discourses about photojournalism, including beliefs about the nature of the medium, that continue to inform photography's positions in the contemporary press.

Beliefs that photographs supply unmediated pictures of actual events could have been the foundation for treating photographs as news by institutions whose credibility rests on the facticity and accuracy of their reports about the world. Yet there is a contradiction, because photography, when constructed as a purely visual medium, is also thought to bypass those intellectual processes that journalism will specifically address and cultivate. Photography's more immediate, direct appeal is seen as a threat to reason, and to the journalistic institution's Enlightenment heritage. The tension inherent in these reconstructions of photography and journalism permeates the discourse in which these practices coexist. Tracing the history of this discourse, and particularly journalism's ambivalence toward photography's popular appeal, one finds patterns of use and journalistic structures that refer to photography and exploit its popularity, while simultaneously insulating the elite segments of the daily press in exclusively verbal forms of journalistic practice.

Analyzing the role of photography in the press can thus help illuminate the simultaneous problems of the 'political' and the 'aesthetic' in contemporary communication studies, and offers insights into the relationships among representation, historical knowledge, and value at the heart of the postmodern debate. This chapter engages these issues first, by examining the historical development of the use of photographs in the Western press, and secondly, by analyzing the tabloid press as the contemporary context in which photography continues to be a primary means of representing the news.

THE EARLY PICTURE PRESS

In the early 1840s illustrated magazines were launched almost simultaneously in several European countries. The *Illustrated London News*, founded in 1842, was a well-written weekly magazine which hired illustrators to portray important current events (Hassner 1977; Taft 1938). Its success[2] was echoed by *L'Illustration* in France

and *Illustrierte Zeitung* in Germany (both founded in 1843) and which were soon followed by others. *Frank Leslie's Illustrated Newspaper* (1855) and *Harper's Weekly—Journal of Civilization* (1857) were the first such publications to appear in North America.

These magazines were all using wood engravings to illustrate the news. Well-known artists were hired to 'cover' events, and competed to be the first with their reports. *Leslie's*, for example, sent an illustrator to the hanging of the anti-slavery movement leader John Brown in 1859, with instructions to take the first train back to New York where sixteen engravers worked through the night to meet the press deadline. The text published with the engraving stated that it was 'from a sketch by our own artist taken on the spot', invoking the authority of the eyewitness (Hassner 1977: 170).

At that time the publication of actual photographs was technically impossible, but wood engravings were preferred for other reasons. The camera's 'likeness' apparently was considered stiff and too dependent on the luck of the machine, in contrast with the hand-drawn image that reflected the artist's perspective and the engraver's craft. When a photograph was used (often quite loosely) as a referent for the engraver, a statement like 'from a photograph' frequently accompanied it, lending the machine's authority to the artist's work. By the 1860s, the engraving was considered 'a meticulously faithful reproduction of reality' within a 'sphere of objectivity around the medium itself' (Johannesson 1982).[3]

Thus, the periodical press had established patterns of visual reporting several decades before the halftone process was developed to facilitate printing photographs and text side by side. The topics that were covered, the ideals of immediacy and accuracy and the competition valorizing both the journalistic process and its product (both the hunt and its trophy), were well established on publications that carried an aura of quality and distinction. The 1890s saw these conventions of illustration gradually being adapted to photography.

Histories of photojournalism trace a heritage to a limited number of prestige periodicals, locating a tradition of photographic reportage in the work of a few editors and photographers (Hassner 1977; Edom 1976; Kobre 1980). *Collier's Weekly*, a 'cultural magazine emphasizing literary material', is often named as one of the first to shift from illustration to photo-reportage. Photographer James Hare, *Collier's'* primary correspondent throughout the Spanish–American War, is seen as the chief reason for the magazine's success.[4] Hare's assignment to investigate the sinking of the battleship *Maine* is among the earliest examples used to present the photojournalist as hero:

> He snapped the wreck of the *Maine* from every point of the compass. He caught divers still busy at the somber task of bringing up the drowned . . . . With the aid of an interpreter, Jimmy prowled through reconcentrado camps. He photographed swollen bodies with bones breaking through the skin; he took pictures of the emaciated living, and of babies ravaged by disease. Every ship that passed Morrow Castle enroute to New York carried a packet of snapshots. Their influence upon public opinion can hardly he overestimated (Carnes 1940: 15; Edom 1976: 38).

The rapid expansion of weekly magazines in the United States was due in part to the overheated atmosphere and competitive coverage of the war with Spain. Technical innovations and new legal privileges were also encouraging growth, and most important, with industrialization and the shift to a market economy, advertising began to provide significant support for the weekly press. As many magazines cut their purchase prices in half, a potentially nation-wide market suddenly opened up and the so-called 'general interest mass circulation magazine' arose. Advertising volume grew from 360 million to 542 million dollars between 1890 and 1900 (Kahan 1968; Hassner 1977: 216–17). The availability of large advertising revenues and the assumption of a mass appeal would become foundations of the picture magazines in the 1930s.

At the turn of the century, however, there are few indications that photography actually increased magazine sales (Kahan 1968: 194;

Hassner 1977: 218). Nevertheless, 'the weekly photo-news magazine concept' had been established, and the heroic construction of its news photographer had begun.

THE TABLOID = SENSATIONALISM = PHOTOGRAPHY

Daily newspapers did not have an established tradition of illustration predating photography, which helps to explain the slow introduction of halftone reproduction in the daily press. Daily deadline requirements also meant that the early halftone process was too cumbersome for newspaper production routines. By the late 1890s, more than a decade after the process was invented, many papers only occasionally published photographs. The exception was the United States' 'yellow press', and particularly the fierce competition between two New York papers, Joseph Pulitzer's *World* and William Randolph Hearst's *Journal*, where pictures were seen as a key to successful and sensational coverage. The *World*, for example, carried what is claimed were 'the first actual photographs of the wreck' of the *Maine* in 1898, and which were in fact drawn simulations of photographs (Time-Life 1983: 16).

It was in the tabloid press of the 1920s that large sensational photographs first appeared, with violence, sex, accidents, and society scandals as the major themes. United States press historians point to this as a low point for the press, an expression of what they consider the loose morals and loss of ethical standards that threatened public and private life. It was a time 'made to order for the extreme sensationalism of the tabloid and for a spreading of its degrading journalistic features to the rest of the press' (Emery 1962: 624). The *New York Daily News* was a primary culprit, and by 1924 had the largest circulation of any US newspaper. Its main competitors were the *Daily Mirror* and the *Daily Graphic*. England's *Daily Mirror* (founded 1904) had established 'a genre making public the grief of private individuals', and in the 1920s was, together with the *Daily Express*, among the newspapers influenced by the US tabloids' use of photographs (Baynes 1971: 46, 51).

'Sensational' journalism breaks the press, as-cribed guidelines of ethical practice with the intention of attracting attention in order to sell more papers. In this process, journalism's audi-ence—its 'public'—is reconstructed as a mass, undifferentiated and irrational. The 'sensational' occurs within journalistic discourses that are also bounded by cultural, historical, and political practices that in turn position the ethical guide-lines around different types of content, an im-portant point to remember when examining the tabloid press of different countries.[5] Yet, a com-ponent common to the various constructions of the sensational is that attracting attention takes precedence over other journalistic values, includ-ing accuracy, credibility, and political or social significance. In the US, the sensationalism of the tabloid press was intensified by 'photographs of events and personalities reproduced which are trite, trivial, superficial, tawdry, salacious, mor-bid, or silly' (Taft 1938: 448). It was not the sub-ject matter, in other words, but the ways the photographs reproduced it which appealed to the emotions and thereby created the sensation.

Herein lies the rationale for prohibiting the photographing of news-worthy events that take place where reason and order are seen as crucial, that is, within most judicial and legislative bod-ies. Newspaper violations of these prohibitions have been held up as examples confirming the need for exclusion (Dyer and Hauserman 1987) or, conversely, within photojournalistic discourse to point to the need for self-regulation (Cookman 1985). One frequently cited case was a New York divorce trial in which the husband, a wealthy white manufacturer, wanted to annul his mar-riage on the grounds that his wife had concealed from him that she was part African-American, which she in turn claimed was obvious to him at the time of their marriage. At one point in the trial, when she was required to strip to the waist, the courtroom was cleared and no photo-graphs were permitted. The *Evening Graphic* con-structed what it proudly called a 'composograph' by recreating the scene using actors, then past-ing in photographs of the faces of actual trial participants (Hassner 1977: 282; Kobre 1980: 17). No discussion of this obvious montage as a

dismantling of photographic truth is offered in today's texts, nor is the outcome of the trial itself. They do note, however, that such practices led to the *Graphic*'s nickname, 'the *Porno-graphic*' (see Time-Life 1983: 17).

The *Daily News* is seen as the leader of that 'daily erotica for the masses' (Kobre 1980: 17), particularly for heating up competition, and thus increasing the excesses of sensationalism among the tabloids. The execution of Ruth Sny-der, found guilty of murdering her husband after a much publicized 'love triangle' trial in 1928, is often given as an example. Although reporters were allowed to witness the electrocution, pho-tographers were excluded (Time-Life 1983: 17). The day before, the *Graphic* had promised its read-ers 'a woman's final thoughts just before she is clutched in the deadly snare that scars and burns and FRIES AND KILLS! Her very last words, ex-clusively in tomorrow's *Graphic*' (cited in Emery 1962: 629).

The *Daily News*, however, had a Chicago press photographer, unknown to New York prison au-thorities and press, in the execution chamber with a camera taped to his ankle. At the key mo-ment be lifted his trouser leg and made an expos-ure using a cable release in his pocket. 'DEAD!' was the simple heading over the photograph in the *Daily News*' extra edition. The caption gave it scientific legitimation as 'the most remarkable ex-clusive picture in the history of criminology', and described details ('her helmeted head is stiffened in death') difficult to distinguish in the heavily retouched photograph. The edition sold a million copies, easily beating the *Graphic*'s non-visual ac-count of the event (Emery 1962: 629).

Within this journalistic discourse, the photo-graph itself had come to mean sensational jour-nalism. In his history of photography in America in 1938, William Taft claimed:

Such prodigious and free use of photographs in picture newspapers and magazines has in a measure defeated their own object, presumably that of disseminating news. Such journals are carelessly thumbed through, the reader glances hastily at one picture—looks but does not see or think—and passes on to the next in the same

manner and then throws the periodical aside—
a picture album with little purpose or reason.

These criticisms and abuses the pictorial
press must meet and correct if it is to command
the respect of intelligent people. (Taft 1938:
448–9)

Here we see, if not the origins, then a full-
blown expression of the historical antagonism
between the liberal and the popular press, and
photography's exclusive identification with the
inferior, the popular, side of that antagonism.

THE DAILY PRESS
'SUPPLEMENTS' THE NEWS

With the exception of the tabloid press, photographs rarely appeared in the daily newspapers of
Europe and North America until 1920. Technical
and time constraints offer a partial explanation
for this delay. However, by the time daily photojournalism became practical, conventions of
press photography had already been established.
On the one hand, the abundant illustration in
the magazines of the late nineteenth century
had a broader content than 'the political, legal
and economic matters [that] constituted the primary news in the traditional newspaper' (Hård
af Segerstad 1974: 143). On the other hand, the
leading role photography was playing in the tabloids' abuses of press credibility made it increasingly difficult to see the photograph as a medium
for serious news.

Photographic realism as an ideal had entered
the *verbal* codes of the daily press shortly after
photography's invention. Metaphors of the
American newspaper as 'a faithful daguerreotype
of the progress of mankind' were common from
the 1850s, with the reporter employed as a 'mere
machine to repeat' each event as a seamless
whole, 'like a picture'. According to Dan Schiller
(1977: 93) photography 'was becoming the guiding beacon of reportorial practice'. Although the
conception of photographic realism had become
intertwined with the roots of objectivity in the
occupational ideology of American journalism,
press photography itself had been enclosed in a
different and conflicting discursive field.

Daily newspapers instead had begun to print
weekly supplements on the new gravure presses.
The first of these appeared in New York and Chicago in the 1890s and were illustrated predominantly with photographs. Many, such as the *New
York Times Midweek Pictorial*, provided substantive
complements to the newspaper's daily coverage
of World War I. By 1920, New York's five major newspapers had rotogravure supplements to
their Sunday editions (Schuneman 1966, cited in
Hassner 1977: 279). Established during the period when halftone reproduction became feasible,
these magazines were a response to the popularity of photography. Material was gathered and
packaged with a weekly deadline in a magazine
format on smooth paper that raised the quality
of reproduction. Within this format newspapers
had succeeded in developing a way to use photography that complemented the structure and appearance of the daily news, while insulating and
protecting the newspaper's primary product from
being downgraded by the photograph. Contemporary examples of this phenomenon persist,[6]
offering a showcase for 'good' photojournalism,
pursued separately from the daily news product.

Photography had followed three distinct routes
in its entry into the Western press, establishing
separate and overlapping discourses of photojournalism which, by the 1920s, were serving as
three models. One may argue that this construction is based on secondary sources, the received
histories of journalism and its photography,
without looking at the primary material, that is,
the press itself. Yet received histories undeniably
serve as models for practice; indeed that is their
power. It is the memory of how things were done
in the past as reconstructed in contemporary
discourse—not the day-to-day production process from any specific or actual period of time—
which informs today's practice.

THE PICTURE MAGAZINES'
LEGACY

Before turning to the specific case of the contemporary tabloid press, it is important to mention
briefly the mass-circulation picture magazines.
Although they have had little direct influence on

tabloid photojournalism, their histories and the trajectories they established continue to inform photojournalistic discourse, including standards of practice and aesthetic value (Becker 1985).

Mass circulation picture magazines emerged between the wars, first in Germany, soon thereafter in other European countries, and by the late 1930s were established in England and the United States (Gidal 1973; Hall 1972; Hassner 1977; Eskildsen 1978; Ohrn and Hardt 1981). Not only did these magazines establish new genres of photoreportage—notably the photo essay and the practice of documenting both the famous and the ordinary citizen in the same light. More important, they emerged during a period when, in various ways in each of their respective countries, what Victor Burgin has described as 'a dismantling of the differentiation between high and low culture was taking place' (Burgin 1986: 5). The notion of 'mass' art—referring to both the production and consumption of the work—had emerged to challenge the notion of 'high' culture as the sole repository of aesthetic value. Photography, in particular documentary photography, became accepted as popular art, and made its first major entry into the museum world.[7]

Walter Benjamin's predictions (1936) that the mass production of photographic images would bring about a defetishization of the art object had very nearly been reversed by the postwar years. Instead, we find an 'aura' reconstructed to privilege particular spheres of mass production and popular culture, including in this case, photojournalism. Within the magazines, photography was bearing the fruits of becoming a mass medium in a form that was popular and respected. Supported by consistently rising circulations and mass-market national advertising, and operating in a cultural climate which could accept the products of mass production as popular art, the status of photojournalism and of the men and women who produced it reached unprecedented heights. Several specific elements of this photojournalism continue to be seen as meriting the institutionalized culture's stamp of value: the formal structural properties of the ideal photo essay; the determination of the single photograph as an idealized moment—fetishized as 'the decisive

moment' either alone or at the centre of the essay; and the reconstruction of the photojournalist as artist.[8]

The elevation of photography's status continued to exclude the tabloid press. The ideology of cultural value which had shifted to admit photojournalistic documents into museum collections, gallery exhibitions, and finely produced books has persisted in treating tabloid press photography as 'low' culture. This meant, with few exceptions, not considering it at all.[9] The vacuum which has persisted around the tabloid press would be reason enough to examine its photojournalism. This is, after all, the daily press where photography continues to play a major role.

THE CONTEMPORARY DOMAIN OF THE TABLOID

Many very different kinds of newspapers are published in a tabloid format. The present investigation, based on examples from the United States, England, Australia, Austria, Norway, Sweden, and Denmark,[10] found wide variation in the degree to which the different papers overlapped with news agendas of the elite press and, in the cases of overlap, distinctly different ways of angling the news.[11] The few characteristics these papers have in common include an almost exclusive reliance on news-stand sales, a front page that seems to work like a poster in this context—dominated by a photograph and headlines referring to a single story—and photographs occupying a much larger proportion of the editorial content than one finds in other segments of the daily press.

The particular 'look' often associated with the photography of the tabloid press—where action and expression are awkwardly and garishly caught in the flat, raw light of bare bulb flash—is relatively uncommon. Far more frequently, one encounters photographs of people posed in conventional ways, looking directly into the camera. Celebrities, including entertainers and sports figures, in addition to the pose, are often portrayed performing. Occasionally famous people are also 'revealed' by the camera, drawing on a set of stylistic features that have long been thought to typify tabloid photojournalism. Coverage of political events, that category of coverage which overlaps most with news in the elite press, is constructed using photographs following each of these forms. But this is also where one is more likely to see photographs that exhibit the traditional look of the tabloid press.

These three broad and occasionally overlapping categories of coverage—of private or previously non-famous persons in circumstances that make them newsworthy, or celebrities, and of events that correspond to conventional constructions of news—provide a framework for analyzing this photography in terms of its style, communicative value, and political implications.

PLAIN PICTURES OF ORDINARY PEOPLE

Most photographs in the tabloid press are in fact very plain. They present people who appear quite ordinary, usually in their everyday surroundings: a family sitting around a kitchen table or on their living room sofa, couples and friends embracing, children with their pets. Sometimes the people in the photographs are holding objects that appear slightly out of place, so that we see the objects as 'evidence': a woman hugging a child's toy, or presenting a photograph to the camera, for example. Sometimes the setting itself is the evidence behind the formal pose: a woman standing next to a grave, or a man sitting in the driver's seat of a taxi. Their faces often express strong emotion, easy to read as joy or sorrow. These are not people whom readers recognize as famous. One would not be likely to pay much attention to them in another context.

From the words we learn what has happened to them, why they are in the newspaper. 'Pals for years', the two happily embracing women never dreamed that they were sisters who had been separated at birth. The family sitting in their kitchen has just had their children's stomachs pumped for narcotics, amphetamine capsules the pre-schoolers had found on the playground. The woman with the child's toy continues to hope her kidnapped son will be returned safely. The little girl hugging her chimpanzee has donated one of her kidneys to save the pet's life. The middle-aged

woman lounging on her sofa in a tight-fitting outfit is upset after losing a job-discrimination suit; despite her sex-change operation, employers have refused to accept that she is a woman.

Sometimes they are people whose lives have been directly affected by major national or international events. Rising interest rates are forcing the family to sell their 'dream house'. A man holds the framed photograph of his daughter and grandchildren who have been held hostage in Iraq for two months.

If one can temporarily disregard the impact of the text on the meanings we construct for these pictures (the impossibility of doing so in practice will be returned to at a later point), they almost resemble ordinary family photographs. Many of the settings and postures are recognizable from that familiar genre. The photographs are also characterized by their frontality, a tendency toward bi-lateral symmetry, and the fact that people are looking directly into the camera. The pictures do not mimic precisely the forms found in family photograph collections: the attention to and control over light and framing give them a more professional look, while the private or informal settings distinguish them from formal portraits with their typical blank backgrounds.

Yet the particular ways that these press photographs resonate with other forms of photography that are private and familiar, make the people in them accessible to viewers. The straightforward frontality of the photographs and, in particular, the level eye-contact between the person pictured and the person looking at the picture establishes them as equals, or at least as comprehensible to each other. The people photographed do not appear to have been manipulated into those postures and settings. Instead the form suggests that the act of making the photograph was co-operative. They seem aware of the way they are being presented, even to have chosen it themselves. It is their story that is being told. And they are not so different from us.

There are two other patterns for presenting photographs of non-famous people in the tabloids, which although less common, are significant. The first is the use of the official identification, or 'i.d.' portrait. Although this is also a frontal photograph with the subject frequently in eye-contact with the camera, it carries none of the connotations of the family photograph. Instead, the tight facial framing and the institutional uses of this form immediately link it to a tragic and usually criminal act.

The second exception appears spontaneous, often candid, and usually portrays action, an event that is underway. Such photographs are part of the tabloids' coverage of news events and usually include ordinary people who have become actors in those events. They are, therefore, considered in the analysis of the tabloids' photographic treatment of conventional news later in this chapter.

CELEBRITIES

Of the several ways that famous people appear in the tabloid press, the plain photograph of the person posing at home is probably the most common. Sports figures, entertainers, and, occasionally, politicians are photographed 'behind the scenes' of their public lives, together with family and loved ones. These pictures, arranged in the same manner that characterizes the pictures of non-famous people, lack only the emotional extremes to be read from the celebrities' faces; these people all appear relaxed and happy. The obviously domestic environments naturalize the stars. The photographs suggest we are seeing them as they 'really' are. At the same time, through angle and eye-contact with the camera, they are brought down to the viewer's level. The photographic construction which presents the private person as someone 'just like us' accomplishes the same task when framing the public figure.

The difference between how these two kinds of domestic pictures work assumes that the viewer can recognize this person as famous. It is not necessary for the viewer to be able to identify the person, only that this recognition takes place. Once it has, however, the home photograph does more than present the person as the viewer's equal, someone 'just like us'. In addition, it has become *revealing*. Recognizing the person's celebrity status establishes the photograph as a privileged look behind the façade of public life.

Performance photographs are also quite common, often published next to the behind-the-scenes photograph of the celebrity at home. The picture of the singer or rock star performing is often a file photograph, and the particular performance is rarely identified. The sports figure's performance, on the other hand, is presented in a recent action photograph usually from the game or competition which provides the reason for coverage.[12] These photographs present the recognizable and familiar public face of the celebrity.

File photographs of celebrities' performances occasionally accompany stories about scandals surrounding them. When a star is arrested on gambling charges or is reportedly undergoing treatment for a drug problem, for example, the performance photograph introduces a discontinuity. The photograph contrasts the controlled public view the star has previously presented with the revelations of the present scandal.

Candid photographs which penetrate the celebrity's public façade form a distinct genre of the tabloid press. However, like the posed photograph at home, many photographs that *appear* candid must be seen as extensions of the institutional edifice constructed around the star.[13] The apparently spontaneous flash photograph of the rock musician leaving a 'gala' event with a new lover at his side, for example, may be a scoop for the photographer or a revelation for fans, but it cannot be read as a penetration of the star's public façade. He has agreed (and probably hoped) to be photographed in this public setting and, as with the photograph at home, we assume he has done all he can to control the picture that is the outcome.

Candid photographs of celebrities' unguarded moments, on the other hand, do appear in the tabloids, although with far less frequency than one is led to expect by the reputation of these newspapers. The *paparazzi*, the name Fellini gave to the celebrity-chasing photographers in his film *La Dolce Vita*, find a larger market for their work in the weekly popular press than in the daily tabloids (Freund 1980: 181). However, the death of a major film star brings *paparazzi* work into the tabloid press. And the film star whose son is on trial for murder or the sports star who was withdrawn from public life following a drug scandal are examples of celebrities the tabloids pursue for photographs.

The look of these photographs is awkward, overturning the classical rules of good composition. Objects intrude into the foreground or background, light is uneven and often garish, and even focus may be displaced or imprecise. The photographs freeze movement, thus creating strange physical and facial contortions. They appear to be the result of simply pointing the camera in the direction that might 'make a picture'.[14] This style of 'candid' photography is grounded, as Sekula (1984) argues, in 'the theory of the higher truth of the stolen image'. The moment when the celebrity's guard is penetrated 'is thought to manifest more of the "inner being" of the subject than is the calculated gestalt of immobilized gesture, expression, and stance' (Sekula 1984: 29). The higher truth revealed in the candid moment is a notion that is repeated and expanded in the tabloids' photographic coverage of news events.

THE NEWS EVENT

'News' is defined and constructed in many different ways within tabloid newspapers, yet there is a core of nationally and internationally significant events that receive coverage across the spectrum of the tabloid daily press. In addition to the posed photographs of people whose lives have been touched by news events (discussed above), photographs are sometimes published from the time the event was taking place. These are usually action photographs and appear candid, in the sense that people are acting as if unaware of the photographer's presence. It is incorrect to think of the events themselves as unplanned, for many are scheduled and the press has mapped out strategies for covering them. These strategies include obtaining spontaneous photographs of people at the moment they are experiencing events that are seen as momentous, even historic (Becker 1984).

Many of the photographs bear a strong similarity to the candid pictures of celebrities. Like those images, these undermine the institutionally accepted precepts of 'good' photography in their awkward composition, harsh contrasts, and uncertain focus. Another similarity is that candid

news photographs are structured to reveal how people react when the comfortable façade of daily life is torn away. Facing experiences of great joy or tragic loss, people expose themselves, and photographs of such moments are thought to reveal truths of human nature. Examples include photographs taken at the airport as freed political hostages are reunited with their families, or those of policemen weeping at a co-worker's funeral.

These candid photographs are typically treated as belonging to a higher order of truth than the arranged pose. Yet to rank them along some absolute hierarchy of documentary truth ignores the cultural practices we use to distinguish between nature and artifice. Examples of these practices within photojournalism include specific technical effects (artifice) that are integrated into the tabloids' construction of realism (or nature).

Extreme conditions, including darkness or bad weather, can reduce the technical quality of news photographs. So can surveillance-like techniques, such as using a powerful telephoto lens to photograph from a distance, or using a still picture from a security video camera to portray a bank robbery. Technical 'flaws' like extreme graininess and underexposure have actually become conventions of the tabloids' style, visually stating the technical compromises the newspaper will accept in its commitment to presenting the 'real' story. The techniques work to enhance the appearance of candour, lending additional support to the construction of these photographs as authentic.

Many of the tabloids have a legacy of active crime reporting, and this style suggests a continuation of that tradition.[15] In contemporary tabloids, however, suspected and convicted criminals are not as common as are the faces and testimony of ordinary people caught in traumatic circumstances not of their own making. Photographs of political leaders are likely to be small portraits and file photographs, while the common people acting in the event receive the more prominent visual coverage. This is particularly marked when a photographer has been sent to cover foreign news.

Political turmoil and natural disasters are reasons for sending photographer–reporter teams on foreign assignments. Earthquakes and famine, elections threatened by violence, the redrawing of national and international borders, popular resistance movements and their repression attract major coverage. The coverage may include photographs of local officials, but the emphasis is on ordinary people, particularly children, who are affected by the events. The photographs establish their perspective, portraying their actions and reactions in the candid style typical of tabloid news photography. Yet the words often transform the style of the coverage into a first-person account, relocating the photographer as the subject or the story. Here again, we encounter the impossibility of seeing the photographs independently from the ways they are framed by the text.

REFRAMING THE PICTURE IN WORDS AND LAYOUT

Photographs attain meaning only in relation to the settings in which they are encountered. These settings include, as this investigation hopefully has demonstrated, the historically constructed discourses in which specific topics and styles of photography are linked to particular tasks or patterns of practice (Sekula 1984: 3–5). The photograph's setting also includes the concrete, specific place it appears in and how it is presented. In the newspaper, photographs have no meaning independent of their relationship to the words, graphic elements, and other factors in the display which surround and penetrate them. It is these elements which are, to borrow Stuart Hall's phrase, 'crucial in "closing" the ideological theme and message' of the photograph (Hall 1973: 185).

In general, the text which frames photographs in the tabloid press is far more dramatic than the photographs alone. Even a cursory analysis indicates that it is the words, in particular the headlines, which carry the tone of 'sensationalism'. 'Thirteen-year-old chopped up watchman' is the headline over a photograph of the victim's widow, posing with his photograph. 'Devil's body guard' are the words next to a photograph of two masked men standing beside a coffin draped with the IRA flag. Over a dark colour photograph of an oil platform, we read 'Capsized—49 jumped into the sea last night'. The text is large in relation to

the page size, generally in unadorned typefaces. Punctuation consists of exclamation points and quotation marks, enhancing both the drama and the authenticity of the words: '"It feels like I'm dying little by little"' is inserted into one of the last pictures of the aged film star [Greta Garbo]. Often headlines are short, as for example, the single word 'Convicted!' over the police photograph of the man found guilty of murdering the prime minister.

The relationship between text and the official i.d. photograph is relatively simple to unwind. The explicit purpose of this tightly framed, frontal portrait with its frozen expression is to identify its subject in the most neutral way possible. Through its instrumental service to institutional needs, it has acquired a primary association with law enforcement and police investigations. Any time a photograph in this form is linked with news, it now connotes criminal activity, tragedy, and death. The words published with the photograph serve to strengthen those connotations by repeating the associations awakened by the photograph alone and adding details that anchor the photograph's meaning in a specific event.

The relationship between text and the photographs most prevalent in the tabloids—of ordinary people posed in domestic settings—is more complex. Typically the text contradicts the 'ordinary' appearance of these subjects; they are not what they seem. The words tell us that their lives have been struck by tragedy, confusion, some unexpected joy, or else that they are deviant, carrying some secret which is not evident on the surface. The disjunction between photograph and text is greatest for photographs that present no 'evidence' that something is out of place, and instead mimic the private family portrait without interrupting its connotations of familiar security.

In these cases the text seems to carry the greater authority; it tells us what we are 'really' seeing in the photographs. The text here *illustrates* the image, instead of vice versa, as Barthes has pointed out, by 'burdening it with a culture, a moral, an imagination'. Whereas in the case of the i.d. photograph the text was 'simply amplifying a set of connotations already given in the photograph', here the text *inverts* the connotations, by retroactively projecting its meanings into the photograph (Barthes 1977: 26–7). The result is a new denotation; we actually locate evidence in the photograph of what lies behind the formal pose. From the photograph and the apparently contradictory text together, we have constructed a deeper 'truth'.

Candid photographs, whether of celebrities or of events conventionally defined as news, offer a third case, for their look of candour depends on visual conventions that connote unreconstructed reality. Their subjects and the messages of the accompanying texts are too varied to reveal one specific pattern capable of explaining how they work together in the construction of meaning. In general, the stylistic features of the candid photograph appear to confer the text with greater authority.

When portions of the text are marked as direct quotations, a technique often used in the tabloids, additional nuances of meaning are constructed. If the quoted text is offered as the words of the person in the photograph, it becomes a testimony of that individual's experience. The quotation bonds with the subject's 'inner being' that we see revealed in the candid photograph, enhancing the connotations of closeness and depth being produced individually within the photograph and text.

Occasionally the text also specifically constructs the tabloid's photographer. Accounts include how a certain subject was photographed, emphasizing the persistence and devotion the work required. The 45-year-old *paparazzo* who took the last photographs of Greta Garbo, 'for ten years lived only for taking pictures of "the Goddess", and now plans to leave New York and find something else to do; "My assignment is finished," he said.'

The photographer becomes a major figure, the public's eyewitness, when the words establish the photographs as first-hand exclusive reports of major news events. The two journalists sent by their newspaper to Beijing in June 1989 found themselves 'in the middle of the blood bath' that took place in 'Death Square'. The tabloid's coverage included portraits of the reporter and photographer, first-person headlines often in the present tense, heightening the immediacy, and enclosed in quotation marks ('"He dies as I take the picture"'), several articles written in the first person and many candid photographs, taken at night, showing the violence and its young victims.

This style of coverage, while it underscores many of the news values of conventional journalism, at the same time contradicts the ideal role of the journalist as one standing apart from the events being reported. Here the photographer is constructed as a subject, an actor in the events. The valorization of the photographer, a common theme in the wider discourse of photojournalism, enters a specific news story. This further heightens the authority of the coverage as an unmediated account: we are seeing events as they happened in front of the subject's eyes, as if we were present.

These specific techniques, the first-person text together with the harsh, high contrast candid photographs, further work to establish this as a sensational story. The events were so unusual that the journalists' conventional rules of news coverage proved inadequate. Their professional role stripped from them by what they were seeing, they were forced to respond directly and immediately, as subjects. The coverage is constructed to bring us closer, through the journalists' subjective response, to the extraordinary nature of these events.

Again, one must remember that what we see in the tabloid is not the work of photographers. Despite the presence of bylines, the photographs bear little resemblance to the photographers' frames. Extreme sizes, both large and small, and shapes that deviate sharply from the originals' rectangular proportions are routine. Photographs are combined in many different ways, creating contrasts and sequences. Graphic elements are imposed over the photographs, including text, directional arrows and circles, or black bands over subjects' eyes. Montages and obvious retouching of photographs are not unusual.

Many of these techniques contradict the conventions for presenting photographs as representations of fact. According to the rules applied in other areas of photojournalism and documentary photography, the integrity of the rectangular frame is not to be violated.[16] With few exceptions (which are often discussed heatedly by photographers and editors), the frame is treated as a window looking out on an actual world. Changes in perspective should be limited to moving the borders in or out: any penetration of the frame is disallowed as a change in the way the frame 'naturally' presents reality.[17]

The tabloid press's consistent violation of these conventions confronts the persistent construction of the photograph as unmediated. Here we see the 'original' image repeatedly manipulated and altered with irreverent disregard for the standards that guide the elite press. At the same time that the text and photographs combine to support the revelation of deeper truths in the tabloid's coverage, the journalistic 'package' continually overturns the guidelines established to protect the notion of photographic truth.

CONCLUSIONS

Contemporary photojournalism has attained the status of popular art, outside the margins of the daily press. Yet those characteristics which have been used to increase photojournalism's cultural capital in other spheres we see confronted and even inverted in tabloid newspapers. Instead of cleanly edited photo essays, the tabloids are more likely to present heavily worked layouts of overlapping headlines, photographs and text. In place of the idealized grace of the 'decisive moment', the individual photograph is generally either a compositionally flat and ordinary pose or a haphazardly awkward candid shot. And instead of the photojournalist as respected artist successfully interweaving realism and self-expression, the photographers who occasionally emerge from the muddled pages of the tabloid are impulsive individuals, consumed by the events they were sent to photograph.

The dichotomies that are usually drawn to distinguish between the tabloid and elite segments of the press cannot accommodate this photography. In the tabloid press, photographs appear to both support and contradict the institutional standards of journalistic practice. The practices used to present major news events are at the same time serious and emotional. Topics that lie well outside the news agendas of the elite press are covered using strategies that conform to standard news routines. Tabloid photojournalism is framed in texts that work to establish the photograph as credible and authentic and simultaneously prevent it from being seen as a window on reality. Such apparent inconsistencies are contained within a journalistic discourse that is irreverent, antagonistic, and specifically anti-elitist.

Sekula reminds us that 'the making of a human likeness on film is a political act' (Sekula 1984: 31), and publishing that likeness in a newspaper compounds the political implications. Within the journalistic discourse of the tabloid press, photography appears anti-authoritarian and populist. There are many ways in which its specific techniques construct photographers, the people in the photographs and the people who look at them all as subjects. These subjects are accessible and generally are presented as social equals. But it is difficult to locate a systemic critique in this work.

The critique that emerges from the tabloid press, and particularly its photography, is directed instead against the institutionalized standards and practices of elite journalism. In the pages of this press, we witness the deconstruction of both the seamless and transparent character of news and the ideal of an unbiased and uniform professionalism. The photographs within the discourse of tabloid journalism work simultaneously as vehicles for news and the means of its deconstruction.

NOTES

1. This essay is a revised version of the paper, 'The simultaneous rise and fall of photojournalism, a case study of popular culture and the western press', presented at the seminar 'Journalism and Popular Culture', Dubrovnik, Yugoslavia, 7–11 May 1990.
2. *Illustrated London News* circulation rose from 60,000 the first year to 200,000 in 1855, the

year the tax on printed matter was repealed (Hassner 1977: 157).

3. Johannesson has also identified competing syntaxes that apparently rendered reality somewhat differently. Whereas in the United States engravings began imitating the syntax of the photograph, in Europe the engraving followed the other visual arts (Johannesson 1982).

4. *Collier's* circulation doubled during 1898, the first year of Hare's employment, and by 1912 had reached one million (Hassner 1977: 224).

5. For several examples from the current investigation see note 11, below.

6. The *New York Times Sunday Magazine* is an outstanding example, frequently commissioning well-known photojournalists to cover specific topics.

7. Maren Stange offers a convincing analysis of the political and aesthetic adjustment that occurred within the Museum of Modern Art in New York as Edward Steichen launched the first major exhibitions in the documentary style, culminating in 1955 with the spectacular popularity of 'Family of Man' and its 'universalizing apolitical themes'. This major cultural institution, she argues, had 'installed documentary photography yet more firmly in the realm of popular entertainment and mass culture' (Stange 1989: 136).

8. The reader is referred to Becker (1990) for a full development of this point. For a discussion of the left-humanist art theory which provides the basis for the reconstruction of the photojournalist as artist, see Burgin (1986: 157).

9. Exceptions include the re-interpretation of a particular style of photojournalism—in which elements are 'caught' in the frame in strange relationships to each other, usually with the added effect of bare-bulb flash—as surrealist art. Photographer Arthur ('Weegee') Fellig's work is the best-known example or art institutional redefinition of this style (Sekula 1984: 30).

The Museum of Modern Art exhibition 'From the Picture Press' is another example of this tendency to 'surrealize' photojournalism. The exhibit consisted primarily of *New York Daily News* photographs selected with the help of photographer Diane Arbus (Szarkowski 1973). Henri Cartier-Besson has long preferred to call his work 'surrealism' instead of 'photojournalism'.

10. I am grateful to Mattias Bergman and Joachim Boes, Peter Bruck, John Fiske, Jostein Gripsrud, John Langer, David Rowe, Herdis Skov, and Colin Sparks for providing copies of many of the tabloids on which this analysis is based.

11. Some contrasts may be explained by national differences in newspaper consumption patterns: in England, tabloid press readership increased during the period when people began to confine their reading to one newspaper, whereas in Sweden the afternoon tabloids continue to be used as a complement to the morning broadsheet papers.

Differences in content also suggest cultural variation in the construction of the sensational. A striking ease is the conditions under which sex becomes an explicit topic, ranging from near-nude pin-ups as a regular feature in British and Danish papers, to unusual cases of sexual preference treated as news, to the virtual absence of sex in the most serious Australian tabloids. Another contrast is the extensive coverage the British and Australian papers devote to the 'private' lives of their royalty, whereas the Scandinavian papers only cover their royal families when one member is seriously ill, is presiding over some official occasion, or has become involved in a political debate. Explaining such differences, significant though they may be, remains beyond the scope of this chapter.

12. The sports action photograph in the tabloid press appears to correspond precisely to the same genre in the sports sections of elite newspapers. If true, this raises interesting issues about why sports photography in particular is found without modification in both classes of newspapers.

13. Here I have drawn on Alan Sekula's discussion of *paparazzi* photography, although my analysis and conclusions are somewhat different (Sekula, 1984).

14. Weegee, one who is credited with creating the style, said of his photograph from an opening night at New York's Metropolitan Opera, that it was too dark to see, but 'I could *smell* the smugness so I aimed the camera and made the shot' (Time-Life 1983: 54).

15. The style was associated with a particular way of working by photographers who chased down

tips from their police radios into places that were dark, crowded, confusing, and where they were not wanted. Although the style is now considered outmoded, a guarded admiration survives for the photographers who still follow this work routine. I wish to thank Roland Gustafsson, who has conducted interviews among the staff of Stockholm's *Expressen*, for drawing this point to my attention.

16. This convention also constructs the photographer as the authority, the intermediary through which this view of reality is refracted.

17. See, for example, the textbook guidelines for creating a 'clean' picture layout in the style of the classic photo essays (Hurley and McDougall 1971; Edey 1978; Kobre 1980: 271–81).

REFERENCES

Barthes, Roland (1977) 'The photographic message', in Stephen Heath (ed. and trans.) *Image, Music, Text*. New York: Farrar, Straus and Giroux. pp. 15–31.

Baynes, Kenneth (ed.) (1971) *Scoop, Scandal and Strife: a Study of Photography in Newspapers*. London: Lund Humphries.

Becker, Karin E. (1984) 'Getting the moment: newspaper photographers at work', paper presented at the American Folklore Society Annual Meeting, San Diego.

Becker, Karin E. (1985) 'Forming a profession: ethical implications of photojournalistic practice on German picture magazines, 1926–1933', *Studies in Visual Communication* 11 (2):44–60.

Becker, Karin E. (1990) 'The simultaneous rise and fall of photojournalism. A case study of popular culture and the western press', paper presented at the seminar 'Journalism and Popular Culture', Dubrovnik.

Benjamin, Walter (1936) 'The work of art in the age or mechanical reproduction' in Hannah Arendt (ed.), *Illuminations*. New York: Schocken, 1969. pp. 217–52.

Burgin, Victor (1986) *The End of Art Theory. Criticism and Postmodernity*. London: Macmillan.

Carnes, Cecil (1940) *Jimmy Hare, News Photographer*. New York: Macmillan.

Cookman, Claude (1985) *A Voice is Born*. Durham, NC: National Press Photographers Association.

Dyer, Carolyn Stewart and Hauserman, Nancy (1987) 'Electronic coverage of the courts: exceptions to exposure', *The Georgetown Law Journal* 75(5): 1634–700.

Edey, Maitland (1978) *Great Photographic Essays from Life*. New York: Little, Brown.

Edom, Clifton C. (1976) *Photojournalism. Principles and Practices*. Dubuque, IA: Wm. C. Brown.

Emery, Edwin (1962) *The Press and America. An Interpretive History of Journalism*, 2nd edn. Englewood Cliffs, NJ: Prentice-Hall.

Eskildsen, Ute (1978) 'Photography and the Neue Sachlichkeit movement', in David Mellor (ed.), *Germany. The New Photography, 1927–33*. London: Arts Council of Great Britain. pp. 101–12.

Freund, Gisèle (1980) *Photography and Society*. London: Gordon Fraser.

Gidal, Tim (1973) *Modern Photojournalism: Origin and Evolution, 1910–1933*. New York: Collier Books.

Hall, Stuart (1972) 'The social eye of the *Picture Post*', in *Working Papers in Cultural Studies 2*. Birmingham: CCCS.

Hall, Stuart (1973) 'The determinations of news photographs', in Stanley Cohen and Jock Young (eds), *The Manufacture of News*. London: Constable. pp. 176–90.

Hassner, Rune (1977) *Bilder for miljoner* (Pictures for the millions). Stockholm: Rabén & Sjögren.

Hurley, Gerald D. and McDougall, Angus (1971) *Visual Impact in Print*. Chicago, IL: Visual Impact.

Hård af Segerstad, Thomas (1974) 'Dagspressens bildbruk. En funktionsanalys av bildutbudet i svenska dagstidningar 1900–1970'. (Photography in the daily press), Doctoral dissertation, Uppsala University.

Johannesson, Lena (1982) *Xylografi och pressbild* (Wood-engraving and newspaper illustration). Stockholm: Nordiska museets Handlingar, 97.

Kahan, Robert Sidney (1968) 'The antecedents of American photojournalism', PhD dissertation, University of Wisconsin.

Kobre, Kenneth (1980) *Photojournalism. The Professionals' Approach*. Somerville, MA: Curtin & London.

Ohrn, Karin B. and Hardt, Hanno (1981) 'Camera reporters at work: the rise of the photo essay in Weimar Germany and the United States', paper presented at the Convention of the American Studies Association, Memphis, TN.

Schiller, Dan (1977) 'Realism, photography, and journalistic objectivity in 19th century America',

Studies in the Anthropology of Visual Communication 4(2): 86–98.

Schuneman, R. Smith (1966) 'The photograph in print: an examination of New York daily newspapers. 1890–1937', PhD dissertation, University of Minnesota.

Sekula, Allan (1984) *Photography Against the Grain.* Halifax: The Press of the Nova Scotia College of Art and Design.

Stange, Maren (1989) *Symbols of Ideal Life. Social Documentary Photography in America 1890–1950.* Cambridge: Cambridge University Press,

Szarkowski, John (ed.) (1973) *From the Picture Press.* New York: Museum of Modern Art.

Taft, Robert (1938) *Photography and the American Scene. A Social History, 1839–1889.* New York: Dover.

Time-Life (1983) *Photojournalism*, rev. edn, Alexandria, VA: Time-Life Books.

16

Miller's Crossing: War, Surrealism, and *Vogue*

KAREN ENGLE

'[The] background and the image couldn't heal together . . .' (Burke 2005: 95)

PROLOGUE: DISSOLUTIONS

In April of 1945, Lee Miller visited Dachau, twelve hours after its liberation by Allied soldiers. She took the photograph in Figure 16.1.

Except for part of the right arm still exposed to air, the body is floating just below the water's surface. It is partial—just a head and torso in profile, their edges bleeding into the water, unless it is the water taking over the body, swallowing it up bit by bit. The shadow at the elbow looks like an open wound from a slash or a slice, suggesting an incomplete severing of the arm. The verticality of the shadow-wound draws the eye down to the base of the image, which cuts off the bottom half of the body, and the slice of concrete bisecting the lower left section of the image makes explicit the operations of framing and cropping.

As we look more closely at the play of light and dark, the camouflage print of the jacket is echoed by the darkened splotches on the face, making the face resemble the uniform. Spots of light on the water, to the right of the torso, also duplicate the camouflage dots, and appear to be moving onto the jacket, eating through it like acid. Or, maybe the camouflage spots are leeching out into the water, draining the jacket of content like a soul leaving a body. In any case, the relation

FIGURE 16.1 Dead SS guard floating in the canal beside the camp

between patches of light and spots of conceal-ment produces an eerie mimetic effect whereby the body seems to be becoming, or dissolving into, water. What we see, preserved here like a fly caught in amber, is a moment of transition from one thing into another.

In June 1945, *Vogue* magazine published sev-eral photographs that Miller had taken during her visit to Dachau and Buchenwald, but this photograph was not among them. This essay is an attempt to imagine why Miller's floating sol-dier was excluded.

'THE ANGLES OF VISION ARE SKEWED'[1]

As the story goes, the first thing American pho-tographer Lee Miller did upon receiving her accreditation as a *Vogue* magazine war corres-pondent in 1942 was to head over to Saville Row and order her uniform (Burke 2005: 213). She had been in London since the war began, alternately documenting the Blitz and shooting the fashion world for *Vogue*. Miller came to photography via her father, who liked to photograph her nude throughout her childhood in Poughkeepsie, New

York, and later through Edward Steichen, who inspired her to become a photographer while he photographed her for *Vogue*.

When she was 22 years old, she moved to Paris and began an affair and apprenticeship with Man Ray, one of surrealism's favourite photographers. Between 1929 and 1932, Miller learned about lighting, shooting, and darkroom processing. While acquiring the techniques of photography, Miller continued her New York career as a *Vogue* model and general object of desire.[2] But as she developed her technical competence, she became a respected photographer in her own right. Miller shot everyone, from Pablo Picasso to Joseph Cor-nell to Charlie Chaplin. Her street scenes reflect a deep understanding of Eugène Atget's studies of Paris, as well as a thorough knowledge of the history of Western art. She also mastered the sur-realist aesthetic of the *informe*—the destabiliza-tion of categories and blurring of boundaries that pervade the images and texts of its practitioners.[3]

A favourite technique for achieving the *informe* among photographers of the period was solar-ization, a process producing shifting tones on a photographic print. When photographic paper is exposed to light during the printing process, the density and intensity of the developed image changes. Solarization can make a positive print re-semble a negative, producing a fragmented effect 'which visually walls off parts of a single space or a whole body from one another, establishing in this way a kind of testimony to a cloven reality' (Krauss, Livingston, and Ades 1985: 28). Because photography is indexical—an 'imprint or trans-fer off the real'—solarization injects uncertainty into a viewer's experience of reality (Krauss 1986: 110). In Man Ray's 1931 solarized photograph, *The Primacy of Matter over Thought*, for instance, the visual laws of reality seem to dissolve. As a black line tracing the woman's limbs highlights the contours of her flesh, the boundary between body and space is blurred, and the body seems to liquefy into its environment. This is the *informe*.

Depending on whose account we read, either Miller and Man Ray invented the method togeth-er, or she caused Man Ray to discover it one day by accidentally exposing some negatives to light.[4] In one version, Miller felt something crawl over her foot while working in the darkroom. She panicked, switched on the light, and exposed the negatives to certain ruin, until Man Ray threw them desperately into the developer, hoping to salvage something.[5] In another version, Miller's role is completely excised and solarization is just another technique she learns from him (Haworth-Booth 2007: 41). In a third account, Miller and Man Ray discover it together, as Miller turned on the light 'forgetting that twelve negatives . . . hung in the developing tank'[6] (Burke 2005: 93). Depending on which account we read, the picture changes.

The subversive quality of solarization, and of other techniques of the *informe*, is precisely its ability to rupture our sense that reality is stable. Krauss describes it thus: 'the photographic medium is exploited [by surrealists] to produce a paradox: the paradox of reality constituted as sign—or presence transformed into absence, into representation, into spacing, into writing'[7] (Krauss 1986: 112). Photography does not present us with a false view of the real; it exposes the fact that 'reality' is never singular, stable, or monocular. Solarization, in this sense, is akin to the writing of history: no single authoritative account of an event can be said to exist. One moment in time can open out to infinite reflection and refraction, providing different angles of vision and superimposing one interpretation onto another. When it comes to depictions of war, whether in picture or in word, we do well to remember this multiplicity of perspective. To paraphrase novelist Tim O'Brien, there is no such thing as a true war story.[8]

When Lee Miller's London editor, Audrey Withers, sent her on assignment to capture the daily lives of nurses in Second World War France, or to cover the liberation of Paris, she had no idea what Miller would turn out until the packet made its way across the Channel and through the censors. If three or four different versions of the solarization scene can be found just by consulting a few history books, imagine how many thousands of images Miller could make of an embattled Europe, and how many different war stories she could write. The job of Withers and American *Vogue* editor Edna Woolman Chase was

to sift through the reams of images and the written dispatches arriving from the Continent and to decide what to include and what to cut[9]—to craft one story out of the myriad possibilities.

Miller's challenge, of course, was to get these images in the first place. Unlike 'ordinary journalists . . . [who] could sit in the safety of a press camp miles behind the action gathering their material at press conferences or from supply teams', photographers had to be in the action, shooting under tremendously dangerous and unpredictable circumstances (Penrose 1985: 131). Under these conditions, Miller alternated between two Rolleiflex cameras to increase the likelihood of producing something usable (ibid., 131). Since there was no light meter, telephoto lens, or automatic advance for the camera, Miller never knew whether or not she had been successful on a shoot until she saw the finished article weeks later (Livingston 1989: 63). She had little contact with Withers, which drove her to distraction, and she had no idea which images would be usable since she sent all of the film to London for processing.[10] As well, Miller wrote the text to accompany images she had not yet seen. She found writing torturous, something she could get down to only after hours of 'boondoggling', a process involving lots of sex, alcohol, and tears. While the published articles certainly made for good reading, they obscure these details that, in retrospect, seem to dominate Miller's day-to-day experiences as a war correspondent.

In a letter to Withers, Miller describes her frustration with the isolation and uncertainty of her war work:

> I have no way of knowing what you like or what you are using and find myself coming to full, unnecessary stops in work because you never comment—good—bad—or indifferent. It could be six weeks before I see what you have published so I barge on, feeling futile, like dropping stones into a well which is so bottomless that there is no returning sound on which to base a calculation. (Penrose and Scherman 1992: 92)

What Withers never saw, and what readers never guessed at, were the countless drafts Miller wrote in this state of isolation. The many versions of her first France story, housed today in the Lee Miller Archives in England, give us a sense of the way she worked (Burke 2005: 222). She photographed and wrote in the dark, not knowing which images had been successful or what narrative detail her editor wanted. How strange the finished product must have looked to her, bound in a beautiful fashion magazine and looking as effortless as a *Vogue* model.

The process seems to me akin to Miller's description of the bewitching results produced by solarization: 'the background and the image couldn't heal together . . . . The new exposure could not marry with the old one' (ibid., 95). The finished magazine story presents a focused picture that does not reflect its complex origins. Were we able to compare the finished articles in *Vogue* with the unedited manuscripts and hundreds of images in archives, the disjunctions between frontline photography and backroom editing would undoubtedly come into view. Although most of us will never make this pilgrimage, we can consult several published volumes on Miller's life and photography that provide a broader picture of her war work. One of these books, *Lee Miller's War*, published in 1992 by Miller's son Antony Penrose, is devoted to her wartime experiences. Said to illustrate the 'full range' of Miller's war work now located in the archives, the book cobbles together her correspondence from fragments and completed drafts, and sets it alongside numerous images, many of which were never published in either British or American *Vogue* (Penrose and Scherman 1992: 205).

IN *VOGUE* IN JUNE

Miller was notoriously restless, a fact covered in great detail by her biographers. When war came, she responded by joining the staff of *British Vogue* (or 'Brogue', as it was often nicknamed) in 1939. After shooting the Blitz in London during 1940 and 1941, Miller managed to become an accredited official war correspondent for Brogue in December 1942[11] (Burke 2005: 213). She alternated between fashion assignments and documenting women's roles in the war, including those of the

Wrens and the Auxiliary Territorial Service, but she was never supposed to see combat. It was illegal for women journalists to travel alone or to visit theatres of operation. Women were supposed to stay well behind the lines and cover women's interest stories (ibid., 221). When Brogue sent her to France in 1944, they wanted her to cover the experiences of American nurses at an evacuation hospital at 'Omaha Beach' (Penrose and Scherman 1992: 9). Miller did this, of course, but she also hitched a ride to a field hospital—much closer to the front—in order to cover seriously wounded or dead soldiers, evacuations, and surgical operations with often cinematic tension.

Her first taste of combat came entirely by accident. She was sent to St Malo in Brittany after the Omaha Beach story to cover the Allied victory, only to learn upon arrival that, contrary to all reports, the Germans had not surrendered (Penrose and Scherman 1992: 33). Though initially punished with house arrest for 'exceeding the limits of her assignment', Miller became the only woman correspondent to see front-line action in the Second World War, and she had an uncanny knack for arriving before any other journalists[12] (ibid., 10). David Scherman, *Life* correspondent and fellow photographer, remembers that 'Marguerite Higgins of the *New York Herald Tribune* once complained to me: "How is it that every time I arrive somewhere to cover a story you and Lee Miller are just leaving?"' (ibid., 12). She was, in other words, in the thick of things.

Both British and American *Vogue* published Miller's photo stories, although Brogue published more of them. The June 1945 issues of US and UK *Vogue* each contain a spread on her visit to Germany, with reference to her trips to Dachau and Buchenwald. Intriguingly, they did not print identical versions of the same story. In the US version, one photo essay, titled 'Germany Today', contains both Miller's dispatch—edited down significantly—and a selection of images. A second photo essay, 'Believe It', contains two double-page spreads of photographs with captions, the second with the subtitle 'Nazi Harvest'. The British version, by contrast, contains only one article entitled 'Germany: The War That is Won'. It has far fewer images, includes much more of Miller's narrative account, and omits the 'Believe It' photo essay. Miller did not have control over layout, captions, or which photographs were used, and the choices made by the respective editors certainly reflect the specific contexts of American and British readers (Sim 2009: 65).

The most striking difference between the UK and US versions is the relative absence of gruesome photographs in Brogue. Featuring only one small shot of bodies from Buchenwald, Audrey Withers explains the London editorial decisions thus: '[the] mood then was jubilation. It seemed unsuitable to focus on horrors' (Burke 2005: 265). A full-page photograph of a Frankfurt monument to Justice, and shots of a destroyed cathedral, a bombed-out chemical works, and German civilians waiting to cross the Main river in Frankfurt constitute the remainder of the Brogue images. The American issue, by contrast, features several grisly images, including pictures of burned bones, furnaces with body parts still visible, a pile of corpses, beaten guards, and the body of a Nazi's daughter who committed suicide. Since America was still heavily engaged in the Pacific theatre, and had not experienced either the Blitz or the Occupation, the liberation in Europe did not register in the same jubilatory way[13] (Haworth-Booth 2007: 189). Chase's decision to print more concentration camp images was undoubtedly connected to the fact that for America, the war was far from over. The enemy still needed a face.

The American *Vogue* team was not only unafraid of publishing scenes of horror, they seem almost to have delighted in it, as the sadistic 'Nazi Harvest' subtitle suggests. Despite this relish for the grotesque, US *Vogue* excluded the dead SS guard floating in the canal at Dachau, arguably one of Miller's most arresting camp images. The image mesmerizes. How entrancing its play of light and form, the way the edges between body and water merge into each other, and how the grasses seem like fingers reaching down. How odd that things seem to metamorphose like this, before our very eyes. How arresting to find something so beguiling in such an ugly place. Writer André Breton, the cranky 'central spokesman' of surrealism, might have recognized it as an example of Convulsive Beauty—something 'that

shakes the subject's self-possession' (Krauss 1986: 92–3; Krauss, Livingston, and Ades 1985: 85). *Vogue*'s chosen images of death, while striking, do not play such tricks with our eyes.

The photographs included in 'Believe It' reflect that Miller's 'aggressive "portraiture" style . . . is, in many ways, organized around the notion of voyeurism as a sadistic act' (Zox-Weaver 2003: 22). This is particularly true of her photographs of beaten or dead SS guards that depict unflinching evidence of violence against Germans, not by them. Miller gets up close and forces us to acknowledge that we are indeed looking at beaten and brutalized bodies—bodies rendered thus by Allied soldiers. She frames them in mug-shot style—profile ('prisoner hanged on iron hook') and frontal ('S.S. Guards who tortured prisoners, beg mercy on their knees, are beaten by ex-prisoners')—an aesthetic effect that reinforces their Nazi criminality, thereby helping to offset the reality that here they have been victims, not agents, of violence.

The pleasure of looking at the defeated enemy, in both the composition and content of the photo essays, simultaneously echoes the sadism of 'Nazi Harvest', *and* the theme of justice. The small photograph of a monument to Justice in Frankfurt, captioned 'Justice amid the ruins' and positioned just to the left of 'Nazi Harvest' makes this theme explicit; it frames the war, as well as Americans' (especially American women's) observation of it, as a just war. Allied audiences could enjoy the horror of looking at these photographs because they were positioned as morally upright. What's more, the 'Believe It' title admonishes us to look, since visual evidence of atrocity is required to counter any claims of fakery or exaggeration.[14] What makes the theme of justice most explicit for *Vogue*'s readers, however, is the editorial addition of captions, those tiny textual clues for pictorial interpretation.

The anxiety generated by an image, as Roland Barthes argued long ago, lies in the multiplicity of its potential interpretations (Barthes 1978). Captions are inserted in order to direct this flow of meaning: 'The caption is the missing voice, and it is expected to speak for truth' (Sontag 2001: 108–9). In the documentary war photograph,

"BELIEVE IT"

Lee Miller cables from Germany

"This is Buchenwald Concentration Camp at Weimar." The photograph on the left shows a pile of starved bodies; the one above, a prisoner hanged on an iron hook, his face clubbed.

Lee Miller has been with American Armies almost since D-Day last June; she has seen the freeing of France, Luxembourg, Belgium, and Alsace, crossed the Rhine into Cologne, Frankfurt to Munich. Saw the Dachau prison camp. She cabled: "No question that German civilians knew what went on. Railway siding into Dachau camp runs past villas, with trains of dead and semi-dead deportees. I usually don't take pictures of horrors. But don't think that every town and every area isn't rich with them. I hope Vogue will feel that it can publish these pictures—"

Here they are.

FIGURE 16.2 Reproductions of US *Vogue* layout, pages 104–5

FIGURE 16.3 Reproductions of US *Vogue* layout, pages 106–7

the caption helps to stabilize meaning, or at least to grant the illusion of such stability.[15] If we remove the captions from the 'Believe It' spread, for instance, we have no guide for labelling individual photographs, or for linking the images together.[16] The captions do work for us: they provide identifying information for each image, and they unify—thematically—the layout. All of the captions in 'Believe It' relate to the theme of 'eye for an eye' justice: 'Like the women of German-invaded countries, German women now cook in the ruins'; 'While Allied soldiers use bridge, German officers, boots pulled off, wade river'; and especially 'Pilloried Nazi labeled as food-thief'. Captions alone cannot frame how we feel about the act of looking, but they certainly influence how we interpret images, and how we understand our relation to those images.

For a caption to be most effective, however, this kind of image must comply with certain conventions. Historically, documentary war photography is meant to be what Rosalind Krauss calls 'straight photography': never reflecting too much (or any) thought on the part of the photographer in its form or composition, and never disrupting the subjectivity of the spectator (Krauss, Livingston, and Ades 1985: 95). Krauss refers, of course, to an ongoing debate about the danger that explicit 'artfulness' poses to the credibility of a medium thought to possess evidential force. In *Regarding the Pain of Others*, Susan Sontag claims that the uglier a photograph of atrocity, the more palatable it is to modern morality: 'Transforming is what art does, but photography that bears witness to the calamitous and the reprehensible is much criticized if it seems "aesthetic"; that is, too much like art' (Sontag 2003: 76). The presence of beauty or aesthetic sensibility in the documentation of death detracts from a photograph's indexicality—its status as a record of something actually existing in the physical world—and thus its ability to serve as a witness for something real.

Vogue certainly printed 'ugly' in its June issue. The beaten and hanging guards, the pile of corpses—these are repulsive images. But strangely, punctum-like,[17] one image in 'Believe It' stands out from the rest in both tone and content: that of the daughter of the burgomaster of Leipzig, a 'victim of Nazi philosophy' who has committed suicide with her parents (*Vogue* [US] June 1945, 106; Penrose and Scherman 1992: 176). Whether or not we recognize Jacques-Louis David's painting *The Death of Marat* (1793) in the girl's classical pose and Miller's attention to lighting, the stillness and theatricality of the image immediately sets it apart from both the everyday scenes and the more violent photographs in the spread. The girl is 'pretty' in her nurse's uniform, and light shining across her face makes her resemble a beatified saint.[18] As a 'victim of Nazi philosophy', her death is Ophelia-like: she succumbed to the madness. Space is granted for pity here, both in the photograph and the caption. And yet, pity does not compromise the documentary need to divide ally from enemy, nor does it collapse the boundary between sanity and insanity.

Max Kozloff tells us that war photography is about the separation of an 'us' from a 'them' via the depiction of 'traumatic content . . . that charges two major categories of the genre: one concerned with images of price, therefore potency; the other with humiliation (Kozloff 1987: 212). Opposite the 'Nazi Harvest' subtitle, a title framing all of the images states: 'Retribution overtakes the Germans: the people shamed, humiliated; the country destroyed, and honour lost' (*Vogue* [US] June 1945, 107). The pretty daughter of the burgomaster of Leipzig has killed herself because she is guilty. She belongs in a spread devoted to retribution, shame, and humiliation. In America, suicide is not heroic; it attests to her complicity and accords with the theme of justice. Ophelia is a figure of pathos, but there is no redemption for her Leipzig double.

While captivating, the image does not confuse the categories of ally and enemy: *Vogue* readers would have known from the uniform, and of course the caption, that this pretty girl was a Nazi. In this sense—and perhaps only in this sense—the photograph works as 'straight photography', which at base is about resolving the anxiety of knowing who is who and how everyone is positioned. For this reason, Krauss argues that 'straight photography' does not disorient the spectator. The same cannot be said of Miller's floating SS guard: his camouflage uniform tells us immediately that we cannot be certain of what we think we see.

If we read Miller's full textual account of this scene in the canal, we obtain a quite different picture than what the photograph suggests: 'The small canal bounding the camp was a floating mess of SS, in their spotted camouflage suits and nail-studded boots. They slithered along in the current, along with a dead dog or two and smashed rifles' (Penrose and Scherman 1992: 182). A teeming mess of bodies slithering like snakes through the water. The slipping of human into snake—that unmistakable representative of evil in Judeo-Christian culture—describes the metamorphoses that Miller captures in her lens. Faced with the evidentiary truth of this 'mess' of bodies, Miller animates the scene with a document that details the collapse of one thing into another.

PRAYING MANTIS

About 10 years before Miller made this image of the floating SS guard, sociologist and avant-garde writer Roger Caillois published two articles in the surrealist magazine *Minotaure*. One of them dealt with the sexual practices of the female praying mantis (a favourite subject for surrealist artists) and the other analyzed animal mimicry.[19] Both essays were extremely influential for artists like Salvador Dali, André Masson, and Max Ernst, and the mimicry essay in particular proved important for philosopher Jacques Lacan's formulation of the 'mirror stage'. For surrealist writer André Breton, mimicry was a primary instance of convulsive beauty (Krauss 1986: 112).

In the praying mantis essay, Caillois examines the bizarre capability of the mantis to mime life when dead. He writes that when decapitated, 'without any center of representation or of voluntary activity . . . [the mantis] can walk; regain its balance; sever a threatened limb; assume the spectral stance; engage in mating; lay eggs; build an ootheca; and (this is truly frightening) lapse into feigned *rigor mortis* in the face of danger . . . the mantis, when dead, [is] capable of simulating death' (Caillois 2003: 79). A dead thing not only can imitate life, it also can imitate death.

Inevitably, a question emerges: How can one tell the difference between the living and the dead? Or, between the living-miming-death, and the dead-miming-life-miming-death? The question is not gratuitously complex, for it addresses what Miller has done in the photograph of the floating soldier, namely, to ask, What is the difference between a German and a non-German?

To accompany her photographs of Germany for the June 1945 British and American issues of *Vogue* magazine, Miller wrote a full-length article. Both Withers and Chase edited it down, but Chase cut it drastically and set it alongside the 'Germany Today' story for her American audience, which appears first in the issue. The 'Believe It' spread, which follows 'Germany Today', does not include any of Miller's narrative; photographs and editorially written captions alone make up the four-page story. *Lee Miller's War* reproduces a full version of her manuscript, which begins thus:

> Germany is a beautiful landscape dotted with jewel-like villages, blotched with ruined cities, and inhabited by schizophrenics. There are blossoms and vistas; every hill is crowned with a castle. The vineyards of the Moselle and the newly ploughed plains are fertile. Immaculate birches and tender willows flank the streams and the tiny towns are pastel plaster like a modern watercolor of a medieval memory. Little girls in white dresses and garlands promenade after their first communion. The children have stilts and marbles and tops and hoops, and they play with dolls. Mothers sew and sweep and bake, and farmers plough and harrow; all just like real people. But they aren't. They are the enemy. This is Germany and it is spring. (Penrose and Scherman 1992: 161)

The text throughout this article, and in all the dispatches Miller provided for *Vogue*, is unambiguous. She didn't like Germany. She didn't like Germans. Her description brings to mind the *unheimlich*—Freud's famous description of the uncanny as that class of the frightening that turns out to be strangely familiar and long known.[20] But it seems to me that Miller is not trying to say that the Germans are secretly like the Allied forces, or vice versa. There is, rather, an attempt to differentiate. The strangeness Miller experiences from surveying the German landscape does not occur from seeing people and things that seem at first unrecognizable but later are clear markers of a common humanity. The strangeness stems specifically from the realness of the scene—from the issue of resemblance, or, in one of the common terms of the day, mimicry.

Surrealist artists and photographers were interested in mimicry for several reasons, including its capacity to blur boundaries and disrupt discrete categories—not a desirable effect in the documentary war photography of the day. Miller's textual narrative, by contrast, seems to use mimicry in order to erect a boundary. She does so by characterizing the relationship between German and Allied as imitation, a deeply ironic assertion given National Socialism's reverence for imitation—of all things classically Greek, that is. As philosopher Philippe Lacoue-Labarthe describes in his study of Heidegger and the work of art, the Nazi drive to emulate the Greek—to become fully and authentically German through imitating the classical, was fundamentally paradoxical. 'At least since Plato', he writes, 'identification or appropriation—the self-becoming of the Self—will always have been thought as the appropriation of a model . . . imitate me in order to be what you are' (Lacoue-Labarthe 1990: 80, 81). The concept 'self', in other words, paradoxically derives from a mimetic operation.

The Nazi desire for aesthetic purity and beauty could never be realized, since it would only ever be a secondary imitation. But Miller's text takes us even further than this: because of the perverse quest for purity, imitation produces not merely secondarity, but unreality. *Imitation* is an important word, particularly in the context of documentary image work, which is always dangling before us the question of reality. Miller tells us that the Germans look real, but they aren't. What they represent is merely a perverse imitation of life. But can we tell this from the image?

The boundaries between face and uniform, between body and environment, have been blurred here—another joke, of course, on the fascist's

dream of machine-like impenetrability. But the precise nature of the blurring in the photograph of the SS guard, the collapse of the body into water, or the water taking over the body, can be read as a form of mimicry. In his praying mantis essay, Caillois describes mimicry as a loss of self-possession and distinctiveness; the mantis becomes a figure through which to interpret 'the human desire to recover its original insensate condition, a desire comparable to the pantheistic idea of becoming one with nature' (Caillois 2003: 79). In his second essay, 'Mimicry and Legendary Psychasthenia', Caillois argues against the conventional wisdom that animal mimicry constitutes an extraordinary defence system, positing instead that it represents a 'disorder of spatial perception' (ibid., 99). Employing biology as a tool for psychoanalytic analysis, animal mimicry is used to explain the schizophrenic's disturbed relation to space: 'the subject crosses the boundary of his own skin and stands outside of his senses . . . He feels that he is turning into space *himself—dark space into which things cannot be put*' (ibid, emphasis in original). As the surrealists knew, the mimicry of the praying mantis could be viewed not only as the insect blending in, but also as the environment taking over. Caillois uses the conceit of mimicry to re-think the field of visuality, suggesting that the schizophrenic 'tries to see *himself, from* some point in space' (ibid, emphasis in original). It is particularly this section that Lacan draws on to develop the model of vision we are now familiar with—visuality is 'imposed on a subject who is [caught] in a cat's cradle of representation' (Krauss, Livingston, and Ades 1985: 78). In other words, we are in the picture and we cannot see ourselves being seen.

Water reflects, somewhat as a mirror does, although it distorts more than glass does. In the tradition of Western art, water and reflection signal (among other things) the myth of Narcissus. Miller's image of the floating guard can be seen as a reflection without its Narcissus—at least until we realize that we occupy the position of Narcissus, gazing into the water to see this reflection. The camera puts us there, hovering on the bank looking straight down. The implications are unsettling, for where can we distinguish between the seeing subject and its reflection, the spectator and the SS officer? This image constitutes a wholesale twisting of representational conventions of the Narcissus myth. In classical versions of the myth, and even in Dali's 1934 painting, the spectator retains full subjective integrity.[21] Gazing at Narcissus gazing at his reflection, observers are typically situated at a distance, wholly outside of the experience. But here in Dachau, Miller projects us into the scene. The perspective from which she shoots places us in the position of a classical Narcissus looking down on our beautiful, deadly reflection.

And yet this doesn't seem quite right, for a true reflection would require that we—as spectators—be also in profile, therefore making us unable to see the image, since our gaze would be pointed in another direction. It's a visual puzzle, for we see something impossible here, or to borrow that old saw of Lacan's, 'You never look at me from the place at which I see you' (Lacan 1998). It was Lacan's analysis of the anamorphic skull in Hans Holbein the Younger's painting *The Ambassadors* (1533) that clarified his theory of the object gaze. One can see the skull properly only by looking at the painting awry, at which point the rest of the picture is skewed. Not only does the skull seem to look back at us, implicating us in the scene, but also the painting teaches us that we cannot see everything. So what are we looking at? What are we unable to fully frame in Miller's image? The position of the soldier's face in profile complicates any conclusion of simple one-to-one reflection, but the camera's perspective insists that some kind of mirroring is at play.

In part, the strange temporality of the photographic image addresses this question of gaze and reflection, for photography, as Barthes observes, ushered in 'a new category of space-time: spatial immediacy and temporal anteriority' (Barthes 1978: 47). He explains that a photographic image paradoxically combines unreality with reality: 'Its unreality is that of the here, since the photograph is never experienced as an illusion; it is nothing but a presence .... Its reality is that of a having-been-there .... We possess, then, a kind of precious miracle, a reality from which we are ourselves sheltered' (ibid., 47). In Miller's photograph, the confusion of self and other, or of Allied and German, stems from this paradoxical combination of unreality and reality. Unreality is produced when the image is experienced as a reflection of the Now, and therefore a reflection of the Self—as a presence. This experience is triggered by the equivalence Miller produces between camera, spectator, and Narcissus. Its reality, by contrast, comes from its indexicality, its status as a trace of something that was there. It seems to me that despite Miller's hatred of the Germans, those schizophrenics parading as real people, her photograph creates a space where identity is put into question and left unresolved.

Taken over by his environment, the floating SS Guard signals a loss of self-possession—on the part of both corpse and spectator. The mimicry we observe in the relation between corpse and water is doubled in our experience of looking. Instead of the classical representational perspective of Narcissus that leaves the spectator intact, here we experience dissolution and a destabilization of the categories 'self' and 'other', dissolution and destabilization being favourite themes in surrealist photography. While war photography of this time does not admit of such aestheticization— and *Vogue* proved no exception—Miller's genius is to blend the two, her surrealist sensibility infiltrating the document and spreading out, like water into a body. As praying mantis, Miller collapses war into beauty. Her photograph renders Dachau beautiful; this makes the photograph a moment of pure danger.

NOTES

1. O'Brien 1998: 78.
2. Discovered in 1927 by Condé Nast in New York, she was photographed by, among others, Steichen, Genthe, and Hoyningen-Huene (Burke 2005: 56–9).
3. Countless histories of surrealism exist. Given

the complex and ever-changing relationships of artists associated, either officially or unofficially, with surrealist ideas, it would be fatuous to attempt any all-encompassing definition of surrealism as a movement. That said, I am partial to Rosalind Krauss's analysis of surrealism as a kind of strategy devoted to the *informe*, a word she takes from Georges Bataille's definition of the term in *Documents* 1, no. 7 (1929): 382. (Krauss, Livingston, and Ades 1985; Krauss 1986).

4. See, for example, Man Ray's *Lee Miller* (1929) and *Calla Lilies* (1930).

5. See Livingston 1989: 35; L'Ecotais and Ware 2007: 89 (although in this last version it is the prints exposed to light, not the negatives, and no mention is made of Man Ray's fury or attempt to salvage the negatives); and Penrose, 30. These accounts all refer to Mario Amaya's 1975 interview with Lee Miller, 'My Man Ray'.

6. Technically, none of these accounts are precisely correct, since records tell us that numerous photographers in the nineteenth century had already discovered the very same effect, and that Man Ray had seen a Sabattier print years before he met Miller. The Sabattier effect refers to the re-exposure of a print during processing, a slightly different procedure than solarization, but one that produces a similar effect. Even if Miller and Man Ray did not invent solarization, or the 'rayograph' as it was then called, they did devote tremendous energy trying to perfect the method (Burke 2005: 93).

7. The terms *spacing* and *writing* here are references to Jacques Derrida's work in *Of Grammatology*.

8. From *The Things They Carried*, cited earlier: 'In any war story, but especially a true one, it's difficult to separate what happened from what seemed to happen. What seems to happen becomes its own happening and has to be told that way. The angles of vision are skewed' (O'Brien 1998: 78).

9. Chase was the editor of American *Vogue* during Miller's war correspondence years. Both American and British *Vogue* published her work, although as we will see, they did not print identical photo stories.

10. Henri Cartier-Bresson called it becoming a '"silkworm"—endlessly loading, exposing, and unloading film, writing data, loading the lot on the plane for New York, and not knowing

until you are three weeks and two thousand miles away from the subject whether the second strobe went off' (Newhall 1998: 138).

11. David Scherman dates her accreditation to 1944, but I imagine he is referring to the date she gets permission to visit the Continent (Penrose and Scherman 1992: 9). In addition to her reports to *Vogue*, two books were also published: *Grim Glory: Pictures of Britain Under Fire* (1941), a propaganda effort to persuade the US to enter the war, contained several of her photographs, and *The Wrens in Camera* (1943).

12. Other women photographers, like Margaret Bourke White and Mary Jean Kempner, were shooting at the same time, but Miller was the only one to see action.

13. As Haworth-Booth also notes, the editorial in the US June issue is titled, 'Halfway to Victory' (2007: 189).

14. As Penrose tells us, the horror of the camps was so great and unimaginable, that many of the visiting American GIs thought at first that they were 'a grotesque propaganda stunt faked by their own side' (1985: 139).

15. Sontag's argument here is that the context of use will always inflect the meaning of an image, and, that contexts are always changing. She notes on the next page how easily 'the caption-glove slips on and off' (2001: 109).

16. The absence of such information can generate genuine anxiety and anger among readers. Writing in 1952, Nancy Newhall recounts one such instance when David Douglas Duncan published his photos of the Korean war without captions: '[they] were outraged to find no identification whatsoever in a whole bookful of "journalistic" photographs of the war in Korea' (1998: 142).

17. Barthes describes the punctum in *Camera Lucida* as that mysterious element in a photograph that pierces or wounds the viewer, eliciting an unexpected emotional response. It is a wholly subjective experience, and speaks to our inability to fix or stabilize photographic meaning.

18. See Miller's full description of the scene in Penrose and Scherman(1992: 176).

19. The titles are, respectively, 'The Praying Mantis: From Biology to Psychoanalysis' and 'Mimicry and Legendary Psychasthenia' (Caillois 2003).

20. Freud 1991.

21. See, for example, Caravaggio's *Narcissus* (1597–1599); John William Waterhouse's *Echo and Nar-* *cissus* (1903); or Salvador Dali's *Metamorphosis of Narcissus* (1937).

BIBLIOGRAPHY

Amaya, Mario. "'My Man Ray": Interview with Lee Miller'. *Art in America* (1975): 55.

Barthes, Roland. *Image, Music, Text*. Hill and Wang, 1978.

Benjamin, Walter. *Walter Benjamin: Selected Writings, Volume 2: 1927–1934*. Belknap Press of Harvard University Press, 1999.

Burke, Carolyn. *Lee Miller: A Life*. Knopf, 2005.

Caillois, Roger. *The Edge of Surrealism: A Roger Caillois Reader*. Duke University Press, 2003.

Carter, Ernestine, ed. *Grim Glory: Pictures of Britain Under Fire*. Lund, Humphries, 1941.

Derrida, Jacques. *Archive Fever: A Freudian Impression*. University of Chicago Press, 1998.

Freud, Sigmund et al. *The Standard Edition of the Complete Psychological Works of Sigmund Freud; Transl. from the German Under the General Editorship of James Strachey*, 1991.

Haworth-Booth, Mark. *The Art of Lee Miller*. Yale University Press, 2007.

Kozloff, Max. *The Privileged Eye: Essays on Photography*. University of New Mexico Press, 1987.

Krauss, Rosalind, Jane Livingston, and Dawn Ades. *L'Amour fou: Photography and Surrealism*. Abbeville Press, 1985.

Krauss, Rosalind E. *The Optical Unconscious*. MIT Press, 1994.

——. *The Originality of the Avant-Garde and Other Modernist Myths*. MIT Press, 1986.

Lacan, Jacques. *The Four Fundamental Concepts of Psychoanalysis*. W.W. Norton, 1998.

Lacoue-Labarthe, Philippe. *Heidegger, Art, and Politics: The Fiction of the Political*. Blackwell, 1990.

L'Ecotais, Emmanuelle de, and Katherine Ware. *Man Ray*. Taschen, 2007.

Livingston, Jane. *Lee Miller Photographer*. California International Arts, 1989.

Miller, Lee. *Wrens in Camera*. Hollis and Carter, 1945.

Newhall, Nancy. *From Adams to Stieglitz: Pioneers of Modern Photography*. 2nd edn. Aperture, 1998.

O'Brien, Tim. *The Things They Carried*. Reprint. Broadway, 1998.

Penrose, Antony. *Lives of Lee Miller*. Thames & Hudson, 1985.

—— and Scherman, David Edward. *Lee Miller's War: Photographer and Correspondent With the Allies in Europe 1944–45*. First American Edition. Bulfinch Press, 1992.

Schwartz, Joan M. "'Records of Simple Truth and Precision": Photography, Archives, and the Illusion of Control'. *Archivaria* 50 (2000): 1–40.

Sim, Lorraine. 'A Different War Landscape: Lee Miller's War Photography and the Ethics of Seeing'. *Modernist Cultures* 4 (2009): 48–66.

Sontag, Susan. *On Photography*. Picador, 2001.

——. *Regarding the Pain of Others*. Douglas & McIntyre, 2003.

Stoler, Ann Laura. *Along the Archival Grain: Epistemic Anxieties and Colonial Common Sense*. Princeton University Press, 2010.

Vogue. New York, Condé Nast Publications. Print.

——. London, Condé Nast Publications. Print.

Zox-Weaver, Annalisa. 'When the War Was in Vogue: Lee Miller's War Reports'. *Women's Studies* 32.2 (2003): 131.

QUESTIONS FOR REFLECTION

1. Analyze the front page images of two major newspapers. What messages are communicated by these images? Do both form and content help to convey this message, and how does the surrounding text work to frame this interpretation?
2. If images in the tabloid press participate in the construction of cultural values and beliefs, what values and beliefs are built through contemporary tabloids? Do these values and beliefs differ in the tabloids of different countries?
3. Look through news magazines and newspapers for stories on war. What types of images are included, and what kind of messages do they communicate? Are the images 'straight' photographs as discussed by Engle? Could the same images have been used to tell a different story?

FURTHER READING

Barnhurst, Kevin G., and John Nerone. *The Form of News: A History.* New York: Guilford, 2001.

Brennen, Bonnie, and Hanno Hardt, Eds. *Pictures in the Public Sphere: Studies in Photography, History and the Press.* Urbana-Champaign: University of Illinois, 1999.

Carlebach, Michael L. *American Photojournalism Comes of Age.* Washington: Smithsonian, 1997.

Carlson, Matt. 'The Reality of a Fake Image: News norms, photojournalistic craft, and Brian Walski's fabricated photograph'. *Journalism Practice* 3.2 (2009): 125–39.

Gross, Larry, John Stuart Katz, and Jay Ruby, Eds. *Image Ethics: The Moral Rights on Subjects in Photographs, Film, and Television.* New York: Oxford, 1988.

Gross, Larry, John Stuart Katz, and Jay Ruby, Eds. *Image Ethics in the Digital Age.* Minneapolis: University of Minnesota, 2003.

Kennedy, Liam. 'Securing Vision: Photography and US foreign policy'. *Media, Culture & Society* 30.3 (May 2008): 279–94.

Perlmutter, David D., and Nicole Smith Dahmen. '(In)visible evidence: pictorially enhanced disbelief in the Apollo moon landings'. *Visual Communication* 7.2 (May 2008): 229–51.

Perlmutter, David D., and Gretchen L. Wagner. 'The Anatomy of a Photojournalistic Icon: Marginalization of Dissent in the Selection and Framing of "a Death in Genoa"'. *Visual Communication* 3.1 (2004): 91–108.

Seelig, Michelle. 'A Case for the Visual Elite'. *Visual Communication Quarterly* 12.3/4 (September 2005): 164–81.

Sontag, Susan. 'The Photographs Are Us'. *New York Times Magazine* 23 (May 2004): 24–49, 42.

Squiers, Carol. 'Class Struggle: The Invention of Paparazzi Photography and the Death of Diana, Princess of Wales'. *Over Exposed: Essays on Contemporary Photography.* Ed. Carol Squiers. New York: The New Press, 1999. 269–304.

Zox-Weaver, Annalisa. 'When the War was in Vogue: Lee Miller's War Reports'. *Women's Studies* 32.2 (2003): 131–63.

PART SIX

COLLECTING CULTURE: THE MUSEUM

The practices of collecting, archiving, and displaying images in public forums such as museums and galleries play an important role in the construction of knowledge as well as of memory, history, and identity. Importantly, collections of artworks, news photographs, architectural drawings, maps, or any other forms of representation can rarely be complete collections. This is especially true in the case of broad subject areas such as modern art, advertisements, or anatomical atlases. The inherent incompleteness of collections highlights the power of both the collector and the collection in the construction of knowledge. Collecting, archiving, and displaying images are acts of choice in which certain images are selected over others. Such choices necessarily impact what can and cannot be known through the collection, both in terms of research based on its contents and through its display in the form of public exhibitions. The essays in this part analyze collecting and displaying as inherently powerful practices that function in the construction of identity, history, and memory.

The first reading in the part, 'The MOMA's Hot Mamas', by Carol Duncan, examines public art museums—specifically the Museum of Modern Art (MOMA), New York—as institutions that are 'prestigious and powerful engines of ideology'.

The author begins the essay by positioning 'modern art' as a cultural construct, stressing that what is commonly understood as the history of modern art is actually highly selective and culturally and historically specific. The author argues that this dominant narrative or 'story' of modern art is centred on a myth of linear progress: that artistic production follows a clean trajectory of one movement succeeding another. Duncan then examines the representation of this story—of modern art—in the Museum of Modern Art, a leading institution in the collection and dissemination of modern art. As Duncan shows, the artists whose work is chosen, the subject matter of their works, and the spatial arrangement of the works in the gallery all help to propel a specific story of modern art.

As the title of Duncan's essay suggests, gender plays a primary part in her analysis of MOMA and its representation of modern art. She argues that modern art (as we know it) is largely conceived by and for men, and that the representation of women is a dominant theme in this work. Importantly, and in a manner reminiscent of the essays by Cregan and Cartwright in this book, Duncan stresses that women are not represented as individuals but as aggregate types identified according to their 'sexually accessible bodies'. She then draws upon a more contemporary example—an advertisement for Penthouse magazine—to suggest that museum spaces, like advertisements, function in the construction of concepts of self and one's position in society. This is a relatively brief but important comparison as it highlights the cultural impact of public museums and the stories that they tell. Duncan's work in this essay, as well as in her numerous other publications, was fundamental in bringing critical, feminist analysis to public institutions such as galleries and museums.

The modernist notion of linear progress is central to the second essay in this part, 'Whiffs of Balsam, Pine, and Spruce: Art Museums and the Production of a Canadian Aesthetic', by the Canadian visual culture scholar Anne Whitelaw. Like Duncan, Whitelaw stresses that the particular strategies of display in a museum or gallery—what gets shown and where—are essential

components in the construction of narratives. Where Duncan highlights the construction of a gendered narrative of modern art, Whitelaw addresses national identity (the subject of the essays in Part Seven). Specifically, the author examines the collection and display of works by the Group of Seven within the permanent collection of the National Gallery of Canada. She borrows from Benedict Anderson to argue that national identity is a subjective, dynamic construct: it is not a transhistorical and inherent phenomena but is something that is produced within historically and culturally specific parameters. Whitelaw's essay highlights the role of cultural production and collecting practices in the construction of Canadian national identity.

Whitelaw analyzes the public discourse around the development of the National Gallery and its purchase and exhibition of works by the Group of Seven. She argues that the Group's work was promoted as representative of Canadianness both within Canada and outside its borders. Key to the narrative was the Group's focus on the northern landscape and the break with European art historical tradition. This message was reinforced through the particular display of the work in the gallery, which literally positioned the work between older, European-influenced Canadian art and more contemporary, abstract work. Thus the Group's work is defined as marking a turning point not just in Canadian art but in the formation of a distinct national culture. And as Whitelaw rightly notes, such a practice presupposes that a single, locatable national identity can exist. She writes: 'underscoring appeals to nationalism is the belief that there is such a thing as "a" (single) "common heritage" that will have meaning across boundaries of race, class, sexuality, and generation.' The National Gallery's portrayal of the Group's work was therefore less representative of Canadianness than it was of a relatively small, homogeneous group of white, affluent art patrons, critics, practitioners, and professionals.

The modernist project of art museums serves as the point of departure for the final essay in this part, 'The Mask Stripped Bare by its Curators: The Work of Hybridity in the Twenty-First Century', by the anthropologist and art historian Ruth B.

Phillips. The author argues that the modernist project is concerned with and built upon key binaries such as art/non-art and Western/Other. For Phillips, such clean categories do not exist in the contemporary world and museums need to account for the increasingly complex and global nature of cultural production. The author stresses the problematic nature of such categorization in her discussion of translation, where the products of one culture are translated into another as they are collected and displayed by museums. Using the specific example of African masks, Phillips notes that, when collected and displayed in modern Western museums, such artifacts are too often 'stripped' of their context and meaning and are repositioned within the exhibition as isolated, purified cultural artifacts.

Phillips borrows from science studies scholar Bruno Latour to introduce the concepts of imbroglio and hybridity as useful tools for new, critical museological practice. Imbroglio and hybridity reference the erosion of traditional, modernist categories (art/non-art, Western/Other) and the 'entanglement' of disparate phenomena. As Phillips notes, museum exhibitions and museological practice increasingly bleed beyond the confines of the institution and engage with 'politics, ethics, and practice'. Rather than attempting to suppress these networks of relations, Phillips stresses that contemporary museums must interrogate them and make them transparent. She concludes: 'We must find better ways to relish difference . . . and to respect separateness while at the same time insisting on interconnection.' Phillips's essay is an important post-colonial analysis of collecting culture and of the role of the museum in society. Her call for a critical museological practice and the recognition of cultural difference is a direct response to the traditional practices of collection and display that were the subject of the essays by Duncan and Whitelaw.

To collect, archive, and display images is to participate in the production of knowledge, memory, history, and identity. This can be seen at both micro and macro levels. In the former, our individual image collections tell a story about us and our lives. In the latter, national galleries and archives contribute to the formation of cultural beliefs and values that come to appear as natural fact. In each case the collection or display only ever presents a partial account. As the essays by Duncan, Whitelaw, and Phillips show, we need to be more critically aware of image collections as *collections*. This is essential in order to evaluate and interrogate the stories that they tell.

17

THE MOMA'S HOT MAMAS

CAROL DUNCAN

The theme of this issue of *Art Journal* is Images of Rule. The objects that my essay discusses, well-known works of art, are not images of rule in any literal sense—they do not depict a ruling power. They are, nevertheless, effective and impressive *artifacts* of rule. Rather than directly picturing power or its symbols, they invite viewers to an experience that dramatizes and confirms the social superiority of male over female identity. This function, however, is obscured and even denied by the environments that surround the works, the physical environment of the museum, and the verbal environment of art history. In what follows, I try to uncover this hidden function.

When The Museum of Modern Art opened its newly installed and much-enlarged permanent collection in 1984, critics were struck with how little things had changed. In the new installation, as in the old,[1] modern art is once again a progression of formally distinct styles. As before, certain moments in this progression are given greater importance than others: Cézanne, the first painter one sees, announces modern art's beginnings. Picasso's dramatically installed *Demoiselles d'Avignon* signifies the coming of Cubism—the first giant step twentieth-century art took and the one from which much of the history of modern art proceeds. From Cubism unfolds the other notable avant-garde movements: German Expressionism, Futurism, and so on, through Dada-Surrealism. Finally come the American Abstract Expressionists. After purifying their work of a residue of Surrealist representation, they made the final breakthrough into the realm of absolute spirit, manifested as absolute formal and non-representational purity. It is in reference to their achievement that, according to the MOMA (in its large, new, final gallery), all later significant art in one way or another continues to measure its ambitions and scale.

Probably more than any other institution, the MOMA has promoted this 'mainstream modernism', greatly augmenting its authority and prestige through acquisitions, exhibitions, and publications. To be sure, the MOMA's managers did not independently invent the museum's strictly linear and highly formalist art-historical narrative; but they have embraced it tenaciously, and it is no accident that one can retrace that history in its galleries better and more fully than in any other collection. For some, the museum's retrospective character is a regrettable turnaround from its original role as champion of the new. But the MOMA remains enormously important for the role it plays in maintaining in the present a particular version of the art-historical past. Indeed, for much of the academic world as for the larger art public, the kind of art history it narrates still constitutes the definitive history of modern art.

Yet, in the MOMA's permanent collection, more meets the eye than this history admits to. According to the established narrative, the history of art is made up of a progression of styles and unfolds along certain irreversible lines: from style to style, it gradually emancipates itself from the imperative to represent convincingly or coherently a natural, presumably objective world. Integral to this narrative is a model of moral action, exemplified by individual artists. As they become liberated from traditional representation, they achieve greater subjectivity and hence greater artistic freedom and autonomy of spirit. As the literature of modern art portrays it, their progressive renunciation of representation, repeatedly and minutely documented in monographs, catalogues, and critical journals, is often achieved

through painful or self-sacrificing searching or courageous risk-taking. The disruption of space, the denial of volume, the overthrow of traditional compositional schemes, the discovery of painting as an autonomous surface, the emancipation of colour, line, or texture, the occasional transgressions and reaffirmations of the boundaries of art (as in the adaptation of junk or non-high art materials), and so on through the liberation of painting from frame and stretcher and thence from the wall itself—all of these advances translate into moments of moral as well as artistic choice. As a consequence of his spiritual struggle, the artist finds a new realm of energy and truth beyond the material, visible world that once preoccupied art—as in Cubism's reconstruction of the 'fourth dimension', as Apollinaire called the power of thought itself; Mondrian's or Kandinsky's visual analogues of abstract, universal forces; Robert Delaunay's discovery of cosmic energy; or Miró's recreations of a limitless and potent psychic field. Ideally and to the extent to which they have assimilated this history, museum visitors re-enact these artistic—and hence spiritual—struggles. In this way they ritually perform a drama of enlightenment in which freedom is won by repeatedly overcoming and moving beyond the visible, material world.

And yet, despite the meaning and value given to such transcendent realms, the history of modern art, as it is written and as it is seen in the MOMA and elsewhere, is positively crowded with images—and most of them are of women. Despite their numbers, their variety is remarkably small. Most often they are simply female bodies, or parts of bodies, with no identity beyond their female anatomy—those ever-present 'Women' or 'Seated Women' or 'Reclining Nudes'. Or, they are tarts, prostitutes, artist's models, or low-life entertainers—highly identifiable socially, but at the bottom of the social scale. In the MOMA's authoritative collection, Picasso's *Demoiselles d'Avignon*, Léger's *Grand Déjeuner*, Kirchner's scenes of street walkers, Duchamp's *Bride*, Severini's Bal Tabarin dancer, de Kooning's *Woman I*, and many other works are often monumental in scale and conspicuously placed. Most critical and art-historical writing give them comparable importance.

To be sure, modern artists have often chosen to make 'big' philosophical or artistic statements via the nude. If the MOMA exaggerates this tradition or overstates some aspects of it, it is nevertheless an exaggeration or overstatement of something pervasive in modern art history—as it is represented and illustrated in the literature. Why then has art history not accounted for this intense preoccupation with socially and sexually available female bodies? What, if anything, do nudes and whores have to do with modern art's heroic renunciation of representation? And why is this imagery accorded such prestige and authority within art history—why is it associated with the highest artistic ambition?

In theory, museums are public spaces dedicated to the spiritual enhancement of all who visit there. In practice, however, museums are prestigious and powerful engines of ideology. They are modern ritual settings in which visitors enact complex and often deep psychic dramas about identity—dramas that the museum's stated, consciously intended programs do not and cannot acknowledge overtly. Like all great museums, the MOMA's ritual transmits a complex ideological signal. My concern here is with only a portion of that signal—the portion that addresses sexual identity. I shall argue that the collection's recurrent images of sexualized female bodies actively masculinize the museum as a social environment. Silently and surreptitiously, they specify the museum's ritual of spiritual quest as a male quest, just as they mark the larger project of modern art as primarily a male endeavour.

If we understand the modern-art museum as a ritual of male transcendence, if we see it as organized around male fears, fantasies, and desires, then the quest for spiritual transcendence on the one hand and the obsession with a sexualized female body on the other, rather than appearing unrelated or contradictory, can be seen as parts of a larger, psychologically integrated whole.

How very often images of women in modern art speak of male fears. Many of the works I just mentioned feature distorted or dangerous-looking creatures, potentially overpowering, devouring, or castrating. Indeed, the MOMA's

collection of monstrous, threatening females is exceptional: Picasso's *Demoiselles* and *Seated Bather* (the latter a giant praying mantis), the frozen, metallic odalisques in Léger's *Grand Déjeuner*, several early female figures by Giacometti, sculpture by Gonzales and Lipschitz, and Baziotes's *Dwarf*, a mean-looking creature with saw teeth, a single large eye, and a prominent, visible uterus—to name only some. (One could easily expand the category to include works by Kirchner, Severini, Rouault, and others who depicted decadent, corrupt—and therefore *morally* monstrous—women.) In different ways, each of these works testifies to a pervasive fear of and ambivalence about woman. Openly expressed on the plane of culture, it seems to me that this fear and ambivalence makes the central moral of modern art more intelligible—whether or not it tells us anything about the individual psyches of those who produced these works.

Even work that eschews such imagery and gives itself entirely to the drive for abstract, transcendent truth may also speak of these fears in the very act of fleeing the realm of matter (*mater*) and biological need that is woman's traditional domain. How often modern masters have sought to make their work speak of *higher* realms—of air, light, the mind, the cosmos—realms that exist above a female, biological earth. Cubism, Kandinsky, Mondrian, the Futurists, Miró, the Abstract Expressionists—all drew artistic life from some non-material energy of the self or the universe. (Léger's ideal of a rational, mechanical order can also be understood as opposed to—and a defense against—the unruly world of nature that it seeks to control.) The peculiar iconoclasm of much modern art, its renunciation of representation and the material world behind it, seems at least in part based in an impulse, common among modern males, to escape not the mother in any literal sense, but a psychic image of woman and her earthly domain that seems rooted in infant or childish notions of the mother. Philip Slater noted an 'unusual emphasis on mobility and flight as attributes of the hero who struggles against the menacing mother.'[2] In the museum's ritual, the recurrent image of a menacing woman adds urgency to such flights to 'higher' realms.

Hence also the frequent appearance in written art history of monstrous or threatening women or, what is their obverse, powerless or vanquished women. Whether man-killer or murder victim, whether Picasso's deadly *Seated Bather* or Giacometti's *Woman with Her Throat Cut*, their presence both in the museum ritual and in the written (and illustrated) mythology is necessary. In both contexts, they provide the reason for the spiritual and mental flight. Confrontation and escape from them constitutes the ordeal's dark centre, a darkness that gives meaning and motive to the quest for enlightenment.

Since the heroes of this ordeal are generically men, the presence of women artists in this mythology can be only an anomaly. Women artists, especially if they exceed the standard token number, tend to degender the ritual ordeal. Accordingly, in the MOMA and other museums, their numbers are kept well below the point where they might effectively dilute its masculinity. The female presence is necessary only in the form of imagery. Of course, men, too, are occasionally represented. But unlike women, who are seen primarily as sexually accessible bodies, men are portrayed as physically and mentally active beings who creatively shape their world and ponder its meanings. They make music and art, they stride, work, build cities, conquer the air through flight, think, and engage in sports (Cézanne, Rodin, Picasso, Matisse, Léger, La Fresnaye, Boccioni). When male sexuality is broached, it is often presented as the experience of highly self-conscious, psychologically complex beings whose sexual feelings are leavened with poetic pain, poignant frustration, heroic fear, protective irony, or the drive to make art (Picasso, De Chirico, Duchamp, Balthus, Delvaux, Bacon, Lindner).

De Kooning's *Woman I* and Picasso's *Demoiselles d'Avignon* are two of art history's most important female images. They are also key objects in the MOMA's collection and highly effective in maintaining the museum's masculinized environment. The museum has always hung these works with precise attention to their strategic roles in the story of modern art. Both before and after the 1984 expansion, de Kooning's *Woman I* hung

at the threshold to the spaces containing *the* big Abstract Expressionist 'breakthroughs'—the New York School's final collective leap into absolutely pure, abstract, non-referential transcendence: Pollock's artistic and psychic free flights, Rothko's sojourns in the luminous depths of a universal self, Newman's heroic confrontations with the sublime, Still's lonely journeys into the back beyond of culture and consciousness, Reinhardt's solemn and sardonic negations of all that is not Art, and so on. And always seated at the doorway to good reason. De Kooning's *Women* are exceptionally successful ritual artifacts and masculinize the museum's space with great efficiency (Figures 17.1, 17.2).

The woman figure had been emerging gradually in de Kooning's work in the course of the 1940s. By 1951–52, it fully revealed itself in *Woman I* (Figure 17.3) as a big, bad mama—vulgar, sexual, and dangerous. De Kooning imagines her facing us with iconic frontality, large, bulging eyes, open, toothy mouth, massive breasts. The suggestive pose is just a knee movement away from open-thighed display of the vagina, the self-exposing gesture of mainstream pornography.

These features are not unique in the history of art. They appear in ancient and tribal cultures as well as in modern pornography and graffiti. Together, they constitute a well-known figure type.[3] The Gorgon of ancient Greek art (Figure 17.4), an instance of that type, bears a striking resemblance to de Kooning's *Woman I*, and, like her, simultaneously suggests and avoids the explicit act of sexual self-display that elsewhere characterizes the type. An Etruscan example (Figure 17.5) states more of its essential components as they appeared in a wide range of archaic and tribal cultures—not only the display of genitals, but also the flanking animals that point to her origins as a fertility or mother goddess.[4] Obviously, the configuration, with or without animals, carries complex symbolic possibilities and can convey many-sided, contradictory, and layered meanings. In her guise as the Gorgon witch, however, the terrible aspect of the mother goddess, her lust for blood and her deadly gaze, is emphasized. Especially today, when the myths and rituals that may have suggested other meanings have been

FIGURE 17.1 Willem de Kooning, *Woman I*, 1952, oil on canvas, 76 x 59", as installed in the Museum of Modern Art.

FIGURE 17.2 Willem de Kooning, *Woman II*, 1952, oil on canvas, 59 x 48", as temporarily installed in the Museum of Modern Art.

FIGURE 17.3 De Kooning, *Woman I*

FIGURE 17.4 Gorgon, clay relief. Syracuse, National Museum.

lost—and when modern psychoanalytic ideas are likely to colour any interpretation—the figure appears especially intended to conjure up infantile feelings of powerlessness before the mother and the dread of castration: In the open jaw can be read the *vagina dentata*—the idea of a dangerous, devouring vagina, too horrible to depict, and hence transposed to the toothy mouth.

Feelings of inadequacy and vulnerability before mature women are common (if not always salient) phenomena in male psychic development. Such myths as the story of Perseus and such visual images as the Gorgon can play a role in mediating that development by extending and re-creating on the cultural plane its core psychic experience and accompanying defenses.[5] Thus objectified and communally shared in imagery, myth, and ritual, such individual fears and desires may achieve the status of higher, universal truth. In this sense, the presence of Gorgons on Greek temples—important houses of cult worship (they also appeared on Christian church walls)[6]—is paralleled by *Woman I*'s presence in a high-cultural house of the modern world.

The head of de Kooning's *Woman I* is so like the archaic Gorgon that the reference could well be intentional, especially since the artist and his friends placed great store in ancient myths and primitive images and likened themselves to archaic and tribal shamans. Writing about de Kooning's *Women*, Thomas Hess echoed this claim in a passage comparing de Kooning's artistic ordeal to that of Perseus, slayer of the Gorgon. Hess is arguing that de Kooning's *Women* grasp an elusive, dangerous truth 'by the throat', 'And truth can be touched only by complications, ambiguities and paradox, so, like the hero who looked for Medusa in the mirroring shield, he must study her flat, reflected image every inch of the way.'[7]

But then again, the image type is so ubiquitous, we needn't try to assign de Kooning's *Woman I* to any particular source in ancient or primitive art. *Woman I* can call up the Medusa as easily as the other way around. Whatever he knew or sensed about the Gorgon's meanings, and however much or little he took from it, the image type is decidedly present in his work. Suffice it to say that de Kooning was aware, indeed, explicitly claimed, that his *Women* could be assimilated to the long history of goddess imagery.[8] By choosing to place such figures at the centre of his most ambitious artistic efforts, he secured for his work an aura of ancient mystery and authority.

The *Woman* is not only monumental and iconic. In high-heeled shoes and brassiere, she is also lewd, her pose indecently teasing. De Kooning acknowledged her oscillating character, claiming for her a likeness not only to serious art—ancient icons and high-art nudes—but also to pin-ups and girlie pictures of the vulgar present. He saw her as simultaneously frightening and ludicrous.[9] The ambiguity of the figure, its power to resemble an awesome mother goddess as well as a modern burlesque queen, provides a fine cultural, psychological, and artistic field in which to enact the modern myth of the artist-hero—the hero whose spiritual ordeal becomes the stuff of ritual in the public space of the museum. As a powerful and threatening woman, it is she who must be confronted and transcended—gotten past—on the way to enlightenment. At the same time, her vulgarity, her 'girlie' side—de Kooning called

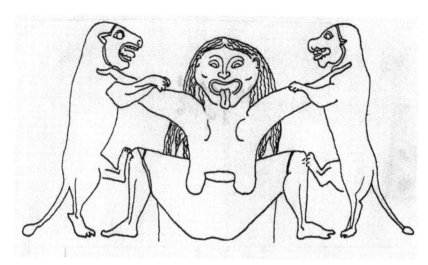

FIGURE 17.5 Etruscan Gorgon, drawing after a bronze carriage-front. Munich, Museum antiker Kleinkunst.

it her 'silliness'[10]—renders her harmless (or is it contemptible?) and denies the terror and dread of her Medusa features. The ambiguity of the image thus gives the artist (and the viewer) both the experience of danger and a feeling of overcoming it. Meanwhile, the suggestion of pornographic self-display—more explicit in his later work but certainly present here—specifically addresses itself to the male viewer. With it, de Kooning knowingly and assertively exercises his patriarchal privilege of objectifying male sexual fantasy as high culture.

An interesting drawing-photomontage by the California artist Robert Heinecken, *Invitation to Metamorphosis* (Figure 17.6), similarly explores the ambiguities of a Gorgon-girlie image. Here the effect of ambiguity is achieved by the use of masks and by combining and superimposing separate negatives. Heinecken's version of the self-displaying woman is a composite consisting of a conventional pornographic nude and a Hollywood movie-type monster. A well-qualified Gorgon, her attributes include an open, toothy mouth, carnivorous animal jaws, huge bulging eyes, large breasts, exposed genitals, and one very nasty-looking claw. Her body is simultaneously naked and draped, enticing and repulsive, and the second head, to the left of the Gorgon

head—the one with the seductive smile—also wears a mask. Like the de Kooning, Heinecken's *Invitation* sets up a psychological unstable atmosphere fraught with deception, allure, danger, and wit. The image's various components continually disappear into and reappear out of

FIGURE 17.6 Robert Heinecken, *Invitation to Metamorphosis*, 1975, emulsion on canvas and pastel chalk, 42 x 42".

FIGURE 17.7 Pablo Picasso, *Les Demoiselles d'Avignon*, 1907, oil on canvas, 96⅜ x 92½". The Museum of Modern Art.

one another. Behaving something like de Kooning's layered paint surfaces, they invite ever-shifting, multiple readings. In both works, what is covered becomes exposed, what is opaque becomes transparent, and what is revealed conceals something else. Both works fuse the terrible killer-witch with the willing and exhibitionist whore. Both fear and seek danger in desire, and both kid the danger.

Of course before de Kooning or Heinecken created ambiguous self-displaying women, there was Picasso's *Demoiselles d'Avignon* of 1907 (Figure 17.7). The work was conceived as an extraordinarily ambitious statement—it aspires to revelation—about the meaning of Woman. In it, all women belong to a universal category of being existing across time and place. Picasso used ancient and tribal art to reveal her universal mystery: Egyptian and Iberian sculpture on the left and African art on the right. The figure on the lower right looks as if it were directly inspired by some primitive or archaic deity. Picasso would

have known such figures from his visits to the ethnographic art collections in the Trocadero. A study for the work in the Musée Picasso in Paris (Figure 17.8) closely follows the type's symmetrical, self-displaying pose. Significantly, Picasso wanted her to be prominent—she is the nearest and largest of all the figures. At this stage, Picasso also planned to include a male student on the left and, in the axial centre of the composition, a sailor—a figure of horniness incarnate. The self-displaying woman was to have faced him, her display of genitals turned away from the viewer.

In the finished work, the male presence has been removed from the image and relocated in the viewing space before it. What began as a depicted male–female confrontation thus became a confrontation between viewer and image. The relocation has pulled the lower right-hand figure completely around so that her stare and her sexually inciting act, although not detailed and less symmetrical than before, are now directed outward. Picasso thus isolated and monumentalized the ultimate men-only situation. As restructured, the work forcefully asserts to both men and women the privileged status of male viewers—they alone are intended to experience the full impact of this most revelatory moment.[11] It also assigns women to a visitors' gallery where they may watch but not enter the central arena of high culture.

Finally, the mystery that Picasso unveils about women is also an art-historical lesson. In the finished work, the women have become stylistically differentiated so that one looks not only at present-tense whores but also back down into the ancient and primitive past, with the art of 'darkest Africa' and works representing the beginnings of Western Culture (Egyptian and Iberian idols) placed on a single spectrum. Thus does Picasso use art history to argue his thesis: that the awesome goddess, the terrible witch, and the lewd whore are but facets of a single many-sided creature, in turn threatening and seductive, imposing and self-abasing, dominating and powerless—and always the psychic property of a male imagination. Picasso also implies that truly great, powerful, and revelatory art has always

FIGURE 17.8 Pablo Picasso, *Study for 'Les Demoiselles d'Avignon*,' 1907, charcoal and pastel, 18½ x 24⅝". Paris, Musée Picasso.

been and must be built upon such exclusively male property.

The museum's installation amplifies the already powerful meanings of the work. Mounted on a free-standing wall in the centre of the first Cubist gallery, it seizes your attention the moment you turn into the room—the placement of the door-way makes it appear suddenly and dramatically. Physically dominating this intimately scaled gallery, its installation dramatizes its role as progenitor of the surrounding Cubism and its subsequent art-historical issue. So central is the work to the structure of MoMA's program that recently, when it was on loan, the museum felt compelled to post a

notice on its wall explaining its absence—but also invoking its presence. In a gesture unusual for the MoMA, the notice was illustrated by a tiny colour reproduction of the missing monument.

The works I have discussed by de Kooning and Heinecken, along with similar works by many other modern artists, benefit from and reinforce the status won by the *Demoiselles*. They also develop its theme, drawing out different emphases. One of the elements they develop more explicitly than Picasso is the element of pornography. By way of exploring how that pornographic element works in the museum context, I want to look first at how it works outside the museum.

FIGURE 17.9 Bus shelter on 57th Street, New York City, with advertisement for *Penthouse* magazine, 1988.

Last year, an advertisement for *Penthouse* magazine appeared on New York City bus shelters (Figure 17.9). New York City bus shelters are often decorated with near-naked women and sometimes men advertising everything from underwear to real estate. But this was an ad for pornographic images as such; that is, images designed not to sell perfume or bathing suits but to stimulate erotic desire, primarily in men. Given its provocative intent, the image generates very different and—I think for almost everyone—more charged meanings than the ads for underwear. At least one passerby had already recorded in red spray-paint a terse, but coherent response: 'For Pigs.'

Having a camera with me, I decided to take a shot of it. But as I set about focusing, I began to feel uncomfortable and self-conscious. As I realized only later, I was experiencing some prohibition in my own conditioning, activated

not simply by the nature of the ad, but by the act of photographing such an ad in public. Even though the anonymous inscription had made it socially safer to photograph—it placed it in a conscious and critical discourse about gender— to photograph it was still to appropriate openly a kind of image that middle-class morality says I'm not supposed to look at or have. But before I could sort that out, a group of boys jumped into the frame. Plainly, they intended to intervene. Did I know what I was doing?, one asked me with an air I can only call stern, while another admonished me that I was photographing a *Penthouse* ad—as if I would not knowingly do such a thing.

Apparently, the same culture that had conditioned me to feel uneasy about what I was doing also made *them* uneasy about it. Boys this age know very well what's in *Penthouse*. Knowing what's in *Penthouse* is knowing something meant for men to know; therefore, knowing *Penthouse* is a way of knowing oneself to be a man, or at least a man-to-be, at precisely an age when one needs all the help one can get. I think these boys were trying to protect the capacity of the ad to empower them as men by preventing me from appropriating an image of it. For them, as for many men, the chief (if not the only) value and use of pornography is this power to confirm gender identity and, with that, gender superiority. Pornography affirms their manliness to themselves and to others and proclaims the greater social power of men. Like some ancient and primitive objects forbidden to the female gaze, the ability of pornography to give its users a feeling of superior male status depends on its being owned or controlled by men and forbidden to, shunned by, or hidden from women. In other words, in certain situations a female gaze can *pollute* pornography. These boys, already imprinted with the rudimentary gender codes of the culture, knew an infringement when they saw one. (Perhaps they suspected me of defacing the ad.) Their harassment of me constituted an attempt at gender policing, something adult men routinely do to women on city streets.

Not so long ago, such magazines were sold only in sleazy porn stores. Today ads for them can decorate midtown thoroughfares. Of course, the ad, as well as the magazine cover, cannot itself be pornography and still be legal (in practice, that tends to mean it can't show genitals), but to work as an ad it must *suggest* it. For different reasons, works of art like de Kooning's *Woman I* or Heinecken's *Invitation* also refer to without actually being pornography—they depend on the viewer 'getting' the reference but must stop there. Given these requirements, it shouldn't surprise us that the artists' visual strategies have parallels in the ad (Figure 17.10). *Woman I* shares a number of features with the ad. Both present frontal, iconic, massive figures seen close up— they fill, even overflow, the picture surface. The photograph's low camera angle and the painting's scale and composition monumentalize and elevate the figures, literally or imaginatively dwarfing the viewer. Painting and photograph

FIGURE 17.10 The cover of *Penthouse* used in the advertisement, with a photograph by Bob Guccione, April 1988.

alike concentrate attention on head, breasts, and torso. Arms serve to frame the body, while legs are either cropped or, in the de Kooning, undersized and feeble. The figures thus appear powerful and powerless at the same time, with massive bodies made to rest on unstable, weakly rendered, tentatively placed legs. And with both, the viewer is positioned to see it all should the thighs open. And of course, on *Penthouse* pages, thighs do little else but open. But de Kooning's hot mama has a very different purpose and cultural status from a *Penthouse* 'pet'.

De Kooning's *Woman I* conveys much more complex and emotionally ambivalent meanings. The work acknowledges more openly the fear of and flight from as well as a quest for the woman. Moreover de Kooning's *Woman I* is always upstaged by

FIGURE 17.11 Willem de Kooning, *The Visit*, 1966–67, oil on canvas, 60 x 48". London, The Tate Gallery.

the artist's self-display *as an artist*. The manifest purpose of a *Penthouse* photo is, presumably, to arouse desire. If the de Kooning awakens desire in relation to the female body it does so in order to deflate or conquer its power of attraction and escape its danger. The viewer is invited to relive a struggle in which the realm of art provides escape from the female's degraded allure. As mediated by art criticism, de Kooning's work speaks ultimately not of male fear but of the triumph of art and a self-creating spirit. In the critical literature, the *Women* figures themselves become catalysts or structural supports for the work's more significant meanings: the artist's heroic self-searching, his existentialist courage, his pursuit of a new pictorial structure or some other artistic or transcendent end.[12]

The work's pornographic moment, now subsumed to its high-cultural import, may (unlike the *Penthouse* ad) do its ideological work with unchallenged prestige and authority. In building their works on a pornographic base and triggering in both men and women deep-seated feelings about gender identity and difference, de Kooning, Heinecken, and other artists (most notoriously, David Salle) exercise a privilege that our society has traditionally conferred upon men only. Through their imagery, they lay claim to public space as a realm under masculine control. Transformed into art and displayed in the public space of the museum, the self-displaying poses affirm to male viewers their membership in the more powerful gender group. They also remind women that their status as members of the community, their right to its public space, their share in the common, culturally defined identity, is not quite the same—is somehow less equal—than men's. But these signals must be covert, hidden under the myth of the transcendent artist-hero. Even de Kooning's later *Women* figures, which more openly invite comparison to pornographic photography and graffiti (Figure 17.11), qualify the reference; the closer to pornography, the more overlaid they must be with unambiguously 'artistic' gestures and philosophically significant impastos.

Nevertheless, what is true in the street may not be so untrue in the museum, even though different rules of decorum may make it seem so. Inside or outside, such images wield great authority, structuring and reinforcing the psychic codes that determine and differentiate the real possibilities of women and men.

NOTES

1. For an analysis of the older MoMA, see: Carol Duncan and Alan Wallach, 'The Museum of Modern Art as Late Capitalist Ritual,' *Marxist Perspectives*, 4 (Winter 1978), pp. 28–51.

2. Philip Slater. *The Glory of Hera*. Boston, 1968, p. 321.

3. See: Douglas Fraser. 'The Heraldic Woman: A Study in Diffusion,' in *The Many Faces of Primitive Art*, ed. D. Fraser. Englewood Cliffs, New Jersey, 1966, pp. 36–99; Arthur Frothingham, 'Medusa, Apollo, and the Great Mother.' *American Journal of Archaeology*, 15 (1911), pp. 349–77; Roman Ghirshman, *Iran: From the Earliest Times to the Islamic Conquest*. Harmondsworth, 1954, pp. 340–3; Bernard Goldman, 'The Asiatic Ancestry of the Greek Gorgon,' *Berytus*, 14 (1961). pp. 1–22; Clark Hopkins, 'Assyrian Elements in the Perseus-Gorgon Story,' *American Journal of Archaeology*, 38 (1934). pp. 341–58, and 'The Sunny Side of the Greek Gorgon.' *Berytus*, 14 (1961), pp. 25–32; and Philip Slater (cited n. 3), pp. 16–21, and 318 ff.

4. More ancient than the devouring Gorgon of Greece and pointing to a root meaning of the image type, a famous Louristan bronze pin in the David Weill Collection honours an older, life-giving Mother Goddess. Flanked by animals sacred to her, she is shown giving birth to a child and holding out her breasts. Objects of this kind appear to have been the votive offerings of women; see: Ghirshman (cited n. 3), pp. 102–4.

5. See: Slater (cited n. 2), pp. 308–36, on the Perseus myth, and pp. 449 ff., on the similarities

between ancient Greek and middle-class American males.

6. Sec: Fraser (cited n. 3).

7. Thomas B. Hess. *Willem de Kooning*, New York, 1959, p. 7. See also: Hess, *Willem de Kooning: Drawings*, New York and Greenwich, Conn., 1972, p. 27, on a de Kooning drawing of Elaine de Kooning (c. 1942), in which the writer finds the features of Medusa—a 'menacing' stare, intricate, animated 'Medusa hair'.

8. As he once said, 'The *Women* had to do with the female painted through all the ages. . . . Painting the *Woman* is a thing in art that has been done over and over—the idol, Venus, the nude.' Quoted in *Willem de Kooning. The North Atlantic Light, 1960–1983*, exh. cat., Stedelijk Museum, Amsterdam. Louisiana Museum of Modern Art, Humlebaek, and the Moderna Museet, Stockholm, 1983. Sally Yard, 'Willem de Kooning's Women,' *Arts*, 53 (November 1975). pp. 96–101, argues several sources for the *Women* paintings, including Cycladic idols, Sumerian votive figures, Byzantine icons, and Picasso's *Demoiselles*.

9. *North Atlantic Light* (cited n. 8), p. 77. See also: Hess, *de Kooning* 1959 (cited n. 7). pp. 21 and 29.

10. *North Atlantic Light* (cited n. 8), p. 77.

11. See, for example: Leo Steinberg, 'The Philosophical Brothel'. *Art News*, September 1972. pp. 25–6. In Steinberg's groundbreaking reading, the act of looking at these female figures visually re-creates the act of sexually penetrating a woman. The implication is that women are anatomically unequipped to experience the work's full meaning.

12. Very little has been written about de Kooning that does not do this. For one of the most bombastic treatments, see: Harold Rosenberg, *De Kooning*, New York, 1974.

18

'WHIFFS OF BALSAM, PINE, AND SPRUCE'[1]: ART MUSEUMS AND THE PRODUCTION OF A CANADIAN AESTHETIC

ANNE WHITELAW

Not all the pioneering in Canada has been done in her forests and plains by any means. The growth of the fine arts from the days of the earliest topographical draughtsmen and water colourists . . . to our own day, when a vigorous and national school of painting is springing up, has been no less heroic and deserving of epics and monuments than the work of her explorers and her statesmen.[2]

Culture has long been the pivotal point around which the contestation of national identity has occurred in Canada. Poised between two major political and cultural powers, politicians and members of the cultural elite have attempted since Confederation to stem perceived encroachments on the nation's autonomy by controlling the import of cultural goods, and by subsidizing local production.[3] As the legislators see it, a strong centralized support of Canadian culture remains the foremost tool in the construction of a Canadian national identity: a tool which has proven useful historically in bringing together the remote regions of the Canadian political landscape, but which has also served as an important mechanism in 'acculturating' immigrant cultures and assigning them a place within the Canadian mosaic. National institutions of culture—the National Film Board, the CBC, the National Museums—function in different ways to ascribe a coherence to, as well as to contain, a diverse set of practices and traditions that may be characterized as 'Canadian', advancing a single unified national culture that would effect a (unified) national identity.

Although the repository of *high* culture, a realm traditionally associated with universal values that transcend national boundaries, the

National Gallery of Canada also figures as an important marker of national culture. This importance goes beyond the gallery's legislated status as a national institution, with a mandate from the federal government to promote Canadian identity. The gallery's fostering of national culture is made visible in the exhibition of its permanent collection, and specifically through the display of the work of Canadian artists. It is through this display that a coherent narrative of Canadian art is constructed, a narrative organized around the contribution of Canadian artistic practice to the nation's growing realization of its status as an autonomous state. Inscribed in the display of Canadian art in the National Gallery's permanent collection, then, is Canada's emergent sense of itself as a nation.

Although the gallery's exhibition of Canadian art is organized as a chronicle of artistic development in Canada, it is motivated by a quest for a specifically Canadian aesthetic vocabulary: an artistic language that would reflect Canada's distinct identity and signal its separateness from the former colonial power.[4] For many historians, this distinct Canadian aesthetic took shape in the work of the Group of Seven, a collective of artists working out of Toronto who, from their first exhibition in 1920, foregrounded a new style in painting that broke with the European picturesque style of their predecessors and set the agenda for the development of Canadian art. The Group's almost exclusive use of the landscape as subject matter contributed to their status as Canada's 'national school'. This essay, however, is not concerned with the nationalism of individual works of art. Rather, it examines the exhibition of works in the permanent collection of the National Gallery, and the production through this display of narratives of nation-ness. As I will argue, the gallery has organized this artistic chronology around particular conceptions of 'Canadian' art and 'Canadian' identity, conceptions that are seen to be epitomized in the paintings of the Group of Seven (and Tom Thomson)[5] during their most cohesive years as a group.[6]

Lawren Harris, J.E.H. MacDonald, Arthur Lismer, A.Y. Jackson, Fred Varley, Frank Carmichael, and Frank Johnston came together through a common dissatisfaction with the state of Canadian art and a desire to 'paint Canada'. On a formal level, these artists broke with the aesthetic conventions of their time, the European-derived romantic and picturesque landscape tradition found in the works of the preceding generation of Canadian painters, preferring the stylized lines of Art Nouveau design and the brilliant colour of the Fauves. As the artists matured, they developed an increasing interest in the use of broad, simplified forms and shapes to represent the massive wilderness of northern Ontario, perhaps most evident in the later work of Lawren Harris (Figure 18.1). In this, the artists have often been regarded as Canada's first modernists: for breaking with prior artistic conventions in Canada, and for introducing abstraction on a wide scale. The principal claim to artistic distinctness of the Group of Seven, however, is their treatment of the Canadian landscape, and the belief that their paintings alone captured the essence of the Canadian spirit. As J.E.H. MacDonald wrote in the *New Statesman* in 1919:

The Canadian Spirit in art prefers the raw youthful homeliness of Canada to the overblown beauty of the recognized art countries. It aims to fill its landscape with the clear Canadian sunshine and the open air, following faithfully all seasons and aspects and it would make its treatment of them broad and rich attempting to convey the sense of rough dignity and generosity which the nature of the country suggests. Let the reader go if he will [to the exhibition] and feel in the pictures the Canadian spirit in art, striving through sincere expression for a self-determination which will enable our people to make their necessary and fitting contribution to the common art treasures of the world.[7]

It is this legacy of the Group of Seven, their preoccupation with the landscape as artistic subject matter and as a philosophy of Canadian distinctness, that has provided coherent material around which a narrative of national identity has been articulated. The centrality of the land figures in other media such as film and literature,[8] but in

FIGURE 18.1 Installation view of paintings by the Group of Seven

the years following the First World War, it was the paintings of the Group that produced the visual vocabulary and conception of territory around which nationhood could be articulated. As British critics' favourable reaction to the work exhibited at the British Empire Exhibition in 1924 testifies, this portrayal of the landscape was seen not only as constitutive of Canada but as the first art form that celebrated Canada's emerging sense of nation-ness:

Canada reveals herself in colours all her own, colours in which the environment of Nature plays no insignificant part. She has mixed her colours with her restless unrestrained energy, her uncontrolled forces. We feel as we look at these pictures, the rush of the mighty winds as they sweep the prairies, the swirl and roar of the swollen river torrents, and the awful silent majesty of her snows. And such is Canada's art—the 'pourings out' of men and women whose souls reflect the expansiveness of their

wide horizons, who dream their dreams, 'and express themselves in form and colour' upon the canvas.[9]

As the above passage suggests, the success of the Group's paintings in Britain was due in large part to the way in which the artists' choice and treatment of subject matter was seen to embody contemporary images of Canada's national character. This also accounts for their later popularity in Canada, and the relative ease with which such paintings of northern Ontario and Quebec functioned to represent the nation both in Canada and abroad. As Benedict Anderson has argued in *Imagined Communities*, the nation is produced less through the defining of territorial boundaries than through the collective imaginings of its inhabitants. Anderson thereby moves the emphasis from an essentialist notion of national identity as something one is born into to a fluid conception of nationhood as a sense of belonging, organized around shifting signifiers that resonate in the experience of a nation's populace. As such, nations are to be distinguished not by their falsity or their genuineness but by the way in which they are imagined. Cultural artifacts, institutions, landmarks, and geographical elements play a central role in the representation of the nation and constitute some of the mechanisms through which an affective relationship between it and its inhabitants is produced. The museum is one such mechanism which makes the nation visible. Through the ascription of symbolic value on certain objects placed on public display, the museum produces a narrative of nationhood within which a national public can inscribe itself. There is thus in the museum's display an attempt to build on the affective relationship of the individual citizen with the nation, isolating those objects that resonate on a national level, obscuring elements that provide conflict. The museum produces a discourse of nation-ness that frames individual objects in terms of collective memory through appeals to a common heritage and shared national values.[10] Through their location in an overarching narrative of national artistic production, objects are mobilized to provide viewers with a sense that they are members of a national public, and that they are participating in a collective endeavour that has meaning beyond the individual experience.

In Canada, the recent construction of two major museum buildings in the capital—to house the Canadian Museum of Civilization and the National Gallery—testifies to the centrality of cultural institutions in the articulation of national identity. The National Gallery was established by the nation's first governor general, the Marquis de Lorne, in 1880, little more than a decade after the founding of a Canadian state to unify Upper and Lower Canada. Both the National Gallery and the newly instituted Royal Canadian Academy of Arts[11] were seen by the governor general and other members of Canada's cultural elite as essential tools in the encouragement of a distinctly Canadian cultural tradition. The promotion of a visual symbolic that was 'native' to Canada was seen as a mechanism that would differentiate Canada as much from the United States as from Great Britain, as well as bring together

under the aegis of a single institution the cultural products of Canada's disparate regions.[12]

Under the terms of the first National Gallery of Canada Act of 1913, the gallery's primary function was educational: its mandate was 'the encouragement and cultivation of correct artistic taste and Canadian public interest in the fine arts, the promotion of the interests of art, in general, in Canada'.[13] The belief in the civilizing powers of high art was central to the formation of many art museums in the New World at the turn of the century,[14] and over the years the National Gallery has actively sought to acquire important works from Europe and the United States in order to present a complete art historical survey.[15] Nevertheless, the work of Canadian artists remains a central component of the gallery's collection, and its quest for a truly Canadian high art tradition has resulted in its promotion of Canadian artists at home and abroad. This position was stated as far back as 1912 by director Eric Brown:

> There is no doubt that Canada has growing along with her material prosperity a strong and virile art which only needs to be fostered and encouraged in order to become a great factor in her growth as a nation. No country can be a great nation until it has a great art . . . . [H]owever, . . . the encouragement of our national art in its broadest and best sense is not achieved by the exclusive purchase of Canadian works of art. The purpose of our National Art Gallery is mainly educative, and as a knowledge and understanding of art is only to be gained by the comparison of one work of art with another, so for this comparison to lead always to higher ideals and understanding we must have in addition to our own Canadian pictures the best examples we can afford of the world's artistic achievements by which we may judge the merit and progress of our own efforts. It is on these lines that the purchase of works for the National Gallery is proceeding.[16]

As a national institution, in addition to acquisition policies, the gallery has had (and continues to have) a commitment to making its works accessible to the entire population of Canada through a program of circulating exhibitions and educational material. There is then in the National Gallery's own policies and internal structure a continuing belief in the centrality of its role in building a national culture, through the presentation of a largely European cultural heritage and through the collection of works by living Canadian artists.

This commitment to a nationalist project, however, is not simply an internal motivation. As one of four national museums in Canada,[17] the National Gallery has a mandate from the federal government, outlined in the 1990 Museums Act, to 'preserv[e] and promot[e] the heritage of Canada and all its peoples throughout Canada and abroad, and [to] contribut[e] to the collective memory and sense of identity of all Canadians'.[18] In recent years, as was particularly apparent in evidence submitted to the Standing Committee on Communications and Culture of the Federal Government in 1991,[19] the National Gallery has stood by this belief in the importance of a national culture, and the centrality of its role in maintaining that culture. To quote from the gallery's submission to the committee: 'As one of the government's national cultural agencies, we will strive as always to make visible to all Canadians the supremely important part artists play in creating our national identity, our "Canadianness".'[20]

The art museum's assigned role in the production of a national culture is not specific to Canada, despite our chronic nationalist malaise. Since its inception as a public institution at the end of the eighteenth century in France, the art museum has functioned as a monument to the nation. As Carol Duncan and Alan Wallach have described in 'The Universal Survey Museum', it functions, both physically through its architecture and symbolically through the display of accumulated objects, as a marker of the state's power. Through the chronological exhibition of a representative selection of works from the history of art that culminates with the greatest achievements of the nation's artists, the art museum serves both as the storehouse of 'official' Western culture and as a monument to the artistic production of the nation itself. As Duncan and Wallach thus argue, it is through the orchestrated

narrative[21] of displayed artifacts in the museum that the state can make visible its adherence to the highest values of Western civilization, while simultaneously positioning itself as the rightful inheritor of those values through the works of the nation's greatest artists. In more general terms, the aesthetic ideology at work in the art museum is one that operates along a modernist notion of art as embodying universal, transcendental values, while at the same time highlighting the production of the nation's artists as emblematic of those universal values.[22]

The permanent display in the Canadian galleries of the National Gallery provides a linear chronology of Canadian artistic production from the late seventeenth century to the 1960s. Traditional in scope and intent, it provides a trajectory of great moments in Canadian art organized around a selection of major artistic movements—for example, the Group of Seven, Painters Eleven, the Automatistes, and the Plasticiens. As in most 'survey' museums throughout the Western world, the traditional art-historical view of the history of art as a linear stylistic trajectory is present in the gallery's display of the permanent collection.[23] This view of the history of art as a progressive artistic development culminating in abstraction is reinforced in the physical layout of the rooms that house the collection of Canadian artworks. The major moments or instances of works that do not fit into the larger teleological narrative of 'Canadian art' are situated in the smaller theme rooms, adjacent to the main rooms, and therefore outside the main exhibition trajectory. One of the most important motivations in this stylistic progression is the development of abstraction, first seen in the stylized landscapes of the Group of Seven, and reaching its apogee in the very disparate work of the Plasticiens and the Painters Eleven in the 1950s and 1960s. The rise of artistic modernism, as it is traced through the trajectory of the permanent collection, signals the abandonment of European-derived realist art forms, and Canada's move towards entry into a universal aesthetic avant-garde. This full participation in the international art world can perhaps best be seen in the shift in the gallery's organization of its permanent collection: from a strictly Canadian history of art up to the 1960s, to the integration of the work of Canadian and international artists in the contemporary galleries.

This stylistic separation of works into those that form the main history and those works that are outside this history must also, however, be seen as part of the larger project of both the National Gallery and the Canadian art historical establishment: namely, the development of an authentically Canadian aesthetic. This quest for a distinctly Canadian artistic vocabulary was the original impetus behind the creation of both the Royal Canadian Academy and the National Gallery, under the assumption that the development of such an aesthetic—and the establishment of a wholly Canadian art movement—would translate into visual terms the affective experience of nationhood. This distinct Canadian aesthetic was seemingly only achieved with the Group of Seven, whose exploration of the Canadian landscape—though that landscape only reflected a small portion of Canadian territory—was seen by both the artists themselves and by posterity as 'a direct and unaffected mode of painting derived from an experience of the Canadian land that all Canadians, if they would only look about themselves, would have to acknowledge as being true and worthwhile'.[24]

The articulation of national identity with the land, however, did not originate with the Group of Seven. Although for many these artists more closely approximated the rough wilderness that was Canada than the picturesque images produced by their predecessors, the work of earlier artists—from Cornelius Krieghoff's paintings of habitants and coureurs des bois in the nineteenth century and Paul Kane's voyages west to capture the 'vanishing Indian', to the romanticized paintings of Lucius O'Brien and Horatio Walker—also took as their subject matter the distinctive elements of the Canadian landscape. These early depictions, however, were poetic and idealized visions of the land, virtually indistinguishable from the picturesque and romantic European paintings avidly collected in Montreal and in Toronto. They nonetheless point to the importance of the landscape in any artistic articulation of national identity in Canada. Art historians

have repeatedly attempted to explain Canadian artists' preoccupation with painting the land. Notes Dennis Reid, 'A number of theories have been advanced to explain this "landscape" fact in Canadian painting, as also in our literature and music. They usually involve the identification of the essentially individualistic, introspective nature of the Canadian psyche, and the consequent need to see oneself in a one-to-one relationship with nature in all its magnitude.'[25] Others see the preponderance of images of the land throughout Canadian art as a mechanism for domesticating what was for early settlers a harsh and difficult landscape, or even as an incentive for European emigration to Canada[26] on the part of late-nineteenth century nationalists (who asked artists to paint pictures with no snow).[27]

The identification of topographical characteristics with national identity, however, went beyond works of art. The rhetoric of many Canadian nationalists in the decades after Confederation sought to establish a close association between Canada's northern location and racial superiority. As Carl Berger has shown, many early nationalists believed that Canada's strength lay in its geographical location and climatic conditions, arguing that the cold climate had fostered the development of a strong and pure race already equipped with an ingrained sense of freedom and the capacity for self-governance.[28] In their arguments for the strong correlation between climate and racial character, these early nationalist tracts manifested in varying degrees a kind of social Darwinism. The more moderate version saw the Canadian climate as conducive to the production of certain characteristics desirable in a free and democratic country. The second, more extreme argument maintained that the climate functioned as a process of natural selection, and that races indigenous to cold climes were inherently superior to those of warmer areas. This belief was often 'proved' in the migration northwards of the human species as it evolved, and in the greater wealth of countries of the North compared with the underdeveloped nations of the South.[29]

In these characteristics of strength, perseverance, and the capacity for self-governance, Canadians were likened to the peoples of Scandinavia

FIGURE 18.2 The Canadian galleries with Lawren Harris's *North Shore Lake Superior*, 1926, in foreground

and Germany, Britain and northern France: all northern 'races' and all seen as the direct ancestors of English and French Canadians. Canada's racial affinity with Britain lay in sharp contrast to the perceived differences between Canada and the United States, a country whose Anglo-Saxon heritage, in the minds of advocates of the more extreme position, was being diluted by an influx of immigrants from warmer climes, races who were inherently lazy and less governable than those individuals of superior northern heritage[30] (Figure 18.2).

Although most Canadians did not take up the extreme views of these post-Confederation nationalists, the landscape, and in particular the mythic North, constituted an important element in the popular imaging of the nation. Members of the Group of Seven recognized the affinity between northern landscapes and popular conceptions of Canada at the same time as they abandoned the picturesque conventions of European landscape painting, a shift which has been chronicled in the Group's mythology as an 'awakening'

to the essential character of Canada, 'the spirit of our native land'.[31] The Group's belief in the superior qualities of the northern climate and the importance of developing an artistic practice that captured the essence of the land were the fundamental elements that banded them together as a group, and which endeared them to promoters of a 'national feeling'.[32] For these artists, the flourishing of Canadian art was only possible once the artistic conventions of Europe lost their dominance. And a truly Canadian art form could only occur out of a spiritual engagement with the environment, an engagement which in the formative years of the Group took place in the Canadian Shield. In an essay in *The Canadian Theosophist*, Lawren Harris describes the impact of the North on the Canadian artist, a description in which can be found echoes of early nationalists' theories of dominant northern races:

We are in the fringe of the great North and its living Whiteness, its loneliness and replenishment, its resignations and release, its call and answer, its cleansing rhythms. It seems that the top of the continent is a source of spiritual flow that will ever shed clarity into the growing race of America, and we Canadians, being closest to this source seem destined to produce an art somewhat different from our Southern fellows—an art more spacious, of a greater living quiet, perhaps of a more certain conviction of eternal values. We were not placed between the Southern teeming of men and the ample replenishing North for nothing.[33]

The centrality of the Canadian Shield in the work of the Group of Seven is consonant with the exalted position of this small area of central Canada within the national symbolic. It is to the Canadian Shield that writers and artists refer when they speak of 'the North',[34] but the contingent nature of this conception underscores the constructed nature of national identity, and the function of narrative in experiences of nationhood. The centrality of the Canadian Shield, and in particular of Algonquin Park, in the visual vocabulary of the Group of Seven highlights the particular origins and interests of Canada's political and cultural elite. The broad success enjoyed by the Group, and the active patronage of the National Gallery, cannot be seen apart from the fact that Group members painted largely what Toronto's wealthy art patrons saw outside the windows of their cottages in the Muskokas. This is made abundantly clear in the National Gallery's inclusion in the Canadian galleries of the murals painted by J.E.H. MacDonald and Arthur Lismer for Dr James MacCallum's cottage on Georgian Bay.

The Group of Seven's status as Canada's 'national school' is reflected in their prominent location within the permanent display of Canadian art. They are accorded several large rooms in the northernmost corner of the Canadian galleries, and are positioned, quite literally, as a turning point in the developmental history of Canadian art. With the European-derived work of the early settler artists and of the Academicians behind them, they point towards the flourishing of Canadian art in the abstract works of the Automatistes and other high modernists. This pivotal position

in the development of a specifically Canadian aesthetic, as well as their established status as the first modernists, underscores the Group of Seven's fundamental importance in the display of Canadian art in the National Gallery and its narrative of national identity. Given the consonance of the goals of the Group and the National Gallery—in particular the fostering of a Canadian aesthetic tradition—it is not surprising to see a strong element of co-operation between them, especially in later years when some of the Group of Seven were sent on Gallery-sponsored lecture tours of Canada in an effort to bring the narrative of Canadian art to a broad public. As Dennis Reid has commented, 'to a large degree the struggles of the Group became the struggles of the Gallery'.[35]

This close relationship and the common goal to produce a distinct Canadian aesthetic is exemplified in the protracted debate between members of the Canadian Academy and members and admirers of the Group of Seven over the National Gallery's strong support of the work of the Group.[36] The debate was occasioned by the gallery's commitment to acquire and exhibit both in Canada and abroad the works of the 'modernist' Group of Seven, at the perceived expense of the traditionalist members of the Academy (who had, moreover, founded the gallery in 1880). The fundamental issue in the debate centred around which aesthetic tradition best embodied the 'Canadian genius', i.e., which work was more 'Canadian'. This contest over representation, over which aesthetic—traditional or modernist— would best represent the nature of Canadian art, not only in the National Gallery but in the eyes of the art world, constitutes a formative moment in the history of the gallery, and of Canadian art history. The debate was a public one, with calls for the gallery's director, Eric Brown, to be 'controlled' by Parliament,[37] and with articles from both sides published regularly in newspapers across the country. The National Gallery felt vindicated, however, by British critics' high praise for the works of the Group of Seven on display at the British Empire Exhibition in 1924, with particular attention paid to the artists' ability to capture the Canadian spirit in their depiction of the landscape. This positive critical reception began the process which established the centrality of the Group of Seven in the Canadian national symbolic and in Canadian art history. The debates that continue to rage over whether the gallery's collection is representative of artistic production in Canada offer a powerful statement about the contested territory of national cultural production and the role of the National Gallery in determining and legitimizing that territory.[38]

In its display the permanent collection presents in material form the moments of progress and development chronicled by Canadian art history. This narrative, like the museum, presents the viewer with a series of artworks that have been divorced from their original setting and exist in a timeless void. 'Everything takes place in the museum in some eternal contemporaneity; all diachrony, all difference, all multivocality is enframed in synchronicity', Donald Preziosi has observed.[39] More importantly, such objects are subject to the infinite manipulation of historical narratives and to the temporal organization determined by those narratives. As Preziosi has argued, the purpose of art history is to organize data and objects, to get them to 'stay' and 'lie orderly'[40]—in other words, to submit to the organizing narrative that will give these objects meaning according to their position within the broader system. In the case of Canadian art history, that system is more often than not the articulation of a distinctly Canadian aesthetic: one that would differentiate our cultural production from that of other nations. And harnessed to this quest for artistic distinctness is the search for a broader cultural identity that could serve as an overarching principle in the definition of a unified national identity.

Most visible in the permanent display of Canadian art, then, is the apparent solidity of the trajectory: More than anywhere else in the museum, this exhibit signifies History, a nation's connection to its past. This is the 'shared cultural heritage' outlined in promotional literature and exhibition introductions, and most clearly stated in evidence submitted by the gallery's director, Shirley Thomson, to the Standing Committee on Communications and Culture in 1991. It is worth quoting this submission at length:

We believe that the National Gallery of Canada in bringing together the best works of artists through time and across the country makes visible both what we hold and value in common and the rich diversity of our viewpoints and traditions. As one form of cultural expression, the visual arts serve as a record of who and where and how we were. Today that record is part of our common heritage, an expression of our national identity in the landscape, peaceful or rugged, majestic or humble, and in the faces of the settlers, ecclesiastics, homesteaders, *coureurs des bois*, soldiers and native people who have preceded us. These images powerfully evoke Canada. The compelling Joseph Brant, the serene Soeur Saint-Alphonse, the enduring jack pine, the mystic totem pole—these images are familiar and common to all of us. By collecting, showing, touring, borrowing and lending the works of say William Berczy, Alphonse Plamondon, Tom Thomson, Emily Carr and many more, the gallery as a federal cultural agency makes a vital and direct contribution to Canadians' sense of themselves. We provide the essential links from coast to coast, from one Canadian to another, and from all Canadians to their visual arts heritage.[41]

What this statement reveals is that the trajectory of Canadian art on permanent display in the National Gallery presents a particular narrative of Canadian nationhood. First Nations peoples are included only as the subjects of representation, and not as cultural producers. Where they are mentioned elsewhere in the gallery's submission it is in relation to the Canadian Museum of Civilization—a more 'anthropological' museum—or, together with the works of 'ethnic' artists, as part of the intriguing diversity of Canada's statistical make-up. What Shirley Thomson's statement does suggest, however, is the solidity of the art-historical narrative reproduced in the gallery and its powerful evocations of a unified affective relationship with the 'masterpieces' of Canadian art—the jack pine, Emily Carr's images of totem poles, and the *coureurs des bois*—images that are 'familiar to all of us'.

These appeals to a common sensibility, to a shared vision, are part of the museum's construction of a unified and homogeneous 'national' public: an assumed self-recognition that is built into the display of objects, suggestive of a sense of appurtenance, a belonging, a 'we'. Through the permanent collection's appeal to the public to identify with the objects ordered for display, there is an inherent inscription of the viewing subject within the national narrative. The assumption is that by subscribing to the display of power/knowledge in the museum, the viewer is acquiescing to the proposed narrative of nationhood. This construction of a unified subject in the museum is mirrored in the way in which the nation continually attempts to construct a unified national population, usually around cultural symbols seen to be invested with meaning for an entire nation. In other words, underscoring appeals to nationalism is the belief that there is such a thing as 'a' (single) 'common heritage' that will have meaning across boundaries of race, class, sexuality, and generation.

Within Benedict Anderson's characterization of the nation as an imagined community lies the fundamentally important assumption that the experience of nationhood is largely subjective: that the communities imagined in the minds of the nation's inhabitants are not undifferentiated across time and geography. In the nationalist rhetoric of the National Gallery, the permanent collection displays a progressive development of Canadian art, a particular vision of Canada as seen through the eyes of its foremost artists, but positioned as embodying the national values of a shared or common heritage of a diverse population. However, what is in effect presented as emblematic of a nation's cultural identity is the hegemonic narrative of national art production found in Canadian art history and forming the basis of the National Gallery's permanent display of Canadian art.

In positioning the Group of Seven as a formative moment in the history of Canada and its aesthetic production, this essay has traced the emergence of the modern as a significant moment in the constitution of Canadian identity. As Canada's first aesthetic modernists, the Group of Seven established a mode of painting in Canada that was formally distinct from the work that preceded it and which served, in the years following the First World War, to reinforce Canada's efforts to establish itself as a distinct and autonomous nation. In foregrounding a new, distinct aesthetic style, the Group was seen to epitomize the foundation of the modern nation. The pivotal role that the Group played in the trajectory of Canadian art is based not only on the formal properties of their work but on the belief that these works represent Canada's 'true' image of itself, in a way unequalled by any other artist or group of artists.

In the rhetoric of nationalism articulated in the National Gallery, the continued popularity of the paintings of the Group is seen as evidence of the centrality of these works in the affective relationship between individual and nation. This relationship is seen to reside in the artists' ability to capture the essential nature of the Canadian landscape, a landscape that is assumed to embody all the characteristics of Canadian identity, and therefore to have great meaning for all Canadians. As a result of their perceived importance within the context of a narrative of Canadian art history, as well as in the emergence of Canadian national autonomy, these paintings of the Canadian landscape occupy a central position in the narrative of national identity on display in the National Gallery of Canada, and form the basis for the gallery's and Canadian art history's quest for a truly 'Canadian' aesthetic.

NOTES

This essay was written prior to Charles Hill's 1995 exhibition *The Group of Seven: Art for a Nation*. For a more detailed analysis of the exhibitionary practices of the National Gallery, please see my 'Exhibiting Canada: Articulations of National Identity at the National Gallery of Canada', PhD Thesis, Concordia University, Department of Communication Studies, 1995.

1. This quote is taken from Housser's celebratory history of the Group of Seven, *A Canadian Art*

Movement: The Story of the Group of Seven, 49.
2. Foreword, *A Portfolio of Pictures from the Canadian Section of Fine Arts; British Empire Exhibition*, London, 1924.
3. In 1951, in a report that has largely shaped the form of Canadian cultural legislation, the Massey Commission emphasized the essential role played by cultural institutions in the maintenance and promotion of a distinctly Canadian cultural identity. The fundamental role of these institutions was to restrict the flow of cultural commodities from the United States and thereby their influence on Canadian life, while at the same time providing centralized sites for the production of distinctly Canadian works of art and culture. In the wake of recent debates over national identity, the policies put forward in the Massey Commission Report continue to resonate in more recent documents produced by the federal government, particularly as Canada's political and cultural autonomy is seen to be under threat from the US (for example, with the Canada–US Free Trade agreements and NAFTA). A recent example is the 1992 Report of the Standing Committee on Communications and Culture drafted in preparation for the Charlottetown Constitutional Accord, *The Ties That Bind*, a document which in its support of the continued protection of national culture through support of centralized federal institutions reiterates many of the recommendations put forward by the Massey Commission.
4. This quest for a distinct Canadian aesthetic can also be found in art-historical survey texts on Canadian art.
5. Although Tom Thomson died in 1917 (appropriately while sketching in Algonquin Park) before the official formation of the Group of Seven, he painted and sketched with them often, and is credited in Canadian art history as being a major influence on the works of the Group.
6. This is roughly delimited as 1920–26. May 1920 marks the date of the Group's first official exhibition at the Art Museum of Toronto; 1926 signals the moment at which individual members began to strike out on their own, and the Group lost its cohesiveness. It is also the date of publication of F.B. Housser's paean to the Group, *A Canadian Art Movement*. The Group did not formally disband until 1933, although their last exhibition was in 1931. See Harper for a brief chronology of the Group's activities, and Reid for a detailed analysis of their lives and works.
7. Housser, *A Canadian Art Movement*, 143–4.
8. See, for example, Peter Morris's *Embattled Shadows* for references to early Canadian filmmaking, and Margaret Atwood's *Survival* for the theme of the land in Canadian prose and poetry.
9. J.M. Millman, quoted in Harper, *Painting in Canada*, 288.
10. Annie E. Coombes describes this process as follows: 'Through transformations in marketing and policy, the museum has become both a vital component in the reclaiming and defining of a concept of collective memory on the local level and, on the national level, an opportune site for the reconstituting of certain cultural icons as part of a common 'heritage'—a 'heritage often produced as a spectacle of essentialist national identity with the museum frequently serving as the site of the nostalgic manufacture of a consensual past in the lived reality of a deeply divided present' ('Inventing the "Postcolonial"', 41).
11. An early function of the National Gallery was to serve as the depository for the diploma works of members of the Royal Academy; hence the Academy's stake in the evolution of the gallery's acquisition policies.
12. Tooby, 'Orienting the True North', 18.
13. National Gallery of Canada Act, 1913.
14. See Michael J. Ettema, 'History Museums and the Culture of Materialism'.
15. This rhetoric was recently used by the gallery to justify the expense of purchasing Barnett Newman's *Voice of Fire* and Mark Rothko's *No. 16*.
16. Cited in Charles Hill, 'The National Gallery, A National Art, Critical Judgement and the State', 70–1.
17. The other three national museums are the Canadian Museum of Civilization (includes the Canadian War Museum), the National Museum of Natural Sciences, and the National Museum of Science and Technology (includes the National Aviation Museum), all located in the Ottawa area.
18. Bill C-12.
19. The evidence submitted by the National Gallery

was in the context of *Culture and Communications: The Ties That Bind*, a document on national identity and unity drafted by the Standing Committee on Communications and Culture in preparation for the Charlottetown Accord, which was signed by representatives of all ten provinces, the two territories, and the Assembly of First Nations in August 1992. It was subsequently put to a national referendum and was rejected by Canadian voters.

20. Government of Canada, 'Evidence Submitted to the Standing Committee', 6.

21. Following anthropologist Victor Turner's research, Duncan and Wallach describe this as a process in which citizens enact a symbolic ritual that reinforces the state's ideological position. Although this essay is very useful in unpacking the physical and symbolic mechanisms through which the museum constructs meaning, I would rather see the visitor's activity in the museum as a process of reading, thereby suggesting an active engagement with the material objects on display, rather than the passive following of an ideological script as Duncan and Wallach seem to suggest.

22. Duncan and Wallach trace out their argument through analyses of the Louvre and the Metropolitan Museum of Art in New York. Both these institutions are more properly 'universal survey' museums because their collections begin with the works of the ancient world (Egypt, Greece) and cover all major periods of art, ending with important works from their nations' artists. Although the National Gallery of Canada does not have the wealth of objects of the Louvre or the Metropolitan, similar concerns with providing a complete 'history of art' govern the organization of the works on display.

23. Douglas Crimp has discussed the legacy of Hegel's aesthetic philosophy in the discourse of traditional art history. The view of the history of artistic production as a linear development from the functionalist to the wholly spiritual was taken from Hegel and adapted to a notion of art history as stylistic succession. This linear and evolutionary conception of the history of art underscores the organization of the traditional museum (and as Crimp argues, is evident in the design of the prototypical art gallery the Berlin Altes Museum) and can also be found

in contemporary art, specifically, Alfred Barr's schematic outline of the genealogy of modern art in the catalogue for the 1936 MOMA exhibition, *Cubism and Abstract Art* (Douglas Crimp, 'The Postmodern Museum' in *On the Museum's Ruins*).

24. Reid, *The Group of Seven*, 13–14.

25. Ibid., 15.

26. Osborne, 'The Iconography of Nationhood', 164.

27. Requests for depictions of Canada without snow were also made to the directors of the early CPR films; see Peter Morris, *Embattled Shadows*.

28. Berger, *The True North*, 15.

29. Ibid., 19.

30. Ibid., 14.

31. Early in his chronicle of the Group, Housser writes: 'The story is unique in the history of art. It is not, however, so much the story of an art movement as the dawn of a consciousness of a national environment which to-day [1926] is taking a most definite form in the life of the nation' (*A Canadian Art Movement*, 32).

32. W. Stewart Wallace wrote of the Group of Seven in 1927: 'The work of this group has attracted international attention, mainly because of its strong native character. It tends at times to the crude and bizarre; but at its best it is instinct with the feeling of Canada's 'great open spaces', from which indeed it draws its inspiration' (*The Growth of Canadian National Feeling*, 77).

33. L. Harris, *Revelation of Art*, 86.

34. Cole Harris has characterized Canadian nationalism as an 'incantation to the north' with 'the north' equalled to the Canadian Shield. 'The Canadian or Precambrian Shield is as central in Canadian history as it is to Canadian geography, and to all understanding of Canada . . . . And this alternate penetration of the wilderness and return to civilization is the basic rhythm of Canadian life, and it forms the basic elements of Canadian character' (William Morton, *The Canadian Identity* [1961] quoted in Harris, 'The Myth of the Land in Canadian Nationalism', 28).

35. Reid, *The Group of Seven*, 11.

36. Charles Hill provides a detailed analysis of this debate in his essay 'The National Gallery, a National Art, Critical Judgement and the State'.

37. Charles Hill cites from the *Vancouver Sun* that

J.A. Radford demanded in 1932 that 'parliament . . . find out what is wrong and . . . correct the error' (Hill, ibid., 65).

38. Debates have occurred in recent years over the lack of contemporary art by First Nations artists on display in the Gallery, and the gallery's lack of attention at various times to francophone artists from Quebec (as in the *Songs of Experi-* *ence* exhibition of 1986) or to artists from the Maritimes (*Canadian Biennial of Contemporary Art*, 1989).

39. D. Preziosi, *Rethinking Art History*, 69.

40. Ibid., 61.

41. Government of Canada, *Evidence Submitted to the Standing Committee on Communications and Culture*, 6.

BIBLIOGRAPHY

Anderson, Benedict. *Imagined Communities: Reflections on the Origin and the Spread of Nationalism*. Rev. ed. London and New York: Verso 1991.

Atwood, Margaret. *Survival*. Toronto: Anansi Press 1972.

Berger, Carl. 'The True North Strong and Free'. In *Nationalism in Canada*, ed. Peter Russell. Toronto: McGraw Hill 1966.

Coombes, Annie E. 'Inventing the "Postcolonial": Hybridity and Constituency in Contemporary Collecting'. *New Formations* 18 (Winter 1992): 39–52.

Crimp, Douglas. *On the Museum's Ruins*. Cambridge, MA: MIT Press 1993.

Duncan, Carol, and Alan Wallach. 'The Universal Survey Museum'. *Art History* 3, no. 4 (December 1980): 448–69.

Ettema, Michael J. 'History Museums and the Culture of Materialism'. In *Past Meets Present: Essays about Historic Interpretation and Public Audiences*, ed. Jo Blatti. Washington and London: Smithsonian Institution Press 1987.

Government of Canada. *Culture and Communications: The Ties That Bind*. Report of the Standing Committee on Communications and Culture, April 1992.

Evidence Submitted to the Standing Committee on Communications and Culture 5 (3 October 1991).

Harper, John Russell. *Painting in Canada: A History*. 2nd ed. Toronto: University of Toronto Press 1977.

Harris, Cole. 'The Myth of the Land in Canadian Nationalism'. In *Nationalism in Canada*, ed. Peter Russell. Toronto: McGraw-Hill 1966.

Harris, Lawren. 'Revelation of Art in Canada'. *The Canadian Theosophist* 7, no. 5 (July 1926): 85–8.

Hill, Charles. 'The National Gallery, a National Art, Critical Judgement and the State'. In *The True North: Canadian Landscape Painting 1896–1939*, ed. Michael Tooby. London: Barbican Art Gallery 1991.

Housser, F.B. *A Canadian Art Movement: The Story of the Group of Seven*. Toronto: Macmillan Company of Canada 1926.

Morris, Peter. *Embattled Shadows: A History of Canadian Cinema 1895–1939*. Montreal: McGill-Queen's University Press 1978.

Osborne, Brian. 'The Iconography of Nationhood in Canadian Art'. In *The Iconography of Landscape*, ed. Denis Cosgrove and Stephen Daniels. Cambridge: Cambridge University Press 1988.

A Portfolio of Pictures from the Canadian Section of Fine Arts; British Empire Exhibition. London 1924.

Preziosi, Donald. *Rethinking Art History: Meditations on a Coy Science*. New Haven and London: Yale University Press 1989.

Reid, Dennis. *The Group of Seven*. Ottawa: National Gallery of Canada 1970.

Stacey, Robert. 'The Myth—and—Truth of the True North'. In *The True North: Canadian Landscape Painting 1896–1939*, ed. Michael Tooby. London: Barbican Art Gallery 1991.

Tooby, Michael. 'Orienting the True North'. In *The True North: Canadian Landscape Painting 1896–1939*, ed. Michael Tooby. London: Barbican Art Gallery 1991.

Wallace, W. Stewart. *The Growth of Canadian National Feeling*. Toronto: Macmillan Company of Canada, 1927.

THE MASK STRIPPED BARE BY ITS CURATORS: THE WORK OF HYBRIDITY IN THE TWENTY-FIRST CENTURY

RUTH B. PHILLIPS

I begin this paper, which addresses relationships among art history, anthropology, and museology in the first decade of the twenty-first century, by recalling an anecdote from my fieldwork in Sierra Leone in the 1970s. It bears retelling three decades later because it suggests what has changed and not changed in the intervening years, both in the practices of academic art historians and anthropologists and in the museum representations for which their disciplines are, ultimately, held accountable. My dissertation on Mende women's masks focused on classical art-historical problems of iconographic interpretation and stylistic development and in preparation for my

fieldwork I studied collections of Mende masks in major European and North American museums. In Sierra Leone, I travelled from village to village, observing masquerade performances, interviewing people about ritual context, and asking to see and document the carved headpieces then in use by Sande Society masqueraders.

My focus on the carved headpiece, however, proved to be very un-Mende, and it immediately led to a problem of translation. The Mende, like most African peoples, do not have a separate word for 'mask', for to speak of the headpiece separately from the rest of the masquerade costume, or to articulate the masked being's identity as an *ngafa*, or spirit, as separable from the material and mechanical components of its dramatic realization by a human impersonator, implies a distinction which the Mende do not verbalize in public discourse.[1] I learned that the phrase that most closely translates the English '*sowei* mask' is *sowo wui* ('the head of *sowei*'). In more 'modern' villages, the Sande women did not object to my seeing, measuring, and studying these 'heads'—although sometimes in an enclosed area that men could not enter. In villages in which traditional protocols were more strictly observed, however, the Sande women brought out the fully masked and costumed figures, each accompanied by her attendants and heralded by the musical, high-pitched chanting of her name. Early on in my fieldwork, I tried to explain to the chief who had arranged my meeting with Sande women in one of these more traditional villages that it wasn't necessary for my needs to go to all the trouble of 'pulling' the whole masquerade. He gently responded that the *ndoli sowei* could only be seen when fully and correctly garbed, and to drive home the point he asked me: 'Could you go out without your head?'[2]

This exchange impressed on me that if I was to appreciate *sowei* masks from a Mende perspective in the same way that I had been taught to appreciate a Botticelli painting by understanding fifteenth-century religious observances, neo-Platonism, and aesthetic ideals, it would be necessary to attend both to the moments when translation proved difficult and to the synesthetic experience of the total performance. It was one of many transformative moments in my practice as an art historian that I owe to dialogue with members of contemporary indigenous communities. Cumulatively, such encounters have led to a conviction that for both cognitive and ethical reasons, the goal of achieving emic, or insider, understanding trumps—although does not necessarily preclude—the subsidiary formal and connoisseurial pleasures of looking at 'heads'. I have never since been able to look at a museum installation in which a *sowei* mask has been stripped bare of her raffia, white head tie, protective amulets, jewellery, and black body costume without feeling that a violation has taken place—a voyeuristic stripping bare, an amputation (Figures 19.1 and 19.2).

For anyone with a training in art history, such an apprehension is inevitably also informed by Marcel Duchamp's fundamental insight that the Western system of art and museums operates as a machine for the production of economies of commodification and desire while at the same time preventing the fulfillment of those desires. Like the Bride in *The Bride Stripped Bare by her Bachelors, Even*, the African mask, displayed as a bare headpiece, cannot satisfy the viewer's hunger to possess the Other. Decapitated and stripped, the mask fatally frustrates access to the knowledge of the Other which is at the heart of the satisfaction of desire. The universalizing process of formalist appreciation that is imposed under the sign of modernist primitivism occludes localized identities, denatures the exotic, and reduces it to sameness. Equally importantly, such modernist installation strategies prevent viewers from recognizing the historical and contemporary networks of interconnection amongst world cultures—whether they be networks of artistic exchange or the underlying political and economic processes which have

FIGURE 19.1 *Sowei* mask, Western or Kpa-Mende style, Sierra Leone, XIXᵉ siècle.

FIGURE 19.2 *Sowei* masker in performance. Sierra Leone, 1972.

delivered up exotic artifacts to the Western gaze. My example of masks from Sierra Leone is particularly compelling in this respect, because the diamond-driven violence suffered by its peoples lends to the words 'amputation' and 'stripping' a literal and tragic resonance. The ethical problem is, however, general, and urgent in this era of speeded up global flows of people, capital, images, and things.

My small epiphany in West Africa is paralleled by the experiences of many other historians of non-Western art who have gone 'into the field' both in distant countries and in their own back yards. In the academy, the transformative power of dialogic encounter has produced a remarkable new art-historical and anthropological literature about non-Western arts. In the museum, dialogue with members of originating communities, activated by post-colonial politics and contestations, has resulted in innovative new collaborative

practices, especially in settler societies such as Canada, Australia, New Zealand, and the United States. Museums have begun to reverse past processes of stripping away, to revise modernist notions of authenticity, and to alter standard Western practices of conservation. The example of masks is, again, emblematic, as demonstrated by three representative examples of restoration projects that have taken place during the past decade or so. At the Fennimore House Museum in Cooperstown, New York, Yupik artist and performer Chuna McIntyre has replaced the feathers and other elements that were lost decades earlier from the Yu'pik masks so beloved of the surrealists and other modernist artists.[3] The University of British Columbia's Museum of Anthropology and the Royal British Columbia Museum regularly lend old masks in their collections for use in potlatches and other events, allowing artists to

FIGURE 19.3 Mende mask installation, Detroit Institute of Arts, 2008.

add new cedar bark fringes and even to repaint them so that they can be returned to a state appropriate for performance. A conservator at the Metropolitan Museum of Art worked with art historian Frederick Lamp, a specialist in Baga art from Guinea, to make a new raffia and fabric body costume for a Baga *D'mba* mask—another African genre canonized by the modernist taste culture—which is displayed in its Rockefeller wing.[4]

Museum installations of indigenous arts have also changed, although in ways that are more uneven and difficult to characterize. There has been a notable merging of the modernist display paradigms of art and artifact; art museums such as the Metropolitan increasingly provide extended labels, maps, and contextual photos that instruct viewers about the meaning of iconographic motifs and ritual contexts (Figure 19.3), while anthropology museums regularly exhibit contemporary art as a way to incorporate indigenous perspectives on history and culture and as cultural artifacts that evidence both living world views and participation in international art markets.

Yet in other museums, such as the Louvre's Pavilion des Sessions, the old paradigms seem to have reasserted themselves in particularly pure forms that seem strangely reactionary following more than two decades of deconstruction and postcolonial critique.[5]

In the remainder of this paper I will interrogate this early twenty-first century tension between hybridity and purity in three different ways. I will look briefly at the hybrid relationship between art history and anthropology which, as I will argue, has not only been increasingly evident in recent years, but was also present in the formative phases of the two disciplines. I will then turn to Bruno Latour's theorization of hybridity and his concepts of imbroglio and translation in order to urge their explanatory force in rethinking the museum representation of indigenous arts in the twenty-first century. In the last section of the paper I will discuss two current exhibitions of African and Pacific Islands art that, in my view, instantiate the attention to hybridity and networks that Latour advocates.

ART HISTORY AND ANTHROPOLOGY—ALWAYS ALREADY HYBRID

The relationship between art history and anthropology has most often been represented as a dialectical opposition: art historians focus on works of art, defined as products of high culture, in order to promote aesthetic appreciation and experience, while anthropologists study material culture as evidence of cultural beliefs and technologies and as mechanisms for social reproduction in order to promote cognitive understandings of the ways of life of entire social groups.[6] This has, in my view, always been something of a false dichotomy, for in their modernist phases both disciplines drew on a common repertoire of aesthetic and scientific constructs in order to contribute to evolutionist and progressivist meta-narratives of human history. Both adopted a comparative methodology based on visual description and analysis that was derived from natural science and for which collections of material objects and visual images were essential.[7] Both judged value in terms of similar standards of aesthetic quality grounded in Kantian aesthetics, and both imposed a characteristically Western hierarchy of fine and applied arts on objects produced in other times and by other cultures. In the early twentieth century, through the parallel projects of Franz Boas and Alois Riegl, both disciplines also began to move toward more historically contingent and relativist modes of analysis and understanding.

It is not accidental that the modernist paradigms of art and artifact were most rigidly imposed on indigenous art forms during the middle decades of the twentieth century, for during this period, the project of historical and cultural contextualization common to art historians and cultural anthropologists was suspended. Academic anthropologists moved away from the study of material culture and the anthropology of art, and art historians adhered to their traditional focus on the European tradition and 'Great Civilizations'. By default, the representation of indigenous arts was left largely to a third discursive community, made up of modernist artists and critics whose deep appreciation of Primitive Art was narrowly defined by their formalist aesthetic concerns and their disenchantment with industrial modernity.

The re-engagement of art history and anthropology in the 1980s was stimulated by a number of interrelated political, economic, and social movements of the postwar period, including the dismantling of colonial empires, the civil- and human-rights movements, identity politics, the growing demographic pluralism of Western nations, and economic and cultural globalization. Arguably, the growing cultural inclusivity of art history and its renewed interest in the social history of art, the revival of material culture studies and the anthropology of art, the interest of both scholarly communities in contact histories, and the emergence of new interdisciplinary fields such as visual studies and critical museology all respond to these global developments.

In keeping with these trends, anthropologists have returned to museum storerooms and archives and study the circulation of 'art' across cultures.[8] Art historians study a broader range of world art traditions and make use of anthropological theory and fieldwork methods. It is often difficult to tell the difference, at least in theory, among visual anthropologists, anthropologists of art, practitioners of the social history of art, and art historians who define their field as visual studies. In their renewed hybridity, art historians and anthropologists are today working out old methodological and conceptual problems within the new frames of post-colonialism, pluralism, transnationalism, and globalization.[9]

WE HAVE NEVER BEEN MODERN: HYBRIDITY AND IMBROGLIO

What, then, has been the parallel history of art and anthropology museums which, in their origins, were controlled by academic disciplinary formations? It is a notable feature of the late twentieth century that a great many of the most ambitious exhibitions of indigenous arts have been attended by controversy and intense critical debates which have been well rehearsed in the critical literature. A partial list would include the Museum of Modern Art's *Primitivism and Twentieth-Century Art* (1984), the Glenbow Museum's *The Spirit Sings* (1988), the Royal Ontario Museum's *Into the Heart of Africa* (1989), the Arts Council of Great Britain's *The Other Story* (1990), the Centre Pompidou's *Magiciens de la Terre* (1989), the US National Gallery of Art's *Circa 1492* (1992), the permanent installations of the Smithsonian's new National Museum of the American Indian (2003), and, most recently, the Musée du Quai Branly (2005).[10]

Each of these museological projects overflowed its boundaries into realms of politics, ethics, and practice to which it had initially seemed unrelated. This kind of excess has been characterized by Bruno Latour, the historian and philosopher of science and co-founder of Actor Network Theory (ANT), as a sign of the breakdown of the categorical separations imposed by modernism. Some of Latour's key concepts seem very useful for our present problem. In particular, I want to make use of his notion of 'imbroglio', defined in his 1991 book *We Have Never Been Modern* as an entanglement of unrelated phenomena.[11] Like Latour's imbroglios of phenomena of the scientific and the social that have been understood as separable and discrete, the museum dilemmas of recent years often occur when categorical distinctions between art and non-art or the West and the rest are revealed as always already fictive.

Latour's understanding of the modern both predicts and explains these museum dilemmas. 'The proliferation of hybrids', he writes, 'has saturated the constitutional framework of the moderns' [italics original].[12] In other words, such blurrings and convergences indicate that our categories can no longer contain the accumulated contradictions bred by their own fictiveness. As he notes, 'when the word "modern", "modernization", or "modernity" appears, we are defining, by contrast, an archaic and stable past. Furthermore, the word is always being thrown into the middle of a fight, in a quarrel where there are winners and losers.'[13] But the response he advocates goes further, for in order to reconnect that which has been severed by the modern 'work of purification' we must substitute what he calls a 'work of translation' in which we engage actively in identifying those networks which have, all

along, connected the multifarious phenomena of the world. In his words:

[T]he word 'modern' designates two sets of entirely different practices which must remain distinct if they are to remain effective, but have recently begun to be confused. The first set of practices, by 'translation', creates mixtures between entirely new types of beings, hybrids of nature and culture. The second, by 'purification', creates two entirely distinct ontological zones: that of human beings on the one hand; that of non-humans on the other . . . . The first set corresponds to what I have called networks; the second to what I shall call the modern critical stance.[14]

As a theorist of science studies, Latour's primary focus here is on the relationship processes purported to belong to incommensurable realms of science and society. I propose a parallel necessity for the work of critical museology, for just as the environmental crisis has made urgent the reconsideration of the nature/culture dichotomy, so has the challenge of learning to live in increasingly pluralist societies made it necessary to revisit the art/culture divide. Indeed, from the perspective of ANT, the science/society and Western/non-Western art and culture issues are themselves part of a large network, for it is often precisely the categorical division of nature from culture that indigenous advocates seek to alter in museum representations. If, in the past, the museum has served as one of modernity's key tools of separation and purification, it is, then, today called upon to serve as a site where the networks that link complex and apparently heterogeneous social, political, economic, and natural events are revealed rather than concealed.

NETWORKING THE OBJECT, AND THE TWENTY-FIRST CENTURY EXHIBITION

Latour's critique of modernity has not only useful explanatory force in helping us to understand the debates that regularly explode around museum representations of non-Western phenomena, but also indicates ways in which museums might work *with* hybridity rather than suppressing or occluding its presence. Such a project would require museums to make evident the way in which categories are networked—for example, the interconnectedness of art history and anthropology and the economic and other relationships among the peoples of the 'West' and the 'non-West' that have been present for centuries. As I learned from the experience of fieldwork, the key is to focus on the processes of translation. Cognitively, attending to the concepts which are most difficult to translate reveals the spaces between different world views that need to be bridged in order to achieve dialogue. Ethically, acts of translation among the different systems of meaning—nature, culture, art, economic exchange—enable us to identify the networks of apparently heterogeneous social, political, economic, and natural events which link peoples together across distances great and small. As noted, translation is a key concept of ANT theory. As John Law has written, it represents the process by which heterogeneous actors form into networks. '"Translation",' he writes, 'is a verb which implies transformation and the possibility of equivalence, the possibility that one thing (for example an actor) may stand for another (for instance a network).'[15] By focusing on the activity of translation, as Law and Latour recommend, we may be better able to reposition museum representations within complex networks of historical and contemporary cultural interaction rather than mystifying them.

How, then, can museums shift in practice to sites of translation in the ANT sense? I would like to conclude this paper by discussing two exhibitions focusing on masks and masquerades. Both, in my view, work with hybridity by attending to translation in the senses I have been advocating. The first is a small temporary exhibit entitled *The Village is Tilting: Dancing aids in Malawi*, which opened in January 2006 at the University of British Columbia Museum of Anthropology in Vancouver.[16] The second is a permanent installation at the National Museum of Australia in Canberra, entitled *Dhari a Krar: Headdresses and Masks from the Torres Strait*, which opened in 2005. Both are relatively small exhibitions, created with modest budgets. Both insist on the dynamic nature

of masquerade traditions as expressive modes that adapt to the changing conditions of life of indigenous people in the contemporary world, rather than freezing them in a past time of cultural purity or fetishizing them as objects of desire. Both exhibitions, furthermore, make the masks available for aesthetic appreciation as products of an individual carver's skill and imagination while also representing them contextually as masquerades comprised of multimedia assemblages of carvings, textiles, dramatic impersonation, sound, and dance.

The Village is Tilting was curated by Douglas Curran, a photographer who has spent 10 years visiting Malawi to create a comprehensive photographic documentation of the Gule Wamkulu, or Great Dance of the Chewa people.[17] The exhibition juxtaposes his large-scale photographs with mask headpieces and costumes. As the title of the exhibition indicates, its thematic focus is the way in which the Chewa address the AIDS pandemic and its devastating impact on their lives through their masquerade traditions. A video monitor placed at the entrance to the exhibition introduces the theme with a series of short statements by Chewa people. Visitors then enter down a ramp lined with a semi-transparent fabric wall through which the masks appear as spectral presences. Excerpts from interviews with Chewa consultants are printed on the fabric, introducing the historical, cosmological, and causal framework through which Chewa villagers speak about AIDS. 'When the men were going to work in the mines, this is when this disease started to come to us,' states Mai Karonga. 'We who don't listen, descend to the silence of our ancestors long ago. AIDS, NO! There is AIDS.' 'There is the slippery slope to the silence,' says Luciano Zagwazatha, a man from another village. Mai Alphonsina Kumilambe elaborates, stating: 'Men, women, and boys and girls are not following the rules of life set out by our ancestors . . . today no young girl runs away from a man.'

The text panels in the exhibition provides an ethnographic account of the Gule Wamkulu and the access provided by the masked spirits, or *nyau*, to the spirits of the ancestors and their power over fertility and life. The texts also recall

FIGURE 19.4 Installation of Chewa mask from *The Village is Tilting*, at the University of British Columbia Museum of Anthropology, 2007.

the attempts of colonial administrators to ban the Great Dance as an obscene 'national evil', and affirm the adaptive capacity of the masquerades to reinforce positive social values and trans-generational continuity. The maskers, we are told,

dance stories old and new that reinforce the consensus on the family and community values that are the cornerstone of Chewa identity. Failure to recognize the role of the spirits . . . the Chewa believe, leads to disruption and a breakdown of the community.

As the AIDS virus has permeated their society, the forms of the Chewa spirits have been regenerated again, providing new contemporary frameworks through which to understand the broader social implications and responses to the pandemic.

Other text panels interpret unfamiliar artistic materials by explaining their significance in Chewa cosmology:

Madzi ndi mayo, the Chewa say, 'water is life', an idea reflected in key elements of *nyau* practice . . . . The idea is borne out by the materials used to create the masks. Water-softened bamboo is bent for ribs, while wetted palm leaves are fashioned into heads and jaws of 30 foot long spirit animals. This sacred application of mud details for the eyes and face is equivalent to *kumwtsera*, to give a drink, and the act of mudding the limbs and goodies of the dancers is *kusamba*, to wash.

Both traditional masquerade characters such as 'Chadzunda, The old deaf man/The chief', who represents ideals of dignity and modesty, and 'Akupha Aonongo, The killers are destroyers' are presented and their attributes explained. Akupha exemplifies the Chewa 'anti-aesthetic': his 'appearance indicates he is a carrier. His face is not smooth and well-oiled as is the Chewa ideal: instead, his dusty, ashen skin is delineated with many wrinkles, and atop his head is a tumor.'

The effectiveness of the exhibition results, as always, from the success of the designer, Skooker Broome, in creating an installation that expresses its central thematic in visual and spatial terms. The walls are painted a deep rusty red, the colour of blood, in keeping with the aura of danger and power invoked both by AIDS and the Gule Wamkulu. This use of colour and the dramatic spotlighting of the individual masks also intensify the sense of enclosure and drama. The juxtapositions of the masks with Curran's large-scale photographic panels and triptychs evoke a sense of human scale and interaction, further enhanced by a video of masquerade performances in Chewa villages (Figure 19.4). Each assemblage of carved headpiece, costume, and photographs is given sufficient space to be appreciated as a unique ensemble; design and installation combine to position viewers as spectators of dramatic performances.

A similar emphasis on context and theatricality characterizes the National Museum of Australia's *Dhari a Krar: Headdresses and Masks from the Torres Strait*, and it, too, emphasizes the role of masquerade traditions in mediating historical and contemporary change. The exhibition is the result of a collaboration between the museum's curator, Anna Edmundson, and two Torres Strait Islanders who are also museum professionals. Brian Robinson, an artist and a curator at the Cairns Regional Gallery, originated the idea for the exhibition while an intern at the museum, and Carly Jia was brought in to liaise with community members in the Torres Straits. Jia commissioned new masks for the exhibition and the Museum's permanent collection and also developed public programming.[18]

Nineteenth-century Torres Strait masks are canonical objects of Primitive Art. The famous tortoise shell and wooden masks left the islands in the late nineteenth and early twentieth century following the 'Coming of the Light' in 1871, when missionaries arrived in the Torres Strait and converted the people to Christianity. Today, none of these old masks remains in Torres Strait communities. Rather, masquerade traditions continued to evolve and adapt in response to new spiritual and political needs. *Dhari a Krar* is remarkable for the clarity with which it explains the relationship of the older masks to these more recent masquerade traditions, and, in so doing, demystifies the 'rare art tradition', to use Joseph Alsop's phrase, of Primitive Art.[19] We learn that masquerades and headdresses remain important symbols of distinct local identities within the Torres Strait region and also serve as a key site for the re-enactment and preservation of historical memory. The opening panel states (both in English and in Kala Lagaw Ya, Torres Strait Islander Western language) that headdresses and masks have distinct local histories and styles within the islands and that they are today 'a source of ongoing identity and pride for Islander people'.

The texts are explicit about the way in which masquerade traditions were adapted after the coming of Christianity. A text panel on 'Old-fashioned Dance' states:

> The arrival of the London Missionary Society on Erub (Darnley) Island in 1871 heralded a number of changes to Torres Strait dance and dance artefacts. While many cultural practices were discouraged, some traditional dances were deliberately maintained as part of secular celebrations.
>
> Dances adhering more strictly to pre-Christian styles are known as 'old-fashioned dance'. Dances incorporating newer elements (such as Polynesian dance styles introduced by missionaries in the late 19th century) are known as *ailan dans* (island dance.)

In explaining how masks and headdresses reflect trade in the islands the exhibition also works to correct widely held dismissal of hybrid forms as inauthentic and, in the process, provides a striking example of how stripping away these added elements denatures the local identity and artistic content of a mask. 'Through trade, Islanders acquire the bases for the masks themselves', the panel on 'Trade' states. 'Wooden masks known as *mawa* or *buk* were traded from Papua New Guinea in an undecorated state. Torres Strait people added ochre designs, human hair, feathers, fibres and seeds.' A piece of information that also suggests in a highly graphic way how stripping away these added elements denatures the local identity and artistic content of a mask.

Another important way in which masquerades facilitate the realities of demographic mobility and migration in the Pacific Islands is stated in the panel on 'Dance and Innovation':

Unlike ceremonial dances, Torres Strait secular dances have always been innovative in their choreography and costume. From the mid 1800s the establishment of missions and the pearling industry brought people from around the globe including Japanese, Malays, Filipinos, Micronesians, Polynesians and Europeans. Torres Strait Islanders took advantage of this mix of cultures to create new repertoires of songs and dances. Today Torres Strait Islander dancers continue to draw on a diverse range of influences.

As in the UBC Museum of Anthropology's Chewa exhibition the design of the National Museum of Australia's exhibition communicates its messages not only through words, but also through the choices of colour, lighting, visual aids, and spatial arrangement. When the curators engaged Merrima Design of Brisbane (whose head is a Torres Strait Islander), they provided a clear brief to the designer. 'We wanted an "art hang",' Edmundson explains, 'whose simplicity would not distract from the masks and headdresses on display. The design would, however, convey the drama of traditional masquerades performed in jungle clearings when, during initiation, masked beings would appear suddenly among the trees, impressing the initiates with their mystery and power.[20]

For visitors to the exhibition, the core of the exhibit is the large screen on which masquerade performances are projected so that the dancers appear close to life size (Figure 19.5). The

FIGURE 19.5 Video installation, *Dhari a Krar*, National Museum of Australia, Canberra.

video projection activates the mask headpieces displayed on the walls and enables visitors to become spectators at a virtual performance. Equally importantly, the contemporaneity of the experience makes clear that the masquerade traditions—transformed by Torres Strait Islanders' success in using this art form to address the enormous changes in spiritual belief and the political and demographic makeup of their society of the past century—is a living art form that will continue to grow and evolve. The walls and cases are painted black, allowing both old and new masks installed in cases to be seen and appreciated for their formal qualities. But as the visitor views them, the music of performance fills the room, emanating from a large video of masquerade and dance performances on a stage, made especially for the exhibition. Like the Curran photographs in *The Village is Tilting*, these images are close to life-size. In the dark room, the electric glow, colour, movement, and sound of the video draw visitors to sit and watch the dancers. As at the UBC Museum of Anthropology, they become spectators at a virtual performance.

Both of these exhibitions make clear that it is not necessary to choose between formal appreciation and contextual understanding, or between knowledge of the historical evolution of an art form and its relevance to contemporary societies. Rather, both successfully translate between the familiar rigour of the Western art gallery's attention to form and the performative aesthetic and cognitive understandings of the originating communities. On a didactic level, both also reveal the global networks of circulation which have carried Christianity, viruses, human diasporas, money, political power—and masks—back and forth across the globe for over a century. To

do less in contemporary exhibitions is to fail to come to grips with the most important challenge that public museums have faced since they emerged as key institutions of geopolitical and historical consciousness and aesthetic experience at the beginning of the nineteenth century. We must find better ways to relish difference without homogenizing it through the very act of recognition, and to respect separateness while at the same time insisting on interconnection.

NOTES

1. Herbert Cole comments: 'In English . . . we interpose an extra word, "mask", for something that to the African is active and powerful and very real. Thus our neutral, inanimate "mask" is for the African a meta human presence, an antelope spirit or a dead "father" returned, even if temporarily, to the village.' Cole 1970, 24.
2. Paramount Chief Karkartuwa (village of Mende, Luawa chiefdom, Kailahun district), November 3, 1972.
3. Chuna McIntyre discussed this project in a talk delivered at the Fennimore House Museum in June 2005. Eva Fognell kindly answered further queries by email in May 2007.
4. Metropolitan Museum Curator of African Art Alissa Lagamma, personal communication, April 2001; and Frederick Lamp, personal communication, May 2008.
5. I have discussed these recent patterns in museum installations of non-Western art in more detail in Phillips 2007.
6. See Dominguez 1992 on the contrast between constructs of Kultur and 'culture' used in modernist art history and anthropology.
7. See Ginzburg 1989.
8. See, for example, Thomas 1991, Marcus and Myers 1995, Myers 2002, and Morphy 2007.
9. For examples of these new anthropological and art-historical approaches, see Westermann 2004. I analyze this overlap further in my essay in that volume, 'The Value of Disciplinary Difference: Art History and Anthropology at the Beginning of the Twenty-First Century'.
10. For *Magiciens de la Terre*, see Buchloh 1989, and

the special issues of *Art in America*, July 1989 ('The Global Issue') and of *Third Text* (vol. 6, spring 1989), containing English translations of articles published on the occasion of the exhibition in *Les Cahiers du Musée National d'Art Moderne*. For the debates sparked by the MOMA show see Foster 1985, 181–210, and Clifford 1988. The published debates around the *The Spirit Sings* and *Into the Heart of Africa* are summarized in Jones 1993. See also the detailed case study in Butler 2007. For the new National Museum of the American Indian see Lonetree and Cobb 2008.
11. Latour 1991.
12. Latour 1991, 51.
13. Latour 1991, 10.
14. Latour 1991, 10–11.
15. Law 1992, 7.
16. The exhibition ran from February 6 to September 3, 2007.
17. See Curran 1999.
18. I am grateful to Anna Edmundson for her account of the development of the exhibition, on which the following discussion is based. Personal communication. June 2007, Canberra, Australia.
19. Alsop 1982.
20. The low budget for the exhibition (only Aus. $75,000) was a help in achieving the desired design as the curators were allowed to reuse and paint black older cases rather than having to conform to the more elaborate 'house style' used elsewhere in the museum.

REFERENCES

Alsop, Joseph. *The Rare Art Traditions: The History of Art Collecting and its Linked Phenomena Wherever These Have Appeared*. New York: Harper & Row, 1982.

Buchloh, Benjamin H.D. 'The Whole Earth Show: An Interview with Jean-Hubert Martin'. *Art in America* (May 1989).

Butler, Shelley Ruth. *Contested Representations: Into the Heart of Africa*. Peterborough, ON: Broadview Press, 2007.

Clifford, James. 'Histories of the Tribal and the Modern'. In *The Predicament of Culture*. Cambridge, MA: Harvard University Press, 1988.

Cole, Herbert. *African Arts of Transformation*. Santa Barbara, CA: The Art Galleries, University of California, 1970.

Curran. Douglas. 'Nyau Mask and Ritual'. *African Arts* 32, 3 (Autumn 1999): 68–78.

Dominguez, Virginia. 'Invoking Culture: The Messy Side of Cultural Politics'. *The South Atlantic Quarterly* 91, 1 (1992): 19–42.

Foster, Hal. 'The Primitive Unconscious of Modern Art, or White Skin Black Masks'. In Foster, Hal, ed. *Recodings: Art, Spectacle, Cultural Politics*. Seattle: Bay Press, 1985.

Ginzburg, Carlo. 'Clues, Roots of an Evidential Paradigm'. In his *Clues, Myths and the Historical Method*. Baltimore: Johns Hopkins University Press, 1989.

Jones, Anna Laura. 'Exploding Canons: The Anthropology of Museums'. *Annual Review of Anthropology* 222 (1993): 201–20.

Latour, Bruno. *We Have Never Been Modern*. Translated by Catherine Porter. Cambridge, MA: Harvard University Press, 1993.

Law, John. 'Notes on the Theory of the Actor Network: Ordering, Strategy and Heterogeneity'. http://www.lancs.ac.uk/fass/sociology/papers/law-notes-on-ant.pdf (accessed March 2008). (Also published in *Systems Practice* 5: 379–93.)

Lonetree, Amy and Amanda Cobb. eds. *The National Museum of the American Indian: Critical Conversations*. Lincoln. NB: University of Nebraska Press, 2008.

Marcus, George E. and Fred R. Myers, eds. *The Traffic in Culture: Re-figuring Art and Anthropology*. Berkeley: University of California Press, 1995.

Morphy, Howard. *Becoming Art: Exploring Cross-Cultural Categories*. New York: Berg, 2007.

Myers, Fred R. *Painting Culture: The Making of an Aboriginal High Art*. Durham, NC: Duke University Press, 2002.

Phillips, Ruth B. 'The Museum of Anthropology: Twenty-First Century Imbroglios'. *Res:Anthropology and Aesthetics* 52 (Autumn 2007): 8–19.

Thomas. Nicholas. *Entangled Objects: Exchange, Material Culture, and Colonialism in the Pacific*. Cambridge, MA: Harvard University Press. 1991.

Westermann, Mariet, ed. *Anthropologies of Art*. New Haven: Yale University Press and Clark Art Institute, 2004.

QUESTIONS FOR REFLECTION

1. Visit a museum and gallery (in person or online) and perform a critical analysis of an exhibition. Is there a specific story being told and, if so, how do the selection, arrangement, and content of the works contribute to that story?

2. Examine your own collection of images (material or digital). Does your collection tell a specific story about you and your life? Why do you choose to keep some images and delete others, and how do your choices impact the story told by your collection?

FURTHER READING

Anderson, Benedict. *Imagined Communities: Reflections on the Origin and Spread of Nationalism.* Rev. edn. New York: Verso, 1996.

Anderson, Gail. *Reinventing the Museum: Historical and Contemporary Perspectives on the Paradigm Shift.* Walnut Creek, California: AltaMira Press, 2004.

Bennett, Tony. *The Birth of the Museum.* London: Routledge, 1995.

Duncan, Carol. *Civilizing Rituals: Inside Public Art Museums.* New York: Routledge, 1995.

Duncan, Carol, and Alan Wallach. 'The Museum of Modern Art as Late Capitalist Ritual'. *Marxist Perspectives* (Winter 1978): 28–51.

Duncan, Carol, and Alan Wallach. 'The Universal Survey Museum'. *Art History* 3.4 (December 1980): 448–69.

Ferguson, Bruce W., Reesa Greenberg, and Sandy Nairne. *Thinking About Exhibitions.* London: Routledge, 1996.

Kirshenblatt-Gimblett, Barbara. *Destination Culture: Tourism, Museums and Heritage.* Berkeley: University of California, 1998.

O'Doherty, Brian. *Inside the White Cube: The Ideology of the Gallery Space.* Berkeley: University of California Press, 2000.

Pollock, Griselda, and Joyce Zemans. *Museums After Modernism: Strategies of Engagement.* Malden: Blackwell, 2007.

Sherman, Daniel J., and Irit Rogoff, Eds. *Museum Culture: Histories, Discourses, Spectacles.* London: Routledge, 1994.

PART SEVEN

IMAGES AND NATIONAL IDENTITY

Images serve to represent us in a diversity of capacities. On driver's licences, passports, student cards, and other identification documents, images are used to verify our identity. In less formal contexts, such as family photographs and the images we collect and share through photo archives and social networking sites, we consciously choose the representations that others will see and that will serve as the basis of our memory and history. In this latter manifestation, and as explored by Wagman in Part Three, we consciously participate in the construction of our identity: actively choosing which images to save, which to share, and which to delete. Just as images help to construct individual identity, so too they function in the construction of national identity. The paintings, photographs, films, television programs, and other forms of a nation's visual culture are often understood to be representative of that nation's character or identity. Similarly, the continued circulation of images about a nation in film, television, magazines, textbooks, travel guides, and other venues help to build cultural attitudes and beliefs about that nation in the minds of its residents as well as those outside its borders.

The role of the image in the construction and shaping of identity has been addressed in various capacities throughout this book. Most notably, the essays in Part Two addressed the roles of visual representation in the construction of knowledge about the body, and specifically in the construction of cultural attitudes towards the male and female bodies. And the essays in Part Eight address the topic in relation to the construction of audience identity. In these and other capacities, visual representation plays a central role in the development of individual and group identity. The essays here in Part Seven highlight the role of the image in the construction of national, and specifically Canadian, identity.

The first essay, 'Through a Canadian Lens: Discourses of Nationalism and Aboriginal Representation in Governmental Photographs', is by the noted photography and visual culture scholar Carol Payne. Payne opens her essay with a discussion of the unique status of the photographic image. Borrowing from Charles Peirce's theory of signs, she identifies the indexical authority of the photographic image, that is, its ability to serve as a direct referent of its subject matter. As the author notes, the photograph's capability in this regard made it particularly well suited for use in scientific practice in the nineteenth century, which was guided by positivism and the belief that truth could be gleaned through the direct observation of the natural world. Payne then explores the use of photographic imagery as produced through three different government agencies: the North American Boundary Commission, the Anthropology Division of the Geological Survey of Canada, and the Still Photography Division of the National Film Board of Canada. Despite their idiosyncrasies, Payne argues that the images produced by these agencies functioned as part of a larger imperialist project. In this way, the images presented a specific story of Canadian identity, one in which the government featured prominently as a patriarch caring for its peoples.

Payne performs a rich historical and archival analysis and makes many provocative observations. She notes that, as it was used in cartographic, geographic, and anthropological contexts of the late nineteenth century, the photograph was ostensibly about research; however, she argues that the use of camera often supported pre-established

beliefs about people and places, such as Canada's First Peoples being 'primitive' compared to the southern, white populations. Such use of imagery therefore contributed to a particular kind of national identity that positioned the white, southern population as the norm, with the various peoples of Canada's North as 'other'. Importantly, although Payne's case study is of Canada, she stresses that such practice is also international in scope. She writes: 'Under the guise of scientific discourse, photographs have been employed variously to map territories, justify invasions, promote colonial settlement, and subjugate Aboriginal peoples throughout the world.' Thus Payne's essay is as much about the power of images—particularly photographic images—as it is about their role in identity construction.

The second essay in the part, 'Votes for Stoves: *Everywoman's World* and the Canadian Citizen–Consumer in the Early Twentieth Century', is by the communication studies scholar and feminist media historian Anne-Marie Kinahan. The essay is a focused analysis of the construction of a particular facet of Canadian identity: the female citizen–consumer of the early twentieth century. Kinahan performs a visual and textual analysis of the Canadian periodical *Everywoman's World* and argues that the periodical 'intervened in political, cultural, and economic domains', and, as such, was not just a reflection of the time, but was an active agent of social change. More specifically, Kinahan stresses the extent to which the magazine focused on issues of woman suffrage and, in so doing, helped to create a generalized 'image' of the Canadian suffragist. Importantly, the author also stresses readers' agency in this process. As Kinahan argues, female readers were not simply passive receivers of the magazine's content; rather, they used the magazine to help negotiate their role in the changing social, political, and economic climate of early twentieth century Canada.

Kinahan's treatment of the visual is particularly interesting. As she shows, the visual functions both literally and figuratively in the process of creating the female citizen–consumer. In the literal function, *Everywoman's World* included photographs and illustrations of key figures in the suffragist movement and, as such, gave a literal face to the Canadian citizen–consumer. Such images worked in concert with advertisements in the magazine to construct the Canadian woman as both politically engaged and in charge of domestic life. In the figurative function, the stories, editorials, and advertisements of the magazine helped to construct a more generalized 'image' of the Canadian citizen–consumer. The essay is a compelling account of the complex negotiation among images, text, writers, publishers, and readers in the creation of the Canadian female citizen–consumer.

The final essay in this part, 'Meatballs Matters', by communication studies and film scholar Peter Urquhart, also examines the notion of Canadianness in popular culture, through an analysis of the film Meatballs. Urquhart notes that by all accounts Meatballs is a Canadian film; yet it is completely absent from the critical and academic discourse on Canadian cinema. The author then asks: 'What explains Meatballs's invisibility in Canadian film culture?' Urquhart's essay answers that question, calling attention to the role of professional discourse—in this case that of the discipline of film studies—in what constitutes good, bad, and Canadian film. And in a manner parallel to Whitelaw in Part Six, Urquhart questions whether the very notion of a national cinema is even feasible. He asks, humorously, what would constitute Canadian cinema: 'Films about winter? Hockey? Doughnuts'?

The author argues that Canadian film studies is dominated by a cultural nationalist perspective which privileges films thought to espouse 'Canadian' ideals. From the 1970s through to the present, the bulk of critical and academic work on Canadian film has positioned it as intellectually challenging and decidedly non-commercial, locating commercially successful and otherwise 'popular' films as American. As Urquhart argues, this dichotomy is both false and limiting. The exclusion of Meatballs from discussions of Canadian cinema reflects an elitist professional discourse that privileges certain films over others. Importantly, and as the author stresses, this discourse is not fixed but is historically and culturally specific. Urquhart therefore calls on scholars to revisit films such as Meatballs that were previously excluded from discussions of Canadian film on the grounds that they were un-Canadian. For Urquhart, Meatballs matters, both because of its commercial success and its role in shaping a genre that has become a mainstay in contemporary film.

The essays in this part cover a broad historical range and an equally broad subject matter. Yet all are united in their emphasis on the role of images in the development of certain conceptions of Canadian identity. Such conceptions are necessarily historically specific, and what constitutes a nation's identity is a deeply complex topic. Indeed, and as stressed by Urquhart, the very notion of national identity can be called into question. Nonetheless, the images that are produced, interpreted, and disseminated by, for, and about a nation are powerful sites where identity is literally and figuratively performed. Critically evaluating such images sheds light both on the process of identity construction—with its attendant implications and ramifications—and on the powerful nature of visual communication.

THROUGH A CANADIAN LENS: DISCOURSES OF NATIONALISM AND ABORIGINAL REPRESENTATION IN GOVERNMENTAL PHOTOGRAPHS

CAROL PAYNE

> Like the state, the camera is never neutral . . . it arrives on the scene vested with a particular authority, authority to arrest, picture and transform daily life . . . . This is not the power of the camera but the power of the apparatuses of the local state which deploy it and guarantee the authority of the images it constructs to stand as evidence or register a truth.
>
> —John Tagg[1]

During one of his terms as prime minister, Sir John A. Macdonald sat for a series of unattributed and undated portraits. Among them was a full view of the prime minister leaning on a table covered by books.

The contrast between this image and photographic portraiture of today is striking. While we might expect a semblance of intimacy and naturalness (whether real or feigned) in our own snapshots, Macdonald's portrait seems formal and rigid. He gazes off into the distance, left hand raised in a stylized gesture familiar to orators of the time. There is a tangible sense of the first prime minister's awkwardness or even discomfort before the lens. Indeed, Macdonald probably was uncomfortable. Although photographers had been active in Canada as early as 1840, photography remained a novelty for most, and technical limitations of the time made the very business of being photographed disquieting.[2] Still, I would argue that for late nineteenth-century viewers, this early portrait effectively imbued Macdonald with a sense of dignity appropriate to his office while presenting him as an embodiment of the dominion's very aspirations.

How does a seemingly simple image like this one confer a sense of national identity? This essay will address that question by examining, through three brief case studies, how photographs commissioned by the government (and those co-opted for governmental use) have historically contributed to official constructions of Canadian identity. Throughout the country's history, still photographs have been deployed to buttress governmental authority. They helped justify Aboriginal acculturation, promote northern and western settlement, establish borders, serve military efforts, advertise Canadian industry, and provide visual endorsements for numerous other bureaucratic initiatives. In short, the Canadian government's use of photography has been varied, extensive, and influential. While a full survey is beyond the scope of this article, I will focus in each case study on one recurrent and acute example of how still photographs support national hegemony with regards to representations of First Peoples. These will be discussed in the context of the rendering of the dominant culture, as in the portrait of Macdonald. Although this essay chiefly scrutinizes the 'official picture', I also acknowledge that dominant discourses are not intractable; they *can* be resisted. To present a governmentally sanctioned and, at times, suppressive view without its alternative would be tantamount to an endorsement of it. Accordingly, this article will also introduce how First Nations peoples, in particular, have resisted dominant visual models of Canadian identity in recent scholarship and art.

Until relatively recently, photographs have typically been presented as neutral and authoritative historical evidence; valued for their 'transparency', they have often been invoked to 'illustrate' or lend credibility to a number of historical and political positions. In contrast, this essay introduces photography as a 'social practice', one which, rather than being detached from social narratives, participates in the naturalization of or resistance to discourse. Accordingly, another aim of this essay is to introduce the reader to the distinctive character of the analog photograph (the non-digital image) and of photographic meaning. Finally, in addition to exploring the specific histories narrated here, this essay offers the reader bibliographical sources for further study.[3]

Any photograph—whether a portrait of John A. Macdonald or a Polaroid snapshot of a friend—is

FIGURE 20.1 Photographer unknown, *Sir John A. Macdonald, c. 1867–1891*

historically inscribed; in effect, the medium is not a neutral device but encompasses the biases and concerns of the culture and times in which it was developed and viewed. The invention of analog photography, which is typically dated to about 1839 in Western Europe, reflected the cultural environment from which it emerged. Nineteenth-century European perceptions of photography still form the foundation for our thinking about the medium today. Western Europeans at that time—living in the cradle of the industrial revolution—invested tremendous authority in mechanical instruments. The camera—like the steam engine, the sewing machine, and the type-writer—was one of the most influential mechanical inventions of the time and, therefore, it crystallized both the authority of science and the cachet of the modern. To photograph a scene was to confer it with (or judge it against) the values of modern progress and power. In addition, the nineteenth century—like our own times—privileged visuality over other sensory experiences. As an implement that provided seemingly consummate visual detail, the camera responded to those biases and seemed to complement one of the key philosophical tenets of nineteenth-century Europe: positivism. With its stress on empirical observation and tangible evidence as the bases of all that was knowable, positivist philosophy, particularly in the writings of Auguste Comte from the 1820s through the 1840s, proposed that knowledge of the 'actual laws of phenomena' alone could be achieved through reason and observation.[4] Photography, it seemed to many nineteenth-century viewers, was an ideal device for merging the rational and the visible. It achieved phenomenal popularity almost immediately.

At the same time, however, nineteenth-century viewers saw the photograph as a distinctive form of visual representation, a new type of realism that surpassed human optics. Not only did it provide heightened visual detail, but also—by merit of being mechanically produced—its images were typically thought to be *unmediated* by human intervention. The language used to describe photography in the nineteenth century reflects this belief in the photograph as an authoritative and neutral form of representation; it was termed variously an 'exact facsimile [of nature]', the 'mirror with a memory', and the 'pencil of nature'.[5]

Semiotics—particularly the approach developed by Charles Peirce—offers us one of the most compelling ways of accounting for photography's particular type of realism. Peirce suggests three classifications of signs: symbols (signs—such as language—developed by cultural convention with no natural relationship to their referents), icons (signs—including representational drawings—that *resemble* their referents) and, lastly, indices (signs—including footprints,

shadows, and the act of pointing—that maintain a physical relationship to their referents).[6] According to this model—as interpreted by scholars of photography—a photograph is both an icon and an index.[7] The portrait of John A. Macdonald noted above, for example, is an icon in that it resembles its referent—in it we can recognize the physical appearance of the country's first prime minister; yet, for many people, this image also surpasses the mimetic by offering a seemingly direct physical connection to this historic figure, that is, an *index*. In effect, the portrait captures an historic moment when Macdonald stood in front of a camera. By looking at the photograph, we feel, in turn, transported back to that time and place, in the prime minister's presence.[8] It is for this reason that, when faced with a photograph, people often seem to forget that they are looking at a representation. This is particularly true of portraiture. Rarely, for example, would we expect someone to say, 'That is how a photographer—within the limits of technology and following conventions of the time—depicted John A. Macdonald.' Instead, without a second thought most of us would simply pronounce, 'That *is* John A. Macdonald.' The slippage in language here is telling. It reveals how pervasive the analog photograph's *indexical* character is, a character that distinguishes it from other forms of visual representation and that is at the root of photographic authority. In short, unlike a drawing or a written account, a photograph is often experienced, in the words of Roland Barthes, as a direct 'emanation of its referent'.[9]

Despite claims of a privileged relationship to the 'real', however, photography is by no means a neutral and objective trace of the world.[10] Instead, it *mediates* the visible through subjective selection of subject matter, vantage point, and framing; alterations in depth, colour, and tone; the extraction of one fraction of time from a temporal continuum; the exclusion of other sensory information and, usually, binocular vision; and recontextualization through placement, accompanying language, and reception. Moreover, it translates the effects of light on silver into the form of a two-dimensional representation employing the conventions of Western Renaissance perspective.

The portrait of John A. Macdonald, for example, conveys coded meaning through props and pose. Books and other accoutrements of scholarship, which appear prominently in the image, were favoured in most nineteenth-century commercial photographers' studios; they were intended to signify the sitter's learnedness.[11] Beyond this unambiguous symbolism, the image is also encoded more subtly through technical devices. The full-length view from a low vantage point, a convention of portraiture, accentuates the subject's height, thereby conferring a sense of respect and reverence. Lighting and the prime minister's preoccupied gaze enhance those implied qualities. But the image, which was intended for public circulation, also reflects the then-emergent cult of celebrity. Middle-class audiences in the nineteenth century enthusiastically collected photographs—often in *carte-de-visite* or other standard formats—of performers, royalty, and, notably, politicians.[12] In the public imagination, the familiar visage of the statesman functioned as synecdoche—that is, he appeared not only as a unique individual but stood for the whole of the nation. Images like this one probably rested like faithful old friends in albums next to those of family members, fostering a sense of personal identification with and commitment to the politician and the Dominion he represented. This seemingly straightforward and utilitarian depiction is coded in a variety of ways; viewers of the time likely perceived Macdonald as a respectful, learned, and yet amiably familiar leader as well as the very embodiment of Canada.

Yet throughout most of its history, photography, as Jonathan Crary has argued, 'masquerade[s] as a transparent and incorporeal intermediary between observer and world'.[13] In short, photographs have been experienced as unimpeachable facts. It is precisely for this reason—because they are at once mediated or malleable carriers of meaning, and yet they almost imperceptibly disguise subjectivity as fact—that photography has become a powerful tool of persuasion, a means of encoding ideology.

Photography not only reflected the nineteenth-century predilection for mechanical innovation and positivist philosophy but also functioned as a handmaid to contemporary Europe's most pervasive cultural program: imperialism. Under the guise of scientific discourse, photographs have been employed variously to map territories, justify invasion, promote colonial settlement, and subjugate Aboriginal peoples throughout the world.[14] As a settler colony, Canada, too, enacted colonial possession in part through photographic representations. Imperialist tendencies in Canadian photography can perhaps be seen nowhere more clearly than in the myriad images produced for the British North American and Canadian governments during the nineteenth century to facilitate northern and western expansion. In Canada, these images contributed to what Edward Said has termed an 'imaginative geography'—as it applies to the construction of nationhood.[15] During the nineteenth century, photography was employed by a number of government-sponsored agencies and programs to document new territories not previously settled by non-Aboriginal peoples.[16] These included expeditions undertaken by the Royal Corps of Engineers, the Canadian Pacific Railway, and the Geological Survey of Canada.[17]

The use of photography by the Royal Corps of Engineers for the North American Boundary Commission provides an instructive example of how photography contributed to an imperialist project in nineteenth-century Canada.[18] As early as 1858, the corps began marking the British side of the forty-ninth parallel between British Columbia and the United States.[19] By 1872, following the American Civil War and after a renewed debate between the Canadian and US governments, a Joint Boundary Commission was established. Work was then resumed identifying and marking the forty-ninth parallel between the Rockies and the Lake-of-the-Woods. At this point, the camera would become, as Andrew Birrell reports, 'an integral part of military intelligence, research and operations'.[20] Four photographers were included among the 44 sappers on the team. Their equipment included a portable darkroom tent, two 12 x 12-inch cameras with rapid rectilinear and wide-angle lenses and two 7½ x 5-inch cameras with stereographic and rapid rectilinear lenses, as well as glass plates and chemicals.[21]

Despite the arduousness of nineteenth-century field photography,[22] by the time the Royal Corps of Engineers ceased work in 1874, after just three seasons in the field, they had produced fully 250 negatives.[23] Photographic prints accompanied the commission's official report and were offered to the Colonial Office, the Foreign Office, the Canadian Department of the Interior, Governor General Lord Dufferin, and members of the expedition as souvenirs. Engravings from individual photographs were also reproduced in non-governmental publications. The images depict landscapes, corps members at work, their encampments, boundary mounds, depots, geological features, and various Aboriginal peoples encountered along the way, among other subjects. While, as Andrew Birrell suggests, the emphasis was on providing legible scientific information, a closer inspection reveals how this work buttressed the colonial project as a whole.

The Boundary Commission frequently used photography as an addendum to the act of mapping, a crucial undertaking in colonization and the construction of nationhood. Photographic images ostensibly documented the forty-ninth parallel and provided information about the surroundings and occupying peoples, information that supplemented cartographic records. Maps, of course, not only offer a symbolic rendering of space; like photographs, they also imprint geographical territory with political meaning. This is often imperceptible, partly because cartography, too, is commonly experienced as an indexical sign and a neutral science.[24] Therefore, within the context of nineteenth-century North America, maps—as used largely by European visitors and settlers—naturalized a Western European hegemony.[25] As Alan Trachtenberg has noted, a crucial component of mapping is the act of naming.[26] Naming, particularly in its ability to recast geographic locales in the linguistic shades of the colonizer, in effect performs appropriation. Photographs, in turn, perhaps because of the authority of their presumed indexical character, became integral to mapping. They buttressed the claim of ownership by, as Trachtenberg argues, attaching 'a possessable image to a place name'.[27] In short, mapping, naming, and photographing enact a sense of cultural and political ownership—through symbolic, linguistic, and scopic means.

At the same time, they also give form to a corollary effect: erasure. For in assessing geography by European measurements, language, technology, and perspectival systems, they also negate Aboriginal culture.[28] This is compounded by the fact that for most Aboriginal peoples of the time, the very notion of possessing land not only constituted trespass but was, within their cultures, an utterly alien—even antithetical—concept.

While much of the Boundary Commission's work enacted colonial possession and Aboriginal erasure, photographic representations of First Peoples were not entirely absent from their archives. Indeed, as noted above, commission photographers also depicted members of various First Peoples living across the Prairies; but rather than asserting their presence, the images offer their subjects as the presumed European viewer's other. For example, one particularly notable and haunting image taken by a member of the Royal Corps of Engineers in 1873 depicts three unnamed Chippewas at a grave site. Wrapped in blankets with their heads bowed, most viewers would assume them to be in mourning.[29] It is, however, hard not to confer the image with broader significance. It reproduces pictorially the trope of the 'vanishing race'—that is to say, it functions as an emblem of Aboriginal annihilation while simultaneously implying colonial ascendency.

We might expect that First Peoples themselves would utterly shun such images, but, surprisingly, increasing numbers of Aboriginal scholars, artists, and communities are revisiting photographic representations like these, finding in them a site within which to reclaim the Native subject. One of the most engaging interventions into Euro-Canadian imaging of the First Peoples of the Prairies is found in the work of the Plains Cree artist George Littlechild.[30]

In his art practice, Littlechild explores questions of identity formation (often with direct autobiographical references) in part through the recontextualization of historic photographs. Littlechild was a member of the generation known colloquially as the 'Sixties Scoop'—a group described by curator Ryan Rice as the thousands of Aboriginal children who, during the 1960s, were seized from their birth communities to be

FIGURE 20.2 Royal Corps of Engineers, Untitled, 1873

raised by non-Aboriginal foster families.[31] The artist was able to reconstruct his family tree by combing various archives and locating hundreds of photographs and textual records pertaining to his birth family. These documents were originally produced under the auspices of several anthropological, governmental, or religious organizations, who typically presented their subjects as anonymous racial types. They initially served as justifications for the very paternalistic control and acculturation that scarred Littlechild's own life; but in the artist's hands, they become emblems of a newly rediscovered heritage. In these works, Littlechild employs collage, colour, and textual amendments to reinscribe the archival material with Cree symbolism, announcing the reclamation of family history while giving form to the tensions between cultures.

Aboriginal representations continued to figure prominently in governmental photography into the twentieth century. Among the most extensive bodies of work depicting First Peoples were those produced under the auspices of the Geological Survey of Canada's Anthropology Division. Like nineteenth-century images promoting western expansion, these visual documents, too, belie an imperialist agenda.[32] The Geological Survey of Canada (GSC) was founded in 1841.[33] It was, according to Christy Vodden, crucial in stimulating the mining industry, then a pivotal part of the colonial economy.[34] Over the following decades, it would be instrumental in establishing the mineral industry, but also in mapping the country, gathering information about flora and fauna, and documenting indigenous inhabitants. In 1910, the last of these concerns was expanded upon when the survey founded an Anthropology Division.[35] The division emerged as the government's most important institution for the study of Aboriginal culture.[36]

The most influential figure associated with the GSC's Anthropology Division was C. Marius

Barbeau (1883–1969). Barbeau remains well known today for his anthropological and folklore studies within both Québécois and Aboriginal cultures (including Huron and Iroquois nations as well as peoples of the Northwest coast). He joined the division in 1911 and continued to be a part of the institution until 1949. Current scholarship identifies his efforts at cataloguing and mythologizing First Peoples' culture as reflective of the 'vanishing race' thesis.[37]

Like most early twentieth-century anthropologists, Barbeau and his colleagues at the GSC's Anthropological Division adopted the camera as an invaluable tool for field research.[38] Photographic technology, at this time, had become increasingly portable and easy to use. It proved particularly helpful in both social anthropology and ethnographic research, the study of racial variations through empirical data. In this capacity, photography was often used alongside an array of other technological implements including calipers, measuring tape, audio recorders and movie cameras in order to support theories of racial difference and study the subjects' cultures. Like the camera, as already noted, these seemingly neutral tools also culturally inscribed. As the products of the (European) interpreting culture, they naturalize Europeanness and implicitly mark their non-Western subject as other. As Elizabeth Edwards has argued, the anthropological uses of photography reflected the colonial encounter in general; they 'represented technological superiority harnessed to the delineation and control of the physical world' and supported anthropology's effect of transforming 'the power of knowing . . . into a rationalized, observed "truth"'.[39] In nineteenth- and early twentieth-century studies of Native North Americans, ethnographic photographs and other materials were often marshalled to support racial and evolutionary theories proposed by such then-influential figures as Henry Rowe Schoolcraft and Lewis Henry Morgan.[40] Photographs, therefore, supposedly offered verifiable proof of racial distinctions and classifications, with their inherent premise of Aboriginal inferiority and need for paternalistic care. In short, these images contributed to a justification for colonial dominance.

Among the groups Barbeau studied and photographed were the Nisga'a people in settlements along the Nass and Skeena Rivers in northern British Columbia.[41] This group is now familiar for its recent precedent-setting land claim case against the BC government.[42] Between 1927 and 1929, Barbeau studied their social organization, arts, mythology, and history along with a Nisga'a colleague, William Beynon.[43] According to Linda Riley, Barbeau's photographs of the settlements were not chiefly concerned with visual ethnography but rather were intended as documents supporting his specific areas of research. For example, exactly one-third of the images depict totem poles, a key subject of study.[44] Others feature views of the surrounding region, housing, grave monuments, petroglyphs and other pictorial forms, social gatherings, fishery, and canning, among other sites and endeavours. However, Barbeau also made a number of portraits of the peoples of the area in both ceremonial and European dress. These portraits reflect conventions in ethnographic photography.

In 1927 and 1928, Barbeau made a series of portraits depicting the Head Chief of the Eagle clan, also known in Barbeau's records as 'Old Menesk'.

These include frontal, back, and profile views of the chief in various forms of ceremonial dress. In the example reprinted here, he wears, according to the field notes, 'a button blanket cape, fringed apron with buttons and puffin beaks, a frontlet of wood with ermine trim, abalone shell inlay, sea lion whiskers and a double border of faces' in addition to carrying a rattle.[45] Nothing could mark a sharper contrast to the portrait of John A. Macdonald with which I began this essay. Although obviously staged, Macdonald's portrait nonetheless presents him as an actor, in effect performing his role of political leader and, as I suggested, embodiment of the Canadian dominion. The chief of the Eagle clan, on the other hand, seems inert. By posing him in a harsh frontal view against the relatively neutral backdrop of a leafy tree—a convention in ethnographic portraiture—Barbeau has removed him from the ceremonial context for which his elaborate garb was intended. The chief is denied

FIGURE 20.3 Charles Marius Barbeau, *Old Menesk*, chief of the Eagles of Gitladamks, 1927

a sense of agency. Instead, the 'real' action progresses behind the lens with Old Menesk serving as little more than a prop.

Like images of western expansion, ethnographic photographs of Aboriginal peoples—such as this example—have also recently come under the scrutiny of Aboriginal scholars, artists, and communities. In 1999, for instance, Onondaga curator/photographer Jeff Thomas, a key figure in re-examining Aboriginal photographic representations in Canada, organized for the Canadian Museum of Civilization an innovative exhibition that addressed photographs made under the auspices of the GSC's Anthropology Division. The exhibition, entitled

'Emergence from the Shadow: First Peoples' Photographic Perspectives', combined two ideologically and historically divergent practices: field photographs by four GSC anthropologists and photo-based work by six contemporary Aboriginal artists. Here, as in Thomas's other curatorial projects and his own photographic practice, imperialist images are not eschewed but are instead juxtaposed with those depicting a vibrant contemporary Aboriginal life. In this way Thomas engages in what Homi K. Bhabha has termed 'hybridity' or 'cultural translation': the space of tension between cultures.[46] For Bhabha, incidents of hybridity not only 'unsettle the mimetic or narcissistic demands of colonial power but reimplicate its identifications in strategies of subversion'.[47] In short, hybridity—or cultural translation—as evident in Jeff Thomas's work operates as a strategy of retranslating or reinscribing the effects of the dominant culture. By demonstrating that the dominant culture can be subverted in this way, hybridity signals the tenuousness of the colonial position and asserts the agency of the colonized. Those assertions of agency can take the form of representational intervention, as in Thomas's work, or in the case of the Nisga'a people, direct political action.

Canadian officials increasingly recognized that photography could also serve as a vehicle for public relations.[48] One of the government's most extensive uses of the promotional photograph appeared under the auspices of the National Film Board (NFB) of Canada's Still Photography Division (1941–84). In its governmentally endorsed portrait of nationhood, representations of Aboriginal peoples also played a telling role.[49]

Today, the NFB's Still Photography Division has been mainly eclipsed from public memory by the board's celebrated Motion Picture units. Nonetheless, the Still Photography Division also achieved an influential program of image production and distribution. It was founded in 1941—two years after its parent agency—under the direction of John Grierson. Like the board as a whole, the Still Photography Division was charged with the task of 'interpret[ing] Canada to Canadians and to other nations'. In short, its mandate called for the development of a visual rhetoric of national hegemony. In the 200,000 images and hundreds of texts it would produce, the division addressed that lofty goal by reinforcing familiar symbols of Canada—including wilderness, the North, and, by the 1960s, multiculturalism—and offering homogenized visions of the country's regions and peoples. It gave form to the 'imagined community' of Canadian nationhood.[50] During the height of its activity from the 1940s to the 1960s, the Still Photography Division's distinctively jingoistic portrayal of nationhood was consumed on a regular basis by millions of Canadians and international audiences through magazines, newspapers, exhibitions, Canadian embassies, and NFB-sponsored books.

Although John Grierson's tenure at the NFB was relatively brief, his approach to documentary would continue to shape the board's cinematic and still photographic production for years. Today, of course, he is regarded as a pivotal figure in the history of non-fiction film. In 1926, Grierson coined the term 'documentary'.[51] While initially employed as a category of cinema, it quickly came to refer to still photographs, too. Grierson defined documentary as the 'creative treatment of actuality', an acknowledgment of the disguised subjectivity of camera-made images.[52] As I have argued elsewhere, his particular approach to documentary is rooted in liberal 'rational reform'—the systematic social control and planning by governments, social scientists, and industry—of the 1920s and 1930s.[53] For Grierson—and indeed, as John Tagg has demonstrated, for most documentary practice of the 1930s and after—documentary films and photographs became privileged forms in the discourse of social management.[54] Within the workings of the National Film Board of Canada, they were unabashedly at the service of governmental propaganda. As Grierson himself stated in 1942, 'The materials of citizenship today are different and the perspectives wider and more difficult; but we have, as ever, the duty of exploring them and of waking the heart and will in regard to them. That duty is what documentary is about. It is, moreover, documentary's primary service to the state.'[55] 'Service to the state' would remain the Still Photography Division's guiding principle throughout its history. The division was staffed by a team of photographers, photo-editors, writers, librarians, and administrators. Its Ottawa office included extensive darkroom facilities and a photography library for use by government departments and the public at large.[56]

Throughout much of its history, the division's chief vehicles for disseminating its work were photo-stories: narrative layouts containing between three and nine images with accompanying captions and text. These were produced as often as weekly for national and international publications.[57] Typically, the layouts translated the linear narrative of board documentary films into pictures. Photographs were privileged over text; one visual 'protagonist' emerged as a figure with whom the viewer was intended to identify, and text remained brief though glowing. Indeed, photo-stories offered an unremittingly cheerful picture of Canadian prosperity. Photo-stories were engaged, above all, with the project of constructing normative models of Canadian identity as a strategy of national unity.

The particular character of 'Canadian-ness' proposed by the Still Photography Division is perhaps nowhere more evident than in photo-stories depicting children, a recurrent motif throughout its history, and particularly those featuring Aboriginal children. Children came to stand—in a variety of complex ways—for the nation itself and its citizenry. From 1955 to 1960, for example, 66 out of 250 photo-stories featured images of children.[58] They surfaced (predictably) in photo-stories addressing leisure and in others where assumptions about childhood innocence and purity were exploited, as well as children's status as embodiments of the nation's future. More surprisingly, images of children were also invoked to promote the Canadian economy in pictorials devoted to everything from agricultural production to the fur trade. They were seen most frequently—particularly in the late 1950s—in instructional settings or other institutional contexts. They were, for example, virtually ubiquitous in photo-stories on health care.

But the kids featured in photo-stories hardly seemed to act like 'kids'. They stoically endured medical and dental examinations, listened obediently to authority figures, and looked up admiringly at all adults. Youths or children who did not fit the division's mould of happy conformity and relentless middle-class normalcy were portrayed as institutionally contained.[59] In short, children served a metonymic function in division photo-stories: they stood for an idealized model of Canadian citizenry, one that relied on a paternalistic relationship with government. In effect, these seemingly malleable kids reflected John Grierson's famous call for documentary to 'mould' the materials of citizenship. In images depicting Aboriginal youth, childhood as a sign of citizenry cared for by a paternalistic government was doubly inscribed. Because Aboriginal adults were frequently described in division publications and archival records as 'childlike'—an evocation of the familiar trope of Native peoples as the 'childhood of mankind'[60]—Native children were presented as the neediest of the needy.

A 16 December 1958 photo-story dedicated to the Charles Camsell Indian Hospital in Edmonton exemplifies the division's treatment of Aboriginal children.

The pictorial includes six photographs prominently featuring young Aboriginal patients seen within the institution and under the direct care of Euro-Canadian nurses.[61] Few of the children are identified by name, as if they represent interchangeable racial types rather than individual kids. Only one image takes the viewer outside the hospital. It portrays a young woman being taken on a shopping spree—apparently for a new hat—under the watch of a chaperone. Hat poised on her head, she smiles awkwardly at herself in a mirror. The emulation of Euro-Canadian middle-class status by Aboriginal peoples, as in this photograph, was another common feature in division images. She is presented as what Homi K. Bhabha terms a figure of the mimic. In addition to subject matter, the message of paternalistic Euro-Canadian authority is also buttressed by the very composition of the images themselves. As in most photo-stories, in these images the photographer adopts what we might call a 'fly on the wall' view. Children and nurses seem unaware of the photographer's—and by implication, our own—presence. When they meet the gaze of the

camera—as does one of the toddlers eating lunch at the lower right—their look suggests deference to authority or perhaps apprehension. As I have noted elsewhere, the all-seeing and all-powerful view became a common stylistic feature in all division photography of the time. It was, in effect, a visual equivalent of the so familiar 'voice of God' narratives from documentary films produced by the board during the same years, providing a second layer of (implied) institutional guardianship.[62] Photo-stories like this one, with its representational reinforcement of institutional authority, provided a visual form for the NFB Still Photography Division's own ideological emphasis on government as paternalistic caretaker for its citizenry, its needy children—particularly Aboriginal citizen/children.

Popular culture depictions of Aboriginal peoples—such as this example from the NFB Still Photography Division, are also being re-examined by Aboriginal peoples. In an essay on popularized images of the Indian Princess typology, prominent Aboriginal scholar Gail Guthrie Valaskakis argues for the importance of engaging with and—like Jeff Thomas—reframing dominant imagery: 'Like our discourse, our communities are not cemented in unity or belonging, but in the transformation and difference which is constructed in our ongoing struggle with power relations. And this dynamic process of building and re-building individual and collective identity centres in conflicting social imaginaries and their competing ideological messages.'[63]

The camera has emerged as a powerful tool of official discourse in Canada. As I have suggested in the brief case studies above, photographic representations of First Peoples—whether produced under the auspices of the North American Boundary Commission, the Anthropology Division of the Geological Survey of Canada, or the National Film Board of Canada's Still Photography Division—effectively define a colonial domain and contain the official other of the nation. Drawing on the parallel assumptions of photographic authority and the logic of imperialism, these diverse historic projects marked consistent sites of Aboriginal subjugation. Yet in the face of this long institutionalized pictorial subjugation,

Charles Camsell Indian Hospital
For an Exclusive Clientele

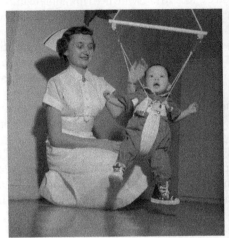

Two-thirds of the hospital's patients suffer from tuberculosis as does the little girl above.

Above, 1-year-old Indian Peter Tingmaniak enjoys a swing under the watchful eye of Nurse Onyshko.

The hospital maintains a varied rehabilitation program which includes educational services and handicraft training. Above, a young Indian girl who has completed her treatment is taken on a shopping tour of local department stores, her first introduction to current fashion styles.

Among the hospital's Eskimo patients is Mary Edetoak from Spence Bay. She belongs to one of the few remaining groups who still use tatoo marks; the custom is losing popularity with the younger generation.

Nurse Gallagher delights two little Eskimo lads with a story about Eskimos. Some members of the staff are themselves of Indian or Eskimo origin.

There's no shortage of hearty appetites in the the tiny tots ward.

FIGURE 20.4 National Film Board of Canada, Still Photography Division, 'For an Exclusive Clientele: Charles Camsell Indian Hospital'. Photograph by Gar Lunney, photo-story No. 188, December 16, 1958

a number of Aboriginal scholars, artists, and communities have developed effective means of resistance against them. As I have briefly noted here, by reframing dominant representations of First Peoples, such figures as George Littlechild,

Jeffrey Thomas, and Gail Guthrie Valaskakis have found a way—in Bhabha's words—to 'turn the gaze of the discriminated back upon the eye of power'.[64]

NOTES

1. John Tagg, *The Burden of Representation: Essays on Photographies and Histories* (Amherst: University of Massachusetts Press, 1988), 63–4.
2. Brian Carey, 'Daguerreotypes in the National Archives of Canada', *History of Photography* 12.1 (1988), 45–60.
3. As a broad survey introducing Canadian photography, I draw extensively on the literature of Canadian photographic history, revisiting and recontextualizing others' research. I am indebted to those scholars and hope that the reader will be encouraged to read their work directly. One invaluable place where the student of Canadian photography can begin their investigation is with the 1996 special issue on Canadian photography edited by Joan Schwartz in the journal *History of Photography* 20.2 (1996).
4. Introduction to Auguste Comte, 'The Nature and Importance of the Positive Philosophy', *Introduction to Positive Philosophy*, ed. Frederick Ferré (Indianapolis/Cambridge: Hackett, 1988), 2.
5. The phrase 'an exact facsimile' is credited to the French Minister of the Interior and is linked to the June 1839 announcement of Daguerre's invention; the American Oliver Wendell Holmes referred to photography as a 'mirror with a memory'; and 'the pencil of nature' was coined by William Henry Fox Talbot, like Daguerre, an inventor of photography. See Vicki Goldberg, ed. *Photography in Print: Writing from 1816 to the Present* (Albuquerque: University of New Mexico Press, 1981), 32, 36–48, 102.
6. Charles S. Peirce, 'What Is a Sign?' *The Essential Peirce*, ed. Nathan Houser and Christian Kloesel (Bloomington: Indiana University Press, 1998), 2: 4–10. Peircian semiotics, because of its inherent visual character, has been embraced by a number of recent scholars of visual culture. See, for example, Michael Leja, 'Peirce, Visuality, and Art', *Representations* 72 (2000): 97–122.
7. See for example, Rosalind E. Krauss, 'Notes on the Index: Part 1', *The Originality of the Avant-Garde and Other Modernist Myths* (Cambridge: MIT Press, 1985), 203.
8. The most important and moving discussion of this effect of portraiture is that proposed by Roland Barthes in his last book. Roland Barthes, *Camera Lucida: Reflections on Photography*, trans. Richard Howard (New York: Hill and Wang, 1981).
9. Barthes, *Camera Lucida*, trans. Richard Howard (New York: Hill and Wang, 1981), 80.
10. In particular, structuralist semiotics of photography reveals how photographic meaning is dependent on a nexus of cultural codes. See Roland Barthes, 'The Photographic Message', *Image/Music/Text*, trans. Stephen Heath (London: Fontana, 1977), 15–31; and Victor Burgin, 'Looking at Photographs', *Thinking Photography*, ed. Victor Burgin (Hampshire, UK: Macmillan, 1982), 142–53.
11. According to William C. Darrah, this austere setting of the studio was known as the 'Brady' or 'American' style of studio decor. William C. Darrah, *The Carte-de-Visite in Nineteenth Century Photography* (Gettysburg: W.C. Darrah, 1981), 26, 132.
12. For a detailed history of the *carte-de-visite*, see Elizabeth Anne McCauley, *A.A.E. Disderi and the Carte-de-Visite Portrait Photograph* (New Haven: Yale University Press, 1985).
13. Jonathan Crary, *Techniques of the Observer: On Vision and Modernity in the Nineteenth Century* (Cambridge: MIT Press, 1999), 136. For an influential discussion of this perception of photography, also see: Roland Barthes, 'The Photographic Message', 15–31.
14. As James R. Ryan states succinctly in his important study of British colonial photography, 'imperialism found sustenance in various photographic practices'. James R. Ryan, *Pictur-*

ing Empire: Photography and the Visualization of the British Empire (Chicago: University of Chicago Press, 1997), 13.

15. Edward Said, Orientalism (London: Routledge, 1978).

16. A detailed historical examination of northern and western consolidation is beyond the scope of this brief study. Nonetheless, it is important to bear in mind that these programs, although various in nature, were provoked in part by a cultural climate characterized by anxieties over United States expansion and Aboriginal presence as well as various economic motivations.

17. Even before Confederation, photography was deployed for such purposes. In the late 1850s, for instance, the Assiniboine and Saskatchewan Exploratory Expedition travelled from Lake Superior to the Red River area. This excursion investigated an expanse of land that British authorities sought to acquire from the Hudson's Bay Company. See Richard J. Huyda, Camera in the Interior: 1858, H.L. Hime, Photographer, The Assiniboine and Saskatchewan Exploring Expedition (Toronto; Coach House Press, 1975).

18. For simplicity's sake, here I use the word 'Canada' to refer to both the Dominion of Canada and the various regions constituting pre-Confederation British North America. My discussion of the Royal Corps of Engineers' use of photography draws extensively on the scholarship of Andrew Birrell. As Birrell has noted, the corps was an early advocate of photography as a scientific aid. Their first known official use of photography dates from 1851. By 1856, a photographic studio was established at their headquarters in Chatham, England, and in 1858, photography was added to the curriculum at the Royal Engineers' School. The camera was used at various times in documenting the corps' work as well as in producing portraits of ethnographic interest. Andrew J. Birrell, 'The North American Boundary Commission: Three Photographic Expeditions, 1872–74', History of Photography 20.2. (1996): 113.

19. In the 1860s, the corps produced an extensive record of over one hundred images documenting the marking of the forty-ninth parallel between British Columbia and the United States. Birrell, 'The North American Boundary Commission', 113–114; and Ralph Greenhill and Andrew Bir-

rell, Canadian Photography, 1839–1920 (Toronto: Coach House Press, 1979), plate 49.

20. The Canadian component of the survey was headed by Captain Donald Roderick Cameron. The scientific work on this survey—including astronomy and photography—was overseen by Captain Samuel Anderson. Birrell, 'The North American Boundary Commission', 114.

21. Birrell, 'The North American Boundary Commission', 114.

22. In the nineteenth century, photographing in the field was laborious. Not only did work have to be limited to the brief warm months, but contemporary photographic technology proved strikingly cumbersome. The Royal Corps of Engineers, like most photographers at this time, used the collodion wet plate process, glass-plate negatives coated with a solution of collodion (diluted gun cotton). Because plates had to be coated with the light-sensitive solution immediately before and developed soon after exposure, the photographer's entire workshop—including fragile glass plates—travelled with him over often-rough terrain. Stories of plates broken or ruined by shoddy processing are legion. For a first-hand account, see William Henry Jackson, 'Time Exposure, 1940: An Excerpt', Photography in Print: Writings from 1816 to the Present, 168–70.

23. In fact, Andrew Birrell reports that through technological improvements and the corps' own expertise, the survey experienced few difficulties with equipment. Birrell, 'The North American Boundary Commission', 119.

24. Peirce, 8.

25. José Rabasa, 'Allegories of Atlas', The Post-Colonial Studies Reader, ed. Bill Ashcroft, Gareth Griffiths, and Helen Tiffin (London and New York: Routledge, 1995), 358–64.

26. Alan Trachtenberg, 'Naming the View', Reading American Photographs: Images as History, Mathew Brady to Walker Evans (New York: Hill and Wang, 1989), 119–63.

27. Trachtenberg, 125.

28. For a discussion of Aboriginal erasure in another area of visual culture, see Jonathan Bordo, 'Jack Pine, Wilderness Sublime—Or the Erasure of the Aboriginal Presence from the Landscape', Journal of Canadian Studies 27.4 (1992–93): 98–128.

29. Birrell, 'The North American Boundary Commission', 119–20. Brock Silversides explains that Aboriginals' frequent lack of co-operation—as seen in Chippewas' bowed heads—was a complex and multivalent response to being photographed. He suggests that it was precipitated variously by misunderstandings about technology, fear that the photograph would strip away part of them, and the antagonism of the photographer. Brock Silversides, *The Face Pullers: Photographing Native Canadians 1871–1939* (Saskatoon: Fifth House, 1994), 6–9. Andrew Birrell also states that the figures here bow their heads 'probably in reaction to the camera rather than in mourning'. Birrell, 'The North American Boundary Commission', 120.

30. For more scholarship offering revisionist examinations of the Aboriginal representation, see, among others, Silversides, *The Face Pullers*; Lucy R. Lippard, *Partial Recall: Photographs of Native North Americans* (New York: The New Press, 1992); and Margaret B. Blackman, 'Copying People: Northwest Coast Native Response to Early Photography', *BC Studies* 52 (1981–1982), 86–112.

31. Ryan Rice, *Decolonizing the Archival Photography: George Littlechild* (Ottawa: Department of Indian and North Development, Indian Art Gallery, 1998).

32. My analysis of the GSC Anthropology Division is indebted to the work of and conversations with Jeff Thomas.

33. It was founded by the Legislature of the Province of Canada (present-day Quebec and southern Ontario).

34. Christy Vodden, *No Stone Unturned: The First 150 Years of the Geological Survey of Canada* (Ottawa: Supply and Services Canada, 1992), 1.

35. It was originally headed by Dr. Edward Sapir. As briefly noted above, anthropological images had appeared in the GSC's work before the formation of the division.

36. From 1911 until the late 1950s, it would be housed in the Victoria Memorial Museum Building (today's Canadian Museum of Nature in downtown Ottawa) and come under the rubric of the National Museums of Canada. Its collections are the foundation of the present-day Canadian Museum of Civilization located in Hull, Quebec. Linda Riley, ed., *Marius Barbeau's Photography Collection: The Nass River*, Canadian Ethnology Service, Paper No. 109 (Ottawa: Canadian Museum of Civilization, 1988).

37. For an excellent discussion of Barbeau's relationship with avant-garde artists in Canada and his efforts to 'indiginize' Euro-Canadian culture, see Sandra Jayne Dyck, '"These Things Are Our Totems": Marius Barbeau and the Indigenization of Canadian Art and Culture in the 1920s', MA thesis, Carleton University, 1995.

38. As R.G. Blackadar has shown, the survey began to employ photography in its work in the 1860s. R.C. Blackadar, *On the Frontier: Photographs by the Geological Survey of Canada* (Canada: Minister of Supply and Services Canada, 1982), 2. By the early twentieth century, field research had become the main approach to anthropological practice. Elizabeth Edwards, Introduction, *Anthropology and Photography, 1860–1920*, ed. Elizabeth Edwards (New Haven and London: Yale University Press in association with the Royal Anthropological Institute, London, 1992), 4.

39. Edwards, 'Introduction', 6.

40. These two figures represented the two dominant American ethnographic theories of the late nineteenth century. Henry Rowe Schoolcraft believed that American natives had degenerated from a higher state to present primitive condition and were therefore incapable of assimilation into North American society. In contrast, Lewis Henry Morgan subscribed to a Social Darwinist theory of the stages of evolution: savagery, barbarism, civilization. He proposed that Aboriginal peoples had achieved barbarism and were capable of reaching the level of civilization, which of course was tantamount to the imitation of European culture. See Brian W. Dippie, 'Representing the Other: The North American Indian', *Anthropology and Photography, 1860–1920*, ed. E. Edwards, 132.

41. For discussions of other photographers and anthropologists depicting Aboriginal peoples of the Canadian Northwest, see, among other titles, Margaret B. Blackman, *Window on the Past: The Photographic Ethnohistory of the Northern and Kaigani Haida*, Mercury Series, Paper 74 (Ottawa: National Museum of Man, 1981); and Margaret B. Blackman, 'Copying People'.

42. For more information, see the Nisga'a Treaty Information, Forum and Voting website at http://www.nisgaa.org/Nisgaa.htm.

43. Riley, v.

44. Riley, v.

45. Riley, 135–36. The photograph described is numbered 69699 in the Canadian Museum of Civilization (Geological Survey of Canada) archives.

46. For a detailed discussion of Thomas's work, see Jeff Thomas and Carol Payne, 'Aboriginal Interventions into the Photographic Archives: A Dialogue', *Visual Resources: An International Journal of Documentation* 18 (2002): 109–25. The term hybridity—with its reverberations of eugenics and genetic modification—has been called into question. See Jamelie Hassan, *Aldin's Gift* (North York: Art Gallery of York University, 1996), 24–28.

47. Homi K. Bhabha, 'Signs Taken for Wonders', *The Location of Culture* (New York and London: Routledge, 1994), 34.

48. As Ellen Scheinberg and Melissa Rombout demonstrate, projects initiated in the 1890s by the Department of Agriculture and the Department of the Interior to promote immigration were among the earliest uses of promotional photography by the Canadian government. Ellen Scheinberg and Melissa Rombout, 'Projecting Images of the Nation: The Immigration Program and Its Use of Lantern Slides', *The Archivist* III (1996): 13–24. The Motion Picture Bureau, which was later folded into the NFB Still Photography Division, was charged with publicizing the country by means of photographic and filmic representations.

49. See Carol Payne, *A Canadian Document: The National Film Board of Canada's Still Photography Division* (Ottawa: Canadian Museum of Contemporary Photography, 1999); Renate Wickens-Feldman, 'The National Film Board of Canada's Still Photography Division: The Griersonian Legacy', *History of Photography* 20.3 (1996): 271–77; Martha Langford, 'Introduction', *Contemporary Canadian Photography from the Collection of the National Film Board* (Edmonton: Hurtig Publishers, 1984), 7–16; and Melissa Rombout, 'Imaginary Canada: Photography and the Construction of National Identity', *Views: The Journal of Photography in New England* 12.2 (1991): 4–9.

50. Benedict Anderson, *Imagined Communities: Reflections on the Origin and Spread of Nationalism*, rev. ed. (London: Verso, 1991).

51. The article—a review of Robert Flaherty's film *Moana*—appeared in the *New York Sun* on 8 February 1926. See Ian Aitken, *Film and Reform: John Grierson and the Documentary Film Movement* (London: Routledge, 1990), 79–80.

52. Forsyth Hardy, Introduction, *Grierson on Documentary*, ed. Forsyth Hardy (London and Boston: Faber and Faber, 1979), 11.

53. Payne, *A Canadian Document.* For a discussion of rational reform, see John M. Jordan, *Machine-Age Ideology: Social Engineering and American Liberalism, 1911–1939* (Chapel Hill and London: University of North Carolina Press, 1994), 4–6, 13, 155–84.

54. Tagg, *The Burden of Representation.*

55. John Grierson, 'The Documentary Idea: 1942', *Grierson on Documentary*, 113.

56. In its first years of operation, during the Second World War, the division was largely occupied with depicting the war effort at home and serving the needs of various government agencies. Following the war, it turned fully to promoting the country's economic prosperity and fostering greater regional understanding within the nation. While the board's film production units—by the mid-1950s housed in suburban Montreal—became increasingly innovative and independent, the Still Photography Division—perhaps because of its proximity to government in Ottawa—did not deviate from its propagandistic function until the mid-1960s, when it gradually turned toward promoting the careers of individual Canadian photographers and a more subjective or 'observational' mode of documentary.

57. As I have discussed elsewhere, these pictorials remained notably uniform. Carol Payne, '"How Shall We Use These Gifts?" Imagining the Land in the National Film Board of Canada's Still Photography Division', *The Virgin Beauty of Mississauga: Canadian Landscape Art and National Identity*, ed. John O'Brian and Peter White (Montreal: McGill-Queen's University Press, forthcoming 2006 [published as *Beyond Wilderness: The Group of Seven, Canadian Identity, and Contemporary Art.* Eds. John O'Brian and Peter White. Montreal: McGill-Queen's (2007): 153–160].

58. However, only 12 division assignment sheets or archival subject categories explicitly deal

with children and their education, literacy, and health as their subject matter.

59. An example of this tendency is a 20 April 1956 photo-story about a school for the deaf. National Film Board of Canada, Still Photography Division papers, Canadian Museum of Contemporary Photography, and the Library and Archives of Canada.

60. Ryan, 153.

61. Captions, however, inform the reader that 'Some members of the staff are themselves of Indian or Eskimo origin.'

62. In fact, images like these relate to what Bill Nichols and Julianne Burton have termed an expository model of documentary cinema. For Nichols and Burton, expository documentary—exemplified by Grierson's own film production—directly address the viewer, are organized around the establishment of a solution to a so-cial ailment, and emphasize unquestioned authority. Bill Nichols, *Representing Reality: Issues and Concepts in Documentary* (Bloomington and Indianapolis: Indiana University Press, 1991), 34–38.

63. Gail Guthrie Valaskakis, 'Sacajawea and Her Sisters: Images and Indians', *Indian Princesses and Cowgirls: Stereotypes from the Frontier*, ed. Marilyn Burgess and Gail Guthrie Valaskakis (Montreal: Oboro, 1992), 15–19.

64. Bhabha, *The Location of Culture*, 35.

This article has been informed by conversations about Canadian photographic representations with Jeff Thomas and Robert Evans. I also gratefully acknowledge insightful feedback from the following graduate students: Jennifer Blunt, Claudette Lauzon, Jaclyn Meloche, and Sandra Fransen.

21

VOTES FOR STOVES: *EVERYWOMAN'S WORLD* AND THE CANADIAN CITIZEN–CONSUMER IN THE EARLY TWENTIETH CENTURY

ANNE-MARIE KINAHAN[1]

> *Everywoman's World* realizes the new place that Canadian women of to-day must take. Its stories, its departments, and its articles keep pace with their forward movements, and even anticipate them. It is alive. It leads in the vanguard of progress. It essentially is an original magazine, quite different from the others, and is, best of all published in Canada, for Canadians, by Canadians (*Everywoman's World*, January 1916, p. 3).

In this editorial column, *Everywoman's World* announced that the magazine had reached a significant milestone in Canadian periodical history: it had attained a circulation of over 100,000 copies in Canada. But in addition to proclaiming this important achievement, the editorial significantly suggests an essential, reciprocal, and symbiotic relationship between the magazine and its readers. *Everywoman's World* did not merely reflect the lives and interests of Canadian women; it was a living, breathing thing, an active agent that both responded to and anticipated the social, political, and legal changes that affected women's lives in the early decades of the twentieth century.

A mass-market magazine aimed simultaneously at female consumers and Canadian manufacturers and advertisers, *Everywoman's World* intervened in political, cultural, and economic domains. In doing so, it helped to create, shape, and define the female citizen–consumer, a particularly salient figure in the magazine's content devoted to woman suffrage. Printing articles, features, editorials, stories, and advertisements that directly addressed woman suffrage, *Everywoman's World* created a discursive, rhetorical, and visual image of the Canadian suffragist. Throughout its 10-year run, the periodical routinely addressed the suffrage movement, and the image of the suffragist that emerges from the magazine is of a married woman, devoted to her family, and heeding the call to involve herself in the world outside her home. Through its visual and discursive representations, including features, fiction, advertisements, and accompanying imagery, the magazine created a figurative and literal image of the emergent female citizen. In this chapter, I examine the way that *Everywoman's World* shaped and represented the issue of woman suffrage, its claims to represent women's public opinion on national issues, and the way it leveraged its status as 'Canada's Greatest Home Magazine' to attract advertisers.

FEMINIST PRINT CULTURE AND WOMEN'S MAGAZINES

The emergence of print culture and periodical history as sites of scholarly inquiry has produced an impressive amount of literature examining women's creation of such media and women's participation in public life and consumer culture (Damon-Moore 1994; Enstad 1999; Gruber Garvey 1996; Scanlon 1995). Examining the history of the suffrage press, the creation of suffrage commodities, and the interplay between the suffrage movement and consumer culture, feminist scholars have critically examined the dialectical relationships among social movements, print media, and consumer culture. Focusing on the suffrage movement in particular, such scholars as Green (2009, 2008), Finnegan (1999), DiCenzo (2000, 2003), and Beetham (1996) argue that consumer culture provided an important public, visual, and tangible resource for suffragists and their message. This participation in consumer culture was not a dilution or co-option of the suffragists' political message. Rather it was an active choice, a self-aware attempt to reach women in various domains, from the local shop (Green 2008) to the street (DiCenzo 2000, 2003) and the department store (Finnegan 1999).

These critical investigations have placed the study of the feminist press, women's periodicals, and suffrage journals within a larger circuit of signification, circulation, and meaning-making. Publications such as *Votes for Women* (DiCenzo 2000; Green 2008) and *The Woman's Journal* (Finnegan 1999), for example, were more than publicity vehicles for the suffrage cause. They testified to women's increasing visibility and influence in public life as women became activists, citizens, and consumers. The publications themselves were more than expressions of pro-suffrage ideology; they were also material objects—'things'—and commodities that circulated within consumer culture. In her article 'Suffrage Things', Barbara Green (2008) analyzes the creation of suffrage artifacts such as badges, ties, brooches, and bars of soap, and examines how such everyday objects were imbued with political significance. She suggests that examining the materiality of suffrage journals, periodicals, and papers may offer unique insights on the function of print as 'thing'—as material culture and as object (p. 77). For many woman suffragists, carrying a copy of a suffrage journal was an overt political statement. In this way, the magazine itself became a visual object that denoted an individual's political beliefs just as a badge or banner did. This attention to the materiality of periodical culture permits an analysis of the multiple ways in which magazines carried and conveyed meaning, and how individuals used such commodities to create new subjectivities (p. 77). Not merely ideological, not merely discursive or rhetorical, the periodical is also a visual medium, to be held, carried, viewed, shared, and used.

In her analysis of women's magazines in the 1920s and 1930s, Fiona Hackney (2008) foregrounds their visuality, and stresses 'while writing itself was of course the central medium of these discussions, much of the meaning of magazines was, and remains, embodied in the genre itself and the particular experiences of looking, reading, dreaming, doing, making, and consuming involved' (p. 119). Rather than dismissing popular women's magazines for their commercial orientation, Hackney examines them as important arbiters of social and cultural change. She finds that women's magazines provided an important resource for their readers: they offered an opportunity to engage with, challenge, or negotiate their roles in an emergent consumer culture. Hackney proposes that women's magazines do not present a wholesale endorsement of private life over the public. Rather, they offer a complicated and contradictory engagement with the changing status of public and private spheres, the development of consumer culture, women's newly recognized status as citizens, and women's recognized roles as domestic consumers (2008, p. 116–17).

With respect to *Everywoman's World*, this engagement not only was discursive, but also operated in and through visual culture. The visual was also a compelling component of the magazine: the use of photographs, images, and drawings in each issue not only served to make the content relatable, but also provided a visible representation of the female Canadian citizen. Additionally, the magazine itself became a visible and visual commodity, circulating in the public domain and creating and reinforcing dialectical relations among women, the home, the market, and the public realm. Indeed, as this chapter demonstrates, *Everywoman's World* positioned itself as a central medium through which women's public opinion became visible, tangible, and commodified.

WOMAN SUFFRAGE AND THE MASS-MARKET MAGAZINE

In this analysis of *Everywoman's World*, I examine the relationship between its treatment of woman suffrage and its function as a mass-market magazine. Through its coverage of woman suffrage, the magazine provided an opportunity for Canadian women to become informed about and engaged in the issue. The visual and discursive representation of the suffrage issue encouraged women to look beyond the confines of the home and participate in public life. In doing so, it defined the suffragist as a relatable, identifiable example of Canadian womanhood. These interventions in the suffrage debate allowed the magazine to present itself as the 'vanguard of women's progress' while creating a positive environment for Canadian advertisers to reach the Canadian housewife.

Most definitely not a 'suffrage periodical', *Everywoman's World* was an advertiser-supported, mass-market magazine, specifically oriented to female consumers, who were addressed as middle-class housewives. Throughout its run, from 1913 to 1923, *Everywoman's World* featured articles on a full range of issues, such as the responsibilities of motherhood, domestic economy, professions for women, raising children, domestic servants, and women's political and legal status. A central component of these features was visual representation: photographs and occasional drawings. In this way, the magazine attempted to provide both a written discussion and a visual representation of the female citizen–consumer.

This mediation between the discursive and the visual also informed the magazine's consumer orientation. For the owners of *Everywoman's World*, Murray Simonski and Charles Nixon, the publication's content was less important than its ability to deliver ads to readers and readers to advertisers. Advertisements were not limited to the back pages, but were incorporated throughout the publication and often echoed the editorial and feature content (Johnston 2001, p. 242). Simonski and Nixon envisioned *Everywoman's World* as an ideal medium through which they could reach the nation's primary consumers, allow advertisers access to this public, and encourage the development of a national market for magazines.

This drive to develop a national market for Canadian periodicals was a significant challenge at the beginning of the twentieth century. As Russell Johnston (2001) explains in his analysis of the history of advertising in Canada, the fledgling domestic magazine industry faced tremendous competition from popular American and British imports. He asserts, 'it would be no exaggeration to state that the market was shaped by the presence of these periodicals, and that Canadian offerings merely filled limited roles not served by their imported counterparts' (p. 229). In order to gain a foothold in the market, Canadian consumer magazines often imitated popular American publications. In addition to competing against American titles, Canadian magazines faced challenges posed by diminished returns on advertising investment. With a population a fraction of the size of its American neighbour, the Canadian market had difficulty sustaining national publications. The dearth of Canadian advertisers wishing to publish in Canadian magazines made it much more difficult for publications to compete with advertiser-supported, and thus cheaper, American titles (Johnston 2001, p. 234).

These challenges notwithstanding, *Everywoman's World* enjoyed widespread circulation throughout Canada, making it a popular and attractive vehicle for advertisers. Created in 1913 and intended as a vehicle to market household products to Canadian women, *Everywoman's World* was, by 1917, the magazine with the largest circulation in Canada with 130,000 subscribers (*Canadian Newspaper Directory*, 1917, p. 105). Simonski and Nixon claimed that the magazine in fact reached 500,000 Canadian readers every month (*EW*, February 1917, p. 3).

However, at the same time that the magazine was valued as a vehicle for advertisers, it also was an important medium in women's self-recognition as consumers and citizens. Through regularly reading the magazine, women could negotiate a changing social and political realm that gave increased opportunities both inside and outside the home, for single, working women, married housewives, and married women who took up paid employment. These opportunities were shaped, challenged, and negotiated through a culture that valued women's 'natural' inclination to marriage and children, and an emergent economic system that valued women as domestic consumers. Through blending these commercial imperatives with the political issue of woman suffrage, the publication politicized women's consumption and marketed women's citizenship.

VOTES FOR WOMEN: *EVERYWOMAN'S WORLD* ON SUFFRAGE IDEOLOGY

Everywoman's World addressed woman suffrage through various methods, from treatises on the philosophical and ideological motivations for women's enfranchisement, to fictional accounts of meetings with suffrage radicals, to profiles of suffrage leaders. In each of these varied treatments, woman suffrage was presented as a reasonable demand, a democratic right, and an

acknowledgment of women's increasing social and political import.

In March 1914, for example, the magazine printed 'Advances being Made by Women', the first in a series of articles which purported to tell readers 'what the women of Canada, United States, and England are doing to advance themselves' (*EW*, March 1914, p. 12). Asserting that the article is 'not partisan', the editor explains that the intent of the series is 'to keep readers of *Everywoman's World* up to date on the coming great movement in world politics' (p. 12). Clearly acknowledging the import of women's political activism and featuring articles supporting woman suffrage, *Everywoman's World* offered a particular perspective on the women's movement. In the article itself, the woman's movement is defined as 'a struggle for recognition of rights, inherent in the woman as one of the race, of the right to *equality of opportunity* and of equal rights *everywhere, irrespective of sex*' (p. 12, original emphasis). Establishing the rational and democratic basis of calls for women's enfranchisement, the article offers an extended discussion on suffrage militancy in England:

Have they been wise or foolish? In so far as they choose to hunger and fast, to suffer imprisonment and to undergo various pains and tortures, it may be in so far sympathy will go out to them and admiration. But when it comes to the destruction of property, to the risk of destroying life and to other forms of destruction, it is a question whether more harm is not done to the cause than any real good. (p. 12)

This potential militancy of women's suffrage appears to have been a concern for the editors and writers at *Everywoman's World*, particularly during the years leading up to women's provincial enfranchisement. In February 1914, Joseph Krauskopf's regular feature 'The Ascendancy of Womanhood' offered a fair-minded and spirited discussion on British suffrage militancy. Addressing the public disapproval of militant actions, Krauskopf writes 'The Parliaments of nations amply illustrate that men have adopted similar courses, and have through them, won great victories' (p. 9). While condemning the specific tactics employed by militants (property destruction, imprisonment, hunger strikes), he admits, 'we cannot but admire that conviction of theirs in the righteousness of their cause that moves them to suffer indignity and imprisonment rather than keep still where their wrongs urge them to speak' (p. 9).

Krauskopf's empathy with militant commitment is accompanied by his analysis of the moderation and rationality of woman's claim to suffrage: 'Woman wants to see the sex element eliminated from the law. Its presence there is a relic of the long ages of barbarism. Having the same responsibilities as men, she wants the same rights. She wants efficiency not sex to be the determining force in legislation, and in the scale of wages. For the same labor she wants the same pay' (p. 9).

These two philosophical arguments in support of woman suffrage lend credence to the magazine's claim to be the vanguard of women's progress. The trope of an ascendant womanhood characterizes each of these articles and is visually represented in the image accompanying Krauskopf's article (see Figure 21.1). The image, taken from a sculpture entitled *The Vision*, portrays a group of women huddled together, shrouded, shadowed, and downtrodden, yet rising and emergent, ready to take their place in the world. The image's caption explains that it is the sculptor's representation of 'the feminine views of the dawn of woman's emancipation' (p. 9). It is a compelling image in its idealized representation of women emerging from subjection and readying themselves to assume their roles as citizens. We can see in this image the visual representation of the magazine's 'call' to women to position themselves at the vanguard of progress, to rise up and assume roles of social prominence. Taking for granted women's 'ascension', *Everywoman's World* further establishes women's public importance through its visual representations: most of the magazine's images and editorial content portray women not as weak, disempowered, downtrodden, or oppressed, but as confident, capable leaders.

The defence of woman suffrage as a reasonable and democratic impulse was consistent with the

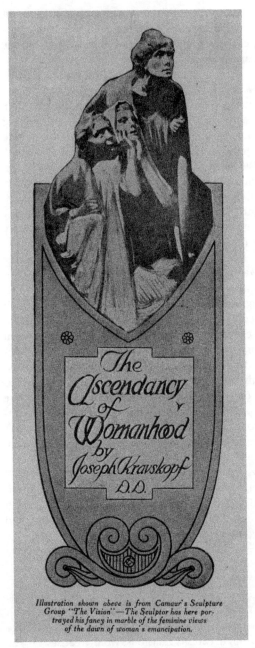

Illustration shown above is from Camaur's Sculpture Group "The Vision".—The Sculptor has here portrayed his fancy in marble of the feminine views of the dawn of woman's emancipation.

FIGURE 21.1 The Ascension of Womanhood

majority of articles on suffrage in the magazine. Clearly grappling with the radical zeal of the British suffragettes, writers in *Everywoman's World* expressed sympathy with women's demands, while seeking to establish the Canadian movement as non-revolutionary. However, rather than assuming that this was a specific attempt to dismiss woman suffrage or to warn female readers about radicalism, we can see that these discourses illustrate the competing tensions that characterized the movement, suffragists' decisions on whether to adopt more militant actions, and concern over the public reception of the movement. While voicing concerns over radicalism, the magazine also promoted a third way, which acknowledged the commitment of radical suffragists and understood the decision to adopt militancy, but counselled the use of moderate and non-violent tactics by Canadian activists.

Another intervention in the suffrage discussion came in the form of a story, 'My Friend the Suffragette' (*EW*, September 1914). The story focuses on two men, one supportive of woman suffrage and the other fearful of women's militancy. Clearly presented as educated members of the leisure class, the men are part of a group sojourning in upstate New York. Upon hearing news that they will be receiving a delegation of militant and non-militant suffrage supporters, the 'fearful' man spends his time avoiding the suffragettes. By chance, as he is visiting with two other guests, a suffragette joins the conversation and enlightens him about woman suffrage generally and militancy in particular. Explaining the reasons for women's militancy, the suffragette states, 'Men inspectors let impure food and milk that was poison to young babies pass. Men talked "wisely" on the terribly high rate of infant mortality, and asked why the children, under the school system managed alone by voting men, were nervous, and had weak eyes, and why the number of mental defectives increased so frightfully' (p. 26). Defending woman suffrage on the 'traditional' grounds of child welfare and the eugenic grounds of mental fitness, the story further illustrates the various perspectives that characterized the issue.

The image accompanying the story portrays the suffragette as a demure, calm, well-dressed, leisured woman, and her explanations clearly illustrate the extent to which she has emerged

FIGURE 21.2 Suffragette as a demure, well-dressed woman

from the home to become more involved, more visible, and more engaged in public life (see Figure 21.2). The story, then, not only functions to dismiss fears over suffrage and establish it as a moderate and reasonable measure, but also provides a snapshot image of who the suffragist is, what she cares about, and how she participates in the world. Oriented to social and moral reform, well-versed in the history of men's failures, and concerned with child health and social welfare, the suffragist is not a property-destroying, hunger-striking militant of the British variety. She is the Canadian citizen–consumer, concerned about children's education and mental health, and the future health and well-being of the nation's young citizens.

I focus on these three examples, the two articles and the story, because they are emblematic of the magazine's approach to women's enfranchisement, and because they collectively present an interesting intervention in the debates by articulating a male perspective on women's political rights. While only one of the articles is 'signed' by its male author (Krauskopf's 'Ascendancy of Womanhood'), each of the pieces 'Advances being Made by Women' and 'My Friend the Suffragette' tells the 'story' of suffrage from a man's point of view. In providing rational and articulate defences of woman suffrage, these pieces also functioned to explain the movement to readers of the magazine. The authors position themselves as allies of woman suffrage and provide calm reassurance that the Canadian movement is unlikely to become militant. However, they also assume that most Canadian women, or at least most readers of *Everywoman's World*, are not already informed about or engaged in the suffrage cause. The assumption here is that *Everywoman's World*'s readers do not expressly identify as suffragists, but should nevertheless be informed about and supportive of women's enfranchisement.

Uniting these articles is an assumption that woman suffrage is a 'new' and potentially destabilizing movement, poised to disrupt and unsettle established boundaries between public and private, radical and reserved, male and female. Furthermore, these articles were written for readers who were assumed to be non-engaged and non-political, but who were also the intelligent, leisured household consumers, encouraged to have an interest in the world outside their doors. These articles inhabit a mediating tension between those supporting the cause and those assumed to be ignorant of it, between women agitating for political rights through suffrage and women politicizing their consumption by reading about suffrage in a mass-market magazine. The images accompanying the articles present woman suffragists as calm and rational subjects. While the articles voice some concern over militancy, the photographs and drawings dismiss these fears by establishing the Canadian suffragist as a reassuring maternal figure, moved to action on behalf of children and the less fortunate, and motivated by a selfless concern for others.

PERSONALIZING WOMAN SUFFRAGE: WOMAN WRITERS ADDRESS WOMAN SUFFRAGE

The articles described above are not the only examples of the magazine's engagement with the suffrage question. At the same time that it addressed the fears attendant upon women's burgeoning political recognition, *Everywoman's World* also ran several features on Canadian women's hopes for the future, their arguments for women's legal and political recognition, and their opinions on Canada's participation in the war and women's work for 'the Empire'. Written by women, and taking women and women's opinions as the central subject matter, these various articles help to form, shape, and define the female citizen–consumer.

A series on the woman suffrage movement, 'What the Women of Canada Want', first appeared in January 1916, as women were beginning to win voting privileges in Canadian provinces. The articles, written by Elizabeth Becker, focus on Canadian suffrage leaders such as Emily Howard Stowe and Margaret Gordon, organizations such as the Canadian Suffrage Association, and the progress of woman suffrage in Canada. Again concerned to explain the objectives of the movement, the 'What the Women of Canada Want' series introduced the magazine's readers to the women who founded various suffrage organizations and seems to have been intended to encourage women's participation in the movement.

Focusing on the moderate and reasonable demands of suffragists, 'What the Women of Canada Want' creates a clear distinction between Canadian, American, and British suffragists: 'The attitude of the Canadian woman toward suffrage is distinctly her own. She is not like the English suffragist, nor yet like the American. She is not likely to ever question whether she will join the forces of militancy, as conditions are so different here, and she has not the reasons to induce militancy, that the English woman has had . . .' (*EW*, January 1916, p. 11). The article goes on to establish the moderation and civility of the Canadian movement and claims: 'If men would only realize that suffrage is not a war against man, but a war with him, for better conditions under which all may have life, liberty, and happiness!' (p. 11).

The second article in the series, called 'What the Women of Canada Need' (*EW*, February 1916, p. 11) provides information about a variety of suffrage organizations and profiles of Canadian women active in the movement. The specific intent of the article, other than publicity for woman suffrage, appears to be to educate, enlighten, and engage the Canadian housewife, who is assumed to be uninterested in the cause. Encouraging housewives to take an interest in the world outside their doors, Becker argues that a danger of the domestic life is loss of interest in social and political issues. Some Canadian women, she suggests, 'have let things domestic, outside of the wise and necessary care of their children, pile up about them so that they cannot see over nor hear the cry of distress from without. They do not feel the need of the vote for themselves or a prompting to help the women who do need it' (p. 11).

Providing a sketch of suffrage leader Dr Margaret Johnston, president of the Toronto Suffrage Association, the article makes a case for women's enfranchisement as a virtuous commitment to social and moral uplift. 'Dr. Johnston believes that as women open their minds to the progressive spirit of the day, and to the needs of those about them, the power of the vote as a lever to lift humanity, will more and more be realized' (p. 11). Indeed, the faith in the Canadian housewife as a capable moral leader characterizes each article in the series.

If there is to be discrimination against any class, it is difficult to understand why the wives and mothers should be the class to be banned, for the capable married women are those to whom we look for intelligent leadership along the various and most necessary lines of social service. Who has so much at stake in the community as the mother? Who is so effected [sic] by environment in her all important work of training her children to be good citizens? Who is so able to judge what is best for the children and young people? And this—the child and the home—is

the real reason of the whole Woman Suffrage Movement' (*EW*, June 1916, p. 11, p. 41).

These discourses can justifiably be interpreted as representing a concerted attempt to 'domesticate' the woman suffrage movement. Linking women's enfranchisement to social and moral reform, child welfare and health, and children's upbringing could be interpreted as effectively de-politicizing a movement thought too radical and revolutionary. Indeed, a recurrent theme in scholarly analyses of woman suffrage revolves around the tension between 'radical' and 'traditional' women, between those who wanted revolution, and those who, fearing such upheaval, de-politicized the more radical elements of the movement (Roberts 1979; Bacchi 1983). But as Hackney (2008) suggests, the discourses in women's magazines also provided women with a valuable resource to learn about political issues, to engage in debate about women's changing social status, and to participate in the creation of new definitions of womanhood. In this view, these discourses on woman suffrage are more than the co-option of political ideals by those wishing to ensure women remain ensconced in the home. Rather, they circulate a definition of Canadian womanhood in which motherhood is invested with national, political, and social significance. No longer 'confined' to the domestic sphere, the Canadian mother must heed the call to be more engaged and active in public life.

The 'What the Women of Canada Want' series, and such regular features as 'Prominent Women', introduced Canadian women to the 'new' woman, who was familiar in many ways: married, well-educated, committed to her family, yet also a force to be reckoned with in her larger community. These articles have multiple functions: to inform a presumably uninformed readership about an important political issue, to encourage Canadian women to take a more active role in issues outside the home, and to defend the legitimacy of calls for woman suffrage. At the same time, they provide an image of who Canadian suffragists are—complete with portrait-style photographs (see Figure 21.3). Reminiscent of official political portraits, these black-and-white medium close-ups present an image of the suffrage leaders as political leaders

"I shall make it the business of my life to see that women have the same educational advantages as men," declared Mrs. Stowe

FIGURE 21.3 Portrait of Dr Emily Stowe

as being fundamentally concerned with the same issues as are most Canadian women—children's health, education, and continued well-being. While these features serve to demystify woman suffrage, the regular appearance of the articles, and the monthly discussions on these topics, make such political issues as woman suffrage a 'normal' and regular aspect of the Canadian housewife's routine. In addition to being concerned about her home and family, the Canadian housewife is, we are to assume, expected to be informed about, supportive of, and engaged in the fight for women's political equality.

Since its creation, *Everywoman's World* purported to represent the public opinion of Canada's women. This assertion animates the April 1915 feature 'What Twelve Canadian Women Hope to See as the Outcome of the War'. Claiming to express the representative public opinion of the nation's women, the feature explains that the magazine had posed the following question to several prominent women: 'What do you as a woman hope to see as the outcome of the war: (1) for the world at large, (2) for women in particular?' (p. 6). The article reprints and summarizes the responses by such women as Nellie McClung, Lucy Maude Montgomery, Katherine Hale, Emily Murphy, and Flora MacDonald Denison. In presenting this 'symposium', *Everywoman's World* also presents itself as the medium of women's public opinion and political expression. Presuming an ongoing conversation on these issues, the magazine places itself and its readers at the centre of debate. Directly addressing the reader, the introduction to the symposium encourages the readers to ' . . . imagine this Symposium, as if these thoughtful women had really met, coming together from the farthest east and west, to talk to each other and to us, expressing their inmost hope for the outcome of war' (p. 6).

This symposium encourages a mediation between visual and discursive imaginings: the reader is invited to visualize a community of prominent women, gathered together to discuss the most pressing political issue of the time. Readers are invited to envision these women together—an invitation supported by the accompanying photos, all extreme close-ups, arranged in a cluster. In

in their own right. Directly addressing the camera or shot in profile, the women in the photos are serious and unsmiling, but clearly portrayed as respected and influential leaders and as role models for 'regular' Canadian women. Combined with the discussion of their commitments, the visual representations provide the image of women who have successfully bridged the divide between the public and the private.

While these women are praised for their dedication and commitment to their families and the cause of suffrage, they are also presented as examples of true Canadian womanhood. Indeed, their accomplishments are significant (forming suffrage organizations, circulating petitions in favour of woman's enfranchisement, going on national speaking tours), but they are portrayed

directly addressing the reader, the magazine acknowledges that the act of reading the opinions
contained in the article is a symbolic participation
in the conversation itself. The readers are not distanced from the discussion, but rather encouraged
to visualize themselves with these women, offering their own wishes and dreams for the future.
With this feature, *Everywoman's World* involves
the reader in the creation of a visual, discursive,
and imaginative bridge between these women, the
magazine, its readers, and Canada as a nation.

SELLING SUFFRAGE AND MARKETING *EVERYWOMAN'S WORLD*

While publishing articles and features that established woman suffrage as a reasonable, moderate,
and even womanly demand, *Everywoman's World*
simultaneously created a discursive arena in
which manufacturers and advertisers could employ suffrage rhetoric in order to target commercial messages to female readers. In the December
1916 issue of the magazine is a full-page ad with
the provocative headline 'Will You Vote?' The ad
encourages women to 'vote' by expressing their
opinion on the 'Lighter Day' kitchen range and
comes with three 'ballots' testifying to the consumer's belief that the range is a 'labor saver' (see
Figure 21.4). The copy begins,

> Some women think for themselves. These
> women lead. They are the women who grasp
> new ideas quickly. Who adopt new labor-saving
> methods in their housework. Who save time
> where others waste it. These are the women
> who investigate new devices and plan to secure
> those that are real helps. To these women who
> think, the others who lack imagination must
> look for guidance. Clare Bros. & Co., Limited,
> now enfranchise the women who think (p. 48).

This advertisement is indicative of the magazine's hybrid political–commercial form of address. On the one hand, it can be interpreted as
a co-option and trivialization of women's emergent political recognition. But on the other, it
suggests the extent to which consumer culture

FIGURE 21.4 Will You Vote?

and women's consumption were key elements in
women's public participation (DiCenzo 2000; Enstad 1999; Finnegan 1999). I would like to move
beyond a dismissal of the ad to consider how it
functions to implicate female consumers within
a new political and commercial order. Engaging
in both class and gender flattery—the 'women
who think' are also the women who can afford
such 'labor-saving devices'—the ad also suggests
an important relationship between female citizen–consumers and manufacturers. In the world
created by the editorial and advertising content
of *Everywoman's World*, it is the manufacturer of
kitchen appliances, not the Canadian government, which enfranchises Canadian women, not
through legislation, but through the pages of a
mass-market magazine.

The dialectical relationship between consumption and citizenship is further established
in an advertorial in the February 1917 issue of

Everywoman's World. Entitled 'The Women's Parliament of Canada', the advertorial claims, 'with 130,000 members', the magazine 'gives the vote to 500,000 women' (p. 3).

> With this issue of *Everywoman's World*, we start a great forward movement. We are mobilizing the vast army of Canadian woman voters. Our belief is that a noble-minded womanhood can make for a purer, nobler national life. The right to vote on national issues has been denied to the women of Canada, while the experience in other countries proves that where women have secured the ballot, the best results have followed (p. 3).

The advertorial introduces a new feature called 'The Women's Parliament of Canada', where proponents and opponents of such issues as conscription and reforming divorce laws present their views. Readers are then encouraged to fill out a ballot, voting 'yea' or 'nay' on the particular question, and asked to mail the ballot to the magazine. The magazine makes this promise to its readers: 'We shall take your case to the foot of the throne—to the Government itself—and there with the thousands of ballots you have cast, we shall present your cause and demand a hearing' (p. 3).

With this feature, *Everywoman's World* tacitly equated women's reading of the magazine to their performance of citizenship. Indeed, the magazine claims that, unlike the government, it actually provides women with the vote. Unfortunately, there is no historical record of whether the magazine actually made good on its promise to represent women's opinion to the government itself, but what remains compelling about this assertion is its suggestion of the important role of the magazine envisioned by its editors. It was not merely something to occupy the housewife's time, to be disposed of once finished. It was the medium through which women could participate in political debate and make their opinions known.

The feature simultaneously functioned as a way to gather information about readers, which could be used to sell advertising space in the magazine. This issue of *Everywoman's World* included a full-page announcement of the debate, the text of the debate itself, and a short editorial discussion. The editorial discussion indicates how the feature served to market the magazine to advertisers. 'After reading the debate, the readers will cast their ballots, and for the first time in the history of Canada a really authentic record of woman's opinion upon great national questions will be polled' (*EW*, February 1917, p. 20). Presuming that a reader followed instructions and mailed a ballot to the magazine, the owners actually received the reader's name, address, and her stated views on such issues as conscription or divorce laws (see Figure 21.5).

'The Parliament of Women' crystallizes the magazine's citizen–consumer mode of address. It asserts the necessity and relevance of political content—and the importance of women's opinions on these issues. It stages a debate on an issue between two individuals, but presumes a much larger, ongoing discussion among the magazine, its readers, and the larger national community. Through this feature, *Everywoman's World* presents itself as providing a space for, and participating in, the public discussion on issues of national importance. But at the same time, it gathers information on the women who read the magazine and what their political views are. 'The Parliament of Women' has multiple functions: an advertisement for the magazine's 'reach', a testament to its purported influence, and a claim to provide women with a public voice and access to power. The copy concludes, 'You cannot in any other way so effectively secure a hearing, or impress your views on those in power. No other publication in Canada could successfully carry such a gigantic undertaking to completion' (p. 3). In the name of providing women with a voice on public issues, the magazine engages in self-promotion and flattery, arguing that it is the only publication in Canada capable of accomplishing such a task. At the same time, it skillfully markets to advertisers its wide availability throughout Canada, and its mechanism for gauging the political beliefs of its readers.

The magazine's simultaneous political and commercial interventions indicate a complex

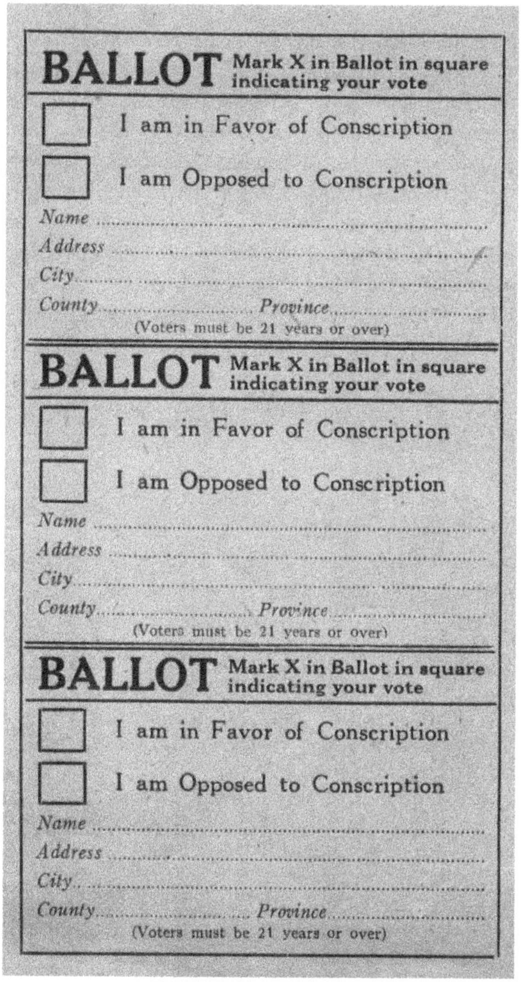

BALLOT Mark X in Ballot in square indicating your vote

☐ I am in Favor of Conscription

☐ I am Opposed to Conscription

Name ....
Address ....
City ....
County .... *Province* ....
(Voters must be 21 years or over)

BALLOT Mark X in Ballot in square indicating your vote

☐ I am in Favor of Conscription

☐ I am Opposed to Conscription

Name ....
Address ....
City ....
County .... *Province* ....
(Voters must be 21 years or over)

BALLOT Mark X in Ballot in square indicating your vote

☐ I am in Favor of Conscription

☐ I am Opposed to Conscription

Name ....
Address ....
City ....
County .... *Province* ....
(Voters must be 21 years or over)

FIGURE 21.5 Ballot

relationship between an advertiser-driven medium, the increasing visibility of women's roles as consumers, and the political and public orientation of the women's movement. These interrelationships created a discursive space in which manufacturers of kitchen ranges could 'enfranchise the thinking women' to support their product, the magazine itself could inform and generate women's public opinion (and claim to represent it to those in power), and female readers throughout the nation could participate in the creation and circulation of new definitions of Canadian womanhood.

In conclusion, I would like to refer to an editorial appearing in the October 1919 issue of *Everywoman's World*, which suggests the potential consequences of this hybrid citizen–consumer mode of address. Discussing the extension of federal voting privileges to Canadian women, the publication claimed 'Labor unrest, incipient Bolshevism—all this can be controlled by women; not from the platform, not by political propaganda, but, in the home' (*EW*, October 1919, p. 3). Once women were federally enfranchised, then, the magazine downplayed the significance of what it previously called the 'great movement in world politics' and encouraged women to invest motherhood with national, political significance. It appears that with the end of the First World War, and with the extension of the federal franchise to Canadian women by 1920, *Everywoman's World* may have lost the political, economic, and discursive grounding on which it addressed its readers. Women's political equality had effectively been achieved, and the cessation of the war meant that their role as consumers, while no less important, was far less politicized. This editorial seems to indicate that the 'great movement in world politics' also functioned as a convenient and socially relevant way for the magazine and its advertisers to attract socially conscious readers, to engage in a form of race, class, and gender flattery, and to publicize household products.

Within the pages of *Everywoman's World*, woman suffrage was as much a commercial strategy as a political issue. Indeed, the magazine not only defined woman suffrage as a reasonable and moderate issue, but also created a discursive and visual arena where suffrage sentiments could be invoked to sell kitchen appliances as well as copies of the magazine. The discursive and the visual worked in tandem to present relatable images of accomplished women, to bring woman suffrage issues into the Canadian housewife's home, and to make suffrage part of her regular routine. The dialectical tensions between politics and commerce and between citizenship and consumerism enabled the magazine to articulate a vision of women's citizenship that was overwhelmingly oriented to domestic issues at the same time that it politicized such domestic concerns. Taken together, the political and commercial content creates an image of the female citizen–consumer: potentially engaged in and certainly informed about woman suffrage, positioned at the forefront of social change through her reading of the magazine, addressed as a 'woman who thinks' through the magazine's advertisements, and flattered as a woman with informed opinions about war, conscription, divorce laws, and other pressing social issues. That each of these issues also provided a skillful way for the magazine to gauge consumer interest for its advertisers testifies to the complex and contradictory relationships between social movements, media, and consumer culture. While the feminist movement was not permanently silenced with the extension of the franchise, it seems that, at this particular historical moment, women's roles as domestic consumers trumped their roles as citizens.

NOTE

1. Anne-Marie Kinahan gratefully acknowledges the financial support of Wilfrid Laurier University and the Social Sciences and Humanities Research Council of Canada, which have provided research grants in support of this project. I'd also like to thank Jonathan Finn for his constructive and considered feedback, and my research assistants, Bibiana Alcala Valencia and Mark Preston, for their patient and careful analysis of materials for this article.

REFERENCES

Bacchi, Carol. 1983. *Liberation deferred?: The ideas of the English-Canadian suffragists, 1877–1918*. Toronto: University of Toronto Press.

Becker, Elizabeth. 1916. What the women of Canada want. *Everywoman's World*. January.

———. 1916. What the women of Canada need. *Everywoman's World*. February.

———. 1916. What the women of Canada need. *Everywoman's World*. March.

———. 1916. What the women of Canada want. *Everywoman's World*. June.

Beetham, Margaret. 1996. *A Magazine of their own?: Domesticity and desire in the woman's magazine, 1800–1914*. London: Routledge.

Blythe, G. 1914. My friend the suffragette. *Everywoman's World*. September.

Canadian newspaper directory. 1917. Montreal: A. McKim.

Damon-Moore, Helen. 1994. *Magazines for the millions: Gender and commerce in the* Ladies' Home Journal *and the* Saturday Evening Post, *1880–1910*. Albany: State University of New York Press.

DiCenzo, Maria. 2000. Militant distribution: *Votes for Women* and the public sphere. *Media History* 6 (2): 115–28.

———. 2003. Gutter politics: Women newsies and the suffrage press. *Women's History Review* 12 (1): 15–33.

Enstad, Nan. 1999. *Ladies of labor, girls of adventure: Working women, popular culture, and labor politics at the turn of the twentieth century*. New York: Columbia University Press.

Finnegan, Margaret. 1999. *Selling suffrage: Consumer culture and votes for women*. New York: Columbia University Press.

Green, Barbara. 2008. Feminist things. In Ann Ardis and Patrick Collier (eds), *Transatlantic print culture, 1880–1940: Emerging media, emerging modernisms*, pp. 66–79. London: Palgrave.

———. 2009. The feminist periodical press: Women, periodical studies, and modernity. *Literature Compass* 6 (1): 191–205.

Gruber Garvey, Ellen. 1996. *The adman in the parlor: Magazines and the gendering of consumer culture, 1880s to 1910s*. New York: Oxford University Press.

Hackney, Fiona. 2008. 'Women are news': British women's magazines 1919–1939. In Ann Ardis and Patrick Collier (eds) *Transatlantic print culture, 1880–1940: Emerging media, emerging modernisms*, pp. 114–133. London: Palgrave.

Horning, Professor L.E. 1914. Advances being made by women. *Everywoman's World*. March.

Johnston, Russell. 2001. *Selling themselves: The emergence of Canadian advertising*. Toronto: University of Toronto Press.

Krauskopf, Joseph, D.D. 1914. The ascendancy of womanhood. *Everywoman's World*. February.

Roberts, Wayne. 1979. Rocking the cradle for the world: The new woman and maternal feminism, 1877–1914. In Linda Kealey (ed.) *A not unreasonable claim: Women and reform in Canada, 1880s–1920s*, pp. 15–45. Toronto: The Women's Press.

Scanlon, Jennifer. 1995. *Inarticulate longings: The Ladies' Home Journal, gender, and the promises of consumer culture*. New York and London: Routledge.

Strictly personal. 1916. *Everywoman's World*. January.

The women's parliament of Canada. 1917. *Everywoman's World*. February.

What twelve Canadian women hope to see as the outcome of the war. 1915. *Everywoman's World*. April.

Women may vote. 1917. *Everywoman's World*. February.

22

MEATBALLS MATTERS

PETER URQUHART

Canadian film studies has, since its emergence in the 1960s and 1970s, been dominated by a critical position we call 'cultural nationalism'. The premise of this position is that any kind of cultural production of a nation should and inevitably does in some way *reflect* something of that nation's history, its sensibilities, its culture. Cultural nationalism further posits that one primary goal of the critic—and of the theorist and historian—is to locate these instances of the nation speaking through a cultural work, be it a painting, novel, song, or film. One result of the dominance of the cultural nationalist paradigm in Canadian film studies is that certain kinds of films are valued over others, simply because of their aesthetic, generic, or thematic approach. As Peter Morris (1994) convincingly demonstrates, even in the realm of popular criticism (as opposed to academic film study), 'canon formation'—i.e., which films we celebrate, place on 'ten best' lists, and so on—is clearly skewed in Canada by the cultural nationalist perspective. Morris shows how demonstrably excellent films are habitually 'underrated', overshadowed, or deemed unworthy of canonization when they do not meet the criterion of excellence (i.e., speaking to, from, or about the nation) assumed by the cultural nationalist position. There are many explanations for this critical paradigm becoming so dominant—chief among these is the apparent persuasiveness of its defensive side, that it protects us from the putative dangers of 'Americanization'. But the goal of this chapter is to examine one Canadian film, *Meatballs* (Ivan Reitman, 1979), not only to demonstrate the limitations of the cultural nationalist position but also to suggest other ways of thinking about film (and other cultural products) within national contexts.

Written, directed, and produced by Canadians, featuring a Canadian cast (American Bill Murray excepted), shot in Canadian 'cottage country' (near Haliburton, Ontario), set in an idyllic outdoor wilderness, and its modest budget of $1 million funded by private Canadian capital (with a small investment from the Canadian Film and Development Corporation, a federal government agency), *Meatballs* is demonstrably a Canadian film by any measure. Released in the summer of 1979, the film became a huge hit internationally, eventually grossing around $70 million in theatrical release and millions more in subsequent video and DVD rentals and sales.

The film is a summer camp comedy, with the plot largely turning on an annual summer 'Olympiad' between two camps situated on either side of a lake—the rich, snooty, and vaguely menacing Camp Mohawk, and our heroes, the ragtag, zany losers of Camp Northstar. Central relationships revolve around senior boys' camp counsellor Tripper Harrison (Bill Murray): his at-first antagonistic relationship with Roxanne (Kate Lynch), the head girls' counsellor, and his father-like friendship with Rudy (Chris Makepeace), an adorable but lonely, bullied, and troubled young camper. Perhaps unsurprisingly, Rudy wins the Olympiad for hapless Northstar in the last minutes of the film, and Tripper and Roxanne fall in love. Subplots involve emergent adolescent romance and sexuality between a number of the so-called CITs (teenaged counsellors-in-training).

With this brief introduction, I want to set the text itself aside for a moment, in order to situate this chapter's argument in broader debates over the place of the popular in cultural analysis, especially in national contexts. But first, I need to tell you that, despite the huge commercial success

of *Meatballs*, despite its clearly, unambiguously, Canadian pedigree, this film has been completely ignored by Canadian film scholars. This chapter questions why this should be. It uses this one film to examine the consequences of a limited critical perspective—in this case, cultural nationalism—in understanding artifacts of visual culture in a national context. In other words, this chapter asks why *Meatballs*, a demonstrably Canadian film, has never counted as such in scholarly and other critical discourses on the nation's cinema.

ORTHODOXIES

Back in 1992, Jim McGuigan described an emerging new orthodoxy in cultural studies in his book *Cultural Populism*: 'the intellectual assumption, made by some students of popular culture, that the symbolic experiences and practices of ordinary people are more important analytically and politically than Culture with a capital C' (3). McGuigan was writing about the then current tendency in cultural studies to focus attention on the culture that people actually consumed in large numbers—popular culture—shifting scholarly attention away from what was seen as the elite practice of high art. McGuigan is pointing to a scholarly trend away from examinations of 'excellence' and 'genius' in the arts and toward examinations of the popular, which was typically understood to be simpler than high art, and even simple-minded. This observation is interesting when thinking about Canadian film studies in that, judging by the extant account of the field, it is not this new orthodoxy that reigns, or has ever reigned, but the old orthodoxy: that artistry and personal expression are what counts, and work aiming at commercial success in popular idioms remains unexamined. The vast majority of Canadian film scholarship specifically venerates artistic personal expression that speaks to or about Canadian culture in some way, while explicitly deriding or more often simply ignoring popular cinema.

I would like to consider *Meatballs* in light of this last statement and analyze the implications of the absence of this film from the historical record for reasons of taste, genre, and historiography. I do not propose to simply turn cultural hierarchies on their head (for example, stating a preference for *Meatballs*'s director Ivan Reitman over the 'auteur' Atom Egoyan or genre films over art films). Instead, I will engage with this disparaged text as an artifact of Canadian culture that can be read both textually and contextually for narrative, formal, and industrial markers of cultural resonance and influence. I will consider the role generic categorization has played in creating tenacious historical assumptions and then examine and attempt to explain the near-complete absence from Canadian film scholarship and from the broader discourse of Canadian film culture of one of the most successful and best-loved Canadian films of all time.

GENRE AND NATION

Structural and historical similarities between the Australian and Canadian cinemas notwithstanding, Canada has never produced a *Crocodile Dundee* (Australia, Peter Faiman, 1986). While it might be argued that national specificity is somewhat evident in, and perhaps a small part of the appeal of, a hit film such as *Meatballs*, it clearly does not carry the same national significance for Canada that *Crocodile Dundee* does for Australia.[1] I begin my discussion of genre in this way because of what this example shows us about the relationships between genre and nation as theoretical ideas. On the emergence of what he calls 'a straightforward genre film', Graeme Turner notes that *Crocodile Dundee* 'speaks from a particular cultural location, and with a recognizable national accent' (107). Many genre films were made in Canada in the 1970s (as well as several before and since), and while some of these speak 'from a particular cultural location, and with a recognizable national accent', and while others have been commercially successful internationally, none have managed the *Crocodile Dundee*–style combination of national specificity *and* international appeal, with the possible exception of *Meatballs*. As the position of *Crocodile Dundee* in Australian film history makes plain, genre films in themselves are not the problem for scholars and critics of minor national cinemas.[2] Rather, what riles the nationalist critic is *either* commercially

successful genre films with little or no trace of national specificity, *or* commercially unsuccessful genre films, of which Canada has produced many. Jim Leach is one film scholar who finds nationally specific genre films such as *Paperback Hero* (Peter Pearson, 1972) satisfying in themselves, and representative of a 'Canadian' aesthetic, even though they did not attract significant audiences. In fact, Leach goes on to blame for the commercial failure of these films the critics who 'constantly bemoan the traditional virtues' of 'a smooth-flowing narrative and aggressive pace' (1986: 362). With Leach's phrase still ringing in our ears, we should remind ourselves of French sociologist and cultural theorist Pierre Bourdieu's observation that it is chiefly because of this 'easiness' that those rich in cultural capital—that is, people with 'good taste'—dislike popular artifacts. He writes,

> The refusal of what is easy—in the sense of simple and therefore shallow and cheap—because it is easily decoded and culturally undemanding, naturally leads to the refusal of what is facile in the ethical or aesthetic sense, of everything which offers pleasures that are immediately accessible and so discredited as childish or primitive (489).

Here, Bourdieu describes a deep divide between, on the one hand, that which is easily understood—in many cases because it is not 'intellectual', often providing 'bodily' pleasures—and, on the other hand, that which is approved by 'good' or cultivated taste, providing thoughtful, reflective distance from the object being consumed. Culinary metaphors are frequently invoked in such debates, with popular culture compared to fast food, sugary breakfast cereal, and other bad-for-us 'junk'. But, as film distributor Daniel Lyon observes, 'to condemn a movie for being dumb and unchallenging is as nonsensical as condemning a doughnut for being round and easy to eat' (B3). Much scholarly and critical writing on Canadian cinema involves a tautology based on these ideas: that popular (easy, junky) forms are American in character, that Canadian film is challenging and therefore good for us, and that

Canadian films can't successfully adopt popular forms because the popular is an American form. I shall elaborate, but this notion—found at the centre of the cultural nationalist perspective in Canada—is, at root, the explanation of why *Meatballs* does not appear as a part of Canadian film history, or even count as a Canadian film, in most accounts of the nation's cinema.

For example, demonstrating Bourdieu's point nicely, and providing a nationalist spin on it as well, Leach argues that genre is essentially a conservative, and American form, and that Canadian genre films can demonstrate their Canadianness only by undermining the principles behind generic film-making. He writes:

The reliance on established genres provides a general security blanket: the producer knows what he or she is investing in, the distributor has an 'angle' to exploit, the director knows the film will find an audience, and the audience knows what to expect and how to respond. This sense of security is precisely what is lacking, almost by definition, in the more traditional (or progressive?) Canadian cinema that explores (often painfully) the uncertainties of the Canadian experience (1986: 358).

In light of such commonly held views circulating in and forming the basis of the nationalist film historiography, here I want to more fully explore the premises that underlie critics' and scholars' dismissal of genre films as somehow un-Canadian, subjecting these premises to a theoretical consideration of genre as a concept. While genre is frequently conceived of as merely a categorical tool, one that in most cases unproblematically lumps together films with similar aspects, recent reconsiderations of genre as a theoretical concept in film studies have turned a corner. Here is one:

. . . genre refers not to just a film type, but to spectator expectations and hypotheses (speculation as to how the film will end). It also refers to the role of specific institutional discourses that feed into and form generic structures. In other words, genres must be seen as part of a

tripartite process of production, marketing (including distribution and exhibition), and consumption. (Hayward 165).

James Naremore agrees, writing that an individual genre

has less to do with a group of artefacts than with a discourse—a loose evolving system of arguments and readings, helping to shape commercial strategies and aesthetic ideologies (14).

These contemporary and compelling theories of genre confirm that the reception of films like *Meatballs*, both within the critical discourse of their day, and in their subsequent treatment by Canadian film histories, is evidence of nothing more than a series of historically specific premises which tell us a great deal more about the period in which they were operative than they do about the texts themselves.

Conceptual frameworks for the application of genre as a useful tool for film studies have dramatically changed since the 1970s. At that time, Canadian genre movies (*Meatballs* is a perfect example), were largely dismissed because of assumptions underlying then-current theories of genre (about the films' conservative nature and simplicity, and about the homogenizing effects of formula). The central theoretical premise of my examination of genre and nation is that no re-evaluation of the dismissed Canadian genre films has been undertaken within the newer conceptual frameworks.

In addition to this temporal aspect, my reconsideration of the relation of genre to nation also has a geographical aspect. It is useful to observe how generic systems function in other national cinemas: for example, the French *policier* and the Italian horror film are central elements of these national cinemas, with the very generic nature of these forms posing no problem for the national specificity of the genre film produced there. But one wonders what should make the teen summer camp comedy necessarily an American form.

As Barbara Klinger notes, 'in the early 1980s, Tony Bennett called for a revolution in literary study, in which one would no longer just study the text, but "everything which has been written *about* it, everything which has been collected on it, becomes attached to it—like shells on a rock by the seashore forming the whole incrustation"' (107). Bennett thus advocates a turn to reception studies and the related privileging of context and intertext over texts themselves. Significantly, this approach, which animates the work of Hayward and Naremore cited above, arrived in humanities scholarship (via cultural studies) shortly *after* the explosion of genre filmmaking in Canada in the 1970s. That Bennett's suggestion, supported by Klinger, comes after the initial release of films like *Meatballs* is particularly useful in this discussion of genre as an evolving discourse. The ways in which films are received, understood, and consumed are changeable, and the current popularity of films such as *Meatballs* that in their day were individually embarrassing to nationalist critics and scholars suggests the importance of reconsidering such films as both artifacts of a time and place, and forever evolving into the future.

Many teen comedies produced in Canada around the time of *Meatballs*—such as *Pinball Summer* (Mihalka, 1979) and *Hog Wild* (Rose, 1980)—share several thematic and stylistic features both among themselves and with the hit generic cousins they resemble. Here I propose to examine how the similarities, as well as the differences, among these texts can help us understand their appearance in Canada at that time. I want to explore this area, because a common critical complaint about Canadian genre comedies like *Meatballs* is that they follow an 'American' formula, with this 'fact' somehow disqualifying them as acceptable representatives of the Canadian national cinema.

The first observation about this cycle of films is that while films about teenagers have long been popular, a new kind of teen comedy emerged in the late 1970s and early 1980s, and the popularity of these films has generated a long series of similar works—a cycle that continues to the present day. Many commentators on the recent popular teen comedies by Judd Apatow, such as *Knocked Up* and *Superbad* (both 2007), remark on the combination of raunch and sweetness that characterizes them, while also noting their debt to the origins of this

generic trope in the late 1970s and early 1980s.[3] Timothy Shary's book *Generation Multiplex: Images of Youth in Contemporary American Cinema* contains many insights into the emergence of youth-oriented films, and he succinctly describes the emergence of this genre cycle:

> . . . a handful of other films truly inaugurated new cycles: two 1978 American films, the low-budget sensation *Halloween* and the college farce *Animal House*, as well as two unassuming Canadian films, *Meatballs* and *Porky's*. These were the starting guns of the new youth subgenres of the 1980s. *Animal House*, *Meatballs* and *Porky's* were raucous comedies featuring goofy and/or hormonal youth pursuing pleasures at college, summer camp, and a 50s-era high school respectively, and their success spawned numerous imitations over the next few years (7).

Let me emphasize here that Shary's persuasive claim is that these films *inaugurated new generic cycles*, not that they imitated existing ones.

These films ordinarily feature characters grouped into factions, one of which is led by a charismatic, often zany, figure, such as Tripper in *Meatballs* or Greg (Michael Zelniker) in *Pinball Summer*. Many teen films are about anxieties over social status and fitting in, and usually side with underdog characters. *Meatballs* sticks closely to this trope, and turns largely on its us-against-them narrative, where the enemies are the spoiled rich kids of Camp Mohawk. Counsellor Tripper fully realizes the inadequacies of his Camp Northstar team and their near-certain defeat in the annual summer camp Olympiad (his kids are losers in just about every way). This realization provokes his inspired pre-Olympiad pep talk. Tripper begins by enumerating what the other team has going for it (a lot) and what their team has working against it (a lot). Gradually escalating, and working himself into a lather, he winds up his talk by shouting 'It just doesn't matter! It just doesn't matter!' The campers all join in, spiritedly. Of course, now that they've acknowledged that 'it just doesn't matter', they eventually do win the Olympiad in a last-minute squeaker. I shall return to this important moment of the film toward the end of the chapter.

The relationship between the troubled boy Rudy and Tripper lends *Meatballs* a degree of warmth. The film never actually tells us what is wrong with Rudy, but he does not seem to belong at Camp Northstar, and tries to leave. As Rudy is making his escape, Tripper bumps into him and convinces him to stay. Rudy ultimately wins the Olympiad for Northstar by winning the cross-country race, the final event. Since few of the other early films from this cycle share such a story element, it is notable how early films in a successful cycle both closely resemble and deviate from each other. For instance, *Pinball Summer* also centres on a contest of competing factions (a pinball contest, of course), but its last-minute underdog saviour is not a hero. He manages only to allow the film's ostensible (but unlikable) heroes to claim the trophy, while remaining, as he had been throughout the film, the butt of joke after joke about his size.[4]

Easily among the most commercially successful Canadian films of all time, *Meatballs* was just one of a series of similar films which emerged in the late 1970s. Its success spawned numerous imitators, and generated a great deal of enthusiasm for the economic potential of the Canadian feature film industry. In some ways not entirely original—it features, for example, comic loudspeaker announcements just like Robert Altman's *M*A*S*H* (1970)—*Meatballs* nevertheless manages that strange alchemy of elements which defines successful genre films. It has familiar elements and novel ones, and as a film set on a forested lake in Canada, it is in many ways among the most obviously 'Canadian' of this genre cycle. And from the distance of some decades, we can see that, rather than slavishly imitating an American formula, it arguably initiated a new cycle of popular comedy films.

WHERE IS *MEATBALLS* IN THE EXTANT ACCOUNT OF CANADIAN CINEMA?

As I said earlier, when we look at the extant historical account of the Canadian cinema, we have an extremely hard time finding any mention of *Meatballs*, one of Canada's most commercially successful feature films. The primary works—no: *all* of the works—of historical and critical scholarship on the English Canadian cinema almost completely ignore this film (and similarly, many others—usually genre films that have been commercially successful). In the last decade, there has been a small flurry of new books on English Canadian film, all of which fall into one of two categories. On the one hand, we have those which allow a one-sentence mention of *Meatballs* (about only its financial performance), including Chris Gitting's *Canadian National Cinema* and George Melnyk's *One Hundred Years of Canadian Cinema*. On the other hand, there are those with *no mention whatsoever* of this important film: Jerry White's *The Cinemas of Canada*; Jim Leach's *Film in Canada*; Eugene Walz's *Canada's Best Features*; Bill Beard and Jerry White's massive and otherwise excellent *North of Everything: English Canadian Cinema Since 1980*; Tom Waugh's gigantic and authoritative *The Romance of Transgression in Canada*: *Queering Sexualities, Nations, Cinemas*; and Malek Khoury and Darrell Varga's *Working on Screen: Representations of the Working Class in English Canadian Cinema*.

Now, some might object to the notion that books like these should necessarily devote some attention to a film like *Meatballs*, although it is difficult to see why the larger surveys should not at least acknowledge its presence. What explains *Meatballs*'s invisibility in Canadian film culture? The answer lies beyond Canadian scholars' simple disagreement with the cultural populists' claim—noted by Jim McGuigan earlier in this chapter—that popular films merit scholarly attention, even if films by, say, Atom Egoyan are typically considered to be 'better', or at least more artful, examples of the medium. But the notion of cultural value clearly does haunt the extant account of English Canadian cinema, where what is popular is associated with America, and what is difficult, challenging, or maybe even off-beat, is associated with Canada. I would like to question this simplistic equation.

This account usually begins with an evocation of Canada's so-called documentary tradition, closely associated with the heroic National Film Board (NFB) and its charismatic founder John Grierson. Grierson, a Presbyterian Scot who was instrumental in founding the leftist-liberal British Documentary Film Movement of the 1930s, is famous for many Arnoldian pronouncements, including his dismissal of the frivolousness of producing films which 'merely entertain'.

Another high-water mark in the Canadian cultural nationalist fear and negation of films in popular idioms is found in the language of the Massey Commission Report of 1951, certainly one of the most important and influential documents in the history of Canadian cultural policy. Consider, for example, this statement:

> The cinema is not only the most potent but also the most alien of the influences shaping our Canadian life. Nearly all Canadians go to the movies, and most movies come from Hollywood . . . Hollywood refashions us in its own image (42).

The report goes on to note that Canadians, at least as judged by their behaviour, certainly want to see commercial feature films, while at the same time they praise the NFB's role as national film educator and recommend an expanded role for the board in order to protect Canadians from 'the effects of commercialization coming from a foreign nation which puts its faith in the machine' (59). This kind of discourse set the parameters of the debate for decades to come. Commercial films—designed to entertain audiences—were an American form. The proper Canadian use of the medium was to educate and enlighten.

Other paradigm-cementing examples abound. Peter Harcourt's enormously influential article entitled 'The Beginning of the Beginning' points to 1963 as a seminal year in the history of the Canadian cinema, with the release that year of both Don Owen's *Nobody Waved Good-bye* and Gilles Groulx's *Le chat dans le sac*, two 'arty' auteur films, each deeply indebted to a filmmaker of the French New Wave: Owen's film to François Truffaut and Groulx's to Jean-Luc Godard. This was the time of the true birth of feature filmmaking in Canada, according to often-cited

piece. The amazing hold of Harcourt's article on Canadian film history has only recently been called into question with researchers' rediscovery of Canadian features like Julian Roffman's horror film *The Mask* (1961) which predates the so-called 'beginning of the beginning' by two years.

Once again, the point here is that a certain kind of Canadian filmmaking— documentary and art films—has been celebrated and canonized, leading to the systematic exclusion of popular works that should clearly be seen as constituent, or even important, elements of the English Canadian cinematic tradition. The treatment of *Meatballs* by Canadian film scholarship is an excellent example of this exclusion. The typical critical biases against it were trotted out in many of the popular reviews of the film in its day, and the film has never yet been given any serious attention since then.

The problem for cultural nationalists, we can assume, seems to be that the film commits the following offences: it has an American star; it was claimed to be somewhat derivative of a popular Hollywood film from the previous year (*Animal House*, which was produced by the same Canadian who directed *Meatballs*—Ivan Reitman); it fails to adequately address 'Canadian themes' (whatever those might be); and finally, it was very popular, which almost by definition excludes it from possibly belonging to the valuable and educative Canadian cinema 'tradition'. This paradox is succinctly described by William Beard, one of the few Canadian film scholars to ever engage with popular cinema (in his case, the horror films of David Cronenberg): 'it remains as difficult as ever to imagine a Canadian *popular* cinema that does not disqualify itself from Canadianness by its very popularity' (148).

In response to these complaints, let me first observe that it is true that the marquee value the then up-and-coming Bill Murray brought to the film probably contributed to its success. But why is this a problem? First, Bill Murray's character is in no way coded as nationally different from the rest of the film's characters, all of whom the astute viewer will recognize as Canadian. Second, foreign-born stars do not seem to taint the purity of other cinemas. Indeed, the entire history of

Hollywood itself is closely tied to non-American labour in every possible facet, from writers, directors, producers, and stars to exhibitors and everything in between.

In considering genre, we must return to the question posed earlier: What makes the teen comedy necessarily an American form? If Canadians have traditionally flocked to genre films in numbers more or less equivalent to their American counterparts, if the 'border' of culture is as transparent and porous as we know it to be between Canada and the United States, on what basis can cultural nationalist critics demand that films from Canada must not entertain in order to count as Canadian? Furthermore, *Animal House*, the film that critics complained *Meatballs* was derived from, was not only produced by *Meatballs* director Reitman; he was also a key creative driver for the project, having worked for years on its development while producing the off-Broadway (and then touring) stage revue called *The National Lampoon Show*. Reitman has since become the most commercially successful director–producer of comedy films in the history of Hollywood, and *Meatballs* should be seen as the Canadian part of the unfolding of his flourishing career.

And finally, we turn to this complete red herring: the issue of so-called 'Canadian themes'. The very notion is so exclusionary as to be ridiculous. What would these films be? Films about winter? Hockey? Doughnuts? Again, this is the heart of the cultural nationalist position: that the cultural artifacts of a nation need to somehow reflect something about the nation. I suggest that the sheer variety of experience of Canadians, based on their ethnic background, where they live, their education, and so on, means that generalizing a 'national experience' is futile and necessarily limiting. That said, if one did seek to analyze *Meatballs* for national themes, it would not be hard to generate a convincing reading which posits the two competing camps as a metaphor for the rich and powerful United States (Camp Mohawk) versus the nicer, politer, much less powerful Canada (Camp Northstar). In fact, one consistent strand of the nationalist thematic film scholarship has its genesis in Robert Fothergill's seminal essay 'Coward, Bully or Clown: The Dream-Life of a Younger Brother' which attempts to explain the profusion of largely ineffectual male protagonists in Canadian films, in contrast to the profusion of heroic ones in Hollywood films. That Camp Northstar is peopled almost entirely by wimps, losers, and nerds would seem to fit this paradigm nicely, and Tripper's 'It just doesn't matter if we lose!' speech could easily be read as a powerful expression of the paradoxically proud feelings of meekness and powerlessness that seem to define so many understandings of the Canadian character, positioned as we are next to such a powerful neighbour.

MEATBALLS MATTERS

The dominance of the cultural nationalist position in Canadian film studies has taught us to think that films like *Meatballs* are American in character, but they are not. All they are is popular, and similarities between life in America and life in Canada—in, say, the imagined experiences of teenagers at summer camp—are manifest, and it is only elitist culturally nationalist critical opinion which denies this is the case. The tradition of cultural value that is claimed to be the defining feature of Canadian cinema—as in documentaries and art films—has been self-perpetuating and has hidden more than it has revealed. A fuller, more accurate and nuanced account of the Canadian cinema is one that includes *Meatballs* and many others like it. We fool no one but ourselves in imagining that the pleasures of truly popular culture are a foreign influence on Canadian life.

NOTES

1. 'National specificity' is of course a difficult quality to measure. In the case of *Meatballs*, some might note the visible Ontario license plates on cars, while others will observe certain American turns of phrase. In any case, the film is not obviously Canadian in the sense that *Crocodile Dundee* is obviously Australian and, at the very least, is almost never discussed as a specifically

Canadian film in the way that *Crocodile Dundee* is almost always discussed as a specifically Australian film. The similarity of American and Canadian accents partly explains this, one presumes.

2. In addition to Turner, see, for example, Stephen Croft's 'Re-imaging Australia: *Crocodile Dundee* Overseas'.

3. See, for example, reviews in www.moviefilm star.com/movie/2005_The_5F40_Year-Old_ Virgin.html *or* www.richardcrouse.ca/page4. html *(accessed July, 2010)*.

4. Fat jokes are another very common trope of this generic cycle, as are 'nerd' characters who lack social graces and often have ill-fitting clothes, runny noses, and tape on their glasses. Arguably, *Meatballs* provided the archetype for these characters in Spaz (Len Blum), versions of which we have seen in countless teen films since then.

WORKS CITED

Beard, William. 'Thirty-Two Short Paragraphs about David Cronenberg'. *North of Everything: English-Canadian Cinema Since 1980*. William Beard and Jerry White (eds). Edmonton: University of Alberta Press, 2002.

Bourdieu, Pierre. *Distinction: A Social Critique of the Judgment of Taste*. Richard Nice (trans). Cambridge: Harvard University Press, 1984.

Croft, Stephen. 'Re-Imaging Australia: *Crocodile Dundee* Abroad'. *Continuum* 2.2 (1989): 129–43.

Fothergill, Robert. 'Coward, Bully or Clown: The Dream-Life of a Younger Brother'. *Canadian Film Reader*. Seth Feldman and Joyce Nelson (eds). Toronto: Peter Martin Associates, 1977: 234–49.

Gittings, Christopher. *Canadian National Cinema*. London and New York: Routledge, 2001.

Harcourt, Peter. 'The Beginning of the Beginning'. *Self Portrait*. Piers Handling (ed.). Ottawa: Canadian Film Institute, 1980: 64–76.

Hayward, Susan. *Cinema Studies: The Key Concepts*. London and New York: Routledge, 2000.

Khoury, Malek and Darrell Varga (eds). *Working on Screen: Representations of the Working Class in Canadian Cinema*. Toronto: University of Toronto Press, 2006.

Klinger, Barbara. 'Film History Terminable and Interminable: Recovering the Past in Reception Studies'. *Screen* 38.2 (1997): 102–22.

Leach, Jim. 'The Body Snatchers: Genre and Canadian Cinema'. *Film Genre Reader*, Barry Grant (ed.). Detroit: Wayne State University Press. 1986: 357–69.

———. *Film in Canada*. Toronto: Oxford University Press, 2006.

Lyon, Daniel. '*Les Boys*' (Letters to Arts). *Globe and Mail* 10 February 1997: B3.

Massey, Vincent. Royal Commission on National Development in the Arts, Letters and Sciences. *Report*. Ottawa: King's Printer, 1951.

McGuigan, Jim. *Cultural Populism*. London and New York: Routledge, 1992.

Melnyk, George. *One Hundred Years of Canadian Cinema*. Toronto: University of Toronto Press, 2004.

Morris, Peter. 'In Our Own Eyes: The Canonization of Canadian Film'. *Canadian Journal of Film Studies* 3.1 (1994): 30–8.

Naremore, James. 'American Film Noir: The History of an Idea'. *Film Quarterly* 49: 2 (1995–96): 12–29.

Shary, Timothy. *Generation Multiplex: The Image of Youth in Contemporary American Cinema*. Austin: University of Texas Press, 2002.

Turner, Graham. 'The Genres are American: Australian Narrative, Australian Film and the Problem of Genre'. *Literature/Film Quarterly* 21.1 (1993): 102–11.

Walz, Eugene. *Canada's Best Features: Critical Essays on 15 Canadian Films*. Amsterdam: Rodopi, 2002.

Waugh, Thomas. *The Romance of Transgression in Canada: Queering Sexualities, Nations, Cinemas*. Montreal and Kingston: McGill-Queens University Press, 2008.

White, Jerry. *The Cinemas of Canada*. London: Wallflower, 2006.

QUESTIONS FOR REFLECTION

1. Look through introductory textbooks, travel guides, or other texts that outline the history and geography of nations. What types of pictures are used in the texts and do those images present a certain identity about nations? How do they do this?
2. Examine the images used by your college, university, or workplace in promotional materials. Do these images help to construct an identity for your school/workplace? What is this identity and how does it compare to your own perceptions?
3. Do contemporary Canadian popular magazines, films, or television shows define a 'typical' Canadian? What are the characteristics of Canadianness as defined in these venues and how do they compare to those described by Payne, Kinahan, and Urquhart?

FURTHER READING

Druick, Zoë, and Aspa Kotsopoulos, Eds. *Programming Reality: Perspectives on English-Canadian Television*. Waterloo: Wilfrid Laurier University, 2008.

Foster, Robert. 'The Commercial Construction of "New Nations"'. *Journal of Material Culture* 4.3 (1993): 263–82.

Geller, Peter. *Northern Exposures: Photographing and Filming the Canadian North, 1920–1945*. Vancouver: University of British Columbia, 2004.

Kaplan, Louis. *American Exposures: Photography and Community in the Twentieth Century*. Minneapolis: University of Minnesota, 2005.

Keller, Wolfram R., and Eugene P. Walz, Eds. *Screening Canadians: Cross-Cultural Perspectives on Canadian Film*. Marburg, Germany: Marburg University, 2008.

Lippard, Lucy R., Ed. *Partial Recall: Photographs of Native North Americans*. New York: The New Press, 1992.

Payne, Carol. 'Lessons with Leah: re-reading the photographic archive of nation in the National Film Board of Canada's Still Photography Division'. *Visual Studies* 21.1 (April 2006): 4–22.

Squiers, Carol. 'Class Struggle: The Invention of Paparazzi Photography and the Death of Diana, Princess of Wales'. *Over Exposed: Essays on Contemporary Photography*. Ed. Carol Squiers. New York: The New Press, 1999. 269–304.

Tejada, Roberto. *National Camera: Photography and Mexico's Image Environment*. Minneapolis: University of Minnesota, 2009.

Urquhart, Peter. 'Cultural Nationalism and Taste: The Place of the Popular in Canadian Film Culture'. *Screening Canadians: Cross-Cultural Perspectives on Canadian Film*. Eds. Wolfram R. Keller and Gene Walz. Marburg, Germany: Universitätsbibliothek Marburg, 2008.

Vettel-Becker, Patricia. *Shooting from the Hip: Photography, Masculinity, and Postwar America*. Minneapolis: University of Minnesota, 2005.

PART EIGHT

IMAGES AND THEIR AUDIENCES

As evidenced throughout this reader, images have both immediate and lasting impacts on their viewers. This final part of readings continues on this theme, specifically addressing the relationship between images and their audiences. Viewing a film in a darkened megaplex with hundreds of other patrons is clearly different from the quiet contemplation of an oil painting in an art gallery, which is different from the consumption of pop culture images (music videos, comic books, advertisements) in the domestic sphere. The differences between these media and the ways in which they are viewed help to frame the audience: They regulate the viewing experience and place certain parameters on the communicative capabilities of the images being viewed. The essays in this part interrogate the relationship between image and audience, drawing specific attention to the materialities of the viewing experience and the influential power of visual communication.

The first essay in Part Eight is by the eminent television studies scholar, Lynn Spigel. The essay, 'Television in the Family Circle', is from Spigel's highly influential book, *Make Room for* TV. In the essay, the author offers a compelling account of television as it existed in postwar America. A central concern of Spigel's is the intersection of television and the spatial arrangement of the home, which includes not just the allocation of viewing space (i.e., where to put the TV), but also the division of labour and power within the domestic sphere. In this sense, television played an active role in constructing its audience.

Spigel performs a thorough analysis of public and professional discourse around television in mid century America and shows the ways in which the TV audience was discussed and constructed in a paradoxical manner. TV was promoted as something that would unify the family, bringing mothers, fathers, and children together in the 'family circle' around the television set. This was particularly attractive in the postwar climate which sought a return to family values after the separation and isolation wrought by war. By contrast, the television also facilitated the division of domestic space along social and sexual lines. In this sense, rather than bringing the family together, television was positioned as a way to uphold traditional gendered roles in the home. Spigel's essay is a fascinating account of the relationship between a mass medium such as television and the political, economic, and social issues of the time. And while the focus is on mid century America, the issues raised in the essay continue to circulate in contemporary discussions about television, computers, and wireless communication devices within and outside the domestic sphere.

The second essay in the part is by the noted Canadian communication scholar, Paul Heyer. The essay, 'Virtually Live: Digital Broadcast Cinema and the Performing Arts', is an examination of an emerging technological and communication phenomenon which Heyer titles 'digital broadcast cinema' (DBC). Introduced at New York's Metropolitan Opera in 2006, DBC is the digital transmission of live, narrative-based performances to movie theatres for simultaneous broadcast. DBC allows viewers worldwide to watch a live event without being co-present with the performers. Heyer's essay is an analysis of DBC as it compares to live theatre, cinema, and television. Audience features prominently in the essay, as what constitutes the viewing audience is challenged by this developing practice.

Heyer addresses the formal qualities of a DBC broadcast, noting that the technology can help to make performances more accessible to a larger, more diversified audience. DBC also brings a level of closeness and allows for attention to detail that would normally be reserved for only those in the most highly prized seats. Heyer's essay concludes with a compelling discussion of the difference between the live experience and its representation, one which parallels Ivins's argument in the opening part of this book. What emerges is a questioning or reformulation of the very notions of audience, live performance, and representation. Who constitutes the audience for a DBC event? Those in attendance at the Met? The viewers in movie theatres who watch the event simultaneously? Or those who are several time zones away and must watch a recorded version of the event? How is watching a live performance in the opera house different from doing so in a movie theatre miles away? Is one viewing experience more 'authentic' or 'real' than the other? As Heyer's essay shows, DBC not only complicates the relationship between the live performance and its representation, but calls the very distinction into question.

Where the first two essays in the part address the spatial and material aspects of the viewing experience, the third stresses the impact of images on their audiences. The essay 'From Counting Calories to Fun Food: Regulating the TV Diet in the Age of Obesity', by Jacqueline Botterill and Stephen Kline, is a critical analysis of television food advertising, specifically that directed at children. Botterill and Kline are internationally recognized for their critical work on advertising, and in this essay they perform a comprehensive visual and content analysis of 1556 North American food advertisements aired between 2003 and 2007. They address what is advertised, how it is advertised, and its impact on the target audience. Their results point to three recurring themes: the representation of food on TV differs dramatically from what is recommended in nutritional guidelines; visual strategies are routinely used to mask the poor nutritional qualities of the food being advertised; and television ads present shifting attitudes towards food and eating, potentially influencing consumer behaviour.

The notion of audience is of primary importance in the essay in two ways. First, Botterill and

Kline point to the growing body of evidence that links television food advertising and childhood obesity. In this way, images have an immediate impact on their audience, literally helping to shape viewers' consumption choices and, ultimately, their health. Second, the debate around children's advertising presupposes certain characteristics regarding audience, specifically, that children are largely incapable of making informed choices when presented with multiple products. Thus for Botterill and Kline, and others concerned with children's advertising, television food advertisements directed at children should not employ the visual and narrative strategies that are present in adult advertising. Further, the authors stress that the effective regulation of television food advertising must recognize the tremendous affective capabilities of images, specifically their ability to shape viewers' behaviour. Botterill and Kline's essay is a reminder of the powerful capabilities of images and visual communication and the subsequent need for a critical, visual literacy.

The once-dominant transmission models of communication in which a message moves seamlessly from sender to receiver have been replaced by a much more nuanced understanding of the complexity of human communication, including the varied role of the audience. As the essays in this part show, the relationship between image and audience is highly complex and framed by numerous factors including the unique features of different media forms (film, television, DBC), the social and spatial parameters of a viewing experience (cinema, theatre, home), and the influential power of images (children's advertising). To critically engage with an object or instance of visual communication, it is therefore essential to recognize the influential and dynamic relationship between images and their audiences.

23

TELEVISION IN THE FAMILY CIRCLE

LYNN SPIGEL

Nicholas Ray's 1955 film, *Rebel Without a Cause*, contains a highly melodramatic moment in which family members are unable to patch together the rift among them. The teenage son, Jim, returns home after the famous sequence in which he races his car to the edge of a cliff, only to witness the death of his competitor. Jim looks at his father asleep in front of the television set, and then he lies down on a sofa. From Jim's upside-down point of view on the sofa, the camera cuts to his shrewish mother who appears at the top of the stairwell. In a 180-degree spin, the camera flip-flops on the image of the mother, mimicking the way Jim sees her descending the stairs. This

highly stylized shot jolts us out of the illusory realism of the scene, a disruption that continues as the camera reveals a television screen emitting a menacing blue static. As the camera lingers on the TV set, Jim confesses his guilt. Moments later, when his mother demands that he not go to the police, Jim begs his henpecked father to take his side. Finally, with seemingly murderous intentions, Jim chokes him. The camera pans across the TV set, its bluish static heightening the sense of family discord. With its 'bad reception', television serves as a rhetorical figure for the loss of communication between family members. In fact, as Jim's father admits early in the scene, he was not even aware of his son's whereabouts during this fateful night, but instead had learned of the incident through an outside authority, the television newscast.

As this classic scene illustrates, in postwar years the television set became a central figure in representations of family relationships. The introduction of the machine into the home meant that family members needed to come to terms with the presence of a communication medium that might transform older modes of family interaction. The popular media published reports and advice from social critics and social scientists who were studying the effects of television on family relationships. The media also published pictorial representations of domestic life that showed people how television might—or might not—fit into the dynamics of their own domestic lives. Most significantly, like the scene from *Rebel Without a Cause*, the media discourses were organized around ideas of family harmony and discord.

Indeed, contradictions between unity and division were central to representations of television during the period of its installation. Television was the great family minstrel that promised to bring Mom, Dad, and the kids together; at the same time, it had to be carefully controlled so that it harmonized with the separate gender roles and social functions of individual family members. This meant that the contradiction between unity and division was not a simple binary opposition; it was not a matter of either/or but rather both at once. Television was supposed to bring the family together but still allow for social and sexual divisions in the home. In fact, the attempt to maintain a balance between these two ideals was a central tension at work in popular discourses on television and the family.

THE FAMILY UNITED

In 1954, *McCall's* magazine coined the term 'togetherness'. The appearance of this term between the covers of a woman's magazine is significant not only because it shows the importance attached to family unity during the postwar years, but also because this phrase is symptomatic of discourses aimed at the housewife. Home magazines

primarily discussed family life in language organized around spatial imagery of proximity, distance, isolation, and integration. In fact, the spatial organization of the home was presented as a set of scientific laws through which family relationships could be calculated and controlled. Topics ranging from childrearing to sexuality were discussed in spatial terms, and solutions to domestic problems were overwhelmingly spatial: if you are nervous, make yourself a quiet sitting corner far away from the central living area of the home. If your children are cranky, let them play in the yard. If your husband is bored at the office, turn your garage into a workshop where he'll recall the joys of his boyhood. It was primarily within the context of this spatial problem that television was discussed. The central question was, 'Where should you put the television set?' This problem was tackled throughout the period, formulated and reformulated, solved and recast. In the process the television set became an integral part of the domestic environment depicted in the magazines.

At the simplest level, there was the question of the proper room for television. In 1949, *Better Homes and Gardens* asked, 'Where does the receiver go?' It listed options including the living room, game room, or 'some strategic spot where you can see it from the living room, dining room and kitchen'.[1] At this point, however, the photographs of model rooms usually did not include television sets as part of the interior decor. On the few occasions when sets did appear, they were placed either in the basement or in the living room. By 1951, the television set travelled more freely through the household spaces depicted in the magazines. It appeared in the basement, living room, bedroom, kitchen, fun room, converted garage, sitting-sleeping room, music room, and even the 'TV room'. Furthermore, not only the room, but the exact location in the room, had to be considered for its possible use as a TV zone.

As the television set moved into the centre of family life, other household fixtures traditionally associated with domestic bliss had to make room for it. Typically, the magazines presented the television set as the new family hearth through which love and affection might be rekindled.[2] In

1951, when *American Home* first displayed a television set on its cover photograph, it employed the conventionalized iconography of a model living room organized around the fireplace, but this time a television set was built into the mantelpiece. Even more radically, the television was shown to replace the fireplace altogether, as the magazines showed readers how television could function as the centre of family attention. So common had this substitution become that by 1954 *House Beautiful* was presenting its readers with 'another example of how the TV set is taking the place of the fireplace as the focal point around which to arrange the seating in the room'.[3] Perhaps the most extreme example of this kind of substitution is the tradition at some broadcast stations of burning Yule logs on the television screen each Christmas Eve, a practice that originated in the 1950s.

More typically, the television set took the place of the piano.[4] In *American Home*, for instance, the appearance of the television set correlates significantly with the vanishing piano. While in 1948 the baby grand piano typically held a dominant place in model living rooms, over the years it gradually receded to the point where it was usually shown to be an upright model located in marginal areas such as basements. Meanwhile, the television set moved into the primary living spaces of model rooms where its stylish cabinets meshed with and enhanced the interior decor. The new 'entertainment centres', comprised of a radio, television, and phonograph, often made the piano entirely obsolete. In 1953, *Better Homes and Gardens* suggested as much when it displayed a television set in a 'built-in music corner' that 'replaces the piano', now moved into the basement.[5] In that same year, in a special issue entitled 'Music and Home Entertainment', *House Beautiful* focused on radio, television, and phonographs, asking readers, 'Do You Really Need a Piano?'[6] One woman, writing to *TV World* columnist Kathi Norris, answered the question in no uncertain terms:

Dear Kathi:
Since we got our television set, we've had to change the arrangement of furniture in our living room, and we just can't keep the piano. I need new pictures, but can't afford to buy them with the expense of television, so I was wondering if I might somehow find somebody who would trade me a picture or two for a perfectly good piano.[7]

This woman and, I suspect, others like her were beginning to think of television as a replacement for the traditional fixtures of family life.[8]

As the magazines continued to depict the set in the centre of family activity, television seemed to become a natural part of domestic space. By the early 1950s, floor plans included a space for television in the home's structural layout and television sets were increasingly depicted as everyday, commonplace objects that any family might hope to own. Indeed, the magazines included television as a staple home fixture before most Americans could even receive a television signal, much less consider purchasing the expensive item. The media discourses did not so much reflect social reality; instead, they preceded it. The home magazines helped to construct television as a household object, one that belonged in the family space. More surprisingly, however, in the span of roughly four years, television itself became *the* central figure in images of the American home; it became the cultural symbol par excellence of family life.

Television, it was said, would bring the family ever closer, an expression which, in itself a spatial metaphor, was continually repeated in a wide range of popular media—not only women's magazines, but also general magazines, men's magazines, and on the airwaves. In its capacity as unifying agent, television fit well with the more general postwar hopes for a return to family values. It was seen as a kind of household cement that promised to reassemble the splintered lives of families who had been separated during the war. It was also meant to reinforce the new suburban family unit, which had left most of its extended family and friends behind in the city.

The emergence of the term 'family room' in the postwar period is a perfect example of the importance attached to organizing household spaces around ideals of family togetherness. First coined in George Nelson and Henry Wright's *Tomorrow's House: A Complete Guide for the Home-Builder* (1946), the family room encapsulated a popular ideal throughout the period. Nelson and Wright who alternatively called the family room 'the room without a name', suggested the possible social functions of this new household space:

> Could the room without a name be evidence of a growing desire to provide a framework within which the members of a family will be better equipped to enjoy each other on the basis of mutual respect and affection? Might it thus indicate a deep-seated urge to reassert the validity of the family by providing a better design for living? We should very much like to think so, and if there is any truth in this assumption, our search for a name is ended—we should simply call it the 'family room'.[9]

This notion of domestic cohesion was integral to the design for living put forward in the home magazines that popularized the family room in the years to come. It was also integral to the role of the television set, which was often pictured in the family rooms of the magazines' model homes. In 1950, *Better Homes and Gardens* literally merged television with the family room, telling readers to design a new double-purpose area, the 'family-television room'.[10]

But one needn't build a new room in order to bring the family together around the television set; kitchens, living rooms, and dining rooms would do just as well. What was needed was a particular attitude, a sense of closeness that permeated the room. Photographs, particularly in advertisements, graphically depicted the idea of the family circle with television viewers grouped around the television set in semicircle patterns.

As Roland Marchand has shown with respect to advertising in the 1920s and 1930s, the family circle was a prominent pictorial strategy for the promotion of household goods. The pictures always suggested that all members of the family were present, and since they were often shot in soft-focus or contained dreamy mists, there was a romantic haze around the family unit. Sometimes artists even drew concentric circles around

the family, or else an arc of light evoked the theme. According to Marchand, the visual cliché of the family circle referred back to Victorian notions about domestic havens, implying that the home was secure and stable. The advertisements suggested a democratic model of family life, one in which all members shared in consumer decisions—although, as Marchand suggests, to some extent the father remained a dominant figure in the pictorial composition. In this romanticized imagery, modern fixtures were easily assimilated into the family space:

> The products of modern technology including radios and phonographs, were comfortably accommodated within the hallowed circle. Whatever pressures and complexities modernity might bring, these images implied, the family at home would preserve an undaunted harmony and security. In an age of anxieties about family relationships and centrifugal social forces, this visual cliché was no social mirror; rather, it was a reassuring pictorial convention.[11]

Much like the advertisements for radio and the phonograph, advertisements for television made ample use of this reassuring pictorial convention—especially in the years immediately following the war when advertisers were in the midst of their reconversion campaigns, channelling the country back from the wartime pressures of personal sacrifice and domestic upheaval to a peacetime economy based on consumerism and family values. The advertisements suggested that television would serve as a catalyst for the return to a world of domestic love and affection—a world that must have been quite different from the actual experiences of returning GIs and their new families in the chaotic years of readjustment to civilian life.

The returning soldiers and their wives experienced an abrupt shift in social and cultural experiences. Horror stories of shell-shocked men circulated in psychiatric journals. In 1946, social workers at VA hospitals counselled some 144,000 men, half of whom were treated for neuropsychiatric diseases.[12] Even for those lucky enough to escape the scars of battle, popular media such as film noir showed angst-ridden, sexually un-stable men, scarred psychologically and unable to relate to the familial ideals and bureaucratic realities of postwar life (the tortured male hero in *Out of the Past* [1946] is a classic example). The more melodramatic social problem films such as *Come Back Little Sheba* (1952) and *A Hatful of Rain* (1957) were character studies of emotionally un-stable, often drug-dependent, family men. Such images, moreover, were not confined to popular fiction. Sociological studies such as William H. Whyte's *The Organization Man* (1956) presented chilling visions of white-collar workers who were transformed into powerless conformists as the country was taken over by nameless, faceless corporations.[13] Even if his working life was filled with tension, the ideal man still had to be the breadwinner for a family. Moreover, should he fail to marry and procreate, his 'manliness' would be called into question. According to Tyler May: 'Many contemporaries feared that returning vet-erans would be unable to resume their positions as responsible family men. They worried that a crisis in masculinity could lead to crime, "per-version" and homosexuality. Accordingly, the postwar years witnessed an increasing suspicion of single men as well as single women, as the au-thority of men at home and at work seemed to be threatened.'[14] Although the image of the swing-ing bachelor also emerged in this period—par-ticularly through the publication of *Playboy*—we might regard the 'swinger' image as a kind of desperate, if confused, response to the enforce-ment of heterosexual family lifestyles. In other words, in a heterosexist world, the swinger image might well have provided single men with a way to deflect popular suspicions about homosexual-ity directed at bachelors who avoided marriage.[15]

Meanwhile, women were given a highly con-straining solution to the changing roles of gender and sexual identity. Although middle- and work-ing-class women had been encouraged by popu-lar media to enter traditionally male occupations during the war, they were now told to return to their homes where they could have babies and make colour-coordinated meals.[16] Marynia Farnham and Ferdinand Lundberg's *The Modern Woman: The Lost Sex* (1947) gave professional,

psychological status to this housewife image, claiming that the essential function of women was that of caretaker, mother, and sexual partner. Those women who took paid employment in the outside world would defy the biological order of things and become neurotics.[17] One postwar mar-riage guidebook even included a 'Test of Neurotic Tendencies' on which women lost points for choosing an answer that exhibited their desire for authority at work.[18] The domestic woman needed to save her energy for housekeeping, childrear-ing, and an active (monogamous) sex life with her husband.[19] The ways in which people inter-preted and applied such messages to their own lives is difficult to discern, but their constant rep-etition in popular media did provide a context in which women could find ample justification for their early marriages, child-centredness, re-luctance to divorce, and tendency to use higher education only as a stepping stone for marriage.[20]

Even if people found the domestic ideal seduc-tive, the housing shortage, coupled with the baby boom, made domestic bliss an expensive and often unattainable luxury. In part, for this rea-son, the glorification of middle-class family life seems to have had the unplanned, paradoxical effect of sending married women into the labour force in order to obtain the money necessary to live up to the ideal. Whereas before the war sin-gle women accounted for the majority of female workers, the number of married women workers skyrocketed during the 1950s.[21] Despite the fact that many women worked for extra spending money, surveys showed that some women found outside employment gave them a sense of per-sonal accomplishment and also helped them en-ter into social networks outside family life.[22] At the same time, sociological studies such as Why-te's *The Organization Man* and David Reisman's *The Lonely Crowd* (1950) showed that housewives expressed doubts about their personal sacrifices, marital relationships, and everyday lives in alien-ating suburban neighbourhoods. Although most postwar middle-class women were not ready to accept the full-blown attack on patriarchy launched in Simone de Beauvoir's *The Second Sex* (1949; English translation, 1952), they were not simply cultural dupes. Indeed, as the work of

FIGURE 23.1 Family members circle around the console in a 1949 RCA advertisement

feminist historians such as Elaine Tyler May and Rochelle Gatlin suggests, postwar women both negotiated with and rationalized the oppressive aspects of the family ideal.

The transition from wartime to postwar life thus resulted in a set of ideological and social contradictions concerning the construction of gender and the family unit. The image of compassionate families that advertisers offered the public might well have been intended to serve the 'therapeutic' function that both Roland Marchand and T.J. Jackson Lears have ascribed to advertising in general. The illustrations of domestic bliss and consumer prosperity presented a soothing alternative to the tensions of postwar life.[23] Government building policies and veteran mortgage loans sanctioned the materialization of these advertising images by giving middle-class families a chance to buy into the 'good life' of ranch-style cottages and consumer durables. Even so, both the advertising images and the homes themselves were built on the shaky foundations of social upheavals and cultural conflicts that were never completely resolved. The family

circle ads, like suburbia itself, were only a temporary consumer solution to a set of complicated political, economic, and social problems.

In the case of television, these kind of advertisements almost always showed the product in the centre of the family group. While soft-focus or dreamy mists were sometimes used, the manufacturers' claims for picture clarity and good reception seem to have necessitated the use of sharp focus and high contrast, which better connoted these product attributes. The product-as-centre motif not only suggested the familial qualities of the set, but also implied a mode of use: the ads suggested television be watched by a family audience.

A 1951 advertisement for Crosley's 'family theatre television' is a particularly striking example. As is typical in these kinds of ads, the copy details the technical qualities of the set, but the accompanying illustration gives familial meanings to the modern technology. The picture in this case is composed as a *mise-en-abyme*; in the centre of the page a large drawing of the outer frame of a television screen contains a sharp focus photograph of a family watching television. Family members are dispersed on sofas on three sides of a room, while a little boy, with arms stretched out in the air, sits in the middle of the room. All eyes are glued to the television set which appears in the centre lower portion of the frame, in fact barely visible to the reader. According to the logic of this composition, the central fascination for the reader is not the actual product, which is pictured only in miniscule proportions on the lower margin of the page, but rather its ability to bring the family together around it. The ad's *mise-en-abyme* structure suggests that the Crosley console literally contains the domestic scene, thereby promising not just a television set but an ideal reflection 'of the family, joined together by the new commodity.[24]

Even families that were not welcomed into the middle-class melting pot of postwar suburbia were promised that the dream of domestic bliss would come true through the purchase of a television set. *Ebony* continually ran advertisements that displayed African-Americans in middle-class living rooms, enjoying an evening of television. Many of these ads were strikingly similar to those used in white consumer magazines—although often the advertisers portrayed black families watching programs that featured black actors.[25] Despite this iconographic substitution, the message was clearly one transmitted by a culture industry catering to the middle-class suburban ideal. Nuclear families living in single-family homes would engage in intensely private social relations through the luxury of television.

Such advertisements appeared in a general climate of postwar expectations about television's ability to draw families closer together. In *The Age of Television* (1956), Leo Bogart summarized a wide range of audience studies on the new medium that showed numerous Americans believed television would revive domestic life. Summarizing the findings, Bogart concluded that social scientific surveys 'agree completely that television has had the effect of keeping the family at home more than formerly'.[26] One respondent from a Southern California survey boasted that his 'family now stays home all the time and watches the same programs. [We] turn it on at

3:00 p.m. and watch until 10:00 p.m. We never go anywhere.'[27] Moreover, studies indicated that people believed television strengthened family ties. A 1949 survey of an eastern city found that long-term TV owners expressed 'an awareness of an enhanced family solidarity'.[28] In a 1951 study of Atlanta families, one respondent said, 'It keeps us together more', and another commented, 'It makes a closer family circle.' Some women even saw television as a cure for marital problems. One housewife claimed, 'My husband is very restless; now he relaxes at home.' Another woman confided, 'My husband and I get along a lot better. We don't argue so much. It's wonderful for couples who have been married ten years or more . . . . Before television, my husband would come in and go to bed. Now we spend some time together.'[29] A study of mass-produced suburbs (including Levittown, Long Island, and Park Forest, Illinois) found similar patterns as women expressed their confidence that television was 'bringing the romance back'. One woman even reported, 'Until we got that TV set, I thought my husband had forgotten how to neck.'[30]

Typically also, television was considered a remedy for problem children. During the 1950s, juvenile delinquency emerged as a central topic of public debate. Women's magazines and child psychologists such as Dr. Benjamin Spock, whose *Baby and Childcare* had sold a million copies by 1951, gave an endless stream of advice to mothers on ways to prevent their children from becoming antisocial and emotionally impaired. Not only was childrearing literature big business, but the state had taken a special interest in the topic of disturbed youth, using agencies such as the Continuing Committee on the Prevention and Control of Delinquency and the Children's Bureau to monitor juvenile crimes.[31] Against this backdrop, audience research showed that parents believed television would keep their children off the streets. A mother from the Southern California survey claimed, 'Our boy was always watching television, so we got him a set just to keep him home.'[32] A mother from the Atlanta study stated, 'We are closer together. We find our entertainment at home. Donna and her boyfriend sit here instead of going out now.'[33] Such sentiments were popularized in a *Better Homes and Gardens* survey in which parents repeatedly mentioned television's ability to unify the family. One parent even suggested a new reason for keeping up with the Joneses. She said, 'It [television] keeps the children home. Not that we have had that problem too much, but we could see it coming because nearly everyone had a set before we weakened.'[34]

TROUBLE IN PARADISE

The ideal of family togetherness that television came to signify was, like all cultural fantasies, accompanied by repressed anxieties that often resurfaced in the popular texts of the period. Even if television was often said to bring the family together in the home, popular media also expressed tensions about its role in domestic affairs. Television's inclusion in the home was dependent upon its ability to rid itself of what *House Beautiful* called its 'unfamiliar aspect'.[35]

At a time when household modernization was a key concern, women's magazines continually examined the relationship between the family and the machine. The magazines were undecided on this subject, at times accepting, at times rejecting the effects of mechanization. On the one hand, they offered their female readers technological fantasy worlds that promised to reduce the time and energy devoted to household chores. Dream kitchens, which had been displayed by women's magazines since the 1920s, resembled Technicolor spectacles found on the cinema screen, only here the bold primary colours depicted a woman's Shangri-la of electric gizmos and sleek linoleum surfaces. Just in case this pictorial display of technological commodity fetishism was not enough, the magazines didactically reminded their readers of the need to 'be up to date'. In 1951, *House Beautiful* provided a list of 'changes and improvements that arrived [after the war] as predicted'. Included were such labour-saving devices as the dishwasher and garbage grinder, but also leisure-enhancing machines, most notably television. In that same year, *House Beautiful* included a quiz entitled 'How Contemporary is Your Life?' Most of the 58 questions had to do with the degree to which the home

was equipped with 'modern' appliances, and the magazine warned its readers that if 'you score less than forty . . . you are depriving yourself of too many contemporary advantages'. Owning a television set was a must, according to this modernity exam.[36]

Whereas in the prewar and war years a fully mechanized household would have been presented in the popular press as a futuristic fantasy, in the postwar years it appeared that tomorrow had arrived. Moreover, living without an array of machines meant that you were anachronistic, unable to keep pace with tomorrow. Still, this rampant consumerism and its attendant 'machine aesthetic' had a dark underside from which the new household technologies and mechanized lifestyles appeared in a much less flattering light.

As numerous cultural historians have shown, since the 1800s American thinkers have exhibited a profound ambivalence toward technology. The idea that people would become prisoners to machines, sacrifice romance for scientific utopias, or trade the beauty of nature for the poisonous fruits of industrialization were central themes for novelists such as Mark Twain, Edward Bellamy, and Henry David Thoreau.[37] With increasing class antagonism and urban strife, this ambivalence grew stronger in the twentieth century, and it was exhibited both in intellectual circles and in popular culture venues. Such sentiments were not only symptomatic of large-scale political fears about industrialization and the urban milieu: they were also expressed in terms of the micropolitics of everyday life and the increasing mechanization of the middle-class household. Machines provided leisure, comfort, and the possibility of progress, but they also suggested an end to nature and the 'natural' order of things both at home and in civic life. By the 1930s, when the American industrial society seemed finally to have collapsed, people were caught between their faith that the wheels of technological progress would transport them out of misery and their bitter resentment toward the mechanized world that had let them down. As Susman has observed, at the same time that Americans were celebrating the technological future in the 'Land of Tomorrow' at the 1939 New York World's Fair, the

Gallup Poll revealed that most people neverthe-less believed technological development caused the unemployment of the Great Depression.[38]

The home magazines of the postwar era adopt-ed this ambivalence toward machines, scrutiniz-ing each step forward in household technology for its possible side effects. *House Beautiful*, the same magazine that tested its readers on their modernity quotients, just as often warned of the dismal future in store for the residents of the mechanized household. In 1951, the magazine asked if the 'houses we live in . . . accustom us . . . to feel more at home in surroundings where everything suggests only machines . . . that do as they are told and could never have known either joy or desire.' And if so, there is an overwhelm-ing threat that 'man is nothing but a machine . . . [who] can be "conditioned" to do and to want whatever his masters decide.'[39] The threat of the 'machine man', couched in the rhetoric of behav-iouralism, gave rise to a host of statements on the relationship between television and the family. Would the television set become the master and the family its willing subject? The adage of the day became, 'Don't let the television set domin-ate you!'

The idea of 'technology out of control' was con-stantly repeated as the language of horror and sci-ence fiction invaded discussions of everyday life. The television set was often likened to a monster that threatened to wreak havoc on the family. *Business Week* called television the 'New Cyclops', while *American Mercury* referred to it as the 'Giant in the Living Room', a kind of supernatural child who might turn against his master at any mo-ment. The essay proclaimed, 'The giant . . . has arrived. He was a mere pip-squeak yesterday, and didn't even exist the day before, but like a genie released from a magic bottle in *The Arabian Nights*, he now looms big as life over our heads.'[40] As such statements suggest, television posed the intimidating possibility that private citizens in their own homes might be rendered powerless in the face of a new and curious machine.

The threatening aspects of television technol-ogy might have been related to its use as a surveil-lance and reconnaissance weapon during World War II. To some degree, the public was aware of this because television's aircraft and military applications had been discussed in popular lit-erature since the 1930s, and after the war, men's magazines such as *Popular Science* and *Popular Mechanics* continued to present articles on tele-vision's wartime uses.[41] Such links between tele-vision and World War II sharply contradicted, however, the images of television and domes-tic bliss that were put forward after the war. It seems plausible that television's military applica-tions created doubts about its ability to enter the home. In fact, television's effect on culture was sometimes discussed in the context of warfare and atomic weaponry. Words such as 'invasion' and 'battle' were often employed in criticisms of the new medium, and a popular assumption was that television would cause cancer by transmit-ting waves of radiation. Later in 1961, when FCC Chairman Newton Minow chided the broadcast industry in his famous 'vast wasteland' speech, he too used the imagery of atomic warfare to sug-gest the powerful effects that television might have on the public. Minow claimed:

> Ours has been called the jet age, the atomic age, the space age. It is also, I submit, the television age. And just as history will decide whether the leaders of today's world employed the atom to destroy the world or rebuild it for mankind's benefit, so will history decide whether today's broadcasters employed their powerful voice to enrich the people or debase them.[42]

Although popular discourses suggested that television technology was out of control, they also provided soothing antidotes to this fear of machines. In 1953, the Zenith Corporation found a way to master the beast, promising consumers, 'We keep them [television sets] in a cage until they're right for you.' A large photograph at the top of the page showed a zoo cage that contained a Zenith scientist testing the inner components of the receiver. On the bottom of the page was the finely constructed Kensington console model, artfully integrated into a living room setting. As this advertisement so well suggests, the unfamil-iar technology could be domesticated by mak-ing the set into a piece of glamorous furniture.[43]

Stromberg-Carlson advertised its console model with 'hand painted Chinese legend on ivory, red, or ebony lacquer', while Sparton television claimed that it was hand crafted by 'trained cabinet makers who can turn a fine piece of wood into a masterpiece'.[44]

Also typically, the home magazines suggested that television be made to mesh with the room's overall decorative style. As *House Beautiful* told its readers in 1949, 'Remember that television can be easily tailored to match the character of your room.'[45] Perhaps a testimony to the contradictory character of postwar domesticity, the two most popular styles were Contemporary and Early American design.[46] The constant associations drawn between television and contemporary living, as well as its most basic box-like form, gave the television set a privileged place in the modern style. The home magazines often displayed model rooms composed of simple geometric shapes where the television set seemed to be a natural addition. Conversely, the new machine was often thought to clash with Early American decor. Out of step with the evocation of a colonial past, the set had to be carefully blended into the overall decorative scheme. In 1955, *American Home* placed a receiver on an Early American table that supposedly established a 'rapport between Colonial decor and television'. In that same year, Zenith advertised its Colonial cabinet by suggesting, 'Early American Charm and present day entertainment are a happy blending in this 21 inch console.'[47] More typically, however, when it came to colonial decor, the television set was shown to be an unrelenting eyesore. The home magazines often resorted to a kind of 'decorative repression' in which the set was placed in a remote corner of the Early American room or else entirely hidden from view.

In fact, this design strategy extended beyond the specific case of Colonial decor. More generally, the decorative attempt to master the machine meant the literal *camouflage* of the set. In 1951, *American Home* suggested that 'television needn't change a room' so long as it was made to 'retire at your command'. Among the suggestions were hinged panels 'faced with dummy book backs so that no one would suspect, when they are closed,

that this period room lives a double life with TV'. In 1953, *House Beautiful* placed a television set into a cocktail table from which it 'rises for use or disappears from sight by simply pushing a button'. Even the component parts had to be hidden from view. In 1953, *American Home* and *Popular Science* each displayed an indoor antenna fashioned to look like a sailboat.[48]

The attempts to render the television set invisible are especially interesting in the light of critical and popular memory accounts that argue that the television set was a privileged figure of conspicuous consumption and class status for postwar Americans. A basic assumption in the literature on television, this argument can be found in standard histories as well as theoretical accounts like Jean Baudrillard's *For a Critique of the Political Economy of the Sign*, in which he discusses television's value as a sign of class status in lower- and middle-class living rooms.[49] The early attempt to hide the receiver complicates such assumptions because it suggests the visual pleasure of interior decor was at odds with the display of wealth in the home. This popular fascination with hiding the receiver should remind us that the accumulation of commodities in the home might also have had attached to it a degree of shame. The kind of commodity exhibitionism that Thorstein Veblen first identified in 1899 could have been tempered by a contradictory impulse to inhibit the new commodity. Such 'commodity inhibitionism' can itself be explained by television's class status during the postwar period. From the point of view of upper-class standards, by the 1950s television might well have been less a status symbol than a sign of 'bad taste'. Although television bad been a rich person's toy in the 1930s and 1940s, its rapid dissemination to the middle and even lower classes after 1948 transformed it into a poor person's luxury. Since middle-class home magazines often reflected upper-class tastes, their decorative suggestions on hiding the television set might have been offered in the context of upper-class prejudices against television.

In addition to offering decorative solutions to the fear of machines, the magazines often associated television with nature. Literally placing the 'machine in the garden', popular magazines showed how plants and floral arrangements could transform an ordinary set into a thing of beauty.[50] Anthropomorphism was another popular strategy. In 1951, *House Beautiful* declared that 'television has become a member of the Family', and *American Home* explained ways to 'welcome' television 'into the family circle'.[51] More generally, the magazines described television as a 'newborn baby', a 'family friend', a 'nurse', a 'teacher', and a 'family pet' (a symbol that had previously proven its success when the Victor phonograph company adopted the image of a fox terrier for its corporate logo). As the domesticated animal, television obeyed its master and became a benevolent playmate for children as well as a faithful companion for adults. A 1952 advertisement for Emerson shows a typical scenario. The immanent pet-like quality of the television set emanates from the screen where a child and her poodle are pictured. Meanwhile, the advertising copy conjures up notions of master-servant relations, reminding consumers, again and again, that the set will be a 'dependable' machine.[52]

Even if anthropomorphism helped to relieve tensions about television technology, the media continued to express doubts. The idea of 'technology out of control' was turned around and reformulated. Now it was viewers who had lost control of themselves. Considering television's negative effects on the family, Bogart claimed in *The Age of Television* that 'the bulk of the disadvantages listed by the TV owners reflect their inability to control themselves once the set has been installed in the house'.[53] At least at the level of popular discourse, Bogart's suggestions are particularly accurate. The media attributed a wide range of human failures to television, failures that were typically linked to problems of family discord.

SEDUCING THE INNOCENT

More than any other group, children were singled out as the victims of the new pied piper. Indeed, even while critics praised television as a source of domestic unity and benevolent socialization, they also worried about its harmful effects, particularly its encouragement of passive and addictive behaviour. In 1951, *Better Homes and Gardens* complained that the medium's 'synthetic entertainment' produced a child who was 'glued to television'.[54] Worse still, the new addiction would reverse good habits of hygiene, nutrition, and decorum, causing physical, mental, and social disorders. A cartoon in a 1950 issue of *Ladies' Home Journal* suggests a typical scenario. The magazine showed a little girl slumped on an ottoman and suffering from a new disease called 'telebugeye'. According to the caption, the child was a 'pale, weak, stupid looking creature' who grew 'bugeyed' from sitting and watching television for too long.[55] Perhaps responding to these concerns, some advertisements presented children spectators in scenes that associated television with the 'higher arts', and some even implied that children would cultivate artistic talents by watching television. In 1951, General Electric showed a little girl, dressed in a tutu, imitating an onscreen ballerina, while Truetone showed a little boy learning to play the saxophone by watching a professional horn player on television.[56]

As the popular wisdom often suggested, the child's passive addiction to television might itself lead to the opposite effect of increased aggression. These discussions followed in the wake of critical and social scientific theories of the 1930s and 1940s that suggested that mass media injects ideas and behaviour into passive individuals. Adopting this 'hypodermic model' of media effects, the magazines circulated horror stories about youngsters who imitated television violence. In 1955, *Newsweek* reported on young Frank Stretch, an eleven-year-old from Ventura, California, who had become so entranced by a television western that 'with one shot of his trusty BB gun [he] demolished both villain and picture tube'.[57] Similar stories circulated about a nine-year-old who proposed killing his teacher with a box of poisoned chocolates, a six-year-old who asked his father for real bullets because his sister didn't die when he shot her with his gun, and a seven-year-old who put ground glass in the family's lamb stew—all, of course, after witnessing murders on television.[58] In reaction to the popular furor, as early as 1950 the Television Broadcasters' Association hired a public relations firm to write pro-television press

FIGURE 23.2 'Telebugeye' afflicts the young in this cartoon from a 1950 issue of *Ladies' Home Journal*

releases that suggested the more positive types of programming that television had to offer.[59]

Of course, the controversy surrounding television was simply a new skirmish in a much older battle to define what constituted appropriate children's entertainment. Such controversies can be traced back to the turn of the century when reformers, most notably Anthony Comstock, sought to regulate the content of dime novels.[60] Similar battles were waged when middle-class reformers of the early 1900s debated film's impact on American youth, and later these reform discourses were given scientific credence with the publication of the Payne Fund Studies in 1933. Broadcasting became the subject of public scrutiny in that same year when a group of mothers from Scarsdale, New York, began voicing their objections to radio programs that they considered

to be harmful to children. The public outcry was taken up in special interest magazines—especially the *Christian Century, Commonweal, New Republic, Outlook Nation,* and *Saturday Review.*[61] In all cases, childhood was conceived as a time of innocence, and the child a blank slate upon whom might be imprinted the evils of an overly aggressive and sexualized adult culture. In her work on *Peter Pan,* Jacqueline Rose has argued that the image of presexual childhood innocence has less to do with how children actually experience their youth than it does with how adults choose to conceptualize that experience. The figure of the innocent child serves to facilitate a nostalgic adult fantasy of a perfect past in which social, sexual, economic, and political complexities fade into the background.[62]

In the postwar years, the urge to preserve childhood innocence helped to justify and reinforce the nuclear family as a central institution and mode of social experience. Parents were given the delicate job of balancing the dividends and deficits of the ever-expanding consumer culture. On the one hand, they had to supply their youngsters with the fruits of a new commodity society—suburban homes, wondrous toys, new technologies, glamorous vacations, and so forth. Early schooling in the good life would ensure that children continued on a life trajectory of social mobility based on the acquisition of objects. On the other hand, parents had to protect children from the more insidious aspects of the consumer wonderland, making sure that they internalized the ability to tell the difference between authentic culture and synthetic commercial pleasures. According to Helen Muir, editor of the *Miami Herald*'s children's books section, there was a difference between the 'real needs and desires of children' and 'the superimposed synthetic so-called needs which are not needs but cravings'.[63] In this context, mass media provided parents with a particularly apt target. More than 20 years before Marie Winn called television 'the plug-in drug', Muir and others likened mass media to marijuana and other narcotics that offered children a momentary high rather than the eternal pleasures of real art.

The most vocal critic was psychiatrist Fredric Wertham, whose *Seduction of the Innocent* (1953) became the cornerstone of the 1950s campaign against comic books. For Wertham, the tabula rasa conception of the child was paramount; the visual immediacy of comics, he argued, left children vulnerable to their unsavoury content. Although most social scientists and psychologists had a more nuanced approach to mass media than Wertham had, his ideas were popularized in the press and he even served as an expert witness in Estes Kefauver's 1954 Senate Subcommittee hearings on juvenile delinquency.[64] The war that Wertham waged against mass culture struck a chord with the more general fears about juvenile delinquency at the time, and parents were given armour in what popular critics increasingly defined as a battle to protect the young from the onslaught of a hypercommercialized children's culture.[65]

Indeed, discussions about children and mass culture typically invoked military imagery. One woman, who had read Wertham's 1948 article in the *Saturday Review*, wrote a letter that explained how her children had become 'drugged' by mass media: 'We consider this situation to be as serious as an invasion of the enemy in war time, with as far-reaching consequences as the atom bomb.' One year later, anthropologist Margaret Mead expressed similar fears to her colleagues, worrying about children who grew up in a world where 'radio and television and comics and the threat of the atomic bomb are every day realities'.[66] If in the late 1940s television was seen as just one part of the threatening media environment, over the course of the 1950s it would emerge as a more central problem.

As Ellen Wartella and Sharon Mazzarella have observed, early social scientific studies suggested that children weren't simply using television in place of other media; instead, television was colonizing children's leisure time more than other mass cultural forms had ever done.[67] Social scientists found this 'reorganization hypothesis' to be particularly important because it meant that television was changing the nature of children's lives, taking them away from school work, household duties, family conversations, and creative play. This hypothesis was also at the core of early studies conducted by school boards around the country, which showed that television was

reducing the amount of time children spent on homework. Researchers and reformers were similarly concerned with television's effects on children's moral and physical welfare. As early as 1949, PTA members voted at their national convention to keep an eye on 'unwholesome television programs'.[68] Religious organizations also tried to monitor television's unsavoury content. In 1950, the National Council of Catholic Women counted violent acts in television programs while Detroit's Common Council (which was composed of religious groups and city officials) drew up a three-prong plan to make the new medium safe for children and teenagers. By 1951, the National Council of Catholic Men had joined the fray, considering a system of program ratings, while Catholic teachers were urging the formation of a Legion of Decency at their annual conference in Washington.[69] Even Wertham, who devoted most of his energy to comic books, included in his book a final chapter on television (appropriately titled 'Homicide at Home'), which warned parents that programs such as *Captain Video* and *Superman* would corrupt the potential educational value of the new medium and turn children into violent, sexually 'perverse' adults.

Such concerns were given official credence as senators, congressmen, and Federal Communications Commission (FCC) commissioners considered the problem. Commissioner Frieda Hennock championed educational television, which she believed would better serve children's interests. Thomas J. Lane, representative from Massachusetts, urged Congress to establish government censorship of television programs, claiming that teachers and clergymen 'have been fighting a losing battle against the excess of this one-way form of communication', and praising parents who were demanding that the 'juvenile delinquent called television' be cleaned up 'before it ruins itself and debases everybody with whom it has contact'.[70] Largely in response to such concerns, the National Association of Radio and Television Broadcasters (NARTB) (following the lead of the film industry and its own experience with radio) staved off watchdog groups and government officials by passing an industry-wide censorship code for television in March 1952, a code that included a whole section on television and children.[71] But the debate persisted and even grew more heated. In that same year, Ezekiel Gathings, representative from Arkansas, spearheaded a House investigation of radio and television programs, which presented studies demonstrating television's negative influence on youth as well as testimony from citizen groups concerned with television's effects on children.[72] By 1954, Estes Kefauver's Senate Subcommittee hearings on juvenile delinquency were investigating television's relationship to the perceived increase in youth crimes, focusing particularly on the 'ideas that spring into the living room for the entertainment of the youth of America, which have to do with crime and with horror, sadism, and sex'.[73] At the beginning of the next decade, Newton Minow incorporated such concerns into his 'vast wasteland' campaign, claiming that children's television was 'just as tasteless, just as nourishing as dishwater'.[74]

While scholarship has centred around the question of how television affects children, little has been said about the way adults have been taught to limit these effects. What is particularly interesting here is the degree to which discussions about television and children engaged questions concerning parental authority. Summarizing parents' attitudes toward television, Bogart claimed, 'There is a feeling, never stated in so many words, that the set has a power of its own to control the destinies and viewing habits of the audience, and that what it "does" to parents and children alike is somehow beyond the bounds of any individual set-owner's power of control.'[75] In this context, popular media offered solace by showing parents how they could reclaim power in their own homes—if not over the medium, then at least over their children. Television opened up a whole array of disciplinary measures that parents might exert over their youngsters.

Indeed, the bulk of discussions about children and television were offered in the context of mastery. If the machine could control the child, then so could the parent. Here, the language of common sense provided some reassurance by reminding parents that it was they, after all, who were in command. As the *New York Times'* television critic Jack Gould wrote in 1949, 'It takes

a human hand to turn on a television set.'[76] But for parents who needed a bit more than just the soothing words of a popular sage, the media ushered in specialists from a wide range of fields; child psychologists, educators, psychiatrists, and broadcasters all recommended ways to keep the problem child in line.

One popular form of advice revolved around program standards. Rather than allowing children to watch violent westerns such as *The Lone Ranger* and escapist science-fiction serials such as *Captain Video*, parents were told to establish a canon of wholesome programs. *Better Homes and Gardens'* readership survey indicated that some parents had already adopted this method of control:

> Forty percent of all the parents answering do not approve of some of the programs their children would like to see—chiefly crime, violent mystery or horror, western, and 'emotional' programs . . . .
>
> About one-fourth of the parents insist on their children viewing special events on TV. In this category they mention parades, children's shows, educational programs, great artists, and theater productions.[77]

In many ways this canon recalled Victorian notions of ideal family recreation. Overly exciting stimuli threatened to corrupt the child, while educational and morally uplifting programs were socially sanctioned. In response to these concerns, magazines such as *Reader's Digest, Saturday Review*, and *Parents* gave their seal of approval to what they deemed as culturally enriching programs (*Ding Dong School, Romper Room, Shari Lewis, Captain Kangaroo*, and even *Huckleberry Hound*). In all cases, critical judgments were based on adult standards. Indeed, this hierarchy of television programs is symptomatic of the more general efforts to establish an economy of pleasure for children spectators that suited adult concepts about the meaning of childhood.

Moreover, the preoccupation with critical hierarchies reflected a class bias. Summarizing numerous social scientific studies, Bogart claimed that it was mainly the middle class who feared television's influence on children and that while 'people of higher social position, income and education are more critical of existing fare in radio, television and the movies . . . those at the lower end of the social scale are more ready to accept what is available.' Even if he believed that discriminating taste was a function of class difference, Bogart still internalized the elitist preoccupation with canon formation, lending professional credence to the idea that adults should restrict their children's viewing to what they deemed 'respectable' culture. He suggested:

If television cannot really be blamed for turning children into criminals or neurotics, this does not imply that it is a wholly healthful influence on the growing child. A much more serious charge is that television, in the worst aspects of its content, helps to perpetuate moral, cultural and social values which are not in accord with the highest ideals of an enlightened democracy The cowboy film, the detective thriller and the soap opera, so often identified by critics as the epitome of American mass culture, probably do not represent the heritage which Americans at large want to transmit to posterity.[78]

Thus, while Bogart noted that working-class parents did not find a need to discriminate between programs, and that the formation of critical standards was mainly a middle-class pursuit, he nevertheless decided that television programs would not please the value systems of 'Americans at large'. Here as elsewhere, the notion of an enlightened democracy served to justify the hegemony of bourgeois tastes and the imparting of those tastes onto children of all classes.

Meanwhile, for their part, children often seemed to have different ideas. As numerous surveys indicated, youngsters often preferred the programs that parents found unwholesome, especially science-fiction serials and westerns. Surveys also indicated that children often liked to watch programs aimed at adults and that 'parents were often reluctant to admit that their children watched adult shows regularly'.[79] Milton Berle's *Texaco Star Theater* (which was famous for its inclusion of 'off-colour' cabaret humour) became so popular with children that Berle adopted the persona of Uncle Miltie, pandering to parents by telling his juvenile audience to obey their elders and go straight to bed when the program ended.[80] Other programs, however, were unable to bridge the generation gap. When, for example, CBS aired the mystery anthology *Suspense*, numerous affiliates across the country received letters from concerned parents who wanted the program taken off the air. Attempting to please its adult constituency, one Oklahoma station was caught in the cross fire between parents and children. When the station announced it would not air 'horror story' programs before the bedtime hour of 9:00 p.m., it received a letter with the words 'We protest!' signed by 22 children.[81]

Perhaps because adult aesthetic hierarchies did not always match children's tastes, popular magazines also concentrated on more forceful methods of ensuring children's proper use of televisions.[82] Drawing on cognitive and behaviouralist theories of childhood that had been popular since the 1920s, and mixing these with the liberal 'hands off' approach of Dr. Spock, the experts recommended ways for parents to instill healthy viewing habits in their children. In 1950, *Better Homes and Gardens* wrote, 'Because he had seen the results of . . . viewing—facial tics, overstimulation, neglect of practicing, outdoor play . . . homework—Van R. Brokhane, who produces education FM programs for New York City schools, decided to establish a system of control.' Brokhane's system was typical; it took the form of a careful management of time and space: 'The Brokhanes put their receiver in the downstairs playroom where it could not entice their teenage daughter away from her homework . . . then they outlined a schedule—their daughter could watch TV before dinner, but not afterward, on school nights.'[83] Faced with the bureaucratized institutions of a mass culture that adults found difficult to change, parents could nevertheless exercise their power by disciplining children through a careful system of reward and punishment. Adopting the language of B.F. Skinner's behaviouralist techniques, magazines discussed ways to control children's viewing through positive reinforcement. In 1955, *Better Homes and Gardens* reported, 'After performing the routine of dressing, tidying up his room . . . Steve knows he can . . . joy of joys—watch his favorite morning TV show. His attitude is now so good he has even volunteered . . . to set the table for breakfast and help his little sister dress.'[84] Thus, discipline was conceived not only in the negative sense, but also in the positive 'prosocial' terms suggested by behaviouralist psychology.

Expert advice also borrowed principles from psychoanalysis to engage in a kind of therapeutic interrogation of family dynamics. Here the television was not so much the cause of aberrant deeds as it was a symptom of deeply rooted problems in the home. As *Better Homes and Gardens* advised in 1950, 'If your boy or girl throws a tantrum when you call him away from the set, don't blame television. Tantrums are a sign that tension already exists in a family.'[85] In 1951, the magazine called in psychologist Ralph H. Ojemann to verify the claim: 'The child who seems permanently enchanted by an electric gadget in the parlor generally gets that way because he has nothing else that challenges him . . . "It's unfortunate but true," Doctor Ojemann says, "that we're just not too good at building the best environments that the human personality needs for growth."'[86] For Ojemann the 'best environment' was a household that provided stimulating activities beyond television entertainment. Like other experts of the period, he turned the problem of disciplining children spectators into a larger problem of cultivating the home for proper socialization.

The paradox of such expert advice on television and children was that the experts—rather than the parents—took on the authoritative role. To borrow Jacques Donzelot's phrase, this expert advice amounted to a 'policing of families' by public institutions.[87] By the turn of the century, American doctors, clergymen, educators, industrialists, architects, and women's groups had all claimed a stake in the management of domestic affairs. One of the central conduits for this was the new mass-circulation women's magazines that functioned in part as a site for reform discourses on the family. During the Progressive era and especially in the 1920s, the public control of domestic life was regularized and refined as outside agencies began to 'administer' private

life. In the 1920s, Secretary of Commerce Herbert Hoover became a housing crusader. His policies encouraged a proliferation of government agencies and civic centres that disseminated advice on subjects ranging from house building to child-rearing. Hoover, in conjunction with private industry and civic groups, thought that outside agencies would help stabilize social and economic turmoil by ensuring a proper home life for all Americans. Women's magazines were closely linked to Hoover's campaigns, most obviously when Mrs. William Brown Meloney, editor of the *Delineator*, asked him to serve as President of Better Homes in America, a voluntary organization that began in 1922 and had 7279 branches across the nation by 1930. More generally, women's magazines were inundated with advice from professionals and industrialists who saw themselves as the custodians of everyday life.[88]

In the postwar period, television became an ideal vehicle through which to regulate family life. As in the case of Dr. Ojemann's advice, watching television was typically figured as a sign of a larger family problem that needed to be studied and controlled by outside authorities.[89] In this sense, it served to support the social regulation of family life. It made parents more dependent upon knowledge produced by public institutions and thus placed parents in a weakened position.[90]

Perhaps because of their admonishing tones, experts were sometimes unpopular with their audiences. In 1951, an author in *House Beautiful* complained about the loss of parental dominion, claiming:

It seems that raising a child correctly these days is infinitely more difficult than it was 30 years ago when no one ever heard of Drs. Kinsey and Gessell, and a man named Freud was discussed only in women's beauty parlors . . . .

20 or 30 years ago when there weren't so many authorities on everything in America, the papas and mamas of the nation had a whole lot easier going with Junior than we have today with the authorities.

The author connected his loss of parental power directly to television, recalling the time when his little boy began to strike the television set with a large stick. Unable to decide for himself how to punish his son, he opted for the lenient approach suggested by the expert, Dr. Spock. Unfortunately, he recounted, 'the next day Derek rammed his shovel through the TV screen [and] the set promptly blew up.'[91]

In part, anxieties about parental control had to do with the fact that television was heavily promoted to families with children. During the 1950s, manufacturers and retailers discovered that children were a lucrative consumer market for the sale of household commodities. An editor of *Home Furnishings* (the furniture retailer's trade journal) claimed, 'The younger generation from one to twenty influences the entire home furnishings industry.'[92] As one of the newest household items, television was quickly recognized for its potential appeal to young consumers. Numerous surveys indicated that families with children tended to buy television more than childless couples did. Television manufacturers quickly assimilated the new findings into their sales techniques. As early as 1948, the industry trade journal *Advertising and Selling* reported that the manager of public relations and advertising at the manufacturing company, Stromberg-Carlson, 'quoted a survey . . . indicating that children not only exert a tremendous amount of influence in the selection and purchase of television receivers but that they are, in fact, television's most enthusiastic audience.'[93] Basing their advertisements on such surveys, manufacturers and retailers formulated strategies by which to pull parents' purse strings—and heart strings as well. In 1950, the American Television Dealers and Manufacturers ran nationwide newspaper advertisements that played on parental guilt. The first ad in the series had a headline that read, 'Your daughter won't ever tell you the humiliation she's felt in begging those precious hours of television from a neighbor.' Forlorn children were pictured on top of the layout, and parents were shown how television could raise their youngsters' spirits. This particular case is especially interesting because it shows that there are indeed limits to which even advertisers can go before a certain degree of sales resistance takes place. Outraged by the advertisement,

parents, educators, and clergymen complained to their newspapers about its manipulative tone. In addition, the Family Service Association of America called it a 'cruel pressure to apply against millions of parents' who could not afford television sets.[94] In the midst of this controversy, the American Television Dealers and Manufacturers discontinued the ad campaign. Although this action might have temporarily quelled the more overt fears of adult groups, the popular media of the period continued to raise doubts that often surfaced in hyperbolic predictions of the end of patriarchal family life.

THE TROUBLE WITH FATHERS

Just as advertisements bestowed a new kind of power upon child consumers, television seemed to disrupt conventional power dynamics between child and adult. Popular media complained that the television image had usurped the authority previously held by parents. As television critic John Crosby claimed, 'You tell little Oscar to trot off to bed, and you will probably find yourself embroiled in argument. But if Milton Berle tells him to go to bed, off he goes.'[95] Here as elsewhere, television particularly threatened to depose the father. Television was depicted as the new patriarch, a threatening machine that had robbed men of their dominion in the home.

Television critics (most of whom were male) lashed out at the appearance of bumbling fathers on the new family sitcoms. In 1953, *TV Guide* asked, 'What ever happened to men? . . . . Once upon a time (B. TV) a girl thought of her boyfriend or husband as her Prince Charming. Now having watched the antics of Ozzie Nelson and Chester A. Riley, she thinks of her man, and any other man, as a Prime Idiot.' One year later, a review in *Time* claimed, 'In television's stable of 35 home-life comedies, it is a rare show that treats Father as anything more than the mouse of the house—a bumbling, well-meaning idiot who is putty in the hands of his wife and family.'[96]

The henpecked male was, of course, a stock character in previous forms of popular entertainment such as twentieth-century vaudeville and film.[97] The kind of criticism directed at television and its bumbling fathers likewise had its roots in a well-established tradition of mass-culture criticism based on categories of sexual difference. Culture critics have often expressed their disdain for mass media in language that evokes contempt for those qualities that patriarchal societies ascribe to femininity. Thus, mass amusements are typically thought to encourage passivity, and they have frequently been represented in terms of penetration, consumption, and escape. As Andreas Huyssen has argued, this analogy between women and mass culture has, since the nineteenth century, served to valorize the dichotomy between 'low' and 'high' art (or modernism). Mass culture, Huyssen claims, 'is somehow associated with woman while real authentic culture remains the prerogative of men.'[98]

The case of broadcasting is especially interesting in this regard because the threat of feminization was particularly aimed at men. Broadcasting quite literally was shown to disrupt the normative structures of patriarchal (high) culture and to turn 'real men' into passive homebodies. The 'feminizing' aspects of broadcast technology were a central concern during radio's installation in the twenties. Radio hams of the early 1910s were popularized in the press and in fiction as virile heroes who saved damsels in distress with the aid of wireless technology (a popular example were the 'Radio Boys', Bob and Joe, who used wireless to track down criminals and save the innocent).[99] But as Catherine Covert has claimed, once radio became a domestic medium, men were no longer represented as active agents. Now they were shown to sit passively, listening to a one-way communication system.[100]

In the early 1940s, the connection between radio technology and emasculation came to a dramatic pitch when Philip Wylie wrote his bitter attack on American women, *Generation of Vipers*. In this widely read book, Wylie maintained that American society was suffering from an ailment which he called 'momism'. American women, according to Wylie, had become overbearing, domineering mothers who turned their sons and husbands into weak-kneed fools. The book was replete with imagery of apocalypse through technology, imagery which Wylie tied to the figure of the woman. As he saw it, an unholy alliance between women and big business had turned the world into an industrial nightmare. Corporations like Alcoa and General Electric had created a new female 'sloth' by supplying the housewife with machines that 'deprived her of her social usefulness'. Meanwhile, claimed Wylie, women had become 'Cinderellas'—greedy consumers who 'raped the men, not sexually, but morally'.[101]

In his most bitter chapter, entitled 'Common Women', Wylie argued that women had somehow gained control of the airwaves. Women, he suggested, made radio listening into a passive activity that threatened manhood and, in fact, civilization. Wylie wrote, 'The radio is mom's final tool, for it stamps everyone who listens to it with the matriarchal brand—its superstitions, prejudices, devotional rules, taboos, musts, and all other qualifications needful to its maintenance. Just as Goebbels has revealed what can be done with such a mass-stamping of the public psyche in his nation, so our land is a living representation of the same fact worked out in matriarchal sentimentality, goo, slop, hidden cruelty, and the foreshadow of national death.'[102] In the 1955 annotated edition, Wylie updated these fears, claiming 'that television would soon take the place of radio and turn men into female-dominated dupes. Women, he wrote, 'will not rest until every electronic moment has been bought to sell suds and every bought program censored to the last decibel and syllable according to her self-adulation—along with that (to the degree the mom-indoctrinated pops are permitted access to the dials) of her de-sexed, de-souled, de-cerebrated mate.'[103]

The mixture of misogyny and 'telephobia' that ran through this passage is clearly hyperbolic; still, the basic idea was repeated in more sober representations of everyday life during the postwar period. Indeed, the paranoid connections that Wylie drew between corporate technocracies, women, and broadcasting continued to be drawn throughout the 1950s as large bureaucracies increasingly controlled the lives of middle-class men. Television was often shown to rob men of their powers and transform them into passive victims of a force they could not control.

FIGURE 23.3 Dad interrupts the family during a TV western in this 1954 episode of *Fireside Theatre*

A popular theme in the fifties was television's usurpation of the father's parental authority. In 1954, *Fireside Theatre*, a filmed anthology drama, presented this problem in an episode entitled 'The Grass is Greener'. Based on the simple life of a farm family, the program begins with the purchase of a television set, a purchase that the father, Bruce, adamantly opposes. Going against Bruce's wishes, his wife, Irene, makes use of the local retailer's credit plan and has a television set installed in her home. When Bruce returns home for the evening, he finds himself oddly displaced by the new centre of interest. Upon entering the kitchen door, he hears music and gun shots emanating from the den. Curious about the source of the sound, he enters the room where he sees Irene and the children watching a television western. Standing in the den doorway, he is literally off-centre in the frame, outside the family group clustered around the television set. When he attempts to get his family's attention, Bruce's status as outsider is further suggested. His son hushes him with a dismissive 'Shh', after which the family resumes its fascination with the television program. Bruce then motions to Irene who finally—with a look of condescension—exits the room to join her husband in the kitchen where the couple argue over the set's installation. In her attempt to convince Bruce to keep the set, Irene suggests that the children and even she herself will stray from the family home if he refuses to allow them the pleasure of watching TV. Television thus threatens to undermine the masculine position of power in the home to the extent that the father is disenfranchised from his family, whose gaze is fastened onto an alternate, and more seductive, authority.

The episode goes on to figure this problem of masculinity through an unflattering representation of the male spectator. Bruce first reluctantly agrees to keep the television set on a 30-day trial basis—so long as it remains in the children's room. But he too soon falls prey to the TV siren; in the next scene we see him alone in his den, slumped in an easy chair, half asleep, watching a western.[104] After Irene discovers him, he appears to be ashamed because he is caught in the act he himself claimed unworthy. Thus, as the narrative logic would have it, the father succumbs to television, and in so doing his power in the home is undermined. Indeed, the act of viewing television is itself shown to be unmanly.

The episode further suggests a waning of masculinity by suggesting nostalgia for the virile heroes of the Hollywood cinema. When a serviceman installs the television set we learn that Bruce used to be a screen idol in film westerns. The serviceman looks with awe at the studio portraits of Bruce that are pasted on the den wall. As Irene explains to the serviceman, Bruce chose to leave the glamour of Hollywood behind for the simple life on their family farm. While Irene boasts about wholesome virtues, the image track shows the serviceman/fan who appears to be lost in a trance of spectator identification as he ogles the photographs on the den wall. This excess of male identification, this nostalgic admiration for the ex-movie star, reminds us of Bruce's decreased authority in the present. As a farmer, Bruce is no longer an idol of spectator admiration; his masculine identity is now at odds with his former pin-up photos. As this story suggests, the images of masculine prowess so much a part of the classical Hollywood era (especially in genres like the western) are now the remnants of a forgotten culture. In place of these heroes, television gives us pragmatic family types—the bumbling but well meaning fathers like Ozzie Nelson and Jim Anderson.[105] Indeed, as audiences must have understood at the time, the larger-than-life cowboy idols of the silver screen were vanishing from the local theatre and reappearing in a debased form on 12-inch television screens. The new western heroes were not the John Waynes of classical A-movie westerns; rather, they were comic book, B-movie heroes who appealed almost entirely to a male juvenile audience—indeed, Bruce's son is shown to be an avid fan of TV westerns.

Fireside Theatre's implicit comparison between masculine ideals in Hollywood and television was more explicitly stated by popular critics who compared television's family men with Hollywood's virile heroes. In a 1953 review of *Bonino*, a short-lived situation comedy starring Ezio Pima, the *Saturday Review* claimed:

Philip Morris doesn't know it, but it's sponsoring a crime show . . . . The crime is 'Bonino', starring Ezio Pima, and the victim is an illusion that is slowly being murdered—a beautiful, vital, and universal illusion, yours and mine. We met it first in 'South Pacific' on that enchanted evening when Pima walked into Mary Martin's life. He was romantic, he was cosmopolitan, he was virile . . . .

And now what have they done to our dream on 'Bonino'? They have emasculated, eviscerated, and domesticated it; Jurgen has come home to his beer and his bedroom slippers. No longer the Phoenix lover, our Pinza is merely a father . . . . Where once was assurance and the comforting touch of power, now there is only the stereotype of *pater americanus*, well-meaning, tenderly stupid, and utterly inadequate in every department of his life except his profession. Weep for Adonis![106]

As the review so pointedly suggested, the Golden Age of masculinity was headed for a fall, and importantly, television itself seemed unable to resist commenting on the situation.

The Adventures of Ozzie and Harriet, whose corny, wishy-washy, do-nothing 'Pop' was perhaps the prime abuser of the masculine ideal, reflected on the relationship between television and male power in a 1953 episode, 'An Evening With Hamlet', which tied the theme of technological emasculation to a more general atrophy of patriarchal culture. The episode opens at the breakfast table as the young son Ricky sadly announces that the television set is broken. As was the case in many postwar households, the father in this home is unable to fix the complicated technology himself. Instead, the family is dependent upon a new cultural hero, the TV repairman, whose schedule is so tight that the Nelsons have to wait patiently for his arrival. Ozzie uses this occasion to assert his parental authority by finding family amusements that compete with television for the boys' attention. His idea of family fun recalls Victorian modes of recreation—specifically, dramatic reading—but his sons are less than pleased. As Ricky says in a subsequent scene, 'Hey Mom, that television man didn't get here yet . . . now we're stuck with that darn Shakespeare.'

This episode goes on to highlight the competition for cultural authority between fathers and television by objectifying the problem in the form of two supporting characters. While the Nelsons recite *Hamlet*, two men visit the family home. The first is a wandering bard who mysteriously appears at the Nelson door and joins the family recital. The bard, who looks like he is part of an Elizabethan theatre troupe, evokes associations of high art and cultural refinement. The second visitor, a television repairman, represents the new electronic mass-produced culture. He is presented as an unrefined blue-collar worker who is good with machines but otherwise inept. A conversation between Ozzie and the repairman succinctly suggests the point:

> REPAIRMAN: Oh a play, huh, I used to be interested in dramatics myself.
> OZZIE: Oh, an actor!
> REPAIRMAN: No, a wrestler.

As this scene so clearly demonstrates, television not only competes with the father at home, but also disturbs the central values of patriarchal culture by replacing the old authorities with a new and degraded art form.

A HOUSE DIVIDED

In a home where patriarchal authority was undermined, television threatened to drive a wedge between family members. Social scientists argued that even while families might be brought together around the set, this spatial proximity did not necessarily translate into better family relations. As Eleanor MacCoby observed in her study of families in Cambridge, Massachusetts, 'There is very little interaction among family members when they watch TV together, and the amount of time family members spend together exclusive of TV is reduced, so it is doubtful whether TV brings the family together in any psychological sense.'[107]

Popular periodicals presented exaggerated versions of family division, often suggesting that television would send family members into separate worlds of pleasure and thus sever family ties, particularly at the dinner table. In 1950, Jack Gould wrote, 'Mealtime is an event out of the ordinary for the television parent; for the child it may just be out.' In that same year a cartoon in *Better Homes and Gardens* showed parents seated at the dining room table while their children sat in the living room, glued to the television set. Speaking from the point of view of the exasperated mother, the caption read, 'All right that does it! Harry, call up the television store and tell them to send a truck right over!' In 1953, *TV Guide* suggested a humorous solution to the problem in a cartoon that showed a family seated around a dining room table with a large television set built into the middle of it. The caption read, 'Your kids won't have to leave the table to watch their favorite programs if you have the Diney model.'[108]

Even more alarming than the mealtime problem, television threatened to cause disputes between siblings and between mates. As *House Beautiful* suggested in 1950, 'Your wife wants to see *Philco Playhouse* and you don't. So you look too, or are driven from the room.'[109] Similarly in 1954, *Popular Science* asked, 'Is it hard to balance your checkbook or read while the kids are watching TV? Ever want to see the fights when your wife is chatting with a friend?'[110] Perhaps the most frustrated of all was the well-known critic and radio personality Goodman Ace, who wrote a satiric essay on the subject in 1953, 'A Man's TV Set Is His Castle'. The irony of this title was quickly apparent as Ace drew a rather unromantic picture of his life with television:

> The big television networks, fighting as they do for the elusive high rating, are little concerned with the crumbling of a man's home. Programs are indiscriminately placed in direct opposition one to the other, regardless of domestic consequence.
>
> That she [his wife] likes Ann Sothern and I much prefer Wally Cox opposite Miss Sothern is of little import to the executive vice presidents in charge of programming . . . . Perry Como sings for our supper while I wonder where John Cameron Swayze is hopscotching for headlines on the competitive network. When I should

be at ringside for a Wednesday night fight, I'm watching 'This Is Your Life'.

The critic concluded with a tip for the prospective TV consumer: 'Don't be misled by advertisements announcing the large 24-inch screens. Buy two 12-inch screens. And don't think of it as losing your eyesight but rather as gaining a wife.'[111]

Harmony gave way to a system of differences in which domestic space and family members in domestic space were divided along sexual and social lines. The ideal of family togetherness was achieved through the seemingly contradictory principle of separation; private rooms devoted to individual family members ensured peaceful relationships among residents. Thus, the social division of space was not simply the inverse of family unity; rather, it was a point on a continuum that stressed ideals of domestic cohesion. Even the family room itself was conceived in these terms. In fact, when coining the phrase, Nelson and Wright claimed, 'By frankly developing a room which is "entirely public" . . . privacy is made possible. Because there's an "extra room", the other living space can really be enjoyed in peace and quiet.'[112]

This ideology of divided space was based on Victorian aesthetics of housing design and corresponding social distinctions entailed by family life. The middle-class homes of Victorian America embodied the conflicting urge for family unity and division within their architectural layout. Since the homes were often quite spacious, it was possible to have rooms devoted to intimate family gatherings (such as the back parlour), social occasions (such as the front parlour), as well as rooms wholly given over to separate family members. By the 1950s, the typical four-and-one-half room dwellings of middle-class suburbia were clearly not large enough to support entirely the Victorian ideals of sociospatial hierarchies. Still, popular home manuals of the postwar period placed a premium on keeping these spatial distinctions in order, and they presented their readers with a model of space derived in part from the Victorian experience.

The act of watching television came to be a central concern in the discourse on divided spaces as

the magazines showed readers pictures of rambling homes with special rooms designed exclusively for watching television. Sets were placed in children's playrooms or bedrooms, away from the central spaces of the home. In 1951, *House Beautiful* had even more elaborate plans. A fun room built adjacent to the home and equipped with television gave a teenage daughter a 'place for her friends'. For the parents it meant 'peace of mind because teenagers are away from [the] house but still at home'.[113]

It seems likely that most readers in their cramped suburban homes did not follow these suggestions. A 1954 national survey showed that 85 per cent of the respondents kept their sets in the living room, so that the space for TV was the central, common living area in the home.[114] Perhaps recognizing the practical realities of their readers, the magazines also suggested ways to maintain the aesthetics of divided spaces in the small home. While it might not have been possible to have a room of one's own for television viewing, there were alternate methods by which to approximate the ideal. Rooms could be designed in such a way so that they functioned both as viewing areas and as centres for other activities. In this sense, television fit into a more general functionalist discourse in which household spaces were supposed to be made 'multi-purposeful'. In 1951, *Better Homes and Gardens* spoke of a 'recreation area of the living room' that was 'put to good use as the small fry enjoy a television show'.[115] At other times such areas were referred to specifically as 'television areas'. While in many cases the television area was marked off by furniture arrangements or architectural structures such as alcoves, at other times the sign of division was concretized in an object form—the room divider.

In some cases the television receiver was actually built into the room divider so that television literally became a divisive object in the home. In 1953, for example, *Better Homes and Gardens* displayed a 'living-dining area divider' that was placed behind a sofa. Extending beyond the sofa, its right end housed a television set. As the illustration showed, this TV/room divider created a private viewing area for children.[116] In

FIGURE 23.4 In this 1955 advertisement, General Electric promises family harmony through separation.

1955, one room-divider company saw the promotional logic in this scenario, showing mothers how Modernfold Doors would keep children spectators at a safe distance. The ad depicts a mother sitting at one end of a room, while her child and television set are separated off by the folding wall. Suggesting itself as an object of dispute, the television set works to support the call for the room divider—here stated as 'that tiresome game of "Who gets the living room"'. Moreover, since room dividers like this one were typically collapsible, they were the perfect negotiation between ideals of unity and division. They allowed parents to be apart from their children, but the 'fold-back' walls also provided easy access to family togetherness.[117]

The swivelling television was another popular way to mediate ideals of unity and division. In

1953, *Ladies' Home Journal* described how John and Lucille Bradford solved the viewing problem in their home by placing a large console set on a rotating platform that was hinged to the doorway separating the living room from the play porch. Lucille told the magazine, 'The beauty of this idea . . . is that the whole family can watch programs together in the living room, or the children can watch their own special cowboy programs from the play porch without interfering with grownups' conversation.'[118]

This sociosexual division of space was also presented in advertisements for television sets. In 1955, General Electric showed how its portable television set could mediate family tensions. On the top of the page a cartoon depicts a family besieged by television as Mother frantically attempts to vacuum up the mess created by her young son who, sitting on his tricycle, changes the channel on the television console. Father, sitting on an easy chair in front of the set, is so perturbed by the goings-on that his pipe flies out of his mouth. The solution to this problem is provided further down on the page where two photographs are juxtaposed. The photograph on the right side of the page depicts Mother and Daughter in the kitchen where they watch a cooking program on a portable tv while the photograph on the left side of the page shows Father watching football on the living room console. This 'split-screen' layout was particularly suited to GE's sales message, the purchase of a second television set. The copy reads: 'When Dad wants to watch the game . . . Mom and Sis, the cooking show . . . there's too much traffic for one TV to handle.'[119]

The depiction of divided families wasn't simply a clever marketing strategy; rather, it was a well-entrenched pictorial convention. Indeed, by 1952, advertisements in the home magazines increasingly depicted family members enjoying television alone or else in subgroups. At least in the case of these ads, it appears that the cultural meanings that were circulated about television changed somewhat over the course of the early years of installation. While television was primarily shown to be an integrating activity in the first few years of diffusion, in the 1950s it came to be equally (or perhaps even more) associated with social differences and segregation among family members.[120]

It is, however, important to remember that the contradiction between family unity and division was just that—a contradiction, a site of ideological tension, and not just a clear-cut set of opposing choices. In this light, we might understand a number of advertisements that attempted to negotiate such tensions by evoking ideas of unity and division at the same time. These ads pictured family members watching television in private, but the image on the television screen contained a kind of surrogate family. A 1953 ad for Sentinel TV shows a husband and wife gently embracing as they watch their brand new television set on Christmas Eve. The pleasure entailed by watching television is associated more with the couple's romantic life than with their parental duties. However, the televised image contains two children, apparently singing Christmas carols. Thus, the advertisement shows that parents can enjoy a romantic night of television apart from their own children. But it still sustains the central importance of the family scene because it literally represents the absent children by making them into an image on the screen. Moreover, the advertisement attaches a certain amount of guilt to the couple's intimate night of television, their use of television as a medium for romantic rather than familial enjoyment. The idea of guilty pleasure is suggested by the inclusion of two 'real' children who appear to be voyeurs, clandestinely looking onto the scene of their parents' pleasure. Dressed in pyjamas, the youngsters peek out from a corner of the room, apparently sneaking out of bed to take a look at the new television set, while the grownups remain unaware of their presence.[121]

The tensions between opposing ideals of unity and division were also expressed in material form. Manufacturers offered technological 'gizmos' that allowed families to be alone and together at the same time. In 1954, *Popular Science* displayed a new device that parents could use to silence the set while their children watched. As the magazine explained, 'NOBODY IS BOTHERED if the children want to see a rootin'-tootin' Western when Dad and Mother want to read, write or talk. Earphones let the youngsters hear every shot, but the silence is wonderful.'[122] DuMont had an even better idea with its 'Duoscope' set. This elaborate construction was composed of two receivers housed in a television cabinet, with two chassis, two control panels, and two picture tubes that were mounted at right angles. Through polarization and the superimposition of two broadcast images, the set allowed two viewers to watch different programs at the same time. Thus, as the article suggested, a husband and

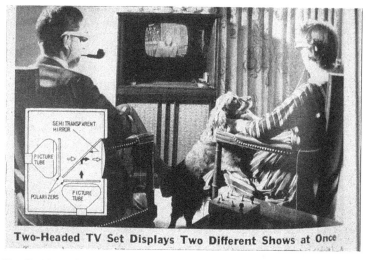

Two-Headed TV Set Displays Two Different Shows at Once

FIGURE 23.5 The DuMont Duoscope promotes togetherness through division.

wife equipped with polarized glasses were able to watch television together but still retain their private pleasures.[123]

While the Duoscope never caught on, the basic problem of unity and division continued. The attempt to balance ideals of family harmony and social difference often led to bizarre solutions, but it also resulted in everyday viewing patterns that were presented as functional and normal procedures for using television. Popular discourses tried to tame the beast, suggesting ways to maintain traditional modes of family behaviour and still allow for social change. They devised intricate plans for resistance and accommodation to the new machine, and in so doing they helped construct a new cultural form.

NOTES

1. *Better Homes and Gardens*, September 1949, p. 38.
2. In some cases, the television set was actually placed in the fireplace. Here, the objects were made to share the same system of meaning so that the familial values traditionally attributed to the fireplace were now also attributed to the television set. See, for example, *House Beautiful*, May 1954, p. 72; *Better Homes and Gardens*, August 1953, p. 10; *American Home*, June 1954, p. 48.
3. *House Beautiful*, September 1954, p. 153.
4. Television sets were often adorned with objects that connoted intellectual pursuits and high art, values traditionally associated with the piano. See, for example, *Ladies' Home Journal*, April 1951, p. 132; *House Beautiful*, November 1954, p. 220.
5. *Better Homes and Gardens*, March 1953, p. 72.
6. *House Beautiful*, January 1953, p. 76.
7. Kathi Norris, 'How Now', *TV World*, August 1953, p. 54.
8. While the home magazines recommended substituting the television set for the piano, other evidence suggests that piano ownership might still have been significant for postwar families. Sales figures for the entire market show that the sale of pianos actually rose from 136,332 in 1940 to 172,531 in 1950, and by 1960 sales had increased to 198,200. Although these sales statistics alone cannot tell us how significant this rise was for the domestic market per se, they do caution us against assuming that the piano was actually phased out during the postwar years. See *Statistical Reference Index*, Music USA: 1982 Review of the Music Industry and Amateur Music Participation/American Music Conference, Report A2275-1 (Bethesda, MD: Congressional Information Service, 1983), p. 4. Also note that the National Piano Manufacturers Association saw radio as largely responsible for a 300 percent increase in sales during the late 1930s. The Association claimed, 'Millions of listeners, who otherwise might never have attained an appreciation of music, are manifesting an interest in musical culture and endeavoring to become participants themselves.' Cited in Davis, 'Response to Innovation', p. 138.
9. George Nelson and Henry Wright, *Tomorrow's House: A Complete Guide for the Home-Builder* (New York: Simon and Schuster, 1946), p. 80.
10. *Better Homes and Gardens*, August 1950, p. 45.
11. Marchand, *Advertising the American Dream*, pp. 248-54.
12. Tyler May, *Homeward Bound*, p. 88.
13. William H. Whyte, Jr., *The Organization Man* (1956; Reprint. Garden City, NY: Doubleday, 1957).
14. Tyler May, *Homeward Bound*, p. 88.
15. See Barbara Ehrenreich, *The Hearts of Men: American Dreams and the Flight from Commitment* (Garden City, NY: Doubleday, 1983).
16. As Maureen Honey shows in her study of women's wartime magazine fiction, the Office of War Information gave suggestions to the magazine editors on ways in which to encourage married middle-class women to work. Honey, however, shows that magazines suggested wartime work for women was temporary, to be discarded when the GIs returned. Still, as Honey also shows, many women did not want to leave their jobs when men returned home. See *Creating Rosie the Riveter: Class, Gender and Propaganda During WWII* (Amherst: University of Massachusetts Press, 1984). Also see Susan M. Hartmann, *American Women in the 1940s: The Home Front and Beyond* (Boston: Twayne, 1982),

pp. 163–205, and Tyler May, *Homeward Bound,* pp. 58–91.

17. Marynia Farnham and Ferdinand Lundberg, *The Modern Woman: The Lost Sex* (New York: Harper and Bros., 1947).

18. Jean and Eugene Benge, *Win Your Man and Keep Him* (New York: Windsor Press, 1948), p. 10. Cited in Tyler May, *Homeward Bound,* pp. 80–1.

19. Although feminine ideals and attitudes toward sexuality had changed considerably since the nineteenth century, the ideal woman of the 1950s shared a common problem with her Victorian ancestors—she was placed in the impossible position of taking on several incompatible roles at the same time. The efficient housewife was somehow supposed to transform herself into an erotic plaything for her husband at night. Even mothering was presented in terms of divided consciousness. In *Their Mothers' Daughters* (1956), psychiatrists Edward Strecker and Vincent Lathbury spoke of the 'dual parental performance' that the working mother had to take on, telling women that 'youngsters of both sexes feel uneasy about their mother's being cast in the father role. We know of one woman, who, since the death of her husband, has been quite successful in the literary field, who makes a point of being very feminine and occasionally even a bit "helpless" with her children.' Edward A. Strecker and Vincent T. Lathbury, *Their Mothers' Daughters* (Philadelphia: J.B. Lippincott Company, 1956), p. 29. Ironically, Strecker and Lathbury were prescribing what psychiatrist Joan Reviere had previously analyzed as a female defence mechanism against negative conceptions about working women. In her seminal 1929 study 'Womanliness as a Masquerade', Reviere showed how successful female professionals felt compelled to adopt a heightened veneer of femininity as a strategy for coping with their 'transgression' of normative gender roles. By posing as super feminine types, these women were able to minimize anxiety about the negative reactions they anticipated from male associates. See the article reprinted in *Formations of Fantasy,* ed. Victor Burgin, et al. (London: Methuen, 1986), pp. 35–44.

20. In the early 1950s, the median marriage age ranged between twenty and twenty-one; the average family started having children in the

beginning of the second year of marriage and had three to four children. For birthrates, see Rochelle Gatlin, *American Women Since 1945* (Jackson, MS: University Press of Mississippi, 1987), pp. 51, 55, 61; Hartmann, *American Women in the 1940s,* pp. 25, 91, 170, 213; Glenna Matthews, *'Just A Housewife': The Rise and Fall of Domesticity in America* (New York: Oxford University Press, 1987), p. 265; and Tyler May, *Homeward Bound,* pp. 7, 136–7; on marriage and divorce rates, see Hartmann, pp. 163–65; Gatlin, p. 51; and Tyler May, pp., 6–8, 21, 59, 117, 185. Hartmann demonstrates that the divorce rate rose among returning veterans and their wives, but levelled off in 1946 (p. 165). Tyler May explains that 'college enrollments increased for women during the postwar years, but not at the same rate as for men.' Since 'college degrees did not guarantee the same entry into well-paying jobs and careers for women as they did for men,' many 'white women were likely to drop out of college in order to marry'. Conversely, while much fewer black women were enrolled in college, those who were enrolled tended to finish their degrees. Black women did so, May argues, because they expected to be employed and expected that college degrees would improve their job prospects (pp. 78–9).

21. For labour force statistics, see Gatlin, *American Women Since 1945,* pp. 24–48; Julia A. Matthaei, *An Economic History of Women in America: Women's Work, the Sexual Division of Labor, and the Development of Capitalism* (New York: Schocken Books, 1982), especially p. 252; Hartmann, *American Women in the 1940s,* pp. 90–5; Tyler May *Homeward Bound,* pp. 76–7; Matthews, *'Just A Housewife',* p. 267.

22. A 1955 survey showed that while most women worked for financial reasons, 21 per cent worked to fulfill 'a need for accomplishment' or to keep busy and meet people; even the women who worked for economic purposes cited the benefits of companionship and a sense of independence. A 1958 survey showed that almost two-thirds of married women cited their jobs as their chief source of feeling 'important' or 'useful' while only one-third mentioned housekeeping. See Gatlin, *American Women since 1945,* p. 33, citing Marion G. Sobol, 'Commitment to Work', *The Employed Mother in America,* ed. F. Ivan Nye and

Lois Wladis Hoffman (Chicago: Rand McNally, 1963), pp. 40–63; Robert Weiss and Nancy Samuelson, 'Social Roles of American Women: Their Contribution to a Sense of Usefulness and Importance', *Journal of Marriage and the Family* 20 (November 1958), pp. 358–66. For more on women's conceptions of work, see Tyler May, *Homeward Bound*, pp. 75–87.

23. Marchand, *Advertising The American Dream*, pp. 335–59; and T. J. Jackson Lears, 'From Salvation to Self-realization: Advertising and the Therapeutic Roots of Consumer Culture, 1880–1930', *The Culture of Consumption: Critical Essays in American History, 1880–1980* (New York: Pantheon, 1983), pp. 1–38.

24. *American Home*, October 1950, p. 25. For other examples of the product-as-centre motif, see *House Beautiful*, November 1949, p. 1; *Ladies' Home Journal*, October 1948, p. 115; *House Beautiful*, February 1949, p. 1.

25. For examples, see *Ebony*, March 1950, p. 7; *Ebony*, August 1953, p. 3; *Ebony*, December 1955, p. 103. Advertisements in *Ebony* also showed white viewers and white actors on screen.

26. Bogart, *Age of Television*, p. 101. As a cautionary note, I would suggest that in his attempt to present a global, synthetic picture of the television audience, Bogart often smoothes over the contradictions in the studies he presents. This attempt at global synthesis goes hand in hand with Bogart's view that the television audience is a homogeneous mass and that television programming further erases distinctions. He writes, 'The levelling of social differences is part of the standardization of tastes and interests to which the mass media give expression, and to which they also contribute. The ubiquitous TV antenna is a symbol of people seeking—and getting—the identical message' (p. 5). Through this logic of mass mentalities, Bogart often comes to conclusions that oversimplify the heterogeneity of audience responses in the studies he presents.

27. Edward C. McDonagh et al., 'Television and the Family', *Sociology and Social Research* 40 (4) (March–April 1956), p. 117.

28. John W. Riley et al. 'Some Observations on the Social Effects of Television', *Public Opinion Quarterly* 13 (2) (Summer 1949), p. 232. This study was cosponsored by Rutgers University and CBS.

29. Raymond Stewart, cited in Bogart, *Age of Television*, p. 100.

30. Harry Henderson, 'The Mass-Produced Suburbs: I. How People Live in America's Newest Towns', *Harpers*, November 1953, p. 28.

31. For more on this and other aspects of the public concern over juvenile delinquents, see James Gilbert, *A Cycle of Outrage: America's Reaction to the Juvenile Delinquent in the 1950s* (New York: Oxford University Press, 1986). Gilbert shows that while public officials, educators, psychologists, and other 'experts' increasingly focused on criminal youth, 'the incidence of juvenile crime does not appear to have increased enormously during this period'. Gilbert goes on to show that crime statistics were imprecise and, since the definition of juvenile crime and the policing of it had changed over the course of the century, it is difficult to prove that the postwar period actually witnessed a substantial rise in teenage crimes. Given this, Gilbert argues that the perception of juvenile delinquency in the 1950s was based less on reality than it was on the way crime was labelled and reported, as well as the general worries about the future direction of American society (pp. 66–71).

32. McDonagh et al., 'Television and the Family', p. 116.

33. Stewart, cited in Bogart, *Age of Television*, p. 100.

34. *Better Homes and Gardens*, October 1955, p. 209. In the 1952 House hearings on the content of radio and television programs, Representative Joseph Byrson from South Carolina testified to a similar domestic situation. He claimed, 'My two younger children spent much of their time watching the neighbor's television. In a year or two, when my youngest son had graduated from a local junior high school, he wanted to go away to school. I believe, if I had purchased a television set at that time, he would have finished high school here in Washington.' House Interstate and Foreign Commerce Committee, *Hearings before a Subcommittee of the Committee on Interstate and Foreign Commerce: Investigation of Radio and Television Programs*, 82d Cong., 2d Sess., 3 June 1952, H. Res. 278, p. 23 (hereafter cited as *Hearings: Radio and Television Programs*). Congressional witness Lloyd C. Halvorson (an economist for the National Grange, a farm organization) stated a similar problem. He told

the Committee, 'You may ask, why don't I turn the television set off or throw it out. If I do, the children will just go over to the neighbors, and to keep them home would make them think I was cruel. It would make an impossible family situation' (p. 93). The hearings reconvened on 4, 5, and 26 June 1952; 16, 17, 23, 24, 25, and 26 September 1952; and 3, 4, and 5 December 1952.

35. 'Television Has Become a Member of the Family', *House Beautiful*, September 1951, p. 118.

36. *House Beautiful*, January 1955, pp. 39–43, 84.

37. See Kasson, *Civilizing the Machine*, pp. 183–234 and Marx, *Machine in the Garden*, pp. 227–353.

38. Susman, *Culture as History*, p. 268.

39. Joseph Wood Krutch, 'Have You Caught On Yet . . .' *House Beautiful*, November 1951, p. 221.

40. 'Television: The New Cyclops', *Business Week*, 10 March 1956, reprinted in *Television's Impact on American Culture*, ed. William Y. Elliot (East Lansing, MI: Michigan State University Press, 1956), pp. 340–54; Calder Willingham, 'Television Giant in the Living Room', *American Mercury*, February 1952, p. 115. This article is especially interesting since Willingham presents a kind of metacriticism of the anxieties about television during the period.

41. For discussions of this, see Jeanne Allen, 'The Social Matrix of Television: Invention in the United States', *Regarding Television*, ed. E. Ann Kaplan (Los Angeles: University Publications of America, 1983), pp. 109–20 and Davis, 'Response to Innovation', pp. 100–1. For examples of postwar articles, see Bill Reiche, 'Television is the Navy's School Teacher', *Popular Mechanics*, November 1948, pp. 125–7, 270, 272; Devon Francis, 'TV Takes over Test Pilot's Job', *Popular Science*, March 1951, pp. 144–8; 'Dismantling Bombs by TV', *Science Digest*, January 1954, inside cover.

42. Newton Minow, 'The Vast Wasteland' (Address to the 39th Annual Convention of the National Association of Broadcasters, Washington DC: 9 May 1961).

43. *Look*, 21 April 1953, p. 18.

44. *American Home*, September 1953, p. 104; *House Beautiful*, March 1955, p. 78.

45. Helen Little, 'How to Decorate for Television', *House Beautiful*. August 1949, pp. 66, 69.

46. It should be noted here that the term 'contemporary' referred to a kind of watered-down modernism that appealed to middle-class tastes in a way that 'highbrow' modernism did not. The furniture trade journal, *Home Furnishings*, was a forum for debates about the public response to modernism. The journal took a conservative attitude toward it, establishing a canon of contemporary design that was an extremely softened version of the idiosyncratic objects made by famous modernist furniture makers. The journal, in this regard, was responding to the popular skepticism about modernism during the period. In the fifties, there were various attempts to mass-produce modernist furniture, and several department stores coordinated their retail efforts with the Museum of Modern Art's furniture exhibits. However, the popular press often scorned the extremism of modern styles, representing modernism as being contrary to middle-class family ideals. Editor Elizabeth Gordon of *House Beautiful* even called modernist design 'The Threat to the Next America' in her bitter essay that argued that modernism was an international conspiracy originating in Nazi Germany with the machine aesthetics of the Bauhaus School. See *House Beautiful*, April 1953, editorial.

47. *American Home*, February 1955, p. 44; *Better Homes and Gardens*, May 1955, p. 28.

48. 'Now You See It . . . Now You Don't', *American Home*, September 1951, p. 49; *House Beautiful*, December 1953, p. 145; *American Home*, November 1953, p. 60; *Popular Science*, March 1953, p. 87.

49. Jean Baudrillard, *For A Critique of The Political Economy of the Sign*, trans, Charles Levin (St. Louis: Telos Press, 1981), pp. 53–7.

50. For examples of this sort, see *House Beautiful*, October 1953, p. 193; Beulah Donohue Hochstein, 'Small Room, but Space for Living, Eating, and Sleeping', *Better Homes and Gardens*, November 1951, p. 197; *American Home*, November 1954, p. 127.

51. 'Television Has Become a Member of the Family', p. 66; *American Home*, September 1951. p. 48.

52. *Better Homes and Gardens*, December 1952, p. 133.

53. Bogart, *Age of Television*, p. 97.

54. William Porter, 'Is Your Child *Glued* to TV, Radio,

Movies, or Comics?' *Better Homes and Gardens,* October 1951, p. 125.

55. *Ladies' Home Journal,* April 1950, p. 237. For a similar cartoon, see *Ladies' Home Journal,* December 1955, p. 164.

56. *House Beautiful,* June 1951, p. 8; *Life,* 26 November 1951, p. 11.

57. 'Bang! You're Dead', *Newsweek,* 21 March 1955, p. 35.

58. See Norman Cousins, 'The Time Trap', *Saturday Review of Literature,* 24 December 1949, p. 20.

59. Edward M. Brecher, 'TV, Your Children, and Your Grandchildren', *Consumer Reports,* May 1950, p. 231.

60. For more on this, see Mark West, *Children, Culture and Controversy* (Hamden, CT: Archon, 1988).

61. Davis, 'Response to Innovation', pp. 209–16, Davis argues that 60 per cent of the discussions on television's effect on children took place in these special interest magazines (p. 170).

62. Jacqueline Rose, *The Case of Peter Pan: The Impossibility of Children's Fiction* (London: Macmillan, 1984).

63. Cited in Fredric Wertham, *Seduction of the Innocent* (New York: Rinehart, 1953), p. 377.

64. Gilbert, *Cycle of Outrage,* p. 102 also observes that the Supreme Court used Wertham's testimony and implicitly accepted his theories of media effects in the 1952 case Beauharnais vs. Illinois, 343 U.S. 250 (1952), which upheld a censorship law concerning negative portrayals of racial groups.

65. A 1954 Gallup Poll showed that 70 per cent of all adults who were questioned thought that crime comics and mystery and crime programs on television were at least in part responsible for the rise in juvenile delinquency. See Bogart, *Age of Television,* p. 273.

66. Agnes Maxwell Peters to Fredric Wertham, 1 August 1948, Wertham MS, cited in Gilbert, *Cycle of Outrage,* p. 105; Margaret Mead, 'Problems of the Atomic Age', *The Survey,* July 1949, p. 385, cited in Tyler May, *Homeward Bound,* p. 27.

67. Ellen Wartella and Sharon Mazzarella, 'A Historical Comparison of Children's Use of Leisure Time', *For Fun and Profit: The Transformation of Leisure into Consumption,* ed. Richard Butsch (Philadelphia: Temple University Press, 1990), pp. 183–5.

68. PTA reform reported in 'Another TV Censor', *Variety,* 5 October 1949, p. 27. For early school board activities, see, for example, 'TV Also Alarms Cleve. Educators', *Variety,* 22 March 1950, p. 29; 'Students Read, Sleep Less in TV Homes, Ohio School Survey Shows', *Variety,* 5 April 1950, p. 38.

69. 'Catholic Council Plans TV Legion of Decency Via National Monitoring', *Variety,* 29 August 1951, pp. 1, 63; 'Catholic Women Attack TV for Crime Overplay', *Variety,* 25 October 1950, p. 1; 'Detroit vs. TV "Kid Abuses": City Fathers in Organized Stand', *Variety,* 20 December 1950, p. 25; 'Catholics Urge Legion of Decency To Clean Up Programs For Kids', *Variety,* 14 March 1951, pp. 1, 18.

70. 'TV Censorship: One Down, More to Go', *Broadcasting,* 5 March 1951, pp. 54–6.

71. The networks also tried to police themselves. As early as 1948, NBC executives considered problems of standards and practices in television. *NBC Standards and Practices Bulletin—No. 7: A Report on Television Program Editing and Policy Control,* November 1948, NBC Records, Box 157: Folder 7, Wisconsin Center Historical Archives, State Historical Society, Madison. In 1951, NBC became the first network to establish standards for children's shows, crime shows, mention of sex on programs, proper costuming, etc. See *NBC Code,* 1951, NBC Records, Box 163: Folder 1, Wisconsin Center Historical Archives, State Historical Society, Madison. For a general explanation of the code, see 'Catholic Council Plans TV Legion', *Variety,* 29 August 1951, p. 63.

72. *Hearings: Radio and Television Programs,* 1952.

73. Chairman Senator Robert C. Hendrickson cited in Committee on the Judiciary United States Senate, *Hearings before the Subcommittee to Investigate Juvenile Delinquency: Juvenile Delinquency (Television Programs),* 83d Cong., 2d sess., 5 June 1954, S. Res. 89, p. 1 (hereafter cited as *Hearings: Juvenile Delinquency (Television Programs)* (Kefauver Hearings). The Committee reconvened on 19 and 20 October 1954, and also met on 6 and 7 April 1955, to continue the debates.

74. Newton Minow, 'Is TV Cheating Our Children?' *Parents,* February 1962, pp. 52–3; 'Minow Magic', *Newsweek,* 14 August 1963, p. 66.

75. Bogart, *Age of Television,* p. 268.

76. Jack Gould, 'What Is Television Doing To Us?'

New York Times Magazine, 12 June 1949, p. 7. *Popular Science*, March 1955, took the logic of human agency to its literal extreme, presenting a 'lock-and-key' TV that 'won't work until Mama sees fit and turns it on with her key' (p. 110).

77. *Better Homes and Gardens*, October 1955, p. 202.

78. Bogart, *Age of Television*, p. 289. In the 1954 Kefauver Hearings, similar findings about the relationship between social class and parents' attitudes toward television were made part of the official record. See Committee on the Judiciary United States Senate, *Juvenile Delinquency (Television Programs)*, 5 June 1954, pp. 21–3.

79. Reverend Everett C. Parker summarizing findings from the Information Service, Central Department of Research and Survey, National Council of the Churches of Christ in the United States of America, *Parents, Children, and Television—The First Television Generation* (New York: n.p., 1954). Reprinted and summarized in Committee on the Judiciary United States Senate, *Hearings: Juvenile Delinquency (Television Programs)*, 5 June 1954, p. 28. The surveys in Bogart's account include a 1955 study from the *New York Herald Tribune* that studied 1200 school children; a 1952 and 1955 study by the American Research Bureau of children ages six to sixteen; H.H. Remmars, R.E. Horton and R.E. Mainer, *Attitudes of High School Students toward Certain Aspects of Television* (Indiana: Purdue University, (953). All are summarized in Bogart, pp. 252–6. See also the *Better Homes and Gardens* survey cited above and summarized in Bogart.

80. For example, in 1952, the American Research Bureau observed that by the age of seven, one child in four had stayed up to watch Berle. Bogart, *Age of Television*, p. 254.

81. 'Kids Not Kidding', *Variety*, 29 March 1950, p. 33.

82. Even researchers at the time interpreted parental control in these terms. Bogart, for example, suggested that 'one reason why high school teen-agers receive less supervision in their TV viewing is that their program tastes apparently are considerably closer to those of their parents' (p. 262).

83. Dorothy Diamond and Frances Tenenbaum, 'Should You Tear 'Em Away from TV?' *Better Homes and Gardens*, September 1950, p. 56.

84. *Better Homes and Gardens*. March 1955, p. 173.

85. Diamond and Tenenbaum, p. 239.

86. Porter, 'Is Your Child *Glued* to TV', p. 178.

87. Jacques Donzelot, *The Policing of Families* (New York: Pantheon, 1979). Donzelot discusses the history of the public regulation of families in France.

88. The housing program of Better Homes in America was formalized in its advice manual of 1931. See Blanche Halbert, *The Better Homes Manual* (Chicago: University of Chicago Press, 1931). The last chapter listed 12 governmental and educational organizations that regulated housing and home improvements. Note too that children were one of the main interests of outside agencies and reform movements. In the 1880s, childhood emerged as a distinct sociological category, something to be studied apart from other family issues, and by 1912 the category was officially recognized by the formation of a Federal Bureau of Children. For more, see Wartella and Mazzarella, 'Historical Comparison'. For a discussion of the development of child psychology see Fass, *The Damned and the Beautiful*.

89. Bogart, *Age of Television*, pp. 283–5 cites various psychologists who also claimed that television was a symptom of wider family problems. See also Eleanor MacCoby, one of the first social scientists to study children's use of television. She argued that 'children will spend more time watching television if they are highly frustrated in real life than if they are not.' See MacCoby, 'Why Do Children Watch Television?' *Public Opinion Quarterly* 18 (3) (Fall 1954), p. 240.

90. This situation was aggravated by the fact that popular experts often blamed parents for their children's fixation to television. In 1950, Jack Gould wrote, 'If they are willing to face up to the truth, the average television parents probably must concede that they themselves in part brought about their child's preoccupation with television. A television receiver becomes an exceptionally handy "baby sitter" if parents want a little relief from youthful spirits . . . . Later they may find the habit difficult to break.' See Gould, 'Video and Children', *The New York Times*, 8 January 1950, sec. X, p. 15. Similarly, in 'The Time Trap', Norman Cousins blamed parents for the 'unspoken parental benediction' of their children's bad viewing habits.

91. Lloyd Shearer, 'The Parental Dilemma', *House Beautiful*. October 1951, pp. 220, 222.

92. Sylvia O'Neill, 'Are You Guilty of Juvenile Delinquency?' *Home Furnishings*, August 1954, p. 14.

93. 'Video's Juvenile Audience', *Advertising and Selling*, August 1948, p. 99.

94. 'Television Tempest', *Newsweek*, 27 November 1950, p. 62.

95. John Crosby, 'Parents Arise! You Have Nothing to Lose but Your Sanity', *Out of the Blue: A Book about Radio and Television* (New York: Simon and Schuster, 1952), p. 115.

96. Robert Lewis Shayon, 'Who Remembers Papa?' *Saturday Review*, 13 October 1951, p. 43; Bob Taylor, 'What is TV Doing to MEN?' *TV Guide*, 26 June 1953, p. 15; 'Daddy with a Difference', *Time*, 17 May 1954, p. 83. For additional examples, see Eleanor Harris, 'They Always Get Their Man', *Colliers*, 25 November 1950, p. 34; 'The Great Competitor', *Time*, 14 December 1953, p. 62; 'Perpetual Honeymoon', *Time*, 22 March 1954, p. 82.

97. For example, vaudeville sketches such as 'A Wife's Strategem' showed women insulting and nagging their male partners. See Staples, *Male-Female Comedy Teams*, pp. 144–5. Such scenarios could also be seen in films such as the Vitaphone serial, *The Naggers*, whose shrewish wife henpecked her ineffectual husband.

98. Andreas Huyssen, 'Mass Culture as Woman: Modernism's Other', *After the Great Divide: Modernism, Mass Culture, Postmodernism* (Bloomington and Indianapolis: Indiana University Press, 1986), p. 47.

99. Douglas discusses this in 'Amateur Operators and American Broadcasting' and in *Inventing American Broadcasting*, pp. 187–215.

100. Covert, 'We May Hear Too Much', p. 205.

101. Philip Wylie, *Generation of Vipers* (1942; Reprint, New York: Holt, Rinehart and Winston, 1955), pp. 199–200.

102. Ibid., pp. 214–15.

103. Ibid., pp. 213–14.

104. As William Lafferty has pointed out to me, Bruce is actually watching the previous week's episode of *Fireside Theatre*, a western melodrama entitled, 'His Name is Jason'.

105. This is not to say that Hollywood movies always presented strong male characters. In fact, the figure of the dandy was a popular male type in twenties and thirties films. What I am arguing here is that the episode represents the dichotomy between Hollywood and television through the opposition between virile and passive male heroes.

106. Robert Lewis Shayon, 'Daddy Pinza and Daddy Thomas', *Saturday Review*, 1 November 1953, pp. 54–5.

107. Eleanor E. MacCoby, 'Television: Its Impact on School Children', *Public Opinion Quarterly*, 15 (3) (Fall 1951), pp. 421–44. This kind of research filtered down to the industry trade journals, which reported on the decline in family interaction in television households.

108. Jack Gould, 'TV Daddy and Video Mama: A Dirge', *The New York Times Magazine*, 14 May 1950, p. 56; *Better Homes and Gardens*, September 1950, p. 56; *TV Guide*, 21 August 1953, p. 11. MacCoby, 'Television', p. 438, and Bogart, *Age of Television*, p. 261, also summarized numerous other studies that suggested television was interfering with meals.

109. John Crosby, 'What's Television Going to Do To Your Life?' *House Beautiful*, February 1950, p. 125. This is one of the rare occasions in which a popular television critic wrote for a woman's home magazine. It is also one of the few articles that was addressed to a male reader.

110. Phil Hiner, 'Television As You Like It', *Popular Science*, May 1954, p. 216.

111. Goodman Ace, 'A Man's TV Set is His Castle', *The Saturday Review*, April 1953, reprinted in Ace, *The Book of Little Knowledge: More Than You Want to Know about Television* (New York: Simon and Schuster. 1955), pp. 165–7.

112. Nelson and Wright, *Tomorrow's House*, p. 76.

113. *House Beautiful*, October 1951, p. 168.

114. Alfred Politz Research, Inc., *National Survey of Radio and Television Sets Associated with U.S. Households* (New York: The Advertising Research foundation, 1954), p. 71.

115. *Better Homes and Gardens*, November 1951, p. 263.

116. *Better Homes and Gardens*, June 1953, p. 126.

117. *American Home*, September 1955, p. 17.

118. Nancy Crawford, 'Young Home Builders', *Ladies' Home Journal*, November 1953, p. 182.
119. *Better Homes and Gardens*, October 1955, p. 139.
120. For examples of advertisements depicting divided families, see *Better Homes and Gardens*. November 1953, p. 40; *Better Homes and Gardens*, December 1952, p. 30; *American Home*, November 1951, p. 10.
121. *American Home*, December 1953, p. 84.
122. Phil Hiner, 'Television As You Like It', *Popular Science*, May 1954, pp. 216–18. A similar device was marketed by Philco.
123. 'Two-Headed TV Set Displays Different Shows at Once', *Popular Science*, March 1954, p. 156.

VIRTUALLY LIVE: DIGITAL BROADCAST CINEMA AND THE PERFORMING ARTS

PAUL HEYER

If I had to choose between paying $80 for a spot in the upper balcony and $22 to sit in the middle of the action, I just might make for the nearest multiplex.

—Justin Davidson (*New York* magazine arts critic)

Regularly seen in movie theatres on wide screens, these productions are not motion pictures. Using the logic of *Jeopardy*, the question might be, 'What are the Metropolitan Opera's live HD broadcasts?' A few years ago this would have been the only correct response. Now it would be equally valid to mention London's National Theatre, Royal Ballet, Royal Opera House, and Covent Garden, and Milan's La Scala. In Canada, the venerable Stratford Theatre made its gala 2008 premiere of George Bernard Shaw's *Caesar and Cleopatra* available to 80 movie screens across the nation (31 January 2009) through a partnership with Cineplex and CTV–Bravo. In response to this proliferation of live broadcasts, *Screen Digest* predicts that within four years income from such sources will amount to 5 per cent of total cinema box office.[1] Using the Met's pioneering efforts as a case study, I want to pose and then tentatively try to answer the question, *When engaging their audiences, how do these broadcasts both resemble and differ from what we experience when viewing live theatre, cinema, or television?*

This format for the outreach of the performing arts, which the Met refers to as 'live cinema', might be more inclusively referred to as 'digital broadcast cinema' (DBC).[2] All of the Met performances are originally broadcast live, though this is not the case with other presenters. But each Met performance is also recorded and later re-trans-mitted as an encore. The production of Georges Bizet's *Carmen* (16 January 2010) received three such encore presentations, adding substantially to a worldwide audience of one-quarter million who viewed the initial live presentation. Countries such as Australia and Japan, in time zones incompatible with the Met's Saturday afternoon broadcast, have to settle for a recording of the opera a day or two later. Since some performing arts companies seeking to enlarge their audience in this way lack the resources to attempt live transmissions, a recorded version must suffice. This was the case with the aforementioned Stratford production of *Caesar and Cleopatra*, which was recorded as it was performed, then edited, and later transmitted to cinemas. Therefore, if we were to define DBC it can be said to include *the broadcast into movie theatres, either live or recorded, of various arts and entertainment productions that, like cinema, have a narrative format.* In other words, opera, ballet, musicals, and stage-plays qualify, but concerts and sporting events, which already have a history of being beamed into movie theatres, do not.[3]

CINEOPERA

Since DBC productions are viewed on wide screens in movie theatres, some resemblance to conventional cinema is to be expected. In the case of the Met broadcasts, the projected images have an aspect ratio of at least 1:85:1. Upwards of 12 cameras capture the performance, which is edited 'in camera', or more precisely at an editing console, using a grid of monitors with the producer using the musical score as a reference. This format can lead us to question media scholar James Monaco's distinction between a performing art, such as theatre or dance, and a recording art, such as film, painting, photography, or sound recording.[4] (Opera is one of the few art forms he does not consider, although its link to what he says about theatre is obvious.) Monaco does concede that recent technological developments have extended the recording arts, turning them into 'a new mode of discourse', whereby 'any performance that can be seen or heard can be recorded on film, tape, or disc'.[5]

Although the Met productions are transmitted live and as recorded encores before being eventually released on DVD, what we are seeing is not cinema, nor is it a faithful replication of what an in-house audience experiences. If there is a precedent, it could be argued that it is the concert film as it emerged in the second half of the twentieth century—*Monterey Pop* (1969) and *The Last Waltz* (1978) being prime examples. Here the gap between what constitutes a performing art and a recording art is substantially narrowed, since the performances in these films were 'captured' by, rather than staged for, the camera. Nevertheless, through post-production, the conventions of a recording art significantly influence what we see in terms of the duration of particular moments in the performances, transitions, and points of view. With DBC, any such editorial choices must be done in real time throughout the whole production.

A live audience at the Met or at London's National Theatre sees the performers and stagecraft from the fixed position of the seats. Is it reasonable to argue, then, that viewing the same live production in a movie theatre offers more? Monaco's position is that 'we watch a play as we will; we see a film only as the filmmaker wants us to see it'.[6] Since DBC presentations use a variety of camera shots, are we therefore constrained to see only what those shots direct us to see? Given the rich field accommodated in many of the shots, some of the freedom of an in-house audience in viewing selected aspects of the mise-en-scène seems possible, and this in turn is augmented by the cameras taking the DBC audience, through the use of close-ups, overhead shots, and the like, to places and points of view that only a recording art such as cinema can provide. Occasionally a camera captures the in-house audience itself as it responds to aspects of a production. These reaction shots are more frequent in broadcasts of comedies, such as Rossini's *The Barber of Seville* (24 March 2007) and Donizetti's *La Fille du Régiment* (26 April 2008) than in those of tragedies. This is unlike anything in theatre or cinema; the only analogy I can think of is a television program sometimes providing us with reaction shots of a live studio audience.

Although, according to Monaco's definition, DBC cannot be considered a recording art per se, such as painting, photography, film, or sound recording, it nevertheless incorporates aspects of film and painting. The camera work and editing, coupled with the widescreen format, create an experience that is often movie-like, until it is punctuated by moments of narrative explanation and backstage interviews. It also becomes readily apparent how important production design is to the staging of a performance. Scene changes, frequent in cinema, are few in opera and theatre, generally ranging from two to five. This gives the DBC audience, perhaps more so than in-house patrons because of the camera shots, a better chance to lavish their attention on details of the visual context of a performance.

We can therefore add production design to Monaco's list of recording arts. Franco Zeffirelli's highly praised sets for Giacomo Puccini's *La Bohème* (5 April 2008) provided a feast for the eye. In Scene II, for almost an hour the audience gazed at a dazzling street scene in mid nineteenth–century Paris—a veritable Renoir painting come to life. Not to be outdone, London's National Theatre's live DBC staging of Mark Ravenhill's *Nation* (30 January 2010), featured a dynamic interplay of illusions and swirling puppets. *Nation*, coming on the heels of James Cameron's film *Avatar* going into wide release, prompted one Toronto commentator to refer to the production as an example of 'the original 3-D'.[7]

DBC productions like those of the Met strive for the precise packaging of a well-edited concert film, despite the fact that the editing takes place during the performance. The result is at times a compromise between shots of the full staging that allow the DBC audience to scan the whole production as if, following Monaco's assertion, they were in the theatre itself, and specific shots chosen by the director, who, in Monaco's argument, creates the point of view for an audience.

Sometimes this point of view is guided through the use of multiple screens. Experimental filmmaker Barbara Willis Sweete, who regularly directs the Met's 'live cinema', employed the technique in a production of Richard Wagner's *Tristan und Isolde* (22 March 2008). In cinema, the technique

goes back at least as far as Abel Gance's *Napoléon* (1927), which divided the screen using a triptych format called polyvision. Although the divided screen technique draws attention to itself, and is therefore used with caution in contemporary cinema—video game–influenced movies excepted—it has become almost naturalized when representing a telephone conversation. Michael Gordon's *Pillow Talk* (1959) is perhaps the most famous, but not the first, example of this usage.

Recent examples of the multiple screen, such as Mike Figgis's intriguing four frames in the film *Time Code* (2000) or in Hans Canosa's *Conversations with Other Women* (2006), have invoked the label 'arty experiment' from critics. A precedent of sorts for the use of multiple screens in a concert film can be found in Michael Wadleigh's *Woodstock* (1970). Clearly the technique when used in DBC shatters the illusion of live theatre—I have yet to see it employed in theatrical productions apart from those of the Met. Reaction from patrons I have interviewed regarding this usage has been mostly negative. Comments such as 'intrusive' and 'distracting' were frequent, especially when the screen within the screen moved across the overall frame during the emotionally stirring finale of *Tristan*. Given the starkness of the set, and with only the two principals on stage, a simple long shot to zoom might have been more effective.

Still, whatever criticisms purists have raised regarding the Met's use of DBC, a definite plus is that to an audience habituated to cinema, opera experienced this way can be more accessible than if viewed in the formal confines of the performance venue itself. Of course, since its beginnings, cinema has been influenced by opera, both in orchestral scoring and narrative, and numerous films have featured opera-singing protagonists. Nevertheless, filmed operas have been few and far between, having rarely enjoyed significant box office success or critical accolades.[8] An exception might be the numerous versions of *Carmen*, given the visual dynamics of its dance numbers—Cecil B. DeMille even filmed a silent *Carmen* in 1915. The Met's three encore presentations attest to this opera's enduring appeal. Despite cinema's reticence to present full operatic productions, opera sequences within movies have yielded many memorable moments. A partial list might include *Citizen Kane* (1941), *Diva* (1982), *Pretty Woman* (1990), *Meeting Venus* (1991), and even a recent James Bond film, *Quantum of Solace* (2008).

Any comparative discussion of the differences between a live theatrical production and cinema would be quick to point out the epic sweep possible in celluloid versus the constraints of the proscenium stage. For the Met, however, that stage can yield possibilities that might amaze anyone not familiar with what state-of-the-art technological resources can bring to a live theatrical presentation. Productions such as Tan Dun's *The First Emperor* (13 January 2007) and Giuseppe Verdi's tale of love and death in ancient Egypt, *Aida* (24 October 2009), were almost DeMilleian in their expansiveness. Having attended *Aida* live while it was being transmitted as a DBC offering, I can attest to the audience's gasps, both when the curtains opened to reveal grandiose hieroglyphed monuments, and again during the victory procession with its endless stream of supernumeraries and menagerie of live animals. Having been privy to a backstage tour at the time, not only did the sets look superb during the performance, it took a lingering touch to discern that they were not stone or computer-generated images.

One area with clear parallels between cinema and theatrical productions such as those of the Met is costume design. Opera is as much a visual spectacle as it is a musical medium. The Met has always prided itself on attire crafted as well as or better than any we might see in a big-budget historical film, despite the fact that to appreciate subtle design detail requires a viewing proximity that excludes most members of the in-house audience. Enter DBC. Using well-chosen close-ups, costume design now becomes a 'recording art' accessible to an international audience. Building on accolades it received in this regard during its first two DBC seasons, the Met's third opened with a prologue gala (22 September 2008) that featured a close look at Renée Fleming's costumes in each of the three segments she would perform—costumes by Christian Lacroix in Verdi's *La Traviata*, by Karl Lagerfeld for Chanel in Jules Massenet's *Manon*, and by John Galliano in Richard Strauss's *Capriccio*.

Psychoanalytical film theory has pointed out that the illusion of cinema often presents us with a dream-like fantasy experience. Opera, especially when transmitted through DBC, can do likewise. The illusion of realism is largely absent, because dialogue is minimal and mostly replaced by singing in a variety of formats, and most opera productions are set in either a vague historical context—*The First Emperor*—or a mythological past—Mozart's *The Magic Flute* (30 December 2006). The dream-like aspects of a production can sometimes take on a nightmarish quality, as with *Hansel and Gretel* or Hector Berlioz's *La Damnation de Faust* (22 November 2008). The former, ostensibly staged as a holiday production for children, featured enough nightmare-inducing ghoulishness, cannibalism, and cruelty to have perhaps elicited approval from that defender of fairy tales in the raw, the late psychoanalyst Bruno Bettelheim.[9] The production of *Faust* was directed by Canada's Robert Lepage, renowned for his work in theatre, film, and Cirque du Soleil. It featured special effects that included projected interactive moving images, something rarely seen on the operatic stage. Lepage will bring his intermediality to a highly anticipated staging of the four operas in Richard Wagner's Ring Cycle, beginning with *Das Rheingold* (9 October 2010), followed by *Die Walküre* (14 May 2011).

In contrasting the way the cameras are used in DBC and in cinema, the latter favours repeated takes and extensive editing after the fact. DBC edits in real time, and although shots are planned in advance, choices sometimes have to be made on the spur of the moment, given the less than 100 per cent predictability of a live performance. It could also be argued that DBC can sometimes be more cinematic than cinema itself. With twelve or more cameras strategically placed, the shot variety at a given moment can exceed what is possible in the average movie scene not dependent on computer-generated imagery.

TELEVISUALITY

Whether a DBC production is seen live or as a recorded encore, the B stands for *broadcast*: productions are transmitted digitally to movie theatres rather than delivered physically to a projectionist. In the case of the Met, resemblances to the format of broadcast television are stronger than might appear at first glance. Unlike previous concert genres or other kinds of theatrical productions beamed into movie theatres, those of the Met loosely constitute an ongoing series since they started in 2006. If we apply Monaco's criteria for broadcast television, we can classify them as an open-ended program with 'static' (versus developing plot) situations—whereas close-ended programming is the realm of the mini-series, one-off special, or made-for-television movie. Occasionally the announcer for the Met or for London's National Theatre might say, 'If you saw the previous broadcast in our series . . .', with respect to a conductor or cast member's earlier appearance; nevertheless, each production is sufficiently self-contained to be accessible on its own terms to the first-time viewer.

The closest parallel to a previous television format suggested by DBC might be the live anthology dramas of the 1950s—*Playhouse 90, U.S. Steel Hour, CBC Television Theatre*, and their kin. These shows sometimes featured a host, as do the Met and National Theatre broadcasts. There are, to be sure, notable differences. The anthology dramas lacked a live studio audience. Production usually employed three large cameras with turret lenses and limited mobility. In contrast, digital technology and robotics have allowed DBC cameras to track, pan, zoom, or cut to almost any aspect of the production and its audience (although in the case of the Met I have yet to see a shot of the prompter). This capacity, which at first glance appears cinematic, is also televisual, since it builds on the Skycam legacy pioneered in television sports coverage—its use gained wide attention beginning with Monday Night Football on ABC in 2001. And if the onstage perfection of a given production lulls the DBC audience into assuming they are experiencing something carefully edited after the fact, moments of live televisual reality occasionally intrude and elicit a chuckle: someone in the balcony stands unexpectedly and partly obliterates a shot, necessitating a quick cut; or a supernumerary, unaware of the shot being selected, makes an out-of-context gesture or expression.

Another staple of the Met and National Theatre broadcasts that is televisual is the postmodern emphasis on the production process itself. The Met intermissions and National Theatre prologues feature interviews with the performers as well as those involved with the technical aspects of a production. At the Met, handheld cameras intrusively follow cast and crew backstage accompanied by a litany of questions—in pop culture, this was a recurring theme in Madonna's concert film *Truth or Dare* (1991). During these interviews, we often get a glimpse of the mechanics involved in staging a given production: behind every impressive facade we see a maze of industrial scaffolding. Each broadcast then, is partly an auto-documentary, recalling those 'how they make it' programs featured on The Learning Channel and the Discovery channel.

According to communication theorist Edmund Carpenter, in contrast to cinema, television has an inherent theatricality.[10] Television programs generally feature a small cast and fewer sets and locations than does cinema. This helps explain the ongoing popularity of sitcoms, soap operas, and law and medical dramas. Opera and theatre also tend to feature a small primary cast and few set changes; for example the National Theatre's staging of Alan Bennett's *The Habit of Art* (22 April 2010) featured just one set. Yet to say that television favours theatricality in its mode of presentation, as both Carpenter and John Ellis argue, is not to suggest that theatre and opera themselves can be successful draws on television. Contemporary culture rather than high culture is television's mainstay; even historically inclined dramas or comedies are rare, with the occasional exception of programs on PBS, CBC, or HBO.

Ellis's position is that while cinema viewing favours the gaze—sustained looking—television, with its lower-quality image viewed in ambient light and accompanied by frequent distractions, favours the glance.[11] How then could the Met's DBC productions, which have obvious cinematic elements, be televisual as well? Ellis provides us with a clue in his claim that television, more than film, is anchored in sound, especially dialogue. An opera provides this very kind of anchoring with its libretto, sung and occasionally spoken.

The libretto, although verbally incomprehensible to non-speakers of the language of a production (and sometimes to its speakers as well), can be followed by the use in DBC of supertitles. Watching a supertitled opera is quite different from watching a subtitled film where there is often a struggle to read the dialogue and see the events at the same time, as anyone who has tried to follow the motor-paced dialogue of a Fellini film can attest. Since to sing a simple declarative sentence in opera takes more time than to read it in a supertitle, a quick glance at the printed text is all that is necessary, after which attention can be turned to the action onstage.

Another area in which DBC productions can be considered televisual is the way they favour more quick cuts and close-ups than we normally find in cinema. In the case of the Met, perhaps the legacy of MTV videos is also an influence. Shots of a duet are just as likely to feature rapid cutting between the singers shown from different angles, as they are to keep both of them in the frame as we might find in a 'filmed' opera; and should something orchestrally distinct emerge, a bass clarinet trill, for example, the camera might cut to a shot of fingers on the clarinet's keys. In National Theatre productions, the camera cuts to close-ups of the speakers with the speed and precision of a television sitcom.

The heavy use of the close-up in DBC productions, especially in theatre and opera, has a clear impact on the way we regard the performers. Normally accustomed to performing onstage where they are viewed from 'public distance', to appropriate Edward Hall's terminology,[12] they are now being seen from 'personal distance' and at times even 'intimate distance'.

Questions have therefore arisen regarding the importance of appearance to performance, just as they have in the realm of pop music. It now seems that performers must look compatible with the roles they play in order to be convincing. Here, DBC has merely exacerbated a long-standing issue. As Hutcheon and Hutcheon show in their comprehensive study of the body in opera, debates about looking appropriate for a role and singing it adequately, versus the power of an extraordinary performance to suspend disbelief over what appears to be a physical miscasting, are nothing new.[13] In theatre, eyebrows have been raised when aging thespians have played younger roles, such as in Shakespeare's *Romeo and Juliet*. In the National Theatre production of *The Habit of Art*, characters in the play even joke about whether they looked enough like the historical persons they are portraying.

With the arrival of DBC, changes appear to be forthcoming, and not just in the casting. In talking

FIGURE 24.1 *La Bohème* (Puccini). Broadcast live, 5 April 2008, Metropolitan Opera. A low angle shot approximating what you would see from the front row of a theatrical production.

FIGURE 24.2 *La Bohème* (Puccini). Broadcast live, 5 April 2008, Metropolitan Opera. A medium-close shot, a staple of television drama and comedy.

FIGURE 24.3 *La Bohème* (Puccini). Broadcast live, 5 April 2008, Metropolitan Opera. A wide-angle shot fully utilizing the aspect ratio of contemporary cinema.

to people at the Met, I was informed that when a production goes DBC, movie make-up people are brought in, the lighting is changed, and performers may position themselves differently onstage for camera access. The renowned opera diva and occasional host of the Met broadcasts Renée Fleming has said she consciously alters her stage persona to accommodate a global audience who now see more of her than Met audiences ever have.[14] Expectations regarding her physical appearance at the 22 September 2008 gala (at least those of people in the New York area) may have also been influenced by a publicity campaign in which a large image of her face was seen on the side of New York City buses, à la Sarah Jessica Parker's Carrie Bradshaw in *Sex and the City*.

VIEWING THE AUDIENCE

Audiences for the Met's DBC productions, although much older than the average movie audience, are not as homogenous, elderly, or affluent as is the case at major opera houses, at least in North America (National Theatre audiences are much younger). Generalizing from a variety of experiences at different venues, the audience breakdown seems roughly as follows: (1) the true and experienced opera fans; (2) those with a basic grasp of what opera is about but who are not necessarily devotees; (3) regular movie patrons largely unfamiliar with opera who have heard about the productions from friends or the media, and are open to the experience. This third category often contains younger people, such as students with an interest in the arts who might find a traditional opera venue unaffordable or overly formal. Not surprisingly the biggest draw for audiences are the famous operas, such as *La Bohème* and *Carmen*. It should also be noted that although DBC operas can attract a diverse audience, this is not necessarily the case for theatre. Productions such as Stratford's *Caesar and Cleopatra* or National Theatre plays generally attract knowledgeable patrons familiar with what to expect from and how to respond to conventional theatre.

With a new medium such as DBC, the audience sees both the live performance and the in-house patrons at the venue in which it is taking place. Reaction shots of the in-house audience are often used when the opera or play is a comedy. With comedic operas, we can observe the Met audience laughing and laugh with them. The audience, either in-house or in movie theatres, is a participant. With tragic operas, the movie theatre audience comprises individual spectators who appear to personalize their responses to the fate of the protagonists. One could sense the cinema audience at *La Bohème* fighting to hold back tears at Mimi's death, as if they were watching 'only a movie', rather than live flesh-and-blood performers exuding a level of emotionality that differs from a performance on film.

With either comedy or tragedy, traditional opera audiences have been renowned for the way they respond to productions, both in terms of felt emotions and overt expression.[15] Tomato-tossing episodes at Milan's La Scala are legendary. (Do they bring the produce because they know the performance might be problematic, or bring it just in case?) Met audiences are somewhat more sedate. They are more likely to express disapproval with brief applause, and respond to a production's ordinariness with no standing ovation. Nevertheless, boos were heard after the production of Verdi's *Macbeth* (12 January 2008) and Puccini's *Tosca* (21 September 2009), not for the performers, but for the production design. The setting for *Macbeth* was transposed from early medieval Scotland to a hypothetical banana republic; *Tosca* featured a stark mise-en-scène that replaced the longstanding and much loved version designed by Franco Zeffirelli.

These points raise the question of how the audience in a movie theatre should respond to a live presentation from far away. Does it make sense to applaud in a movie theatre in Toronto, Vancouver, or Waterloo, when the performers in a production are privy to reactions only from within the house? Newspaper reviews of the Met's first DBC season indicate, as do my experiences, that in smaller municipalities less familiar with opera custom, sporadic applause suggests a largely passive audience that is slightly less passive in their response when the production is a comedy. In other words, they behave more like movie patrons than theatre patrons. In larger centres, where many in the audience have previous opera- or theatre-going experience and can imagine themselves at the performance venue, reactions are more overt.

Recently, Martin Barker, Research Professor at Aberystwyth University in Wales, has made considerable headway in understanding the audience's response to what he has called 'live-streamed performances' or 'alternative cinema content'.[16] He has produced a detailed UK-based study that is both quantitative, drawing from 644 questionnaire responses, and qualitative, containing informed analysis and interpretation. In the 'new kind of cultural occasion' that he attributes to the live-streamed format, opera emerges as the clear winner in popularity over theatre and ballet. It has also attracted the most diverse audience. Viewers responded to his questionnaire with a 94 per cent 'excellent' or 'good' rating of the live-streamed experience. Patrons were influenced by the affordability of the productions, proximity of the venues, and the visual presentation of performances. Although 'experts tended to be skeptical, the general audience assumed "the virtual invisibility of the medium."'[17] In other words, for many it was almost like being at the performance venue; and for a number of respondents who had attended performances at the Met, the live-streamed alternative was preferred.

An interesting complement to Barker's report is the question of how knowledgeable students of opera might respond to a DBC performance. I was able to do a field study in this regard by leading the University of Toronto's Operatics Workshop in a viewing and subsequent discussion of Richard Strauss' *Der Rosenkavalier* (9 January 2010). The responses varied. At the extremes, a few thought it trivialized opera and detracted from the authenticity of the experience, while several were enthralled with the idea and saw it as a kind of McLuhanesque 'global village' future. Some complained that the auditory quality was adversely affected by the type of sound system used in the cinema multiplex. (One person was quick to note that the Met Opera Orchestra was not up to the challenge of this particular work, which is of course not a DBC problem.) There was, nevertheless, virtual unanimity on two points. First, these productions are worthwhile, *on occasion*, but cannot substitute for a live in-house experience. Second, they employ too many close-ups and quick cuts, which tend to lead the audience rather than allow it to selectively scan aspects of a production in a more personalized way (there was a small but vociferous opposition to shots of particular instrumentalists in the orchestra). In other words, these students thought that DBC should strive to be more theatrical and less cinematic and televisual in its presentation. This runs completely counter to the preferences of the general public attending these performances, according to the Barker study.

FINALE

When the Met's general manager, Peter Gelb, launched the HD broadcasts in 2006, performing

arts and film critics were skeptical. The success of the first season still did not guarantee that the format would have staying power. Fortunately, the even more ambitious second season secured the concept and inspired other performing arts companies to follow suit. The 2009–2010 season featured a series of popular operas—in addition to *Carmen*, productions of Puccini's *Tosca* and *Turandot* (7 November 2009), and Verdi's *Aida*—which led to more encore broadcasts than in any previous season. For those who either were enthralled by these productions and wanted to see them again, or were unable to experience them at the Met or on screen, reasonably priced HD versions are available through the Met's online service.

The 2009 Stratford production of Shaw's *Caesar and Cleopatra*, although not a live transmission, was inspired by the Met's format for capturing a performance, but used nine HD cameras to the Met's twelve. Several theatres in the Toronto region were sold out, and reviews were uniformly positive, especially regarding Christopher Plummer's performance in the lead. Renowned theatre critic Richard Ouzounian was quick to note that Plummer's skill as a performer on both stage and screen makes him a natural for this new media format.[18]

A recurring question with respect to DBC is, How does the camera set-up intrude on the in-house patrons' view of a production? Hardly at all, from my own experience of Met productions, except from near the front of the orchestra, where the camera tracking back and forth across the front of the stage can be a distraction. In the smaller National Theatre venue, the situation is different. Cameras are always visible—those on-stage even show up occasionally in the DBC transmissions. As a consideration, in-house patrons for those performances are charged the same price as those who view the production in a movie theatre.

DBC endeavours not only to close the gap between what constitutes a performing art and a recording art, but also tries to bridge the divide that has traditionally separated high art from popular culture. The cost of attending a broadcast, the casualness of the venues, and the explanations that accompany the performances all contribute to the format's accessibility. The question is whether the 'virtual' compromises the 'authentic', tarnishing what Walter Benjamin might call its 'aura'. How are we to regard DBC in light of his observation that 'even the most perfect reproduction of a work of art is lacking one element: its presence in time and space, its unique existence at the place where it happens to be'?[19] Yet the condition of the postmodern DBC viewer involves a situation Benjamin probably never imagined, wherein that viewer is far from the event being staged, yet experiences it as it is taking place, and therefore becomes part of it, a phenomenon media historians sometimes call 'co-presence'.

Benjamin, writing in 1935, before the age of television broadcasting, is comparing theatre only to film and argues that the camera's selection of what we see does not respect the performance as a whole; also, the film actor cannot adjust to the audience as a stage actor can. While Benjamin's point regarding the actor's relationship to an audience in theatre versus film is certainly valid, the case is less clear-cut when applied to DBC. True, the performers cannot see their virtual audience, but they can respond to the in-house audience. The virtual audience can respond both to the performance and to the in-house audience's reaction to it, thereby gaining a sense that they are sharing an experience, or an 'aura' if you will, that is closer to watching live theatre than to watching a film. Martin Barker has even suggested that the virtual audience be encouraged to behave as if they are at the actual performance venue.

As this new media format continues into the future, which seems quite likely, more questions are destined to emerge. Will Broadway follow with broadcasts of live theatre? My sense is that its ties to New York tourism are too strong for this to happen often. What about local performing arts companies? Will they benefit through a kind of trickle-down effect from the increased arts appreciation and growing audiences created by DBC, or will A-list cinema broadcasts trump B-list local productions? At the moment the answers are unclear, although some evidence suggests that attendance for local companies may be up slightly. Clearly, DBC is physically and financially creating new possibilities for public access to the performing arts.

At a time when traditional movie attendance is facing increased competition from technological innovations, such as new HD disc formats and the latest in-home and mobile screen options employing the Internet, DBC represents an intriguing counter-current (as no doubt does the return of 3-D film extravaganzas, such as *Avatar* and *Alice in Wonderland*). Perhaps it should come as no surprise that opera is a major player in this regard. Over a century ago, Richard Wagner referred to it as total art; but film soon usurped that mantle, given its capacity to assimilate other performing and plastic arts, including theatre, dance, photography, and painting. Yet DBC, through the Met operas or National Theatre productions such as *Nation*, can do likewise. By using new and old technologies to create intermedia spectacles that rival cinema, performance companies can then go movies one better by doing it live.

NOTES

1. This is primarily a UK estimate and was forwarded to me by Martin Barker (personal correspondence, 4 January 2010).
2. Portions of this chapter previously appeared in 'Live from the Met: Digital Broadcast Cinema, Medium Theory, and Opera for the Masses' (*Canadian Journal of Communication* 33, 4, 2008).
3. Although this is the case, CTV nonetheless, in deciding to make the 2010 Winter Olympics available in movie theatres across the country, cited the success of the Met's opera transmissions as influencing their decision.
4. James Monaco, *How to Read a Film: Movies, Media, Multimedia* (New York: Oxford, 2000).
5. Monaco, *How to Read a Film*, 38.
6. Monaco, *How to Read a Film*, 48.
7. Elizabeth Renzetti, 'Dazzling effects—in the original 3-D' (*The Globe and Mail*, 30 January 2010). DBC has also entered the world of real 3D, no doubt inspired by the success of *Avatar* and films that followed in its wake. On 23 Feb-

ruary 2011, London's English National Opera broadcast Donizetti's *Lucrezia Borgia*. Not to be outdone, the following month on 5 March, the Royal Opera House offered Bizet's *Carmen* in 'RealD 3D'. Reviews were not encouraging and it is uncertain if DBC will continue to experiment with 3D.

8. Ingmar Bergman's highly regarded production of Mozart's *The Magic Flute* is one of several productions that have drawn accolades. For extensive commentary regarding opera on film see Ken Walschin, *Opera on Screen* (Los Angeles: Beachwood Press, 1998), and David Schroeder, *Cinema's Illusions, Opera's Allure* (New York: Continuum, 2002).

9. Bruno Bettelheim, *The Uses of Enchantment: The Meaning and Importance of Fairy Tales* (New York: Knopf, 1976).

10. Edmund Carpenter, 'The New Languages', in Edmund Carpenter and Marshall McLuhan (Eds), *Explorations in Communication* (Boston: Beacon Press, 1960).

11. John Ellis, *Visible Fictions: Cinema, Television, Video* (London: Routledge, 1992).

12. Edward Hall, *The Hidden Dimension* (New York: Doubleday, 1966).

13. Linda Hutcheon and Michael Hutcheon, *Bodily Charm: Living Opera* (Lincoln, Neb.: University of Nebraska Press, 2000).

14. From an interview cited in Justin Davidson, 'The Sopranos on the Big Screen' (*New York*, 28 December 2007).

15. The former is discussed in Hutcheon and Hutcheon, *Bodily Charm*, and the latter in Joseph Wechsberg, *The Opera* (New York: MacMillan, 1972).

16. Martin Barker, 'Report to Picturehouse Cinemas/City Screen on the Findings of a Research Project into Audience Responses to Streaming of Live Performances ("Alternative Content") to Cinemas'. Unpublished report. I am grateful to Professor Barker for making this report available to me.

17. Martin Barker, personal correspondence, 4 January 2010.

18. Richard Ouzounian, 'Caesar and Cleopatra: Play even better on the big screen' (*The Toronto Star*, 30 January 2009). Plummer's recent performance in the Stratford production of Shakespeare's *The Tempest* will be seen in movie theatres sometime in early 2011.

19. Walter Benjamin, 'The Work of Art in the Age of Mechanical Reproduction', in Gerald Mast and Marshall Cohen (Eds), *Film Theory and Criticism: Introductory Readings* (New York: Oxford University Press,1985).

25

FROM COUNTING CALORIES TO FUN FOOD: REGULATING THE TV DIET IN THE AGE OF OBESITY

JACQUELINE BOTTERILL AND STEPHEN KLINE

INTRODUCTION

Consumer sovereignty is at the root of the neo-liberal economists' account of how to democratize the distribution of social resources and ensure economic growth. But their celebration of the individual's rational choice in competitive markets depends on the assumption of a perfect distribution of product information. Rational choice is possible only if all consumers have complete and accurate information about the qualities, risks, and costs of competing goods. This assumption ensures that communication occupies a privileged place in the politics of neo-liberal markets, in which advertising is justified in that

it provides information to enable consumers to make the best choices. Yet as John Kenneth Galbraith (1957) notes, when the assumption of 'autonomous rational consumers' is in doubt, there is no reason to believe that the 'invisible hand' of the free market will work towards improving our collective well-being. For this reason, since the 1930s, policy-makers have seen the need to regulate commercial media, to ensure that marketers' communications about product benefits, risks and costs are neither 'deceptive or misleading' (Leiss et al. 2005).

During the 1970s, child-targeted advertising raised doubts about young people's capacity for rational choice. In the United States, the Federal Trade Commission (FTC) worried that the food and toy ads that punctuated children's TV could unduly influence children because of their developmental immaturity. Since research showed that children under eight years of age seemed not to understand the persuasive intent of TV advertising (Ward et al. 1977), the FTC imposed strict regulatory guidelines on children's marketers. These guidelines required 'bumpers' to separate advertisements from programming and limits on the use of popular TV characters in advertising, and included cautions about unrealistic claims. In Canada, similar concerns justified the CRTC's code for TV advertising, which called on advertisers to be mindful of the limitations of child audiences—particularly their limited ability to distinguish fantasy from reality—and to critically evaluate persuasive appeals embedded in imaginary stories. Quebec banned food advertising to children for the same reason. Yet in 1981, US President Ronald Reagan cast aside the FTC's precautionary approach to children's vulnerability, transforming American TV into a cultural laboratory for experimentation in synergistic promotion: animated toys and product placement, cross-promotion, celebrity endorsements, and brand characters became common elements in the marketers' fantastic story-telling that inundated the screen (Kline 1993). Toy and food promotions entered Canada thereafter via cable television.

Children's advertising became the focal point in the policy debates about advertising for a very simple reason: research suggests children are not capable of 'rational consumer choice' until they are fully informed, able to make complex product comparisons, and recognize and filter the persuasive techniques used by advertisers (Roedder-John 1999). Justifying the return of advertising regulation in the US during the 1990s, FTC commissioner Mary Azcuenaga (1997) argued that market regulation is called for when the assumption of 'informed choice' is in doubt.

It is hardly surprising, then, that the World Health Organization's 2004 report implicating soft-drink advertisers in the weight gains of child population reignited the 25-year-old controversy about the unhealthy nature of TV food advertising targeting children (Kline 2005). As anxiety about child obesity grew, so too did the public debate about the unhealthy biases of the food marketing system (Kline 2010), challenging policy-makers to judge not only what constitutes deceptive and misleading claims in children's food advertising, but also how far food advertisers could be deemed responsible for children becoming obese.

The obesity crisis forced advertising regulators to revisit the rationale for regulating children's food marketing on TV (Kline 2004). UK researchers launched a series of policy reviews looking at the content of advertising to children. The Hastings et al. (2003) report, one of the most comprehensive studies, suggests that what matters is not just what is advertised excessively, but what is missing. The authors find that advertising targeting children 'was lacking in meats, fruit and vegetables (especially fresh, non-processed meat, fruit and vegetables)' (ibid., 84). Products were often shown in their most unhealthy form—'pre-sugared breakfast cereals, sweetened dairy products, processed meat (burgers), breaded fish, canned fruit and deep-fried vegetables' (ibid., 85). Healthier products were also used to boost the perceived nutritional value of food products providing little nutrition. The Hastings report also examines the various creative strategies employed in children's food advertising. Animation, a common device, is 'particularly strongly associated with children's food advertisements compared with non-food . . . . Breakfast cereal advertisements were identified as more likely to involve a mixed animation/live action format in which children encounter fantasy cartoon characters' (ibid., 95). The report concludes, therefore, that 'creative appeals in children's food advertising concentrated on "fun" and "taste", rather than on health or nutrition' (ibid., 100).

A subsequent review of the impact of food advertising on children's consumption (Livingstone and Helsper 2006) resulted in the UK regulator, OFCOM, banning advertising of unhealthy foods to children and youth on children's TV dayparts in 2007. As David Buckingham (2009) states, 'The debate about children and food advertising in the UK provides an illuminating case study of the some of the broader forces at play in the making of contemporary cultural policy, particularly the field of media regulation', because it highlights the issue of children's 'competences' in mediated markets (p. 218). But it was not just children's 'advertising literacy' that propelled this debate, but also the evidence that exposure to food marketing constituted a risk to children's health and well-being.

In the US, reviews of epidemiological and consumer research literatures (Kunkel et al. 2004; Kaiser Family Foundation 2005; Holt et al. 2007) pressured Congress to threaten the food industry with new advertising regulations beyond the Food and Drug Act's requirement of truthful product claims. Mobilized by former president Bill Clinton, American food makers responded by acknowledging their ability to influence children's health and promised that, if allowed to 'self-regulate', they would promote good nutrition and active living.

In 2003, Canadian advertising regulators also reminded Canadian food marketers that they must not exploit children's 'credulity, lack of experience or their sense of loyalty' or present information or illustrations that 'might result in their physical, emotional or moral harm'. They warned that humour and flights of fantasy were problematic ways to convey a message about an unhealthy product (Advertising Standards Canada 2003).

Although misleading advertising has been much debated, the global obesity crisis exposed the limitations of the regulatory framework for preventing 'systemic risks'. In this chapter, we explore three ways in which accumulated evidence of a link between advertising exposure and weight gain (Dietz 1986; Zimmerman and Bell 2010) presents a profound challenge for the regulation of child-targeted advertising. First, we argue that the potential harm done to children is linked not to a single advertisement, but to a *biased food system on commercial TV* that deviates from the nutritionally recommended diet. To explore this 'promotional cultural system' we report a textual analysis of 1556 North American food advertisements shown in the fall and spring on commercial TV between 2003 and 2007 during

prime time and children's dayparts (Saturdays, mornings, after school, and during children's specials). Second, after analyzing the social communication of advertising, we suggest that scientifically accurate nutritional claims can still be *misleading within the context of the visualized narratives* of branded food promotion. Given the doubts about young children's advertising literacy, we suggest that regulatory guidelines must better address whether the audio-visual techniques used in brand promotion facilitate or sidetrack 'rational choice'. Third, by examining the scenes of eating in food commercials, we explore how the advertisers' *skewed representation of food culture* could influence consumption behaviours and ultimately children's health.

THE TV DIET DEBATE

Studies have repeatedly shown that the diet promoted on TV is 'unhealthy' and 'energy dense', consisting of high-calorie foods with little nutritional value. Products high in salt, sugar, and fat predominate on TV, contrary to nutritional guidelines. Reviewing the 44 extant content analyses of food advertising, the Hastings Committee's 2003 review for the UK Food Standards Agency notes that an over-representation of the 'Big Five' food types—salty snacks, confections, sweetened cereals, soft drinks, and foods found in fast-food restaurants—and an under-representation of fruits, vegetables, and whole foods in children's TV dayparts mean that children are habitually presented an unbalanced dietary array. A number of subsequent studies have confirmed the nutritional shortcomings of the TV diet (Neville et al. 2005; Harrison and Marske 2005; Wilson et al. 2006; Roberts and Pettigrew 2007). For example, Mink et al. (2010) compare the nutritional value of foods advertised in 84 hours of prime time and 12 hours of Saturday morning television during the fall of 2004. They found that overall, when compared to the national nutritional guidelines, the TV diet contained '2,560% of the recommended daily servings for sugars, 2,080% of the recommended daily servings for fat' but just '40% of the recommended daily servings for vegetables, 32% of the recommended daily

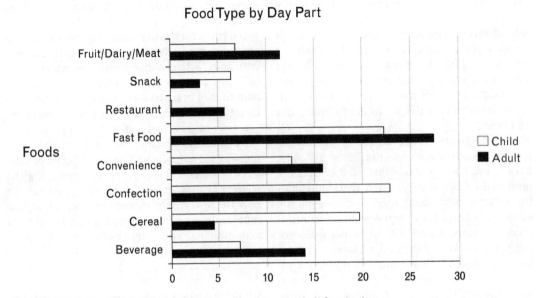

Food Type by Day Part

Foods

- Fruit/Dairy/Meat
- Snack
- Restaurant
- Fast Food
- Convenience
- Confection
- Cereal
- Beverage

☐ Child
■ Adult

0 5 10 15 20 25 30

FIGURE 25.1 Food type by day part as a percentage of all food ads

servings for dairy, and 27% of the recommended daily servings for fruits' (ibid., 904). They concluded that food promotion highlights protein, fat, cholesterol, and sodium, while overlooking 'fiber, vitamins A, E, and D, pantothenic acid, iron, phosphorous, calcium, magnesium, copper, and potassium'(Ibid.).

Our content analysis of North American ads similarly reveals that high-calorie, low-nutrient foods dominate the sample—fast food (26 per cent), sweets (21 per cent), and sugary cereals (13 per cent). The major whole-food groups—fruits, meats, dairy, and vegetables—appeared in under 14 per cent of the adult ads but less often in children's TV time. Cereals, confections, and snacks were the food types disproportionately advertised on children's dayparts, while fast food and beverages were more advertised in prime time. Fast food was the most-advertised category overall, but confections (candy, cookies, cakes) slightly edged out fast food in children's time TV.

We also analyzed the nutritional content of advertised food, noting the extent to which the recommended healthy foods (fruit, vegetables, diary) were missing in the kids' dayparts. As Figure 25.1 demonstrates, we found that not only

did representations of junk food and products of limited nutritional value dwarf those of healthy food, food of low nutritional value appeared more often on children's time than on adult time. The problematic food types identified by nutritionists for limited consumption accounted for 66 per cent of adult ads, but for 80 per cent of child-targeted advertising. These findings confirm that although the TV diet is skewed towards the unhealthy, the food ads targeting children are nutritionally more questionable.

REGULATING VERBAL HEALTH CLAIMS

Given the unique health risks associated with edible products, the accuracy of health and utility claims in food advertising has long been regulated by food and drug legislation—the Food Standards Agency in the UK, the Food and Drug Administration in the US, and Health Canada. Yet, food and drug regulation assesses 'information communicated' in commercials based on the scientific validity of verbalized product claims (e.g., 'low-fat', 'cholesterol-free', 'healthy'). Legislation insists that all claims made in ads about a product's ingredients and effectiveness (e.g., 'builds strong bodies', 'full of vitamin or minerals', 'alleviates the symptoms of allergies') be scientifically justified. In this context, a misleading claim is one that deviates from 'accuracy'. For example, the US consumer group the Center for Science in the Public Interest (CSPI) recently employed a misleading claims analysis to support a legal challenge against Coca-Cola Co. Pointing to written claims, CSPI argued that Coca-Cola marketed its Vitaminwater as a 'healthy alternative' to soda. The group identified the use of health buzzwords like *defense, rescue, energy,* and *endurance,* and claims that Vitaminwater would address specific illnesses. Having scientifically evaluated the content of Vitaminwater, CSPI nutritionists argued that Coca-Cola's health rhetoric was misleading. With 33 grams of sugar per bottle, Vitaminwater was more likely to promote obesity and diabetes than to promote wellness and 'perform the advertised benefits listed on the bottles' (Reuters 2009). Coca-Cola retorted that it was not deceiving the public, because every bottle clearly stated the sugar content. The company claimed that it was up to consumers to search out the nutritional information on the package, and that it did not need to address health risks in its advertising.

Regulating food advertising based upon the scientific validity of explicit health claims is an ineffective policy, however, because it discourages advertisers from addressing nutrition and health. In our sample of North American food ads, less than 25 per cent explicitly stated a health claim. Although they sometimes mention the health qualities associated with their products, food advertisers are reluctant to invoke the 'health risks' associated with inappropriate consumption of the product, such as exceeding the recommended daily intake of grams of fat or salt. Less than 4 per cent of all ads gave warnings about overconsumption, and very few of these cautions were directed at children. Moreover, while verbal claims and health messages were equally distributed among messages aimed at adults and at children, nutrition messages were qualitatively different when children were addressed. Prime-time ads received more detailed and specific phrasing such as 'contains 6 essential vitamins and minerals', whereas

children heard more general and vague messages about food value and contents in their advertising, such as 'bursting with 5 summery fruit flavours and vitamin C'.

BEYOND VERBAL CLAIMS: DISCOURSE ANALYSIS OF SOCIAL COMMUNICATION IN ADVERTISING

Other health messages in many food advertisements are often communicated through techniques of visual association. In her study of US food advertising, Byrd-Bredbenner (2002) found that healthy foods are used to provide 'symbolic health' to unhealthy foods: 'The most common misleading image was fresh fruit shown in advertisements for fruit-flavoured candy and beverages. Through visual images of fruits, advertisers conveyed a false impression of the fruit content of foods even though they did not make any false verbal statements' (ibid., 394). In our study too, we found that many advertisers used images of fruit and nature to imply that wholesome ingredients are used in the product.*

A common trope is the sugar-laden cereal shown with fruit in the bowl surrounded by a large jug of milk, a glass of milk, whole wheat toast, and orange juice, accompanied by the nutritional claim 'part of a balanced breakfast'. Other visual associations include showing children eating apples or carrots along with highly processed or sugar-dense foods. By inserting their products into an ensemble of whole grains, milk, and fruit, advertisers make implied claims about wholesomeness, which are echoed in the verbal reference to a 'healthy' or 'balanced' breakfast, while failing to state that it is the milk and fruit that make it healthy. Just as toy advertisers are required to state 'batteries not included', children's advertisements might benefit from the warning 'strawberries not included'.

There are several well-known techniques that make foods visually attractive including staging, makeup, and airbrushing. Nutritionists admonish the food marketers for using these techniques to promote excessive consumption, recommending instead showing serving sizes far more modest than the plate-overflowing images. Food stylists forge enhanced depictions of food—known in the advertising industry as 'food porn'—sculpted for maximum visualized taste: the whipped cream is impossibly fluffy and white; the steaks juicy, dripping, and deeply, darkly crusted; the chocolate impossibly velvety; the cheese fantastically melted and perfectly stretchy. Frequently, ingredients are artfully blended or carefully separated—thus the crisp, green lettuce is unaffected by the thick steaming beef patty on top. Such images appear frequently in store posters and street billboards. These food models are as aesthetically exaggerated, pumped up, coloured, shadowed, and photographed from the most flattering camera angles as are human ones. Most ads contain a product 'beauty shot' that shows the real product without backdrop or setting. Although luscious images of stacked lettuce, tomato, and sauce stay on the screen for only a few seconds, a child may not be able to judge relative size when the camera cuts from a wide-angle shot to a close-up.

Many TV ads embed product beauty shots in narratives describing consumers' motivations and pleasures. The adult ad sample featured a trope of visual storytelling, which, as Jean Kilbourne (1999) notes, depicts female eaters in a state of sensual self-indulgence. For example, an ad asks which is better—sex or chocolate—although the scenes of erotic eating imply the question is rhetorical. In another ad, waves of chocolate, caramel, and nougat undulate temptingly across the screen to the beat to an exotic chant overwritten by the words *drool, pant,* and *lick the screen*. The dripping streams of carnal temptation fold together into a chocolate bar shape as a female voice taunts 'What are you going to do with your energy?' The repetition of the food porn trope across the adult sample constantly positions snacking as a sinful yet decadent luxury, part of a hedonistic pampered life that females especially deserve.

Yet, we noted that advertisers generally avoid using the food porn approach in children's time. The camera rarely dwells on the sensuousness of kids' food or explores the dimensions of taste metaphorically other than the way food 'bangs', 'bursts', 'crackles', 'pops', and 'explodes' in children's mouths. References to decadence, sinfulness, and hedonism were notably absent from the children's sample. The only connotation of sexuality in children's advertising is the occasional use of treats in depicting innocent childhood crushes. Rather, the metaphors of children's taste is action-packed—personified, animated, or turned into a toy, a game, or a lively brand character. On kids' TV, foods come alive rather than being objects of visual desire. In children's ads, chewing gum jumps out of planes (Extra), candies race (M&M's), cookies attend dinner parties (Chips Ahoy), and brand characters jump into the shopping basket of their own volition.

The unrealistic claims often embedded in imaginative brand narratives in children's food advertising present another hard-to-regulate dimension of communication. Animated consumption scenes are especially problematic when scenes are intercut with 'realistic' product shots. For example, a Nestlé's Quick ad cuts from real children to an animated character drinking a swimming pool full of chocolate milk. Alternatively, humorous exaggeration defies the notion of portion size when teenage boys order a cement truck full of macaroni and cheese to fill a kitchen, or avoid interrupting their hockey game by taping to their heads huge jugs of liquefied pasta, which they drink through tubes while they skate. We do not deny that adolescent boys require considerable calories and that Kraft Dinner can supply them. But we take issue with how, in the name of imaginative overstatement, implicit messages about gluttony are normalized.

FEEDING THE IMAGINARY

Elsewhere we have argued that targeted brand promotion evolved with strategic appeals to segmented audiences (Botterill and Kline 2007). Since President Reagan's deregulation of children's TV in the 1980s, marketers have developed a synergistic approach to targeting that favours the cartoon stylization of popular children's films and TV shows. Currently, food advertisers target children not only through TV campaigns but also through in-school marketing, product placements, kids' clubs, online media, free toys, cross-marketing, tie-ins, and sweepstake prizes (Story and French 2004). Cross-marketing is rampant. The UK Food Commission (2005) reported on 41 non-broadcast food marketing techniques aimed at children, observing that:

> Marketing campaigns aimed at children and young people move smoothly between different formats, perhaps combining product placement in blockbuster films; which in turn feature characters who will appear on food products and in interactive games; backed by websites offering music downloads and movie clips, containing yet more inducements to buy ... (ibid., 3).

Table 25.1 compares the branding strategies in prime time and in children's advertising, indicating that cross-marketing and animated stories are preferred by kids' marketers. Contemporary children's campaigns reveal a range of targeting techniques, including product placement, brand characters, cross-marketing, animated fantasy, and celebrity endorsements. Not surprisingly, therefore, we found twice as much cross-marketing in kids' ads as in prime-time ads (36 per cent versus 19 per cent).

While celebrity endorsements are more common in prime-time ads, animated brand characters and cross-marketing are the easily identifiable techniques used for cereal, snack, and fast-food brands in children's dayparts. Brand characters are ambiguous metaphors in kids' ads—they are intermediaries between the imaginary world of popular culture and the real world of children's daily lives. In a Frosted Flakes ad, for example, a young boy's solo basketball game is disturbed by Tony the Tiger loudly crunching his breakfast cereal. Tony apologizes for disturbing the boy's practice, but continues to eat his cereal. The boy is sympathetic to Tony's plight, perhaps because the basketball court seems an odd place for even an animated character to eat breakfast.

Food marketers also use gifts and games as inducements to purchase their products, as exemplified in the McDonald's Happy Meals cross-marketing. Another example is seen in a recent Kinder Surprise ad, which depicts a rosy-cheeked cherub

TABLE 25.1 Cross-marketing in Ads for Kids Compared to Prime Time Ads

	Total	Adult	Kids
Cross-marketing	30	19	36
Celebrity	3	5	2
Animation	34	13	46

Source: Steven Kline and Jacqueline Botterill

who returns from a family shopping expedition proudly proclaiming to his mother that his recently purchased chocolate egg treat contains a secret code for playing a computer game. The ad cuts to mother and child in front of the computer as the son explains how much he enjoys playing this video game. Transfixed by the screen, he distractedly munches on the chocolate egg while his mother smiles approvingly. The ad closes with the tag line 'It's all about spending time together.' Whatever this ad implies about the sorry state of 'quality time', the fact remains that in many children's ads, the toy and not the food is the dominant selling point. Scenes of children playing with the toys convey the idea of 'fun' associated with the food brand but also marginalize the nutrition, taste, and health aspects of eating. Kline (2010) argues that synergistic selling strategies such as the marketing tools thinly disguised as programs, product placements, gifts, promotional toys, and cross-marketing campaigns in different media make it harder for children to understand the selling intent or sponsorship of ads. Even children who understand the selling intent of the food advertiser may find their savvy tested by the offer of a 'free' gift in every box.

Despite the injunction to be mindful of children's vivid imaginations, one-fifth of the ads we studied emphasized the power of imagination, dreams, and fantasy to transform children's lives. We should not be surprised that children don't know where their milk comes from: food ads rarely show its source, or how real grains, nuts, and fruits grow, either. Perhaps the most egregious abuse of the confusion of the imaginary and the real is exemplified in a Cap'n Crunch's Choco Donuts ad. It starts with a scene of real children in a supermarket where the shelves are empty of their favourite chocolate cereal. Cap'n Crunch sails into the store and transports their animated selves to an imaginary ship where they power-lick the chocolate decks clean with big slurps of their animated tongues. The last shot shows them at home, their oversized animated tongues licking their real lips while the announcer tells viewers that 'Choco Donuts' are 'part of a balanced chocolatey breakfast'.

Ads like this one raise serious questions about children's ability to be sovereign consumers: How are they to make reasoned choices about food when the acts and consequences of eating are imaginary? How is information about nutrition distorted when it is reworked within the imaginary space of humorous brand narrative? To contribute to this debate, advertising analysis must move beyond examining truth and falsehood to consider the values and attitudes conveyed by brand narratives.

FUN FOOD AND ACTIVE LIFESTYLES

Accused of contributing to obesity, food marketers have pledged to be responsible advertisers by promoting active and healthy lifestyles. Fast-food advertisers are especially adept at finding techniques to make their offerings appear more healthy and more socially palatable. In terms of general values, three times as many adult ads made verbal reference to 'health' and 'vitality' (16 per cent) as did children's ads (5 per cent). But what children's ads lack in verbal claims is made up for in the dynamism of images and aesthetics. Almost universally, children's animated food ads emphasize humour, fun, and action in building a symbolic bridge between children's lives and the brand narrative. The rapid cutting style and pulsing music gives a high-energy feel, with 40 per cent of children's food ads emphasizing fun, play, and leisure as their core value: children are dancing, playing, skateboarding, and singing with Ronald McDonald—instead of eating.

Indeed, actual eating is half as likely to appear in children's ads as in adult ads. Instead, kids are in a constant state of movement and very seldom

sedentary (e.g., sitting at the table, reading, watching TV). In kids' time TV, 42 per cent of ads depicted moderate activities (walking, slow movement) and 20 per cent showed high-intensity activities (running or great physical exertion). The motion is almost frenetic, conveying a sense of non-stop active lifestyles, high-energy pursuits, and vitality. In contrast, 53 per cent of the adult ads depicted repose and only 4 per cent high-activity pursuits. It is the adults who engage in sedentary activities like watching TV. Creators of ads can rightly claim that they show images of active children, although we must qualify this statement with the observation that activity turns eating into snacking while masking the nutritional deficits of the products.

VISUALIZING THE CULTURE OF THE TABLE

Whether realistic or animated, food advertising also conveys ideas about eating behaviours and more broadly about the attitudes to food in our promotional culture. Nutritionists have shown that it is not only *what* one eats that is associated with weight gain, but also *how* one eats: a constellation of eating behaviours is linked with obesity, including eating in front of the TV, eating alone, skipping breakfast, and frequent snacking. Likewise, leisurely meals and family meals together seem to help protect against obesity (Taylor et al. 2005). In order to understand the visual biases of the TV diet, we analyzed the modelling of food behaviours by noting how eating rituals and habits are represented in advertising. Our analysis examined not only the culturally embedded claims about health but also how food is eaten—where, when, and with whom. In about 20 per cent of ads, there is no clear reference to eating (food is shown it is a 'beauty shot' only). On kids' TV, 12 per cent of ads show breakfast and only 6.5 per cent show dinner, whereas 17 per cent of prime-time ads show dinner and 6.8 per cent show breakfast. Eating at home is mostly depicted in the kitchen or dining room, but appears in only 6 per cent of ads. The adult ads were three times more likely to depict eating in a restaurant than were the children's ads (21 per cent versus 7 per cent), but the children's ads were more likely to show eating outdoors (21 per cent versus 10 per cent). Most often, however, snacking is depicted, which takes place in almost half of the kids' ads and a third of prime-time ads. Children's eating often takes place on the run, spliced into play and leisure activities. When children eat however, they rarely do so alone (8 per cent), but rather with peers (40 per cent), with their families (26 per cent), or with adults other than relatives (14 per cent).

A Quaker Oats ad provides a clue to the changes taking place in family meals. The theme, of course, is that instant Quaker Oats has changed little since it first appeared in 1901. It is nutritious, healthy, and natural. The durability of this brand is set against the changing family breakfast: first, we see a shot of a large extended family eating outside at a long wooden table laden with large quantities of food, presumably the food needed to fuel the family for energy-intensive agricultural labour. Both mother and daughter serve the food, while father sits at the head of the table. Food is passed around, symbolizing a nostalgic blend of wholesome, social family interaction. In the second vignette, with styling suggesting the 1930s, father has changed out of his overalls into white collar and tie, illustrating the transition from rural to urban labour. The family is now nuclear rather than extended, permitting father to take more interest in his individual children, indicated by his deep bend forward as he cranes to listen to the children's soft voices. Mother stands and serves. This family-around-the-table arrangement is repeated in the third scene, but mom's beehive hair and dress suggests the early 1960s.

The last scene deconstructs family eating behaviours with amazing acuity: mom and dad are at a counter, instead of a table, poised on tall stools that allow each an easy return to their busy lives. Moreover, in a post-feminist world, gendered food preparation is replaced by a convenient self-serve mode of eating on the run. The ad's tagline is 'Wholesome goodness that fits your life'. Yet when the ad is examined more closely, there are no children seated at the counter; instead, a young boy puts on his bicycle helmet and passes quickly across and out of the frame, while his parents stop their conversation and turn briefly to say goodbye to their offspring. Kids are

'on their own on the go'. In this 30-second ad, the advertiser has identified several profound social changes in our rituals of the table: snacking, eating on the run, and the fragmentation of family life are acknowledged and reflected back in these scenes. Thus, the Quaker Oats ad suggests that family size, gender roles, active living, individualism, and time pressures have all contributed to changes in domestic consumption.

Several ads suggest that family dining has become a problem. Eating scenes in children's ads are anything but family oriented. Rather, the food itself becomes a magic wand that lifts children out of the humdrum of home-cooked meals. For example, tacos transform the dreariness of everyday meals into a festive occasion accompanied by up-beat music—the children dance, elated that dinnertime is 'fun' again. In another ad, the crabby babysitter who scolds the children for jumping on the furniture and eating their favourite cereal is reprimanded by Cap'n Crunch, who whisks them away to a party on his cool ship where they eat cereal and dance to disco music. A third ad suggests that mom is a bad cook until she becomes a DJ and boogies with the kids. As food advertisers assimilate the ethos of MTV, the family dinner is replaced by snacking at pool parties, sports events, picnics, and street concerts.

We also detected notable differences in the emotions in scenes depicting the family meal. Family eating is a source of longing and anxiety for adults. As the extended family of the past disappeared, it became a powerful resource for advertiser's romantic re-creations, such as the trope of the sun-dappled Italian family enjoying a leisurely alfresco lunch, during which a son serenades his mother (as in a McCain pizza ad). Marketing foods as a remedy for presumed social discontents about family eating, a KFC ad depicts two confused children at the dinner table with their parents and wondering why they have been summoned to this unfamiliar social gathering. 'What are we doing here?' asks one: 'Is this a family meeting?' chimes the other. Mother tells them that they are at the table to eat a meal together—a bucket of deep-fried chicken.

Some ads suggest that individual choice and taste pose a challenge to traditional family meals, but food products bridge the differences with, for example, pizzas comprising four mini pizzas, each with a family member's favoured toppings. In an ad for Lean Cuisine, the voice-over announces that the manufacturer has heard women's concerns about the individualization of diets, and thus provides special easily prepared meals for children and a hearty bowl of healthy food for mother. A cereal manufacturer suggests that eating their product in the morning would prevent family members from making silly mistakes and provide a less frantic start to the day (Kellogg's Fruit Harvest). At its most extreme, the will of the sovereign consumer contradicts the principles of communal eating, and several ads privilege individual gratification. Thus, to keep the food for himself, an adult son tells his aging father that he would not like the cereal he himself is eating (Oatmeal Crisp), and likewise a hostess transgresses the rituals of politeness when she eats all the cookies on the plate offered to her guest (Peek Freans).

New products may also rework traditional table manners, stressing playfulness in eating. Cheestrings, a processed cheese product that can be pulled apart and shaped, and Go-Gurt, a yogurt product that can be eaten squeezed out of a tube instead of scooped with a spoon, are just two examples of how eating is changing. Mobile eating is a matter of grabbing, squirting, throwing, or dancing with your foods. Children's foods are also shaped like animals, letters, toys, or even bugs (think of prized candy worms for dessert). In critically examining the fun-food aspect of children's advertising, we are not advocating a reactionary return to the traditional family meal. The loosening of patriarchal family ties has been progressive particularly for women and children. But we want to emphasize that the under-socialized, grab and go, on-the-run eating rituals promoted to children are directly correlated with poor nutrition and obesity, and thus need to be acknowledged in the regulatory debates about food marketing to children.

CONCLUSION

We have discussed how the targeted approaches of North American food marketing between 2003 and 2007 sidestepped the prohibition of deceptive nutritional claims. We have argued that visual analysis of advertising reveals problems for policy approaches that so far have been limited to debates about the 'scientific accuracy' of claims made in individual ads. In assessing the undue influence of food advertising on children's immature powers of judgment, communication researchers have used content analysis to demonstrate that food marketing on TV targeting children is a biased promotional discourse, not only in depicting nutritional content, but also in how the risks, costs, and benefits of the products are communicated. In the US, where commercial free speech is protected by the Constitution, First Lady Michelle Obama continues to appeal to food marketers to be responsible, because a policy that recognizes the special developmental status of child consumers is seen to be at odds with freedom of commercial speech. In contrast, a ban on unhealthy food advertising directed at children was enacted in the UK, based on the argument that children cannot be assumed to exercise rational choice in their consumer decisions. Although the ban avoids the problem of distinguishing persuasion from information in commercial speech, it drives unhealthy food marketing into prime time, where children also see it, and drives it online, where so far it escapes the ambit of the regulation of commercial persuasion directed at this class of vulnerable consumers.

Recognizing that calls for industry self-regulation are not adequate, Canada's position lies somewhere between that of the US and the UK. In 2007, recognizing the difficulty of judging the animated storytelling so common in contemporary children's marketing, Canadian regulators proposed further interpretive guidelines for children's food marketers: depictions of excessive food consumption were frowned upon, product claims could not be exaggerated, snacks had to look like snacks and not meal substitutes, and visual exaggerations in size or consequence were to be limited to be more in keeping with *Canada's Food Guide to Healthy Eating*. Given doubts about children's capacity to make sense of visualized narratives and product claims, we feel that an even more robust definition of misleading visual claims is required to take account of the cultural practices and values of eating that are found in food advertising that children are exposed to. Yet, without further study, we have no way of evaluating to what extent these new guidelines

have moderated the TV diet or altered the representation of food and eating in Canadian advertising, or modified children's risk of exposure to the biased promotional system.

NOTE

*Permission to publish images of the advertisements described in this article was not granted at the time of publication.

REFERENCES

Advertising Standards Canada (2003). 'The 14 clauses of the Canadian Code of Advertising Standards'. http://www.adstandards.com/en/standards/the14Clauses.aspx.

Azcuenaga, M. (1997). 'The role of advertising and advertising regulation in the free market', Federal trade commissioner speech, Turkish Association of Advertising, Istanbul, April 8.

Botterill, J., and Kline, S. (2007). 'From mcLibel to mcLettuce', *Society and Business Review* 2, 1: 74–95.

Buckingham, D. (2009). 'The appliance of science: The role of evidence in the making of regulatory policy on children and food advertising in the UK', *International Journal of Cultural Policy* 15, 2: 201–15.

Byrd-Bredbenner, C. (2002). 'Food safety: An international public health issue', *International Electronic Journal of Health Education* 5: 59–74.

Dietz, W. (1986). 'Prevention of childhood obesity', *Pediatric Clinics of North America* 33, 4: 823–33.

Galbraith, J.K. (1957/1998). *The affluent society*. Boston: Houghton Mifflin.

Harrison, K., and Marske, A. (2005). 'Nutritional content of foods advertised during the television programs children watch most', *American Journal of Public Health*, 95: 1568–74.

Hastings, G., Stead, M., McDermott, L., Forsyth, A., MacKintosh, A., Rayner, M., Godfrey, C., Caraher, M., and Angus, K. (2003). *Review of Research on the Effects of Food Promotion to Children*, Report commissioned by Food Standards Agency, September. http://www.food.gov.uk/multimedia/pdfs/food-promotiontochildren1.pdf.

Holt, D., Ippolito, P., Desrocher, D., and Kelley, C. (2007). *Children's exposure to TV advertising in 1977 and 2004: Information for the obesity debate*. Federal Trade Commission, Washington, DC: US Government Printing Office.

Kaiser Family Foundation (2005). 'Generation M:

Media in the lives of eight to eighteen year olds'. Menlo Park California. www.kff.org/entmedia/entmedia030905pkg.cfm. Accessed October 2006.

Kilbourne, J. (1999). *Deadly persuasion: The addictive power of advertising*. New York: Simon and Shuster.

Kline, S. (1993). *Out of the garden: Toys and children's culture in the age of TV marketing*. London: Verso.

Kline, S. (2004). 'Sedentary lifestyle or fast food culture? Lessons from the battle of the bulge', in Umashankar Shastri (ed.), *Fast food industry—issues and implications*. Executive Reference Books Institute of Chartered Financial Analysts of India (ICFAI University).

Kline, S. (2005). 'Countering children's sedentary lifestyles: An evaluation study of a media risk education approach', *Childhood* 12, 2: 239–58.

Kline, S. (2010). 'Children as competent consumers', in Marshall, D. (ed.), *Understanding children as consumers*. London: Sage, 239–57.

Kline, S. (forthcoming). *Globesity, food marketing and children*. Palgrave: London.

Kunkel, D., Wilcox, B., Cantor, J., Palmer, E., Linn, S., and Dowrick, P. (2004). *APA task force report on advertising and children: psychological issues in the increasing commercialization of childhood*. Washington: American Psychological Association.

Leiss, W., Kline, S., Jhally, S., and Botterill, J. (2005). *Social communication in advertising: Consumption in the mediated marketplace*. New York: Routledge.

Livingstone, S., and Helsper, E.J. (2006). 'Relating advertising literacy to the effects of advertising children's food choice: An integration of two research literatures', *Journal of Communication* 56, 3: 560–84.

Mink, M., Evans, A., Moore, C.G., Calderon, K.S., and Deger, S. (2010). 'Nutritional imbalance endorsed by televised food advertisements', *Journal of the American Dietetic Association* 110, 6: 904–10.

Neville, L., Thomas M., and Bauman, A. (2005). 'Food advertising on Australian television: The extent of children's exposure', *Health Promotion International* 20, 2: 105–12.

Reuters (2009). U.S. group sues Coke over Vitamin-Water health claims. Reuters: New York, 15 January. http://www.reuters.com/article/2009/01/15/us-cocacola-vitaminwater-idUSTRE50E54L20090115.

Roberts, M., and Pettigrew, S. (2007). 'A thematic content analysis of children's food advertising', *International Journal of Advertising* 26, 3: 357–67.

Roedder-John, D. (1999). 'Through the eyes of a child: Children's knowledge and understanding of advertising', in M. Carole Macklin and Les Carlson (eds), *Advertising to children*. Thousand Oaks, Calif.: Sage Publications.

Story, M. and French, S. (2004). 'Food advertising and marketing directed at children and adolescents in the US', *International Journal of Behavioral Nutrition and Physical Activity* 1: 3.

Taylor, J., Evers, S., and MacKenna, M. (2005). 'Determinants of healthy eating in children and youth', *Canadian Journal of Public Health* 96, 3: S20–S26.

UK Food Commission (2005). 'Marketing of foods to children'. http://www.which.co.uk.

Ward, S., Wackman, D.B., and Wartella, E. (1977). *How children learn to buy: The development of consumer information processing skills*. Beverly Hills, Calif.: Sage.

Wilson, N., Signal, L., Nicholls, S., and Thomson, G. (2006). 'Marketing fat and sugar to children on New Zealand television', *Preventive Medicine* 42: 96–101.

World Health Organization (2004). *Marketing food to children*. World Health Organization: Switzerland.

Zimmerman, F., and Bell, J. (2010). 'Associations of television content type and obesity', *American Journal of Public Health* 100, 2: 334–40.

QUESTIONS FOR REFLECTION

1. Where is the television in your home or residence? How does its placement impact the viewing experience and the communicative capabilities of what you watch?

2. On what types of screens do you watch television and film? How do these viewing experiences differ from those described by Spigel and Heyer? Why might such differences matter?

3. In the research cited by Botterill and Kline, children are identified as incapable of making informed consumer decisions. Are you, as an adult, able to interrogate the visual strategies used by advertisers and make informed consumer decisions? Should food advertisements to adults be further regulated? How and to what effect?

FURTHER READING

Brooker, Will, and Deborah Jermyn, Eds. *The Audience Studies Reader*. London: Routledge, 2002.

Ellis, John. *Visible Fictions: Cinema, Television, Video.* London: Routledge, 1982.

Heyer, Paul. 'Live from the Met: Digital Broadcast Cinema, Medium Theory, and Opera for the Masses'. *Canadian Journal of Communication* 33.4 (2008): 591–604.

Jancovich, Mark, Lucy Faire, and Sarah Stubbings. *The Place of Audience: Cultural Geographies of Film Consumption*. London: British Film Institute, 2003.

Leiss, William et al. *Social Communication in Advertising: Consumption in the Mediated Marketplace*. New York: Routledge, 2005.

Mayne, Judith. *Cinema and Spectatorship*. London: Routledge, 1993.

Monaco, James. *How to Read a Film: Movies, Media, Multimedia*. New York: Oxford, 2000.

Muller, Floris and Joke Hermes, 'The Performance of Cultural Citizenship: Audiences and the Politics of Multicultural Television Drama'. *Critical Studies in Media Communication* 27.2 (June 2010): 193–208.

Nightingale, Virginia and Karen Ross, Eds. *Critical Readings: Media and Audiences*. Maidenhead, Berkshire: Open University, 2003.

Schudson, Michael. *Advertising, The Uneasy Persuasion: Its Dubious Impact on American Society*. New York: Basic, 1984.

Spigel, Lynn. *Make Room for TV: Television and the Family Ideal in Postwar America*. Chicago: University of Chicago, 1992.

Stacey, Jackie. *Star Gazing: Hollywood Cinema and Female Spectatorship*. London: Routledge, 1994.

Staiger, Janet. *Media Reception Studies*. New York: New York University, 2005.

CREDITS

Grateful acknowledgement is made for permission to reproduce the following:

Arnheim, Rudolph. 'Vision in Education.' From Arnheim, Rudolph. *Visual Thinking*. Berkeley: University of California, 1969, pages 294–315.

Becker, Karin E. 'Photojournalism and the Tabloid Pres.' From *The Photography Reader*. Ed. Liz Wells. New York: Routledge, 2003. 291–308.

Cartwright, Lisa. 'A Cultural Anatomy of the Visible Human Project.' From *The Visible Woman: Imaging Technologies, Gender, and Science*. Ed. Paula A. Treichler, Lisa Cartwright and Constance Penley. New York: New York University Press, 1998. 21–43.

Cregan, Kate. 'Blood and Circuses.' From Klaver, Elizabeth. *Images of the Corpse: From Renaissance to Cyberspace*. © 2004 by the Board of Regents of the University of Wisconsin System. Reprinted by permission of The University of Wisconsin Press.

Duncan, Carol. 'The MoMA's Hot Mamas.' *Art Journal*, 48.2 (1989), pages 171–178.

Finn, Jonathan. 'Powell's Point: Denial and Deception at the U.N.' From *Visual Communication* 9.2 (February 2010): 25–49, Sage Publications.

Goodwin, Charles. 'Professional Vision.' Reproduced by permission of the American Anthropological Association from *American Anthropologist*, Volume 96, Issue 3, pp 606–633, 1994. Not for sale or further reproduction.

Harley, J.B. 'Deconstructing the Map.' From *Cartographica* 26(2) 1989: 1–20. Reprinted with permission from University of Toronto Press Incorporated (www.utpjournals.com).

Ivins, Jr., William M. 'Recapitulation.' From *Prints and Visual Communication*, pp. 158–160. © 1969 Massachusetts Institute of Technology, by permission of The MIT Press.

Payne, Carol. 'Through a Canadian Lens: Discourses of Nationalism and Aboriginal Representation in Governmental Photographs.' From *Canadian Cultural Poesis: Essays on Canadian Culture*. Eds. Garry Sherbert, Annie Gérin and Sheila Petty. Waterloo, Wilfrid Laurier University Press, 2006. 421–442.

Phillips, Ruth B. 'The Mask Stripped Bare by its Curators: The Work of Hybridity in the Twenty-First Century.' From *Histoire de l'art et anthropologie*. Paris: INHA / musée du quai Branly, 2009. pp.379–396 (or 257–273).

Schwartz, Dona. 'To Tell the Truth: Codes of Objectivity in Photojournalism.' From *Communication* 13(2) 1992: 95–109.

Sherwin, Richard K. 'Visual Literacy in Action: Law in the Age of Images.' From *Visual Literacy*. Ed. James Elkins. New York: Routledge, 2007. 179–194.

Sontag, Susan. 'In Plato's Cave.' Excerpt from ON PHOTOGRAPHY by Susan Sontag. Copyright © 1977 by Susan Sontag. Reprinted by permission of Farrar, Straus and Giroux, LLC.

Spigel, Lynn. 'Television in the Family Circle.' From *Make Room for TV: Television and the Family Ideal in Postwar America*. Chicago: University of Chicago Press, 1992. 36–72.

Vance, Carole S. 'The Pleasures of Looking: The Attorney General's Commission on Pornography vs. Visual Images.' From C. Squiers (Ed.), *The Critical Images*. Bay Press: Seattle, pp. 38–58, 1990.

Vertesi, Janet. 'Mind the Gap: The London Underground Map and Users' Representations of Urban Space.' From *Social Studies of Science* 38(1) 2008: 7–33.

Whitelaw, Anne. '"Whiffs of Balsam, Pine, and Spruce": Art Museums and the Production of a Canadian Aesthetic.' From *Capital Culture: A Reader on Modernist Legacies, State Institutions, and the Value(s) of Art*. Ed. Jody Berland and Shelley Hornstein. Montreal: McGill-Queens University Press, 2000. 122–137.

Figure Credits

Figure 2.3: Paul Klee, Contributions to a Theory of Pictural Form, p. 93. Zentrum Paul Klee, Bern

Figure 4.1: The Anatomy Theatre at the Worshipful Company of Barber-Surgeons, London, cross-section of the interior, from Isaac Ware's Designs of Inigo Jones and others (ca.1731). RIBA Library Photographs Collection.

Figure 4.2: The Anatomy Lesson given by John Banister (1533–1610) at the Barber Surgeons Hall in 1548. Frontispiece of 'De re anatomonica' (Paris, 1562) by Matteo Realdo Colombo (Renaldus Columbus) (1516–1559). 2nd edition, ca. 1580. Location: Bibliotheque Nationale, Paris, France. Photo Credit: Scala/White Images / Art Resource, NY.

Figure 5.1: The Visible Human Project ® From the National Library of Medicine.

Figure 5.2 The Visible Human Project ® From the National Library of Medicine.

Figure 5.3 The Visible Human Project ® From the National Library of Medicine.

Figure 12.1: LondonTown.com